W9-COX-967

LIEBERT & SPIEGLER'S
PERSONALITY
STRATEGIES AND ISSUES

EIGHTH EDITION

AS REVISED BY LIEBERT & LIEBERT

LIST OF RELATED TITLES

SOCIAL PSYCHOLOGY

Group Dynamics (2nd ed.), by Donelson Forsyth
Health Psychology (3rd ed.), by Linda Brannon and Jess Feist
Health Psychology, by Phillip Rice
Our Social World, by Donelson Forsyth
Psychology Applied to Modern Life (5th ed.), by Wayne Weiten and Margaret Lloyd
Social and Personality Development (3rd ed.), by David Schaeffer

CLINICAL PSYCHOLOGY

Abnormal Psychology: An Introduction, by V. Mark Durand and David H. Barlow
Abnormal Psychology: An Integrative Approach, by David H. Barlow and V. Mark Durand
Casebook in Abnormal Psychology, by Timothy Brown and David H. Barlow
Clinical Psychology (5th ed.), by E. Jerry Phares and Timothy J. Trull
Culture and Mental Illness, by Richard J. Castillo
Meanings of Madness: Readings in Culture and Mental Illness, by Richard J. Castillo
Seeing Both Sides: Classic Controversies in *Abnormal Psychology*, by Scott O. Lilienfeld

FORTHCOMING TITLES

Abnormal Child Psychology, by David Wolfe and Eric Mash
Casebook in Child Behavior Disorders, by Christopher Kearney
Looking into Abnormal Psychology: Contemporary Readings in *Abnormal Psychology*, by Scott O. Lilienfeld

LIEBERT & SPIEGLER'S PERSONALITY STRATEGIES AND ISSUES

EIGHTH EDITION

AS REVISED BY LIEBERT & LIEBERT

Robert M. Liebert
State University of New York at Stony Brook

Lynn Langenbach Liebert
State University of New York at Stony Brook

Brooks/Cole Publishing Company
I(T)P® An International Thomson Publishing Company

Pacific Grove · Albany · Belmont · Bonn · Boston · Cincinnati · Detroit · Johannesburg · London · Madrid · Melbourne · Mexico City · New York · Paris · Singapore · Tokyo · Toronto · Washington

Sponsoring Editor: *Marianne Taflinger*
Marketing Team: *Lauren Harp, Alicia Barelli, Jean Thompson*
Editorial Assistant: *Scott Brearton*
Production Editor: *Nancy Velthaus*
Editing and Production: *Graphic World Publishing Services*
Permissions Editor: *Linda Rill*
Interior Design: *Graphic World Publishing Services*
Cover Design: *Laurie Albrecht*
Cover Art: *Bob Western*
Photo Researcher: *Roberta Spieckerman, Bob Western*
Typesetting: *Graphic World, Inc.*
Cover Printing: *Phoenix*
Printing and Binding: *Courier*

For more information, contact:

BROOKS/COLE PUBLISHING COMPANY
511 Forest Lodge Road
Pacific Grove, CA 93950
USA

International Thomson Publishing Europe
Berkshire House 168–173
High Holborn
London WC1V 7AA
England

Thomas Nelson Australia
102 Dodds Street
South Melbourne, 3205
Victoria, Australia

Nelson Canada
1120 Birchmount Road
Scarborough, Ontario
Canada M1K 5G4

International Thomson Editores
Seneca 53
Col. Polanco
11560 México, D. F., México

International Thomson Publishing GmbH
Königswinterer Strasse 418
53227 Bonn
Germany

International Thomson Publishing Asia
221 Henderson Road
#05–10 Henderson Building
Singapore 0315

International Thomson Publishing Japan
Hirakawacho Kyowa Building, 3F
2-2-1 Hirakawacho
Chiyoda-ku, Tokyo 102
Japan

Printed in the United States of America.

10 9 8 7 6 5 4 3 2 1

Library of Congress Cataloging-in-Publication Data

Liebert, Robert M., 1942–
[Personality]
Liebert & Spiegler's personality : strategies and issues / Robert M. Liebert, Lynn L. Liebert.—8th ed.
p. cm.
Includes bibliographical references and index.
ISBN 0-534-26418-2
1. Personality. I. Liebert, Lynn Langenbach. II. Title.
BF698.L465 1997 97-44686
155.2—dc21 CIP

Robert M. Liebert and Lynn Langenbach Liebert

Robert M. Liebert received his Ph.D. in clinical psychology from Stanford University, after study at Tulane University and University College, London, England. Author or co-author of 9 books and well over 100 journal articles and book chapters, he has been Professor of Psychology at the State University of New York at Stony Brook since 1973. He is currently Area Head of Clinical Psychology at Stony Brook, where he also directs The Psychological Center and serves as Director of Clinical Training. Professor Liebert is an avid reader of poetry and philosophy and is a particular admirer of the poems of W. H. Auden and the thinking of Heinz von Foerster.

Lynn Langenbach Liebert received her Ph.D. in clinical psychology from the State University of New York at Stony Brook and is currently Research Associate in the Department of Neurology at University Hospital, Stony Brook. She has expertise in the psychological effects of neurological disease and trauma, particularly as they relate to individual differences in personality. She has long-standing interests in cognitive rehabilitation and psychological adjustment to neurological insults and impairment, as well as professional ethics. When not working or writing, Lynn can often be found on the tennis courts (though not as often as she would like). She also has deep appreciation for art, music, and fine chocolate.

Bob and Lynn were married in 1993 and have previously collaborated on a number of research and writing projects, including the most recent edition of the well-known text *Science and Behavior.* Other joint projects have included the design of their current home and parenting their daughter, Rachel, now 3 years old, who is a precocious redhead with a winning smile and a loving heart. The Lieberts make their home in the seaside village of Port Jefferson, Long Island, where they live with Rachel, Bob's 13-year-old son, Alex (creator of the widely admired video games *Barney Blast, Barney Blast II: The Revenge,* and *SpinBall*) and 93-year-old mother, Minnie (who expresses her Romanian heritage by reading cards on Friday nights).

To Herbert and Joan Langenbach,
for your continued support and encouragement,
(not to mention a lot of Mee-ma and Pee-pa services
throughout the writing of this book!)
—with love, Lynn and Bob

Contents in Brief

Contents

Chapter Four Freud's Psychoanalytic Theories 75

Chapter Five Post-Freudian Perspectives 109

Special Features

PREFACE

Writing this eighth edition of *Personality: Strategies and Issues* has been like running an intellectual marathon for us. In reviewing the previous edition and the current state of the field of personality psychology, we realized that the existing text was in need of an entire overhaul and reorganization. Some exciting and current research areas were not even represented in the previous edition and needed to be incorporated. In other areas, the research focus seems to have shifted over time to present a slightly different picture than was apparent in our last review effort. This necessitated a reconceptualization of the overall organization of the book and its major components. Like running, this provided an intellectual "high" that comes of total absorption in an engaging pursuit. (On a related note, we have now included a discussion on the concept of "Flow" in Chapter 16.)

We are pleased and gratified by our new understanding and hope to have conveyed it effectively throughout this text. Like runners at the end of the race, though, we find ourselves exhausted from the effort. We are in need of a respite, but look forward to the opportunity to further refine our current understanding, as well as our presentation, through the opportunity to revise this text in the future. For now, our hope is that we have accomplished our goal reasonably and that present and future adopters share enough of our view to appreciate our conceptualization.

OUR AIM

Our aim in writing this edition, as in previous editions, was to capture the essence of the field of personality at a level appropriate for a first undergraduate introductory course. Toward that end, we have continued to avoid jargon where possible and define terms clearly throughout the text. We have also substantially revised the glossary at the end of the text, so that it is now comprehensive and fully cross-referenced. We have also made every effort to employ examples that capture concerns familiar to most undergraduates. This allows students to effectively relate the material to their own day-to-day experiences, thus enhancing processing and ultimately retention and recall of the material.

We feel it is very important to expose first-time students to the broad theoretical underpinnings of the field in a sound historical context, with links to contemporary research efforts and theory. Toward that end, we present each of the four strategies with explicit attention to both its earliest roots and its links with theorizing from other strategies. We have also described the broader historical, cultural, and scientific context from which each strategy emerged. We have tried to weave together coverage of the most up-to-date research with currently important theoretical issues and significant practical applications.

ORGANIZATION

The text is organized into six parts. The first part provides the groundwork of the field of personality psychology as it exists today. Here we introduce the basic ideas and questions of the field, as well as the methods of research used by personality psychologists. Parts II–V each present one of the major theoretical strategies used to address questions about personality. Within each of these parts are four chapters. The discussion of each strategy opens with an introduction to the major assumptions and common themes that link the theories within it. This overview chapter is followed by two theory chapters, which review major theoretical approaches and contemporary research related to them. We wrap up each strategy with a chapter that examines the applications derived from the theories of the strategy, and we conclude by turning a critical eye on the strategy in noting its inherent limitations. Part VI, the end of the basic text, contains an integrative epilogue intended to lead readers to reflect on the material as a whole and to heighten awareness of the areas of overlap among the strategies.

NEW TO THIS EDITION

Applied Material Pulled Together

Past adopters will recognize some organizational changes from previous editions. Like earlier editions of Liebert and Spiegler, this edition continues to focus on four strategies, within which four distinct issues are examined. However, in this revision we saw the need to make these four issues somewhat more conspicuous. Thus, *theory, research, assessment,* and *personality change* are all still given significant coverage. However, the applications of the theories (in the form of specific assessment tools and procedures, as well as therapy techniques) have now been gathered together and are presented within the final chapter of each major part, followed by presentation of the limitations of the strategy. This modification was undertaken for two reasons. First, some strategies focus more on assessment than on change (the Dispositional Strategy being the prime example), whereas others present a wider range of applications. With the new organization, these applied elements can be compared across strategies more directly. Second, some instructors feel strongly that applications are beyond the scope of a first introductory course. While we sympathize with this opinion, it is also clear to us that students find applications particularly interesting. By separating the applications from the presentation of the basic theories we have allowed instructors to easily choose to include or pass over this material, making it optional for the student or the instructor.

Reconceptualized Strategies

Two of the previous strategies have been reorganized substantially, and renamed to reflect their new emphasis. Thus, the earlier Behavioral Strategy has been re-cast as the *Environmental* Strategy. This strategy is defined by its focus on the impact of forces *external* to the person in the form of both environmental contingencies and the rules and examples provided by the immediate and extended family and by the wider social and cultural world in which each person lives. Similarly, the Phenomenological Strategy of the previous edition has been transformed into a subset of the *Representational* Strategy, which is defined by a focus on how each of us thinks about and construes ourselves and our social and physical worlds. The strategy includes a single chapter covering the important contributions of phenomenological theorists, followed by a chapter covering the contributions of cognitive and social-cognitive theories to the understanding of personality.

Limitations as a Section of the Closing Chapter

As before, limitations continue to appear at the end of each strategy. However, instead of appearing in very short, free-standing chapters, limitations now constitute the *final section* of the closing chapter of each strategy, following the presentation of the strategy's applications. We present each strategy and its component approaches in a positive light, as its adherents and proponents would. But, for instructors who choose to employ a more critical approach, the limitations sections can easily be assigned at any point, such as preceding the entire strategy, immediately following the introductory chapter, or following the entire strategy presentation.

Balance and Flexibility for the Instructor

These various organizational changes, in combination, allowed us to consolidate material effectively, so that the strategy presentations are more balanced than in the preceding editions. Each strategy now contains the same basic four chapter structure, providing increased flexibility for instructors in terms of order of presentation of the material.

Chapters within strategies can now more easily be assigned or omitted as per instructor preferences, as can entire strategies. Each strategy is free-standing (although our emphasis on historical and cultural roots did guide our order of presentation). We have come to recognize that not all instructors will choose to cover every strategy and that time constraints may necessitate omitting or glossing over some material. The organization of this edition was purposely designed to create maximum flexibility in course structure.

Revamped Demonstrations of Personality Principles

Boxes are now used to highlight material of particular interest to students, as well as to present the best of the demonstrations from preceding editions. Many of the demonstrations have been modified to enhance their clarity and pedagogical function. Some demonstrations from previous editions have been omitted from the basic text but are all reprinted in the instructor's manual and are still available for use. (The former tear-out pages for demonstrations no longer appearing in the basic text are included in the instructor's manual, so they can be photocopied and distributed in class.)

Attention to Biology, Cognition, Ethics, Culture, and Gender

Several contemporary research areas were underrepresented in the previous edition. Specifically, we have included an entirely new chapter on the *biological approach,* as well as the *social cognitive approach.* A new section on ethical concerns particularly related to psychological research is included in Chapter 2. *Gender, social* and *cultural issues* and their impact on personality have been included for the first time; they are a major focus of Chapter 13.

Every effort has been made to replace dated material with current material. This applies equally to the research base of the text and to the examples and illustrations employed throughout. Illustrations have been modified, replaced, and supplemented to increase clarity and understanding. To the extent possible, examples were written with an eye toward experiences and concerns common to students and their everyday experiences.

Finally, we have added a final wrap up chapter in the form of an epilogue (Chapter 19). Although this chapter does not represent a comprehensive effort to tie up all of the loose ends of the field, it does serve as a starting point for this endeavor. We highlight some of the most interesting areas of overlap between strategies, the controversies that continue to exist between them, and importantly, both the present direction of movement within the field and the great promise for the future of personality psychology. This chapter picks up our "journey" analogy from Part I and is intended to provide a sense of structure, integration, and closure for the student.

WHY FOUR STRATEGIES?

We divide the field of personality into four relatively distinct theoretical strategies for several reasons. First and foremost, we believe this provides students with a meaningful framework (a personality schema) within which to appreciate, understand, and integrate the diverse content of the field. Second, we believe that for this framework to adequately serve our pedagogical purposes, it must be limited enough for easy retention and recall, while being clear and distinct enough to offer meaningful connections and associations between related theories. And last, we believe that the four strategies as they are now conceptualized and presented *do* adequately encompass all of the most important theories within contemporary personality psychology.

Clearly, the strategies are to some extent our own construction; however, that does not imply that they are arbitrary. Rather, they are based on our best understanding of the state of the field, and in many cases our reinterpretation of older theories in light of recent research related to them.

PEDAGOGICAL FEATURES

- Clear, accessible writing style
- Comprehensive, fully cross-referenced glossary
- Detailed outlines precede each chapter
- Chapters close with point-by-point summary of contents
- Central strategy themes are emphasized, reiterated, and also captured by a concise "catch phrase" featured at the opening of each part to enhance understanding and retention
- Clear, relevant examples drawn from experiences common to students
- Graphics are generously employed to illustrate key ideas visually

- Each new text is accompanied by a complimentary study guide
- Boxes are used both for demonstrations and for presentation of current material of particular interest to student readers
- All key terms are presented in boldface and accompanied by explicit definitions in the text; these terms all appear in the glossary, with paraphrased or complementary definitions to further clarify meaning

ACKNOWLEDGMENTS

Producing a text of this type clearly requires the talents and efforts of many people beyond the authors. We have been particularly fortunate in having received the assistance and support of many hard-working and extremely talented individuals. Our deepest gratitude to Marianne Taflinger of Brooks/Cole, who served not only as editor of this project, but also cheering section and advocate. Marianne supplied crisp, constructive, and much needed editorial and artistic feedback, along with a tremendous amount of guidance and support. Her confidence in our abilities never flagged. She also provided the critical reviews, direction, encouragement, and resources to see this job to completion.

Scott Brearton (also of Brooks/Cole) deserves special mention. He provided incredibly efficient responses to requests of all kinds. He managed to provide every type of answer or resource we needed quickly, accurately, and always with a pleasant tone. Thanks also to Nancy Velthaus, Faith Stoddard, and Vernon Boes of Brooks/Cole. The entire Brooks/Cole team managed to comply with even our most trying requests, and received them as if they were commonplace and expected. (We often knew, in fact, they were quite unprecedented and frequently made enormous time demands.) Yet on no occasion were we disappointed by the results!

Thanks are due to Suzanne Copple of Graphic World Publishing Services, for her continued support and tolerance of the (sometimes conflicting) demands of those involved with this book. She managed to juggle the specifications and always produce a gem, with never a harsh word. Thanks, too, are owed to the entire team at Graphic World for their dedicated effort and meticulous care in the preparation of this manuscript. We also thank Roberta Spieckerman (and associates) for securing photos of every sort to our specifications, from the most exacting to the most obscure, without complaint or compromise. Thank you also to Linda L. Rill for her meticulous research efforts.

We owe a tremendous debt of gratitude to Dr. James Jay Johnson of Illinois State University, who committed much of his summer to (multiple) detailed reviews of our manuscript. His input was invaluable and often profoundly insightful. Without Jim's prudent guidance, we would surely have wandered astray in many locations. He demonstrated patience (with our multiple drafts and last-minute revisions) and incredible perseverance. He also managed (in keeping with our very tight schedule) to maintain a very fast turn around time without losing sight of the "big picture," or compromising his meticulous eye for detail.

We also extend our thanks to the many others who served as reviewers of the manuscript at various stages, including Dr. Susan E. Beers of Sweet Briar

College, Dr. James A. Cranford of the State University of New York at Albany, Dr. Louis R. Franzini of San Diego State University, Dr. Diane Friedman of Radford University, Dr. Barry Fritz of Quinnipiac College, Dr. Kathryn Graff Low of Bates College, Dr. John P. Hall of Texas Wesleyan University, Dr. Benjamin Harris of University of Wisconsin—Parkside, Dr. Margaret Kasimatis of Hope College, Dr. Peter K. Miene of Winona State University, Dr. John Moritsugu of Pacific Lutheran University, Dr. Tom Randall of Rhode Island College, Dr. John Seta of the University of North Carolina at Greensboro, Dr. John Shepherd of New Mexico Junior College, Dr. Rhea E. Steinpreis of The University of Wisconsin—Milwaukee, Dr. Susan C. Tobin of California State University—Chico, Dr. Teddy D. Warner of the University of New Mexico, Dr. R. Douglas Whitman of Wayne State University, and Dr. John P. Wilson of Cleveland State University. Thank you also to Dr. Everett Waters of the State University of New York at Stony Brook for generously sharing with us his extensive knowledge of the history and literature on attachment theory.

Special thanks to our team of research assistants at Stony Brook—Robin L. Leake, Tara West, and Christy Lennington—who proved able to perform minor miracles under intense time pressure. Thanks also to Carol Carlson for assistance typing various parts of the manuscript. We are indebted also to Alex Liebert for the contributions of his time, effort, and creativity in the production of the "subculture" cartoon in Chapter 13. Thank you to Dawn Sweet, who not only assisted with research and resources as needed, but helped keep our family and household running in the process. And particular thanks to Pat Urbelis who oversees scheduling and campus commitments with such precision that appointments were never missed or obligations overlooked in the race to complete this project.

Heartfelt thanks to Dr. Mark J. Kropf for all of his patience and support during the preparation of this manuscript (not to mention the rest of our lives). Thank you, too, to Herbert and Joan Langenbach for the tremendous amount of support, patience, and childcare assistance they provided this year and throughout all the tough times. Thank you to Rachel Liebert for the inspiration she provides daily, as well as tremendous patience and sacrifice in allowing Mommy and Daddy to work on "the book." (We fear she's going to ask us to read it to her at night-night time.) Thank you also to Minnie and Alex Liebert for forgiving us our absences and distraction at times. Thank you also to the rest of our family members for their patience and endurance through this grueling process.

Robert M. Liebert
Lynn Langenbach Liebert
Port Jefferson, NY

PART ONE

INTRODUCTION

The Faces We Wear

CHAPTER ONE

Overview

magine that you have just confided to a close friend that you and your steady partner of 2 years have split up. After expressing sympathy and concern about your situation, your friend begins to offer a brief description of someone else who might interest you. The description begins with some basic physical characteristics, but they are only a small part of the story. What you *really* want to know is what this new "someone else" is like, to hear about the individual's **personality.** Will you like the same activities? enjoy the same movies? eat the same foods? share the same basic values? In other words, how can one person decide who will or will not be a compatible partner? Which characteristics are more important and which less so? How enduring are these characteristics? How are they formed and by what means? All these questions are addressed by modern personality psychologists.

This book introduces personality psychology as it exists today and shows how it evolved as a product of what has been thought, written, and practiced over time. Our journey begins with a brief look at the history of the term *personality* and the evolution of personality psychology as a field of formal study.

THE SEARCH FOR THE "REAL" PERSON

In ancient Rome, actors used no makeup. Instead, each player wore a **persona,** a full-face mask that told the audience to expect a particular set of attitudes and behaviors. Various personae came to refer not only to the masks but also to the roles they implied (Burnham, 1968).

Although *persona* is the source of the English word *personality,* the concept of personality as we use it today (as something more than a set of actors' roles) did not emerge until the 18th century. Sampson (1989) traces the term to the modern idea of a *real person.*

> In premodern society . . . roles were the elements that constituted the person as such. Roles were not appended to the "real" person who somehow continued to dwell authentically behind them. There was no stepping outside one's community and one's roles in order to act differently. . . . To be outside was in effect to be nonexistent, a stranger, or dead. (p. 915)

Sampson concludes that it was only with the emergence of the modern concept of *personality* about 200 years ago that "seeking to understand the individual became a highly cherished cultural project" (1989, p. 916). This cultural project gives rise to two important questions: "What am I *really* like" and "What is the other person *really* like?"

In the theater of ancient Rome, actors wore a mask, called a persona, to indicate the personality characteristics of the role they played.

There is certainly more than one way to answer these questions. This book provides an introduction to the *scientific* study of personality. It deals with the issues involved in developing a formal scientific approach to understanding ourselves and others. Our primary aim is to provide a general picture of the diversity of existing knowledge and thinking about personality, including both the assumptions personality psychologists have made and the evidence they have considered important. We endeavor to explain the central ideas underlying significant theoretical positions and, at the same time, to summarize the often dramatic advances of recent years.

THE NATURE OF PERSONALITY PSYCHOLOGY

Modern psychology is a very broad field, comprising many specialized areas. Interpersonal relations, attitude change, and the influence of social forces are typically the domain of social psychology. Developmental psychology emphasizes the historical antecedents of a person's behavior; it is concerned with the interplay of maturational and social influences as people advance from childhood to adulthood to senior status. "Deviant" behavior (behavior markedly different from the norms of society, especially behavior that proves maladaptive for the person or others) is of particular interest to abnormal psychology. This field includes the theoretical and experimental work of psychopathology as well as the applied work of clinical and counseling psychology.

Specific human enterprises are the focus of fields such as biopsychology, health psychology, industrial and organizational psychology, educational psychology, and school psychology. Experimental psychology involves the study of single aspects of the organism, such as sensation, perception, learning, and emotion. Cognitive psychology concentrates on how human beings think and mentally process information.

In many ways, **personality psychology** is at the crossroads of these other fields. One personality psychologist gives this view of the "big picture."

> To me, the most fruitful definition of the goal of scientific psychology is to understand and explain why individuals think, feel, act, and react as they do in real life. The special contribution of personality psychology to this effort is to develop theories and conduct empirical research on the functioning of the individual as a totality. (Magnusson, 1989, p. 1)

Defining *Personality*

Can we define the term *personality* more precisely? In fact, personality psychologists use many definitions. Which definition particular psychologists select depends in part on their theoretical orientation. (See Table 1.1 for a sampling of "classical" definitions.) For the purpose of this book, we have in mind the following working definition:

> **Personality** is the unique, dynamic organization of characteristics of a particular person, physical and psychological, which influence behavior and

Table 1.1 Some classical definitions of personality

Allport: Personality is the dynamic organization within the individual of those psychophysical systems that determine his unique adjustments to his environment. (pp. 494–495)

Cattell: Personality is that which permits prediction of what a person will do in a given situation. [It] is concerned with *all* the behavior of the individual, both overt and under the skin. (p. 496)

Eysenck: Personality is the more or less stable and enduring organization of a person's character, temperament, intellect and physique, which determines his unique adjustment to his environment. (p. 496)

Sullivan: Personality is the relatively enduring pattern of interpersonal situations which characterize a human life. (p. 497)

Source: Based on "Personality: Its Place in Psychology," by N. Sanford, 1963, pp. 488–592. In S. Koch (Ed.), *Psychology: A Study of a Science, Study II, Vol. 5., The Process Areas, The Person, and Some Applied Fields: Their Place in Psychology and Science.* McGraw-Hill.

responses to the social and physical environment. Of these characteristics, some will be entirely unique to the specific person (i.e., memories, habits, mannerisms) and others will be shared with a few, many, or all other people.

STRATEGIES: THE PRECURSORS OF A "PARADIGM"

The ultimate goal of science is theory development; a scientific field is generally considered mature when most of its practitioners accept and operate within the same theoretical framework, or **paradigm** (Kuhn, 1970). Present-day psychology remains in a "preparadigmatic" state. There is no consensus yet in the field as to a single unifying theoretical framework to guide psychologists' work. The "hard" sciences of physics and chemistry, which date back not hundreds but thousands of years, are much closer to and now approximating a mature state. An acceptable theory in these fields today requires a formal statement that must meet rigorous criteria to be taken seriously by peers. Personality psychology and the other social sciences have thus far not reached the stage of substantial theoretical agreement, but as would be expected, *they are progressing in that direction.*

We refer to the major theoretical orientations to personality psychology as **strategies.** In our view, strategies have been the most fundamental "guiding lights" in the scientific work on personality for the past century and remain so today. Specifically, we focus on four broad fundamental strategies, each of which has served as a starting point for approaching personality scientifically.

Each of the specific viewpoints we discuss within any strategy shares with the other theories of the strategy a basic assumption in its approach to personality. These assumptions contrast with the fundamental assumptions of the other three strategies. It is shared assumptions—and typically a focus on specific aspects of personality—that link the approaches *within* strategies together while *distinguishing* them from the others. Nonetheless, it is wrong to consider the four strategies to be mutually exclusive, so that each in some way denies or refutes all the others. Figure 1.1 shows the simplistic view of strategies as wholly independent, competing systems and contrasts it with what we believe is a more valid picture of the consensus, independence, and disagreement that exist among the four strategies today.

Overview of the Four Strategies

The four strategies around which this book is organized are the Psychoanalytic Strategy, the Dispositional Strategy, the Environmental Strategy, and the Representational Strategy.

The Psychoanalytic Strategy

The Psychoanalytic Strategy is probably the most familiar to the general public. Its guiding assumption is that personality is driven by one or more underlying forces within the person. Theorists of this strategy have divided views on particular issues (e.g., the number and nature of specific drives), but they all focus ultimately on the idea of driving forces that motivate all human behavior.

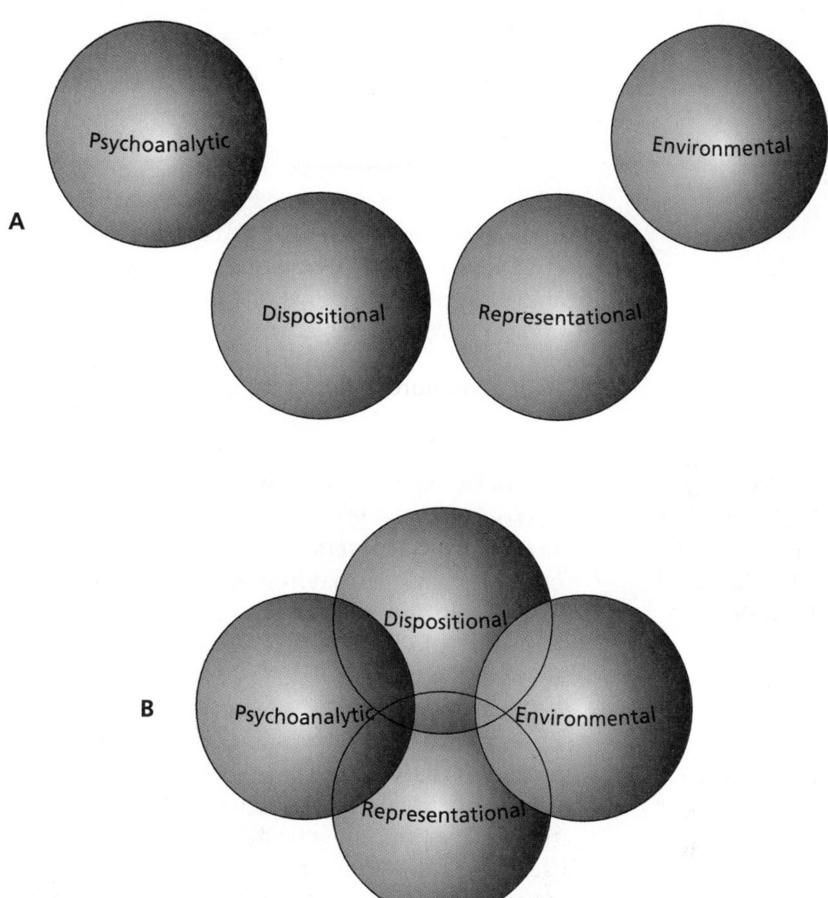

Figure 1.1
The four strategies are *not* wholly independent of one another as depicted in **A.** Rather, they share some common elements as depicted in **B.**

The Dispositional Strategy

The Dispositional Strategy has roots that go back at least to early Greek philosophy. Its basic assumption is that personality is a set of enduring characteristics, with individuals differing on how much of each characteristic they possess. This assumption is shared by an array of specific biological viewpoints and forms the basis for sophisticated mathematical studies aimed at the identification and measurement of individual differences among people.

The Environmental Strategy

The Environmental Strategy assumes that personality is shaped by an enormous set of external conditions and circumstances impinging on the individual. It concerns itself with both *how* and *what* the individual learns through interactions with the environment. Both *processes* by which personalities are shaped (e.g., conditioning and observing others) and the *content* of what is learned (e.g., the specific language, practices, and beliefs of the surrounding culture and subculture) interest psychologists who espouse the Environmental Strategy.

The Representational Strategy

The basic assumption of the Representational Strategy is that personality is a reflection of the ways individuals mentally represent themselves and the people, objects, and events they experience. The foundation of this strategy was laid in the 1950s by the writings of Carl Rogers, George Kelly, and Julian Rotter. This particular strategy has grown in popularity to the point that psychologists now recognize and acknowledge that a "cognitive revolution" reverberated throughout psychology in the 1970s. The Representational Strategy is also distinctive in that it is now embraced by many who were formerly environmentally oriented (e.g., erstwhile "social learning theorists"). These converts expanded or changed their viewpoints during or in response to the cognitive revolution.

ISSUES: FOUR FUNDAMENTAL CONCERNS IN THE STUDY OF PERSONALITY

Each of the strategies just introduced must address the same four underlying issues: (1) a theory of personality, (2) an approach to the assessment (or measurement) of personality, (3) research procedures for testing hypotheses (or implications derived from the theory), and (4) applications derived from the theory including methods of personality change (i.e., psychotherapy). The strategies differ in *how* and *to what extent* each of these particular issues is addressed.

There is considerable overlap in the roles played by each issue. Theories suggest ideas or hypotheses that are then tested in research. At the same time, the nature of the research is determined by what the particular theory leads the researcher to expect. And to conduct research, aspects of personality that are of interest must first be measured. Before measurement can be executed, assessment techniques that conform to the theory's assumptions about personality must be developed. The success of personality-change techniques and other applications serves to partially validate the principles derived from the theory.

In sum, theory, assessment, research, and applications are intricately linked elements of every strategy. In fact, discussing one issue is often difficult without referring to one or more of the other three (Tjeltveit, 1989). Thus, coverage of all of these elements is often woven throughout the strategy-specific parts of this book.

The strategy-specific parts of the book are all constructed so that each strategy contains one introductory chapter emphasizing the links that tie the theories into a distinct strategy, two chapters covering the theories and related research of the strategy, and a final chapter devoted to an examination of the applications derived from the theories and the limitations of the strategy overall. First, though, we will examine each of these four underlying issues and their importance to the scientific study of personality.

PERSONALITY THEORIES

We have already used the word **theory** on several occasions. Now we will take a closer look at this important word and its meaning in personality psychology. A "true" scientific theory, in the philosophy of science sense, must meet a stringent set of criteria. Although dozens of descriptions and explanations of personality have been put forward and discussed as "theories," none of them (with the notable exception of the theory of George A. Kelly, a master of the philosophy of science) is a true theory in the classical sense of being fully and precisely explicated.

Scientific Theory

A **scientific theory** is an explanation, but not all explanations are scientific theories (Hesse, 1963). Scientific theories have two components: theoretical constructs and relational propositions.

Theoretical Constructs

Theoretical constructs (CON-structs) are the basic terms and building blocks of a theory. *Energy* is a theoretical construct in physics, *oxidation* is a theoretical construct in chemistry, and *natural selection* is a theoretical construct in evolutionary biology. Personality psychologists use a wide variety of theoretical constructs; among the more familiar are *anxiety, self-concept, extraversion,* and *ego.*

One characteristic distinguishes all theoretical constructs. They have been *invented* to describe and explain observations. Thus, theoretical constructs do not actually exist; they are entirely abstract and cannot be seen, touched, or heard.

Why are theoretical constructs desirable or even necessary? A major reason is that they economically tie together meaningful relationships among observations that would otherwise soon become a hopeless quagmire of raw facts. In other words, they allow for efficient organization and communication of ideas.

Figure 1.2 illustrates the advantage of using the theoretical construct *anxiety* to link various events and observations. Even in the case of only three events and three observations, a single concept that unites each of the three events with the three observations (Figure 1.2*B*) is more economical, manageable, and comprehensible than descriptions of nine separate relationships (Figure 1.2*A*).

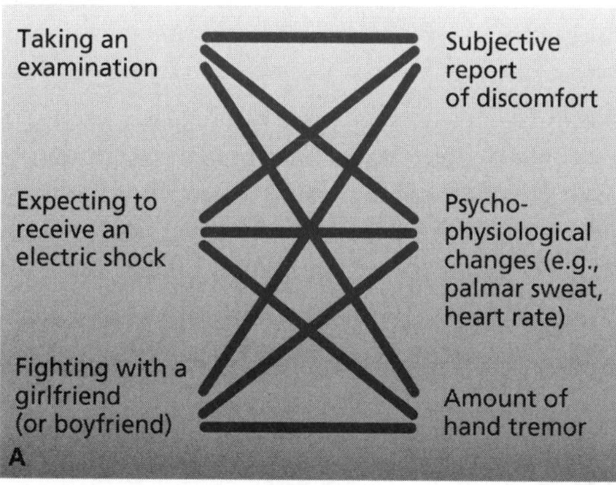

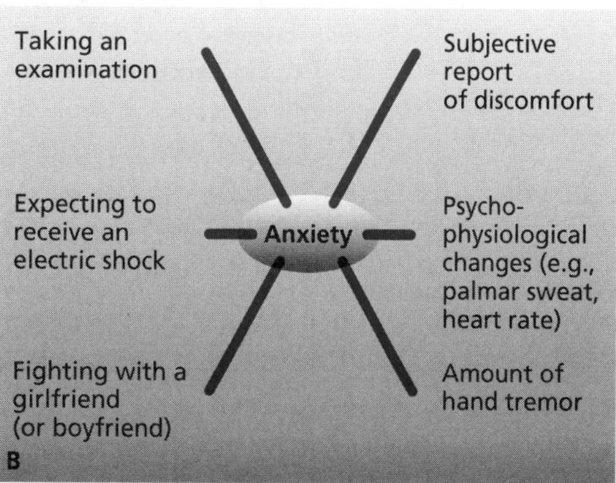

Figure 1.2
An illustration of the advantages of using *anxiety* as a theoretical construct, operating differently in a number of circumstances **(B),** over a mere listing of observed, separate relationships **(A).**
Source: Modified from "Liberalization of Basic S-R Concepts: Extensions to Conflict Behavior, Motivation, and Social Learning" by N. E. Miller, 1959. In S. Koch (Ed.), *Psychology: A Study of a Science* Vol. 2. McGraw-Hill.

Relational Propositions

The constructs of a scientific theory are related to one another by statements (sometimes called *laws*) that describe the relationships among the constructs. These are the theory's **relational propositions.** For example, Einstein's famous theory uses (among others) the constructs energy *(E)*, mass *(m)*, and a constant *(c)*, which is the speed of light. The best-known relational proposition of the theory is $E = mc^2$. The exact relationship of each construct to the others is explicitly and precisely described through the relational statements expressed by the mathematical symbols.

Personality theories contain many relational propositions, but they are rarely quantified in the precise way propositions in physics are. Psychoanalytic theory, for example, tells us that frustration leads to aggression, dispositional theory tells us that similarity in genetic makeup leads to similarity in personality, and environmental theory tells us that a response that has been occasionally rewarded will be more difficult to extinguish (eliminate) than one that has been rewarded invariably.

Functions of Theory

Theory serves three general purposes in science: (1) to organize and clarify observations, (2) to provide a sense of understanding of the subject matter, and (3) to guide future research.

Organizing and Clarifying Observations

The classic example of how a scientific theory can organize and clarify observations is Nicolaus Copernicus's heliocentric theory of the solar system, which posits that the sun (not the earth) is the center of our planetary system. Copernicus considered the whole set of observations that had been made about the positions of the planets and stars in the sky, the diurnal cycle of the sun, the changing of the seasons, and so on and found them a confusing hodgepodge. The prevailing *geocentric theory* (earth as the center of the universe) was based on presumptions and speculation.

By postulating the *heliocentric theory*, Copernicus brought a new order to otherwise seemingly unrelated observations. Movement of the heavenly bodies became increasingly predictable once they were construed as orbiting the sun rather than the earth.

Providing a Sense of Understanding

Freud's concept of transference illustrates how theories can provide a sense of understanding. We often notice that people show an immediate attraction or repulsion to someone they have never before met. Freud's notion is that these feelings have been *transferred* from a person (mother, for instance) in their past to the new person because of some perceived similarity between the mother and the stranger.

Guiding Future Research

Finally, the way theories can generate intriguing new research is demonstrated by Leon Festinger's (1957) *theory of cognitive dissonance.* Festinger claimed that whenever we experience inconsistency between our actions and our thoughts, a state of imbalance (dissonance) is created. To restore the balance, we must find some reasonable way to justify our own behavior to ourselves.

This proposition led to dozens of experiments demonstrating such effects as (1) underpaid subjects evaluate the research project they are working on more highly than subjects who are adequately paid and (2) harshly treated fraternity pledges place higher value on fraternity membership than those treated with more respect.

Criteria for Evaluating Theories

We can identify seven major criteria for evaluating a theory: empirical validity, parsimony, comprehensiveness, coherence, testability, usefulness, and acceptability. Existing personality theories fulfill many of these criteria to a greater or lesser extent. No current personality theory yet fulfills all the criteria adequately.

Empirical Validity

Empirical validity is the degree to which a theory is supported by evidence derived from observations. Theories are not themselves directly proved or disproved by research. Rather, more specific propositions, called **hypotheses,** are derived from the general theory. These specific hypotheses may then be empirically tested through research. Technically, even hypotheses cannot be proved or disproved absolutely. Rather, research may either *support* or *fail to support* a particular hypothesis derived from a theory. When research provides regular support for the hypotheses derived from a particular theory, scientists tend to accept the theory as useful. In contrast, theories that generate hypotheses that research consistently fails to support tend to be discarded.

Parsimony

Parsimony refers to simplicity or conciseness. Any observed phenomenon can be described and explained in different ways. Theories concerning the same phenomenon differ in the complexity and in the number of fundamental assumptions they require. When all else is equal, theories that involve simpler explanations and fewer assumptions are considered better—they are more parsimonious.

Comprehensiveness

Comprehensiveness refers to the breadth of the phenomena that a theory encompasses. All other things being equal, the more phenomena a single theory can account for, the better the theory is. (Recall how Copernicus's heliocentric theory allowed for understanding of the movement of virtually all of the then-visible heavenly bodies within one comprehensive system.) Broader theories also inspire more research than narrow ones. In fact, restrict*ed* theories tend to be restrict*ive* theories. They often arbitrarily exclude important phenomena and problems with which they are unable to deal effectively.

No theory of personality has yet been advanced that can explain the whole range of human psychological and social functioning. Thus, most of the personality theories we discuss deal with only some aspects of personality;

that is, no one personality theory has yet been able to encompass the entire field.

Coherence

Coherence refers to the degree to which the propositions and assumptions of a theory fit together into an internally consistent, larger explanation. In other words, a theory should be free of internal contradictions. Some personality theories are, on close examination, such a loose confederation of ideas and concepts that the parts do not mesh. These theories are obviously limited in explanatory power and are thus not "true" theories.

Testability

Testability refers to how well or easily a theory can be supported or refuted through research. (Formal hypothesis testing relies on refutation rather than substantiation of hypotheses generated by theories.) Testability is enhanced when a theory's concepts are so clearly defined that hypotheses derived from the theory can be stated precisely and unambiguously.

Until well into the 20th century, it was assumed that scientific propositions were testable to the extent they could be verified. Philosopher of science Karl Popper (1959) took issue with this so-called *principle of verification* by complaining that it is too easy to obtain verifications for a theory. Confirmations, argued Popper, are impressive only when they arise from *"risky" predictions.*

Suppose, for example, that a meteorologist has a theory that explains rainfall on the basis of moisture in the soil rather than in the atmosphere. This meteorologist predicts that it will rain in Seattle tomorrow (based on analysis of local soil samples)—and it does. Inasmuch as it rains on most days in Seattle, verification in this case is not very impressive evidence. The theory has predicted an outcome that might well have occurred even if the theory is all wet. In short, this is not a *risky* prediction.

Now suppose instead that the meteorologist predicted exactly 3.6 inches of rain for Seattle, a rare occurrence and thus a much riskier prediction. So, if the rainfall in Seattle is exactly 3.6 inches on the date predicted, we are impressed. The likelihood of this outcome occurring by chance alone is much less than that of the earlier prediction (simply that it would rain). In other words, it is the potential for *falsification* that makes a theory testable.

Usefulness

"Theory," wrote the Irish poet James Stephens, "is but the preparation for practice." Scientists may balk at public demands for practical applications of their ideas, but theories that survive often lead to important practical applications, at least in the long run. Methods of personality assessment and techniques for inducing personality change provide a measure of the practical usefulness of personality theories.

Acceptability

To be influential, a theory must be known and taken seriously by others. Theories proposed before or after "their time" do not fare well. A theory must have some acceptability among scientists if it is to be tested through research and applied in practice. Public tolerance and funding of research require a belief in the theory's worth. The most brilliant theory cannot thrive in a social climate that does not find it acceptable and plausible.

For example, as early as the third century B.C., some Greek philosophers had suggested that the sun rather than the earth was the center of the universe (Oldroyd, 1986). But their idea could not gain broad acceptance then and had to lie dormant for almost two millennia until Copernicus (re)proposed the theory.

On the Correctness of a Theory

Theories are theories; that is, they are speculations about the nature of phenomena. Facts (actual observations) are used to generate, bolster, and support theories. But theories are not facts. They cannot logically be firmly substantiated. Therefore, strictly speaking, theories cannot be right or wrong, true or false. They can, however, be more or less "useful," depending on their intended purposes. Thus, correctness is ***not*** one of the accepted criteria for evaluating theories.

Implicit Theories of Personality

As you read this book, you are likely to find some theoretical propositions that you immediately agree with; others will seem obviously wrong to you. These reactions occur because you already have a set of ideas about how your own personality and the personalities of others work. You have an **implicit theory of personality** (Kemp, 1988).

Implicit personality theories differ from the theories developed by personality psychologists. Despite their limitations, the personality theories we will examine have been communicated openly to others (especially to peers in the scientific community). In contrast, implicit theories of personality often are not communicated to others at all (Furnham, 1988). They are implicit because they are private and never stated explicitly. (They may, however, play a prominent role in your own life as well as in the lives of most other people.)

PERSONALITY ASSESSMENT

Modern psychology is said to have begun in 1879. In that year, Wilhelm Wundt established a psychological laboratory at the University of Leipzig. Only 5 years later, Francis Galton proposed formal personality measurement. Galton (1884) wrote: "The character which shapes our conduct is a definite and durable 'something,' and therefore . . . it is reasonable to attempt to measure it" (p. 179). Toward that end, Galton made a number of specific proposals about how to assess personality, including ratings by teachers and peers and direct observation of the person in social situations.

Modern personality psychologists still rely on many sources of information—self-reports, tests, direct observation, impressions of others, detailed personal histories and life records—to draw inferences about personality. Researchers often seek converging lines of evidence from different sources to bolster their conclusions.

Self-Reports: Interviews and Questionnaires

One way to find out something about a person is to ask the person directly through an interview, a questionnaire, or a combination of the two. **Self-report** data have been widely used in studies of personality. They have the advantage of providing information quickly and easily. Moreover, they are our only access to the person's subjective internal experiences (e.g., "How are you feeling today?").

Despite their appeal, self-reports alone provide an incomplete picture. What people say about themselves is subject to memory lapses, misunderstandings, and a variety of other distortions, especially when "sensitive" content is involved. If it seems that direct self-reports may be invalid or inaccurate, *in*direct assessment techniques may be used. In some cases, these techniques are "disguised" so those being assessed cannot readily distort their responses. However, as we will see, the difficulty with disguised assessment methods is that responses must then be "interpreted." Psychologists may disagree on how to interpret what a person reports, such as what the person sees in an inkblot.

Direct Observations of Behavior

A second way to learn about people is to **observe them directly** in particular situations. The situations may be contrived (in laboratories) or natural. These situations may also include observations of a subject's responses to the testing situation itself, as well as responses to specific test items.

For example, in some well-known studies of aggression, the test situation involved leading subjects to believe they were "teachers" in an experiment on the effects of punishment on learning. Subjects administered electric shocks to a "learner." (In fact, the learner was a confederate of the experimenter and no shock was given.) The severity of shock administered served as the measure of aggression.

In contrast, a psychologist interested in aggression might simply observe children on a playground to note and record the nature, severity, and circumstances of various acts of aggression that occur spontaneously. Such **naturalistic observation** (whether by a clinician or a researcher) may have more credibility than interviews or questionnaires. But naturalistic observation is often expensive or otherwise impractical; observation of even a single individual in more than a small number of situations is usually out of the question for personality assessment.

Impressions of Others

Sociologist Erving Goffman (1959) suggested that personality includes both how people *express* themselves and how they *impress* others. How people are seen by others, including friends, family, and employers, is an important part of who they are. Using the impressions of others to judge personality has a subtle implication, though: It blurs the line between objective judgment and mere opinion. Psychiatrist Thomas Szasz (1960), for example, has argued that terms such as *mental illness* and *abnormal personality* are really only value judgments. They are used to describe persons whose values, thoughts, and actions simply differ from those of most other people in their environment.

Personal Histories and Life Records

Finally, much information can be found in a person's **history** and **life records.** Educational, employment, and marital histories, as well as personal accomplishments, can reveal a great deal about a person. Such data have the advantage that they can be obtained or confirmed objectively by consulting local *archives,* such as government statistics agencies.

Bogus Personality Assessment

So far, our discussion has focused on personality assessment from the assessor's viewpoint. An equally interesting aspect is the point of view of the person being assessed.

Popular "personality" assessment techniques include everything from numerology to handwriting analyses. These techniques have never been shown to be scientifically valid, yet they continue to enjoy enthusiastic endorsements by many.

Box 1.1 is a demonstration of how personality assessments may seem to be true to the person who is offered them when, in fact, much like cotton candy, they have little substance. Box 1.1 will also allow you to try your hand at some actual research, the next issue we will consider in this chapter.

Box 1.1
DEMONSTRATION: THE CREDIBILITY OF BOGUS PERSONALITY ASSESSMENTS

Most people have read horoscopes in newspapers or magazines at one time or another. Close examination of these predictions reveals them to be very general descriptions, lacking any specificity. They typically describe, in vague terms, behaviors that commonly occur to most people, in other words, high **base rate** phenomena. The predictions themselves are left open to a wide range of interpretations and appear (at least minimally) applicable to all readers. Yet most consumers of horoscopes probably recognize the lack of specificity, realize the breadth of the audience at which these predictions are aimed (all Sagittarians for the week of January third, for instance), and therefore do not accept them wholeheartedly. A more sophisticated version of the same kind of generalized description can be extremely convincing, however, and can even lead people to believe that it is a unique description of their own personalities. The context in which the information is provided plays a role, as well as the apparent credibility of the source, but perhaps not to the extent you might expect.

Testing this hypothesis, Ulrich, Stachnik, and Stainton (1963) asked students in psychology classes to take two personality tests. A week later, the students were given written interpretations of their test scores. Each interpretation was presented as the result of careful effort on the part of the professor. As a second part of the study, other students were taught how to administer the same two personality tests to a friend. For both phases of the study, the people whose personalities were being "assessed" were asked to rate the accuracy of the "interpretation" (on a scale ranging from excellent to very poor) and to comment on it. Despite the individualized appearance of the personality description, all persons were given exactly the same "interpretation" (although the order of the statements varied), and in fact, no interpretations of the students' actual responses were made. The "interpretation" read:

> You have a strong need for other people to like you and for them to admire you. You have a tendency to be critical of yourself. You have a great deal of unused capacity which you have not turned to your advantage. While you have some personality weaknesses, you are generally able to compensate for them. Your sexual

Box continued on following page

Box 1.1 *Continued*

DEMONSTRATION: THE CREDIBILITY OF BOGUS PERSONALITY ASSESSMENTS

> adjustment has presented some problems for you. Disciplined and controlled on the outside, you tend to be worrisome and insecure inside. At times you have serious doubts as to whether you have made the right decision or done the right thing. You prefer a certain amount of change and variety and become dissatisfied when hemmed in by restrictions and limitations. You pride yourself as being an independent thinker and do not accept others' opinions without satisfactory proof. You have found it unwise to be too frank in revealing yourself to others. At times you are extroverted, affable, and sociable, while at other times you are introverted, wary, and reserved. Some of your aspirations tend to be pretty unrealistic. (p. 832)

Virtually all the students who had been administered the personality tests by the professor rated the "interpretations" as good or excellent. In the second phase of the study, approximately 75% of the subjects tested by admittedly inexperienced students also rated the assessments as good or excellent. Furthermore, the subjects' comments clearly indicated an acceptance of these "interpretations" as accurate and individualized descriptions of their own personalities. One subject who had been given the tests and "interpretation" by the professor said: "On the nose! Very good. I wish you had said more, but what you did mention was all true without a doubt. I wish you could go further into this personality sometime." A subject who had been given the tests and "interpretation" by a student commented: "I believe this interpretation fits me individually, as there are too many facets which fit me too well to be a generalization" (p. 833).

Snyder and Larson (1972) replicated this study, extending it to show that college students accept these global evaluations as relevant, regardless of whether they are presented by a psychologist in an office or a graduate student in the laboratory. Indeed, even among students who had been led to believe that their tests had been scored by a computer (rather than evaluated by a human scorer), most rated the statements as between good and excellent. From their own and earlier experiments of this sort, Snyder and Larson concluded that the evidence provides

> an object lesson for the users of psychological tests. People place great faith in the results of psychological tests, and their acceptance of the results as being true for them is fairly independent of test setting, administrator, and scorer. Furthermore, it must be realized that presentation of the results of psychological tests, typically represented to the individual as being for him personally, maximizes the acceptance of the psychological interpretation. Thus, the individual's acceptance of the interpretation cannot be taken as a meaningful "validation" of either the psychologist or his tests. (p. 388)

This clearly presents a serious problem for psychological researchers to overcome.

To replicate this experiment for yourself, tell a friend that you are learning how to use personality tests in class. Ask the person to make two different drawings for you: (1) a self-portrait and (2) a picture as the friend would like to look. (The Draw-a-Person Test is a projective technique used to assess personality; we will have more to say about projective techniques in Chapter 6.) In your own handwriting, copy the "interpretation" on page 15. After you offer this assessment and your friend has had an opportunity to read it, ask him or her to rate the "interpretation" as excellent, good, average, poor, or very poor. Then ask for some feedback as to how well you are doing as a "psychological examiner."

Finally, after obtaining the feedback, make sure you explain to your friend the *actual nature and purpose* of the demonstration. Complete explanation of the purpose and any deception involved in research, called **debriefing,** should remove the possibility that permanent misconceptions about psychological testing will result. It also may evoke further comments of interest. We will have more to say about deception in psychological research and the ethics of concern to practicing researchers in Chapter 2, where we examine more closely the methods of conducting personality research.

PERSONALITY RESEARCH

As stated earlier, each strategy for studying personality includes a statement of theory, procedures for assessment, methods of research, and applications derived from the theory. The importance of theory and assessment, introduced previously, are obvious to most beginning students of personality. We all have implicit personality theories, and we have informally assessed other personalities (and our own) long before studying personality psychology. Often, the importance of research seems less obvious.

Until about 100 years ago, the formal study of personality was rooted in philosophy; it proceeded almost entirely on **rational** grounds. Discussion, argument, the opinions of various authorities, and a general appeal to "reason" were the bases for settling disputes among adherents of differing viewpoints. People often cannot agree on what is reasonable, however, so the rational approach to the study of personality, by itself, offers no solid way of resolving differences of opinion. What one person regards as a great insight may seem to others like a preposterous fantasy.

An alternative to the **rational approach** is the **empirical approach,** which can be traced at least to the 17th century and John Locke. According to the empirical approach, disputes can be settled by admitting as "fact" only what is verifiable by *direct observation*. Thus, the empirical approach demands objectively verifiable data rather than circumstantial or subjective evidence. Rational considerations may give rise to theories, but they are not potent enough to contribute to validation of theories.

Empirical research involves systematic attempts to gather evidence through observations and procedures that can be repeated and confirmed by others. The four strategies we will consider (psychoanalytic, dispositional, environmental, and representational) are all committed to supporting the validity of their theories, assessment procedures, and applications through empirical research. This commitment to research distinguishes the **scientific approach** to knowledge from other approaches (Liebert & Liebert, 1995).

Scientific personality research is not a stereotyped or rigid enterprise, however. There are many scientifically legitimate ways of investigating personality. In Chapter 2, we discuss three basic methods of investigation: experimental, correlational, and case study.

We will also see, throughout this book, how research has helped dispel an intuitively obvious but incorrect idea or establish a principle or process that seemed implausible until the evidence was obtained and evaluated. Empirical demonstration is really never superfluous.

APPLICATIONS AND PERSONALITY CHANGE

The fourth issue that personality psychologists deal with is applications of their theories. Applications typically include specific assessment devices used to guide decisions about placement and treatment of individuals and techniques for personality change. Change in personality actually has two meanings: (1) naturally occurring developmental changes over time and (2) planned changes when personality "problems" arise. Natural changes, or personality development, are covered as we discuss theories. In this book, the term

personality change most commonly refers to *planned* personality change. For the most part, this term is synonymous with *psychotherapy* and is discussed in the context of describing specific techniques and methods aimed at personality change.

Personality psychology, as distinguished from abnormal psychology, primarily deals with normal personality. However, normal and abnormal personality are closely related, and personality theorists often link the two. In fact, many personality theorists began their professional careers as "clinically trained" psychologists or psychiatrists. Their theories arose from observations of their patients or clients and dealt with the development and treatment of abnormal personality and of problems in daily living. These psychologists then turned the insights they had gained from dealing with clients to their understanding of human personality in general.

A vast body of empirical evidence now exists in the field of psychopathology, so our discussions often draw on research findings from this field for support. Psychopharmacology has also contributed a great deal to our understanding of the operation of the human brain and nervous system. This area, too, is drawn on extensively throughout parts of our discussion to illustrate what we have learned about the anatomy and physiology of the human nervous system.

Running through the material presented in this book are several recurring philosophical questions. Each has been raised and addressed to varying degrees (in different ways) by both personality psychologists and philosophers. Before proceeding, we will briefly describe these issues.

RECURRING PHILOSOPHICAL QUESTIONS

Specifically, five recurring philosophical questions are embedded in the psychological study of personality.

Free Will versus Determinism

Do we have free choice, or are our actions and thoughts determined by forces and factors that are out of our control? On this fundamental matter, personality psychologists are divided. Sappington (1990) argued that the question often posed as free will versus determinism can be better understood as a continuum, ranging from hard determinism to free will, with "soft" determinism falling in between.

Proponents of hard determinism say that human behavior is entirely determined by factors beyond the control of the person. They assume that all phenomena in the universe are determined by immutable "laws" and that "the mind is governed by the same laws that govern billiard balls or fish" (Sappington, 1990, p. 1). This captures the position of the famous behaviorist B. F. Skinner, who argued that all our actions result from environmental factors and our prior experience (or learning history).

At the other end of the continuum, the free will position asserts that we control our own destinies. Free will implies that human beings are a special case, unique in nature because of our potential for self-determination. Humans, alone of nature's creatures, are seen as able to generate their own alternatives, set their own goals, and gauge their own performances. This is the view taken by personality theorist Albert Bandura, who wrote: "The capacity to exercise control over one's thought processes, motivation, and action is a distinctly human characteristic" (1989a, p. 1175).

Objective versus Subjective Aspects of Personality

Philosophers have long understood that we can never know directly what is "inside" another person; we can neither witness nor feel another's subjective experience of thoughts, objects, and events. For example, people may say that "Tom is happy" to label his smile, laughter, and jocularity, but they are really addressing only Tom's overt behavior and not necessarily any private, internal state that he is experiencing.

Some personality psychologists hold that psychology's sole concern should be with observable behavior. They argue that the scientific study of personality must rest entirely on objective evidence. However, most personality psychologists argue that the field must acknowledge and explain private, subjective experiences as well. Although Tom appears happy, he may, in fact, be miserable. Likewise, Sophie, who seems to be self-assured and "together," may have doubts and fears about her adequacy and competence. In general, outward appearances may not adequately reflect a person's "real" personality. Which view is right? That depends to some extent on how personality is defined in the first place.

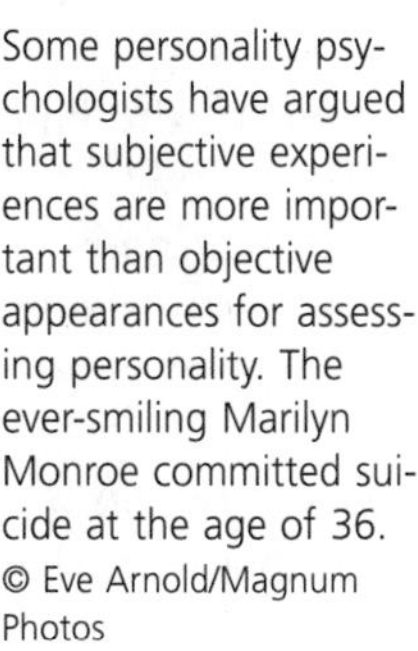

Some personality psychologists have argued that subjective experiences are more important than objective appearances for assessing personality. The ever-smiling Marilyn Monroe committed suicide at the age of 36.

The Person/Situation Controversy

To what extent are people consistent in the way they think, feel, and act in various situations? One often hears descriptions such as "John is quiet" or "Sharon is irresponsible." People speak as though these are properties of individuals, like the color of their eyes, that are always apparent and virtually unchangeable. But personality is plainly not as consistent as eye color. John, the quiet one, may be very outspoken about his hobby, stamp collecting. Sharon, the irresponsible one, may keep meticulous financial records (although she has not finished a single class assignment on time for at least 3 years).

Definitions and theories of personality differ in the way they deal with the inconsistencies in a person's behavior in different situations or at different times. Some theorists have minimized the importance of such inconsistencies, whereas others focus directly on this issue and emphasize its significance (Emmons & Diener, 1986).

Human Nature and Individuality

Henry Murray, a personality psychologist whose work we discuss in some detail in Chapter 5, noted that there are three levels to the question of human nature and individuality. The modern version of "Murray's dictum" is as follows:

> In some ways each person is like all other persons.
> In some ways each person is like some other persons.
> In some ways each person is like no other person.
> (cf. Kluckhohn & Murray, 1953; Runyan, 1983)

Personality theories differ in the degree to which they address each of these three levels. Statements at the first level relate to universals in human nature. They address primarily the mechanisms and processes of personality—that is, how personality *works*. In psychoanalysis, for example, every human being is presumed to be driven by the same underlying forces and to pass through the same sequence of stages in the development of personality. In a parallel fashion, radical behaviorists believe that we are all shaped by the rewards and punishments doled out by our environments.

At the second level, we try to categorize people according to the type of personality or array of personality traits they possess; that is, the *content* of personalities is considered. Thus, psychoanalysts speak of an "anal triad" of personality characteristics occurring in those who were especially stressed by toilet training, whereas dispositional theorists distinguish groups of people such as introverts or neurotics.

Only at the third level do we confront the idea of *uniqueness in personality*. At this level, it is the *specific* content (traits and characteristics) that is critical. Personality psychologists generally agree that every human being is unique in some way, but the implications of this uniqueness for the study of personality are controversial. One view is that each of us is so distinctive as to be understood only in terms of one particular life and set of experiences. Comparison with others, according to this approach, is not meaningful. This view, called the **idiographic approach** by personality psychologist Gordon Allport (from the Greek *idios,* meaning "personal"), has inspired extensive detailed studies of particular individuals with the aim of achieving a unique understanding of each person (Hermans, 1988).

The alternative view Allport called the **nomothetic** (no-mo-THET-ik) **approach,** which assumes that each person's uniqueness is a product of general biological and psychological laws (*nomos* is the Greek word for "law"). According to this approach, each person is a unique combination of "ingredients." Each ingredient, though, is a product of general processes. The processes can be understood by investigating specific aspects of personality in a wide variety of individuals. The goal is to formulate laws of behavior that hold for people in general.

Goals of Personality Psychology: Description, Prediction, Control, and Understanding

The goals of personality psychology are description, prediction, control, and understanding. **Description** involves effectively measuring and communicating about important personality dimensions. **Prediction** is accurately anticipating the likelihood of occurrence of various behaviors. **Control,** as used here, means influencing behavior.

Suppose a theory suggests that "conscientious" people tend to earn higher GPAs in college. If a means of assessing the variable called conscientiousness is provided, we can now assess and describe subjects' relative positions on this dimension. We then can begin to make comparisons, yielding the potential for prediction. If we know that Barbara is very conscientious, we can predict (based on our working theory) that she will earn better grades than less conscientious students. We might even begin to exert some control (influence) over her behavior by emphasizing the importance of, say, being "responsible" (a variable presumed to be related to conscientiousness) about her coursework and study habits.

Description, prediction, and control are more or less straightforward ideas. The meaning of *understanding* is elusive and more ambiguous. **Understanding** usually refers to comprehension of a particular process and the ability to provide an explanation of it. But the level of comprehension and explanation sufficient for a person to say "I understand" varies from individual to individual. For most automobile drivers, it is enough to know that their cars will not start due to mechanical failure. Others might require further explanation, such as an electrical short in the ignition, but mechanically inclined drivers may not be satisfied with this information. Some may want to know exactly where the short was and what caused it—as well as precisely how to fix it and prevent recurrence. Understanding can thus mean very different things to different people.

People vary in the extent or amount of information they want or can handle in any particular situation. Consider the most "mechanically minded" people who needed to know exactly what prevented the car from starting. When seeking the opinion of an internist about a persistent sore throat, these same people may have no interest in the specific bacterium that caused the irritation. They may only care that it can be effectively treated and relieved.

What people mean when they say they adequately "understand" a phenomenon may be dramatically different, and the amount and specificity of the information they require to say this may well vary by subject area, previous exposure and knowledge, as well as other specific circumstances. Whether they perceive some degree of control over future occurrences and whether they actually believe the current circumstances will ever recur may influence the amount of information people desire at any particular time.

PLAN OF THIS BOOK

This book is divided into six parts. Part I includes this overview chapter and Chapter 2, which deals with the most common methods of personality research that will be drawn on for the remainder of the book. The next four parts are devoted to descriptions of the theories, research, applications, and limitations of each of the four strategies for the study of personality: psychoanalytic, dispositional, environmental, and representational. Thus, we present the study of personality in terms of a 4×4 matrix, as illustrated in Figure 1.3.

Each strategy section opens with an introductory chapter that should be read first. You may also want to reread it after you complete the entire section to help you integrate what you have learned about the specific strategy.

Our aim is to convey a sense of the nature of these strategies. The formats, emphases, and writing styles of Parts II through V vary somewhat to be consistent with the flavor and customs of each strategy. Each strategy is presented in a generally positive light that serves to highlight its strengths and assets. In essence, each strategy is described from the viewpoint of its own

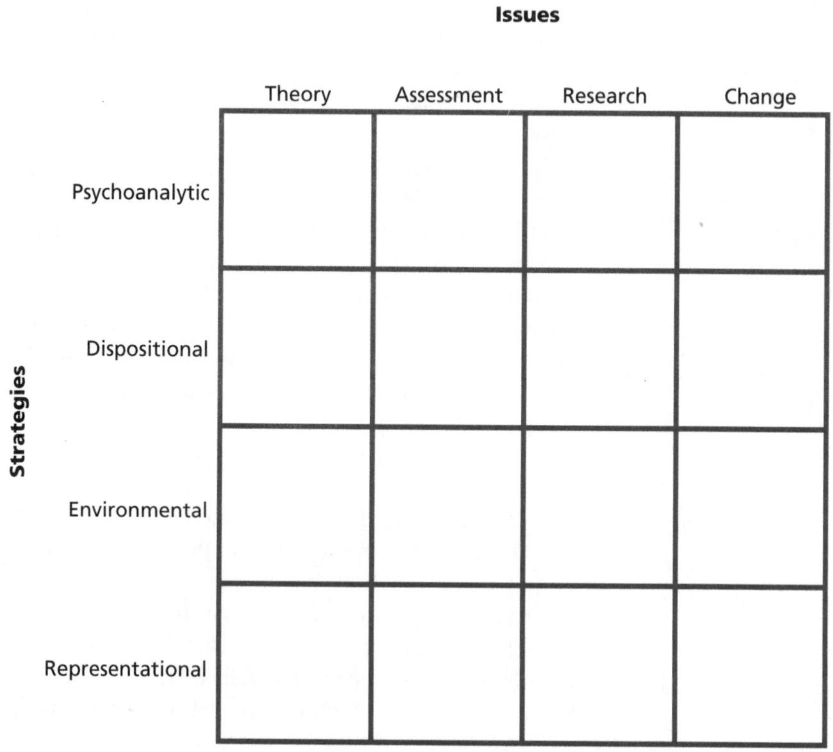

Issues

Strategies	Theory	Assessment	Research	Change
Psychoanalytic				
Dispositional				
Environmental				
Representational				

Figure 1.3
Personality can be studied from the perspective of four different strategies, each of which is concerned with the same four issues.

adherents, which we believe is the best way to learn about each strategy and to allow for the most objective evaluation of the overlap and contrasts between the various strategies.

The last section in each part deals with the strategy's applications and limitations. Applications include both specific techniques for assessment of personality and methods and therapies for personality change derived from the theories of the strategy to the extent that the proponents actually address them. In the limitations sections, we adopt the stance of a harsh critic to emphasize each strategy's particular weaknesses. Many of our criticisms can be leveled at more than one strategy, and no strategy is free of critics. Again we try to present the limitations of each strategy objectively to complement the positive light in which each strategy was presented in the preceding chapters. The limitations sections are not intended as complete critiques or thoroughly evenhanded evaluations; rather, they illustrate the range of limitations and problems of each strategy when applied to the full scope of the study of human personality. Overall, our aim is to give readers an opportunity to evaluate the merits and liabilities of each strategy, thereby providing an optimal introduction to the entire field of personality psychology.

The final part of this book contains a brief epilogue that attempts to integrate the earlier material into a meaningful whole. Here, we focus most intensively on the areas of overlap and reiterate the contrasts between the four strategies. We also try to provide a framework from which to view and evaluate the many theories presented in the earlier chapters. We hope to leave you with a coherent overview of the field of personality psychology as it looks today.

SUMMARY

1. The modern idea of personality and the concept of the "real" person are only about 200 years old.
2. Personality psychology is the study of the totality of the individual, including common and unique features and how they impact on and influence people's behavior relative to their environment; a more specific definition of personality depends on theoretical considerations.
3. Empirical research is the hallmark of the scientific study of personality. Such research involves systematic attempts to gather evidence through observations and procedures that can be repeated and verified by others.
4. Personality psychology is really the intersection of many branches of psychology. It draws on and integrates findings from numerous sources.
5. Strategies represent broad assumptions underlying the orientation and approach to personality adopted by psychologists. We identify four basic strategies as the starting point for the scientific study of personality.
6. Each of the four strategies can be captured by its central underlying assumption. The Psychoanalytic Strategy focuses on drives as the most important determinant of personality. The Dispositional Strategy emphasizes differences in the quantity of each of the innate

characteristics of the person. The Environmental Strategy emphasizes aspects of the external world (social and physical) and their impact on the person. The Representational Strategy looks to private mental representations of people, events, and things as they are experienced by the person as determinants of personality.

7. Four fundamental issues concern all those interested in the scientific study of personality: theory, research, assessment, and applications of theory to personality change.
8. Scientific theories serve several important functions. They organize and clarify observations and communication, produce a sense of understanding, and guide future research.
9. Evaluation of theories involves seven major criteria: empirical validity, parsimony, comprehensiveness, coherence, testability, usefulness, and acceptability.
10. Theories are better judged based on their utility than on such criteria as right or wrong or true or false.
11. Theory, assessment, research, and applications are all heavily interdependent. Each often serves to define and inform the others over time.
12. Personality assessment may take many forms. Self-reports, accounts of others, direct observation, and archival records are all used by personality psychologists.
13. Applications of theory most often take the form of either (1) specific assessment devices used to direct treatment and placement in educational and vocational settings or (2) methods of treatment aimed at personality change and alleviation of problems in daily living.
14. The philosophical question of free will versus determinism divides personality theorists. Personality psychologists also differ in the degree of emphasis they put on the subjective and objective aspects of human functioning, on the relative emphasis they place on the person versus the situation, and in their approach to the study of personality (nomothetic or idiographic). Finally, there is the question of whether description, prediction, and control are the only goals of personality psychology or whether "understanding" is or should be a major goal in itself.

CHAPTER TWO

Methods of Personality Research and Assessment

ersonality research involves asking and answering questions about why people act, feel, and think as they do. In this chapter, we describe how personality psychologists carry out their research and assessment efforts. You have probably already encountered most of these topics and issues if you have taken an introductory course in psychology or research methods.

THREE BASIC APPROACHES TO PERSONALITY RESEARCH: OVERVIEW

Three major research approaches have been used to gather information about personality: case studies, correlational studies, and experiments. **Systematic observation** of behavior is the element that the three methods have in common. Systematic observation entails carefully monitoring or measuring and recording behavior in prescribed ways—that is, observing behavior of subjects at precise points in time, at prescribed intervals, or under specified conditions or circumstances.

The major differences between the three methods are found in (1) the types of observations made, (2) the circumstances in which the observations are made, and (3) how the data from the observations are examined.

A **case study** involves a detailed qualitative description of the behavior of a single individual. Case studies yield a depth and richness of information that cannot be obtained with correlational studies and experiments.

A **correlational study** examines the quantitative relationship between two or more **variables** (factors, characteristics, or events that may assume a range of values) for a group of people observed under the same conditions. An **experiment** looks at the quantitative relationship between conditions that are systematically varied and are expected to cause specific changes in people's behavior.

In principle, most research questions can be answered by using any of the three basic methods. How the questions are stated and the type of answers sought determine the method used. In addition, considerations of ethical issues, feasibility, and economy also influence the choice of method.

Before examining each of the methods in detail, we will take a single, broad question—Does viewing violence on television affect the aggressive behavior of children?—and see how it has been investigated with each method. This comparison will illustrate how the same basic question can be approached in different ways.

Televised Violence and Aggression: Case Studies

The earliest investigations of TV violence and children's aggressive behavior were case studies of individual youngsters who had apparently been deeply influenced by events they had seen depicted on television. Following are two excerpts from case studies involving TV and aggressive behavior (Schramm, Lyle, & Parker, 1961).

> In Los Angeles, a housemaid caught a 7-year-old boy in the act of sprinkling ground glass into the family's lamb stew. There was no malice behind the act. It was purely experimental [not in the scientific sense!], having been inspired by curiosity to learn whether it would really work as well as it did on television. . . . (p. 161)

> A 13-year-old . . . boy who said he received his inspiration from a television program, admitted to police . . . that he sent threatening notes to a . . . school teacher. [The idea] for the first letter came while he was helping the pastor of his church write some letters. When the minister left the office for an hour, the boy wrote his first poison-pen letter. "I got the idea when I saw it happen on TV," he told Juvenile Sergeant George Rathouser. "I saw it on the 'Lineup' program." (p. 164)

These reports are of isolated incidents, but they certainly raise the possibility that TV violence could inspire aggressive acts. (In fact, in several recent incidents children emulated the behavior depicted in the TV program *Beavis and Butthead*, resulting in loss of life and property.) More children must be examined in a systematic manner to determine whether such a relationship exists for the general population and not just for the few children described in the case studies. Furthermore, if researchers want to know how strong the relationship is between TV violence and aggression among children in general, they need *quantitative data* (numbers) and a relatively large number of youngsters to supplement the qualitative descriptions that case studies provide. The correlational method can satisfy these additional requirements.

Televised Violence and Aggression: Correlational Studies

Numerous correlational studies have provided quantitative evidence of a relationship between viewing TV violence and aggression for children in general (Centerwell, 1989; Liebert & Sprafkin, 1988). For example, one study correlated the viewing habits and antisocial behaviors of 2300 junior and senior high school students in Maryland (McIntyre & Teevan, 1972). First, the students were asked to list their four favorite TV programs, "the ones you watch every time they are on the air." A numerical rating of violence was assigned to each program, and an average violence score was computed for each subject. Second, the students completed a self-report checklist of various antisocial behaviors (e.g., serious fights at school). The subjects indicated how often they engaged in each behavior using a simple numerical scale (0 = never, 1 = once, 2 = twice or more).

The researchers now had two numerical scores for each of the 2300 students. One score was the degree of violence in their preferred TV programs; the other score was a measure of their antisocial behavior. It was thus possible to statistically examine the nature of the relationship *(correlation)* between these two sets of scores. The correlation in this study indicated a direct relationship between the antisocial behavior and program violence ratings: The more violent the programs watched, the greater the incidence of antisocial behavior.

Televised Violence and Aggression: Experiments

The correlational evidence does not prove that violence depicted on television *caused* any aggressive behavior. It reveals only that the amount of TV violence watched is *related* to the frequency of exhibiting some antisocial behaviors. It is possible that performing deviant behaviors makes youngsters more interested in watching violent TV programs, rather than vice versa.

Cause-and-effect relationships can be demonstrated most clearly by the experimental method. For example, Liebert and Baron (1972) hypothesized that children who saw violent TV programs would be significantly more willing to hurt other children than would children who saw nonviolent programs. To test this hypothesis, boys and girls ages 5 through 9 were left alone to watch television briefly. The TV episodes they saw came from actual television shows. Half of the children saw an episode with a chase, two fist fights, two shootings, and a knifing. The other half of the children saw an exciting (high-action but nonviolent) sports episode of equal length.

After watching television, each child was brought to another room and seated in front of a large box with wires leading into the next room. On the box were a green button, labeled HELP, and a red button, labeled HURT. Over the two buttons was a white light. The experimenter explained that the wires were connected to a game a child in another room was going to play. The game involved turning a handle; each time the child started to turn the handle, the white light would come on.

The experimenter explained that by pushing the buttons, the subject could either help the other child by making the handle easier to turn or hurt the other child by making the handle hot. The subjects were told that the longer they pushed the buttons, the more they helped or hurt the other child. Finally, the experimenter said that they had to push one of the two buttons every time the light came on. The experimenter then left the room, and the light came on 20 times. (In fact, there was no other child, and the subjects' responses had no effect on anyone.)

How long a child pushed the HURT button was the measure of aggression. The investigators found that children who had viewed the violent

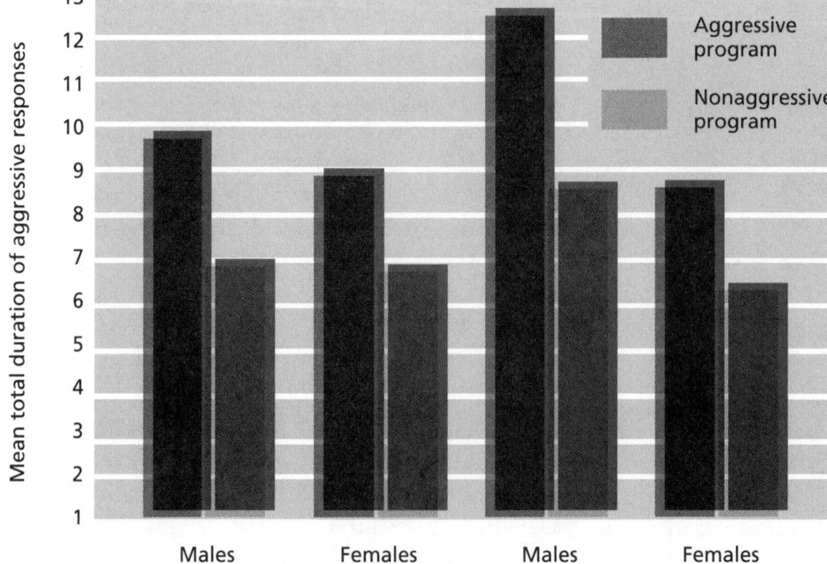

Figure 2.1
Mean total duration of aggressive responses in Liebert and Baron's (1972) experiment.
Source: "Some Immediate Effects of Televised Violence on Children's Behavior" by R. M. Liebert and R. A. Baron, 1972, *Developmental Psychology, 6,* pp. 469–475.

programming were significantly more willing to "hurt" another child by impeding their success than were those who saw the sports episode. As Figure 2.1 shows, this finding appeared for boys and girls in both age groups. Because the only difference between the two groups of children at the outset was the TV episode they saw, it is reasonable to conclude that watching the violent TV episode caused the greater willingness to hurt other children.

The same basic question can be approached with different methods of research, as you have just seen. Each strategy for the study of personality may favor a particular type of research for one reason or another, but all three basic research methods are at times used within each strategy. Before proceeding with a detailed discussion of each research approach, a brief overview of the ethical rules that guide research in psychology is warranted (Box 2.1).

Box 2.1
ETHICAL CONSIDERATIONS IN PSYCHOLOGICAL RESEARCH

The conduct of psychological research is in part guided by the ethical standards of psychologists spelled out in detail in the 1992 American Psychological Association's (APA) code of ethics (American Psychological Association Ethics Committee, 1992). This document addresses the basic responsibilities of all psychologists, as well as expectations for their professional behavior. It also describes in detail the specific standards of behavior to be adhered to within a variety of professional and scientific roles and activities, including the conduct and reporting of research. Most of the details of this document do not concern us now, but you must understand the basic gist of the guidelines to appreciate the influence they exert over the quest for knowledge about personality.

Broadly speaking, researchers in psychology must design research to maximize the information gained while minimizing the risk of harm to subjects. Here are the major principles.

Confidentiality of subjects must be respected and protected at all times.

Deception is to be avoided wherever possible. When deception of any sort is used, subjects must be informed of the nature of the deception at the earliest possible time. Subjects must also be restored to their previous state as quickly and effectively as possible by the researcher. Deception is justifiable only when other methods are not feasible and the potential scientific gains of the research outweigh the risks involved.

Informed consent means subjects must be informed of the nature of the research and their rights and responsibilities as subjects (including the right to withdraw from participation at any time without risk of penalty or prejudice). It includes full disclosure of any potential risk of harm or aversive experiences involved in participation.

Debriefing is a formal procedure at the end of subjects' participation in a research project when researchers reveal to them the nature of the project and the methods employed (including any deception used). Subjects must also be provided with some means of contacting the researcher should future problems arise and to learn the outcome of the research at its conclusion.

Before a research project can be initiated, the researcher must formally propose the project to a review board (usually referred to as an IRB, for *I*nstitutional *R*eview *B*oard). The IRB is composed of research peers and community mem-

Box continued on following page

Box 2.1 *Continued*
ETHICAL CONSIDERATIONS IN PSYCHOLOGICAL RESEARCH

bers who review the planned research and determine its potential worth and risks before allowing it to proceed.

These various precautions have a cost, however. If subjects are fully informed about the purpose of the research, they may produce biased results by responding differently than they might in the natural environment. Also, it is often impossible to inform subjects, such as with "naturalistic" observation of people in their own environment. These and similar considerations represent a challenge for researchers. Not only must their research be designed to provide an adequate test of the hypotheses of interest but it also must not unduly harm or deceive the subjects involved. These requirements, combined with methodological constraints, determine and restrict the type of research conducted.

THE EXPERIMENTAL METHOD

The **experimental method,** sometimes called "the *true* experiment," requires that two criteria be met: (1) A factor that is hypothesized to cause the behavior being studied is systematically varied, while (2) all other possible causative factors are held constant.

In an experiment, the factor that is varied systematically is the **independent variable.** In the Liebert and Baron experiment we discussed earlier, TV violence was the independent variable; it was varied by being either present (for experimental subjects) or absent (for control subjects) in the content of the program they saw.

The behavior that is to be observed is the **dependent variable.** The dependent variable is expected to be *caused by,* or *depend on,* the independent variable. Total time pressing the HURT button was Liebert and Baron's dependent variable.

In the simplest experiment, two groups of otherwise similar subjects are used. Subjects in an **experimental group** are exposed to the independent variable (the hypothesized causal factor or treatment), and subjects in a **control group** are not. In all other respects, the groups are treated alike. If the two groups differ on the dependent variable (the behavior being measured), the difference must be due to the independent variable. In our example, the only difference between the two groups was the television episode they watched.

Suppose the experimental group happened to have a higher proportion of "naturally aggressive children" than the control group. In that case, the greater aggression observed in experimental subjects might not have been due to a difference in the TV episodes they watched. To eliminate the possible effects of such **confounding variables** (factors inadvertently allowed to co-vary with group assignment), groups in an experiment must be equivalent in such matters as subjects' personal characteristics. Usually, this is done by assigning subjects to the groups *randomly.*

Random assignment means that every subject has an equal chance of being placed in each group. The intended result is that differences in subjects' personal characteristics, such as "natural aggressiveness," will tend to equalize across groups. Thus, no group has a disproportionate number of subjects with *any* particular characteristic.

Matched random assignment is a way to enhance our confidence that subjects' personal characteristics are equally distributed in each group. Relevant subject characteristics (i.e., those that may cause changes in the behavior being studied) are assessed before the subjects are assigned to groups. Then, subjects are paired so that each member of a pair has the same value of the characteristic. Finally, one member of each pair is randomly assigned to each group.

The experimental method provides a high degree of **control** over the context, environment, and subject characteristics. (Control in this context refers to systematically varying, randomizing, or holding constant the conditions under which observations are made.) It increases the probability that treatment groups are equivalent across conditions *on all but* the presence of the variable(s) of interest. Such control makes the logical demonstration of cause-and-effect relationships more plausible. The presence of these controls contributes to the confidence we have in our conclusion that the variables under study, and not some other extraneous factor, caused the observed effect.

In studies that use groups of subjects, average performance is examined. Liebert and Baron found that on average, children exposed to a violent TV program were more aggressive than children who were exposed to a nonviolent sports program. However, the amount of aggression among subjects in each group varied. Thus, some experimental subjects may have exhibited less aggression than some control subjects.

True experiments can have more than two groups, and a no-treatment control group is not always required. Instead of just having the independent variable present or absent, different amounts or levels of the independent variable can be examined. For example, a logical next step to Liebert and Baron's experiment might be to examine the hypothesis that the more TV violence children observe, the more aggression they exhibit. Testing this hypothesis would require three or more groups, each watching a different amount of TV violence (e.g., 10, 30, and 60 minutes). In this experiment, comparisons would be between groups exposed to different amounts of TV violence. A no-violence control group is not necessary because the hypothesis concerns only varying degrees of TV violence. Like the simpler experiment, however, it would be necessary to assign children to groups randomly, so that the only difference among the groups was the independent variable (amount of TV violence watched).

Evaluation of the Experimental Method

The major advantage of the experimental method is that it increases our confidence that the relationships observed are, in fact, cause-and-effect relationships. Changes in the dependent variable can be *causally* linked to the independent variable because all other relevant variables (influences) are controlled.

Experiments often are conducted in a psychological laboratory, where tight control over conditions is possible. The price paid for such control may be **artificiality** because the context is so different from real life. For example, watching TV in a psychology laboratory is not exactly the same as watching TV at home. Similarly, pushing a HURT button is obviously different from physically assaulting another child on the street. For conclusions to be meaningful, the experimental conditions must be similar enough to the real-life circumstances of interest. Most experimentalists want to *generalize* from what is found in the experiment to real life.

As you will see, the correlational and case study methods involve less control over relevant variables, but they often preserve a more natural environment and thus make generalization more plausible.

THE CORRELATIONAL METHOD

Correlational studies answer questions about the relationship between variables. **Correlation** means co- or joint relationship. Questions of relationship between two measures are often asked about personality. (Are problems in toilet training related to compulsiveness in adulthood? Is the frequency of dating in college related to marital satisfaction?) The correlational method makes observations of all subjects under the *same conditions.* (Note the contrast with the experimental method, in which the conditions under which subjects are observed are systematically varied.)

In a correlational study, a pair of observations is collected for each member of a group of subjects. Suppose, for example, Professor Curious is interested in whether a relationship exists between how close students sit to the front of the classroom and course grade. The professor could list the number of the row in which each student chose to sit at the beginning of the semester and each student's final grade in the course, as in Table 2.1. These data could be used to correlate seating and final grade. Notice that all the subjects in this correlational study were observed under the same conditions. (An experiment might have been conducted here by *randomly assigning* students to seating at the start of the course.)

Knowing that two variables are correlated is usually not sufficient. We also want to know (1) the strength of the relationship and (2) the way the variables relate. The *magnitude* (strength) of a correlation tells us how well one variable

Table 2.1 Data from a hypothetical study of the relationship between how close a student sits to the front of the classroom and final course grade

SUBJECT	ROW	FINAL GRADE	SUBJECT	ROW	FINAL GRADE
Andy	2	76	Linda	5	71
Ann	5	60	Mary	1	95
Bill	4	79	Pam	1	87
Bob	3	67	Pat	3	80
Eric	1	82	Quiana	3	75
Hector	2	91	Robert	4	81
Jerry	2	86	Sal	2	82
Joan	5	64	Sheila	5	55
Juan	4	62	Shelley	3	90
Ken	4	66	Steve	1	99

can predict the other variable. The higher the numerical magnitude of the correlation, the more accurate the prediction.

Two variables can be related directly or inversely, which is referred to as the ***direction of the correlation***. A **direct** or **positive correlation** between variable *X* and variable *Y* means that high scores on *X* tend to be associated with high scores on *Y*, and low scores on *X* tend to go with low scores on *Y*. For example, a positive correlation is regularly found between the IQs of parents and children; generally, brighter parents have brighter children.

In contrast, in an **inverse** or **negative correlation,** high scores on *X* are associated with low scores on *Y*, and low scores on *X* go with high scores on *Y*. Age and quickness of reflexes are negatively correlated; the older people are, the slower their reflexes.

The correlation between two variables can be visually represented by plotting the scores to make a **scatter diagram** (or scatter plot). Look at the scatter diagrams in Figure 2.2. One variable is plotted on the horizontal axis, and the other on the vertical axis. Each point represents one subject's scores on each of the two variables.

The ***magnitude of the correlation*** is reflected by how closely the points in the scatter diagram conform to a straight line, the line of perfect correlation. In a perfect correlation, all the points fall on a single straight line (Figures 2.2*A* and 2.2*B*). Knowing a person's score on one of the variables (it makes no difference which one) enables perfect prediction of the person's score on the other variable (as Figure 2.3 depicts).

With high or strong (but not perfect) correlations, there is some "scatter" (deviation) around the line of perfect correlation (Figures 2.2*C* and 2.2*D*), but the points tend to fall within a narrow ellipse, making prediction of one variable from the other reasonably accurate. The lower or weaker the correlation, the more scatter there is. Figures 2.2*E* and 2.2*F* show a moderately strong correlation. When no systematic (linear) relationship exists between the variables, the points are scattered all over, making it impossible to predict one variable from the other (Figure 2.2*G*).

The direction of the correlation is determined by the direction in which the points are oriented. If the points plotted generally converge around a line that goes from *bottom left to top right,* the correlation is *positive* or direct (Figures 2.2*A*, 2.2*C*, and 2.2*E*). If the points travel from *top left to bottom right,* the correlation is *negative* or inverse (Figures 2.2*B*, 2.2*D*, and 2.2*F*). The data from Professor Curious's study of the relationship between seating and grades (Table 2.1, p. 32) are plotted in Figure 2.4. Most of the data points fall in a narrow ellipse, indicating a high-magnitude correlation or strong relationship. The points are oriented from upper left to lower right, indicating a negative correlation. Thus, there is a general tendency for students who sit close to the front of the room (i.e., lower row number) to earn higher grades.

The **correlation coefficient** (abbreviated *r*) is a numerical index of the correlation between two variables. It is calculated by means of a mathematical formula. Correlation coefficients range from +1.00 to −1.00. The direction of the correlation is indicated by the algebraic sign, plus (+) for a positive correlation and minus (−) for a negative correlation.

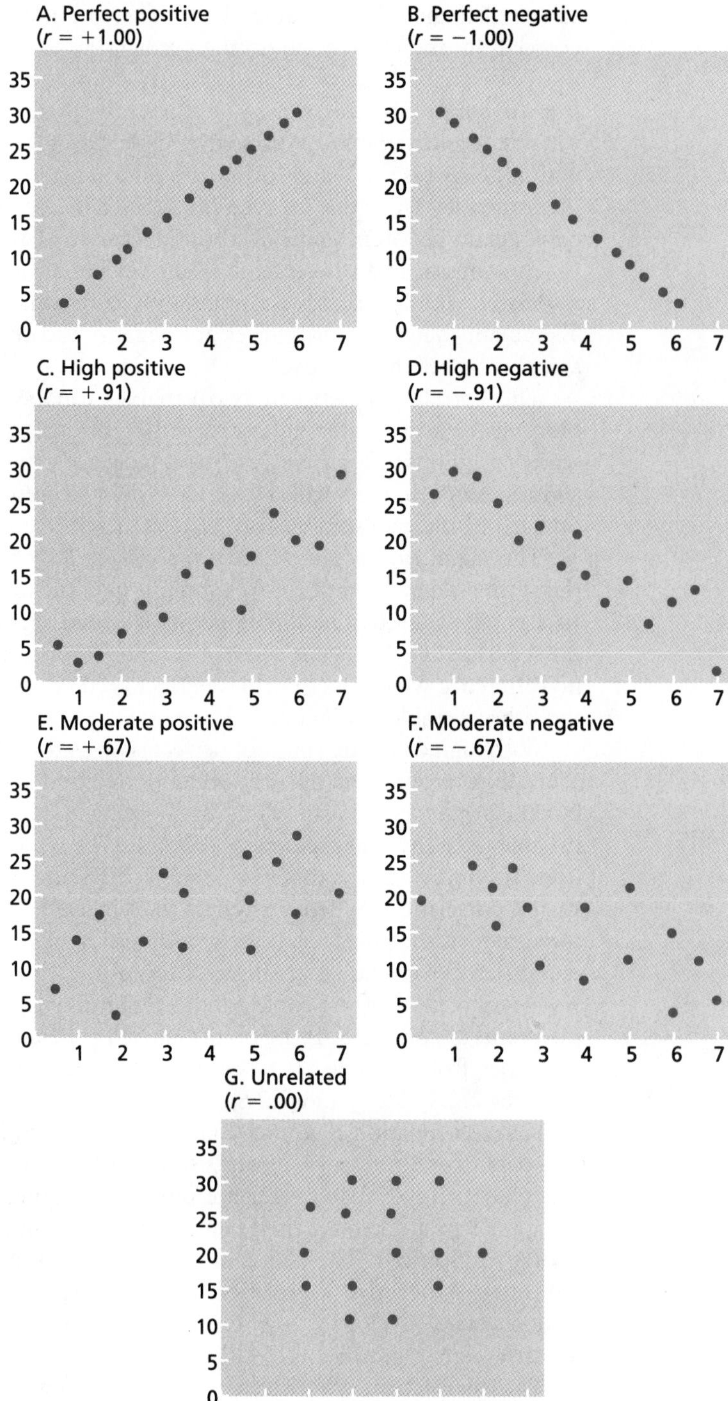

Figure 2.2
Scatter diagrams showing various degrees of relationship between two variables.

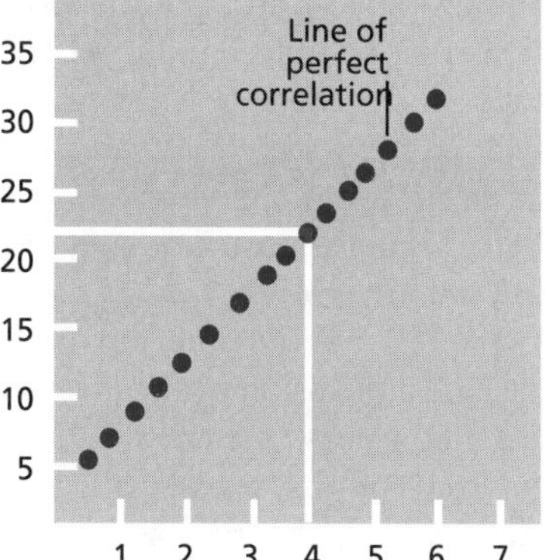

Figure 2.3
In a scatter plot of correlational data, the intersection of the line of perfect correlation of two lines drawn at right angles to each axis allows prediction of one variable from another. For example, a person obtaining a score of 4 on variable *X* would obtain a score of 22 on variable *Y*.

The magnitude of correlation is indicated by the absolute (numerical) value of the correlation coefficient. A correlation coefficient of 1.00 (+ or –) indicates a perfect correlation; either variable can be exactly predicted from the other. As the coefficient decreases in absolute value from 1.00 to 0, the ability to predict one variable from the other decreases. In the extreme, a correlation of 0 indicates that the variables are not linearly related; with a zero correlation, knowledge of one variable would not assist at all in predicting the other. (More complex or *curvilinear* relationships might exist, but they cannot be detected and measured with this technique.)

How closely two variables are related depends only on the absolute size of the correlation coefficient. Thus, correlation coefficients of +.60 and –.60 are equivalent in their ability to predict one variable from the other. The correspondence between correlation coefficients and scatter diagrams can be seen in Figure 2.2 (p. 34), where the correlation coefficient is provided (in parentheses) for each diagram.

Let us return one last time to the research conducted by Professor Curious. The resulting correlation coefficient for the data collected is $r = -.79$. This correlation coefficient reflects a high degree of association and an inverse relationship between the two variables measured. Again, no variable was manipulated in this study: Students were free to choose their own seats

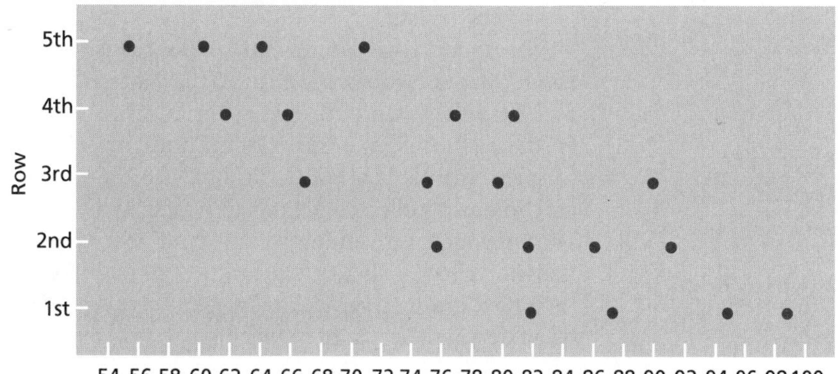

Figure 2.4
Scatter diagram of data (presented in Table 2.1) from a hypothetical study of the relationship between how close a student sits to the front of the classroom and final course grade ($r = -.79$).

at the outset. However, some arbitrary decisions were made by Professor Curious, and these decisions did indeed influence the resulting data. Professor Curious counted the rows of the lecture hall numbering from the front of the room toward the back of the room. Thus, in the resulting data set higher grades were associated with lower row numbers yielding a *negative* (inverse) correlation ($r = -.79$). He might, instead, have counted rows from the rear toward the front, *which would have resulted in a correlation coefficient of exactly the same magnitude* ($r = .79$), but the *direction* of the relationship would have been *positive* (direct). The conclusion drawn from the data and the resulting correlation coefficient might be worded somewhat differently: Students who sit farther from the front of the room tend to earn lower grades. The implications of the results, though, are exactly the same. There is, indeed, a strong relationship between seating and grades earned, and the closer a student sits to the front of the room, the higher the grades earned tend to be! It is extremely important that researchers (and consumers) are aware of any decisions made explicitly or implicitly in the course of designing research or collecting data and how these decisions influence the results obtained.

Evaluation of the Correlational Method

The correlational method involves making observations without controlling the subjects' behaviors or varying the circumstances under which the subjects are observed. The natural environment of the situation is preserved, which may bring the research closer to real life than is possible with the experimental method.

Generally, the correlational method has four advantages over the experimental method. First, some variables of interest to personality researchers are difficult or impossible to vary systematically. A researcher simply cannot vary sex, age, or birth order, for example, and it would be clearly *unethical* to induce traumatic experiences such as rape and kidnapping to study their effects on people (see Box 2.1).

Second, collecting data on a variable as it naturally occurs—as is done in correlational studies—may allow a researcher to examine the variable over a broader range than is possible in experiments. For instance, in studying the effects of stress, it is not ethical to induce more than brief, mild stress in research subjects, but in externally induced stressful situations (e.g., disasters, naturally occurring or human-made), personality psychologists can collect data that may help them learn what factors are associated with severe and prolonged stress.

One such correlational study was carried out during a massive power failure that encompassed much of the Eastern Seaboard of the United States on November 9 and 10, 1965. The blackout occurred in New York City at 5:30 P.M., the height of rush hour. Thousands of people using mass transit had to spend the night in public facilities. In the early morning hours, a team of psychologists collected data from people in a bus terminal and a hotel lobby, both of which were illuminated by emergency power (Zucker, Manosevitz, & Lanyon, 1968). They asked people to complete a questionnaire asking for their birth order, their feelings about being stranded for the night, their level of anxiety, and their preference for being alone or with other people. In addition, before approaching a subject, the investigators noted whether the person was talking to or standing with someone else.

Previous laboratory experiments that created mild stress in subjects had indicated that firstborn persons tend to show more anxiety and a greater preference to be with other people when confronted with stress-inducing conditions than do persons lower in birth order. The data collected during the blackout generally confirmed the previous findings and extended them to a real crisis situation.

A third advantage of correlational investigations over experiments is that correlational studies allow researchers to examine a large number of variables simultaneously. This is important because, in real life, people's behaviors are always influenced by multiple factors. In experiments, the number of independent variables usually is limited to one or two. A fourth advantage is that correlational studies are often more economical than experiments in terms of time, effort, and expense. Correlational data frequently are collected under conditions that already exist, so there is no need to "set up" situations.

Correlation and Causation

The major limitation of correlational research relative to experimental research is that conclusions about cause-and-effect relationships usually cannot be convincingly drawn. Knowing that two variables are correlated does not tell a researcher which is the cause of the other; this dilemma is known as the **directionality problem.** Consider the positive correlation often observed between grades and class attendance in college. One possible explanation is that attending more classes increases the amount learned and thus results in higher grades. An equally plausible interpretation is that good grades enhance a student's feelings about a particular course or subject matter, which encourages students who earn them to attend class more often. Other possibilities exist as well; for example, differences in available time might also account for the observed differences.

In many correlational studies, the problem of directionality cannot be resolved. There are exceptions, however. Some relationships can be logically conceptualized in one direction only. For instance, there is a negative correlation between the amount of alcohol consumed and the speed of one's reflexes. Obviously, this relationship makes sense only in one direction; the speed of your reflexes is not likely to influence how much you drink (except perhaps in a drinking contest).

Longitudinal studies (research in which data are collected over time from the same subjects) may also address the directionality problem. **Temporal precedence** is accepted as one criterion for causality; that is, for one factor to *cause* (or effect a change) in another factor, the first factor must *be present* in time *before* the dependent change occurs. This fact alone does not rule out the possibility of some other variable intervening to cause the effect, though.

It is still possible that both variables could be caused by some other common factor; this possibility is referred to as the **third-variable problem.** Consider, for example, the positive correlation observed between the number of churches in a city and the number of crimes committed in that city; the more churches a city has, the more crimes are committed in it. Does this mean that religion fosters crime? Probably not. That crime fosters religion? Unlikely. The relationship is due to a *third variable*—population. The more people there are in any particular city, the more churches *and* the more crimes.

That causation cannot be inferred directly from correlational evidence does not mean that a cause-and-effect relationship does not exist. It merely means that the correlational method by itself does not permit the identification of the nature of the causal relationship.

Sometimes it is unnecessary to know whether one variable causes the other or whether a third variable is responsible, particularly in applied areas of psychology in which only prediction of a criterion is required. For instance, college admissions committees use high school grades as one criterion to predict success in college. Typically, there is a moderate to high positive correlation between grades in high school and academic achievement in college. Thus, admissions committees can do their jobs without being concerned with the underlying causes of college (or, for that matter, high school) achievement. To gain firsthand experience with correlational research, see the demonstration contained in Box 2.2.

Box 2.2
DEMONSTRATION: CORRELATION: IT'S A PLOT

The best way to gain an understanding of the basics of correlational research is to do some yourself, which is easier than it might sound.

Correlational data consist of pairs of observations gathered from a number of subjects. You can quickly gather such data by asking 15 to 20 people of the same gender for their height and weight.

Once you have collected 15 or more observation pairs, the next step is to make a scatter diagram of them. Remove the graph for Demonstration 2.1 from the Demonstration Materials section at the back of the book (or use a piece of graph paper). Looking at your data, determine the range of weights by finding the highest and lowest. Make these the end points of the horizontal axis. Then divide the axis into equal units. Next, find the range of heights in inches and set up the vertical axis in the same way.

Now plot a single point to represent each person's height *and* weight by finding the point on the graph where these two values intersect for each.

Finally, examine the scatter diagram of your points to determine the nature and strength of the correlation. How are the points oriented? You will no doubt find that they go from bottom left to top right, which indicates a positive correlation (taller people generally are heavier). The points should roughly fall in the shape of an ellipse. Compare your scatter diagram to Figure 2.2*C* (p. 34). If the points make a tighter (flatter) ellipse than that shown in the figure, then you have obtained a strong correlation. If the points make more of a circle (as in Figure 2.2*G*) than an ellipse, you need to collect more data. Adding five to ten more points should make your scatter diagram more elliptical. (If most of the points fit with an ellipse and just a few points are clearly out of the bounds of the ellipse, you can safely ignore the "outliers" for our purposes.)

STATISTICAL SIGNIFICANCE AND PRACTICAL IMPORTANCE

In an experiment or correlational study, a small group of people (subjects), called a **sample,** is selected from a much larger group of people, called a **population.** Personality researchers usually study a sample—a subset of the relevant population—because it is not feasible to deal with an entire population, such as all children who watch television.

However, the researcher usually wants to be able to draw conclusions about the population, not just about the particular sample under investigation); that is, the researcher wishes to *generalize.* To do so, the researcher makes *inferences* about the population based on observed characteristics of the sample. For the inferences to be meaningful, the findings from the sample must be *reliable.* In other words, the researcher must be able to count on the findings occurring again, with a different sample from the same population.

Statistical significance is the standard measure of the probability of obtaining the results of quantitative research based on chance. It is computed mathematically through the application of *statistical tests,* which provide the researcher with an estimate of the probability that the finding from a sample is due to chance alone. The *lower* that probability, the more likely the finding is due to some factor *other than mere chance.*

In psychological research, a finding is usually considered statistically significant if the odds are less than 5 in 100 that it is due to chance alone. This is written "$p < .05$" and is read "probability less than 5% (or, 5 in 100)." Statistical significance can be computed for either experimental or correlational findings.

Statistical significance refers *only* to the probability of a given finding (failing any actual effect of variables under investigation); it does *not* imply that the finding is important, socially relevant, or practically meaningful. It is possible that a statistically significant finding may have little or no practical import. This applies equally to findings at the $p < .05$ *and* $p < .00001$ level of statistical significance.

To use a somewhat whimsical example, suppose a sample of able-bodied people were randomly assigned to an experimental group in which subjects had their feet tied together and a control group in which they did not. Both groups are asked to climb three flights of stairs as fast as they can. Not surprisingly, the experimental group is found to climb significantly more slowly (at the $p < .0001$ level) than the control group. Clearly, this statistically significant finding has little or no practical importance.

THE CASE STUDY METHOD

Case studies provide rich, detailed accounts of significant events in an individual's life. You can see this in the excerpt from Oscar Lewis's (1961) classic case study of family life in a Mexico City slum, *The Children of Sanchez;* the study is based on extensive interviews in which the then-grown children were asked to relate their own life histories.

> Manuel, the eldest son, came closest to the pattern of traits held to be typical in a disorganized slum environment. He recalled little about his home life, though his brother and sisters remembered all too well his crude assertions of authority when father was not at home. Having an "aversion to routine," as

> he put it, he remembered only "the exciting things," and these occurred mainly with his gang of friends who soon became the most important part of his life. Stocky and strong, he was from the first a good fighter and earned the other boys' respect. One of his fiercest fights, started to defend his brother, led oddly to a firm friendship; he and his new companion became inseparable, exchanged many confidences, and for years supported each other during emotional hard times. Manuel did poorly in school, which after the sixth grade he gladly gave up in favor of jobs, pocket money, and girls. At 13 he was inducted into sexual intercourse, after which "the fever, this sex business," got hold of him "in such a way that all I did was to go around thinking about it. At night my dreams were full of girls and sex. I wanted every woman I saw." Presently he fell into the grip of another fever, gambling at cards. "If a day passed without a game," he said, "I was desperate." This fever soon mounted to a point where he would bet a whole week's pay, but when he won he would go out with his friends and "throw it all away." Regretfully he recalled that he "never did anything practical" with his winnings.
>
> There is a certain charm about Manuel. His narrative is full of vitality and drama, and he sometimes reveals generous impulses, especially toward male friends. On one occasion he took over a sick friend's job to hold it for him, thereby sacrificing a much better job of his own. On another occasion, he set up in a small business making shoes; he paid his three helpers so well that he went bankrupt. This mishap extinguished an already feeble spark: "I lost the little confidence I had in myself and lived just from day to day, like an animal. I didn't have the will power to carry out plans." At 15 he started a family and presently had four children. He never provided a home for his family, which finally became part of his father's household, and he increasingly neglected his wife, staying away and having a torrid affair with another woman. When his wife died he was grief-stricken. With his boyhood companion he departed for some months to work and gamble elsewhere, leaving the children to his father's support. No doubt this behavior contained some element of revenge for the humiliations and belittlements received from his father, but there was a strong undertone of shame and sadness in Manual at having led a life "so sterile, so useless, so unhappy." (White, 1976, pp. 132–133)

The case study is mainly descriptive, and its data are qualitative. It is the least systematic and least controlled research method. As we will discuss shortly, this characteristic has both advantages and disadvantages.

Many case studies deal with abnormal personality, where they are used to present data concerning unusual cases. "A Case of Multiple Personality" is the well-known account of a 25-year-old married woman, "Eve White," who displayed three very distinct personalities (Thigpen & Cleckley, 1954, 1957). Eve White had been in psychotherapy for several months because of severe headaches and blackouts. Her therapist described her as "retiring and gently conventional." One day during an interview,

> As if seized by a sudden pain she put both hands to her head. After a tense moment of silence, her hands dropped. There was a quick, reckless smile and, in a bright voice that sparkled, she said, "Hi there, Doc!" The demure and constrained posture of Eve White had melted into buoyant repose. . . . This new and apparently carefree girl spoke casually of Eve White and her problems, always using she or her in every reference, always respecting the strict bounds

of a separate identity. When asked her own name she immediately replied, "Oh, I'm Eve Black." (1954, p. 137)

Following this startling discovery, Eve was observed over 14 months in a series of interviews totaling approximately 100 hours. During this time, a third personality emerged. Later, she exhibited other personalities, 22 in all (Sizemore & Huber, 1988). This case study was especially valuable because, 40 years ago, it was one of only a small number of well-documented cases of a rare phenomenon, a true multiple personality (Comer, 1992). In the past 15 years, reports of cases of multiple personality have increased dramatically, which has led to increased interest in the study of this fascinating phenomenon (e.g., Kluft, 1991; Ross et al., 1990). (In fact, although the rate of reports of this phenomenon has increased, we do not know if this change reflects increased incidence of multiple personality disorder, increased sensitivity of clinicians to the signs and symptoms of the disorder, or some other factor such as greater likelihood of people seeking treatment for this problem. Most likely, the increased rate of reporting reflects a combination of factors operating together.)

Case studies are sometimes used to support theories. Psychoanalysts use case studies extensively to support their theoretical claims. But because case studies are completely uncontrolled, using them in this way is dubious.

Life Histories

A special type of case study is the **life history** or **narrative** approach. This method uses the descriptions provided by subjects (as opposed to direct observations) of their personal histories. The data consist of past events as recalled by the individual and are by their nature more subjective than the accounts described (usually by professional observers) in the form of case studies. Yet, some theorists argue that to try to understand the complexity of the person through only objective and abstract techniques is to overlook subtle but very important features of the individual's self-perception and perception of his or her life (Coles, 1989).

The fact that life events as recounted by the individual are biased (Ross, 1989) can be viewed as providing valuable information about the person, rather than as limiting the accuracy of the reports. How particular people perceive their lives and which events are recalled, elaborated on, or suppressed reflect their own subjective views of themselves and the world around them. Indeed, adequately processing and formulating an account of one's own life may provide an individual with a sense of unique identity and continuity throughout evolving life circumstances (Bruhn, 1990; McAdams, 1985; McAdams, Lensky, Daple, & Allen, 1988). Thus, these qualitative approaches provide a complement to more rigorous quantitative approaches in the type and quantity of information they allow.

However, quantifying the information derived from life histories can be as challenging as with any other version of the case study approach. As valuable as they may be for information about subjective experience, for actual research applications, life histories suffer all of the shortcomings of the case study method.

Other research methods focus on single subjects yet allow for reasonable experimental control **(time series designs).** They are used only rarely in personality research. The interested reader can find an overview of these designs in Liebert & Liebert (1995).

Evaluation of the Case Study Method

As a method of personality research, the case study has several advantages. It is an excellent way of examining the personality of a single individual in great detail. A closely related advantage is that the case study allows an individual's idiosyncrasies and contradictions to show up. These features are masked or minimized in other (group comparison) approaches. No matter how general the laws of human behavior, each person remains unique.

Case studies can reflect the richness and complexity of personality, which makes them a fertile source of hypotheses about human behavior. Hypotheses formulated from case study material then can be tested with more controlled and rigorous methods.

Because the case study allows circumstances to vary naturally, it offers greater potential for revealing new and surprising findings. With the other research methods, the variables measured are specified in advance and only those variables are assessed. As a result, the investigator may miss some vital observations. In contrast, the case study does not specify the observations to be made; instead, as much as possible of the entire situation is recorded.

Another advantage of case studies is that they typically deal with people in their natural environments, not in artificial laboratory settings. In the final analysis, theories of personality are intended to explain behavior in real life. Case studies therefore directly examine the phenomena of ultimate interest.

The case study method has five important limitations. First, because case study observations are not made under controlled conditions, they cannot be directly repeated by independent investigators. As we will see, replication of research is an essential feature of science.

Second, as with correlational studies, definitive statements about cause-and-effect relationships cannot be made from case studies because there is inadequate or no control over other variables that may influence the behaviors being studied.

Third, the data for case studies often come from *retrospective reports* by the subject and other people, such as family members. Retrospective reports are notoriously *in*accurate. Observers (the subject and others) tend to forget what happened and how they felt. Moreover, with the passage of time, observers may see events in a different perspective, as memories become mixed with present thoughts and feelings. (The case of Eve White/Black is an example of a *non*retrospective case study and is an exception; the data were systematically collected as Eve was exhibiting her multiple personalities.)

Fourth, the data from case studies are usually qualitative rather than quantitative. Qualitative data provide less precise measures of behavior than quantitative data. Qualitative data do not allow for simple, direct comparisons across groups of subjects or people.

Finally, it is difficult to generalize from a single case study to people in general, or even particular groups of people, because there is usually no way to compare the subject of a case study to the relevant characteristics of the group of interest. We are left guessing as to how alike or dissimilar from other people the case subject may be on a wide range of measures.

Whether the disadvantages of the case study method outweigh its advantages depends on the purpose of the investigation. At the very least, it is reasonable to use the case study in preliminary research, which may then generate intriguing hypotheses. (Indeed, researchers often do so informally when they derive research ideas from their own personal experiences or casual observation of others.) The validity and generality of such hypotheses then can be tested in more controlled correlational studies and experiments.

META-ANALYSIS: EVALUATING REPLICATIONS

One key idea in the philosophy of science is *replication*. An observation or result is taken more seriously the more consistently it can be repeated at other times, in other places, and by other investigators. Indeed, in a sense *replicability* is a key requirement for reaching a conclusion scientifically. And when it comes to some "big" questions, there will not just be two or three pertinent studies, but many.

Meta-analysis refers to any technique that combines and evaluates the results of a number of related studies. This process begins with an exhaustive search of the literature, with the variables of interest specified at the outset. Computers using keywords related to the variables of interest can then be used to search existing data bases for research reports. (The increased speed and efficiency obtained through the use of computers has contributed enormously to the growing popularity of meta-analysis.)

Once all of the relevant articles are assembled, statistical techniques are used to convert the reported outcomes into a common format and scale of measurement. This process usually involves determining *statistical significance* and a measure of *effect size* for each study. These measures are now weighted and combined to evaluate the overall strength and probable reliability of the effect of interest. Meta-analyses can contribute a great deal to our understanding by dramatically boosting confidence in the existence of reported effects. Although any single study fails to rule out the possibility of findings occurring by chance alone, the accumulated evidence of large numbers of studies all reporting similar results can be very convincing.

The meta-analytic approach is not without its critics, however. A clear threat to the outcome of a meta-analysis is that psychological journals are biased toward publishing *only* statistically significant results. Thus, studies that fail to achieve statistical significance (whether because the observed effect was too small, nonexistent, or simply measured badly) will not be published or circulated. These studies will simply not make it into anyone's meta-analysis. This problem has come to be known as the **file drawer problem** (Rosenthal, 1979) because that is where null results usually land. (Statistical techniques also exist for computing the number of null results that would have to exist to convincingly refute the results of a meta-analysis.) Although meta-analysis can be a powerful tool for demonstrating the existence and magnitude of a particular relationship, it remains limited as a tool for disconfirming reported findings.

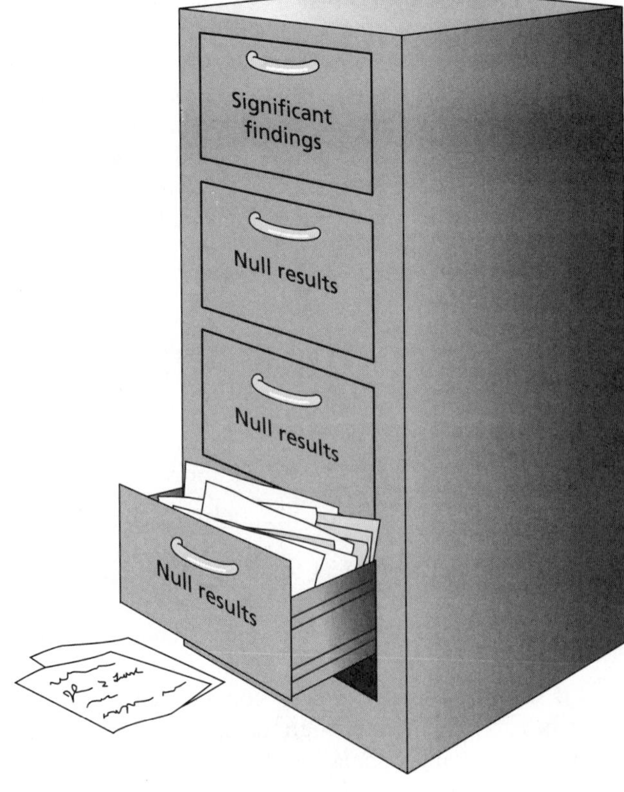

The file drawer problem: We can never know how many studies may exist for every significant finding published.

PERSONALITY ASSESSMENT: SOURCES OF DATA

The primary (or sole) source of information about an individual's personality is often the *self-report personality inventory.* The construction and evaluation of such inventories are important enough to be examined in some detail.

Self-Report Personality Inventories

A **self-report personality inventory** is, in essence, a specialized questionnaire made up of statements that might or might not apply to any person. Taking a self-report inventory involves responding to a large number of statements such as:

I often get mad when things don't turn out as planned.
I enjoy music and dancing.
I am afraid of high places.
I have trouble falling asleep at night.

Respondents indicate whether each statement is generally true or false for them or the degree to which they agree or disagree with the statement. (Occasionally, there is a "cannot say" choice.) The statements are usually printed in a booklet with a separate answer sheet.

Self-report personality inventories are widely used; almost two-thirds of the U.S. population will be asked to take a personality inventory at some time in their lives. One reason for their popularity, of course, is convenience: You just give the questionnaire to a person, who fills it out (typically without any supervision or assistance), and you then score the test by using answer keys provided by the test publisher.

Personality inventories are often scored for a number of different dimensions or scales, although some are designed to measure just one or a few aspects of the person. Each scale of a multiscale inventory involves some subset of the items on the inventory, so the overall inventory provides a set of scale scores that, taken together, reveal the "personality pattern" of a particular individual.

The scale scores are interpreted by the application of **norms,** indicating the range of scores obtained by a large number of individuals who are demographically similar to the person who is being tested. This is the so-called **normative sample.** By consulting a table of norms, the researcher or clinician learns where individuals stand relative to other individuals in the population to which they are being compared.

In addition, most inventories are supported by reliability and validity data, provided by the creators or publishers of the inventory. **Reliability** refers to the degree to which the scales yield information that is consistent or stable over time, whereas **validity** refers to whether the scale measures what it purports to measure.

Hundreds of self-report inventories have been published over the past 50 years. Most of them never become widely used. If an inventory comes to be widely accepted, it is typically revised periodically to update the language and improve reliability or validity based on empirical studies. Revisions may add new scales, improve the wording of items, and provide updated or extended norms. We will illustrate the nature of self-report inventories by describing one of the oldest and most famous inventories, the Minnesota Multiphasic Personality Inventory.

The Minnesota Multiphasic Personality Inventory

Constructed in 1942 by S. R. Hathaway, a clinical psychologist, and J. C. McKinley, a neuropsychiatrist, the Minnesota Multiphasic Personality Inventory (MMPI) filled a need for a practical and valid test to screen patients for various psychiatric disorders. Hathaway and McKinley began with a pool of 1000 self-descriptive statements collected from various psychiatric examination forms and procedures, psychiatric textbooks, and previous inventories. The 1000 statements were given to groups of diagnosed psychiatric patients (who had been classified based on clinical judgments) and to groups of normal individuals. A tabulation was then made of how often subjects in each group agreed with each item. Only items that clearly differentiated between a diagnostic group and the normal group were retained. For instance, a statement became an item on the depression scale if, but only if, patients with a depressive disorder agreed (or disagreed) with the statement significantly more often than did nondepressed persons. This method of choosing scale items is called **empirical keying.**

The MMPI consists of more than 500 statements about attitudes, education, general physical health, sex roles, mood, morale, vocational interests, fears, and preoccupations. A revision of the MMPI, the MMPI-2, appeared in

Table 2.2 Validity and clinical scales of the Minnesota Multiphasic Personality Inventory-2

SCALE NAME	ABBREVIATION	INTERPRETATION
CANNOT SAY	?	One of four validity scales. It is the number of items in the "Cannot Say" category or that the respondent leaves blank.
LIE	L	The second validity scale. It measures the subject's attempt to put himself or herself in a favorable light (e.g., by answering *false* to items that are true for just about everyone, such as "I get angry sometimes.").
FREQUENCY	F	The third validity scale; it is a measure of carelessness or confusion. One item scored on this scale, if the subject answers *true*, is "Everything tastes the same."
CORRECTION	K	The fourth validity scale; often taken as defensiveness.
HYPOCHONDRIASIS (1)	Hs	The tendency to complain of numerous physical symptoms. High scores often have a defeatist attitude.
DEPRESSION (2)	D	The tendency to experience depression or pessismism.
HYSTERIA (3)	Hy	The tendency to express psychological conflict through unbased physical complaints.
PSYCHOPATHIC DEVIATE (4)	Pd	The tendency to be antisocial, rebellious, and impulsive.
MASCULINITY-FEMININITY (5)	Mf	The tendency to have attitudes or feelings often associated with the opposite sex (e.g., sensitivity in males or aggressiveness in females).
PARANOIA (6)	Pa	The tendency to be suspicious or place excess blame on others.
PSYCHASTHENIA (7)	Pt	The tendency to be rigid, phobic, and self-condemning.
SCHIZOPHRENIA (8)	Sc	The tendency to have peculiar thoughts or ideas.
HYPOMANIA (9)	Ma	The tendency to be energetic, optimistic, and flighty.
SOCIAL INTROVERSION/ EXTROVERSION (0)	Si	The tendency to be shy and self-effacing. Low scorers tend to be sociable and outgoing.
ANXIETY*	A	The tendency to become apprehensive.
REPRESSION*	R	The tendency to keep problems from conscious awareness.
EGO STRENGTH*	Es	The ability to maintain well-integrated responses under stress or when in conflict.
MACANDREW ALCOHOLISM SCALE*	MAC	The tendency to abuse alcohol or to become addicted to it.

*The scales were not part of the original MMPI but were incorporated into the latest revision.

1982. It is scored for 4 validity scales and 14 basic clinical scales (University of Minnesota, 1982). Table 2.2 shows the scale names, their customary abbreviations, and a brief characterization of the disposition each scale appears to measure.

The *validity scales* provide information about the trustworthiness of responses on the clinical scales. For example, elevated Lie (L) scales usually mean that respondents are trying to answer the items to present themselves in a favorable light.

Scoring the MMPI is straightforward. Scoring keys indicate the items that make up each scale and the direction (true or false) of each item. The test can be scored by hand in less than 10 minutes; scoring is even faster with a computer. Interpreting the scores is not as simple. Experience has shown that most of the scales cannot be interpreted literally; that is, a person who scores high on the schizophrenia scale is not necessarily schizophrenic. For this reason, the original scales are usually designated by code number (0–9) rather than by the names of psychiatric categories. (Note the numbers in parentheses in Table 2.2.)

To reach a clinical diagnosis, the pattern of scores on the scales is examined and often depicted graphically in a **personality profile.** An example is shown in Figure 2.5. *MMPI atlases* assist in interpreting profiles; they contain typical profiles and descriptive information about samples of subjects producing each profile (e.g., Marks & Seeman, 1963). For example, the atlases list typical and atypical symptoms and behaviors for people with a given profile. They provide information about the most common diagnostic category for these people, their personal histories, and courses of treatment.

It is rare to find a perfect match of profiles with one in an atlas. Therefore, the atlases also provide criteria for determining whether two profiles can be considered similar. These criteria help the examiner find the profile in the atlas that is most like the respondent's profile. An updated set of norms, based on a large sample of subjects ranging in age from 18 to 99, is also available (Colligan, Osborne, Swenson, & Offord, 1984). The MMPI-2 has also

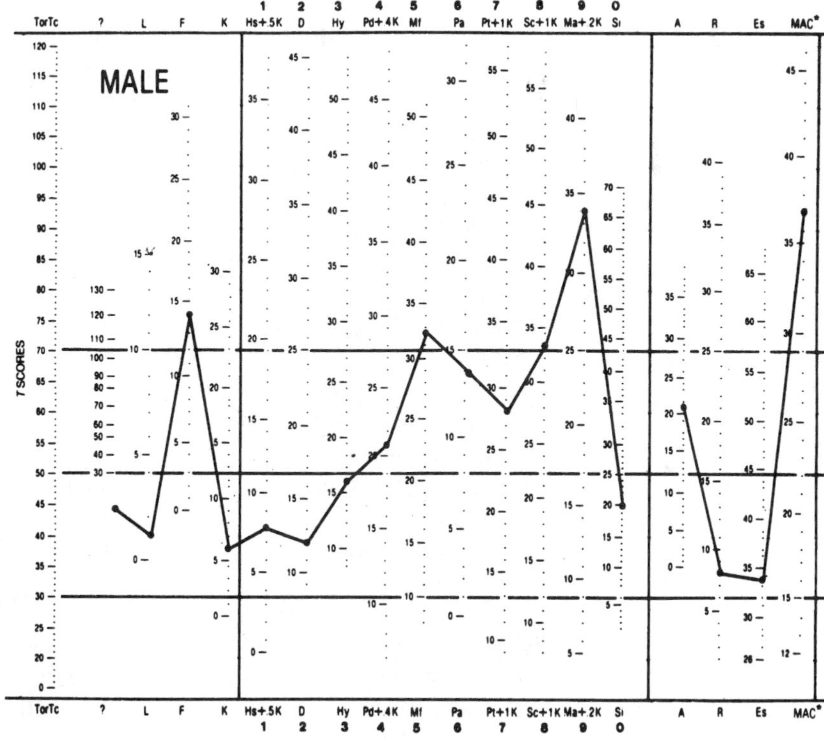

Figure 2.5
Sample MMPI-2 profile.
Source: MINNESOTA MULTIPHASIC PERSONALITY INVENTORY. Copyright © 1942. Renewed 1970. This Profile From 1948, 1976, 1982. All rights reserved. Distributed Exclusively by NATIONAL COMPUTER SYSTEMS, INC. Under License from U of Minnesota.

been shown to be appropriate for use with college students (Butcher, Graham, Dahlstrom, & Bowman, 1990), and separate norms are available for adolescents (Pancoast & Archer, 1988).

What about the reliability and validity of the MMPI? The MMPI seems to be more useful for adults than for teenagers, and college graduates reply in a more consistent fashion than those with less education (McFarland & Sparks, 1985). Nonetheless, a comprehensive review of more than 40 years of research suggests that overall, the MMPI is an adequate instrument in terms of reliability and validity (Parker, Hanson, & Hunsley, 1988). To be sure, critics have found fault with the MMPI (Pancoast & Archer, 1989) and the MMPI-2 (Duckworth, 1991), but the MMPI and MMPI-2 continue to be widely used (Popham & Holden, 1991).

The MMPI has been employed in personality research to predict both undesirable and desirable behavior. Hathaway and Monachesi (1952), for example, predicted delinquent behavior using the MMPI. Harrell (1972) successfully predicted subjects' speed of advancement in business and income 10 years after they had taken the MMPI. More recently, Goldwater and Duffy (1990) showed that the MMPI can be used to detect women who were abused, sexually as well as nonsexually, as children. And, interestingly, the MMPI can be used to predict marital satisfaction. Couples who have similar MMPI profiles are the most happily married (Richard, Wakefield, & Lewak, 1990).

There is also no doubt that the MMPI can still predict a variety of psychiatric symptoms (Kolotkin, Revis, Kirkley, & Janick, 1987; Waiters & Greene, 1988). The MMPI scales can even be used to predict outcomes related to people's health with reasonable accuracy. A 20-year longitudinal study of more than 2000 men revealed that Depression scores on the MMPI predict the long-term likelihood of developing cancer. In fact, individual differences on the MMPI Depression scale predict the likelihood of getting cancer *even after* statistically removing the effects of other predictors including number of cigarettes smoked, alcohol intake, family history of cancer, and serum cholesterol (Persky, Kempthorne-Rawson, & Shekele, 1987).

A note of caution is in order here. When we say "predict," we mean make guesses about what a *group* of people will do (e.g., become juvenile delinquents or not become juvenile delinquents) at better-than-chance level. However, critics have pointed out that MMPI scores or even combinations of scores are *never* accurate enough as predictors to make significant decisions about particular individuals (Colligan & Offord, 1987, 1988). The potential problem is illustrated by the story of the ill-fated MAC scale.

Secondary Scales Derived from the MMPI: The Case of the MAC

Because the MMPI has such a large and diverse item pool, there have been a number of efforts to derive *secondary scales* from it. Essentially, a theoretical personality construct to be measured is identified and then a subset of MMPI items is found that discriminates between those with and without (or high and low on) the characteristic in question. Following this procedure, investigators have derived scales of anxiety (Taylor, 1953), alcoholism (MacAndrew, 1965), narcissism (Wink & Cough, 1990), and limited emotional awareness (Bagby, Parker, & Taylor 1991) among others.

Typically, these scales never gain wide use, but the MacAndrew Alcoholism scale (or MAC) was an exception. MacAndrew's (1965) scale was developed to discriminate between male alcoholic outpatients and nonalcoholic psychiatric outpatients. Over the course of 20 years, it came into wide clinical use as a technique for identifying alcoholics; in fact, the MMPI-2 actually incorporated the MAC as a new primary scale (see Figure 2.5). Accumulating evidence has demonstrated, however, that the MAC is not nearly as potent a measure of alcoholism as was previously thought.

One team of researchers scored the MMPIs of almost 15,000 men and women from a variety of backgrounds for the MAC and then determined the alcoholic or nonalcoholic status of each person by independent means. Overall, the MAC correctly identified only 71% of the alcoholic men and a mere 38% of the alcoholic women. By way of contrast, the single MMPI item "I have used alcohol excessively" *identified 95% of the men and 94% of the women alcoholics* (Davis, Colligan, Morse, & Offord, 1987).

Shortly thereafter, Gottesman and Prescott (1989) published a review of 74 studies on the MAC. Their conclusion was that

> only 15% of individuals identified by the [MAC] scale as alcoholics are correctly classified, while 85% of those called "alcoholic" are not actually affected. The data are so clear that we call for a suspension of the use of the MacAndrew Alcoholism scale outside of research settings. (p. 223)

Alternatives to Traditional Personality Inventories

Self-report inventories are not the only way to assess personality characteristics. We will consider three alternatives: ratings, nominations, and composite profiles.

Ratings

Perhaps the most obvious alternative to self-reports is to observe the person directly in many situations. Whether someone "gets mad often" or "tires easily" can be determined by direct observation. However, in most assessment efforts, it is impractical to observe the person over a range of situations and long enough time to allow for a proper assessment. One practical alternative is to obtain observational data indirectly through the reports of individuals who know the person well. Assessment data obtained in this way are given the general name **ratings.**

Ratings of one kind or another enjoy extremely wide use. Almost everyone has been a rater and has been rated by others. Ratings are often used, for example, in letters of recommendation from former employers and teachers. Mental health workers may use ratings in reports of a client's behavior or progress. Formal rating scales are used in personality assessment and research. Typically, the psychologist will ask a person who knows the subject well (e.g., as a teacher, friend, or spouse) to indicate whether the subject has a particular characteristic, or to assign a number (say, from 0 to 10) that indicates how much of a given characteristic the subject has.

A strong word of caution needs to be introduced about ratings, however. Unless rating scales are designed carefully, they are open to serious biases and distortions. These biases come from the rater and distort the picture given about the subject of the assessment. Several major types of bias are shown in Table 2.3.

Nominations

In contrast to evaluations by one or two raters, **nominations** involve a variety of people and situations. Nominations are based on observations made over extended periods by a number of observers who see the subject from a variety of perspectives and with whom the subject has had different relationships. Neale and Weintraub (1977), for example, collected peer nominations for a large number of children of schizophrenic parents. The subjects were assessed in part using a 35-item peer nomination procedure (Pekarik, Prinz, Liebert, Weintraub, & Neale, 1976).

The procedure involves distributing the 35-item Pupil Evaluation Inventory to all the children in the subject's classroom. The inventory asks the children to name (nominate) other children in the class who have various characteristics (e.g., "those who can't sit still," "those who are liked by

Table 2.3 Possible sources of bias in personality rating scales

SOURCE OF ERROR	EXPLANATION
Error of leniency	When raters know a person well, as they must to offer an informed evaluation, they tend to rate the person higher (or sometimes lower) than they should.
Error of central tendency	Raters are often reluctant to use the extreme ends of a rating scale even when these are appropriate, preferring to stick closer to the middle range of descriptions. (We all do this when we describe a very ugly person as "not being that attractive.")
Halo effect	Raters tend to permit their *general* impression of a person to influence their ratings for most of the person's specific characteristics, just as a halo casts a pleasant, diffuse light over an angel or cherub.
Contrast error	Raters often describe others as being less like themselves than is actually the case. A relatively submissive rater, for example, may see others as being considerably more dominant than they really are.
"Logical" error	Raters often assume that two characteristics should be related ("it seems logical") and bias their evaluations accordingly. For example, a rater who believes that *hostility* and *abrasiveness* go together may rate people who are abrasive as being more hostile than they really are.
Proximity error	When a standard rating form is used, characteristics that are near one another on the list often receive similar ratings just because they are close together. This is a type of response set problem.

Source: Based on the analysis offered in *Psychometric Methods,* 2nd ed., by J. P. Guilford, 1954, New York: McGraw-Hill.

everyone," and "those who make fun of people"). A subject's score for any category is the percentage of the possible nominations in that category; thus, a child in a class of 50 who was nominated by 10 classmates as among "those who can't sit still" would receive a score of 20%; a child in a class of 25 who was nominated by 20 classmates would receive a score of 80%.

The procedure's usefulness has been clearly demonstrated (Pekarik et al., 1976), but the cost of using it is high because the inventory must be administered to an entire class to assess a single child. In fact, to assess a single individual, gathering data through an adequate nomination technique is often out of the question except in the case of schoolchildren.

The "Composite Profile" Approach to Assessment

Rather than rely on one method of personality measurement, some investigators have proposed *a multimethod approach* to ensure that the findings are valid (Campbell & Fiske, 1959; Harris, 1980). As many different measures of the same characteristic as possible are used. It is assumed that the measurement error associated with any one method will be less likely to distort the final measure when many methods of assessment are combined.

An example is assessing an individual's generosity. People may want to present themselves in a favorable light, and therefore overestimate their generosity in a self-report questionnaire. However, peers could also be asked to rate these individuals for the trait in question. When the two different measures are combined, a more accurate picture will emerge.

Following this rationale, Harris (1980) proposed using three methods of assessment to approximate an individual's "true" personality profile. He suggested (1) starting with a carefully constructed personality inventory that objectively assesses formally defined variables, (2) obtaining both peer ratings and self-report ratings on the variables assessed by the inventory, and (3) averaging the three separate assessments to produce a composite profile.

Harris demonstrated that such composite profiles are considerably more stable over time than single-method profiles. Furthermore, composite profiles yield valid measures of personality. If the time and budget are sufficient, Harris' three-method approach offers an alternative that is clearly better than the single-method approach to personality assessment.

Problems with Self-Report and Rating Data

In 1934, Richard LaPiere, a sociologist, wrote letters to 250 hotels and restaurants across the United States asking, "Will you accept members of the Chinese race as guests in your establishment?" A majority of the proprietors answered LaPiere's letter. More than 90% of the respondents replied that they would *not* serve Chinese guests. This should not have been surprising because there was a good deal of anti-Chinese sentiment in the United States in the mid-1930s. What was surprising was that the proprietors did not mean it, as LaPiere well knew. Six months earlier, he had toured the country with a Chinese couple. They had stopped at each of the 250 establishments to which LaPiere had written, and the Chinese couple had, in fact, been served in 249 of them, for the most part with very pleasant treatment!

More recent studies have repeatedly confirmed LaPiere's basic finding. People's stated attitudes or intentions may tell us little or nothing about how they will actually behave. A law-and-order political attitude does not necessarily go along with adherence to certain municipal laws (Wrightsman, 1969); church attendance cannot usually be predicted from expressed attitudes toward church (Wicker, 1971); it is almost impossible to predict how often individual students will cut classes from their attitudes toward their professors (Rokeach & Kliejunas, 1972); and attitudes toward tax evasion do not appear to predict who will actually cheat on taxes (Hessing, Elffers, & Weigel, 1988).

There is a general point underlying these findings. The answers received in personality assessment often depend on the method of inquiry or test used. Many innkeepers might have been labeled harsh bigots based on their written sentiments, but they would have been perceived as fair-minded and unbiased on the basis of their observed actions. This finding—a person's stated attitudes may reveal little about his or her behavior—has led many investigators to try to identify the weaknesses in various personality inventories.

Faking on Personality Inventories

People taking tests such as the MMPI devise various schemes for faking their answers. They may want to make a good impression when applying for a job, or they may want to give a bad impression when being tested for sanity in connection with a murder trial. How successful are these conscious efforts to achieve a desired impression?

The attitudes that people express do not always correspond to or predict their behavior.
Photo by Gary D. Clark

Some fakers, particularly those who overdo it, will be detected by one or more of the validity scales included in most self-report personality inventories (Gillis, Rogers, & Dickens, 1990; Grossman, Haywood, Wasyliw, & Cavanaugh, 1990). Still, on average, people seem to get "better" scores on self-report personality inventories when told to simulate a "nice personality" (Helmes & Holden, 1986; Krahe, 1989).

In general, faking can be detected only imperfectly. The detection rate is probably no higher than 80% with most inventories, and there appear to be as many as 10% false positives—that is, individuals who did not fake but appear to have done so on the basis of validity scales (Schretlen, 1988; Schretlen & Arkowitz, 1990). Not surprisingly, faking is more apparent on the most transparent or obvious items (Schretlen, 1990). Many personality psychologists therefore fear that undetected faking is quite common with self-report personality inventories (Cernovsky; 1988; Wetzler & Marlowe, 1990). Finally, other kinds of test-taking attitudes, known as response sets, may distort the personality picture presented by self-report inventories.

Response Sets

Psychologists often assume that a person's response to any item on a personality inventory is a reaction to the content of the item. For example, they assume that a person who responds "true" to the statement "I like parties" often attends social functions. Is this a valid assumption? Perhaps not.

People with particular test-taking attitudes may not be answering the items in terms of content. **Response sets** are characteristic and consistent ways of responding to a test regardless of what the items say. For instance, **response acquiescence** is the tendency to agree with items, no matter what their content. **Response deviation** is the tendency to answer items in an uncommon direction, such as answering "true" to the statement: "I always like everyone, no matter how they treat me."

Social Desirability as a Response Set

The response set that has received the most attention is **social desirability,** which means answering items in the most socially accepted direction, whether the answers are correct for the respondent or not. For example, people who prefer to be alone and dislike social gatherings might answer "true" to the statement "I like parties." The response is given because they feel that it is socially desirable to enjoy parties, or that there is something wrong with anyone who does not like parties.

Several methods have been devised for controlling the influence of social desirability (O'Grady, 1988). One method is to measure the respondent's tendency to answer self-report inventory items in the socially desirable direction. The person's score on the inventory is then adjusted to take the degree of this tendency into account.

Another approach uses items that are neutral with respect to social desirability. These statements are rated in the middle of the social desirability-undesirability scale. An example is "I am easily awakened by noise." It is often difficult, however, to find or rewrite items that meet the requirement of neutrality and simultaneously capture the necessary content (Fristad, 1988). Imagine how hard it would be to rewrite "Most of the time I wish I were dead" to make it more socially desirable without changing the meaning substantially. (This is an actual MMPI item that is rated as extremely undesirable.)

A third approach for controlling the effects of social desirability is to use a **forced-choice inventory,** in which respondents must choose which of two statements is more characteristic of them. All statements in the inventory are first scaled for social desirability and then paired according to their scale values. The choices in each pair have approximately the same social desirability scale value but different content. Therefore, when respondents choose the statement in each pair that is more characteristic of them, the choices cannot be based on social desirability. Edwards (1953) constructed his Personal Preference Schedule in this way to control for social desirability. The *Personal Preference Schedule* is a self-report personality inventory developed for counseling and research with nonpsychiatric individuals. Examples of items appearing on it are given in Table 2.4.

Response Styles: An Alternative View of the Data

Some psychologists try to rid self-report inventories of the distorting influence of response sets. Other psychologists claim that these characteristic ways of responding might not be sources of error at all (e.g., Edwards & Edwards, 1991). The latter group suggests looking at test-taking attitudes as personality traits rather than as situation-specific reactions. The important measures of personality in self-report inventories might actually be *how* someone responds rather than *what* they respond to (i.e., the content of the items).

Response tendencies can be viewed either as a source of distortion (error) *or* as an indication of existing personality characteristics. Assigning different terms to describe each situation is useful. *Response sets,* as we have said, are sources of distortion. **Response styles** are personality dimensions (Jackson & Messick, 1958). We have already examined social desirability as a response set. Now, we will consider it as a response style—that is, a personality dimension in its own right.

Social Desirability as a Response Style

Edwards (1953) developed the best-known measure of social desirability. He chose 150 items from the MMPI and asked 10 judges to respond to each of them in the socially desirable direction. The judges agreed perfectly on 79 of

Table 2.4 Examples of items from the Edwards Personal Preference Schedule

ALTERNATIVES	ITEMS
A B	A: I like to tell amusing stories and jokes at parties. B: I would like to write a great novel or play.
A B	A: I like to have my work organized and planned before beginning it. B: I like to travel and see the country.
A B	A: I feel like blaming others when things go wrong for me. B: I feel that I am inferior to others in most respects.
A B	A: I like to avoid responsibilities and obligations. B: I feel like making fun of people who do things that I regard as stupid.

Source: From *Manual for Edwards Personal Preference Schedule* by A. L. Edwards, 1953, Psychological Corporation.

the 150 items; these 79 items formed the first Social Desirability (SD) Scale. Later, Edwards reduced the SD scale to 39 items by selecting those items that showed the greatest differentiation between subjects who had high and low total scores. He hypothesized,

> If the SD scale does provide a measure of the tendency of subjects to give socially desirable responses to statements in self-description, then the correlations of scores on this scale with other personality scales, given under standard instructions, should indicate something of the extent to which the social desirability variable is operating at the time. (1957, pp. 31, 33)

Studies by Edwards and other investigators support this hypothesis (e.g., Edwards, 1953, 1957; Edwards & Edwards, 1991; Merrill & Heathers, 1956). Scales measuring socially desirable traits—such as dominance, responsibility, status, cooperativeness, agreeableness, and objectivity—correlate positively with the SD scale. In contrast, scales measuring socially undesirable traits—such as social introversion, neuroticism, hostility, dependency, insecurity, and anxiety—are negatively correlated with the SD scale (Edwards, 1970).

What are the implications of the correlations between Edwards's SD scale and other personality scales? One implication is that the traits these scales measure may be, despite their names (e.g., dominance and introversion), only different aspects of social desirability. It might be more fruitful from the standpoint of prediction and explanation, as well as parsimony, to view the traits that correlate strongly with the SD scale as measures of social desirability. For example, Edwards believed that the trait measured by the Taylor Manifest Anxiety (MA) scale (Taylor, 1953), a measure of the disposition to be anxious derived from the MMPI, should be interpreted as social desirability-undesirability.

The MA scale is negatively correlated with the SD scale. High anxiety tends to be associated with low social desirability; low anxiety tends to be associated with high social desirability. This finding is not surprising if we look at the actual items. Statements like "I am a very nervous person," "I am certainly lacking in self-confidence," and "I cry easily" appear on the MA scale. These characteristics are unquestionably socially undesirable in our society. Thus, high scores on the MA scale can be viewed as endorsing socially undesirable statements. Low scores on the MA scale can be seen as denying socially undesirable characteristics. (For certain subgroups of our culture—such as residents of psychiatric hospitals or homes for the aged—these characteristics are less undesirable and may even be construed as socially desirable because they lead to attention and care.)

The MA scale has been used to select subjects with high and low anxiety. One finding is that for certain kinds of verbal learning, low-anxiety subjects make fewer errors and learn faster than high-anxiety subjects (Montague, 1953; Ramond, 1953; Taylor & Spence, 1952). Edwards (1957) explained these results in terms of social desirability.

> I believe it possible . . . to describe the low group on the Taylor scale as those who desire to make a good impression on others and the high group as those who are less interested in what others may think of them. I would predict that the group desiring to make a good impression on the Taylor scale, that is to say,

> those with low scores, might also desire to make a good impression in terms of their performance on the learning task. They are, in other words, perhaps more highly motivated by the desire to "look good," not only in their responses to the Taylor scale, but also in their performance in the learning situation itself. Surely, to be able to learn fast is, in our society, a socially desirable characteristic. If a subject has a strong tendency to give socially desirable responses in self-description, is it unreasonable to believe that he may also reveal this tendency in his behavior in a learning situation where he is aware of what would be considered socially desirable, namely to learn fast, to do his best? The high group, on the other hand, being less interested in making a good impression, showing less of a tendency to give socially desirable responses in self-description, caring less about how others may value them, does not have equal motivation with the low group in the learning situation. (p. 89)

The arguments favoring a response-style or response-set interpretation of self-report inventories are interesting, but they have certainly not gone unchallenged. In fact, several psychologists argue that the tendency to respond to items on the basis of characteristics other than content may be minimal (Block, 1965; McCrae & Costa, 1983). Recently, in addressing this threat as it applies to their own personality inventory, Costa and McCrae reported that "socially desirable responding is not a threat to the validity of the NEO-PI-R scales in most cases" and add that "[using] social desirability scales to screen or correct NEO-PI-R or NEO-FFI scales is *not* recommended" [italics added] (1992, p. 42).

LOOKING AHEAD: ADVICE TO THE TRAVELER

Learning about personality in terms of the four strategies is analogous to visiting four very different countries. Your tour of each strategy begins in an introductory chapter, You may become aware of the strategy's unique structure almost immediately, just as you would notice the landscape of a new country as your plane comes in for a landing and your tour guide previews what you will be seeing. As you enter the strategy, you will become aware of its distinctive language. You will have to acquaint yourself with new terminology and with common words sometimes used in novel ways. Moreover, the personality psychologists in each strategy often express themselves with a unique style. The presentation style itself can tell you much about the approach to personality.

Foreign travelers are advised to immerse themselves in a new culture, leaving behind their own customs, assumptions, and values. Your understanding and appreciation of each strategy will be enhanced if you temporarily adopt its approach. This includes suspending your critical evaluation until you prepare to depart. In this way, you will be able to put the frequently voiced criticisms discussed at the end of each strategy in proper perspective.

Travel is educational because it exposes the traveler to new ideas about human existence, thought, values, and behavior. You will have a similar experience in learning about personality through the perspective of four diverse strategies that aim to study the same phenomenon—human personality—in quite different ways and respecting different traditions and cultures. Your journey begins in the birthplace of the scientific study of personality, the Psychoanalytic Strategy. Bon voyage!

SUMMARY

1. All methods of personality research involve observation of behavior. The methods differ in the types of observations made, the circumstances in which they are made, and the manner in which the data are examined.
2. Ethical concerns require that researchers make every effort in designing and executing research to maximize the information gained while minimizing the risks to their subjects and their deception of them.
3. In the experimental method, an independent variable hypothesized to be causing the behavior being studied (dependent variable) is systematically varied while all other possible causative factors are held constant. Typically, an experimental group in which the independent variable is present is compared with a control group in which the independent variable is absent. When the two groups are equivalent except for the presence of the independent variable, observed differences between the groups on the dependent variable can be confidently attributed to the effect of the independent variable.
4. Experiments allow cause-and-effect relationships to be established. However, the controls that must be exerted to provide such information make experiments narrow in scope and often limit the ability to generalize from results to real-life situations.
5. Correlational studies examine the degree to which two variables are related. The data consist of pairs of observations collected from each member of a group of subjects under the same conditions. Correlations may be positive (direct)—the variables change in the same direction—or negative (inverse)—the variables change in opposite directions. The magnitude (strength) of the correlation indicates how accurately one variable can be predicted from the other. The higher the correlation, the greater the predictive power of each variable involved.
6. Correlational data can be plotted as a scatter diagram. The direction of the line around which the points fall indicates whether the correlation is positive (moving from lower left toward upper right) or negative (moving from upper left to lower right). The degree of deviation of the points from the line of perfect correlation indicates the magnitude of the correlation (little scatter reveals a high degree of association; greater scatter indicates a weaker association). Correlation coefficients are mathematically determined indexes of the direction and magnitude of a relationship; their values range from zero (no correlation) to ±1.00 (perfect correlation).
7. Correlational research allows observation in existing, natural situations because the variables are simply measured and not systematically varied or manipulated. Definitive cause-and-effect relationships usually cannot be determined from correlational data alone. Either variable may cause the other, or a third variable may cause both.
8. Statistical significance is an estimate of the probability of a quantitative finding occurring by mere chance. Statistical significance is expressed as the probability that the results are due to chance alone. Very low probabilities (generally 5 in 100 or less) are accepted as reflecting real

effects (probably not due simply to chance) and would therefore be expected to occur again under the same or very similar conditions. Replications are attempts to duplicate the findings of others by following their procedures and methods as closely as possible.

9. Case studies and life histories involve qualitative, detailed descriptions of single individuals. They can provide a picture of the richness and complexity of personality that neither the experimental nor the correlational method can.
10. Problems with case studies are that they cannot be replicated, cause-and-effect statements cannot be made from them, they are usually retrospective, they are qualitative rather than quantitative, and generalizations to other people are tenuous at best.
11. Meta-analysis provides a means of mathematically combining and evaluating the accumulated evidence for a given relationship from the available published literature.
12. One source of data for the assessment of personality is the self-report personality inventory, which yields scale scores based on normative samples.
13. Personality inventories should be supported by reliability data (which tell us the degree to which the scales yield information that is consistent or stable over time) and validity data (which tell us whether the scale actually measures what it purports to measure).
14. The Minnesota Multiphasic Personality Inventory (MMPI) was developed by criterion keying for the purpose of distinguishing between diagnostic and normal groups. The MMPI-2's 18 scales (including 14 clinical scales and 4 validity scales) are often plotted as a personality profile, which can be compared with the profiles of various types found in MMPI atlases.
15. The MMPI can predict what groups of people with different profiles will do or be like but is almost never accurate enough to make significant decisions about particular individuals.
16. The MacAndrew Alcoholism Scale (or MAC) is a secondary scale derived from the MMPI-2, which has failed to prove itself very useful in predicting alcoholism.
17. Alternatives to self-report personality inventories include ratings, nominations, and composite profiles.
18. Attitudes assessed by questionnaires and rating scales do a relatively poor job of predicting actual behavior.
19. To some extent, self-report inventories can be "faked" by respondents. Inventories are also plagued by the potential of response sets, which are characteristic ways of responding to questions; response sets include response acquiescence, response deviation, and social desirability.
20. Social desirability (the tendency to give socially approved answers regardless of whether the answers are true) can also be viewed as a response style—that is, as a real personality trait rather than as a source of error.

PART TWO

THE PSYCHOANALYTIC STRATEGY

The Forces Within

CHAPTER THREE

Introduction to the Psychoanalytic Strategy

efore reading any further in this chapter, try something. Write down the words or phrases you think of when you hear the word *psychoanalysis.*

What did you come up with? You may have thought of Freud, unconscious, sex, libido, Oedipus complex, repression, id, ego, superego, defense mechanism, dreams, or "the couch." Most people know more about the Psychoanalytic Strategy than about the other three personality strategies. Psychoanalytic concepts have become part of our popular culture as well as part of a variety of academic disciplines other than psychology, such as literature, philosophy, and history (Arlow & Brenner, 1988; Elms, 1988; Runyan, 1988).

WHAT IS PSYCHOANALYSIS?

Psychoanalysis refers technically to psychoanalytically oriented psychotherapy (the change process) guided by psychoanalytic theory. Psychoanalysis thus encompasses a theory of personality, an approach to studying personality, and procedures for assessing and changing personality (Michels, 1988).

All of the theories of the Psychoanalytic Strategy emphasize the primacy of driving forces within the person that motivate them to display consistent patterns of behavior and interpersonal relations. The emphasis placed on these internal forces distinguishes psychoanalytic approaches from those of the other strategies.

Like the theories of the other strategies, though, there are subtle differences and disagreements between the specific views on some issues, including the number of fundamental human drives and their specific nature. Many of these theorists also share some other assumptions about personality (which overlap to some extent with theories of the other three strategies as well). Most psychoanalytic theorists contend that motivating forces derive from processes that occur beyond the conscious awareness of the individual. Most also believe personality develops over the course of progression through an invariant sequence of stages characterized by intrapsychic conflict. Through the course of this unit we will examine these ideas and the variations on them characteristic of particular theories and theorists.

The four basic issues in personality psychology—theory, assessment, research, and application—are highly intertwined in the Psychoanalytic Strategy. Most psychoanalysts are therapists and are directly involved with personality change, which requires assessment of people's intrapsychic processes. Observations made in psychoanalytic therapy form both the basis of personality theory and the research evidence in support of the theory's validity.

The Psychoanalytic Strategy has been dominated by the work and writings of a single individual: Sigmund Freud. He was the founder of psychoanalytic thought (theory, research methodology, and psychotherapy) and also the first modern personality psychologist.

Freud's theory of personality consists of a number of separable but interrelated minitheories, which he revised a number of times over the course of some 45 years of theorizing that began in the mid-1890s (Gay, 1988).

Freud proposed an organizational framework of the mind, describing different mental structures (**id, ego,** and **superego**) and their relationships

Text continued on page 66

Box 3.1
THE LIFE OF FREUD

On May 6, 1856, at the age of 20, Amalie Freud gave birth to her first child. Although the delivery itself was unremarkable, the baby boy was greeted with particular astonishment and delight because he was born with a *caul*, a thin layer of amniotic sac that covered his head in a manner resembling a monk's hood. Cauled infants are very rare but not unheard of among midwives. Julius Caesar was said to have been born with one, and the belief that any infant born with a caul was destined for greatness was widely held in central Europe. So it was that Sigmund Freud grew up with the conviction that he would become a famous man and leave an indelible mark on the world.

The second half of the 19th century, when Sigmund was a student, was a time of great intellectual excitement. In particular, two daring new ideas influenced Freud's thinking.

The first was that human beings are a natural result of evolution and therefore not fundamentally different from other animals. Charles Darwin (1809–1882) reached this conclusion in 1871. He believed that humans gradually evolved from other life forms through random variation and environmental pressures. Darwin's theory accounts for the appearance, disappearance (extinction), and evolution of species. Darwin claimed that all life forms are motivated by two forces: the will to survive and the urge to reproduce. (Darwin's theory is discussed ingreater detail in Chapter 9.) Darwin stopped short of providing a scientific analysis of the mind, but he set the stage for this task, and Freud accepted the challenge.

The other revolutionary idea affecting Freud's thinking was that unconscious, irrational, and primitive forces play a central role in human motivation. Philosophers Arthur Schopenhauer (1788–1860) and Friedrich Nietzsche (1844–1900) observed that human behavior is often driven by unconscious and irrational forces. Both emphasized how easily the intellect can be self-deluding. Schopenhauer considered sex to be the most important human instinct. Nietzsche suggested that people forget certain memories, turn aggression inward as a basis for ethics and conscience, and derive their ultimate strength from the most primitive part of themselves. By the late 19th century, these ideas held sway among many intellectual Europeans (Ellenberger, 1970; Kern, 1973; Sulloway, 1979). There is little doubt that 19th century thought provided the bedrock upon which Freud's ideas were built (Sand, 1988).

Young Sigmund proved to be an outstanding student, with a special aptitude for science, and entered the University of Vienna at the age of 17 to study physiology and medicine. His first important discovery involved the use of cocaine as an anesthetic, but he was robbed of the credit for this accomplishment by an unscrupulous colleague.

Angered but not disheartened, Freud sought a new avenue for accomplishment through study abroad. At age 29, he won a travel grant to study in Paris with Jean Charcot, a French neurologist whose clinical demonstrations of the hypnotic treatment of hysteria were attracting worldwide attention. (*Hysteria* was the name given to physical symptoms, such as paralysis of the limbs, for which no physical causes could be found.) Charcot had discovered that he could hypnotize patients with hysterical symptoms and, under hypnosis, order them to overcome their disabilities. He also found that he could *produce* neurological symptoms, such as the loss of feeling in an arm or leg.

Freud's experience with Charcot turned his interest to the mind, especially the idea that physical symptoms that could not be explained in physical ways might have mental causes. If true, such patients would need to undergo mental cures. Such cures would depend on a deep understanding of how the mind works; no such understanding was available in Freud's time. So,

Box continued on following page

Box 3.1 *Continued*
THE LIFE OF FREUD

Sigmund Freud (1856–1939) founded psychoanalysis. He introduced the idea of unconscious motivation and offered descriptions of the organization and development of personality.
© Mary Evans Picture Library/Sigmund Freud

ARCHIV/Photo Researchers, Inc.

© ARCHIV/Photo Researchers, Inc.

© Mary Evans Picture Library/Sigmund Freud

in his early 30s, Sigmund Freud followed his destiny and embarked on his quest for understanding the nature and workings of the mind.

Freud first theorized that "hysteric symptoms" are defense mechanisms to protect the individual from repressed memories. In 1895, in collaboration with Josef Breuer, he published *Studies on Hysteria*. The book described a treatment of hysteria in which the patient "talks out" and ultimately sees and consciously understands the repressed memories. Freud and Breuer reported that many patients came to recall childhood sexual seductions, which appeared to be repressed events that a talking cure for hysteria would bring to light. Freud later concluded that these seductions may not have actually occurred and that, instead, they were fantasies of the patient. Much controversy, then and now, surrounded Freud's thinking about seduction reports.

Between 1900 and 1939, Freud wrote 21 books, reflecting developments and changes in his view of how the mind worked. These books and his other works led to his being the most frequently cited psychologist of the 20th century. Table 3.1 lists Freud's most famous books (including original German titles and English translations), along with synopses of their major themes.

Box continued on following page

Box 3.1 *Continued*
THE LIFE OF FREUD

Table 3.1 Partial list of Freud's books, 1900–1939

ENGLISH TITLE	GERMAN TITLE	YEAR PUBLISHED	DESCRIPTION
The Interpretation of Dreams	*Die Traumdeutung*	1900	Freud, primarily using self-analysis, asserts his theory that all dreams represent "wish-fulfillments." He provides analyses of actual dreams and symbols.
The Psychopathology of Everyday Life	*Zur Psychopathologie des Alltagslebens*	1901	Freud uses case examples to illustrate his theory that errors in speech are due to unconscious motivations.
Jokes and Their Relation to the Unconscious	*Der Witz und seine Beziehung zum Unbewussten*	1905	Freud classifies jokes and explains his theory that they are expressions of repressed thoughts that otherwise would not have been expressed.
Three Essays on the Theory of Sexuality	*Drei Abhandlungen zur Sexualtheorie*	1905	Freud describes the course of human sexual development, beginning in infancy and passing through distinct stages. Mastery of repressed sexual feelings about parents is necessary for maturity.
Leonardo da Vinci and a Memory of His Childhood	*Eine Kindheitserinnerung des Leonardo da Vinci*	1910	Freud proposes that Leonardo is a passive homosexual, partly based on an early childhood memory of Leonardo's that Freud interprets to represent a desire to perform fellatio.
Totem and Taboo	*Totem und Tabu*	1912–1913	Freud compares the psychology of "primitive peoples" and neurotics, asserting that they both exhibit "incestuous fixations of the libido." He holds that "primitive fears" are the motivation behind religion.
Introductory Lectures on Psycho-Analysis	*Vorlesungen zur Einfuhrung in die Psychoanalyse*	1916–1917	Freud published his lectures (I–XXVIII), covering topics of "Freudian slips," dream analysis, and his general theory of neuroses.
Beyond the Pleasure Principle	*Jenseits des Lustprinzips*	1920	Freud proposes the theory that two opposing instincts—Eros, the drive toward pleasure, and Thanatos, the death instinct—are the governing forces in human lives.
The Ego and the Id	*Das Ich und das Es*	1923	Freud proposes his theory that the mind is composed of the id, the ego, and the superego.
An Autobiographical Study	*Selbstdarstellung*	1925	Freud's brief autobiography.
Inhibitions, Symptoms, and Anxiety	*Hemmung, Symptom und Angst*	1926	Freud revised his theory on the etiology of neuroses to incorporate his new structural theory of the mind (including the id, ego, and superego).

Box continued on following page

Box 3.1 *Continued*
THE LIFE OF FREUD

Table 3.1 Partial list of Freud's books, 1900–1939 *Continued*

ENGLISH TITLE	GERMAN TITLE	YEAR PUBLISHED	DESCRIPTION
The Future of an Illusion	*Die Zukunft einer Illusion*	1927	Freud criticizes religion (particularly Christianity) as a wishful attempt to "master the sensory world," blatantly contradicting science and experience.
Civilization and Its Discontents	*Das Unbehagen in der Kultur*	1930	Freud theorized that civilization resulted from humankind's need to sublimate unsatisfied wishes. As instincts were repressed, "psychic energy" became available to create cultural artifacts.
New Introductory Lectures on Psycho-Analysis	*Neue Folge der Vorlesungen zur Einfuhrung in die Psychoanalyse*	1933	Freud published his lectures XXIX–XXXV, covering revised theories on topics such as dream analysis and feminine sexuality. He also discussed the Weltanschauung of psychoanalysis, or "view of the universe."
Why War?	*Warum Krieg?*	1933	Freud published an exchange of letters between himself and Einstein regarding avoidance of war. Freud concluded that suppression of the aggressive instinct was not likely.
Moses and Monothesim	*Der Mann Moses und die Monotheistische Religion*	1939	This book was an attempt to show the roots of monotheism and hence undermine it. Freud proposed that Moses was an Egyptian who imposed monotheism on the Hebrews.

to one another. Freud also described three levels of consciousness, the **unconscious,** the **preconscious,** and the **conscious.** In Freud's view, behavior is determined by conflict between forces within the mind. These forces are often operating *un*consciously (beyond the awareness of the person).

All psychoanalytic thinking is based to some extent on Freud's ideas. Chapter 4 focuses in detail on Freud's writing and theories, which lay the foundation for all later psychoanalytic theorizing.

Many followers of Freud diverged somewhat from his original theories and varied greatly among themselves. Some of them offered ideas that are direct outgrowths of Freud's theories. Others suggested major modifications or expansions of Freud's ideas. A few could even be considered *anti*-Freudian. But even the most radical dissidents carried forth some basic underlying elements that warrant their continued membership within the psychoanalytic strategy. Typically, these later theorists agree at least to some extent with Freud about one or more of his basic assertions regarding (1) the concept of driving forces, (2) the operation of the unconscious, (3) conflict between the individual and society, and (4) the need for a developmental scheme to understand personality. These common ties guide our presentation of the major post-Freudian positions described in Chapter 5.

Psychoanalytic theorists fall into five broad camps: Freudians, who closely subscribe to Freud's ideas; revisionist stage theorists, who expand on or alter Freud's developmental scheme; motivational theorists, who expand on the number of basic drives described by Freud and his early followers; ego psychologists, who focus more on ego processes and adaptation in the "healthy" person; and object-relations theorists, who emphasize interpersonal issues and the concept of self. Revisionist stage theorists, motivational psychologists, ego psychologists, and object relations theorists are all considered post-Freudians. All of these theories, as well as those of Freud, are sometimes also called **psychodynamic** theories.

For the purposes of this chapter, we would like to briefly introduce Freud's ideas and the context in which they developed. Chapter 4 will then present a more complete discussion of Freudian theory, with the major post-Freudian schools of thought being elaborated further in Chapter 5.

SEARCH FOR THE DRIVING FORCE(S)

Physicists in the 18th and 19th centuries identified two forces in physical nature (the gravitational force and the electromagnetic force), and Darwin theorized that two forces drove biological life (survival of the individual and survival of the species). Freud reasoned that psychological life was also driven by universal forces.

A **drive** in the Psychoanalytic Strategy is an inborn force built into the human mind. One or more drives are presumed to direct the overall tone of our thoughts, feelings, and activities. When drives are not satisfied, we experience tension. The need is not satisfied or the tension relieved until the drive is allowed some form of expression.

Freud's View

Freud's early theory had two classes of drives: *self-preservative* and *sexual*. The self-preservative drive encompasses all our physical needs, including breathing, thirst, hunger, and excretion. The second drive in Freud's scheme was the *sex drive*. Freud's ideas about sex were more encompassing than ours today. Almost anything experienced as sensuous would probably have been considered sexual by Freud (languidly petting a cat's soft hair, for instance, while the cat purrs gently back at your "advances").

Libido

The great inventions and discoveries of scientists' times combine to produce a particular spirit or atmosphere *(zeitgeist)* in which scientists live and work. This spirit—or the discoveries that contribute to it—often evolves into metaphors on which the scientists of the day build their theories. So it was with Freud.

The most important metaphor of Freud's day was the complex but essentially inert *machine*. (Newton had likened the whole universe to a giant clock.) Machines were then known as inanimate things, which remain immobile unless energized in some way.

The sexual drive was Freud's answer to the need for energy with which to mobilize his proposed system. (Recall that Schopenhauer considered sex to be the most important human instinct.) The system would be static without the presence of *psychic energy.* The English-language word for this form of energy is **libido** (lih-BEE-doe). This libidinal energy was cast by Freud as the ultimate source of energy for all mental activity, including all the activities that modern personality psychologists call *cognitive* (thinking, perceiving, imagining, and problem solving). A great deal of Freud's theorizing was based on his concept of libido, which came to be challenged by even some of his most ardent followers.

Conflict

Conflict plays a central role in personality development within Freud's scheme. Conflict exists both within the individual (e.g., between a moral choice and a selfish choice) and between the individual and society (e.g., society must control an individual's raw impulses toward sex and aggression).

THE BRANCHING PATH

Post-Freudians (by definition) all diverge from Freud's thinking on one issue or another. Some disagreed with very little of Freud's theory but simply extended or modified the developmental scheme he presented.

Revisionist Stage Theories

Many of those who have proposed developmental progression theories that differ from Freud's invariant psychosexual stages diverge relatively little from Freud. Unlike other post-Freudians, Jung and Erikson accepted the bulk of Freud's theory, but extended his view of personality development (which Freud believed was completed by the fourth or fifth year of life), modifying it to some extent. These theories are described in some detail in Chapter 5. Margaret Mahler, by contrast, came out of the object relations movement to propose a radically different developmental scheme. Her theory and other object relations theories are also discussed in detail in Chapter 5.

Alternative Views of Basic Human Motivation

Mention Freud, and many people's initial association is sex. Freud's insistence on the preeminence of the sexual drive in human motivation ultimately made his views unacceptable to many, both within and outside the psychoanalytic circle. His basic conception of drive theory and his emphasis on the sex drive (libido) as the *fundamental* drive underlying human motivation stirred the most disagreement among his immediate followers, including two of his most prominent early followers, Carl Jung and Alfred Adler.

Early in their relationship, Jung (pronounced YUNG) wrote Freud to ask:

> Is it not conceivable, in view of the limited conception of sexuality that prevails nowadays, that the sexual terminology should be reserved only for the most extreme forms of your "libido," and that a less offensive collective term should be established for all the libidinal manifestations? (Freud & Jung, 1974, p. 25)

Jung believed that the sexual drive is an important source of motivation but not the only source.

Adler's disagreement with Freud over the importance of the sexual drive is sharper. Adler believed the fundamental human motive is **striving for superiority,** as compensation for feelings of inferiority. Adler's own life was the basis of the idea. As a child, Adler was continually sick and weak. Adler became a physician, and later a psychoanalyst, in response to his deprived and unsatisfying childhood experiences. Thus, his personal history led him to a different perspective on human motivation, emphasizing superiority and power over the sex drive of Freud.

Ego Psychology

According to Freud, the id (the most primitive aspect of the self) is the dominant force in personality. A major role of the ego—and, to some extent, of the superego—is ensuring that id impulses are held in check. Without the ego, personality would be overwhelmed by basic, instinctual desires.

As psychoanalysis developed, the id-dominated view of the dynamics of personality began to fade. A conflict-ridden personality was a reasonable explanation for the development of psychopathology, but it was inadequate to explain normal, adaptive personality. From this perceived deficit, ego psychology arose as a new branch of psychoanalysis (Blanck & Blanck, 1974).

Ego psychology emphasizes (1) adaptive control rather than defense; (2) general motives, such as mastery and competence, rather than limiting itself to sexual and aggressive drives; and (3) conscious determinism rather than unconscious determinism (Klein, 1976; Levine & Slap, 1985).

Object Relations

Object relations theorists in the main hold that yet another distinct drive motivates human behavior. They contend that striving for contact with others, a *social need,* drives people. The resulting shift, away from the basic drives of Freud and toward an examination of the patterns of thought and feeling that underlie interpersonal behavior, produced the so-called object relations theories. (In psychoanalysis, the term *object* generally refers to persons, not things.) **Object relations** is currently seen as "a set of cognitive and affective processes in close relationships" (Westen, 1991a, p. 211).

The principal claim of object relations theories is that people develop internal working models of self and others. In turn, these models govern feelings and reactions toward the self (e.g., self-esteem) and feelings and reactions toward other people. The mental representations of particular people are called **object representations.**

Of the various object relations theories, none is complete. Current thinking about object relations can be traced to a variety of psychoanalysts, spanning a period of more than 50 years (Westen, 1991b). Our major goal at this point is to synthesize the work of a number of theorists into a coherent whole.

Two major differences between object relations theories and Freudian theory can be distinguished. One difference concerns the basic nature of human motivation. Instead of believing in drive reduction, object relations theorists hold that human beings are primarily motivated by the need to establish and maintain relationships with others. In other words, the primary drive is for human contact (Cashdan, 1988). The second major difference is that all object relations theories focus on the earliest mother-child relationship as the key to psychological growth (Sayers, 1991). In contrast, Freud also emphasized the role of the father and thought that the major turning point in development occurred during the Oedipal years (between the ages of 3 and 5).

PSYCHOANALYTIC PERSONALITY ASSESSMENT

Psychoanalytic theory assumes that our motivations are often unconscious; that is, we are often unaware of why we act the way we do. Assessing motives that you are partially or completely unaware of is complex and difficult. To appreciate the complexity, ask yourself the following questions:

1. Why am I going to college?
2. Why do I like (or dislike) my roommate (friend, relative)?
3. Why do I enjoy my favorite activity?

If the answers to these questions seem obvious at first, try inserting the word *really* in front of the words *going, like,* and *enjoy.* Is answering the questions more difficult?

Psychoanalytic personality assessment is indirect in two respects. First, because unconscious phenomena cannot be observed directly by others, they must be assessed by indirect methods. Second, according to psychoanalytic theory, personality characteristics may appear as either direct or indirect expressions of underlying drives. We normally expect direct expression. For example, we expect an individual who feels hostile to attack another person, either physically or verbally. However, the underlying motives may be expressed indirectly instead. Thus, hostility may be disguised, such as by ignoring others. The most indirect way to express a motive is as its opposite. Hostility may emerge as friendly and loving acts. The more socially unacceptable a motive, the more likely it is to be expressed indirectly. Indirect expression gives a person with unacceptable motives an outlet without the resulting anxiety or guilt normally associated with socially unacceptable motives.

Another vehicle for the expression of unconscious material is through symbols. They can appear through dreams reported by patients or observed in some behaviors in the context of therapy or assessment. They may also be apparent in a person's choice of occupation, hobbies, and leisure activities.

Psychoanalytic Symbols

The mind works in symbols. (As we will see, this idea resurfaced in the 1980s and 1990s in modern theory and research on cognitive processes; see Chapter 17.) A **symbol** is a verbal or pictorial representation that stands for something else. Freud was interested in symbols as a route to unconscious material. Our hidden conflicts, pressing endlessly for expression, might reveal themselves symbolically rather than directly and openly. The trick, of course, is to be able to accurately decipher the "true" meaning of the symbols as they appear.

Freud focused on symbols that he felt conveyed sexual meaning, the most pressing of human drives and the most likely to leak out in symbolic form. Freud believed that, in general, dreaming or fantasizing about elongated or pointed objects usually represents the penis or male sexuality and related themes. Freud also believed that the most pressing conflicts would become evident through *repetition* (often in symbolic form). He originally referred to this phenomenon as **repetition compulsion** and believed that the repetition would continue until the underlying conflict was recognized or resolved.

Symbols are common in art and literature as well. Many of Freud's original symbols pervade Western literature and have achieved wide recognition and acceptance. Almost any element reported from a person's dreams might be subject to symbolic interpretation by an analytically oriented therapist. (Freud's theory of dreams is discussed in Chapter 6.)

PSYCHOANALYTIC RESEARCH

Freud relied entirely on the case study method. He used the extensive information he gathered about the patients in his clinical practice both as the source of his personality theory and as evidence for the theory.

Psychoanalytic case studies include more than just a detailed description of the patient-subject's behavior. The observations must be *interpreted*. These interpretations become an integral part of the case study (Steele, 1986). Any behavior during the psychoanalytic session, including the patient's reports of behavior outside the session, may be interpreted. Before making an interpretation, the analyst waits until a similar observation is made several times, so that a theme is established. An interpretation is validated partially by the degree to which the patient accepts it as true and partially by whether it leads to changes in the patient's behavior. Psychoanalysts also interpret their patients' free associations and dreams, which are assumed to be valuable sources of unconscious material that have become conscious in disguised or symbolic form.

Many psychoanalysts believe that psychoanalytic concepts can be validated only through interpretation of material obtained from case studies. Freud wrote to some researchers who had attempted to validate psychoanalytic concepts through laboratory-type experiments:

> I have examined your experimental studies for the verification of psychoanalytic assertions with interest. I cannot put much value on these confirmations because the wealth of reliable observations on which these assertions rest make them independent of experimental verification. Still, it can do no harm. (quoted by MacKinnon & Dukes, 1962, p. 702)

Case studies, more than any other research method, allow psychologists to explore the richness and complexity of human personality. Interpretative case studies are still the main (although clearly not the *only*) method of research in the Psychoanalytic Strategy (Langs, 1987, 1988). Post-Freudians have increasingly used correlational and experimental methods to test psychoanalytic propositions (e.g., Fisher & Greenberg, 1977; Kline, 1972; Masling, 1983, 1985).

PSYCHOANALYTIC PERSONALITY CHANGE

Psychoanalytic theory, assessment, and research began with attempts to change abnormal personality. Most psychoanalysts are practicing psychotherapists ("personality changers") first and theorists, assessors, and researchers second (Michels, 1988). Psychoanalytic personality change (psychotherapy) involves indirect methods, just as psychoanalytic assessment does. These methods are used because the conflicts causing patients' problems are primarily unconscious. A major aim of psychoanalytic personality change is to make patients aware of their unconscious processes and motives—that is, making conscious what is unconscious.

Personality change comes about primarily through the lengthy process of patients' discovering and understanding the underlying causes of their feelings and behavior. This process is sometimes accompanied by intense emotional release. Patients often discover, in the course of psychoanalysis, that their present behaviors and motives are based on early childhood adjustment problems and conflicts. They must learn that such factors are no longer relevant to their lives and are therefore unrealistic guides for their present behavior.

TRENDS IN THE EVOLUTION OF THE PSYCHOANALYTIC STRATEGY

Psychoanalysis has been evolving ever since Freud and his early followers first charted its course. This evolution has taken five broad directions.

First, there has been increasing recognition of social determinants of personality (especially within the ego psychology and object relations camps). This approach contrasts with the predominant role assigned to biological drives and instincts in Freudian psychoanalysis. Furthermore, whereas Freudian psychoanalysis is a "one-person psychology," more recent psychoanalytic approaches have been "two-person psychologies," in the sense of assuming that individuals can be understood only in the context of another person (e.g., Modell, 1984). Object relations theories are prime examples of this growing recognition among psychoanalysts (Leichtman, 1990).

Second, the time frame of personality development has been expanded and elaborated. Many psychoanalysts today view personality development as lifelong rather than, as Freud believed, virtually completed by age 5. "Whereas the formation of psychic structure in a child is like broad strokes painted on a bare canvas, the evolution of psychic structure in adulthood is equivalent to fine, nearly invisible strokes on a complicated background" (Colarusso & Nemiroff, 1979, p. 62). This broader concept of personality has implications for personality change as well (Gedo, 1979). "The analytic patient, regardless of age, is considered to be still in the process of ongoing development as opposed to merely being in possession of a past that influences . . . present conscious and unconscious life" (Shane, 1977, pp. 95–96).

Third, many psychoanalysts, particularly ego psychologists, consider conscious aspects of personality to be important (Robbins, 1989). This view contrasts with the central role given the unconscious in Freudian theory. It is still true, however, that psychoanalysis emphasizes unconscious motives and conflicts more than any of the other three strategies.

Fourth, contemporary psychoanalysis emphasizes normal personality more than does classical psychoanalysis. This is true in terms of devoting more study to normal personality functioning, as ego psychologists do; it is also true in terms of viewing normal personality as worthy of detailed analysis. Classical psychoanalytic theory focuses on intrapsychic conflict, anxiety and defense, and psychopathology. Ego psychologists examine the other side of the coin: the conflict-free sphere of personality. This part of personality allows people to remain relatively healthy by coping successfully with the inner and outer forces that shape their personalities. Still, psychoanalysis remains a strategy that tends to proceed from abnormal personality to normal personality because most psychoanalytic theorists and researchers are psychotherapists by training and profession.

Fifth, psychoanalysis has increasingly been related to basic theory and research in mainstream psychology. Psychoanalysis began outside traditional academic circles, in Freud's private psychoanalytic sessions. The methods of psychoanalysis—dream analysis, free association, interpretation of mistakes and symbolism—are not those considered acceptable to many academic psychologists. Since the 1930s, however, numerous attempts have been made to relate psychoanalysis to theories and research in the mainstream of academic psychology and to try to validate psychoanalytic concepts empirically through correlational and experimental research. There has even been an effort to relate psychoanalysis to one of the most talked-about recent developments in physics, chaos theory (Moran, 1991).

SUMMARY

1. Psychoanalysis refers to procedures for changing personality based on a comprehensive theory of personality and a related approach to research. Freud was the originator of psychoanalysis, and his ideas dominate the Psychoanalytic Strategy.
2. Sigmund Freud, born on May 6, 1856, wrote 21 books and remains the most cited and probably most influential psychologist of all time. He was the first to popularize psychotherapy as a form of treatment.
3. Freud conceptualized the framework of the mind in two ways: functions of personality (id, ego, and superego) and levels of awareness (unconscious, preconscious, and conscious).
4. Psychoanalytic theorists fall into five broad camps: Freudians, revisionist stage theorists, motivational psychologists, ego psychologists, and object relations theorists.
5. Psychoanalytic theory posits that inborn forces, or drives, direct our thoughts and behavior. Unsatisfied drives result in tension, relieved only when the drive is expressed.
6. The two classes of drives that Freud identified as motivating virtually all human behavior are the self-preservative and sexual drives.
7. Classification of the sex drive (libido) as the fundamental drive created much disagreement among post-Freudians, including Carl Jung and Alfred Adler.

8. Ego psychology is concerned with how the ego copes adaptively with reality through perception, cognition, language, creative production, attention, and memory.
9. Object relation theorists believe that people are primarily driven by social needs rather than basic instinctual drives.
10. Psychoanalytic personality assessment uses indirect methods because personality is presumed to operate primarily at an unconscious level beyond the awareness of the individual.
11. Case studies, usually of patients in psychoanalysis, are the primary research tool of this strategy. Case studies continue to provide the major source of evidence for psychoanalytic personality theory, although other research methods are now also being applied to psychoanalytic theories.
12. Most psychoanalysts are practicing psychotherapists. Psychoanalysis is usually a long process during which the patient is made aware of the underlying, often unconscious determinants of his or her behavior and personality.
13. Modern psychoanalysis has placed increasing emphasis on social relations, lifelong normal personality development, conscious motives, and scientific research methods.

CHAPTER FOUR

Freud's Psychoanalytic Theories

s stated in Chapter 3, Freud initially believed all human motivation was broadly sexual. In other words, all human behavior is motivated by pleasure seeking, involving the release of *libidinal energy.* Yet societies place obstacles in the way of completely or even predominantly satisfying our pleasure-seeking drives. In capsule form, Freud's theory of personality deals with how people handle their sexual needs in relation to society, which often prevents the direct expression of those needs. Each individual's personality is therefore a result of a unique compromise between satisfying sexual drives and conforming to society's restraints.

FREUD'S DUAL DRIVES

Around 1920, shortly after experiencing and observing the tragedy of World War I, Freud revised his theory of motivation to include the *aggressive drive,* in addition to the *sex drive* fueled by libido. (Freud also called the aggressive drive the *death drive, death instinct,* or *Thanatos,* in opposition to the *life drive,* or *Eros.*)

The **aggressive drive** accounts for the destructive aspects of human behavior and has its own kind of psychic energy. However, Freud did not give a specific name to this energy. The development and function of the aggressive drive and the sexual drive are parallel. Freud's **dual theory of drives** assumes that both the sexual and the aggressive drives are involved in motivating behavior.

The contributions of the two drives are not necessarily equal, however. Freud did not describe the aggressive drive as fully or clearly as the sex drive. Freud always considered the sex drive to be paramount. Accordingly, our discussion focuses on the sexual drive.

FOUR CHARACTERISTICS OF FREUD'S THEORIES

Freud's theories all share some common characteristics and assumptions, including that (1) there is a *dynamic* flow of psychic energy among "structures" of personality, (2) human behavior is *determined* by innate drives, (3) personality is *organized* in several layers of "structure" and functions, and (4) all people progress through a *fixed developmental sequence* of psychosexual stages. We will next examine these characteristics in some detail.

Dynamic

Dynamic, as applied to psychoanalytic theory, refers to the exchange and transformation of energy within the personality. Like most later psychoanalysts, Freud believed that the source of human motivation was **psychic energy.** (An alternative name for psychic energy is **libidinal energy.**) He theorized that people have a fixed amount of psychic energy that is used for all psychological functions.

Freud's psychic energy system is a closed system; that is, energy cannot be added to the system, and no existing energy can escape or be depleted. Each person has a fixed quantity of psychic energy that is invested in (devoted to) various behaviors (e.g., one's artistic performance), people (e.g., a parent), and ideas (e.g., philosophic or religious principles). An investment of psychic energy is known as a **cathexis** (*cathexes* is the plural form); to *cathect,* the verb form, is the process of investing psychic energy.

Psychic energy cannot actually be invested in (attached to) people or activities, but in the mind psychic energy can be cathected to mental representations in the form of thoughts, images, and fantasies. The strength of a cathexis is the amount of energy invested in it. The greater the amount of energy devoted to one cathexis, the less psychic energy available for other cathexes and mental activities. A young man who is constantly thinking of a woman friend has difficulty doing other things (e.g., reading an assignment in his personality textbook). Cathexes are not permanent. When we turn our attention to another activity or person, the energy transfers to the new focus.

You may be wondering whether some people have more psychic energy than others. The concept of psychic energy has never been quantified, so the question cannot be answered. What is important is that each person has a *fixed amount* of psychic energy, which places limits on actions, thoughts, and feelings.

Reduction of psychic tension (internal pressure to satisfy drives) is necessary for a person to function. Because tension is unpleasant or painful, reducing tension produces a highly pleasurable experience. The tendency to reduce tension immediately is known as the **pleasure principle.** If the individual's psychic energy does not have an opportunity to discharge in normal or socially acceptable ways, the pressure will increase.

Freud used an analogy to explain the nature of psychic energy: The pressure of psychic energy builds in the same way water pressure builds in a hydraulic system. Take, for example, a series of water-filled pipes, in which the external valve is closed. If pressure increases and there is no outlet for the water, the pipe will burst at its weakest point to reduce the pressure.

Deterministic

According to Freud, all behavior is **determined,** or caused, by some force within the person. Thus, all behavior has meaning; no behavior occurs by chance. Even the simplest actions can be traced to complicated psychological factors of which the person may be totally unaware. Perhaps the best-known occurrences are "Freudian slips"—errors made in speech, writing, and reading that presumably reveal something about the person's "inner" thoughts or "real" intents. Here are three simple examples:

A psychologist was preparing an article condemning Freud's ideas. She began by writing: "Fraud's theory. . . . "

A man was examining the centerfold of *Playboy* magazine. A friend asked what magazine he was reading. He responded, *"Playbody."*

A student told her boyfriend that she was "getting rid of" a statistics examination when she meant to say "getting ready for" the examination.

Other examples of Freud's (1963) thoroughgoing determinism relate to "accidentally" forgetting something or losing an object. He wrote:

> If anyone forgets a proper name which is familiar to him normally or if, in spite of all his efforts, he finds it difficult to keep it in mind, it is plausible to suppose

> that he has something against the person who bears the name so that he prefers not to think of him. . . . (p. 52)

> We lose an object if we have quarreled with the person who gave it to us and do not want to be reminded of him; or if we no longer like the object itself and want to have an excuse for getting another and better one instead. The same intention directed against an object can also play a part, of course, in cases of dropping, breaking, or destroying things. . . . (p. 54)

Freud analyzed and interpreted incidents like these to understand facets of personality that would not otherwise be accessible. He first wrote about them in *The Psychopathology of Everyday Life* (1901), from which the preceding excerpts are taken. (The book is easy to read and is available in paperback.) Freudian slips and related phenomena are particularly appealing ideas because they make psychoanalytic concepts part of daily life (Turkle, 1988).

These examples are also noteworthy because they imply that some of our feelings can be hidden from consciousness. Slavin (1990) commented:

> The underlying notion that there is some important set of desires or perceptions missing from the central conscious personality is, almost by definition, a universal psychoanalytic observation. (p. 308)

Organizational/Structural

Freud divided personality into three separate structures: **id** (primitive, pleasure-seeking impulses), **ego** (rational self), and **superego** (internalized values of society). According to Freud, natural biological instincts (id), such as the need for food, elimination, and sexual gratification, are inevitably in conflict with the restraints of reality (ego) and the rules of society (superego). These conflicts determine an individual's specific actions.

Developmental

The importance of early childhood development in determining adult personality is a cornerstone of Freud's theory. In fact, Freud believed that adult personality is established by approximately 5 years of age. In Freud's own words, "The little creature is often completed by the fourth or fifth year of life, and after that merely brings gradually to light what is already within him" (quoted by Roazen, 1975, p. 106). All psychoanalysts agree that early childhood experiences are important.

Freud theorized that personality development follows a more or less set course from birth. He divided development into a series of discrete stages through which every human being passes. Most post-Freudians agree with Freud that personality development follows a course of discrete stages. However, they have suggested various sets of stages that differ as to when they occur and what transpires in them (as discussed in Chapter 5).

FREUD'S LEVELS OF CONSCIOUSNESS

Freud divided the mind into three levels of awareness: *conscious, preconscious,* and *unconscious.* The **conscious** includes what we are aware of at a given point in time. This definition is close to the everyday use of the term. However, Freud contended that only a small fraction of a person's thoughts, images, and memories is conscious. The Freudian mind, like an iceberg, is nine-tenths below the surface.

The **preconscious** includes thoughts of which we are not immediately aware (conscious) but that can easily be brought to awareness. You may have had the experience of concentrating on a topic, as in an intense conversation, and suddenly finding yourself thinking about a completely unrelated topic. These unrelated thoughts were present but had been in your preconscious. By definition, the content of the preconscious is accessible with minimal effort. By contrast, a great deal of mental content is *not* readily accessible (see Figure 4.1).

Mental content that is not available for conscious recall is stored in the **unconscious,** the dominant part of the mind. According to Freud, most behavior is motivated by forces of which the person is totally unaware. Impulses, memories, and feelings that might be harmful or threatening to us are actively kept out of conscious awareness through a process called *repression*. (Repression is an ego defense mechanism that is discussed at some length later in this chapter.) These unconscious thoughts enter consciousness only in *disguised* or *symbolic* form.

Freud held that these parts of the mind are universal; all people possess a vast unconscious realm within. In *The Psychopathology of Everyday Life,* Freud

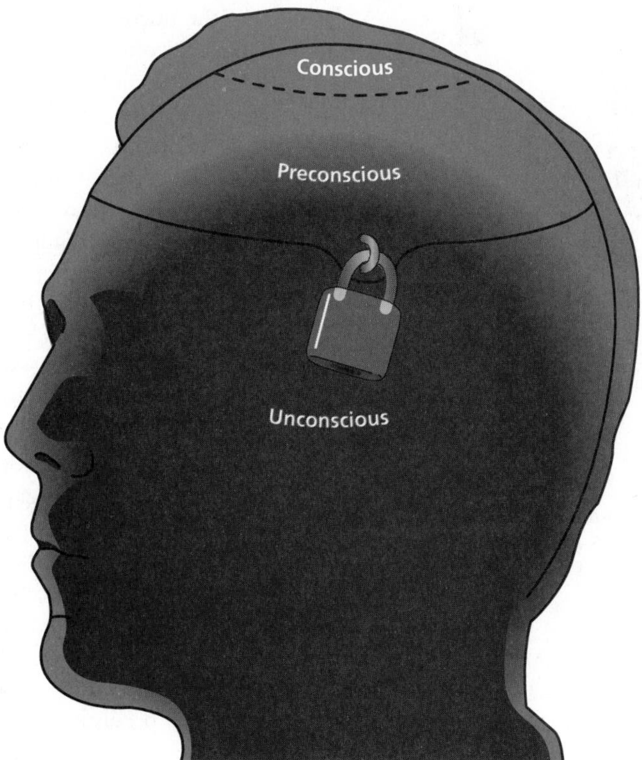

Figure 4.1
Only a small fraction of mental material is available to or retrievable in consciousness.

(1901) argued that the unconscious is an important and influential part of every mind (not just of those who are "sick" or neurotic). In fact, psychoanalysis is sometimes called **depth psychology** because a primary aim is to plumb the depths of the mind to unearth material previously "hidden away" in the unconscious. Carl Jung, a prominent follower of Freud, proposed a variation on Freud's levels of consciousness (see Box 4.1).

Box 4.1
JUNG'S DIVISIONS OF CONSCIOUSNESS

Jung also divided the personality into three levels of consciousness: conscious ego, personal unconscious, and collective unconscious. The **conscious ego** includes perceptions, thoughts, feelings, and memories of which a person is aware. It is essentially equivalent to Freud's conscious.

Carl Jung (1875–1961) challenged Freud's emphasis on the sexual drive. He later introduced the idea of a collective unconscious furnished with archetypes from our ancestral past.
Courtesy of National Library of Medicine, Bethesda, Maryland, 20014

The **personal unconscious** contains some mental images that we are not immediately aware of but that can readily become part of the conscious ego as well as other mental images that are being repressed. We are unaware of some unconscious material because we are attending to other matters. In other cases, images in the personal unconscious are actively repressed because they are threatening to the conscious ego. Jung's personal unconscious has features similar to Freud's preconscious and unconscious.

However, Jung's ideas about the personal unconscious diverge from Freud's in three important ways. First, Jung rejected the idea that the unconscious is "monstrous" (Roazen, 1975). Second, Jung believed that the personal unconscious not only stores past experiences but also anticipates the future. Third, Jung argued that the personal unconscious serves an adaptive function by balancing out conscious attitudes that lean too heavily in one direction. This adjustment is accomplished by allowing the appropriate opposite tendency to occur in dreams and fantasies (Jung, 1969).

Jung believed that personality is more than just a product of personal experiences and memories. Individuals also think and act in ways shaped by experiences common to all humans throughout the evolution of the species. Jung called this part of personality the **collective unconscious.** He considered the collective unconscious to be the dominant aspect of personality. This concept has no direct parallel in Freud's theory and is Jung's most original and controversial idea (Badalamenti, 1988).

The collective unconscious contains **archetypes,** or predispositions to think and act in

Box continued on following page

Box 4.1 *Continued*
JUNG'S DIVISIONS OF CONSCIOUSNESS

particular ways. Archetypes are inherited, general tendencies to form representations of mythological themes. The specific content of each theme (archetype) varies considerably according to time and place but always retains its fundamental pattern. How a person's thoughts and actions are influenced by any given archetype depends on where and when the person lives. The Hero archetype, for example, could assume the form of a medieval knight, a Chinese warlord, an explorer, a basketball player, a civil rights leader, or an astronaut. The Hero archetype can be considered a flexible mold underlying the idea of hero; the archetype requires a culture to fill it with a myth (Storr & Kermode, 1973).

Jung devoted much of his career to discovering the archetypal images that frequently appear in myths from diverse cultures, in dreams and fantasies (including his own), and in art (Figure 4.2). We have already mentioned the Hero archetype. It embodies the generally agreed on meanings of heroism: courage, vanquishing evil or the unknown, and serving noble ends, often for the good of others.

Mother is an archetype that may be elicited by any "mothering" figure. This includes real people, such as one's mother or grandmother, and *mother symbols*, such as the Virgin Mary, one's alma mater (Latin for "other mother"), the Church, and Mother Earth. The Mother archetype has a dual nature: positive (good,

Figure 4.2
Star Wars is a mythical tale in which each of the main characters represents an archetype. Darth Vader represents the *Shadow* and Ben Kenobi represents the *Wise Old Man*.

Box continued on following page

Box 4.1 *Continued*
JUNG'S DIVISIONS OF CONSCIOUSNESS

light) and negative (evil, dark). The Evil Mother often appears in myths and fairy tales as the Wicked Witch (Ulanov & Ulanov, 1987).

The *Shadow* archetype represents the "dark side" of personality—the side people do not like to acknowledge in themselves. It is the model for people's animal instincts and for evil and unacceptable ideas. Shadow images appear in myths as evil, the devil, monsters, and demons (Bly, 1988).

Animus is the archetype of the "masculine" aspects of women; **Anima** is the archetype of the "feminine" aspects of men. (Jung, like Freud, believed in the *bi*sexuality of human personality.) The difference between Animus and Anima is that Animus produces opinions (solid conviction) in women: Anima produces moods (often expressed as sudden changes) in men.

Jung's ideas about archetypes and the collective unconscious came from his extensive study of universal myths and symbols. Contemporary scholars have found that there are indeed common themes in myths and fairy tales, such as the struggles of mythical heroes, across cultures separated geographically and temporally (Campbell, 1988).

ID, EGO, AND SUPEREGO: A CLOSER LOOK AT THE THREE STRUCTURES OF PERSONALITY

Initially, Freud organized personality in terms of levels of consciousness, emphasizing the role of the unconscious. Later, around 1920, he described id, ego, and superego. He proposed that the ego and superego function at all three levels of awareness, but *mainly* at the unconscious level. The id, however, is entirely unconscious. The three personality functions in relation to the three levels of awareness are shown schematically in Figure 4.3.

The id, ego, and superego are theoretical constructs; they do not physically exist within the brain. They represent the desiring and pleasure-seeking (id), realistic and rational (ego), and moral and ideal (superego) aspects of human behavior.

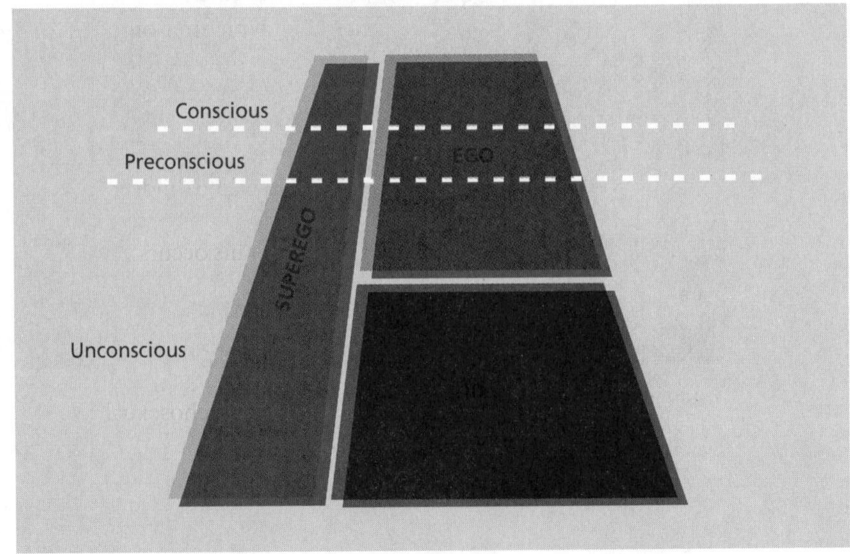

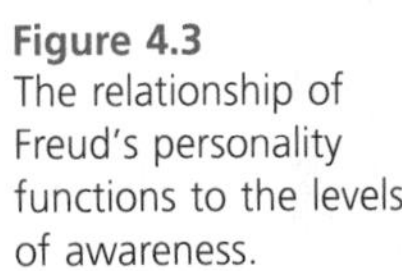
Figure 4.3
The relationship of Freud's personality functions to the levels of awareness.

Id

Freud viewed the newborn as more akin to a demon than an angel. At birth, the personality consists of a single structure, the id. The term (which rhymes with *kid*) comes from the German *das Es,* meaning "the It." The id is a reservoir for all drives and derives power directly from bodily needs and processes. As bodily needs such as hunger and thirst build up, they must be satisfied. The resulting increase in tension must be discharged. When the id governs this discharge, gratification is *immediate.* The id cannot tolerate any delay in gratification. The id is regulated by what Freud called the *pleasure principle,* which demands immediate tension reduction—in other words, instant pleasure and no pain. The priorities of the id are well captured by the phrase "I want what I want—and *I want it NOW!*"

The id uses two basic techniques to reduce tension: reflex action and primary process. At its most primitive level, the id works by **reflex action.** It reacts automatically and immediately to internal and external irritants to the body. Tension or distress from the irritants is thus quickly removed. Reflex actions include inborn mechanisms such as sneezing, blinking, and coughing.

Because the id cannot tolerate any delay of gratification or any tension, we would expect very young children to "cry" the instant an appetite or need arises. This seems to be just what happens. (Infants, of course, can satisfy some of their own needs independently, such as elimination.) The child often requires something tangible from the outside world, however, such as food or water. If the needed object is not immediately available, the id forms a mental image of it. This imagery production aimed at gratification is termed **primary process.** When the infant is hungry, for example, primary process can instantly supply an image of food. This experience is called **wish fulfillment** because the desire is (temporarily) fulfilled. Adult dreams in which a fond desire is met (e.g., a sexual encounter with a movie star) are remnants of infant wish fulfillment.

Primary process is a crude mechanism. No distinction is made between what is actually required and a mere mental image of what is required. Thus, food and a mental picture of food are accepted as equivalent. The id is satisfied with the image, but the image obviously does not actually reduce tension. One cannot survive long on mental pictures of food. If the infant's real needs were met immediately, as they were before birth, primary process would be satisfactory. But inevitably, in life after birth, gratification must be delayed. No mother can be constantly available to tend her baby.

Infants' capacities to tolerate delay of gratification develop as they become aware of a separate external world. Children grow aware of something that is "not me" that must be taken into account and considered apart from, but interrelated with, themselves. This occurs with the development of the second aspect of personality, the ego.

Ego

The ego emerges, in rudimentary form, during the first 6 months of life while the infant is in the oral stage of psychosexual development. (Freud's stages of development are detailed later in this chapter.) Freud called this structure of personality *das Ich,* literally, "the I" in English. (Although "the I" is a literal translation of "das Ich," the Latin word *ego* has been adopted as the accepted English translation.)

The ego "borrows" some of the id's psychic energy for its own functions. Because there is only a limited amount of psychic energy, transfer of energy to the ego means that *less* energy is left for id functions. One consequence is that the child becomes more willing to wait for gratification.

In contrast to the id's pleasure principle, the ego is governed by the **reality principle,** which postpones the discharge of energy until an appropriate situation or object in the real world appears. Whereas the pleasure principle is oriented *inward,* the reality principle is oriented *outward,* toward the constraints of the "real" world. The ego does not challenge the id's pleasure-seeking motivation. Instead, it temporarily suspends pleasure for the sake of realistic constraints.

The ego is the representative of the external world. Whereas the id's primary process identifies the object or situation necessary to satisfy a particular need (e.g., an image of food), the ego's **secondary process** creates a strategy for obtaining the actual object or situation (e.g., going to the cookie jar). The ego, then, is characterized by realistic thinking and problem solving. It is the seat of intellectual processes. Daydreaming is an example of a secondary process and illustrates the reality-bound nature of the ego. People enjoy the pleasurable fantasy of a daydream, but they do not mistake the fantasy for reality as they do with a nocturnal dream (which is a primary process).

Human beings function both as individuals and as members of society. To do so, they must learn not only to deal with the direct constraints of physical

The ego's secondary process plans a reality-based strategy for obtaining gratification demanded by the id.

reality but also to follow social norms and prohibitions. Furthermore, they must conform to society's "laws," even in the absence of external monitors or immediate threats of apprehension, punishment, or failure. Around age 3 or 4, children begin to evaluate their own behavior independently of immediate threat or reward. This is the function of the third structure of personality, the superego.

Superego

The last of Freud's personality structures he termed *das Uberich* (literally "the over-I"), called the superego in English. The superego is the internal representative of the values of parents and society. It strives for the *ideal* rather than the real. The superego judges an act as right or wrong—as consistent or inconsistent with moral values—independent of its usefulness.

When our actions and thoughts are acceptable, we experience pride, satisfaction, and worthiness. When our behavior is unacceptable, we experience guilt.

Superego functions can be divided into two spheres: conscience and ego ideal. The **conscience** fosters morally right behavior. It does so in two ways: (1) by inhibiting id impulses for pleasure and (2) by persuading the ego to attend to moral concerns. The **ego ideal** promotes idealistic and perfectionistic goals (Edwards, 1987).

The superego develops through the process of **incorporation:** "taking in" the values of parents in a manner analogous to the way we take in food. Incorporation begins about the fourth year of life. Through a process Freud termed **defensive identification,** the child absorbs and internalizes the moral values of the same-sex parent. Children also come to value both parents because of the love, warmth, and comfort they provide. By association, children also come to value their parents' moral standards and ideals.

Interaction Among the Id, Ego, and Superego

To summarize the Freudian view of the development of the three structures of personality, at birth only the id exists. Later, in response to the demands of reality, the ego develops. Finally, the superego emerges as the societal representative in the personality. When all three aspects have developed, the psychic energy that once belonged solely to the id is divided among the id, ego, and superego and flows and fluctuates among them. The ego serves as a mediator among three basic forces: (1) the demands of the id, (2) the requirements of reality, and (3) the limitations imposed by the superego (Figure 4.4). The ego ensures that instinctual needs are met in a realistic *and* socially approved manner.

Intrapsychic conflict arises when the aims of one aspect of personality are at odds with the aims of one or both of the other aspects. Most often, intrapsychic conflict erupts because of id demands pressing for immediate satisfaction. But the aims of all three aspects of the personality can be in conflict (Rangell, 1988). Examples appear in Table 4.1

How are intrapsychic conflicts resolved? Logically, three possibilities exist: (1) eliminating the drive, (2) directly expressing the drive, or (3) redirecting the drive. It is assumed that a drive can never be *completely* eliminated; it can be banished from consciousness but not from the total personality. Direct expression rarely occurs; if an id drive were allowed total expression, the ego

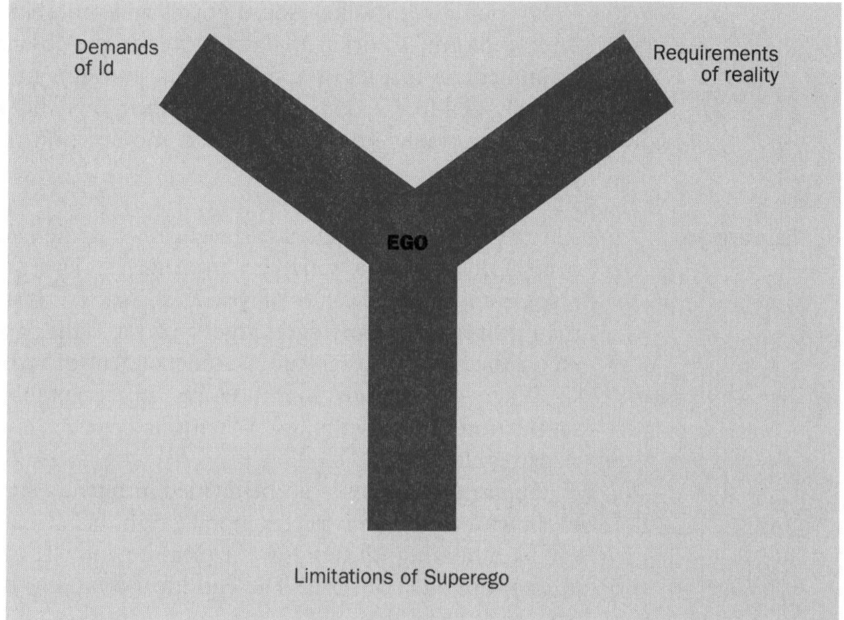

Figure 4.4
The ego as the mediator of personality.

would be overwhelmed with excitation and the person would experience intense anxiety. (The defensive processes the ego uses to prevent this anxiety will be discussed shortly.) Therefore, most intrapsychic conflicts are handled by redirection of a drive, which entails a compromise between the personality structures involved. For example, in an id-ego conflict over your desire to hit someone who has made you angry, you may choose to say something nasty instead.

Intrapsychic conflicts are part of normal personality functioning. Their resolution is a defensive process performed by the ego, which requires psychic energy. The more successfully the ego minimizes intrapsychic conflicts, the

Table 4.1 Possible conflicts among the aspects of personality

CONFLICT	EXAMPLE
Id versus ego	Choosing between a small immediate reward and a larger reward that requires some period of waiting (i.e., delay of gratification)
Id versus superego	Deciding whether to return the difference when you are overpaid or undercharged
Ego versus superego	Choosing between acting in a realistic way (e.g., telling a "white lie") and adhering to a potentially costly or unrealistic standard (e.g., always telling the truth)
Id and ego versus superego	Deciding whether to retaliate against the attack of a weak opponent or to turn the other cheek
Id and superego versus ego	Deciding whether to act in a realistic way that conflicts with both your desires and your moral convictions (e.g., the decision faced by devout Roman Catholics regarding use of contraception)
Ego and superego versus id	Choosing whether to act on the impulse to steal something you want and cannot afford; the ego would presumably be increasingly involved in such a conflict as the probability of being apprehended increased

more energy remains for the ego's higher mental functions, such as problem solving and creative pursuits.

ANXIETY AND DEFENSE

Anxiety is all too familiar to each of us. Freud suggested that anxiety is a signal of impending danger. The source of the danger can be either external or internal. As you probably can guess, Freud thought that anxiety is usually the result of something internal—an id impulse seeking expression.

Freudian theory distinguishes three types adult anxiety:

1. **Neurotic anxiety** results from an id-ego conflict. The id seeks to discharge an impulse, and the ego tries to impose realistic restraints on the impulse. An example would be fending off your impulse to respond angrily when a professor criticizes you in class.
2. **Moral anxiety** is generated by an id-superego conflict. Here the id impulse (e.g., to shoplift) is in opposition to the moral and ideal standards of society ("Thou shalt not steal") and is experienced by the individual as guilt or shame.
3. **Objective anxiety** is produced when a realistic, external threat is present, such as a fire or a street thug.

In each case, anxiety signals impending danger. In objective anxiety, the danger is external. It can be dealt with by taking realistic steps to eliminate or reduce the actual threat. Neurotic and moral anxiety are due to an impending *intrapsychic* danger. They must be coped with by internal means—namely, the defense mechanisms of the ego.

Ego Defense Mechanisms

Ego defense mechanisms are *un*conscious ego processes that keep disturbing and unconscious thoughts from being expressed directly. We are unaware of these processes as they operate in ourselves (because they are, by definition, unconscious operations), but we may be able to detect their operation in others.

The material being defended against can be an impulse, an object loss, or a failure experience (Cooper, 1988). A fundamental assumption of the psychoanalytic view is that conscious awareness of all of our myriad conflicting motives, impulses, and feelings would overwhelm us. Thus, the defense mechanisms of the ego protect the individual from being immobilized by unmanageable dread and anxiety.

Freud viewed defense mechanisms as an *absolute necessity* for survival in human society. He believed that at the most basic level the interests and drives of the individual are in constant conflict with the needs of civilized society. Thus, to avoid total anarchy, the needs of the individual must be expressed only through restricted and socially approved outlets. (Consider what might happen if at a party everyone felt entirely free to grab food, drinks, *and* mates from one another as the mood strikes!)

In learning about defense mechanisms, it is helpful to examine them separately. Bear in mind, though, that people rarely defend themselves against anxiety with a single mechanism; typically, defense mechanisms operate in combination. Furthermore, as will become apparent, there is considerable overlap in the way defense mechanisms protect the ego from overwhelming anxiety.

Repression

Repression involves actively and totally excluding threatening thoughts from consciousness. This does not mean that the thoughts are no longer influencing the individual—quite the contrary. Repressed thoughts exert a powerful influence on behavior, as do *all* unconscious impulses. However, because they are unconscious, the person is not directly aware of them. Repression is characterized by a continual struggle to contain primitive desires. A large investment of psychic energy is required to repress threatening information. A person's ability to repress unconscious impulses successfully may at times be incomplete, leading to some "leaking" into conscious awareness. Thus, individuals may have vague recollections that can be brought out under appropriate conditions (e.g., while undergoing psychoanalysis).

Like all defense mechanisms, repression may occur in "healthy" or "normal" individuals. A price is always paid when defense mechanisms are operative, however. Psychic energy used to defend the ego is unavailable for more adaptive functions such as intellectual and social pursuits. In the case of repression, the price is particularly severe. Repressed impulses may be healthy or adaptive, yet they may be permanently excluded from the development of the personality. For example, exclusion of all aggressive impulses is likely to result in undue passivity.

Daniel Wegner (1994) recently outlined a somewhat different theory to explain why mental content that we desire to keep from expression (repress)

Keeping the "psychic lid" on repressed material requires effort!

sometimes leaks out. He termed these **ironic processes,** meaning that they result in our thinking or doing things that are the precise opposite of what was consciously intended. Wegner's basic idea is that we all have a limited amount of mental capacity (not unlike Freud's idea that we each have a limited amount of psychic energy). When mental capacity is taxed in other ways, repression is less successful or complete than when it is fully available for the task of mental control. Wegner's theory is discussed in greater detail in Chapter 19.

Repression is the most fundamental defense mechanism, and it is also the crudest. In Freud's early writings, he used repression as a general term, synonymous with ego defense. In a sense, other defense mechanisms could be viewed as subtypes of repression. Repression as an idea has received a great deal of attention and been investigated empirically to some extent.

Davis and Schwartz (1987) devised an interesting way to study repression. They asked undergraduate women to recall personal experiences from childhood associated with specific emotions (happiness, sadness, anger, fear, and wonder). The women were classified as "repressors" (based on test scores indicating low anxiety and high defensiveness), high anxious, or low anxious. Repressors recalled fewer negative memories than either high anxious or low anxious subjects. Repressors were also substantially older at the time of their earliest recalled negative memories. Based on these data, Davis and Schwartz concluded that repression limits access to negative affective memories (see Figure 4.5).

Repression can also be used to cope with other negative emotions. For example, cancer patients who appear to repress pain experience fewer and less severe side effects from medication than do nonrepressors (Ward, Leventhal, & Love, 1988).

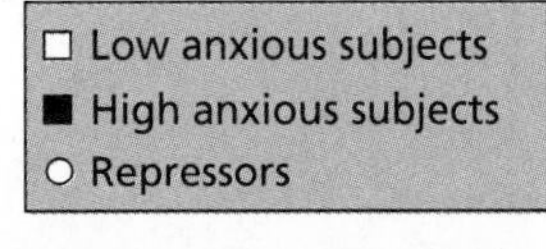

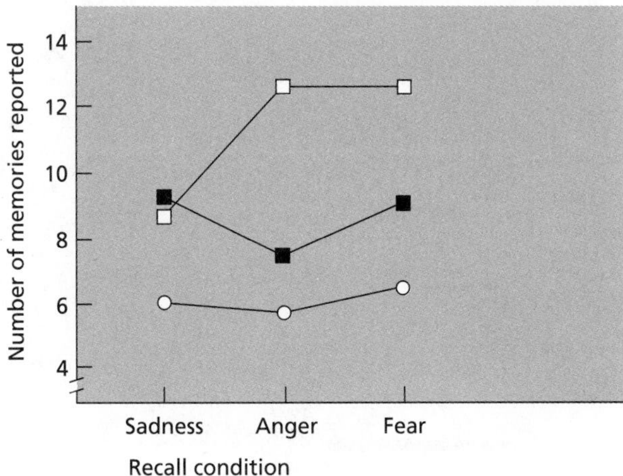

Figure 4.5
Recall of negative memories.
Adapted from "Repression and the Inaccessibility of Affective Memories," by P. J. Davis and G. E. Schwartz, 1987, *Journal of Personality and Social Psychology, 52,* (1) pp. 152–162. Copyright © the American Psychological Association. Reprinted by permission of the author.

Repression remains a central issue in psychoanalytic thinking. Recent claims of the "reemergence" of previously "repressed" memories have generated controversy. This battle is being fought now in American courtrooms over allegations of crimes committed decades before. This topic is of particular interest to psychologists because these previously repressed memories are often revealed through psychotherapy. The accuracy of retrospective reports is always of concern to psychologists and will be addressed repeatedly throughout the text.

Denial

Denial of painful experiences and thoughts is one of the earliest defense mechanisms a person develops (Cramer, 1987; Cramer & Gaul, 1988). Sometimes denial reaches frightening proportions, as when a bereaved parent believes that a deceased child is still alive. A more common form of denial involves fantasy or play, which most of us engage in from time to time (Cohen, 1987). People find temporary relief from reality by daydreaming about how their lives might have been different if some unpleasant event had not occurred. Children deny feelings of inferiority through play, as when a young boy becomes a strict father while playing "house."

Regression

Regression is engaging in behavior associated with the pleasure and satisfaction of an earlier developmental period. Common examples of regression include fingernail biting, using baby talk, overeating, and losing one's temper.

Denial is a powerful defense mechanism that protects us from becoming aware of disturbing events.
© Jan Lukas/Photo Researchers

Fingernail biting is an example of the defense mechanism called regression. To deal with anxiety or frustration, the person reverts to a mode of behavior that was comforting at an earlier stage of psychosexual development—in this photograph, the oral stage.
Photo Source Inc./St. Louis

Undoing

Undoing involves making symbolic retribution for an unacceptable impulse or act. Suppose a woman has been unscrupulous in business dealings. She could undo this behavior by involvement in civic and charitable organizations. Undoing often involves a ritual act that symbolically compensates for an id impulse that is threatening to the ego. A classic example is Shakespeare's Lady Macbeth, who compulsively washes her hands as if to cleanse herself of Duncan's blood.

Reaction Formation

One way of warding off an unacceptable impulse is to overemphasize its opposite in both thought and behavior. Thus, a man who is threatened by his desire to dominate and be aggressive in social situations may think of himself as timid and shy and act passively. Timidity and passivity are then a **reaction formation** against a strong aggressive drive.

It is often difficult to tell whether an act is a manifestation of an impulse or of its opposite. An important hallmark of reaction formation is the persistence or excess of the behavior (going overboard). The behavior may be *repeated* or *exaggerated*. As Shakespeare's Hamlet observed, "The lady doth protest too much." From this viewpoint, the apparently puritanical person who responds to sexual advances with intense alarm may be seething with erotic desire. Similarly, an individual's intensely avowed love for a sibling or spouse may sometimes indicate profound, disguised hatred.

Defensive Projection

Defensive projection is attributing one's own unacceptable impulses or wishes to someone or something else. Freud used the example of the jealous husband who accused his wife of infidelity. In fact, it was the husband who wanted to have an affair but could not face this desire in himself. Defensive projection involves three steps: (1) repressing the threatening impulse, (2) projecting the impulse onto another person, and (3) distancing oneself from the other person (Kernberg, 1987).

Note that defensive projection occurs when an individual is *unaware* of having a negative characteristic. To defend against becoming aware, the person attributes the characteristic to someone else, usually someone whom the person dislikes. Freud thought *scapegoating* to be an example of defensive projection on a mass scale.

Research over several decades has shown that defensive projection does occur in some circumstances (Bramel, 1963; Halpern, 1977; Shulman, 1990b). In one study, female undergraduates were given false feedback indicating that they had a tendency toward "neuroticism" (Sherwood, 1979). The women then rated both a favorable and an unfavorable target person on neuroticism. As the theory of projection would predict, women who denied the higher level of neuroticism in themselves tended to attribute neuroticism to the unfavorable target person.

Displacement

Displacement involves shifting an impulse provoked by an unacceptable, threatening object toward a more acceptable, less threatening object. A common example is the person who is criticized at work by a superior and later gets angry at a family member at home for no apparent reason. Expressing hostility toward the superior is obviously a threatening and maladaptive strategy. Consequently, the person redirects the anger toward a family member who is less likely to retaliate. All this is said to occur outside one's conscious awareness.

Rationalization

A person who performs an unacceptable act or thinks a threatening thought might eliminate the anxiety or guilt by finding a "perfectly reasonable" excuse for the impulse. This defense mechanism is called **rationalization.** People often use rationalization to preserve their self-esteem. If you are stood up by a date, you may tell yourself and friends that you "really didn't want to go out with that loser." This particular rationalization is known as *sour grapes,* after the fable of the fox who, unable to reach some grapes, concluded that they must be sour. Rationalization is an unconscious process, as are all the ego defense mechanisms; it is not the same as consciously making excuses—sometimes called intellectualization.

Fido is the innocent victim of displaced aggression.

Defensive Identification

Defensive identification is taking on other people's characteristics to reduce one's anxiety or other negative emotions.

Defensive identification is a common means of dealing with envy (Rosenblatt, 1988). For example, a younger child identifies with an older sibling to defend against hostile envy. This identification eliminates envy because the younger child now "possesses" the personal characteristics of the older sibling and no longer feels inadequate. Similarly, the envy of college students toward star athletes can be alleviated by identifying with team members. Often we hear someone say, "Didn't 'we' play great tonight?" when, in fact, the speaker is not even a member of the team! Identifying with others in this way gives people feelings of pride and affiliation.

Sublimation

Sublimation alters unacceptable impulses by channeling them through completely acceptable, even admired, outlets. Sublimation allows an impulse to be expressed directly because the expression is socially acceptable and therefore nonthreatening (Vaillant & Vaillant, 1990). Freud considered

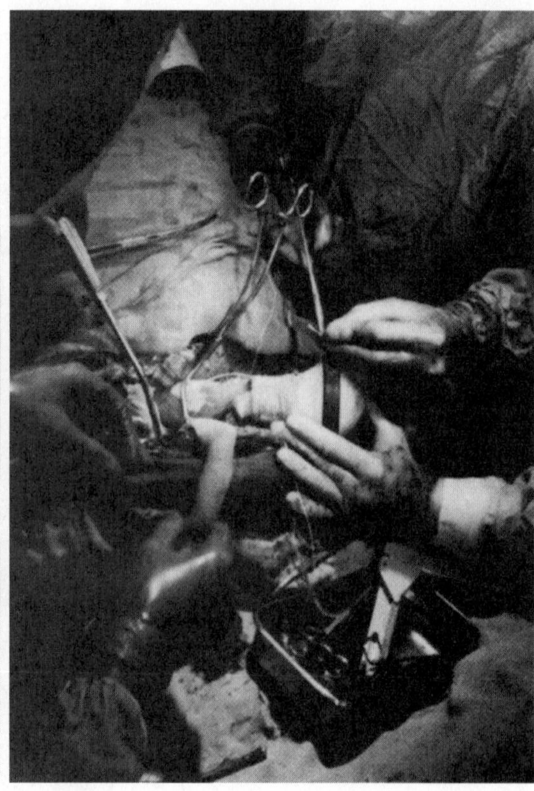

According to psychoanalytic theory, artistic work is a sublimation for the sexual drive, and surgery is a sublimation of the aggressive drive. Both are socially acceptable ways of expressing id impulses.
Left: Courtesy of John May; right: © Owen/Black Star

religion, science, and art to be the major avenues of sublimation (Muller, 1987).

Creative endeavors (e.g., painting and writing poetry) are common sublimations of the sex drive; playing or even watching contact sports like football and boxing are common sublimations of aggression (Golden, 1987). Freud believed our highest virtues are sublimations of our most base characteristics. The surgeon, for example, has found a socially acceptable outlet for aggressive impulses; the romance novelist may be expressing sublimated sexual drives.

Sublimation is the only truly *successful* defense mechanism because it permanently redirects undesirable impulses. All other defense mechanisms are, to some degree, unsuccessful. They must continually ward off the threatening impulses, which requires expenditure of psychic energy that is usurped from other functions.

Projective Identification

One further defense mechanism, **projective identification,** that has been discussed in the psychodynamic literature was originally described by Melanie Klein rather than by Freud. It involves rejecting threatening features of the self and "projecting" them onto another. It is a three-stage process paralleling some other object relations processes and is discussed in detail in Chapter 5.

Choice of Defense Mechanisms

Many factors combine to determine which defense mechanisms a person will use to fend off anxiety. Age is an important factor (A. Freud, 1966; Valliant, 1971, 1977). Early in life, people develop primitive or "immature" defenses, such as denial and repression. Later, they develop more complex and "mature" defenses, such as defensive identification and rationalization.

Cramer (1987) provided empirical evidence for a developmental hierarchy of defense mechanisms. Four age groups were studied: preschool, elementary school, early adolescence, and late adolescence. Subjects' use of three different defense mechanisms—denial, projection, and defensive identification—were assessed from stories they made up about two ambiguous pictures from the Thematic Apperception Test (TAT). (See Chapter 6 for a description of the TAT.) It was predicted that denial would be the most primitive defense and identification the most mature; projection was predicted to be intermediate. As Figure 4.6 shows, the results of the study were consistent with the predicted pattern.

Adults tend to have characteristic ways of defending themselves. These "defensive habits" develop in early childhood, when instinctual conflicts first

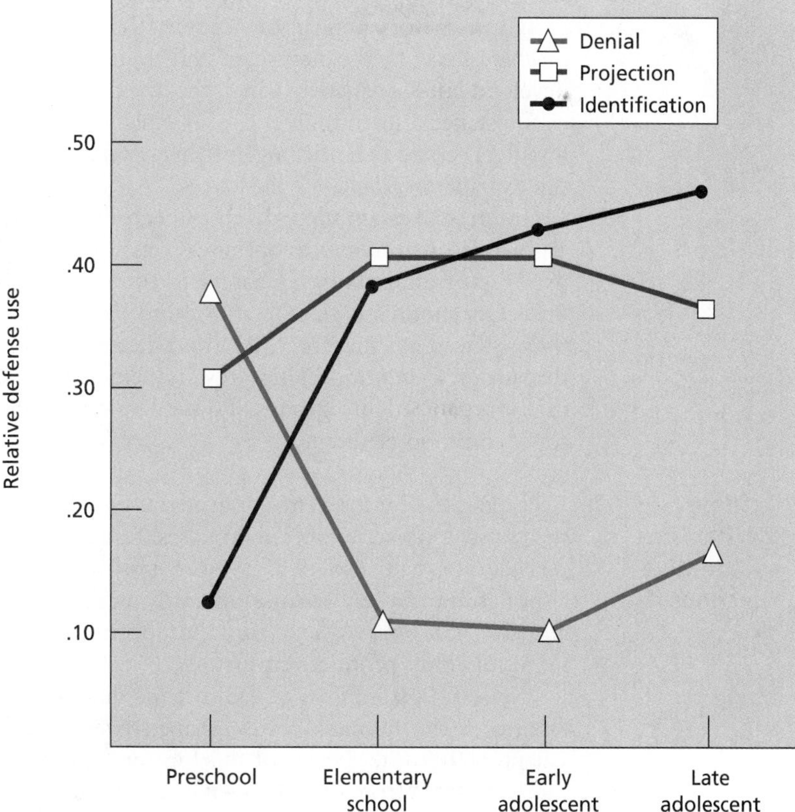

Figure 4.6
The relative use of three defense mechanisms—denial, projection, and identification—among children of four age groups.
Source: Data from "The Development of Defense Mechanisms" by P. Cramer, 1987, *Journal of Personality, 55,* p. 607. Duke University Press.

Table 4.2 How the same unacceptable impulse, negativity, can be defended against by different defense mechanisms

UNACCEPTABLE IMPULSE: **NEGATIVITY**

Defense Mechanism	Examples of Its Use
Sublimation	Being a movie or restaurant critic; reviewing scientific studies for publication
Reaction formation	Expressing optimism and finding worthwhile aspects in any situation
Projection	Being sensitive to negativity in others
Rationalization	Believing that the world is in a dismal state and therefore negativity is "legitimate"
Undoing	Working for positive, optimistic causes (e.g., a world peace organization)
Regression	Doing sloppy work or sulking
Denial	Not being aware of one's negativity

arise, and remain and continue to operate in all of us. Without these defenses, we would be quite literally *"defenseless."*

Three factors appear to account for a person's characteristic defense mechanisms: (1) the nature of the original conflicts, (2) the time in the developmental sequence when the conflicts arise, and (3) the particular circumstances surrounding the original conflicts (Fenichel, 1945). Most impulses can be defended against by any number of defense mechanisms, as the example in Table 4.2 illustrates.

Interest in examining defense mechanisms and categorizing them into more or less mature types continues even now. Muris and Merckelbach (1996) used **factor analysis** (see Chapter 8) to examine responses to the Defensive Style Questionnaire (DSQ) and found three basic groups of defenses: (1) those viewed as "mature," (2) those that were "less mature," and (3) those that avoided emotion. These results demonstrate that defense mechanisms can be organized into groups of several specific mechanisms that tend to share some common elements.

Defense Mechanisms as Adaptive Functions

According to Freud, the main purpose of ego defense mechanisms is to defend the ego from unacceptable id impulses. Ego psychologists believe that defense mechanisms can also play a more positive, adaptive role. For instance, although indefinitely putting off studying for a final examination is far from adaptive, *temporarily forgetting* the upcoming test (denial) may clear one's mind for other productive pursuits.

Nesse (1990) has suggested that the defense mechanisms are an adaptive feature of the human species, shaped over time by natural selection (see Chapter 9). The heart of his argument is that concealing our true motives—even from ourselves—is often in our best interests: "Being aware of one's own motives might make it difficult to hide them adequately . . . the capacity for repression may, therefore, offer a selective advantage by increasing the ability to deceive others about the pursuit of covert selfish motives" (p. 263).

A person who unconsciously hates an exploiting superior, but consciously experiences only admiration and feelings of inadequacy, will have a considerable advantage over someone who is aware of rage and competitive feelings. We tend to assume that the brain has been shaped for accurate perception of reality, but in some situations distorted perceptions of reality may enhance fitness, and selection will tend to favor those tendencies to distortion. (These ideas resurface in Chapter 17.)

The use of defense mechanisms is therefore part of normal personality functioning. No problem arises as long as the defensive processes do not radically distort a person's perceptions of the world or preclude effective action in dealing with the source of anxiety. When distortion is too extreme, problems develop. Persons with extremely distorted perceptions are likely to exhibit abnormal behavior.

FREUD'S STAGES OF PERSONALITY DEVELOPMENT

Most psychoanalysts divide personality development into a number of discrete stages that are considered to be universal, or relevant to all people. However, as we saw in Chapter 3, considerable controversy exists about the nature of these stages.

One controversy involves the role of biological factors versus social factors in development. Freud believed that biological factors are paramount. His developmental stages are biologically determined. Many contemporary psychoanalysts emphasize social factors and minimize the role of biology; the developmental stages they propose are based primarily on social phenomena. Another controversy concerns the extent to which early experience determines adult personality. All psychoanalysts consider early experience important. Freud believed that adult personality is relatively fixed by about age 5. Many analytically oriented theorists agree that early experiences can have a profound impact on later personality, but they also believe that later experiences can also have important effects. These issues are developed further in Chapter 5.

Freud's stages of personality development are called **psychosexual** because they are concerned with the psychological manifestation of the sexual (pleasure) drive. At particular times in the development sequence, one body area—specifically, the mouth, anus, or genital region—is especially sensitive to erotic stimulation. These areas are called **erogenous zones.**

While in a given psychosexual stage, much of the individual's libido is invested in behavior involving the primary erogenous zone. To progress to the next stage, the libido must be freed from the primary erogenous zone of the present stage and reinvested in the primary erogenous zone of the next stage. (Recall that each individual has only a fixed amount of libidinal energy.)

The ability to transfer libido from one stage to the next depends on how well the individual has resolved the developmental conflict associated with each psychosexual stage. The conflict is always between free expression of biological impulses and societal constraints.

Freud used the analogy of military troops on the march to explain this process. As the troops march, they are met by opposition (conflict). If they are highly successful in winning the battle (resolving the conflict), virtually all troops (libido) will be free to move on and ample libido is available to deal with the conflict of the next stage. If the troops experience difficulty in winning the battle, more troops will be left behind and fewer troops will be available to move on. In other words, less libido will be available to cope with the next conflict.

People have difficulty leaving one stage and proceeding to the next when they have been either frustrated or overindulged in the present stage. *Frustration* occurs when the person's needs relevant to the psychosexual stage have not been met. *Overindulgence* occurs when relevant needs have been so well satisfied that the person is reluctant to leave the stage. In both cases, a portion of libido remains permanently invested in a previous developmental stage; this is known as **fixation.** Inevitably, some libido is fixated at each psychosexual stage. The more difficult it is for a person to resolve the conflict of a given stage, the more libido remains fixated at that stage.

Fixation, which occurs in childhood, influences adult personality. If there is little fixation, only vestiges of earlier ways of obtaining satisfaction are seen in later behavior. If the fixation is strong (a substantial amount of fixated libido), the individual's adult personality is dominated by seeking satisfaction through means that were used in that earlier stage. As a result, the individual develops an adult character type (e.g., an "anal character") reflecting the poorly resolved conflict. Once formed, character types are believed to be stable and to greatly influence a person's choice of mate and occupation (Baudry, 1988).

Oral Stage

During the first year of life, the mouth is the most important source of tension reduction (e.g., eating) and pleasure (e.g., sucking). This is the **oral stage.** Weaning is the crucial conflict. The more difficult it is for the child to leave the mother's breast (or bottle) and its accompanying sucking pleasure, the more libido is fixated at the oral stage. Freud focused on the biological ramifications of the oral stage. Post-Freudians emphasize the psychological aspects. As Strupp (1967) put it:

> The focal point of the child's personality organization at this period is not necessarily the mouth per se but the total constellation of immaturity, dependency, the wish to be mothered, the pleasure of being held, the enjoyment of human closeness and warmth. (p. 23)

Karl Abraham (1927) expanded on this idea by further dividing the oral stage into two phases. The early phase is **oral eroticism,** characterized by the pleasure of sucking or taking things in through the mouth *(oral incorporation)*. The later phase he labeled **oral sadism,** which begins as teeth emerge and represents the development of the aggressive drive. The child is now capable of biting and chewing—and therefore of behaving aggressively and destructively.

Gratification through the mouth, especially nursing, is the focus of the oral stage.
Courtesy of Kelly Cameron

The Oral Character

Fixation at the oral stage is presumed to result in an oral character (Abraham, 1927). Some of the major characteristics of the oral character are:

1. Preoccupation with issues of giving and taking
2. Concern about dependence-independence and passivity-activity
3. Special attitudes about closeness and distance to others—being alone versus attachment to the group
4. Extremes of optimism and pessimism
5. Unusual ambivalence (especially true of the oral sadistic character)
6. Openness to novel experiences and ideas
7. A hasty, restless, impatient orientation—wanting to be continuously "fed" with events and things
8. Use of oral channels for gratification for coping with frustration (e.g., overeating, not eating enough, smoking, excessive talking) (Fisher & Greenberg, 1977, p. 88)

These characteristics are general. The specific group of traits a person manifests depends on two factors: (1) whether the person is fixated at the oral erotic or oral sadistic phase and (2) whether the fixation is due to frustration or overindulgence.

Table 4.3 Development of optimism/pessimism as an oral character trait

TIME OF FIXATION	CAUSE OF FIXATION: OVERINDULGENCE	CAUSE OF FIXATION: FRUSTRATION
	Passive Optimism	**Passive Pessimism**
Oral erotic (early)	Believing the world will always provide for one's needs, no matter what one does *Example:* Students do not study because they expect tests will be easy, teacher will understand	Behaving as if one can do nothing to improve one's lot in life *Example:* Students do not study because they feel it is no use; nothing can help; they will inevitably do poorly
	Active Optimism	**Active Pessimism**
Oral sadistic (late)	Aggressively taking (in) from the world to provide for one's needs *Example:* Students study diligently; seek special help; do additional reading and extra credit assignments	Behaving cynically and hostilely toward perceived harsh world; striking out at others indiscriminantly *Example:* Students devote time to criticizing teachers, classes, examinations; bad grades attributed to system

How might the general characteristics be manifested differently? Consider optimism versus pessimism as an example. People who were frustrated would be expected to be pessimistic; those who were overindulged would be expected to be optimistic. The specific form of optimism or pessimism could be broadly passive or active, depending on whether the individual was fixated early (erotic phase) or late (sadistic phase) in the stage. The four possible outcomes are shown in Table 4.3.

Joseph Masling and his associates have correlated a variety of behaviors with oral fixation (Masling, 1985). They measured oral fixation using Rorschach inkblots—ambiguous figures that look like spilled ink (see Chapter 6 for a more detailed description). Subjects were asked to say what they saw in the blots. Examples of Rorschach responses that are taken to indicate oral-dependent behavior appear in Table 4.4.

Table 4.4 Examples of oral-dependent Rorschach responses

CATEGORY	SAMPLE RESPONSES
Food and drink	Milk, whiskey, boiled lobster
Food providers	Waiter, cook, bartender
Food organs	Mouth, stomach, lips, teeth
Oral instruments	Lipstick, cigarette, clarinet
Nurturers	Jesus, mother, father, doctor, God
Good luck objects	Wishbone, four-leaf clover
Oral activity	Eating, talking, singing, kissing
"Baby talk" responses	Patty-cake, bunny rabbit, pussy cat
Negations of oral percepts	No mouth, not pregnant, woman without breasts

Source: Based on "Orality and Latency of Volunteering to Serve as Experimental Subjects: A Replication" by R. R. Bornstein and J. Masling, 1985, *Journal of Personality Assessment, 49,* p. 307.

One direct prediction from Freud's theory is that people fixated at the oral stage will tend to eat and drink excessively. A positive correlation has been found between subjects' reporting oral imagery in Rorschach inkblots and both obesity and alcoholism (Bertrand & Masling, 1969; Masling, Rabie, & Blondheim, 1967).

Dependency is a central trait of the oral character. One study found that college students who depend on others to make decisions for them in ambiguous situations report more oral imagery than do students who make their own decisions (Masling, Weiss, & Rothschild, 1968).

Complying with rules is another indication of dependency on others (authorities) for approval. A positive correlation has repeatedly been found between oral fixation and compliance (Bornstein & Masling, 1985; Ihilevich & Gleser, 1986; Masling, O'Neill, & Katkin, 1981).

Anal Stage

When a child is weaned, libido shifts from the mouth to the anus. Pleasure is obtained at first from expelling feces—the **anal sadistic** phase. Later, pleasure comes from retaining feces—the **anal erotic** phase. This is not to say that the child did not derive similar pleasure during the oral stage. However, during the second and third years of life, anal pleasure predominates, just as oral pleasure did in the first year.

Parents make few demands on children in the first year of life. Starting in the second year, however, parents in most Western cultures begin to place restrictions on their offspring's behaviors, especially regarding bladder and bowel control. The conflict in the anal stage pits the sexual drive for pleasure (from the tension reduced by elimination of bodily wastes) against the social expectation that children develop self-control with respect to urination and defecation.

Bowel and bladder control become the prototype for self-control in general, just as weaning is a prototype for dependency. If children easily accede to their parents' toilet-training demands, they will develop the basis for successful self-control. A child who has difficulty developing control and meeting parental demands will become an anal character.

The Anal Character

When children find their parents' demands for toilet training difficult, they will show *resistance*. Resistance can be either active or passive.

Active resistance entails direct opposition (a "you can't make me do that" attitude). For instance, there may be attempts to counterattack by defecating at especially inopportune moments, such as immediately after being taken off the potty. Children who discover that direct opposition is a successful means of social control will adopt it as a strategy for handling frustration in general. This results in the development of an anal expulsive character. **Anal expulsives** are fixated at the anal sadistic phase. They are expected to rebel or to express anger by becoming wasteful, disorderly, or messy. It is interesting that our colloquial expressions of extreme anger and hostility—"pissed off" or "oh, shit," for example—often refer to elimination.

Passive resistance to toilet training demands involves retaining feces. Gentle pressure against the intestinal walls can be pleasurable. Furthermore,

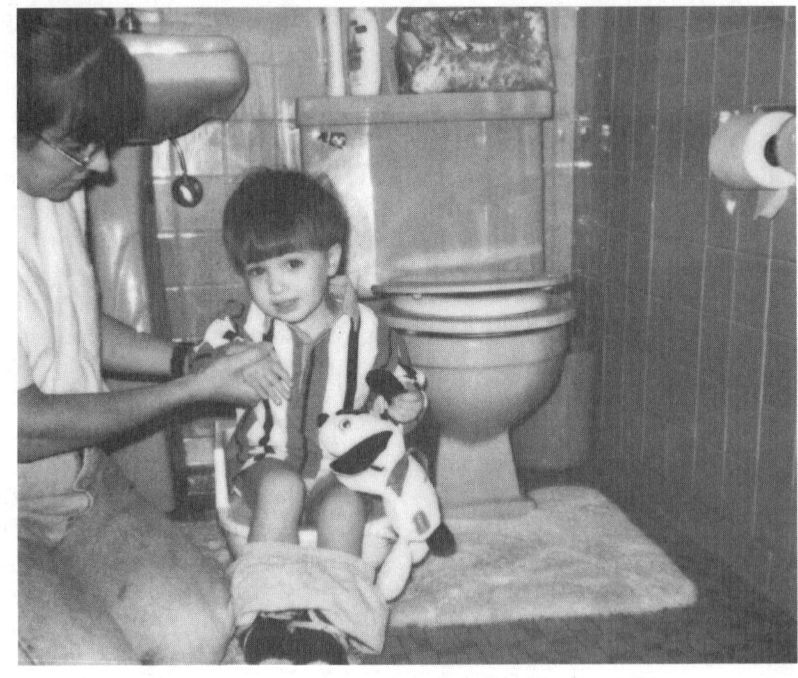

In the anal stage, toilet training is the critical conflict.
Courtesy of Marybeth and Tyler Kozikowski

children can indirectly strike back at their parents by simply not having bowel movements (which creates a serious danger to a child's health). When this tactic is successful, it may set the stage for retentive behavior patterns in later life. This pattern results in the development of an anal retentive character. **Anal retentives** are fixated at the anal erotic phase. They are neat, careful, systematic, and orderly. They may be upset or even revolted by a mess of any kind, including a room in disarray or poorly organized plans that lead to confusion and uncertainty.

Fixation at the anal stage can result in two contrasting character types: the anal expulsive and the anal retentive character. Can you tell which office goes with each type?
Left: © Steve Niedorf/Image Bank; right: © David Lawrence/Image Bank

Table 4.5 The anal character

CHARACTER TYPE	EXAMPLES OF ADULT BEHAVIOR
Anal expulsive	Messy; disorderly; disorganized; careless Wasteful; extravagant; reckless; tardy Defiant; aggressive
Anal retentive	Neat; orderly; organized; careful Parsimonious; hoarding; precise; prompt Withholding; passive-aggressive

Anal expulsiveness and anal retentiveness are two sides of the same fixation; both are responses to being controlled and forced. Examples of behaviors that epitomize the two anal character types are presented in Table 4.5.

Many correlational studies have examined whether the three basic anal retentive character traits—orderliness, stinginess, and stubbornness—tend to occur together (Fisher & Greenberg, 1977). The evidence largely supports Freud's proposed *"anal triad"* (Freud, 1959). The strongest direct association is between orderliness and stinginess. For example, people who are overly neat also tend to be miserly.

Evidence for the anal character also comes from some cleverly designed experiments. In one study, male college students identified geometric forms under two conditions: while their hands were immersed in a smelly, fecal-like substance and while they were immersed in clean water (Rosenwald, 1972). Comparison of performance in the two conditions was used as a measure of anal anxiety; the greater the difference in performance, the greater the anal anxiety. Men who had the most difficulty in dealing with the fecal-like material tended to be the most stubborn and the neatest.

Studies of the origin of the anal character have failed to support the idea that it is related to difficulty in toilet training, however (Fisher & Greenberg, 1977). Thus, empirical evidence does not support Freud's hypotheses that fixation causes either the anal or oral character. This does not mean that the concept of an anal or an oral character is not valid. Freud's observations of certain basic traits associated with various adult behaviors may be accurate. However, his theory (inference) that character type is *caused* by fixation at a psychosexual stage has not received empirical support.

Phallic Stage

During the fourth and fifth years of life, libido is centered in the genital region. Children at this age are frequently observed examining their genitals, masturbating, and asking questions about birth and sex. According to Freud, the conflict in the phallic stage is the last and most crucial conflict with which the young child must cope. The conflict involves the child's unconscious wish to possess the opposite-sex parent and at the same time to do away with the same-sex parent. Freud called this situation the **Oedipus complex** (pronounced ED-ipus). The name is derived from the Greek myth in which the hero, Oedipus, kills his father and marries his mother. Freud, incidently, was well read in classical mythology (Glenn, 1987), and the Oedipus myth seems to have been particularly salient for him (Rudnytsky, 1987).

The Oedipus Complex

The Oedipus complex operates somewhat differently for boys and girls. We will address the male Oedipus complex first.

The boy's first object of love is his mother. As libido centers in the genital zone, his love for his mother becomes erotically tinged and therefore incestuous. Naturally, the boy's father stands in the way of his sexual desire for his mother. The boy sees his father as his rival, someone he would like to eliminate. These aggressive desires make the boy afraid that his father will retaliate. The fact that the little boy knows from casual observations that women lack penises suggests to him that his father may retaliate by castrating him (which is what he thinks happened to women). Because *castration anxiety* is stronger than the boy's desires for his mother, the boy ultimately abandons his wish to possess her.

Resolution of the Oedipus complex entails two processes: repression of his incestuous desires and defensive identification with his father. Repression is putting a thought or feeling completely out of consciousness. Defensive identification involves becoming like a threatening person ("if you can't beat him, join him"), sometimes known as *identification with the aggressor* (Porder, 1987). The boy unconsciously "reasons": "I cannot directly possess my mother, for fear of being castrated by my father. I can, however, possess her vicariously. I can get some of the joy of possessing my mother by becoming like my father." The boy resolves his conflict by identifying with his father's behavior, attitudes, and values. Defensive identification allows the boy to (1) possess his mother vicariously, (2) eliminate his castration anxiety, and (3) assimilate appropriate sex-role behavior. This identification also forms the rudiments of conscience.

The female version of the Oedipus complex is called the **Electra complex** or the female Oedipus complex. (In Greek mythology, Electra persuades her brother to murder their mother, who had killed her father unjustly.)

A girl's first object of love is also her mother. However, during the phallic stage, the little girl is likely to discover that her father and other men have penises, whereas she and her mother (and other women) do not. She reasons that she must have had a penis at one time, and she blames her mother for her apparent castration. These feelings, along with other inevitable disappointments in her mother, lead to some loss of love for her mother and increased love for her father. Her love for her father is erotically tinged as well as envious because he has a penis.

Freud considered *penis envy* the counterpart of *castration anxiety*. But penis envy carries no threat of retaliation, whereas castration anxiety is very threatening and motivates the boy to renounce his incestuous desires. However, the little girl fears loss of her mother's love, which ultimately motivates her to resolve the Electra complex.

Freud was vague about how the Electra complex is resolved. He did state that the resolution occurs later in life than for boys and is never complete.

(This implies that women always remain somewhat fixated at the phallic stage.) The mother does not hold the threat of castration over her daughter. However, she would not tolerate incestuous relations between her husband and daughter.

Presumably, the impracticality of fulfilling her Oedipal wish causes the girl to repress her desires for her father and defensively identify with her mother. This protects the girl from losing her mother's love. It also allows her to possess her father vicariously. We should note that Freud's concept of penis envy and its supposed role in female psychosexual development are among his *least* accepted ideas today (Wilkinson, 1991).

We have presented the general formula for the Oedipus complex. The exact pattern for each individual depends on development in the prephallic stages and on specific family circumstances during the phallic stage. For example, if one parent is absent, the child will presumably substitute a surrogate, such as an aunt or uncle.

Freud considered resolution of the Oedipus complex the most critical aspect of personality development. Normal adult personality requires a successful resolution. Unsuccessful resolution inevitably leads to psychopathology. The phallic stage is also important because the child's moral principles (conscience) develop through identification with parents at this stage.

The Phallic Character

Fixation at the phallic stage results in a **phallic character.** The phallic character is reckless, resolute, and self-assured (Fenichel, 1945); there is also a *narcissistic* element, involving excessive vanity and pride. Phallic characters have not successfully resolved their Oedipus complexes. Because they still have castration anxiety, they tend to be afraid of closeness and love. They also appear courageous and are prone to show off; these behaviors serve as a partial defense against castration anxiety.

Latency Period

Following the resolution of the Oedipus complex, children pass into a period known as **latency.** Latency is not a stage of psychosexual development because the sexual drive does not continue to develop during this time. (The term *latency* refers to the fact that the libido remains dormant.)

According to Freud, latency involves massive repression of all sexual impulses. Libido is rechanneled from sexual pursuits to activities such as school and cognitive development, friendships with children of the same age and gender, sports, and hobbies (Sarnoff, 1976). As discussed in Chapter 5, post-Freudians who focus on social and cognitive aspects of development and deemphasize sexual issues consider the so-called latency period to be a critical time for the child's personality development (e.g., Erikson, 1963, 1968; Sullivan, 1953).

Genital Stage

Freud's final stage of psychosexual development begins at puberty, when the young adolescent starts to mature sexually, and lasts through adulthood. In the **genital stage,** libido is again focused in the genital area. Now, however, it is directed toward heterosexual, rather than autoerotic (masturbatory),

Anna Freud (1895–1982) extended her father's work to the examination of the adolescent years. © Corbis-Bettmann

pleasure. The greater an individual's success in reaching the genital stage without large amounts of libido fixated in pregenital stages, the greater the person's capacity to lead a "normal" life, free of neurosis, and to enjoy heterosexual relationships.

Freud had little to say about adulthood, which is consistent with his belief that the first 5 years of life are paramount in determining personality. Other psychoanalysts, for example, Freud's daughter, Anna, theorized more about entry into the genital stage. Anna Freud was among her father's most devoted colleagues and his constant companion in his later years. She continued to work within her father's classic psychoanalytic framework until her death.

Anna Freud (1958) observed that adolescence brings an onslaught of sexual and aggressive impulses. Indeed, she wrote that "there are few situations in life which are more difficult to cope with than an adolescent son or daughter during the attempt to liberate themselves" (p. 323). (Ask your parents if they would agree.) Anna Freud identified two major strategies that adolescents use to gain a sense of control. One is *asceticism,* in which the adolescent tries to abandon physical pleasure, such as through strict diets or vigorous exercise. The other strategy adolescents use to cope is *intellectualization,* in which they develop personal theories about the nature of love or of life itself.

Anna Freud contributed some new concepts to classical Freudian theory but did not stray far from her father's original ideas. In Chapter 5, we examine more closely the theorizing stemming from Freud but with some significant shifts in emphasis or underlying assumptions in the context of the post-Freudian approaches.

SUMMARY

1. All of Freud's theories are characterized by four basic principles: (1) the dynamic flow of psychic energy in a closed system is responsible for human motivation; (2) all behavior is caused by internal forces; (3) there are three structures and functions of personality—the id, ego, and superego—that are always in conflict; and (4) early childhood development determines adult personality, which progresses through a series of specific stages.
2. Freud divided the mind into three levels of awareness: conscious, preconscious, and unconscious. Personality functioning is dominated by the unconscious.
3. Jung proposed an alternative division: conscious ego, personal unconscious, and collective unconscious. Jung emphasized the influence of the collective unconscious, which contains archetypes that are universal predispositions to think and act in common ways.
4. Freud divided personality according to three basic organizational structures. The id is concerned with pleasure seeking and is the reservoir of biological drives. It operates through the pleasure principle, which requires immediate gratification of needs. This gratification is accomplished through primary process, in which memory images of goals are formed.

5. The ego is the rational aspect of personality and operates according to the reality principle—the gratification of needs is delayed until an appropriate actual goal can be obtained. This delay of gratification is accomplished through secondary process, which involves problem solving and other intellectual functions.
6. The superego is the moral aspect of personality. It is the internal representative of the values of society and guides the individual toward ideals.
7. The ego serves as a mediator among the pleasure demands of the id, the moral strictures of the superego, and the requirements and limitations of the real world. Intrapsychic conflicts among the id, ego, and superego play a major role in determining one's personality.
8. Freud believed that anxiety is a signal of impending danger. He distinguished three types: neurotic anxiety (from an id-ego conflict), moral anxiety or guilt (from an id-superego conflict), and objective anxiety (from actual external dangers).
9. Unconscious ego defense mechanisms keep people from being overwhelmed by unacceptable impulses that are the basis for neurotic and moral anxiety. Repression, in which unacceptable impulses are totally excluded from one's consciousness, is the most fundamental defense mechanism. Other defense mechanisms include denial, regression, undoing, reaction formation, defensive projection, displacement, rationalization, defensive identification, projective identification, and sublimation. Of these, only sublimation is considered a wholly successful defense mechanism.
10. Freud described four basic stages of psychosexual development. The stages are named after the erogenous zones that predominate at various ages: oral, anal, phallic, and genital. At each stage, one erogenous zone is the focus of libido (sexual energy). Each stage has a conflict that must be successfully resolved to proceed to the next stage. When people have difficulty moving to the next stage (because of frustration or overindulgence in the present stage), they leave more libido fixated at the earlier stage. Fixation results in adult character types.
11. In the oral stage (the first year of life), pleasure is derived from sucking, eating, and biting. The conflict is weaning. The oral character centers on dependency. Post-Freudians have broadened Freud's theoretical ideas about the oral stage to focus on its social aspects.
12. In the anal stage (second and third years), pleasure is derived from the retention and expulsion of feces. Toilet training is the conflict. The anal character involves three basic traits: orderliness, stinginess, and obstinacy.
13. In the phallic stage (ages 4 and 5), pleasure focuses in the genital region. The Oedipus complex, the conflict in the phallic stage, involves the child's sexual attraction to the opposite-sex parent. Freud considered resolution of this conflict to be critical for normal personality development.

14. Between the phallic stage and puberty, the child enters a period of latency that involves no psychosexual development. Post-Freudians, however, stress important social developments that occur at this time.
15. The genital stage begins at puberty and lasts through adulthood. Again, the libido is focused in the genital area, but now it is directed toward heterosexual rather than autoerotic pleasure.

CHAPTER FIVE

Post-Freudian Perspectives

roadly speaking, there are two primary areas of disagreement between Freud and the major post-Freudians. Some take exception to his developmental scheme or to the limits of it; others disagree with the one or more premises of Freud's drive theory. The aim of this chapter is to examine the contributions of the most important of these later theorists to the Psychoanalytic Strategy. We begin with an examination of some post-Freudian developmental schemes.

REVISIONIST STAGE THEORIES

Several post-Freudian theorists offered their own views on the development of personality. Some offered only minor extensions or elaborations of Freud's scheme. Jung's conceptualization of the midlife crisis represents one such elaboration.

Jung's Concept of the Midlife Crisis

Jung (1933) targeted middle age (beginning in the late 30s and lasting until the mid-50s) as a critical period in a person's life. Several contemporary writers have expressed agreement with this view (Levinson, Darrow, Klein, Levinson, & McKee, 1978; Sheehy, 1976, 1981; Vailliant, 1977).

Jung described this period as a major transition: from youthful impulsiveness and extraversion to thoughtfulness and introversion, from interests and goals that have their roots in biological urges to interests and goals that are based on cultural norms. The person's values become more social, civic-minded, and philosophical or religious. In short, the middle-aged individual develops into a spiritual being.

These changes precipitate what Jung referred to as a **midlife crisis.** The crisis occurs even among successful people as they realize many of their goals have been set for them by others. "The achievements which society rewards are won at the cost of diminution of personality. Many—far too many—aspects of life which should have been experienced lie in the lumber room among dusty memories" (Jung, 1933, p. 104).

Jung believed that if the transformation of energy during midlife does not occur smoothly, one's personality may be seriously and permanently crippled. Jung was very successful in treating individuals who were having difficulties with this transition. He believed that the midlife crisis can be resolved only through **individuation,** or finding one's own way. The process begins by "turning our energy away from the mastery of the external world . . . and focusing on our inner selves. We feel inner urgings to listen to the unconscious, to learn about the potentials we have so far left unrealized. We begin to raise questions about the meaning of our lives" (Crain, 1980, p. 194).

An interesting aspect of Jung's theory is that it may explain why so many people experience "burnout" at middle age. It also suggests that burnout can be viewed as a positive development (Garden, 1991). Evidence suggests that, consistent with Jung's idea, as the midlife crisis is resolved, both men and women experience an increase in positive emotions and renewed enthusiasm for their careers (O'Connor & Wolfe, 1991).

While Jung offered a view of one stage of development (far beyond the point where Freud believed personality development was complete), others offered more complete life-span schemes. The most elaborate and well developed is the psychosocial theory of personality development of Erik Erikson.

Erikson's Eight Stages of Psychosocial Development

The best-known alternative to Freud's psychosexual stages was proposed by Erik Erikson. Erikson was a student of Freud's daughter, Anna. Erikson did not discount biological and psychosexual influences on the developing individual, but he emphasized the influence of *society* and *culture,* as well as the importance of *ego development* throughout the life span. (Erikson is usually considered part of the ego psychology movement.)

Erikson (1963, 1968) believed that there are eight critical developmental issues in life. Each issue becomes the central focus of attention at a specific period, leading to eight stages of **psychosocial** development. The stages are named for the central issue during that period of life.

Each stage involves conflict between an adaptive and a maladaptive approach to the central issue, such as between basic trust and mistrust. A conflict must be successfully resolved in the period when it predominates to enable the person to be fully prepared to deal with the conflict that follows. Successful resolution is relative and involves developing a "favorable ratio" between the adaptive and maladaptive alternatives (such as considerably more trust than mistrust).

In contrast to Freud's concept of psycho*sexual* stages, the issues involved in Erikson's eight psycho*social* stages are present at birth and remain throughout the life span. For example, during the first year of life (Erikson's first stage), the child's major problems center on developing basic trust. However, the child is also struggling to develop autonomy—the central issue in Erikson's second stage—as when it wriggles to be set free if held too tightly. Similarly, adolescents are primarily concerned with identity, but they also encounter autonomy issues as they struggle to be confident rather than self-conscious.

Erik H. Erikson (1902–1994) introduced a life span perspective in personality development, which encompasses eight stages from infancy to old age.
Photo by Jon Erikson

Erikson's concept of development is illustrated in Figure 5.1, a diagram of Erikson's psychosocial stages plotted against periods of physical and psychosexual development. Each vertical column represents one of the eight developmental issues. The period in life when that issue becomes the central conflict is enhanced with dark shading. These darkly shaded boxes form the diagonal of the diagram. The form of one developmental issue—identity versus role confusion—in other periods of development is spelled out in the diagram. To see the interrelationships, follow the fifth vertical column up from the oral-sensory period to maturity. The nature of each of the other seven developmental issues (that are not the central conflict during puberty and adolescence) is shown in the fifth horizontal row in the lightly shaded boxes.

We now examine the stages in order. Keep in mind that Erikson's description of his eight stages of psychosocial development focuses on the way the person deals with the issue that is the *central conflict* of the stage.

Basic Trust versus Mistrust

Initially, infants must develop sufficient trust to let their mothers, who provide food and comfort, out of sight without experiencing anxiety or rage. Such trust involves not only confidence in the predictability of the mother's

Developmental period	1	2	3	4	5	6	7	8
VIII Maturity					Objective view of accomplishments vs. Distorted view of accomplishments*			Ego integrity vs. Despair
VII Adulthood					Role diversity vs. Burnout*		Generativity vs. Stagnation	
VI Young adulthood					Role acceptance vs. Role rejection*	Intimacy vs. Isolation		
V Puberty and adolescence	Temporal perspective vs. Time confusion	Self-certainty vs. Self-consciousness	Role-experimentation vs. Role fixation	Apprenticeship vs. Work paralysis	Indentity vs. Role confusion	Sexual polarization vs. Bisexual confusion	Leader- and followership vs. Authority confusion	Ideological commitment vs. Confusion of values
IV Latency				Industry vs. Inferiority	Task identification vs. Sense of futility			
III Locomotor-genital			Initiative vs. Guilt		Anticipation of roles vs. Role inhibition			
II Muscular-anal		Autonomy vs. Shame and Doubt			Will to be oneself vs. Self-doubt			
I Oral-sensory	Basic trust vs. Mistrust				Mutual recognition vs. Autistic isolation			

Psychosocial stages

Erikson's diagram of the eight stages of psychosocial development.

*Conflict conceptualized by authors, extrapolating from Erikson's theory.

Source: Adapted from *Childhood and Society* by E. H. Erikson, 1963, New York: W. W. Norton; and *Identity, Youth, and Crisis* by E. H. Erikson, 1968, New York: W. W. Norton.

behavior but also trust in oneself. This conflict dominates during Freud's oral stage.

Autonomy versus Shame and Doubt

Next, the child must develop a sense of autonomy, which is originally accomplished with respect to bladder and bowel control. This stage, not surprisingly, parallels Freud's anal stage. If the child fails to meet parental expectations for bladder and bowel control, shame and doubt may result. The shame of being unable to demonstrate the self-control expected by parents becomes the basis for later problems with independence. In contrast, the experience of attaining adequate self-control with respect to toilet training results in feelings of autonomy in later life. Erikson (1963) noted:

> This stage . . . becomes decisive for the ratio of love and hate, cooperation and willfulness, freedom [and] self-expression and its suppression. From a sense of self-control without loss of self-esteem comes a lasting sense of goodwill and pride; from a sense of loss of self-control and of foreign overcontrol comes a lasting propensity for doubt and shame. (p. 254)

Initiative versus Guilt

Initiative versus guilt is the last conflict experienced by the preschool child. It occurs during Freud's phallic stage. The child must learn to control feelings of rivalry for the mother's attention and develop a sense of moral responsibility. During this stage, children may outwardly indulge in fantasies of grandeur while they may actually feel meek and dominated. To overcome the latter feelings, the child must learn to take role-appropriate initiative by finding pleasure in socially and culturally approved activities, such as creative play and caring for younger siblings.

Industry versus Inferiority

The conflict between industry and inferiority begins with school life. If children are to emerge as healthy individuals, at this stage they must apply themselves to their learning, begin to feel competent relative to peers, and face their own limitations. Note that these important developments occur during the time when, from Freud's point of view, the child is in a period of latency.

Identity versus Role Confusion

With the advent of puberty, the adolescent's attention turns to developing a sense of identity. For Erikson, identity refers to confidence that others see us as we see ourselves. The selection of an occupation or career is particularly important for identity. If an identity is not formed, *role confusion* may occur; this state is characterized by an inability to select a career or to further educational goals and by overidentification with popular heroes or cliques. Role confusion now often extends beyond adolescence and well into young adulthood (Cote & Levine, 1989). It has become more common for young adults (into their 20s and even 30s) to remain in the homes of their parents. And even by young adulthood, identity formation is by no means complete. Rather, as predicted by Erikson's theory, it has been shown to be continually refined and expanded over the entire life span (Berzonsky, 1990).

Intimacy versus Isolation

For Erikson, intimacy is the capacity to commit to a relationship without losing one's own identity (Prager, 1986). By young adulthood, people are expected to be ready for true intimacy. They must develop cooperative social and occupational relationships with others and choose a mate. If they cannot develop such relationships, they will remain isolated (cf. Storr, 1988).

There is evidence consistent with Erikson's claim that identity must precede intimacy. Adolescents and young adults who lack a firm sense of self are typically also unable to commit to another person (Dyk & Adams, 1990).

Generativity versus Stagnation

According to Erikson, a mature person must do more than establish intimacy with others. The individual "needs to be needed" and to assist younger members of society. Generativity involves guiding the next generation through childrearing, teaching, civic activities, and the like. If this need is not fulfilled, the individual may feel stagnant and personally impoverished.

Ego Integrity versus Despair

Despair in later life results from not suitably handling the preceding conflicts. People feel disgusted with themselves and correctly realize that it is too late to start another life. Such individuals remain in a state of incurable remorse for the rest of their days. In contrast, developing adaptive qualities in the other seven stages leads to becoming psychosocially adjusted and having a lasting sense of integrity. Erikson believed that everyone, regardless of capabilities, *can* achieve such adjustment.

Erikson believed that mature people must seek generativity, which involves concern for the development of the young.
© Margaret W. Peterson/ The Image Bank

Table 5.1 Sample items from the Inventory of Social Balance (ISB)

TASK	SAMPLE ITEM*
Trust	"I can usually depend on others."
Autonomy	"I am quite self-sufficient."
Initiative	"When faced with a problem, I am very good at developing various solutions."
Industry	"I genuinely enjoy work."
Identity	"In general, I know what I want out of life."
Intimacy	"I have experienced some very close relationships."
Generativity	"I derive a great deal of pleasure from watching a child master a new skill."
Ego integrity	"Life has been good to me."

*Responses are made on a 5-point scale, from strongly agree to strongly disagree.
Source: Adapted from "A Personality Measure of Erikson's Life Stages: The Inventory of Social Balance," by G. Domino and D. D. Affonso, 1990, *Journal of Personality Assessment, 54,* 580.

A Measure of Psychosocial Development

The Inventory of Social Balance (ISB) is a paper-and-pencil measure of the degree to which a person has resolved the eight Eriksonian conflicts (Domino & Affonso, 1990). Sample items from the ISB are shown in Table 5.1, above, which also serves as an overview and summary of Erikson's theory.

HUMAN MOTIVATION

Many prominent followers of Freud developed theories of human motivation that diverged sharply from Freud's early ideas. Some expanded the number of basic human drives; others emphasized the centrality of drives other than the life drive or libido. In this section, we examine some of the most influential of the post-Freudian drive theories.

Adler's Theory of Human Motivation

Alfred Adler was a weak and sickly child. He had twice been run over in the street, and he almost died from pneumonia (Orgler, 1963). He suffered from rickets (a disease that softens the bones), which made engaging in physical activities with his peers very difficult. In later years, Adler recalled his feelings of inferiority:

> I remember sitting on a bench bandaged up on account of rickets, with my healthy elder brother sitting opposite me. He could run, jump, and move about quite effortlessly, while for me, movement of any sort was a strain and an effort. (quoted in Bottome, 1957, pp. 30–31)

As a consequence of his early life experiences, Adler decided to become a physician in an effort to overcome his maladies and his personal fear of death (Ansbacher & Ansbacher, 1956).

Adler practiced general medicine before turning to psychiatry. In 1907, he presented the intriguing theory that people develop a disease or malfunction in their weakest organ or body part. Furthermore, Adler believed that people deal with such weakness by compensating and even overcompensating. For example, a person born with weak legs might spend many hours developing

Alfred Adler (1870–1937) claimed that the primary human motivation is striving for superiority in an effort to compensate for feelings of inferiority.
Courtesy of the Alfred Adler Institute of Chicago

the leg muscles (compensation). As a result, the individual might eventually become a long-distance runner (overcompensation).

When Adler began to practice psychiatry, he broadened his theory to all feelings of inferiority, including those arising from psychological or interpersonal weaknesses. The individual's perceived inferiority—be it biological, psychological, or social—leads to striving for superiority as a form of compensation. Adler (1964) believed that all people are motivated by two forces operating in cyclic fashion: (1) the need to overcome inferiority and (2) the desire to do so by becoming superior. In normal development, striving for superiority compensates for feelings of inferiority. In the resulting compensatory lifestyle that the individual adopts, feelings of inferiority, which are most prominent in childhood, may be forgotten.

When feelings of inferiority or strivings for superiority become exaggerated, abnormal behavior (neurosis) can result. **Inferiority complex** was Adler's term for such an exaggerated, neurotic reaction. Current thinking among Adlerians has further refined the concept of inferiority complex as having three features:

1. It develops in early childhood and forms the foundation of an emerging lifestyle.
2. It is a subjective perception of the self that results from a comparison of beliefs about others in one's primary group, most notably siblings.
3. The comparison is made regarding three sets of characteristics: physical, social, and goals and standards. The inferiority (and the comparisons) may not be consciously experienced (Strano & Dixon, 1990, p. 29).

Although psychoanalysis was born in Europe, the psychoanalytic circle began to spread to North America in the first years of the 20th century. Whereas Freud's first followers (and critics) were people who knew him personally, second- and third-generation adherents to the Psychoanalytic Strategy had had no real contact with Freud. One of the first of these to make a lasting impact in the United States was Henry Murray.

Murray's Multiple Drive/Needs Model

Henry A. Murray (1893–1988) was an American psychologist and Harvard scholar who offered a somewhat different answer to the question: "What is (are) the fundamental force(s) or needs behind all human existence?" When Murray himself was psychoanalyzed, the experience convinced him at a deep personal level that Freud was correct in focusing on unconscious motivational forces (Anderson, 1988).

Murray's unique theoretical contribution was his conclusion that there are not just one or a few driving forces (e.g., sex, superiority) but *many* (Murray, 1936). Murray himself undertook to study the full pattern of needs and environmental pressures; those who followed him selected one or a few drives to study (e.g., the drives for achievement and power, to be discussed later).

In Murray's writings, the terms *needs* and *drives* are used interchangeably. Both refer to unconscious motivational forces—to what *really* makes the individual "go." Murray himself spoke of 39 human needs, which could be divided into *viscerogenic* (biological) and *psychogenic* (psychological) needs.

Henry A. Murray (1893–1988) considered the father of modern need theory, insisted that both forces within the individual (needs) and environmental factors (press) combine to determine how a person will behave.

Biological needs represent the organism's physical requirements. There are 12 such needs, including those for air, water, food, sex, and physical safety. It is relatively easy to agree on the external or internal conditions that will arouse one of these needs (e.g., when we are thirsty, we are motivated to seek a drink).

There is less agreement on Murray's 27 psychological needs (Table 5.2). Murray believed that the individual and the environment must be considered together—*a person-environment interaction*—in analyzing personality. However, to analyze this interaction, he first had to separate forces within the individual (**needs,** often abbreviated *n*) from environmental forces, called **press.** (Note: The plural of *press* is *press,* not *presses.*) Although all psychologists agree with Murray that environmental forces are important, the term *press* never caught on. So, here our discussion is limited to Murray's work on needs and thus to his ties to (the drive theories of) the Psychoanalytic Strategy.

Table 5.2 Murray's list of psychological needs

MAJOR CATEGORY	NEED	BEHAVIORAL EXAMPLE
Ambition	*n* Achievement	Overcoming obstacles
	n Recognition	Boasting
	n Exhibition	Making efforts to shock or thrill others
	n Acquisition	Acquiring things by working or stealing
	n Conservance	Repairing possessions
	n Order	Tidying up
	n Retention	Hoarding
	n Construction	Organizing or building something
Defense of status	*n* Inviolacy	Maintaining psychological "distance"
	n Infavoidance	Concealing a disfigurement
	n Defendance	Offering explanations or excuses
	n Counteraction	Engaging in acts of retaliation
Response to human power	*n* Dominance	Dictating to or directing others
	n Deference	Cooperating with others
	n Similance	Imitating others
	n Autonomy	Manifesting defiance of authority
	n Contrariance	Taking oppositional views
	n Aggression	Assaulting or belittling others
	n Abasement	Apologizing, confessing, or surrendering
	n Blamavoidance	Inhibiting unconventional impulses
Affection between people	*n* Affiliation	Joining groups
	n Rejection	Discriminating against or snubbing others
	n Nurturance	"Mothering" a child
	n Succorance	Crying for help
	n Play	Seeking diversion by "having fun"
Exchange of information	*n* Cognizance	Asking questions
	n Exposition	Lecturing to, or interpreting for, others

Source: Information from *Explorations in Personality* by H. A. Murray, 1962, New York: Science Editions.

Many of the needs on Murray's list have received little attention since he first wrote about them in the 1930s. In the section that follows, we discuss the two needs that have received the most attention in research: the need to achieve and the need for power.

The Need to Achieve

For more than 30 years, David McClelland investigated the need to achieve, much as it was originally described by Murray. McClelland (1953) defined the need to achieve as "a concern with doing things better, with surpassing standards of excellence" (p. 228).

The McClelland-Atkinson Approach to Measuring Motives

The first step in studying achievement or any other personality construct is to define and measure it. The approach devised by McClelland and his colleague John Atkinson is the basis for the Thematic Apperception Test, or TAT (Atkinson, 1958; Atkinson & McClelland, 1948; McClelland, Atkinson, Clark, & Lowell, 1953), a projective technique we discuss in more detail in Chapter 6.

In brief, the McClelland-Atkinson approach involves the following steps. First, subjects are exposed to a motive-arousing experience. They might be told they are taking an important examination to arouse the achievement drive, or they might watch a stirring political film to arouse the power drive. A control group is exposed to a neutral experience that presumably does not arouse the motive in question. Subjects in both groups then write stories about standard pictures. The differences in the imagery produced by the motive-aroused and nonaroused group in the stories are taken as evidence that the drive, when aroused, manifests itself in particular kinds of imagery.

To develop a scoring system for the need for Achievement, McClelland and his colleagues exposed college students to either achievement-arousing situations (e.g., they were given success or failure experiences) or to situations that did not arouse achievement (e.g., the experimental tasks were presented in a casual, relaxed way). The students were then asked to write stories about four pictures that were especially pertinent to achievement strivings. Stories were scored for a number of different categories related to achievement. Categories that differentiated subjects exposed to varying degrees of achievement arousal were defined as measures of achievement motivation.

David McClelland chose to focus on individual motives (particularly achievement motivation), rather than to examine a person's entire motivational structure.
Courtesy of David McClelland

The Nature of Achievement Motivation

As a first step, McClelland and his associates compared people with high and low achievement TAT imagery scores. They found:

> In general, people with a high achievement imagery index score complete more tasks under achievement orientation, solve more simple arithmetic problems on a timed test, improve faster in their ability to do anagrams, tend to get better grades, use more future tenses and abstract nouns in talking about themselves . . . and so on. (McClelland et al., 1953, p. 327)

The beauty of these imagery measures of latent motivation is that the scoring system for stories can be used with any written material. McClelland could therefore study achievement motivation by examining political documents, novels and stories, letters, and so on. For example, McClelland and his associates studied the relationship between independence training and achievement motivation in Native American tribes by scoring their folktales for achievement themes (McClelland et al., 1953; Winter & Carlson, 1988).

An even more ambitious task involved McClelland's (1967) attempt to "search for the broadest possible test of the hypothesis that a particular psychological factor—the need for Achievement—is responsible for economic growth and decline" (p. vii). Specifically, McClelland tried to "predict" the economic growth of 23 countries from 1929 to 1950 based on the amount of achievement imagery in children's stories in those countries in the preceding decade (1920–1929). He found an impressively high positive

Achievement motivation may be manifested in different ways. Academic excellence is one way, but so too is being a skilled welder, a star athlete, or a computer wiz. Top left: © Christopher O'Keefe; top right: © Erik Leigh Simmons/Image Bank; bottom left: Courtesy of Bobby Doyle; bottom right: Courtesy of Alex Liebert.

Table 5.3 Characteristics of high need achievers at work

Report pushing themselves to their fullest potential[1]
Prefer achievement-oriented supervisors to "supportive" supervisors[2]
Pass quickly over easy tasks to reach more difficult ones[3]
Show increased effort on tasks as time runs out[4]

[1]Emmons and McAdams (1991).
[2]Matheiu (1990).
[3]Slade and Rush (1990).
[4]Beh (1989).

correlation (+.53) between achievement emphasis in children's stories and economic growth. This association across time suggests that a society's aspirations may be found in the stories that it offers its children. Independent experiments suggest that such stories do seem to influence children who hear them (McArthur & Eisen, 1976).

McClelland's earliest work showed that individuals high in achievement motivation (1) like challenges in their work and prefer moderate risk, (2) want concrete feedback on how well they are doing, and (3) like to take personal responsibility for meeting work goals.

Over the past 15 years, research on *n* Achievement has shed further light on the work characteristics of individuals who are high in achievement need. Some of these findings are shown in Table 5.3, above.

Power: The Anatomy of a Motive

David Winter is the leading theorist and researcher on the need for power. Winter (1973) viewed "the striving for power as one important motive . . . in individuals." He defined *power* as a person's ability or capacity to produce intended effects on the behavior or emotions of someone else. Winter's research tried "to determine whether there are differences in the extent to which people want power, or strive to affect the behavior of others according to their own intentions; to measure these differences; and to determine their further consequences and associated characteristics" (p. 5). In fact, Winter (1967, 1968, 1972, 1973; Winter & Carlson, 1988) and other investigators have gathered an enormous amount of evidence indicating that there are individual differences in power motivation (often referred to as *n* Power).

David G. Winter extensively studied the various manifestations of the power motive.
Courtesy Wesleyan University

The Measurement and Meaning of Power Motivation

According to Winter (1973), the goal of the power motive is the status of having power. He wrote:

> By the power motive, I mean a [tendency] to strive for certain kinds of goals, or to be affected by certain kinds of incentives. People who have the power motive, or who strive for power, are trying to bring about a certain state of affairs—they want to feel "power" or "more powerful than." Power is their goal. We would expect that they tend to construe the world in terms of power and to use the concept of "power" in categorizing human interaction, but they do more than that. Not only do they categorize the world in terms of power, but they also want to feel themselves as the most powerful. (p. 18)

As with achievement motivation, power motivation can be measured either by the use of specially created pictures or by thematic analysis of almost any verbal material (Winter, 1987b).

What themes in imagery and prose indicate a high power motive? According to Winter, there are three: (1) strong, vigorous actions expressing power; (2) actions that produce strong emotional reactions in others; and (3) statements expressing concern about a person's reputation or position.

The Hope and Fear of Power

The use of power-related themes in a person's stories or writings does not always imply a hope of power. Sometimes the reaction expressed in such themes seems riddled with conflict or doubt.

Winter believed that there are two aspects to the power motive: **Hope of Power** and **Fear of Power.** Hope of Power and the overall power motive are positively correlated, but Hope of Power and Fear of Power show a slight negative correlation; that is, people with high Hope of Power tend to have low Fear of Power, and vice versa.

Fear of Power: A Closer Look

Fear of Power is simultaneous interest in and worry about power, especially when the individual fears being the *victim* of (others') power. Winter claims that the autonomy concerns of those high in Fear of Power derive from a fear of structure, especially structure that is imposed by someone else of high status or power (e.g., a professor or university administrator). Specified programs, assigned work, lectures, and "objective" examinations are all constraints on behavior that originate from the "outside." Fearing the structure that someone else imposes is thus one manifestation of a fear of the potential power of other people (Winter, 1973, p. 149).

This analysis was supported by two studies that showed that students high in Fear of Power were more likely to be late with major term papers, even in the face of warnings (e.g., the papers would be graded down for lateness). They were also more likely to take "incompletes" in their courses.

A clear implication of these findings is that Fear of Power is often *not* adaptive. Winter has other evidence pointing in this direction. For example, college students high in Fear of Power tend to have more automobile accidents than other students. They are also relatively less efficient when playing a competitive bidding game. When their power is threatened, those with high Fear of Power seem to become debilitated.

Action Correlates of the Power Motive

A major part of Winter's research has involved looking for what he called the "action correlates" of individuals who are high in the power motive; that is, he asked: "What are the overt manifestations of the power motive?"

Presentation of Self

Both women and men with high *n* Power tend to have more "prestige possessions" than those with a low *n* Power (Winter, 1968, 1972; Winter &

Barenbaum, 1985)—even when income or spending money is held constant. Students high in *n* Power are more likely to put their names on the doors of their dormitory rooms, and they tend to report their college grades in a "favorable" light. For example, Winter (1973) asked students to indicate the lowest final grade they had received thus far in college. Those students high in *n* Power tended to lie and report their lowest grade as higher than it really was.

There is a bit more to the picture, though. Winter (1973) asked middle-class business executives and college students which automobile they would most like. He found that individuals high in *n* Power did not want the most expensive cars; they chose cars that handled best. This finding was true for the students, the executives, and those who chose American cars as well as those who chose foreign cars.

Apparently, *control*—of people, possessions, and situations—is a central concern of people driven by power motivation. Such control may be gained through force, prestige possessions, or the embellishment of one's products. Here is an interesting example:

> At Wesleyan University as elsewhere, students submit term papers in a great variety of formats, bindings, and conditions of neatness. Some hand in a few ragged sheets of paper full of typing mistakes and bound precariously with a paper clip. Others submit neatly typed, carefully proofread papers which are impressively bound in colored plastic covers with plastic grips running along the left margin.
>
> To the extent that professors judge a paper by its cover—a misleading but human tendency—the paper that is neatly and impressively bound will fare a little better or at least get a favorable first reaction. In a small way, such bindings use prestige to enhance reputation—they are an "impressive show." In one introductory psychology course, those thirteen students who bound their term papers in colored plastic or colored paper binders were significantly higher in Hope of Power than those fifty students who turned in ordinary papers. (Winter, 1973, p. 133)

In a related study, it was found that college men high in *n* Power tended to be argumentative in class. They were also eager to convince their instructors or fellow students of their point of view (Veroff, 1957). This may be why men high in power motivation do well in those college courses that require classroom participation (McKeachie, 1961).

Selection of Friends

Surprisingly, individuals high in *n* Power tend to prefer friends who are not popular or well known. Winter explained:

> To a power-motivated person, such friends are attractive because they are presumably not a threat, since they do not compete for power and prestige. Being less well known, such friends are also more disposed to form strong ties of friendship, regard, and support for the power-motivated "leader." (1973, p. 114)

One of the most remarkable characteristics of individuals high in power motivation is that they gather a group of followers to whom they are both generous and understanding. At the same time, they display a competitive stance toward people outside the circle. Winter (1973) asked students: "Do you generally like to do things in your own way and without regard for what other students around you may think?" Most students low in power motivation answered yes, whereas a majority of those high in power motivation answered no. To be powerful, you must have a following; to maintain a following, you must show consideration toward those who follow you—or so it seems.

Then again, people high in power motivation have a rough-and-ready attitude toward those who oppose them. For example, Winter (1973) asked students: "If you could say one sentence—any sentence—to anyone, anywhere in the world, in person and without fear of reprisal, what would you say?" Students high in power motivation were significantly more likely to say something with a strong negative effect, usually something obscene, than were those low in power drive.

Reactivity to Power Stresses

McClelland (1982) hypothesized that individuals high in power drive would react more to "power stresses" than those low on this dimension. In situations that arouse power motivation but do not allow power to be exercised, he predicted that the power-motivated individual will experience a high degree of emotional arousal.

Fodor (1984) tested this hypothesis by creating an industrial simulation in which college students (who were either high or low in power motivation) acted as "supervisors" of a work crew. During the experiment, members of the work crew either expressed no work concerns or expressed increasing concerns about their performance. (Crew members were, in fact, confederates who were told what to say by the experimenter.)

The concerns were expressed in comments made to the supervisor: "We're trying to outdo the other groups but we're getting all upset because we're not doing well." "What stress! I never realized money could mean so much to people." "I think we're not really making the grade. Bad scene" (Fodor, 1984, p. 855). The supervisors could do little to change the crews' attitudes or performance, thus creating considerable power stress. They were monitored for emotional arousal as they got feedback from their crews.

Supervisors high and low in power motivation had almost identical levels of arousal when their groups expressed no concern about performance. However, consistent with McClelland's prediction, when the crew *did* express performance concerns, supervisors high in power motivation became much more aroused. The pattern of results is shown in Figure 5.2.

Sexual Behavior and Power

Sexual behavior and power drive have been closely related both in literature and in psychology. The suggested link has some basis in fact. Male students who report having had sexual intercourse before entering college have appreciably higher power motivation scores than those who do not (Winter,

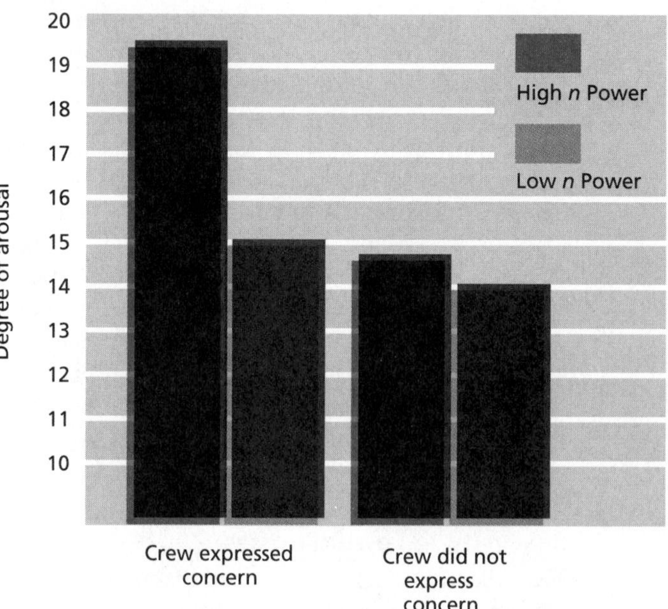

Figure 5.2
Degree of arousal displayed by supervisors who were high and low in *n* Power in Fodor's experiment, as a function of the concern expressed by their work crews about how the work was going.
Source: From data presented in "The Power Motive and Reactivity to Power Stresses," by E. M. Fodor, 1984, *Journal of Personality and Social Psychology, 47,* pp. 853–859.

1973). Men high in *n* Power have also been found to be more likely to physically abuse their partners (Mason & Blankenship, 1987).

Finally Winter found that college men high in power drive were more likely to say that they considered a woman who was dependent an "ideal wife."

> While a dependent wife may interfere with her husband's power, she probably enhances his feelings of power; presumably he then thinks that he is not dependent on her. Thus this combination of qualities is attractive to high *n* Power men because it gives them . . . feelings of superiority. (1973, p. 178)

(The astute reader may have already noticed the similarity between the power drive and the motivation Adler called *striving for superiority.*)

Heinz Hartmann (1894–1970)
emphasized the adaptive functions of the ego in the normal personality.
© UPI/Bettmann Newsphoto

Alcoholism and the Power Drive

McClelland and his co-workers have proposed that the need for power plays a major role in problem drinking (McClelland, Davis, Kalin, & Wanner, 1972). In a 10-year research program, these investigators found that men's feelings of power increased after drinking alcohol. In addition, men with an intense need for power drank even more to satisfy that need. The investigators concluded that dependence on alcohol to satisfy the need for power is the basis of alcoholism. Other research suggests that men's power drive is distinctly high at midlife, which may be when their real power starts to dwindle (Veroff, Reuman, & Feld, 1984). So, the high incidence of alcoholism in middle-aged men can be understood (at least in part) in terms of a need for power.

EGO PSYCHOLOGY

Recall from Chapter 3 that ego psychologists focus more on the *adaptive functions* of the ego and on the personality functioning of "normal" healthy individuals than do classical Freudians. Ego psychology emphasizes the study of well-functioning people to better understand the adaptive role of the ego.

Hartmann's Ego Psychology

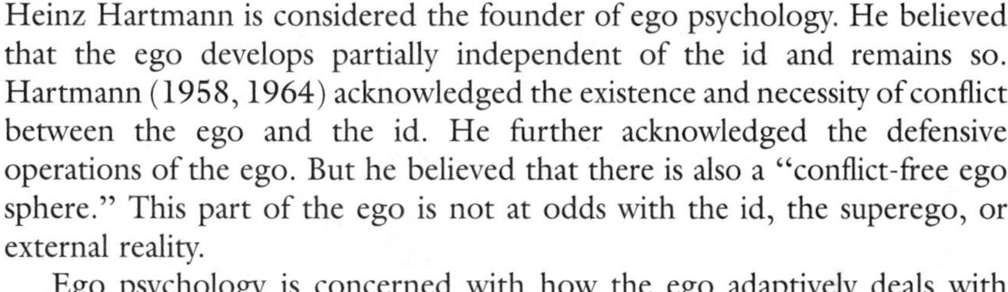

Heinz Hartmann is considered the founder of ego psychology. He believed that the ego develops partially independent of the id and remains so. Hartmann (1958, 1964) acknowledged the existence and necessity of conflict between the ego and the id. He further acknowledged the defensive operations of the ego. But he believed that there is also a "conflict-free ego sphere." This part of the ego is not at odds with the id, the superego, or external reality.

Robert White focused on competence as opposed to drive reduction within the framework of ego psychology. Photo by Paul Koby

Ego psychology is concerned with how the ego adaptively deals with reality through perception, thinking, language, creative production, attention, and memory. In this regard, ego psychology comes closer to contemporary mainstream psychology than does classical psychoanalytic theory. It also provides a more complete account of the full range of psychological processes (Friedman, 1989; Loewenstein, Newmann, Schur, & Solnit, 1966; Siskind, 1987).

Hartmann (1951) believed that ego psychology should investigate "how psychological conflict and 'peaceful' internal development mutually facilitate and hamper each other" (p. 368). Fantasy, for example, is a secondary process that can have definite adaptive features. Hartmann (1951) contended that "fantasy can be fruitful even in scientific thinking, which is the undisputed domain of rational thinking" (p. 372). Other ego psychologists, such as Ernest Kris (1950), argued that the role of fantasy in creative and artistic thinking can be fully explained only if the ego is considered an autonomous part of the personality.

"Drives" of the Ego

Robert White developed an ego psychology theory in which *competence,* not drive reduction, is the major motivation. Sex and aggression, the primary drives in Freudian theory, are satisfied by drive reduction. In contrast, competence drives are satisfied by *stimulation* of the drive. Competence means an organism's "fitness or ability to carry out those transactions with the environment which result in its maintaining itself, growing, and flourishing." White (1959, 1963) buttressed his ideas with research showing the importance of motives like exploration, manipulation, and curiosity in human behavior.

The difference between White's ego psychology and Freud's "id psychology" is illustrated by White's reconceptualization of Freud's psychosexual stages. White (1960) traced the development of competence, in its various forms, just as Freud did with the sexual drive. Table 5.4 summarizes White's view of development. Note the similarities with the psychosocial stages described by Erikson, who may also be considered an ego psychologist.

Table 5.4 White's reconceptualization of Freud's psychosexual stages

FREUD'S STAGE	FREUD'S THEME	WHITE'S THEME (COMPETENCY)	EXAMPLE OF COMPETENCY
Oral stage	Feeding	*Coping with environment*	Infant playing with any and all objects it comes in contact with
Anal stage	Elimination	*Independence*	Two- to three-year-olds' negativism: not wanting to do what they are told and wanting to do things on their own
Phallic stage	Oedipal situation	*Locomotion*	Moving about freely and at will
		Language	Communicating needs verbally and influencing other people through language
		Imagination	Taking on imaginary roles, especially those of adults
Latency period	No psychosexual development	*Social skills*	Making and keeping friends; coping with social rejection
		Meeting realistic challenges	Doing well with schoolwork and athletics
Genital stage	Heterosexual behavior	*Sense of identity*	Defining oneself in terms of strengths and weaknesses and developing self-confidence
		Life skills	Developing intellectual skills that will be used in lifelong pursuits

OBJECT RELATIONS

Modern cognitive psychologists have found it useful to posit that thought involves the interplay of our *mental representations* of things, events, and people. We react not to things as they are but to things as we have represented them in our heads. (These ideas are discussed at length in Part V.) An early version of this idea appeared within the Psychoanalytic Strategy, under the label *object relations.*

In the psychoanalytic literature, the word *object* does not refer to inanimate things but rather to the important people in one's life—including oneself. Each such object in a person's life exists mentally as an **object representation.** We react to people not as they are (in some external "reality") but as we perceive and experience them.

Melanie Klein

There is no single object relations theory. Freud himself was the first to speak of intrapsychic objects, but for him the object was important only as a "target" for the sex or aggressive drive. The object relations approach within

Melanie Klein (1882–1960) founded object relations theory, focusing attention on internal representations of self and others. Wellcome Institute Library, London

psychoanalysis today is an amalgam of ideas, beginning with the writings of Melanie Klein (1882–1960), an English psychiatrist.

Unlike Freud, who studied adults and examined their childhoods retrospectively, Klein worked directly with children. She concluded that children are much more concerned about building social relationships than they are about controlling libidinal impulses. However, Klein (who was nearly a contemporary of Freud's) endeavored in her theorizing to derive the origins of interpersonal difficulties from Freud's original sex drive model. Later object relations theorists deviated more sharply from Freud, suggesting that the need for contact and relatedness to others is *the* primary force behind personality development and *not* merely a product of the sex drive.

Object relations theorists all place great emphasis on dependency on others, which characterizes the human condition. Initially, we all experience *infantile dependency,* which might be thought of as "all take and no give." Development involves a transition from this immature form of social relationship toward *interdependency,* which, in its mature form, involves mutual give-and-take so that we feel that we can rely on others *and* that they can rely on us.

Sullivan's Contributions

In the 1930s, a distinct alternative to Freud's sex drive theory and his mode of treatment began to be formulated in the United States. This alternative to Freudian psychoanalysis, **interpersonal psychoanalysis,** ultimately gave rise to **interpersonal therapy (IPT).** The founder of this approach was an American psychiatrist, Harry Stack Sullivan (1892–1949). Like Erikson and the ego psychologists, Sullivan argued that classical Freudian theory gave too little attention to the larger social and cultural context in which personality develops. Sullivan resolutely believed that mental life is characterized by intense conflict, but he also believed the nature of the conflict arose from the nature of the person's relationship with others.

Harry Stack Sullivan (1892–1949) emphasized the importance of being able to "read" others' feelings as a basis for adequate social adjustment. Courtesy of William Alanson White, Psychiatric Foundation, Inc.

Sullivan spoke of **personifications,** which in his theory were mental representations of self and others similar in many ways to the objects of other object relations theorists. However, Sullivan's personifications are more complex, as self (and others) may be represented by *multiple* personifications. For example, there may be separate representations for the "good me" and "bad me." This "splitting" of mental objects is an important theme that recurs in the writings of many object relations theorists. (This also parallels some contemporary cognitive ideas about the nature of self representations—see Chapter 17.)

Sullivan argued that dependency longings were not derived from the sex drive but, rather, that sexual interests were derived from dependency longings. Anxiety about the deterioration or loss of our relationships with others gives rise to **security operations;** efforts to protect and preserve significant relationships. The pursuit of interpersonal security thus became for Sullivan the central driving force in psychological life. One manifestation of our anxiety about social insecurity is what Sullivan called the ***delusion of unique individuality.*** As Greenberg and Mitchell (1983) explain:

> Sullivan uses the phrase "delusion of unique individuality" in reference to the claim to "specialness" with which the individual adorns itself in its struggle against anxiety. Each of us, he suggests, considers himself as uniquely special, self-contained, different from others by virtue of a particular wisdom, talent, deficit, or victimization. (p. 113)

W. R. D. Fairbairn

W. R. D. Fairbairn (1889–1964), a Scottish psychoanalyst, agreed with Sullivan that what develops in personality development is the need for contact and relatedness with others. "It is not the libidinal attitude which determines the object-relationship," Fairbairn wrote, "but the object-relationship which determines the libidinal attitude" (1946, p. 34). Thus, whereas classical Freudian theory views sexuality as an end in itself, Fairbairn views sexuality as a means to a more fundamental aim, namely, contact with others. The fundamental drive behind human motivation is "object-seeking." According to Fairbairn, then, the most frightening thing that could happen to an individual would be to be left entirely alone.

W. R. D. Fairbairn (1889–1964) emphasized the centrality of interpersonal needs and the quest for meaningful social relationships. Courtesy of Mrs. Marian Fairbairn

Fairbairn was convinced that children need to feel loved as individuals in their own right and also that the love they offer is welcomed and valued by others. He envisioned a gradual developmental process that begins with infantile, dependent relating to the mother and gradually evolves into the capacity for adult mutuality—relationships based on exchange. The child must renounce infantile attachments and dependency on the parents in order to achieve ***mutual dependency.***

Sometimes the anxiety over altering the existing relationship with the parents is too great, and psychopathology enters the picture. Fairbairn stated that "the core conflict of all psychopathology is between the developmental urge toward mature dependence and richer relations, and the regressive reluctance to abandon infantile dependence to undifferentiated objects (both internal and external), for fear of losing contact of any sort" (Greenberg & Mitchell, 1983, p. 162). Thus, each of us desperately needs relationships with other people. If the only way to relate to another person is by adopting a role that produces pain or discomfort, the person will do that because even the apparently painful relationship is better than losing contact with others entirely.

Margaret Mahler

Margaret Mahler (1897–1985) made a major contribution with her elaborate description of the development of personality in very early childhood. Mahler is considered primarily an object relations theorist because of her emphasis on mental representations of self and others and her focus on interpersonal aspects of development.

Mahler, a pediatrician, became interested in the very close relationship between mother and child, which led to her ultimately becoming a psychoanalyst. She relied primarily on naturalistic observations to provide information about the early childhood experiences on which she based her theory. These observations were made in a large indoor playroom where

Margaret Mahler (1897–1985) provided a detailed analysis of object relations development.
The Margaret S. Mahler Psychiatric Research Foundation

children were free to use various toys. The room was divided by a low, fencelike barrier. Mothers sat and watched their children from the other side of the barrier. Research assistants interacted with both children and mothers and later made detailed records of their observations (Bergman & Ellman, 1985).

Mahler believed that personality begins in a state of fusion with other people, especially the mother. Newborn infants do not appear to make a distinction between themselves and others. They seem to consider self ("me") and nonself ("not me") the same. Mother at first appears to them as a part of the self. Mahler's theory focuses on the process by which the infant assumes its own physical and psychological identity, distinct from that of other people (Mahler, 1968; Mahler, Bergman, & Pine, 1975). Development of the self involves separating from the state of total fusion and becoming an independent individual.

Mahler divided the child's development into three phases (stages): (1) normal autism, (2) normal symbiosis, and (3) separation-individuation. These phases are summarized in Table 5.5. The manner in which children "negotiate" each of these phases determines to a great extent the nature of their interpersonal relations as adults. This aspect is similar to Freud's scheme, in which the degree of success in getting through psychosexual stages of development influences later personality. The major difference is that, for Freud, personality development involves channeling sexual energy toward pleasurable goals. For Mahler, development involves the investment of psychic energy in relations with other people.

Table 5.5 Mahler's stages of object relations development

PHASE	APPROXIMATE TIME FRAME	DEVELOPMENTAL PROCESSES
Normal autism phase	Birth–1 month	Completely within self; unresponsive to external stimuli
Normal symbiosis phase	2–3 months	Undifferentiated self and nonself; fusion with mother; vague awareness of need-satisfying objects
Separation-individuation phase		
Differentiation subphase	4–8 months	Initial attempts at separation; sensory exploration of external environment; frequent checking back to mother
Practicing subphase	9 to 15 or 18 months	Locomotion allows further exploration of world; increased temporary separation from mother
Rapproachement subphase	15 or 18 to 24 months	Conflict between independence and dependence; child wants to be with mother yet fears being engulfed by her; critical period for future development
Individuality and emotional object constancy subphase	24 months on	Development of permanent sense of self and permanent emotional and mental representations of others

Separation-Individuation

True object relations are not achieved until **separation-individuation** begins. This third and final phase of the developmental sequence commences in about the fifth month and in some sense continues throughout life. It reflects every person's conflict between the desire for autonomy and the desire to be linked with others.

Separation-individuation involves two developmental processes that are closely related and occur simultaneously. *Separation* is the process whereby the child achieves intrapsychic distinctiveness from the mother. In other words, the child comes to clearly differentiate intrapsychic representations (as opposed to the actual objects) of the self and others (Tuttman, 1988). *Individuation* is an early stage of identity. "To be individuated is a feeling that *I am*—an early awareness of a sense of being, of entity—while identity is the later awareness of *who I am*" (St. Clair, 1986, p. 106).

Splitting

The concept of splitting plays a central role in several object relations theories (Cashdan, 1988; Fairbairn, 1952; Winnicott, 1971). **Splitting** is the mental separation of objects into their "good" and "bad" aspects. (Recall that Sullivan's personifications could represent discrepant elements of a single object, including the self.)

The first splitting occurs because the mother is experienced as inconsistent. Sometimes she is "good," meeting all the infant's needs. Sometimes she is "bad," failing to respond as completely or as quickly as the infant desires. The infant is not mentally equipped to think of the same person as good *and* bad and is thus faced with a dilemma. The dilemma is resolved by dividing the mother into good and bad components and then mentally separating one from the other. In this way, infants maintain their dependent ties without constantly feeling threatened.

Splitting is not by itself abnormal, nor is the process limited to the mother or to early childhood. Rather, carving experience up evaluatively, into good versus bad, is a pervasive way of processing information for adults as well as children (Osgood, Suci, & Tannenbaum, 1957). The critical question is not whether there is splitting, because invariably there is. The question is, "How is initial splitting resolved in later development?"

Reintegration versus Fragmentation

When the beliefs of several object relations theorists are integrated, the resultant developmental path of splitting is an eight-stage process. The stages are diagrammed in Figure 5.3.

Stage I. This is Mahler's normal autism phase. Experience is undifferentiated. Stage I is presumed to be the original state of being.

Stage II. Vague awareness of a possible differentiation of experience begins by the second month. This is Mahler's normal symbiosis phase.

Stage III. There is a dramatic division of experience between "self" and "other."

Stage IV. The "other," mainly composed of mother at this stage, is split into good and bad. This is the "good mother"–"bad mother" split referred to by many object relations theorists.

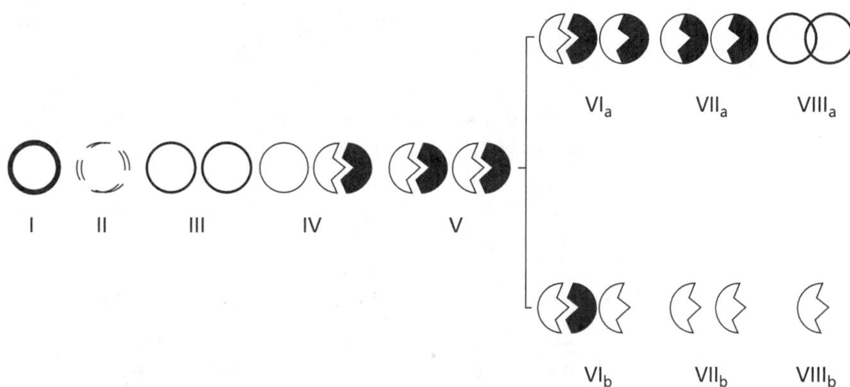

Figure 5.3
Stages of splitting.

Stage V. "Self" is also split into good and bad, as a result of the mother object having been partly "incorporated" into the self.

Stage VI. This is the critical juncture for all later object relations. Essentially there are two ways to go.

VIa. Mothering has been *"good enough."* The individual begins to fuse (co-accept) both aspects of mother into an integrated whole. (Many object relations theorists emphasize the concept of the **good enough mother.** No mother is perfect and invariably available to her infant; however, what is critical for normal development is satisfactory attention to the demands and needs of the child. If the basic needs of the child, physical and emotional, are adequately met, mothering has been good enough.)

VIb. If the mother is very rejecting or extremely ungratifying, it becomes necessary to push the bad mother completely out of awareness. Should this happen, the individual will have trouble dealing with self-splitting and is in for considerable trouble in all future relationships (Kernberg, 1975, 1976; Kohut, 1977, 1984).

Stage VII. The path is now set toward (a) integration or (b) complete fragmentation.

VIIa. Acceptance of mother's dual nature permits acceptance of one's own dual nature.

VIIb. Bad mother and bad self are now both repressed (pushed out of awareness).

Stage VIII. This is the terminal condition of each path.

VIIIa. The person is now capable of relationships characterized by mutual interdependence, which represents psychological maturity.

VIIIb. The person is unable to deal with others in cooperative, sustaining ways. Neither self nor any other can be accepted. The individual is prone to **projective identifications** (see detailed discussion later).

Levels of Object Relations

Object relations theorists believe that people can be understood in terms of the *level* of object relations they have attained (Blatt & Lerner, 1983; Hamilton, 1989; Westen, 1991b). Recall that the basic idea behind object relations theories is that we have internal working models of self and others;

these internal "objects" greatly influence our feelings about ourselves and our dealings with other people. The more advanced our level of object relations development, the better our self-concept and our interpersonal relationships. Consistent with this view, the level of adults' object relations has been shown to be a good predictor of their interpersonal functioning (Mayman, 1967; Piper et al., 1991).

Westen (1991b) has suggested that a person's level of object relations has four aspects: (1) complexity of representations, (2) emotional tone, (3) capacity for emotional investment, and (4) understanding of social causality. Westen's scheme involves five levels, as shown in Table 5.6. At any given level, the four components fit together to form a coherent whole. Also note that very few people are likely to operate at Level 5 *consistently.*

One appealing feature of this object relations model is that it can map the level of object relations onto the type of psychopathology to which a person may succumb. Individuals at Level 1 are likely to be autistic or schizophrenic. Individuals at Level 2 may develop personality disorders. Those at Level 3 tend to have anxiety disorders. Those who attain Levels 4 and 5 are usually free of significant interpersonal psychopathology.

Table 5.6 Five levels in the development of object relations

	COMPLEXITY OF REPRESENTATIONS OF PEOPLE	EMOTIONAL TONE OF REPRESENTATIONS OF PEOPLE
Level 1	People are not clearly differentiated; confusion of points of view.	Malevolent representations: gratuitous violence or gross negligence by significant others.
Level 2	Simple, unidimensional representations; focus on actions; traits are global and univalent.	Representation of relationships as hostile, empty, or capricious but not profoundly malevolent; profound loneliness or disappointment in relationships.
Level 3	Minor elaboration of mental life or personality.	Mixed representations with mildly negative tone.
Level 4	Expanded appreciation of complexity of subjective experience and personality dispositions; absence of representations integrating life history, complex subjectivity, and personality processes.	Mixed representations with neutral or balanced tone.
Level 5	Complex representations, indicating understanding of interaction of enduring and momentary psychological experience; understanding of personality as system of processes interacting with each other and the environment.	Predominantly positive representations; benign and enriching interactions.

Source: Modified from "Social Cognition and Object Relations," by D. Westen, 1991, *Psychological Bulletin, 109,* pp. 429–455.

Projective Identification

Contemporary object relations theorists discuss a defense mechanism called **projective identification** (Cashdan, 1988; Ogden, 1982), which largely parallels the "splitting" process discussed earlier in this chapter. Projective identification is a three-stage process. In the first stage, the individual has a wish to get rid of a "bad" part of the self and so projects it onto another person. In the second stage, the individual pressures the recipient to behave in ways that conform to the bad self—that is, to become like the bad self being projected onto her or him. In the third stage, the recipient responds to the pressure by finally acting as the bad self.

Consider the example of projective identification referred to as *ingratiation.* This phenomenon has its roots in the parenting style in which the parent conveys to the child, "If you don't appreciate all I've done for you, I won't love you." According to object relations theory, repeated exposure to this message causes a split between the side of the child that feels "I *do* appreciate all you do" and the side of the child that says "I *don't* appreciate all you do." The side of the child that says "I do appreciate all you do" is consistent with the parent's demand for gratitude and becomes the displayed *good self.*

CAPACITY FOR EMOTIONAL INVESTMENT	UNDERSTANDING OF SOCIAL CAUSALITY	PSYCHIATRIC APPEARANCE
Need-gratifying orientation: profound self-preoccupation.	Noncausal or grossly illogical depictions of psychological and interpersonal events.	Autism/schizophrenia
Limited investment in people, relationships, and moral standards; conflicting interests recognized, but gratification remains primary aim; moral standards immature and unintegrated or followed to avoid punishment.	Rudimentary understanding of social causality; minor logic errors or unexplained transitions; simple stimulus-response causality.	Personality disorders
Conventional investment in people and moral standards; stereotypic compassion, mutuality, or helping orientation; guilt at moral transgressions.	Complex, accurate situational causality and rudimentary understanding of the role of thoughts and feelings in mediating action.	Anxiety disorders
Mature, committed investment in relationships and values; mutual empathy and concern; commitment to abstract values.	Expanded appreciation of the role of mental processes in generating thoughts, feelings, behaviors, and interpersonal interactions.	Adequate functioning
Autonomous selfhood in the context of committed relationships; recognition of conventional nature of moral rules in the context of carefully considered standards or concern for concrete people or relationships.	Complex appreciation of the role of mental processes in generating thoughts, feelings, behaviors, and interpersonal interactions; understanding of unconscious motivational processes.	Superior functioning

The "I don't appreciate all you do for me" side is repressed because it threatens the loss of parental love. It is the *bad self.* In subsequent relationships, the bad self will be projected on significant others. The person projects: "*You* do not appreciate *me*." The projector then endeavors to force the other into the role of *in*gratitude (e.g., by showering them with gifts and favors so that the other can never be grateful enough), so as to mesh with their own good (grateful) side. Thus, projective identification involves maneuvering others into doing the very things we have repressed in ourselves.

Box 5.1
HORNEY AND THE FEMINIST REACTION TO FREUD

The first prominent psychoanalyst to express feminist views in response to Freud was Karen Horney (pronounced HORN-eye). She reinterpreted the Oedipus complex in terms of interpersonal dynamics.

> The typical conflict leading to anxiety in a child is that between dependency on the parents . . . and hostile impulses against the parents. Hostility may be aroused in a child in many ways: by the parents' lack of respect . . . by unreasonable demands and prohibitions; by injustice; by unreliability; by suppression of criticism; by the parents dominating . . . and ascribing these tendencies to love. . . . If a child, in addition to being dependent on . . . parents, is grossly or subtly intimidated by them and hence feels that any expression of hostile impulses against them endangers security, then the existence of such hostile impulses is bound to create anxiety. . . . The resulting picture may look exactly like what Freud describes as the Oedipus complex: passionate clinging to one parent and jealousy toward the other or toward anyone interfering with the claim of exclusive possession. . . . *But the dynamic structure of these attachments is entirely different from what Freud conceives as the Oedipus complex. They are an early manifestation of neurotic conflicts rather than a primarily sexual phenomenon.* (1939, pp. 81–83; italics added)

Karen Horney (1885–1952) challenged Freud's claim that women experience penis envy and introduced the feminist perspective in psychoanalysis.

Horney was most emphatic in challenging Freud's use of *penis envy* to explain feminine inferiority; at the same time, she intensely disputed Freud's claim that motherhood's greatest psychological importance for women is as a means of compensating for that inferiority. Horney believed that Freud's image of women was distorted and biased because he based it exclusively on observations of *neurotic* (as opposed to healthy and well-functioning) women.

Horney was the first feminist voice in psychoanalysis. Her theorizing was based largely on the bias she perceived as inherent in the

Box continued on following page

Box 5.1 *Continued*
HORNEY AND THE FEMINIST REACTION TO FREUD

patriarchal (father- or male-dominated) view of Freudian theories. In response to this male-dominated perspective, Horney and her followers adopted a **matriarchal** (mother- or female-dominated) posture. The Horney school of thought is distinct from other object relations theories in its thoroughgoing, activist feminism; in fact, some see her strict matriarchal posture as an overreaction to Freud's patriarchal bias (Barrett, 1992; Barratt & Starus, 1994; Young-Bruehl, 1994). Young-Bruehl (1994) refers to this type of reactionary thinking as a "pendulum effect" endemic to social science theorizing. Western society today is neither matriarchal *nor* patriarchal; it is typically one of shared control by women and men, fathers and mothers. More specifically, *both* parent figures are important in a child's personality development.

The fervor of the feminist position escalated beyond the first writings of Horney on the topic. The feminist movement of the 1960s and 1970s in the United States contributed to a close examination of the role of women in a wide variety of contexts, including psychoanalysis. The appearance in 1974 of Juliet Mitchell's *Psychoanalysis and Feminism* marked the beginning of an era of close scrutiny of psychoanalytic thinking by feminist writers (Waddell, 1995).

The past 25 years have seen increasing recognition of women as an oppressed group despite their majority in numbers. The 1980s and early 1990s witnessed an entire academic field, women's studies, spring up in response to the perception that women had been overlooked for too long. Both the American Psychological Association and the British Psychological Society also created special Psychology of Women divisions or sections (Finchilescu, 1995, p. 133). Finally, the recent debate over the apparent rise in reported sexual abuse, especially reports of incest and the media attention it commands, has served to fuel the controversy over the oppression of women by Freudians and others.

Several contemporary writers have suggested that the intensity of the feminist reaction to traditional psychoanalytic thought is now beginning to subside (Barratt & Starus, 1994; Young-Bruehl, 1994). But the feminist movement has clearly brought an awareness to the psychoanalytic community that was lacking at the time of Freud's original contributions. Further criticisms arising from the feminist perspective are discussed in Chapter 6, which examines the limitations of the Psychoanalytic Strategy.

Kohut's Self Psychology

Heinz Kohut has come to be associated with what has been termed *self psychology.* He, like the other object relations theorists, focused on object representations and interpersonal relationships in the formation and functioning of personality. He specifically emphasized the importance of relationships with others for the development of the sense of self. Specifically, Kohut referred to others who serve important needs in the young child (most often the parents) as **selfobjects,** because to the young child they are originally perceived as extensions of the self.

Kohut believed that children gain a sense of self through interactions with their parents and other people by a process of **mirroring.** Mirroring involves responding appropriately and effectively to the needs of children, which reassures them of their own importance and centrality in the world.

Children originally experience the self as the center of the universe. Significant others serving their needs are seen as mere extensions of self.

Heinz Kohut (1913–1981) founded the self-psychology movement. Courtesy of Susan Kohut/ Photo by Fabian Bachrach

Young children do not yet have the mental capacity to view the world from any perspective but their own. For healthy psychological development, this view must gradually be tempered. The child must begin to recognize the distinction between self and others, which is accomplished through an ongoing interactive process of mirroring in which parental responses are adequate, but not excessive.

Either catering too intensely to the child or failing to respond adequately to the child's needs may prevent adequate development of the self-concept, yielding a grandiose and narcissistic personality. The individual will continue to make excessive demands for attention and nurturing from others. The process described by Kohut parallels in many ways the process of separation-individuation described earlier. Like Mahler, Kohut believed that these early interactions with parents set the stage for all future interpersonal relationships. The formation of an adequate self allows mature interdependent relationships to be formed. Inadequate self-development, however, will produce a pattern of relationships characterized by inequality, excessive demands, and intense frustration.

Kohut (1977) contends that mature adult love relationships allow each partner to serve as a selfobject for the other, in ways reminiscent of the early parent-child relationship. Each partner mirrors the other, adequately fulfilling each other's narcissistic needs (for attention, affection, and understanding) without making undue demands on the other person. Thus, mature interpersonal relationships may include elements of early parent-child relationships but in the context of reciprocal *inter*dependence rather than self-centered, demanding dependence.

Attachment Theory

The primacy of interpersonal relationships and a recognition of the relationship with the mother as the first important and enduring relationship have led other theorists to focus on features of the child-parent bond. Research guided by **attachment theory** began as an attempt to scientifically explain observations made by Sigmund Freud regarding the bond between infant and caregiver. Freud believed that the infant-caregiver relationship served as a prototype for all subsequent love relationships. Freud's theories regarding the development and maintenance of this bond could not be scientifically substantiated; therefore, other explanations for this phenomenon were proposed and investigated.

John Bowlby (1958) pioneered work in this field by examining the way infants use their primary caregivers as sources of comfort and safety when stressed or frightened. Bowlby defined **attachment** as *"an emotional bond that ties the child to one or a few figures across time and space"* (emphasis added) (Waters, Kondo-Ikemura, Posaaa, & Richters, 1990, p. 217). Bowlby saw attachment as a goal-directed control system, motivated by the infant's need for perceived safety. He believed that this behavior reflected the operation of a biologically influenced process that evolved to protect the infant from harm. By maintaining proximity to the caregiver, the immediate risk of physical harm to the child is minimized. The child can seek comfort and protection from the parent when confronted by frightening situations or feelings of distress.

For attachment to serve this purpose, the caregiver must be *available* and *dependable;* that is, more than merely being physically proximate, the caregiver must be responsive to the needs of the child for comforting and protection. The child is presumed to monitor the availability and accessibility of the caregiver, which influence the child's behavior.

An available and responsive parent provides a **secure base** from which the child moves outward to explore the environment. The child who is confident that the caregiver remains continuously accessible feels comfortable exploring new territory. In this ongoing interactive system, the infant uses the parent as a source of comfort, affection, help, and information. Children regulate their behavior to maintain adequate proximity to the caregiver. Adequate proximity is relative, though, and is always defined by immediate circumstances. In a safe, familiar environment, the child may move freely about some distance from the parent. In an unfamiliar environment, the child may be reluctant to relinquish close—or perhaps even physical—contact with the parent. In addition, the child's internal states (e.g., hunger, illness) and other contextual cues (e.g., presence of strangers) play a role in the distance the child will travel from the mother and the amount of time elapsed before seeking some sort of contact with her.

Four Styles of Early Attachment

Although the evolutionary function of attachment involves maintaining a balance between environmental stimulation (e.g., exploration) and feelings of safety, the attached person experiences attachment as a psychological bond with the attachment figure. An important tenet of attachment theory involves individual differences in the ability to use the attachment figure as a secure base, and a great deal of attention has been directed toward the identification and study of differences in **attachment style.**

Mary Ainsworth and her colleagues developed a standard procedure for assessing attachment styles. The "strange situation" involves interactions between the child (about 1 year old), parent, and an adult previously unknown to the child. For two brief periods, the child is left in the presence of only the "stranger." The child's reactions to the situation and particularly to the return of the parent are carefully observed and rated (Ainsworth, Blehar, Waters, & Wall, 1978). Studies using this technique have revealed four distinct types of attachment patterns.

Mary Ainsworth studied attachment styles in infants and developed a standard assessment procedure.

Courtesy of Mary Ainsworth/University of Virginia

Secure attachment is characterized by an appropriate display of distress when caregivers depart and then a warm and enthusiastic greeting upon their return. Parents of securely attached infants tend to respond quickly and appropriately to the behaviors of the child. Distress signals are met with comforting behavior, and positive behaviors are met with playful interaction (Isabella, Belsky, & von Eye, 1989). These children have apparently learned that their parent is available *and* dependable.

Other children display some type of *insecure attachment.* Three types of insecure attachment have been identified: ambivalent, avoidant, and disorganized. **Ambivalent attachment** is characterized by intense clinging and resistance to separation on the part of the child. Upon the return of the caregiver, the child may vacillate between approach and avoidance. For example, a child may allow the mother to approach but then have a tantrum and reject the mother's efforts to offer comfort and reassurance. Parents of insecurely attached children appear inconsistent in their responses to their child. At times, they may respond appropriately; at other times, they may respond inappropriately or fail to respond at all to their child's signals.

Avoidant attachment is characterized by a failure to express distress on departure of the parent and then active avoidance of the parent when he or she returns. Parents of avoidant babies appear aloof and detached and are often rejecting or neglectful as well. Children who display avoidant attachment appear to have learned that their caregivers are *not* available to them and cannot be trusted.

The final attachment style has been termed **disorganized** or disoriented (Main & Solomon, 1986). The behavior of these children is highly variable and, at times, even inconsistent and contradictory. The child may begin to approach the returning parent and then turn away or behave as though confused by the parent's return, neither actively approaching nor avoiding, but rather "freezing"; that is, the child fails to respond at all despite having obviously noticed the parent's return.

These attachment patterns have been demonstrated to remain stable over time (despite changes in the specific overt behaviors). Main and Cassidy (1988) found consistency in the attachment-related behavior of 6-year-old children who had been assessed originally at about 1 year of age. Although the nature of the behavior changed, the tone of the response to the parent—avoidant, ambivalent, secure, or disorganized—remained.

Interestingly, the behavior of the group labeled disorganized at age 1 took on a new complexion at age 6. These children had become controlling and now either seemed to be assuming a caring, parentlike style with their parents or became punitive in style, engaging in behavior aimed at humiliating the parent. Some evidence suggests that the parents of children with a disorganized attachment style were more likely than others to have suffered some childhood abuse. These "traumatized" parents may be providing confusing or frightening cues to their children, thus evoking unusual responses (Main & Hesse, 1990).

Attachment Patterns and Adult Personality

Attachment patterns evidenced in childhood continue to influence social relationships throughout the life span. Longitudinal research on attachment has established high reliability over time. Eighty percent of the infants identified as securely attached at 12 months maintained their status at age 21 (Waters, Merrick, Albersheim, & Treboux, 1995). Attachment status has also been shown to correlate with a variety of other characteristics including mastery motivation, cognitive development, peer relations, eating disorders, and behavior problems in school.

Early attachment has been investigated as a prototype for future love relationships. Work done in this area has demonstrated that adults who were securely attached as infants are better able to use their romantic partners as a secure base *and* to serve as a secure base for their partners, than adults who were not securely attached as infants (Gao, Waters, & Crowell, 1997). Attachment difficulties in childhood were also found to be related to problematic romantic relationships and to depression in adulthood (Carnelley, Pietromonaco, & Jaffe, 1994).

Early work in this area conducted by Hazen and Shaver (1987) correlated attachment styles (based on questionnaire data) with descriptions of the subjects' most important romantic relationship. Attachment styles were related to features of the romantic relationship, with securely attached individuals reporting the most happy and trusting relationships. Ambivalent subjects reported experiencing extremes of emotion related to the romantic partner and relationship, as well as intense jealousy, and obsessive preoccupation with the relationship. Others have found similar results (Collins & Reed, 1990; Simpson, 1990).

Still other research has examined the attachment styles of partners to seek patterns in the mates they choose. Some interesting results have emerged. It appears that secure individuals tend to pair with one another, while avoidant and ambivalent types tend to avoid partners with attachment styles similar to their own (Collins & Reed, 1990; Kirkpatrick & Davis, 1994). Thus, attachment style affects both the choice of romantic partners, and the quality and emotional tone of the resulting relationship.

Another line of research has investigated correlations between insecure attachment status and abuse in intimate relationships. Dutton, Saunders, Starzomski, and Bartholemew (1994) investigated attachment status as a precursor to intimacy anger and subsequent partner abuse. These researchers hypothesized that interpersonal anger is a result of frustrated attachment needs. The anger is expressed in an attempt to regain contact with the attachment figure when perceived threats of abandonment arise. They investigated this theory by examining correlations between a personality constellation of physical and emotional abusiveness and ratings of insecure attachment in domestically violent men. Analyses demonstrated a significant relationship between attachment status and abuse of romantic partners. These researchers conclude that their findings suggest a potential pathway from insecure infant attachment to partner abuse via personality characteristics leading to greater anxiety, jealousy, and intimacy rage.

Early attachment style appears to be one important determinant of later personality and interpersonal functioning. Object relations theorists construe interpersonal relationships as a primary human need. Recent work extends some of these theories to postulate a feeling of "belongingness" as critical for normal adjustment.

Belongingness: A Fundamental Need

Baumeister and Leary (1995) reviewed a large body of research to support their theory that people indeed have a need to belong to social groups and that this need is probably innate, universal, and fundamental to humans. By *fundamental*, the authors mean that the need affects a wide range of human behaviors and does not merely represent the manifestation of other underlying needs but is, in fact, basic to human existence.

These authors contend that people have the need "for frequent, nonaversive interactions within an ongoing relational bond" (p. 497). They further contend that this need will not be adequately fulfilled by either frequent contact with unrelated others or intimate social bonds that include only limited contact. The necessity for both elements—contact as well as mutual relatedness and caring—distinguishes this theory from those offered by preceding object relations theorists.

As evidence to substantiate their claim that belongingness needs are fundamental, Baumeister and Leary offer the following observations: Communal living seems to confer adaptive advantages and therefore may have been favored through evolutionary processes. Substitution and satiation effects appear to operate in the drive for social relationships; that is, the drive must be fulfilled, but individual others may be to some extent interchangeable (e.g., new spouses may be sought to replace former ones, and new friendships may be established to replace ties severed through relocation). And, people do appear to need a small number of close affiliations, but beyond this number, the drive to seek more affiliations tends to diminish. Most people claim to favor having a few close friends over having a wide array of acquaintances (Caldwell & Peplau, 1982; Reiss, 1990). A good deal of cognitive activity seems to surround people's interpersonal relationships and those with whom they are intimate. Both formation of new bonds and intensification of existing bonds are inherently positive, evoking feelings of joy, elation, and happiness. Loss or dissolution of social ties is usually accompanied by distress, including anxiety and grief. These reactions follow loss through physical separation, death, and divorce (Holmes & Rahe, 1967; Weiss, 1979) and commonly result even in the dissolution of a *bad* marriage. People for whom the need to belong is thwarted or frustrated (e.g., prisoners, perpetual singles, and the widowed) often suffer greater stress, immune dysfunction and illness, and die younger (Cohen & Wills, 1985; DeLongis, Folkman, & Lazarus, 1988; Goodwin, Hunt, Key, & Samet, 1987; Lynch, 1979).

Baumeister and Leary (1995) extend their observations to social institutions, including religion and marriage practices as well as to psychology and related fields. They conclude by stating: "The desire for interpersonal attachment may well be one of the most far-reaching and integrative constructs currently available to understand human nature" (p. 522). We believe this position has some merit and fits neatly with the thinking of theorists from other strategies. These instances of overlap are a focus of attention in Chapter 19 and are addressed as we proceed with the presentation of the strategies to follow.

SUMMARY

1. Jung was the first to discuss the midlife crisis, which must be resolved by individuation (finding one's own way).
2. Erikson's eight psychosocial stages provide an alternative to Freud's developmental scheme; they emphasize the influence of society and culture, as well as the importance of ego development.

3. Each of Erikson's eight stages involves the resolution of a central conflict that is present at birth and continues throughout the life span: trust versus mistrust, autonomy versus shame and doubt, initiative versus guilt, industry versus inferiority, identity versus role confusion, intimacy versus isolation, generativity versus stagnation, and ego integrity versus despair.
4. Murray is the father of modern need and motive theories. His theory states that behavior is determined both by needs within the individual and by environmental pressures ("press").
5. McClelland picked up on Murray's broad scheme but focused his attention on an in-depth analysis of one motive—the need to achieve. McClelland found that individuals scoring high in *n* Achievement fantasy tend to perform better on a variety of measures than those scoring low on achievement need.
6. Winter studied the need for power. People high in the need for power tend to cultivate a group of followers toward whom they are generous and understanding, while taking a competitive stance toward outsiders. Individuals with a high need for power become emotionally aroused when they feel powerless.
7. Object relations refers to one's relationships with persons, not things. Object relations are mediated by intrapsychic images of ourselves and significant others. This idea was first introduced by Melanie Klein, who argued that children are more concerned with developing social relationships than with controlling libidinal impulses.
8. Harry Stack Sullivan developed interpersonal psychoanalysis as an alternative to Freud's sex drive model. According to Sullivan, individuals are driven to find interpersonal security, and failure to do so results in feelings of conflict and anxiety.
9. According to Fairbairn, human sexuality is the means by which individuals develop successful relationships with others. Children need to feel loved and valued to have relationships based on mutual dependency later in life.
10. Mahler elaborated the process of the child's separation from the mother by using natural observations of mothers and their babies in the laboratory. She characterized child development as three stages: normal autism, normal symbiosis, and separation-individuation.
11. According to several object relations theories, splitting (separating of the good and bad components of an object) invariably occurs. Whether splitting ultimately leads to reintegration or complete fracturing will greatly influence the person's later relationships.
12. Karen Horney challenged Freud's use of the Oedipal conflict and penis envy and reinterpreted these theories as early manifestations of neurotic conflict that children experience about their parents.
13. The early feminists adopted a matriarchal stance in reaction to Freud's patriarchal (male-dominated) psychoanalytic perspective. The more extreme aspects of the feminist movement have been criticized as a

reactionary attempt to overcompensate for the old, traditional school of thought that viewed women as the inferior sex.

14. Attachment theory relates styles of infant caregiver relationships to later personality and interpersonal functioning.
15. The need to belong has been posited as a fundamental human need that might be used to understand a wide range of social behavior.

CHAPTER SIX

Applications and Limitations of the Psychoanalytic Strategy

So far, we have explored the major theoretical ideas of the Psychoanalytic Strategy. Now we will look at applications of the strategy. We conclude the chapter, and this part, with a brief discussion of the strategy's limitations.

PSYCHOANALYTIC PERSONALITY ASSESSMENT

Most psychoanalytic personality assessment procedures are indirect because they are designed to assess unconscious processes that cannot be directly observed. We will discuss two indirect assessment methods: dream interpretation and projective techniques.

Dreams: The Royal Road to the Unconscious

We spend a third of our lives sleeping, and as we sleep we often dream. Humans have always been intrigued by their dreams and wondered what they meant. One ancient view is that every dream has a secret meaning that can be interpreted by an expert. Joseph, in the Bible, was considered such an expert. A second ancient view is that dreams represent wishes in disguised form. Finally, it has long been suspected that dreams result from experiences and ideas in waking life.

What is a dream? Technically, a dream is a mental experience during sleep that involves mainly visual images. The images are often vivid and considered "real" when they occur (Hobson & McCarley, 1977). They have been called cinematographic because they are like movies that pass through our minds while we sleep (Shannon, 1990).

Psychoanalytic Dream Theory

Freud was not the first to call attention to the psychological meaning of dreams (Resnik, 1987), but his theory was the first comprehensive account of

Henri Rousseau's "The Dream" (1910) depicts the rich visual imagery in dreams.
Oil on canvas, 6′8½ × 9′9½. Collection. The Museum of Modern Art, New York. Gift of Nelson A. Rockefeller.

dreaming. Freud believed that dreaming obeys the same underlying psychological laws as all other mental functions. He considered *The Interpretation of Dreams,* first published in 1900, his most significant work (recall Table 3.1), and many commentators agree with his evaluation. Freud revised this book a number of times, and it has been translated into many languages (Bloom, 1987; Porter, 1987).

Freud's dream theory is largely based on his analysis of his own dreams. In fact, the germ of many of Freud's ideas came from his self-analysis, which he began in 1897 by examining a dream. (Freud continued self-analysis throughout his lifetime, usually his last activity each day [Jones, 1953].)

Freud believed that dreams are highly significant mental products. They result from the dynamic interaction of (1) unconscious wishes, (2) the censoring mechanisms of the ego, and (3) events in waking life. Although the dream itself occurs in sleep, the origins and preparation of the dream reflect all aspects of the dreamer's psychological experience.

Dreams, for Freud, are carefully constructed camouflages; there is always a concealed wish and a true meaning to be found. Dreams are subtle and profound reflections of intrapsychic processes. Freud likened a dream to a fireworks display, "which takes hours to prepare but goes off in a moment." He considered dreams the single best source of information about a person's unconscious; he called dreams "the royal road to the unconscious."

Manifest versus Latent Content of Dreams

Freud distinguished two levels of dream content. **Manifest content** is what a person can remember about a dream. **Latent content** is the set of underlying intrapsychic events that led to the manifest content. The latent content is composed primarily of unconscious thoughts, wishes, fantasies, and conflicts, which are expressed in translated or disguised form in the manifest content.

The relation of manifest and latent dream content is like a rebus, such as the one in Figure 6.1. In these puzzles, pictures suggest the sounds of words or syllables they represent. Latent meaning cannot directly enter consciousness because it is threatening; it can, however, be disguised. Manifest content

Figure 6.1
An example of a rebus in which the pictures depict the syllables of a word.

A simpler rebus would be a picture of a coffee mug (cup) followed by one of a plank of wood (board) to represent the word *cupboard.* The reader who is unable to decipher the word that is visually represented above should see the first page of this book, on which the word appears.

is the "dressed-up" version of the threatening determinants of the dream. Like the symbols in a rebus, the images in manifest content "stand for" something else. Latent content becomes manifest through two basic processes: dream work and symbolization.

Dream Work

Dream work refers to the processes by which latent dream content is transformed into manifest content. Freud believed that condensation and displacement are the major processes in dream work. He also identified two other processes: visual representation and secondary revision.

Condensation combines and compresses separate thoughts. The resulting manifest content is a much abbreviated version of the latent content. An example would be a man dreaming of being affectionate with a woman who looked like his wife, who acted like his ex-wife, and whom he believed in the dream to be his mother. The wife, ex-wife, and mother are condensed into a single person. One implication of condensation is that all elements in the dream result from more than one latent source. Thus, dreams are *multiply determined;* they are the product of many sources. Condensation, like all forms of dream work, disguises threatening latent content so that its threat is not apparent in the manifest dream.

Displacement involves shifting emphasis. Often an important element of the dream is changed to an unimportant element. Consider the example of a woman who received a telegram saying that her son had been killed. That night she dreamed of receiving a telegram stating that her son would not be coming home for the weekend. In this dream, a critical aspect of the latent content appears as a trivial aspect of the manifest content.

Abstract wishes, urges, and ideas that make up latent content may be translated into concrete pictures or images by the dream work process known as visual representation. A rebus (see Figure 6.1) is a crude example of visual representation. A more sophisticated example would represent the concept of possession by the act of sitting on an object, much as children do to keep other children from having a prized toy. Note the similarity between displacement as dream work and displacement as a defense mechanism. Both dream work and defense mechanisms keep individuals from becoming conscious of unacceptable and threatening material.

When we awaken after dreaming, we often try to reconstruct our dreams. Attempts at reconstruction often lead to the discovery that the parts of the dream do not logically fit together, which is not surprising. The meaning of the dream (latent content) has been distorted and disguised through condensation, displacement, and visual representation. "Dreams, like symptoms," said one contemporary analyst, "are compromises simultaneously expressing wish and resistance, subjective need and its repression" (Gallego-Mere, 1989, p. 97).

Symbolization

Dream work changes *unacceptable latent* content into *acceptable manifest* content. **Symbolization** allows latent content to become part of the manifest content directly, but in an unrecognizable and, therefore, nonthreatening form. Symbols are objects or ideas that stand for something else. Freud believed that some symbols have universal meanings and therefore represent the same thing in all dreams.

Examples of symbols and their meanings according to psychoanalytic theory appear in Table 6.1. Symbols do not occur only in dreams; they also appear in myths, fairy tales, literature, and other aspects of mental life. For example, one of Freud's patients hallucinated that his finger had been severed; Freud took this to be a sign of castration anxiety (Schmukler & Garcia, 1989).

A quick look at Table 6.1 shows that most of the symbols refer to sexual objects and activities, which is consistent with the central Freudian idea that human motivation is primarily sexual. Freud believed that although there are many symbols, only a few concepts are important enough to be symbolically represented.

What evidence exists for sexual symbolism? Do people connect sexual symbols with sexual objects, as psychoanalysis proposes? One line of research has had people classify psychoanalytic symbols of male and female genitals as either masculine or feminine. In general, these studies show that adults—and sometimes children—can group sexual symbols according to the gender predicted by psychoanalytic theory at a better-than-chance level (Kline, 1972). For example, fruit is considered feminine and snakes masculine. However, people may use cultural associations to make the classification even though their responses are consistent with psychoanalytic theory.

Table 6.1 Common psychoanalytic symbols and their "latent meanings"

SYMBOL	LATENT MEANING
House	Human body
Smooth-fronted house	Male body
House with ledges and balconies	Female body
King and queen	Parents
Little animals	Children
Children	Genitals
Playing with children	Masturbation
Beginning a journey	Dying
Clothes	Nakedness
The number three	Male genitals
Elongated object (e.g., snake, gun, necktie)	Penis
Balloon, airplane	Erection
Woods and thickets	Pubic hair
Room	Woman
Suite of rooms	Brothel or harem
Box	Uterus
Fruit	Breast
Climbing stairs or ladder	Sexual intercourse
Baldness, tooth extraction	Castration
Bath	Birth

For instance, a gun is a masculine symbol both in our culture and in psychoanalysis.

Contemporary psychoanalysts do not agree that all symbolism is sexual. For example, Turkel (1988) believes that dreaming about money is symbolic of internal conflicts over dependency, responsibility, exploitation, and pride, which is considerably different from Freud's original view that money almost always symbolizes feces and the "anal pleasure" of bowel movements.

Freudian Dream Interpretation

Freud's method of dream interpretation begins with the person's report of the dream (the manifest content). The person is then asked to make associations to the dream (e.g., Smith & Andresen, 1988). Dream reports are often relatively short, but the associations to them are generally quite extensive. In the final step, the psychoanalyst uses the principles of dream work and symbolization to interpret the latent meaning of both the manifest content and the associations. The interpretation also takes into account information the analyst has about the individual, such as events in the person's life that appear to be related to the dream.

Thus, Freudian dream interpretation involves analysis of more than just the dream and is admittedly subjective. Its validity cannot be judged against any objective standards of right or wrong. The validity of an interpretation is more a matter of how useful it is in providing the psychoanalyst with information about the individual's personality. Thus, there may be more than one "correct" (useful) interpretation of a dream (Fosshage, 1987; Warner, 1987).

The following dream interpretation by Freud (1961a) illustrates the use of condensation, displacement, and symbolization to understand the latent meaning of the dream. The dreamer was one of Freud's patients. Although the woman was still quite young, she had been married for a number of years. She had recently received news that a friend, Elise L., who was about the same age, had become engaged. Shortly thereafter, she had this dream:

> She was at the theater with her husband. One side of the stalls [theater boxes] were completely empty. Her husband told her that Elise L. and her fiancé had wanted to go too, but had only been able to get bad seats—three for one florin fifty kreuzers—and of course, they could not take those. She thought it would really not have done any harm if they had. (p. 415)

Freud began his interpretation of this rather brief dream by analyzing the symbolic meaning of the monetary units. This particular symbol was, in part, determined by an unimportant event of the previous day. The dreamer had learned that her sister-in-law recently had been given a gift of 150 florins (exactly 100 times the amount dreamed of) and had quickly spent this gift on jewelry.

Freud noted that three tickets were mentioned in the dream. Elise L. and her fiancé would have needed only two tickets for themselves. Examination of previous statements made by the dreamer revealed a connection: "her newly engaged friend was the same number of months—three—her junior" (p. 415).

That one side of the theater boxes was entirely empty is significant. Recently, the patient had wished to attend a play. She had rushed out to buy tickets days ahead of time. In doing so, she had incurred an extra booking fee. When the patient and her husband arrived at the theater, they found that only half the seats were taken. This bit of information accounts in part for the appearance of the "empty stalls" in the dream.

More important in terms of psychoanalytic theory is the underlying meaning of the empty stalls. The patient's actual experience with the theater tickets could clearly lead to the conclusion that she had been too hasty about running out to buy tickets and therefore had to pay an additional, unnecessary price. Freud assumed that she might have had the same hidden feelings concerning her own marriage; in symbolic form, these feelings are revealed by the dream. Thus, Freud offered the following summary interpretation of the dream: "It was absurd to marry so early. There was no need for me to be in such a hurry. I see from Elise L.'s example that I should have got a husband in the end. Indeed, I should have got one a hundred times better" (a treasure) "if I had only waited" (in antithesis to her sister-in-law's hurry). "My money" (or dowry) "could have bought three men just as good" (p. 416).

The Functions of Dreaming

Why do people dream? Freud discussed three interrelated functions of dreaming: (1) wish fulfillment, (2) the release of unconscious tension, and (3) preservation of sleep. He believed that every dream is an attempt to fulfill a wish. The wish may be a conscious desire that is not fulfilled during the day (e.g., wishing to be skiing rather than studying) or an unconscious desire that is an expression of a repressed impulse (e.g., to hurt a friend). Most dreams represent a combination of the two. Furthermore, events and thoughts that occur while awake, called **day residues,** combine with unconscious impulses to produce the dream. In effect, the unconscious impulses provide the psychic energy for enactment of the day residues in the form of a dream. The result is that each of the three functions of dreaming is satisfied.

First, the wish is fulfilled in the dream. Dreams are a *primary process.* Therefore, the mental representation of the behavior needed to satisfy a wish is not distinguished from the actual behavior. When a wish "comes true" in a dream, it is as if the wish were actually fulfilled. While dreaming, we usually believe that the events are really happening, which is why nightmares can be so frightening.

Second, the unconscious impulse is allowed expression. However, this expression is in a disguised and acceptable form, as a result of the dream work process and symbolization. Thus, dreams allow the release of tension that has built up in the unconscious.

Third, the individual remains asleep even though unconscious threatening impulses are becoming conscious in the manifest dream. If threatening impulses begin to enter consciousness during waking periods, anxiety is generated. If such anxiety were present while dreaming, the dreamer would wake up. However, through dream work and symbolization, the threatening aspects of the latent material are disguised. The result is that overwhelming anxiety is not generated, and the person can continue to sleep.

The Importance of Manifest Content

An essential element of Freud's dream theory is its emphasis on the latent content relative to the manifest content. Indeed, Freud considered manifest content important only insofar as it reveals latent content. Contemporary psychoanalytic researchers do not deny the significance of the latent content, but they have found manifest content itself to be rich with psychological meaning. Dream reports clearly indicate that people tend to dream about matters that concern them (McCann, Stewin, & Short, 1990).

Here is a poignant dream of a still grieving widow: "I dreamt that I wanted to tell my husband something but there is nobody there. I was somewhere and I was looking for him, but could not find him. So many people were around and still he was not there. I was very upset, astonished that everyone was there, but he was not" (Prince & Hoffmann, 1991, p. 5).

Consider a few other examples of the effects of everyday life on dreams from a wide array of findings (Fisher & Greenberg, 1977; Zayas, 1988): Pregnant women are significantly more likely than other women to report dreams involving babies or children. Men are more likely than women to report dreaming about aggression. Women are more likely to report dreams relating to sex or hostility during their menstrual periods than at other times. Older people (over 65) are more likely than younger individuals to report dreams involving loss of resources and strength or death-related topics. Expectant fathers tend to dream about loneliness and exclusion.

In a study in Germany, subjects were shown either a film depicting violence, humiliation, and despair or a neutral film (Lauer, Riemann, Lund, & Berger, 1987). Subjects who had seen the disturbing film reported dreams with considerably more manifest aggressive and anxious content than subjects who had viewed the neutral film. Furthermore, a third of the initial dreams of the subjects exposed to the upsetting film included specific content from the film itself. Not only does this study indicate the significance of manifest content but it also indicates that the manifest content of dreams can be influenced by our experiences while awake, further validating the idea of ***day residue*** appearing in dreams.

Dreaming as Problem Solving

In ancient Greece, troubled "patients" were treated by priests. Part of the treatment was administering drugs to induce dreams that were expected to provide the solutions to problems (Marcus, 1988). Many post-Freudian analysts think that dreaming helps people solve problems, particularly interpersonal problems, and plan future actions (e.g., Adler, 1973; Erikson, 1954; French & Fromm, 1964; Miller, 1989; Resnik, 1987; Winson, 1985). For example, dreaming may "integrate current stressful experiences with similar experiences from the past, thus enabling the individual to use . . . basic coping mechanisms (defenses) to deal with the current stressful situation" (Grieser, Greenberg, & Harrison, 1972, p. 281).

Freud's dream theory and the post-Freudians' problem-solving theory are psychological accounts of why people dream, and they relate dreaming to emotional factors. There are also physiological theories of dreaming that essentially ignore the role of emotions. For example, one theory proposes that dreams are by-products of spontaneous brain activity (Lavie & Hobson, 1986).

PROJECTIVE TECHNIQUES

Projective techniques are another method of indirect personality assessment arising from the Psychoanalytic Strategy. Subjects are presented with ambiguous stimuli and asked to impart meaning to them. By doing so, the subject presumably reveals unconscious motives, ideas, and feelings.

Ambiguity and the Projective Hypothesis

Projective techniques are based on the **projective hypothesis:** When individuals must impose meaning or order on an ambiguous stimulus, their responses will project or reflect their feelings, attitudes, desires, and needs; that is, it is assumed that when confronted by stimuli for which there is no obvious right, wrong, or best response, the individual must respond based on wholly subjective interpretations and personal needs. (The unconscious is presumably free to *project* meaning onto the stimulus and the situation.) People must formulate their own personal interpretation of the stimulus, as well as the assessment situation, to produce a response. It is assumed that this response will reflect the expression of unconscious processes because the individual would have no clear conscious guidelines for responding. Observing both their formal responses and their reactions to the unstructured and novel situation provides the skilled clinician with a rich source of information about a subject.

The Nature of Projective Techniques

Some projective techniques appear similar to a test, but calling them techniques or methods is more accurate. Most projective techniques do not meet the generally accepted criteria for tests, such as being standardized and having *norms* (normative data based on performance of large groups of subjects; see Chapter 2) (Anastasi, 1988a). Even where some norms and standard scoring criteria do exist (e.g., for the Rorschach), the primary purpose of projective-based assessment is not to characterize the subject in terms of a standardized score, ranking, or diagnostic classification. Rather, projective results are used as a means of identifying patterns of consistent themes that may reflect personality structure or unconscious conflict within the individual.

The different types of projective techniques vary in the nature of the stimulus presented to subjects and the nature of the response required. Most projective techniques fall into one of four categories: (1) association, such as to inkblots or words; (2) construction, often of stories about pictures (e.g., the Thematic Apperception Test); (3) completion, usually of sentences fragments (e.g., "I often feel . . . ") or stories; or (4) free expression, in drawings (e.g., Draw-a-Person Test) or through acting out a loosely specified role (e.g., in psychodrama). Table 6.2 provides a summary of the most common forms of projective techniques and examples of each.

Table 6.2 Common types of projective techniques

TYPE OF TASK	STIMULUS MATERIALS	INSTRUCTIONS	EXAMPLE
Association	Word (e.g., man)	"After hearing each word, say the first word that comes to mind."	Word association
Construction	Picture	"Tell a story about the picture."	Thematic Apperception Test (TAT)
Completion	Sentence stem (e.g., "I want . . .")	"Complete the sentence."	Sentence completion
Expression	Paper and pencil	"Draw a picture of yourself and a person of the opposite sex."	Draw-a-Person Test

All projective techniques share five important characteristics: (1) The stimulus is relatively unstructured and ambiguous, which compels subjects to impose their own order, structure, and meaning; (2) the purpose of the test and how responses will be scored or interpreted are *not* disclosed to the subject; (3) the subject *is* told that there are no correct or incorrect answers; (4) responses are assumed to reveal something valid and significant about the subject's personality; and (5) scoring and interpretation are generally lengthy and relatively subjective procedures, heavily dependent on the skill and experience of the examiner.

We will focus our further discussion on several examples of the most common projective techniques. We begin with the earliest formal projective technique, which remains among the most common in use today, the Rorschach inkblots.

The Rorschach inkblots are the most frequently used projective technique. This subject is showing the examiner where on the inkblot she saw a particular concept.
Photo by Gary D. Clark

The Rorschach Inkblots

The use of inkblots to reveal something about an individual was not a new idea when Hermann Rorschach began his experiments in the early part of the 20th century. But Rorschach, a Swiss psychiatrist, was the first to use a *standard set* of inkblots to assess personality. In 1921, Rorschach published the results of his work. His monograph, *Psychodiagnostik*, bore the informative subtitle *Interpretation of Accidental Forms.* A year later Rorschach died, and it was left to others to elaborate on the basic procedures he had outlined.

There are 10 nearly symmetrical Rorschach inkblots; five have some color, and five are limited to black and white. The blots are printed on white cardboard (about 7 × 10 inches). Figure 6.2 shows inkblots similar to those used in the Rorschach. The blots were originally made by spilling ink on a piece of paper and then folding the paper in half (something you might enjoy trying yourself).

The Rorschach inkblot technique (or the Rorschach, as it is commonly called) is administered individually in two phases. The first is performance proper, which begins with simple instructions from the examiner: "I am going to show you a number of inkblots, and I want you to tell me what you see in each of them." The examiner records exactly what the subject says about each blot (e.g., "That reminds me of a rabbit running").

When the subject has responded to all 10 inkblots, the second phase—inquiry—begins. Starting with the first card, the examiner reminds the subject of each response made. The examiner asks the subject where on the inkblot the response was seen ("Where did you see a rabbit running?") and what made it look like that ("What about the inkblot made it look like a rabbit running?").

There are a number of different systems for scoring and interpreting Rorschach responses (Exner, 1986; Klopfer & Davidson, 1962). In one of the most widely used systems, each response is scored for five characteristics that focus on how the response was generated: (1) location, where on the card the concept was seen; (2) determinant, the qualities of the blot that led to the formation of the concept (e.g., shape, color, and apparent movement); (3) popularity-originality, the frequency with which particular responses are given by people in general; (4) content, the subject matter of the concept; and (5) form-level, how accurately the concept is seen and how closely the concept fits the blot.

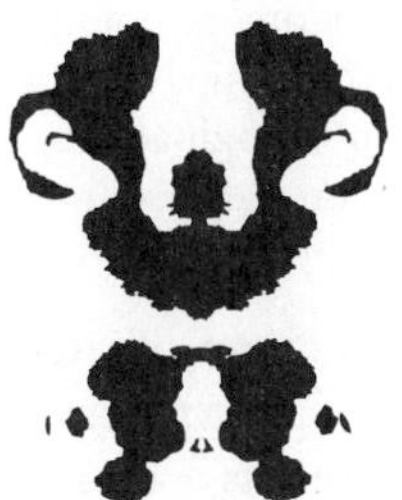

Figure 6.2
Inkblots similar to those used by Rorschach.

Table 6.3 Examples of scoring and interpreting the Rorschach inkblots

SCORING CHARACTERISTIC	EXAMPLES OF SCORING CATEGORY	SAMPLE RESPONSES	EXAMPLES OF INTERPRETATIONS*
Location	Whole	Entire blot used for concept	Ability to organize and integrate material
	Small usual detail	Small part that is easily marked off from the rest of the blot	Need to be exact and accurate
Determinant	Form	"The outline looks like a bear"	Degree of emotional control
	Movement	"A flying hawk"	Level of ego functioning
Popularity-originality	Popular	Response that many people give	Need to be conventional
	Original	Response that few people give (and that fits blot well)	Superior intelligence
Content	Animal figures	"Looks like a house cat"	Passivity and dependence
	Human figures	"It's a man or a woman"	Problem with sexual identity
Form-level	High form-level	Concept fits blot well	High intellectual functioning
	Low form-level	Concept is a poor match to blot	Contact with reality tenuous

*Interpretations would be made only if the type of response occurred a number of times (not just once). See text for further precautions regarding interpretations of Rorschach responses.

Interpretation of the Rorschach requires extensive knowledge of psychoanalytic concepts (Exner, 1986). The interpreter looks for *patterns* of responses or *consistent themes* rather than interpreting single responses. Rorschach interpretations are admittedly subjective. Table 6.3 presents examples of possible interpretations.

The Thematic Apperception Test (TAT)

Recall from Chapter 5 that Henry Murray, David McClelland, and David Winter all used the Thematic Apperception Test (TAT), originally developed by Murray and his colleague, Christiana Morgan. Murray and Morgan assumed that needs are sometimes manifest (observed in overt behavior) and sometimes latent (inhibited, covert, or imaginal). The TAT is concerned with uncovering latent needs.

According to Murray:

> The chief differences between an imaginal need and an overt need is that the former enjoys in reading, or represents in fantasy, in speech or in play what the latter objectifies in serious action. Thus, instead of pushing through a difficult enterprise, a subject will have visions of doing it or read books about others doing it; or instead of injuring an enemy, he will express his dislike of him to others or enjoy playing an aggressive role in a play. . . . The term "imaginal need" is convenient for the expression "the amount of need tension that exhibits itself in thought and make-believe action." (Murray, 1962, p. 257)

Assessment of latent needs follows from this description. A strong latent need "is apt to perceive . . . what it 'wants.' . . . A subject under the influence of a drive has a tendency to 'project' into surrounding objects some of the imagery associated *with the drive that is operating*" (Murray, 1962, p. 260, italics added; note the interchangeability of the words *need* and *drive* in Murray's own writing). This reasoning led to the development of the TAT.

The original TAT consists of a set of 20 pictures. There are multiple variations on the TAT pictures. Sets have been devised specifically for use with men, women, children, and various racial and ethnic groups. Most of the pictures show at least one person, thereby providing someone with whom the respondent can identify. (Some sets geared for children depict cartoon-type animals rather than people.) Figure 6.3 is an example of a TAT picture from the original set.

The TAT cards are presented to subjects with instructions to tell a story about the image. These stories (like all projective techniques) are analyzed for recurrent themes and images. Murray himself stated in the TAT manual that "the conclusions that are reached by an analysis of TAT stories must be regarded as good 'leads' or working hypotheses to be verified by other methods, rather than as proved facts" (1943, p. 14).

Figure 6.3
Example of a TAT-like picture. (Note: TAT is used as an abbreviation, *not* an acronym; thus when spoken, it is pronounced as three letters—T-A-T, not "tat.")
Harvard University Press

Other Projective Techniques

The Rorschach and TAT are among the most commonly used projective techniques. These measures are usually employed in combination with other assessment devices, including but not limited to other projective measures and standardized psychological tests of personality.

Freud himself commonly used "free association" (which is discussed in detail later) to gain access to unconscious material. Word association is still often used today. Subjects are provided with a word and asked to respond with the first word or thought they experience. Responding quickly and freely is assumed to cause defensive processes to interfere less and to allow the unconscious to respond through symbolism that can then be interpreted by the analyst.

The Draw-a-Person Test requires subjects to produce line drawings in response to very simple, limited instructions. The subject is asked to "draw a person" with no specification as to whom to draw and no guidance as to level of detail to be provided. The resulting picture yields information about the person's interpretation of the task, degree of planning in execution (e.g., how well the image fits on the page and uses the space available), attention to instructions (e.g., whether the image represents an *entire* person or only a face or body parts), and attention to detail (whether all features are adequately represented). All of these points reveal important aspects of the subject's personality, as may the specific nature of the drawing produced: Is the image produced a well-integrated human? Is the face smiling or scowling? Other "expression" tasks may include producing drawings of objects (e.g., house, tree) or specific types of people (e.g., man, woman, child).

Completion tasks also enjoy continued popularity. Sentence completion involves providing the beginning few words for a sentence to be completed by the subject. Multiple sentence openings are provided (e.g., "I always wanted to . . . "), and the responses are again interpreted in light of recurrent themes and images. Although psychoanalytic assessment may be undertaken for its own sake, the most common use is to diagnose themes that can be addressed through psychoanalytic psychotherapy.

PSYCHOANALYTIC PSYCHOTHERAPY

For Freud, the practice of psychotherapy was more than just a way to help his patients. His clinical cases provided both the data and the evidence for his theory of personality. Based on what he learned from his patients, Freud formulated his theory. He then gathered support for the theory from further clinical observations. In addition, psychoanalytic psychotherapy involves both personality change and assessment because psychoanalysts consider discovering what is in the patient's unconscious central to the therapy process.

Most of Freud's patients suffered from hysteria (known today as conversion disorder)—a psychological disorder characterized by a physical ailment, such as paralysis of the legs, in the absence of a physiological basis. Hysteria was common at the end of the 19th century, but physicians had little success treating it. For example, Jean Charcot, the neurologist in Paris with whom Freud studied (see Box 3.1 in Chapter 3), hypnotized his hysteric patients and then directly instructed them to renounce their symptoms. This hypnotic suggestion was generally effective as long as the patient remained hypnotized, but when the patient awoke, the symptoms almost invariably returned.

After studying with Charcot, Freud began a private medical practice in Vienna and became associated with Josef Breuer, a prominent Viennese physician. Breuer also used hypnosis in treating hysteria. Breuer, however, did not tell his hypnotized patients to make their symptoms disappear. Instead, he asked the patient to vividly recall the traumatic experience that had first led to the hysterical symptom. The patient's recall of the trauma was accompanied by a great emotional release **(catharsis),** which seemingly produced a cure. In contrast to Charcot, Breuer obtained changes that endured beyond the patient's awakening.

Breuer and Freud concluded that hysterical symptoms arise from painful memories and emotions that have been repressed. The symptoms are relieved when the repressed memories and associated painful emotions are finally permitted open expression. Freud later generalized the theory to all neuroses. Neuroses (plural of neurosis) are psychological disorders characterized by anxiety and abnormal behavior, such as phobias, obsessions, and physical complaints without a clear physical cause.

The Process of Psychoanalysis

In a nutshell, the basic aim of psychoanalysis is to make conscious what is unconscious. More specifically, patients must become aware of unconscious desires and the conflicts that result from them because they are presumed to cause the suffering and functional difficulties of which they complain.

Four fundamental processes are involved: free association; resistance, including transference; interpretation; and insight. The patient talks and freely associates to anything that comes to mind. The therapist listens carefully to identify themes and symbols that might reveal underlying conflicts. At the appropriate time, the therapist offers interpretations. Patients are expected to gradually accept and gain insight about the causes of their problems, which is possible only when the patient's inevitable resistance to gaining insight (and being cured) is overcome (see Figure 6.4).

Figure 6.4
Steps in the process of psychoanalytic psychotherapy.

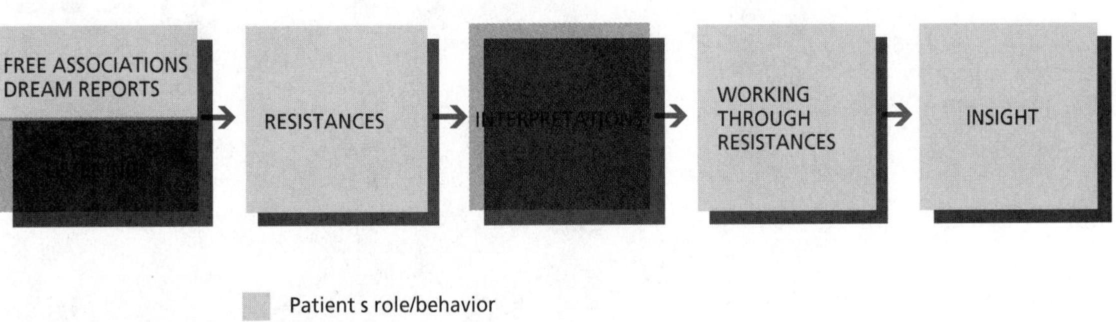

Free Association

When Freud first began his practice, he hypnotized his patients to help them recall events that might have been related to the onset of their disorders. Soon, however, Freud began to urge patients to recall repressed events without hypnosis. He found that, given sufficient freedom, patients wandered in their thoughts and recollections, which allowed him to understand their unconscious conflicts.

Free association became one of the cornerstones of psychoanalysis. The patient is encouraged to say anything that comes to mind. Social convention, logic and order, seeming importance, or feelings of embarrassment must all be set aside. Freud had his patients free associate while lying on a couch. Freud sat behind the couch where patients were seated, out of their direct view (Figure 6.5). Free association is easier for the patient when the patient is not constantly reminded of the therapist's presence. (But free association is not easy. You can demonstrate this for yourself by trying to tell a friend or even just a tape recorder everything and anything that you are thinking of for 5 minutes.)

Resistance

Freud's patients sought treatment for their neuroses, but they often seemed to resist being cured (e.g., Finell, 1987). Broadly speaking, **resistance** refers to anything that impedes the progress of therapy. Resistance can be conscious or unconscious (Strean, 1985). Conscious resistance occurs when patients are aware of impeding the progress of the analysis. Patients may have a disturbing

Figure 6.5
Freud's consulting room in Vienna, with his chair and patient's couch. Truly it may be said psychoanalysis was born here.
© Mary Evans Picture Library/ Sigmund Freud

dream and decide not to report it or actively censor what they say. Patients may also deliberately miss therapy sessions.

In unconscious resistance, the patient is not aware of "fighting" the treatment; thus, unconscious resistance is more difficult to overcome than conscious resistance. Unconscious resistance is also more significant because it indicates the patient's unconscious strivings and thereby provides the analyst with clues about the patient's personality (e.g., Thompson, 1987). Thus, resistance always has a dual nature: (1) It frequently interferes with treatment, but (2) it also provides a source of important information about the patient and is used as a tool for change (e.g., Levenson, 1988).

Transference: A Special Form of Resistance

The patient's inappropriate feelings toward the psychoanalyst are products of an unconscious ego defense process called **transference** (transference is a special case of displacement; see Chapter 4). Feelings that are actually distorted *displacements* from significant others in the patient's life (usually in the past) are "transferred" onto the analyst. Patients may begin to relate to the therapist as they would to their mothers, fathers, or other significant people. Transference can be *positive* (e.g., love, respect, and admiration) or *negative* (e.g., hatred, jealousy, and disgust). Transference is considered the most important form of unconscious resistance (Grubrich-Simitis, 1987; Singer, 1985; Stolorow, 1988). Moreover, the development of transference in a patient is taken as evidence that the psychoanalytic process is actually underway (Renik, 1990).

Are all feelings that a patient has about the psychoanalyst instances of transference? Is it possible for a patient to like or dislike the analyst as a person rather than as a representation of a significant other in the patient's life? Some psychoanalysts would say no, but others would say that transference distinguishes itself from "real" feelings by *inappropriateness* and *repetition* (Schimek, 1983). One of the keys to identifying transference is the intensity of the patients emotions: "transference is not a slice of life; it is a highly intensified . . . version of what the patient is exploring" (Levenson, 1988, p. 14).

At times, transference is an impediment to psychoanalysis because it is an inappropriate reaction. For instance, although the analyst is not the patient's father, a patient who had a strict father may respond to the analyst's interpretations as if they were criticisms. This reaction would make it more difficult for the patient to accept and understand the interpretations.

Transference can also facilitate the therapeutic process. Analysts use such inappropriate behavior to point out to patients the nature of their relationships to significant people in their lives. The interpretation of transference is an integral part of psychoanalysis. Indeed, Freud believed that the patient has to experience transference toward the analyst and work through it if psychoanalysis is to be successful (Osman & Tabachnick, 1988).

Psychoanalysts may experience distorted displacements toward their patients (Gorkin, 1987). This **countertransference** may adversely affect the critical patient-analyst relationship by hampering the analyst's objectivity. Two major controls have been established to deal with countertransference. First, psychoanalysts themselves must undergo psychoanalysis as part of their training. Having insight into their own unconscious processes and conflicts helps analysts recognize and deal with inappropriate countertransference reactions (e.g., Marcus, 1988). Second, analysts regularly review their cases with a supervising analyst who may notice countertransference that the analyst overlooked (e.g., Novick, 1987).

Like transference, countertransference can be therapeutically beneficial (e.g., Drell, 1988). Analyzing countertransference can provide the analyst with useful information. Patient behaviors that trigger emotional reactions in the analyst may affect other people in the patient's life similarly.

Interpretation

Patients provide the analyst with a wealth of information. However, unconscious material becomes conscious only in disguised or symbolic form (e.g., Shear & Kundrat, 1987); the analyst's job is to discover the hidden meanings of what the patient does and says. The analyst then communicates these meanings to the patient as interpretations, which help patients understand how their problematic behavior developed. Freud likened this process to the excavation and reconstruction of an archaeological ruin.

Schwaber (1990) has distinguished two kinds of interpretations used by contemporary analysts. One type of interpretation is aimed directly at helping patients understand and acknowledge something about themselves. The other is aimed at directing patients' conscious and unconscious thoughts toward a question to which the analyst does not yet have an answer.

Interpretations cannot be forced on a patient. It is important that the analyst does not advance an interpretation until the patient is "ready" to hear it. The patient often must work through resistances to be able to accept an interpretation as personally meaningful.

Insight

Analysts' interpretations help patients gain insight into the nature and origin of their neuroses. **Insight** involves more than an intellectual understanding; it also requires emotional acceptance. The patient must think and feel that the new self-knowledge is personally "right" or that it "fits." This sort of understanding and acceptance develops gradually and often painstakingly. Insight, the final goal of classical psychoanalysis, is expected to result in a cure.

Post-Freudian Therapy

Post-Freudian psychoanalysts have made changes in psychoanalytic psychotherapy that are consistent with their modifications in the underlying personality theory. Although there are many forms of post-Freudian therapy, some overall themes can be abstracted.

The most general of these themes is that post-Freudian analysis is more flexible and broader than Freudian analysis (Modell, 1988), a theme that is manifested in many specific ways.

Post-Freudian psychoanalysis focuses on the present as well as the past. Post-Freudians consider it important to explore the ways the patient is functioning effectively as well as to analyze problem behaviors that bring the patient to therapy. The individual's strengths are used to devise a treatment plan. The patient's interpersonal relations are emphasized, and situational stresses are considered along with intrapsychic conflicts.

Analysts who do focus on the past are rethinking the purpose of this practice. Freud hoped to obtain historically true pictures from the memories of his patients (Bloch, 1989). Modern analysts measure the validity of reconstructions of the patient's past created in psychoanalysis by how convincing the reconstructions are to the patient and the analyst. Reconstructions are only narratives, a search for meaning in the present, and, of course, there is no one truth about a person's past. Multiple narratives are possible (Leichtman, 1990). What a good narrative truth must do is provide an "assured conviction," which is as therapeutic as a memory truly recaptured (Roth, 1991). (See Chapter 17 for further discussion of narratives and retrospective recall.)

Interaction between therapist and patient is less formal and restrictive in post-Freudian analysis. The patient often sits facing the therapist. The goal of therapy can be providing support as well as insight (e.g., Bemporad, 1988; Josephs, 1988; Wallerstein, 1989). The patient-therapist relationship is considered important independent of, but not excluding, transference. Post-Freudian analysts specifically attempt to foster a **therapeutic alliance**—that is, a stable, cooperative relationship between patient and therapist (e.g., Novick, 1987; Safran & Muran, 1995). This is considered a necessary (but not a sufficient) condition for effective therapy (Greenson, 1965, 1967; Hartley & Strupp, 1983; Zetzel, 1956). Post-Freudian analysts tend to talk more and to be more *directive* than strict Freudians. Post-Freudian interpretations are likely to be (1) psychosocial as well as psychosexual, (2) more concrete and practical, and (3) less abstract and theoretical.

Psychoanalysis is now applied to a wider range of patients and problems than in Freud's day (Rockland, 1989). Freud himself thought psychoanalysis was useful primarily for adult neurotic problems. Melanie Klein and Anna Freud were both instrumental in beginning the practice of child analysis, a specialty that has flourished (Fonagy & Moran, 1990). Psychoanalysis has proven adaptable to group and family therapy (McCallum & Piper, 1988; Scharff & Scharff, 1987) and substance abuse (Brickman, 1988). Also, traditional analysis typically requires three to five sessions per week over the course of 3 or more years. Post-Freudian therapy often is briefer, involving fewer sessions per week and much shorter duration (Arlow & Brenner, 1988).

Finally, the purpose of psychoanalysis has expanded. Fromm went so far as to say that people should undergo psychoanalysis "not as a therapy but as an instrument for self-understanding" (quoted by Bacciagaluppi, 1989, p. 230).

Object Relations Therapy

Some psychoanalysts feel that contemporary object relations theory suggests a new approach to therapy (Arcaya & Gerber, 1990; Cashdan, 1988; Ogden, 1982). Recall that according to object relations theory, personality is thought to evolve out of human interactions rather than out of biologically derived tensions. Instead of tension reduction, human beings are primarily motivated by the need to establish and maintain relations with others.

What if people question their own ability to form meaningful relationships and sustain them? For such individuals, human relationships are at best tenuous. They cannot assume that others will become or stay involved with them. They may search desperately for means to "cement" relationships. The results are seen in maladaptive patterns of adult object relations (Cashdan, 1988).

Object relations therapists attempt to understand and then modify these maladaptive patterns of relating through means that parallel classical psychoanalysis. The therapist first understands the patient's subjective worldview and object representations by carefully attending to how the patient describes experiences. Therapists are mindful of the ways the patient relates to them, as this reveals some things about the patient's object relations generally.

The object relations therapist must become a significant person for the patient. The therapist is not just another professional, but is a person who empathizes with and can reflect the patient's emotions. This requires demonstrating interest in the details of the patient's life and emotionally linking these details to the patient's current feelings and experiences.

The therapist attempts to modify the maladaptive patterns of object relations by confronting and challenging them directly. This practice parallels the interpretations offered by other therapists, particularly cognitive therapists—see Chapter 18. The object relations therapist must also work toward the patient's acceptance of responsibility for the ultimate resolution of their interpersonal problems.

Interpersonal Therapy (IPT)

Interpersonal therapy (IPT) is an outgrowth of the object relations approach. Its roots can be traced to the writings of Harry Stack Sullivan and Adolph Meyer, who are considered the founders of the interpersonal school of psychotherapy (Klerman, Weissman, Rounsville, & Chevron, 1984).

Today, most practitioners of interpersonal therapy continue to come from psychoanalytic backgrounds. They typically consider early childhood experiences and unconscious processes to be important elements in determining people's personality characteristics. However, these issues are *not* a central focus of concern within the interpersonal approach to therapy.

Interpersonal therapy is distinguished from other forms of psychotherapy by its emphasis on current interpersonal relations in the context of focused and time-limited (short-term) therapy. Although past relationships with significant others are considered relevant, they are not the prime focus of IPT. In IPT, the therapist attends to descriptions of interpersonal relations with an eye toward understanding the patient's *role expectancies* as they apply to both self and significant others. The goal of IPT is to modify the existing interpersonal relationships so as to minimize their continued contributions to symptom formation and maintenance.

Interpersonal therapy has been demonstrated effective for the treatment of depression (Elkin, 1994; Klerman et al., 1994; Weissman, 1979; Weissman, Myers, & Thompson, 1981). The underlying assumption for the application of IPT to depressed patients is found in their interpersonal environments.

When a patient begins to experience depressive symptomatology, the initial reaction from the environment is often one of sympathy and support. Over time, however, this response is likely to shift toward one of impatience and hostility as the depressed individual continues to exert a negative impact on those around him or her (Klerman et al., 1984). It is expected that focusing on and altering the patient's interpersonal interactions will cause the social environment to shift in response. The interactions between the patient and significant others will move toward a more positive state, thereby reducing the resulting negative affect and thoughts of the depressed patient and further enhancing the likelihood of future positive social interactions. Besides alleviating current depression, these effects, combined with the newly acquired skills of the patient, should help further protect the patient from relapse. This, in fact, appears to be the case.

In a study of the efficacy of IPT, IPT alone was compared to amitriptyline (a common antidepressant drug) alone and to the combination of IPT and amitriptyline (as well as a waiting list control group). Both groups treated with a single type of therapy (IPT versus drug) showed greater improvement in reported symptoms than the untreated group, and the combined treatment proved more effective than either treatment alone. The two treatments appeared to have somewhat different effects (DiMascio et al., 1979). The IPT improved mood and work performance and reduced apathy and guilt; the amitriptyline seemed to have its greatest effect on "physical" signs of depression—sleep and appetite disturbances. Thus, IPT seems to contribute something unique, above what can be gained through medication alone, and can be used to enhance pharmacologic treatment (Rounsville, Weissman, & Prusoff, 1979).

LIMITATIONS OF THE PSYCHOANALYTIC STRATEGY

Each strategy has strengths and weaknesses. In the preceding chapters, we have tried to present the substance and flavor of the Psychoanalytic Strategy primarily in terms of its strengths. In this "limitations" section, we discuss the strategy's major weaknesses. (A parallel limitations section concludes the discussion of each of the other three strategies.)

Bear in mind that the criticisms we discuss have been made mainly by proponents of other strategies. (However, the feminists who have criticized Freud and his theories are often psychoanalysts themselves.) Also, as you will see, it is typical for a given limitation to plague more than one strategy. Finally, it would not be surprising if some of these reservations have already occurred to you.

We will consider eight of the most commonly voiced criticisms of the Psychoanalytic Strategy: (1) Psychoanalytic assessment has low reliability and validity; (2) many psychoanalytic concepts are poorly defined; (3) some psychoanalytic hypotheses are untestable; (4) psychoanalytic reasoning is prone to logical errors; (5) classical psychoanalytic theory is sex biased; (6) psychoanalytic case studies are unduly biased; and (7) psychoanalytic treatment does not recover historical truth. The final limitation we will discuss is posed as a question: (8) Is psychoanalysis a science?

Psychoanalytic Assessment Has Low Reliability and Validity

Several thousand studies have examined the reliability and validity of projective techniques (Buros, 1965, 1972). Interrater reliability (agreement among raters) and internal consistency (agreement among the items or stimuli used with a given technique) are usually low. Retest reliability (consistency over time) is equally poor when responses or the themes based on those responses are compared in two separate test administrations.

For example, Lindzey and Herman (1955) gave the same subjects the TAT twice. For the second administration, they told the subjects to write different stories. If the TAT was effective in assessing the subjects' personality dynamics, then the *themes* of the stories would be the same for each subject in the two administrations, even though the specific stories were different. There was no support for this hypothesis.

The validity of projective techniques is also largely unsubstantiated by empirical research (Anastasi, 1988a; Cronbach, 1949). In one of the more common types of validity studies, experienced clinicians write personality descriptions about subjects based on responses to a projective technique such as the Rorschach. The judges are "blind" in terms of other information about the subjects. In such studies, agreement between the judges' descriptions has been low. Also, the judges' descriptions are often so general that they could apply to almost anyone.

Another source of negative evidence casts doubt on the very basis of the techniques, namely, the projective hypothesis (Anastasi, 1988a). According to the hypothesis, responses to ambiguous stimuli will be projections of a person's enduring personality characteristics. Rather than assessing underlying personality dynamics and motivational dispositions, projective techniques may be measuring individual differences in immediate perceptual and cognitive factors.

Some problems with projective techniques stem from a lack of standardization of administration, scoring, and interpretation. Subtle changes in how a projective technique is presented to the subject, including the relationship between the examiner and the subject, influence responses (e.g., Masling, 1960).

Subjectivity is another factor that may account for the low reliability and validity of projective methods. Scoring projective techniques requires at least some subjective judgment, even when placing responses in predesignated categories. Free interpretations of projective responses vary widely according to the skill and experience of the examiner. They also vary among examiners of comparable ability. Projective techniques may be as much a projection of the examiner's own biases, hypotheses, favorite interpretations, and theoretical persuasions as an indication of the characteristics of the subject (Anastasi, 1988a).

Despite their problems, projective techniques are still used extensively in clinical settings. What accounts for this popularity, given the negative evidence for reliability and validity? The simplest explanation can be summarized in one word: Tradition! Compared with other methods of personality assessment, projective techniques have the longest history. Such a huge investment of time and effort is difficult to discard. Moreover, projective techniques are used mainly to assess unconscious motives, conflicts, and thoughts. Few alternatives for assessing the unconscious have been developed.

Both the reliability and validity of dream interpretation suffer from a related problem. Different analysts looking at the same data should reach similar interpretations. As it turns out, though, such agreement is rare. The same dream report is likely to be interpreted in different ways by independent, highly competent psychoanalysts (Lorand, 1946; Schafer, 1950). Furthermore, little empirical evidence supports the symbols and interpretations originally proposed by Freud. Psychoanalytic interpretations have low reliability partially because the data and interpretations are qualitative. If they were quantified, even in the basic sense of categorizing, greater agreement might be possible (Shulman, 1990a). As it stands now, however, results of projective assessment and dream interpretations probably reflect the perspectives and orientation of the examiner as much or more than that of the subject.

Psychoanalytic Concepts Are Poorly Defined

Read Freud's writing closely, and you will find that many psychoanalytic concepts are never defined. Instead, they are merely described, usually in vague, nonspecific, and ambiguous terms. This tendency is apparent even within the contemporary psychoanalytic community. For example, writing in the *Psychoanalytic Review,* Shulman (1990a) reported: "To some psychoanalysts the concept of orality may refer to an instinctual regression to the bodily zone, while to others this concept may refer to interpersonal dependence" (p. 256).

As a result, researchers who wish to test the claims of psychoanalytic theory have no concrete guidelines for determining when a phenomenon discussed by the theory is actually occurring. Consider the case of reaction formation. When does affection reflect underlying hate as opposed to love, for instance? According to psychoanalytic theory, persistence and excess are two possible signs that reaction formation is operating. How much love must a husband show a wife before his expressed feelings and actions are considered a reaction formation to his underlying hate?

This problem and the difficulties it engenders are recognized by research-minded analysts who have begun to call for the establishment of a quantitative approach within psychoanalysis (Eagle & Wolitzky, 1985; Masling & Cohen, 1987; Shulman, 1990b). Some have attempted to formulate operational definitions for Freudian concepts. This approach is not without its difficulties, though.

A study of penis envy illustrates the problem. The study was aimed at testing the seemingly straightforward prediction that more women than men would exhibit penis envy (Johnson, 1966). Penis envy was operationally defined as "keeping a borrowed pencil" (some consider a pencil to be a phallic symbol). In fact, significantly more women than men did fail to return pencils that had been loaned to them. "Keeping a borrowed pencil" is an objective and reliable measure; the researcher has only to count the number of pencils lent to each gender and the number returned by each gender. It could be argued, however, that pencil hoarding is not a *valid* measure of penis envy because it is too remote from the theoretical concept. In fact, no one has devised an adequate means to test whether a pencil is actually a phallic symbol.

Psychoanalytic Hypotheses Are Untestable

A fundamental requirement of any scientific theory is that its propositions be testable—that is, open to verification or falsification through research (see Chapter 1). Critics of psychoanalytic theory claim that some of its most important propositions are not testable because the theory can be stretched to fit any outcome. For this reason, psychoanalytic theory is sometimes accused of being a "rubber sheet" theory. As one analyst concedes:

> Psychoanalysis is hard to test because it allows for the existence of contraries [and because] the psychoanalytic model of mind asserts that there will be a variety of conflicting and complementary unconscious forces that, depending on their combinations and permutations, may result in very different observable manifestations. (Wallace, 1986, p. 381)

To illustrate the problem, suppose one investigates the hypothesis that "oral characters" are dependent in their relationships. If the results of the study show that oral characters are dependent, then obviously the hypothesis is supported. But suppose the results indicate that oral characters are not dependent. In this case, the underlying theory may still not be convincingly refuted because *in*dependence can be a defense (a reaction formation) against dependence. Finally, oral characters might be found to be both dependent and independent. This result could still be consistent with the theory because vacillating between dependence and independence can be viewed as the result of the conflict between the drive and its defense.

Freud himself postulated that all dreams fulfill a hidden wish. Yet dreams are often unpleasant and disturbing. It is difficult to understand how such dreams can be wish-fulfilling. Freud (1961a) explained that these are counterwish dreams that satisfy the dreamer's masochism. This type of reasoning led an early critic to comment that psychoanalysis "involves so many arbitrary interpretations that it is impossible to speak of proof in any strict sense of the term" (Moll, 1912, p. 190).

Psychoanalytic Reasoning Is Prone to Logical Errors

Psychoanalysts commit three logical errors in presenting research evidence for their theory. First, they fail to distinguish between *observation* and *inference*. Consider the Oedipus complex. Freud observed that, at around age 4, boys are affectionate toward and seek the attention of their mothers; to some degree, they also avoid their fathers. To explain these observations, Freud conjectured that a boy's feelings for his mother are due to sexual desires; his feelings for his father are related to the rivalry due to this sexual attachment and the implicit threat of castration. This inference has the status of a *hypothesis*—one possible explanation and nothing more.

To say "4-year-old boys experience an Oedipus complex" is to replace an observation with an inference. It would be a different matter to say "4-year-old boys show behavior consistent with the Oedipus complex." Presenting inferences as observations when they represent only one possible explanation is a logical error. The seriousness of this error becomes even more salient because nonpsychoanalytic theories can sometimes provide equally good, and often better, explanations of the observed facts (e.g., Sears, 1943; Wolpe & Rachman, 1960).

A second logical error that psychoanalysts often commit is confusing correlation and causation. For instance, it is legitimate to report that during the first year of life infants engage in many behaviors involving the mouth (e.g., eating, sucking, and crying). Infants are also dependent on others for most of their needs. Thus, oral behavior and dependency occur together (at the same time), and we can legitimately say that they are correlated. However, we cannot legitimately conclude that dependency is caused by orality. It is entirely possible that a third variable accounts for both dependency and orality—in this case, immaturity of the organism. (See Chapter 2 for a discussion of correlation and causation.)

Psychoanalysts often use analogies to describe their observations, and herein lies a third logical error. *Analogy is not proof.* An analogy may help describe or illustrate a new or complex concept, but it cannot be considered verification of the concept. For example, troops left in battle are used to help explain fixation. It is true that military troops may be permanently lost for future battles in a difficult skirmish. This fact, however, does not in any way validate the claim that libido is a finite entity that, once fixated, is no longer available for future investment.

Classical Psychoanalytic Theory Is Sex Biased

By today's standards, Freud's theory appears blatantly sexist (Frosh, 1987; Sagan, 1988; Sayers, 1991), as is much post-Freudian theorizing. The theories are based on males and then extended to females. For example, Freud attempted to make the Electra complex fit the model of the Oedipus complex. The fit is none too snug (Person, 1988).

Similarly, Freud's concept of castration anxiety follows from the notion that the little boy wants to have sex with his mother. Freud considered penis envy to be the female counterpart of castration anxiety. But penis envy is not directly parallel, and it does not serve the same purpose as castration anxiety—namely, to prevent incest. This part of Freud's theory is poorly formulated because he used male personality development as the basis for female development. It is curious that Freud was not better at theorizing about females in that most of his early patients were women. It may be that, in fact, Freud based most of his theory on his own self-analysis (Anzieu, 1986; Hardin, 1987, 1988a, 1988b).

Freud used male personality as a *prototype* and considered it the ideal. Quite bluntly, in Freud's view, women are inferior to men. He believed that the part of their personality that is different from men's comes from defending against and overcompensating for their inferiority. Consider three of Freud's ideas about female sexuality and personality:

1. *Females are castrated.* Obviously, this concept assumes that women once had a penis, which implies the superiority of the male sexual anatomy. In Freud's (1964b) words: "Her self-love is mortified by the comparison with the boy's far superior equipment" (p. 126). There is no evidence that women feel inferior because they have a vagina rather than a penis or that a penis is in any way superior to a vagina.
2. *Females have more difficulty establishing a sex role than males.* Freud derived this proposition from the view that the girl has a more

complicated Oedipal situation. Although the mother is the first object of love for both sexes, the girl must switch her love to her father, whereas the boy continues with his mother as his primary love object. The additional step for the girl could make her sex-role identification more troublesome. "But the empirical literature suggests that, if anything, the female has less difficulty than the male in the process of evolving a sex role" (Fisher & Greenberg, 1977, p. 220).

3. *Vaginal orgasm indicates sexual maturity.* Freud believed that a woman needs to relinquish her desire for a penis (penis envy) to successfully resolve her Electra complex and to function as a mature adult. According to Freud, the mature woman derives sexual pleasure primarily from penile stimulation of the vagina rather than the clitoris. Freud viewed the clitoris as a woman's penis. Therefore, "no longer deriving sexual pleasure from clitoral stimulation" means relinquishing penis envy. This minor aspect of Freud's theory has been widely accepted as fact. The existing evidence, however, contradicts it. Fisher (1973) obtained ratings from several samples of married women on the degree to which they prefer clitoral to vaginal stimulation in the process of attaining orgasm. He found no indications that women with a clitoral orientation were inferior in their psychological adaptation.

> Surprisingly . . . it was not the clitorally-oriented woman who was most anxious, as would be expected within the Freudian framework, but rather the vaginally-oriented one. (Fisher & Greenberg, 1977, p. 212)

Many of Freud's views of women have not been substantiated, which is not, in itself, an indictment. Theories are developed to be tested. The telling criticism of classical psychoanalytic views of women is that they assume men are the model for all human personality and that women should strive to be like men. Not surprisingly, women writers have begun to voice serious objections to some of the assumptions underlying Freudian psychoanalysis. What is somewhat surprising is the extent of criticism leveled at Freud and his theories by women who consider themselves psychoanalysts. These women do not necessarily wish to abandon psychoanalysis and psychoanalytic thinking; rather, they hope to revise and refine some of Freud's biases and assumptions about women.

Contemporary Feminist Objections to Freud's Theories

The primary points of divergence from Freud by the feminist movement in psychoanalysis today are (1) objection to the male centered *(androcentric)* focus in psychoanalysis and (2) the absence of direct study of women in their own right. Finchilescu (1995) describes these issues pointedly as the "invisibility and marginality of women in psychology" (p. 135).

Continued reliance on a patriarchally biased scheme (especially in the absence of overt recognition and acknowledgment of this fact) serves to perpetuate and justify continued male dominance (Rhode-Dachser, 1992). The centrality of the Oedipal conflict to Freud's theory and his emphasis on the male child's need to recognize his separateness and distinctness (difference) from the mother yield an impoverished and biased psychology of gender differences, based on rejection and contrasts (Caputi, 1993).

A related criticism has come to be termed the **container function of women** (Bion, 1965; Young-Bruehl, 1994). Women are cast as ancillary to the study of men. They therefore become the receptacle for all that is negative, undesirable, or simply not embraced by the (superior) male character. For lack of a better understanding, women are construed as *being whatever men are not* (Bion, 1965; Caputi, 1993; Rhode-Dachser, 1992). Thus, oversimplifications and binary thinking have governed psychoanalytic theorizing about women by Freud and many of his followers (Lacan, 1966; Bennett, 1993).

Early feminist analysis (e.g., Horney, 1939; Jones, 1927; Thompson, 1941, 1942, 1943, 1950) primarily involved a critique and reformulation of classical psychoanalytic ideas. Recently, feminist analysis has gone beyond criticism of Freud's position to present a more balanced view of female personality (e.g., Buie, 1989b; Cantor & Bernay, 1988; Gilligan, 1982; Sayers, 1991). Mitchell (1974a, 1974b), for example, used classical psychoanalysis as a starting point. She argued that classical psychoanalysis need not be viewed as "a recommendation for a patriarchal society," but rather as "an analysis of one. If we are interested in understanding and challenging the oppression of women, we cannot afford to neglect it" (1974b, p. xv).

Psychoanalytic Case Studies Are Unduly Biased

Case studies remain the primary method of research in the Psychoanalytic Strategy (Freud, 1955; Levenson, 1988). These studies are almost invariably conducted with patients during the process of psychoanalysis. The limitations of the case study method were discussed in Chapter 2; here, some specific problems with psychoanalytic case studies are addressed.

The psychoanalytic session is private. Yet it is during these sessions that the data for case studies are gathered. This situation raises a serious problem. Because of theoretical bias, the analyst may selectively recall certain aspects of the case while forgetting other aspects (Grünbaum, 1984). This process, in turn, may result in the analyst's reconstructing earlier material based on later observations. "Thus, the psychoanalyst's theoretical commitment can influence both the patient's utterances themselves and the manner in which they are organized, written up, and interpreted" (Sherwood, 1969, p. 71).

Evidence suggests that analytically oriented therapists may be more likely to succumb to observer bias than therapists of other orientations. In one experiment, psychoanalysts and behavior therapists interviewed people who were presented as either "patients" or "job applicants" (Langer & Abelson, 1974). The analysts were significantly more likely to vary their clinical observations based on the labels alone. They tended to find the "patients" more disturbed than the "job applicants."

Psychoanalytic case studies are not generalizable because they are based on small, atypical samples. Freud's own theorizing is very susceptible to this criticism. A good deal of Freud's original theory is based on his own self-analysis (Gay, 1988). In all of his writings, Freud describes only 12 cases in detail.

Size alone, however, does not determine the suitability of a sample. The critical criterion is whether the sample is *representative* of the population to which the generalizations will be made. Freud believed that few people are suitable for analysis. His requirements for a suitable patient included maturity, courage, education, and good character, as well as the intellectual ability to understand the complexities of psychoanalytic theories (Roazen, 1975).

However, the subjects of published psychoanalytic case studies almost all suffered with some form of psychopathology (Tuttman, 1988). How can one justify generalizing to normal personality from a sample characterized by abnormal personality? The restricted nature of Freud's sample makes it difficult to justify his sweeping generalizations to all humanity.

Contemporary psychoanalytic cases present the same problem. The samples from which generalizations about human personality are made are not representative. Today, patients in psychoanalysis are typically young or middle-aged and white; they are above average in intelligence, highly articulate, and have relatively high incomes. (Psychoanalysis can easily cost $25,000 per year.) They are typically Jewish or Protestant, almost never Catholic. They are also unusually psychologically minded. In fact, many are workers in mental health fields (Grünbaum, 1984; Knapp, Levin, McCarter, Wermer, & Zetzel, 1960; Masling & Cohen, 1987; Wallace, 1986).

Psychoanalytic Treatment Does Not Recover Historical Truth

Freud's good friend and faithful critic, Wilhelm Fliess, posed what is perhaps the most serious challenge of all back at the turn of the 20th century. It specifically dealt with psychoanalytic therapy, but it had implications for psychoanalytic theory, assessment, and research as well.

> During the summer of 1900, in a small resort in what was then western Austria, Wilhelm Fliess suggested to Freud that he [Freud] merely read his own thoughts into the minds of his patients. As Freud realized, the challenge put to him by Fliess in the Achensee was a serious one, striking at the very heart of psychoanalysis. It challenged the therapeutic claim that lasting and significant gains in psychoanalysis result from insight into the cause of the illness; moreover, it threatened the allied diagnostic claim that psychological disorders are rooted in repressed memories and desires. (Richardson, 1990, p. 668)

Freud's clinical experience and that of his immediate followers led to the belief that psychoanalytic treatment is successful ("produces lasting and significant gains") in some patients, but not all. Many of these patients had come in with symptoms (e.g., hysterical paralysis, phobias, impotence) that Freud believed to have deep causes. Thus, "successful" can be viewed in two different ways. One way is to ask if the symptoms are gone. (This result is, after all, what the patient has come in for.) The other way is to ask about underlying process: Have the intrapsychic causes of these symptoms been identified and exposed?

Freud believed a symptom might be banished merely by suggestion. He had seen Charcot order a hypnotized patient with hysterical paralysis to stand up and walk, whereupon she apparently did so. But such cures never lasted; when the patient was awakened from hypnosis, she was again paralyzed. So ridding the patient of the symptom would most likely not be Freud's criterion. Rather, Freud was totally convinced that the analyst had to expose the truth, make the causes of the neurosis visible to the patient's conscious ego, and thereby release the underlying repression at the root of the patient's problems. This criterion is a good deal more problematic than determining the presence or absence of symptoms (Spence, 1984).

Fliess's challenge was to ask: In the practice of psychoanalysis, how do analysts know when they have discovered the truth? Freud's answer was that only the truth would be accepted by the patient as a basis for real insight to occur. An interpretation had to "tally" with the truth. Only a true interpretation would trigger the healing process. Here is the way Freud put his argument: "[The patient's] conflicts will only be successfully solved and his resistances overcome if the anticipatory ideas he is given [by the analyst] tally with what is real in him" (Freud, 1955, pp. 452–453).

Critics beginning with Fliess have suggested that psychoanalysis may offer little more than a good story to the patient. Such a story will have narrative truth (it will be coherent, convincing, and believable), but it will not necessarily have historical truth, and it may be as much the analyst's invented yarn as anything else. As Siegert (1990), himself a psychoanalyst, argued,

> Free association is anything but free. . . . [I]n practice, analysts actually discourage truly free association. . . . What we listen for are stories or narratives, and relatively organized and edited associations to those stories, not to a random collection of disconnected words. . . . Our listening is always and inevitably shaped by what we expect to hear [and] one can only hear after one has a framework. . . . What we listen for is to a very great extent theoretically determined. That is why Freudians tend to hear oedipally, Kleinians tend to hear preoedipally, and Sullivanians tend to hear interpersonally. Our listening isn't unbiased. Our patients don't associate freely. And we do not listen without preconception. . . . In other words, when we believe we are reconstructing the past, *we are actually creating or constructing a past that often has never occurred* [emphasis added]. (pp. 163–164)

Is Psychoanalysis a Science?

Defenders of psychoanalytic theory argue that psychoanalysts, as much as other personality psychologists, care passionately for the truth, but conceive of it in a different way (Langs, 1987). According to this view, different is not necessarily less valid. Objectivity and repeatability appear to be logical and even "right"; still, they are, in the end, as they were when they were adopted, *arbitrary* standards.

The goal of the Psychoanalytic Strategy is also somewhat different from the goal of mainstream psychology, which emphasizes prediction and control of groups of people. Psychoanalysis is concerned mainly with understanding individual patients, which is subjective and often incomplete and ambiguous (Steele, 1979). The primary researchers in the Psychoanalytic Strategy are analysts engaged in full-time psychoanalytic therapy. As such, they are often more interested in helping their current patients than in researching the theoretical foundations on which they base their clinical practice (Michels, 1988; Wallerstein, 1988).

The issue of the relation of psychoanalysis to science is as old as psychoanalysis itself. Freud often considered calling psychoanalysis *meta-*

psychology—meaning that it goes beyond psychology—thereby removing it from psychology defined as the science of behavior. In 1900, Freud wrote:

> I am not really a man of science . . . I am nothing but by temperament . . . an adventurer . . . with the curiosity, the boldness, and the tenacity that belongs to that type of being. Such people are apt to be treasured if they succeed, if they have really discovered something; otherwise they are thrown aside. And that is not altogether unjust. (quoted in Jones, 1953, p. 348)

SUMMARY

1. Freud considered dreams to be a rich source of information about personality. He felt that manifest content—what the dreamer recalls about events and objects in a dream—reveals through its symbolism latent content. Latent content results from unconscious processes and conflict, which can be interpreted by a skilled analyst.
2. In Freudian dream interpretation, both manifest content and patients' free associations to the dream are analyzed and interpreted according to the principles of symbolization and dream work.
3. Projective assessment techniques all use ambiguous stimuli and context that compel subjects to impose their own structure, order, and meaning on the situation to produce a response. These "projections" are assumed to be the product of the subjects' (often unconscious) feelings, thoughts, and desires. The several broad categories of projective tasks include association, construction, completion, and free expression.
4. The Rorschach inkblots and various versions of the TAT are among the most common (standard stimulus) projective techniques. An array of other less structured techniques also exist. Projective data are generally not scored against normative data; rather, they are interpreted and examined for the presence of patterns of recurrent themes.
5. In Freudian psychoanalysis, patients talk about their past, problems, and dreams. Free association is encouraged throughout to allow for expression of unconscious impulses and processes. The analyst interprets all of this information in an effort to provide patients insight into their difficulties. "Cure" is expected to result from gaining adequate insight into these unconscious processes.
6. Insight is possible for a patient only after working through the various forms of resistance that may be operative. Transference represents an important form of resistance in that it often informs and guides the therapist (although it may also at times impede treatment).
7. Post-Freudian therapy is distinguished by its greater emphasis on current functioning, interpersonal issues, shorter duration, and use of direct feedback and suggestions for change. Post-Freudians also emphasize the importance of the therapeutic alliance for the process of therapy. The effectiveness of the interpersonal approach to therapy has been demonstrated for depression.
8. Projective techniques generally have low reliability and validity. Nonetheless, they continue to remain popular as assessment procedures

for clinical practice. The reliability of psychoanalytic dream interpretations is also generally low.

9. Many psychoanalytic concepts are defined in vague, nonspecific, and ambiguous terms. Inadequate definitions make measuring the concepts problematic. Many Freudian concepts cannot be falsified because the theory can be stretched to fit any observed outcome.
10. Psychoanalysts often commit three logical errors in presenting evidence for their theories: (1) They fail to distinguish between observation and inference; (2) they confuse correlation and causation; and (3) they rely on analogy as evidence.
11. Freud's theorizing is plagued by a deep-rooted gender bias. Freud viewed male personality as both prototype and ideal.
12. Feminist psychoanalysts argue that Freud's inattention to female personality and functioning has produced a theory of personality in which women are relegated to assume all characteristics considered not masculine. This produces a theory of gender differences and contrasts, as well as an impoverished view of women.
13. Psychoanalytic case studies may be unduly biased because of the highly private nature of the observations and because these case studies are based on small, atypical samples of people. Also, psychoanalysts may be more biased in their observations than other therapists.
14. It is questionable whether practicing psychoanalysts discover the historical truth about their patients, as Freud had supposed.
15. Psychoanalysis has been criticized as being unscientific. It has been suggested that psychoanalysis should not be judged by the standards of mainstream scientific psychology.

PART THREE

THE DISPOSITIONAL STRATEGY

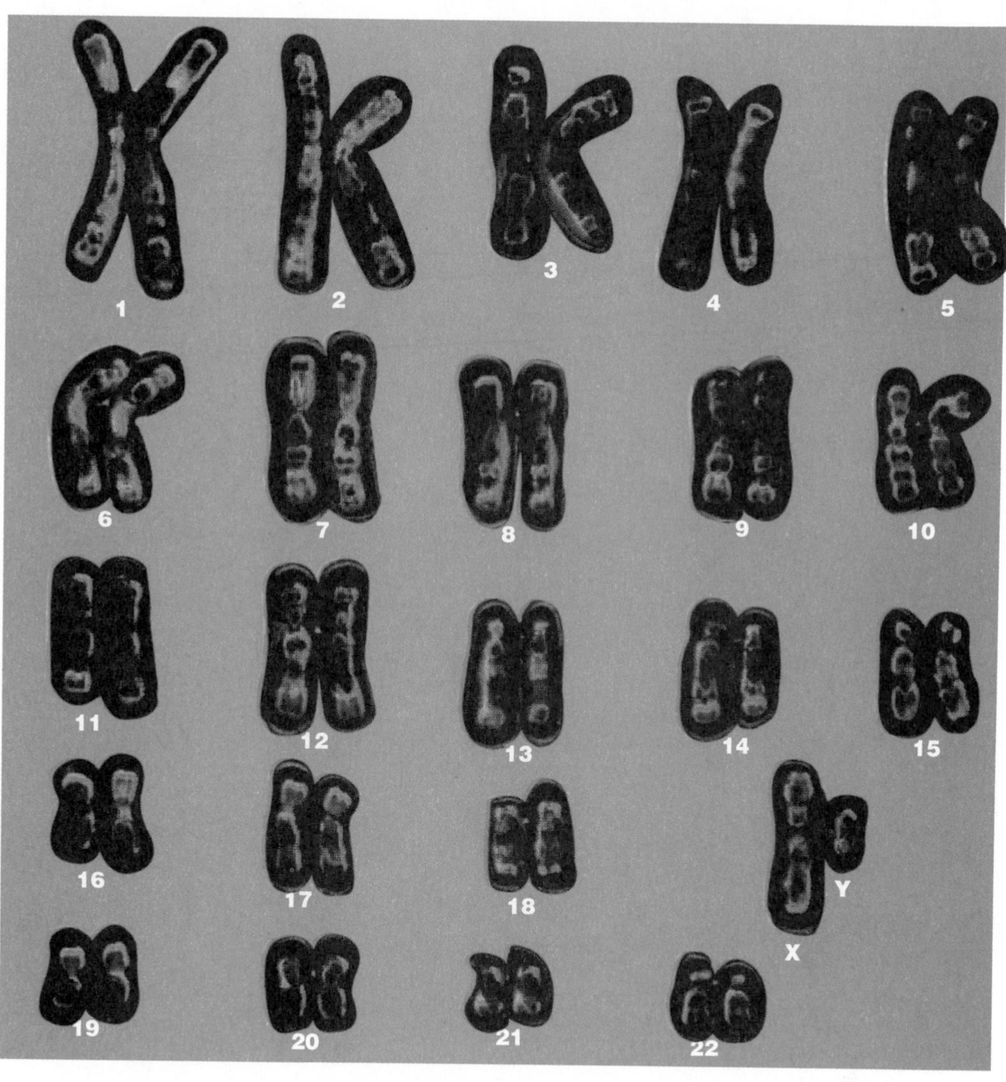

It's All In There

CHAPTER SEVEN

Introduction to the Dispositional Strategy

> She was totally unconcerned about how she appeared to people . . . She was strong and secure and graceful, almost aloof. I always felt a little uncomfortable around her. She was a tough competitor and formidable. (Morris, 1996, p. 117)

hese descriptions convey some "sense" of the woman described. There is a hint of the enduring qualities that set her apart. These qualities might help identify her or predict what she would do in various situations. The woman described is Hillary Rodham Clinton, as she was perceived by two former classmates. The description might, of course, apply to many other people as well, and there is much that it does not tell us. Still, a mere few sentences provide some sense of her basic characteristics and the way she was usually disposed to behave.

In this section, we consider the Dispositional Strategy for understanding human personality. The major idea behind the strategy is found in the definition of a **disposition:** an enduring, relatively stable personality characteristic. According to the Dispositional Strategy, people differ in the way they are generally disposed to behave. Describing individuals, groups, and even nations in dispositional terms seems almost to "come naturally." Before proceeding further, you may wish to try the demonstration in Box 7.1. Most students find completing this demonstration easy; people are very accustomed to thinking of others in dispositional terms.

Box 7.1
DEMONSTRATION: DESCRIBING PEOPLE IN DISPOSITIONAL TERMS

We are accustomed to using dispositional notions in describing and attempting to explain other's behavior. These notions usually take the form "So-and-so is a _______ person" or "So-and-so acts that way because he or she is _______." For example, we might say, "Harry is a meek person" or "Susan acts that way because she is proud."

The purpose of this demonstration is to give you an opportunity to describe people you know in dispositional terms. It will allow you to compare your use of dispositions with the way personality psychologists use the Dispositional Strategy. The demonstration also introduces some of the methods, predictions, and general findings of the strategy.

Procedure

1. Take six sheets of lined paper and write one of the letters *A* through *F* at the top of each sheet. Then remove Work Sheet 7.1, which you will find in the Demonstration Materials section at the back of the book. The work sheet will be used later in the demonstration. (Table 7.1 shows a sample work sheet.)
2. For each of the following categories, designate a particular person of your own sex. Write each person's name at the top of the appropriate sheet of paper.
   A. Your same-sex parent or, if you never knew this person, a close biological relative of the same sex (ideally a blood relative)
   B. A close friend who is not related to you
   C. Someone not related to you with whom you are somewhat friendly (a more casual relationship than you have with person B)

Box continued on following page

Box 7.1 *Continued*

DEMONSTRATION: DESCRIBING PEOPLE IN DISPOSITIONAL TERMS

Table 7.1 **Sample work sheet for demonstration**

RANK	NAME	NUMBER OF ADJECTIVES USED	PERVASIVENESS ALMOST ALWAYS 4	FRE-QUENTLY 3	OCCA-SIONALLY 2	RARELY 1	PERCENTAGE OF SIMILARITY
	Self						
Know best 1st							%
2nd							%
3rd							%
4th							%
Know least 5th							%
	Σ = Sum (total)	Σ =	Σ =	Σ =	Σ =	Σ =	
	M = Mean	*M* =	%	%	%	%	

D. Someone not related to you whom you know only in one specific context (a schoolteacher)
E. A historical figure whom you admire
F. Yourself

Write down as many or as few adjectives as seem necessary to fully describe your same-sex parent (person A). (The order of the adjectives does not matter.) Repeat this procedure for the people in categories B through F, in that order.

Look over the adjectives you have listed for person A. Are any similar or redundant? (For example, *clumsy* and *awkward* have similar meanings.) If you are unsure of any of the definitions, double-check them with a standard dictionary. Condense any redundant adjectives by either eliminating or combining them (e.g., *clumsy-awkward*). Repeat this procedure for persons B through F, in that order.

Now rate each of the adjectives or adjective combinations according to the degree to which each characterizes person A. Use the following scale:

4 = Almost always characterizes the person
3 = Frequently characterizes the person
2 = Occasionally characterizes the person
1 = Rarely characterizes the person

Write the scale number that is most applicable next to each of the adjectives or adjective combinations. Repeat this procedure for persons B through F, in that order.

Box continued on following page

Box 7.1 *Continued*
DEMONSTRATION: DESCRIBING PEOPLE IN DISPOSITIONAL TERMS

Rank persons A through E (excluding yourself) in terms of how well you know them. The person you feel you know best should be given the "first" rank, the person you feel you know second-best should be assigned the "second" rank, and so on until the person whom you feel you know least well has received the "fifth" rank. Write the rank in the upper right-hand corner of each sheet.

In the first column of the work sheet, list the names of the five people other than yourself (persons A through E) in order of familiarity—that is, according to the rank you assigned them in step 6. The person you ranked "first" (the one you feel you know best) should be listed first, the person whom you ranked "second" should be listed next, and so on.

On the work sheet, in the "Number of Adjectives Used" column, put the total number of adjectives or adjective combinations you used to describe each person (A through F).

Next, at the bottom of the column, put the total number of adjectives or adjective combinations you used to describe all the people other than yourself (sheets A through E). Divide this total by 5 to obtain the mean number of adjectives you used to describe the other people, and enter this number in the appropriate space at the bottom of the work sheet.

In the "Pervasiveness" columns, record the number of adjectives for each person (A through F) that fall in each of the four categories. These are the numbers you wrote next to the adjectives in step 5.

At the bottom of the column, put the total number of adjectives in each of the four pervasiveness categories for the five persons other than yourself.

Compute and record at the bottom of the work sheet the percentage of adjectives that fall into each of the pervasiveness categories. To do this, divide the total number of adjectives for each category by the total number of adjectives used to describe the other persons (i.e., combined across all categories), and then multiply by 100.

Looking at all six sheets (A through F), check to see whether any of the adjectives are similar or redundant across persons. For example, if you described yourself as generous and your parent as giving, condense these adjectives into one term, either by changing *generous* to *giving* or vice versa or by hyphenating the two adjectives whenever they both appear (i.e., *generous-giving*). This step is similar to step 4, and you may find a thesaurus helpful. On sheets A through E (every sheet except yours), circle each adjective or adjective combination that is the same as one you used to describe yourself (on sheet F).

Compute the percentage of adjectives used for each of the other people (A through E) that corresponds to your own, and record it in the "Percentage of Similarity" column. That is, divide the number of adjectives that are the same for you and the other person—the ones you have circled—by the total number of adjectives used to describe the other person, and then multiply by 100.

Discussion

You may have already noticed a number of interesting features and patterns in your use of dispositional descriptions for others and yourself. We will mention a few of the findings of dispositional psychologists that are related to the demonstration.

Number of Descriptive Adjectives Used

Gordon Allport (1937) was one of the first to examine the range of dispositional terms, or "trait names," that people use to describe others. He found that people often use a large number of descriptive adjectives but many are synonymous and thus the total number can be reduced. To the extent that your own experiences in this demonstration parallel Allport's findings, you would have been able to substantially reduce the size of your initial lists of descriptive adjectives.

Box continued on following page

Box 7.1 *Continued*
DEMONSTRATION: DESCRIBING PEOPLE IN DISPOSITIONAL TERMS

After condensing redundant adjectives, Allport found that most people actually use a fairly small number of adjectives in describing others they know; the usual range is between 3 and 10. Does your mean number of adjectives fall within this range? How does the number of adjectives you used to describe yourself compare with the mean number of adjectives you used to describe other people?

Dispositions and Genetics

Dispositional psychologists who adopt a biological approach have found evidence suggesting that certain dispositions may be transmitted genetically. Evidence of genetic dispositions might show up in this demonstration in the degree of similarity between you and your parent ("Percentage of Similarity" column on the work sheet). Is this similarity greater than the similarity between you and a close friend?

Relationship to People

Many people believe that the closer their relationship is to someone, the better they know that person. Yet psychological studies provide some evidence that people often feel more comfortable assigning dispositional adjectives to those they know less well.

Examine the relationship between the number of adjectives you used to describe a person and how well you feel you know that person. The five people other than yourself are listed on the work sheet in descending order of familiarity, so you can look down the "Number of Adjectives Used" column to see whether a pattern emerges. Is "secondhand" information, such as that used to describe the historical figure, sufficient to adequately characterize the person? How well were you able to describe the person you know in only a single context?

Pervasiveness

Allport and others have noted that dispositions vary in the degree to which they pervade a particular personality. Not many people have dispositions that pervade all that they do and dominate their entire personality ("Almost Always" category). Did any of the people on your list appear to have a highly pervasive disposition? Did most have a few dispositions that characterize them in many situations ("Frequently" category)?

Other Issues

You might find it interesting to consider some further analyses of your own. What are the qualitative differences among the adjectives you use to describe various individuals you know? What differences would you expect if you repeated the demonstration but described people of the opposite sex? Examining questions like these will help you understand the Dispositional Strategy. Save the demonstration materials and inspect them again as you read the chapters in this section.

Dispositional labels serve as organizing concepts that may explain a person's behavior in a variety of situations. Stagner (1976) gives this example:

> If a young man refuses an invitation to a party, drops a course that requires group discussion, and takes his vacation hiking alone in the mountains, we begin to get the idea that there is an inner consistency that involves the avoidance of situations that require close contact with other human beings. . . . The idea of a trait makes sense as a unifying concept here. . . . (p. 112)

EARLY DISPOSITIONAL CONCEPTS

Dispositional concepts in one form or another have been used to organize and explain the actions of others for thousands of years. Early dispositional views assumed that people could be divided into a relatively small number of types, according to their personalities. By knowing an individual's type, you could predict the way that individual would behave in a variety of circumstances.

The ancient Hebrews used this perspective for what may have been the first formal personality assessment, shown in the following quotation from the Old Testament. The goal was to identify two types of people, those who should fight and those who should not.

> And the LORD said unto Gideon, The people that are with thee are too many for me to give the Midianites into their hands. . . .
>
> Now therefore go to, proclaim in the ears of the people, saying, Whosoever is fearful and afraid, let him return and depart early from Mount Gilead. And there returned of the people twenty and two thousand; and there remained ten thousand.
>
> And the LORD said unto Gideon, The people are yet too many; bring them down unto the water, and I will try them for thee there. . . .
>
> So he brought down the people unto the water: and the LORD said unto Gideon, Every one that lappeth of the water with his tongue, as a dog lappeth, him shalt thou set by himself; likewise every one that boweth down upon his knees to drink.
>
> And the number of them that lapped putting their hand to their mouth, were three hundred men: but all the rest of the people bowed down upon their knees to drink water.
>
> And the LORD said unto Gideon, By the three hundred men that lapped will I save you, and deliver the Midianites into thine hand: and let all the other people go every man unto his place. (Judges 7:2–7, KJV)

A second historic view, the **theory of the four temperaments,** is close to several contemporary theories and many everyday conceptions of personality. This view is based on the ancient Greek idea that the universe can be described in terms of four basic elements: air, earth, fire, and water. The Greek physician Hippocrates, the father of medicine, extended this argument to people. He suggested that the body contains four "humors"—blood, black bile, yellow bile, and phlegm—that correspond to the four elements. The Roman physician Galen later suggested that an excess of any of these humors leads to a characteristic temperament or "personality type": sanguine (hopeful), melancholic (sad), choleric (hot-tempered), or phlegmatic (apathetic).

This ancient theory of personality has been discarded, but another theory of the "ingredients" of personality evolved to replace it. Specifically, the widely accepted notion today is that there are (at least) two broad, distinct ingredients in personality, on which people differ in amount: **extraversion** and **neuroticism** (Stelmack & Stalikas, 1991). These two ingredients play a central role in several contemporary personality theories, as we shall see.

Clearly, one can distinguish many types of people. This fact was obvious even to the ancients, and extensive catalogs of types emerged. With few changes, identifying types of people continued to be popular for thousands of

An ancient woodcut depicting the four temperaments.
© Corbis-Bettmann

years. Perhaps the most striking idea was that physical appearance indicated personality. In Shakespeare's play *Julius Caesar,* for example, Caesar tells Marcus Antonius:

> Let me have men about me that are fat;
> Sleek-headed men, and such as sleep o' nights.
> Yond Cassius has a lean and hungry look;
> He thinks too much: such men are dangerous. (act 1, sc. 2)

The belief advanced by Shakespeare's Caesar is still popular. Many people believe that they can identify a "criminal type" by physical appearance, perhaps "beady" eyes or an ever-shifting gaze. Similarly, people may associate a frail physique and thick glasses with characteristics like intelligence and scholarliness. You may be able to think of many other cases in which judgments are based on first impressions and appearances.

So far, we have used the terms *characteristics* and *type* almost interchangeably. Issues of terminology crop up in even the most formal writing of the Dispositional Strategy. Before proceeding further, we should take a closer look at this issue.

Dispositional Terminology

Several language problems plague this strategy. First, there is no consensus among theorists and researchers as to the exact definitions of many technical terms. Although this problem alone does not distinguish the strategy (note that lack of precise definitions was a criticism of the Psychoanalytic Strategy in Chapter 6), the problem here extends beyond the absence of clear definitions. Theorists within this strategy often apply different terms to the same concepts (*trait* and *disposition* are used interchangeably by most), and one theorist may apply the same term to slightly different concepts than those described by another theorist. For example, *types, trait clusters,* and *factors* may all be used in different ways by some theorists, yet other writers may make no discrimination among them. As Zuckerman (1995) recently stated, "In personality psychology, things called by the same name are not necessarily the same thing, and things called by different names are not necessarily different" (p. 74).

This lack of shared definitions creates confusion both between and within theories and theorists of the Dispositional Strategy. For the purpose of clarity and effective communication, we are choosing to adopt some explicit definitions in this book. These definitions are not arbitrary; they are based on our best understanding of each term's most common use in the current literature. You may recognize some overlap and, redundancy in our definitions. Currently, this is unavoidable. In some cases the use of a particular term has shifted over time. The application of a mathematical tool, factor analysis, to this area of research has also served to introduce a number of new terms for phenomena similar to those previously observed or assessed through other means. Our working definitions are presented in Table 7.2. (These terms also appear in the comprehensive glossary at the end of the book.)

We have attempted throughout our discussion to use these terms in ways consistent with the table's explicit definitions. At times, we will adopt the original phrasing of particular theorists as we describe their work. Where the theorist's definitions deviate from our own, or generally accepted ones, we will point that out to you in the text.

Table 7.2 **Terms of the Dispositional Strategy**

Disposition	Enduring characteristics on which individuals differ; often used synonymously with *traits*
Domain	Broad personality factor; sometimes called *supertraits,* domains each encompass a number (six in Costa & McCrae's scheme) of narrower traits or facets
Facet	Narrow elemental personality features of which personality characteristics (dispositions or traits) are compromised
Factor	Broad domains or "supertraits" often identified through factor analysis
Temperament	Broad dimensions of personality that can be observed, measured, and used to classify individuals from early infancy; three temperaments have been distinguished—emotionality, activity level, and sociability (It appears that these broad dimensions serve as the foundation for the development of later adult personality, including specific dispositions or traits.)
Trait	Synonymous with *disposition,* but often used in combination with other terms to convey somewhat different ideas or to convey the enduring nature of a characteristic that might in other people appear to be a transient "state" (e.g., the term *trait anxiety* is used to convey the idea that in some individuals proneness to anxiety is a stable feature of their personality)
Type	Cluster of characteristics (or dispositions or traits) that tend to occur together in some people; these can range from a small number (three to five) of characteristics to large groupings of distinguishable patterns of characteristics sometimes referred to as *supertraits* or *personality factors* (especially when derived through factor analysis)

THEORETICAL ASSUMPTIONS OF THE DISPOSITIONAL STRATEGY

The defining assumption of the Dispositional Strategy is that personality is the set of enduring characteristics innate to the person. These characteristics influence people's interactions with others and their environment. Individuals differ primarily in the amount of each of these characteristics that they possess. (In some cases, the amount of any particular characteristic possessed by an individual may be, for all practical purposes, none.) These dispositions are presumed to be relatively enduring and stable, producing some degree of consistency in behavior across time and circumstance.

Relative Stability of Dispositions

If individuals are truly disposed to act in particular ways, then personalities should be fairly stable over time. However, dispositional psychologists often caution that this assumption must be understood in the light of several further distinctions.

Most dispositional psychologists conceptualize an individual's **enduring dispositions** as permanent, inherent elements of personality and distinguish them from temporary conditions, or **states.** The latter result from transient situations or conditions like illness, fatigue, stress, or sudden changes in life circumstance. The difference between these two types of "dispositions" can be illustrated by using the construct anxiety. Spielberger described *trait anxiety* as "the disposition to respond with anxiety to situations that are perceived as threatening." This is different from state anxiety, which is "a condition of the organism characterized by subjective feelings of apprehension and heightened autonomic nervous system activity" (Spielberger & Gorsuch, 1966, p. 33).

Note that trait anxiety is only a predisposition to be anxious. People high in trait anxiety will not necessarily be anxious all the time, but they will become anxious *more often* and *more readily* than a similar person who is low in trait anxiety. A person low in trait anxiety may exhibit state anxiety *only* under highly stressful conditions. Research suggests that the trait-state distinction is valuable for clinical as well as normal populations and for dispositions other than anxiety (Oei, Evans, & Cook, 1990). As would be expected, state measures vary more than trait measures from one situation to another (Zuckerman, 1983).

Dispositional psychologists also point out that a **disposition** is a general mode of functioning. The disposition may take different concrete behavioral forms as the individual matures. Thus, a psychologist must know what to look for in order to tell whether a person's behavior has been "stable" over time. Dispositions are not merely habits; instead, they reflect an inner consistency. However, discovering this consistency often takes more than a simplistic analysis of overt acts (Buss, 1989).

Pediatric psychologist Michael Lewis (1967) clearly illustrates this point in his article "The Meaning of a Response, or Why Researchers in Infant Behavior Should Be Oriental Metaphysicians." Briefly, Lewis was interested in the consistency of infants' responses to frustration, which he measured in a group of babies at 1 month of age and then again when they were 12 months old. At 1 month, the procedure consisted of removing a nipple from the infants' mouth for 30 seconds; at 12 months, a physical barrier blocked the youngsters from reaching either their mother or some attractive toys. Crying was the measure of frustration.

Responses to the two situations were negatively correlated; that is, the babies who cried at 1 month were *not* the ones who cried at 12 months. However, as Lewis pointed out, this behavior should not mask a deeper consistency. Specifically, *some of the babies were consistently active and others were consistently passive* in their responses. At 1 month, motor skills are not yet developed. Thus, the active baby can do nothing but cry—which the active baby does. But at 12 months of age, crying is a relatively passive response. At this age, the active babies did not cry; rather, they took some physical action to change the frustrating situation. Thus, developmental issues and other practical constraints on their expression must be considered in the search for stable personality characteristics.

Because these characteristics are construed as permanent and enduring, many researchers have begun to look toward the individual's physical attributes and hereditary endowment for the roots of personality dispositions. The biological approach to personality addresses the underlying biological bases of behavior, as well as the search for evidence to support the role of heredity in complex behaviors as reflected by personality dispositions. Everything from behavioral similarity between parents and offspring to actual shared genetic material is combining to suggest that biological factors *do* contribute to behavior and may account for the relatively stable, enduring quality of personality dispositions.

Consistency and Generality of Dispositions

The second major assumption of the Dispositional Strategy is related to the first. Dispositions have some consistency and generality within a person. Consistency and generality refer to the extent to which a disposition affects behavior. A man who is ambitious in his work is also likely to be ambitious and striving in his recreational activities. He will probably have high ambitions for his children as well.

No disposition is expected to appear all the time or in every situation. One reason is that a person has many dispositions. Different demands and circumstances can bring a somewhat different set of dispositions into play.

Nonetheless, some aspects of behavior are consistent across situations (e.g., Diener & Larsen, 1984; McCrae, 1996; Woodruffe, 1985) and time (e.g., Conley, 1984; McCrae, 1996; Siegler et al., 1990; Staw & Ross, 1985). Woodruffe (1985), for instance, found a high degree of consistency across situations in the tendency to be outgoing or reserved. Conley (1984) showed that introversion-extraversion and emotionality remain moderately consistent across a 45-year period—a substantial part of the adult life span!

Individual Differences

We have all noticed clear differences in abilities, interests, and social responses among adults we know. Even from birth, infants differ in the vigor and style of their responses to frustration and reward (Buss & Plomin, 1984a). Clearly, every individual is unique, different from others. Describing and explaining individual differences is a major goal of the Dispositional Strategy. How does the Dispositional Strategy account for individual differences? The answer is found in the third major assumption of the strategy: Individual differences arise from differences in the strength or pervasiveness of particular dispositions. Most major dispositions are construed as *bipolar* dimensions that are *normally distributed;* that is, people fall everywhere along the continuum from one extreme to the other, and it is in their *specific location* along these (multiple) dimensions that people differ.

The biological approach has demonstrated individual differences in the behaviors of various other species. Theories advanced to account for these (intraspecies) individual differences center around the theory of evolution and natural selection as mechanisms of achieving and maintaining individual differences within species in both appearance and behavioral tendencies.

DISPOSITIONAL PERSONALITY RESEARCH

Dispositional personality research assumes many forms. Of central concern to all is the quest for major dimensions on which people differ. These dimensions are assumed to be enduring, so focus is on personality characteristics that can be assessed over time and demonstrate *intra*individual *stability* as well as *inter*individual *variability* between members of a species; that is, to be important to dispositional psychologists a characteristic must remain relatively stable (character*ize* some people) and yet vary considerably *across* different people to be meaningful. (Without evidence of substantial variation across members of a species, a disposition to behave some particular way tells us little specific to the individual. Understanding of universal, species-specific behavior patterns is in the realm of ethology rather than personality psychology, but we examine the implications of some species-wide behavior patterns in Chapter 9.)

Some researchers seek to identify the origin of these characteristics and so focus on genetic factors or evolutionary processes that might influence human behavior. These issues are examined in Chapter 9. Most dispositional psychologists seek to define and refine what is known about broad and enduring personality characteristics. These researchers focus on traits and dispositions as they emerge over the course of development and impact on behavior.

Identifying Personality Dispositions

Human behavior can be ordered and divided on a nearly infinite number of dimensions. An individual can be known as a happy person, an aggressive person, a person who needs to be loved, a benevolent person, a stingy person, and so on. Which of these dimensions is important? Which dimensions will most likely meet the theoretical assumptions of the Dispositional Strategy?

As Box 7.1 reveals, most people describe themselves and others with a relatively small number of dispositions. However, the total number of traits, types, motives, and needs suggested as human dispositions is vast—perhaps as many as 30,000 by some counts. Therefore, modern dispositional psychologists are actively searching for a set of underlying personality dimensions that "captures" all other essential traitlike characteristics. Much recent debate centers around the required number and best labels for a set of personality dimensions that can adequately accomplish this goal.

The search is akin to early efforts by psychologists interested in visual perception and color vision. These investigators wanted to identify the primary colors from which all other colors could be derived by appropriate combinations and mixtures. It is now common knowledge that just three colors of light—red, green, and blue—can produce any one of the vast array of colors that a normally sighted person can see. Many dispositional psychologists believe that personality can also be cast into a small set of primary, underlying dimensions from which all others can be derived.

A major task of dispositional psychologists is to identify important dimensions, or dispositions, that describe and explain human personality. To do this, some fairly clear indicators, or criteria, must exist that can test whether a given dimension—a prospective psychological disposition—will be useful. One such indicator involves meeting the assumptions of consistency and generality. But consistency and generality are not sufficient. As we saw in the earlier demonstration, the dimension must also clearly distinguish one person from another. If everyone were happy (or aggressive or ambitious), this dimension would be of little use as a psychological disposition; it could not be used to predict or explain any of the *individual differences* in people's behavior.

Dispositional approaches are, in fact, very much psychologies of "amount." Dispositions that do not permit us to say that one person has more or less of some durable characteristic than another person add little to predictive power.

DISPOSITIONAL PERSONALITY ASSESSMENT

The Dispositional Strategy uses almost all the major personality assessment techniques. Interviews as well as projective and situational tests are used to identify various characteristics. However, reporting (as opposed to observing directly) plays a central role in most dispositional assessments. A wide range of "paper-and-pencil" self-report tests are used, as are "reputational" reports in the form of descriptions given by friends, acquaintances, and, sometimes, biographers.

Dispositions are *theoretical constructs.* It is therefore not possible to measure them directly. Instead, dispositional researchers must devise measures of behavior that yield indicators of various underlying dispositions. Most often these measures are self-report inventories or questionnaires. At the same time, it is presumed that there is no one absolute measure of a disposition; in fact, there should be several different indexes. The dispositional psychologist

> explains the behavior of an individual by the *values assigned* to the person on dimensions considered relevant to the behavior in question. These values may be expressed numerically as scores on a test, or they may be represented by labels that stand for different positions on the dimension. A psychologist might, for example, explain an individual's pattern of deference to certain people and hostility to others in terms of authoritarianism, by saying that he is an extremely *authoritarian type* of person. Or the psychologist might predict a person's success as a business executive from his scores on measures of intelligence, aggressiveness, and sociability. The use of these and other dimensions implies that the values obtained on them by individuals have

implications for a fairly wide range of behavior and that these dimensions exist independently of any single method of measurement. Therefore, although a particular test may be the one most frequently used in the measurement of some dimension, it is assumed that there may be other, equally valid measures. Like other theoretical constructs, ***dispositions are inferred;*** their definition rests not on any single set of operations but on the ***convergence of a set of operations*** [italics added]. (Levy, 1970, p. 200)

A related characteristic of dispositional personality assessment is the assumption of additivity. The strength of any disposition is assumed to be the "sum" of various individual response tendencies. Consider Sean, a student who likes to meet strangers, easily approaches teachers to dispute grades on examinations, and is often outspoken in class discussions. Sean would be considered somewhat more extraverted (outgoing) than Marvin, another student who likes to meet strangers and argue about grades but prefers not to take part in class discussions.

A good example of "adding" behaviors to infer a disposition can be seen in the work of Robins (1966), who used a combination of aggressive symptoms in childhood to predict criminal behavior in adulthood. Robins found that summing all the early signs and symptoms suggesting a disposition toward aggressiveness predicted later criminal behavior considerably better than any single aggressive or delinquent behavior during childhood.

Two formal criteria have been adopted for measuring the adequacy of a dispositional assessment procedure: **convergent validity** and **discriminant validity** (Campbell & Fiske, 1959). Measures of presumably the *same* disposition may have quite different forms—such as paper-and-pencil, projective, and situational measures—but they should *converge* and thus *correlate highly* with one another. In contrast, tests designed to measure *different* dispositions should discriminate between them; they should *not* be highly correlated. Thus, a single measure of a personality disposition has convergent validity to the degree that it is found to be positively correlated with other measures of the same disposition; it has discriminant validity to the extent that it is unrelated to measures of other constructs.

Take, for example, the construct "gregarious." One measure of this construct might be a score derived from a gregariousness questionnaire. Other (behavioral) measures of the same construct might be initiating conversations in social settings, approaching strangers to engage in conversation, or preferring group activities over solitary ones. We would expect the person who receives a high gregariousness score from the questionnaire to also be more willing than others to engage in these social behaviors (convergent validity). And if this construct is indeed a distinct and meaningful personality dimension, we would expect it *not* to be strongly associated with other (presumably unrelated) constructs, like conscientiousness or intelligence. Demonstrating the independence of measures of the construct of interest from measures of other distinct constructs contributes to discriminant validity.

A statistical technique called *factor analysis* has proven a very useful tool for dispositional psychologists. It has allowed researchers to determine empirically what behavioral measures do, indeed, "go together," suggesting a common underlying trait or disposition, as well as highlighting divergence among measures of different traits or dispositions. This technique and contributions derived through its use are a major focus of Chapter 8.

Dispositional psychologists readily acknowledge that their tests are imperfect. Every personality test score is assumed to include error, or "noise," as well as true information about the disposition being measured. So these tests probably underestimate the actual stability and generality of the underlying dispositions they tap.

APPLICATIONS OF THE DISPOSITIONAL STRATEGY

For the most part, the underlying assumptions of the Dispositional Strategy (that personality dispositions are inherent and enduring elements of the person) argue against the malleability of personality. Thus, many applications of this strategy focus more on identifying suitable environments—career choices, personnel selection, and program admissions and placements—for the constellation of characteristics displayed by a given individual.

However, the biological approach has produced a number of avenues for change. Psychopharmacology (drug treatment) is ever expanding and can often alleviate difficulties with anxiety, depression, and other psychological disorders that may stem in part from inherited dispositions or tendencies. Genetic engineering offers hope for the future of people afflicted with some inherited diseases, and there is increasing evidence that at least some psychological problems have a genetic basis. The biological approach has also produced a variety of assessment tools now used in research that are finding increasing applicability to problems of everyday life beyond the laboratory.

With the exception of gene therapy (see Box 10.2 in Chapter 10), the applications derived from the Dispositional Strategy aim primarily at symptom relief rather than enduring personality change. Applications derived from this strategy are discussed in Chapter 10.

SUMMARY

1. A disposition is an enduring, relatively stable personality characteristic. We are accustomed to speaking about people in dispositional terms in our daily lives.
2. Dispositional concepts have been around for thousands of years. Dispositional personality psychology endeavors to identify the "ingredients" that make up human personality and to determine how these ingredients combine and interact with one another and the environment.
3. The Dispositional Strategy is plagued by language problems. There are failures to define terms clearly, and the same given term may be used for slightly different ideas by different theorists. This is a serious and continuing problem for the strategy.
4. Dispositional psychologists look for general modes of functioning that tend to be stable or consistent across situations and time and that seem to reflect an inner consistency in the person. Such traits are to be differentiated from states, which are, by their nature, temporary.

5. Some dispositional personality psychologists have turned to biology to explain characteristics shared by all humans, as well as to explain personality differences between one individual and another.
6. Most dispositions are normally distributed, like a bell-shaped curve. Any particular individual can be placed on the particular location they occupy on the curve, such as very high or very low on a particular disposition; because of the way the bell is curved, however, most people will fall in the broad average range on most traits.
7. It is important to keep in mind that a person may be average on one trait and extremely high on another. Thus, personality is patterned by our position on each of the important trait dimensions. In a sense, then, each of us has a personality "profile."
8. Dispositional psychology roughly falls into two groupings of researchers: those who seek to understand human traits through individual differences in the biological and genetic makeup of the person or humans in general and those who use mathematical techniques (particularly factor analysis) to try to identify the number, nature, and structure of personality dispositions.
9. Dispositional assessment uses a wide range of techniques, including direct observation, interviews, and projective techniques. However, paper-and-pencil reports (usually completed on specialized questionnaires) by the person and others constitute the primary source of assessment information.
10. Dispositions are theoretical constructs, not real structures like body organs. For this reason, it is not surprising that differences in opinion among dispositional psychologists still abound.
11. Every disposition is generally assumed to be comprised of more specific response tendencies. These tendencies are presumed to be additive, which means that the strength of a particular disposition in a particular person is the sum of the strength of all their relevant response tendencies.
12. An important research question for dispositional psychologists is to demonstrate the theoretical superiority of the trait structures they propose over those proposed by other theorists.
13. The two major criteria by which the scientific adequacy of a proposed dispositions are measured are convergent and discriminant validity. Measures of a given trait or response tendency should correlate highly with conceptually related traits or tendencies (convergent validity) but show low or zero-order correlations with traits and tendencies to which it is conceptually unrelated (discriminant validity).
14. Inasmuch as the measures used are only indirect reflections of their theoretical constructs (dispositions), any given measure of personality dispositions will have a degree of "noise"; that is, all measures are assumed to be imperfect (relative to, say, the precision of an ordinary ruler when used by an experienced adult).

15. The Dispositional Strategy has been applied to identifying suitable environments for people with particular dispositions. It is also linked to pharmacotherapy (drug treatment) for people who exhibit too much or too little of a disposition to be adaptive for them. For example, a particularly excitable person can be treated with a medication that works at the level of the nervous system to reduce excitability.

CHAPTER EIGHT

Evolution of the Trait Concept

In this chapter, we examine the development of current thinking about *traits.* What these perspectives have in common is that they all consider traits to be real, psychologically meaningful entities. The founder of the modern Dispositional Strategy, Gordon Allport, described this approach as *heuristic realism.* Heuristic [your-IST-tick] has Greek and Latin roots and means "to find out or discover." Allport (1966) meant the term to convey that "the person who confronts us possesses inside his skin generalized action tendencies (or traits) and that it is our job scientifically to discover what they are" (p. 3).

Allport did not believe that traits are physical entities, like glands or organs. He did, however, believe that psychological traits are real attributes of people; they serve to explain behavior rather than merely to describe it. Suppose, for example, a 5-year-old girl and a 25-year-old woman are given a 50-pound barbell to lift. Assuming that both subjects are motivated, it is a safe bet that the woman will succeed but the girl will fail. Most people would say this is because the woman is stronger than the girl. The difference in strength is a real characteristic of the people involved. Therefore, pointing out that the woman is much stronger than the girl explains why she succeeded and the girl failed. In much the same way, trait theorists believe it is legitimate to say that people behave aggressively because they have an aggressive trait.

THE SEARCH FOR IMPORTANT DISPOSITIONS

Hundreds of words can be used to describe human personalities: *aggressive, friendly, warm, pleasant, hostile, eager, bold, intense, irritable, callous, arrogant, serious*—the list goes on and on. Which are the important traits? How do they work together? A fundamental task of the trait approach is to bring some order to the enormous number of possible human traits (Buss & Craik, 1985). Dispositional psychologists have tried to identify the most basic or important traits and types by using three broad approaches: the lexical approach, the theoretical approach, and the statistical approach.

Gordon Allport (1897–1967) is considered the founder of the modern Dispositional Strategy. His philosophy, heuristic realism, is that traits should be considered real characteristics, residing within the person.
Harvard University Archives

The **lexical approach** is based on the assumption that the more important a disposition is, the more often it will be referred to in ordinary language. (*Lexical* derives from *lexicon,* which means "dictionary.") Following this approach, many researchers consider aggressiveness an important disposition. The word *aggressive* and its synonyms are common in everyday language, and used often for describing and comparing people.

As the name suggests, the **theoretical approach** looks to theory to suggest which human dispositions are most central or important. For example, psychoanalytic theory suggests that ego strength is a dimension on which people differ. Similarly, some dispositional theorists propose as traits tendencies that seem to them to have important implications for personality and understanding individual differences.

Finally, there is the **statistical approach,** which analyzes very large collections of data about many people to identify the basic factors that underlie the data set. Factor analysis (discussed later in this chapter) has been a favorite tool of researchers who use the statistical approach.

In this chapter, each of these approaches are discussed as we trace the history of the trait concept. Chapter 9 picks up on many of these themes in an examination of the existing evidence for biologically based contributions to many of these personality dimensions.

ALLPORT'S TRAIT APPROACH

Gordon Allport spent virtually his entire career trying to understand human personality. For more than 35 years, he adhered to the idea of heuristic realism. Allport insisted that the task of finding out "what the other person is really like" should not be abandoned, even though it is difficult.

Traits as the Units for Studying Personality

Allport believed that traits are the basic units of personality. His eight theoretical assertions are as follows:

1. *Traits have more than nominal existence.* They are not just summary labels of observed behavior. Rather, traits are part of the person.
2. *Traits are more generalized than habits.* Brushing one's teeth, Allport noted, may well be a habit, but it is not properly called a trait (although an underlying trait, such as cleanliness, might account for it).
3. *Traits are dynamic and determine behavior.* Traits direct action and are not mere structural artifacts. Unlike the intrapsychic structures posited by Freud, traits do not require energizing from somewhere else.
4. *Traits may be established empirically.* Allport was steeped in the tradition of scientific psychology and unequivocally acknowledged that psychologists must finally defer to their data.
5. *Traits are only relatively independent of other traits.*
6. *Traits are not synonymous with moral or social judgments.*
7. *Traits may be viewed either in the light of the personality that contains them (idiographically) or in the light of their distribution in the population (nomothetically).*
8. *Acts, and even habits, that are inconsistent with a trait are not proof of the nonexistence of the trait.* For example, passive behavior on the part of a person with a trait of assertiveness does not indicate that the person lacks the trait of assertiveness. It simply means that, in this instance, the person's trait is not being expressed.

Allport's eight assertions have been a guiding light for trait psychology ever since (Funder, 1991).

Pervasiveness of Specific Traits

Allport proposed that traits differ in the extent that they pervade any given individual's personality. He called the most pervasive traits cardinal dispositions. A **cardinal disposition** dominates the individual. It cannot stay hidden; it often makes its possessor famous. For example, consider Mother Teresa of Calcutta. Her philanthropic attitude pervaded her entire life, as evidenced by her commitment to improving the living conditions of those around her. She established the Missionaries of Charity organization in 1950, and devoted her life to the service of the sick and needy worldwide. Her efforts were recognized in 1979, when she was awarded the Nobel Peace Prize for her enormous contributions to humanity.

Mother Teresa devoted her life to alleviating the suffering of the sick and poor.
© Camera Press/Archive Photos

Central dispositions are the relatively small number of traits that tend to be highly characteristic of a person. They might be thought of as the characteristics we would mention when writing a detailed letter of recommendation. According to Allport, everyone has a few central dispositions that characterize them; the typical number is between 3 and 10.

Secondary dispositions are characteristics that operate only in limited settings. Preferences for particular kinds of food, specific attitudes, and other peripheral or situationally determined characteristics are included in this category.

Allport described two distinct perspectives from which to view human psychological traits. One view is to think of traits as characteristics that allow comparison of one person with another (much like comparing body weights). The other view is to think of traits as characteristics that are unique to a person and do not invite, or even permit, comparison with other people. In essence, this is the *nomothetic-idiographic* distinction (see Chapter 1).

Common Traits

Trait comparisons across people presume that there are **common traits.** Life situations often compel us to compare people. Business executives must choose among candidates for a particular job, colleges must identify the best applicants for entrance, and you will, during your life, have to choose the "best" person to fill a number of roles relative to yourself (e.g., personal physician, spouse, and attorney). Whenever the job or role is fixed, someone must identify the personality or person who best fits it. Most individuals make rough, approximate comparisons among people daily. The researcher committed to discovering common traits must formalize the criteria for identifying a common trait and also specify the procedures for measuring it.

According to Allport, when scaled for the population at large, common traits often have a normal distribution; that is, scores of a large sample that are plotted on a graph produce a bell-shaped curve. The majority of cases pile up as average scores in the middle; the high and low scores taper off at the more extreme positions. Such a distribution is seen, more or less, in all the "supertraits" we discuss at length later in this chapter (Figure 8.1).

"Patterned Individuality"

Allport acknowledged the merits of comparing personalities along common dimensions (the nomothetic approach), yet he insisted that people can really be understood only by coming to grips with the uniqueness of personality (the idiographic approach). Each person, Allport believed, has a unique inner organization of motives, traits, and personal style. The result is a **patterned individuality** that will never again be repeated exactly.

Some personality psychologists favor a nomothetic approach and seek general principles of behavior. These psychologists often argue that uniqueness merely reflects the combination of common traits in varying strengths. Allport disagreed, claiming that a person's traits always interact to form a unique pattern that cannot be fully explained by its separate parts. As an analogy, he compared a molecule of water with a molecule of hydrogen peroxide. They "have the same universals—hydrogen and oxygen; they differ only quantitatively (H_2O versus H_2O_2), but a small quantitative difference leads to totally unlike products. Try them on your hair and see" (1961, p. 10).

Allport used the term **individual traits** to refer to those important characteristics of the individual that do not lend themselves to comparison across persons. Most of Allport's research focused on common traits and was

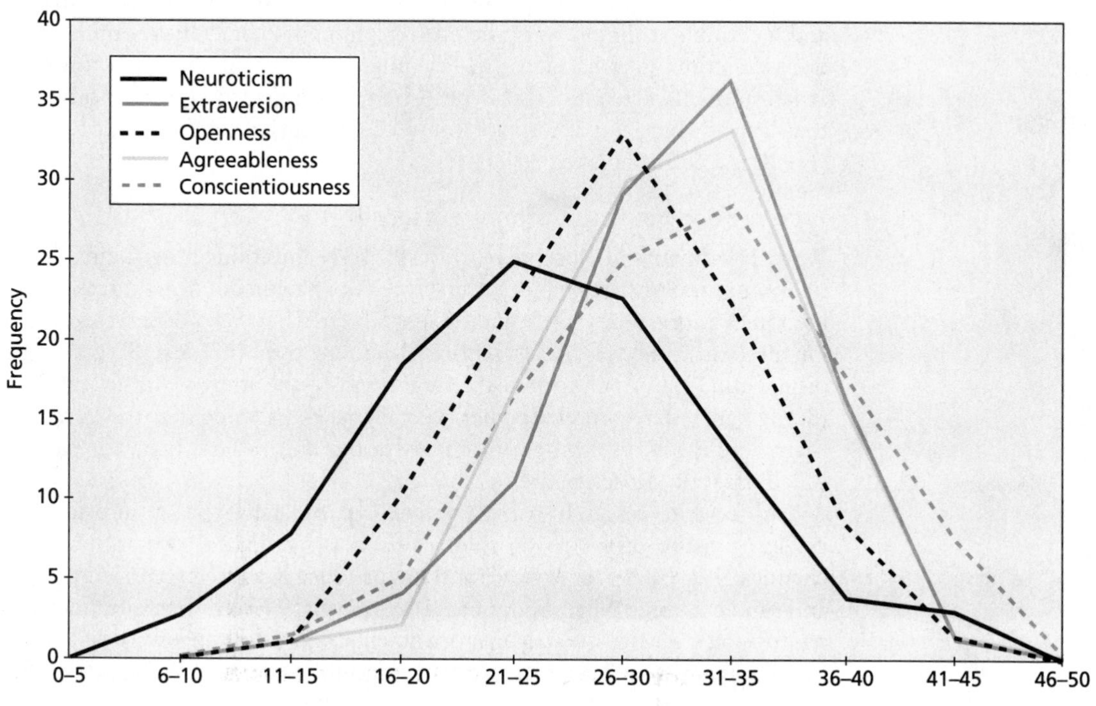

Figure 8.1
Measures of common traits from large samples tend to "pile up" to form a bell-shaped distribution.
Source: Data from "Normal Personality Assessment in Clinical Practice: The NEO Personality Inventory," by P. T. Costa, R. R. McCrae, 1993, *Psychological Assessment, 4,* pp. 5–13.

nomothetic. But he believed that such studies provided only an approximation of what people are really like: All of an individual's behavior and thought is unique to that person. "Even the acts and concepts that we apparently 'share' with others," he wrote, "are at bottom individual. . . . It is true that some acts and concepts are more idiosyncratic than others, but none can be found that lacks the personal flavor" (1961, p. 29).

TWENTIETH-CENTURY TYPOLOGIES

The idea that people can be categorized by a small number of **types** has been popular since ancient times. This idea remains common in 20th-century personality psychology. One typology, discussed in some detail in Chapter 9, originated from the fact that people have noticeably different physiques or body builds. This typology relates physical differences to differences in personality. A second current typology began with the observation that people who have heart attacks seemed to share some behavioral characteristics. This typology has been used to examine differences between people who do and do not display the behavior pattern in an attempt to understand its relationship to health factors.

The Type A Behavior Pattern

Physicians have long noted that the personalities of individuals with heart problems appear to differ from those without such problems. In the late 1950s, the contribution of psychological and behavioral variables to the development of coronary problems began to be examined systematically.

At that time, two cardiologists, Meyer Friedman and Ray Rosenman, sent a questionnaire to 150 businesspeople in San Francisco. The questionnaire asked for information about the behavior of friends who had had heart attacks. More than 70% of the respondents said "excessive competitive drive and meeting deadlines" were the most prominent characteristics of the heart disease victims they had known. Friedman and Rosenman called this combination of characteristics the **Type A behavior pattern.** They hypothesized that Type A behavior is a major cause of coronary artery and heart disease (Friedman & Rosenman, 1974).

Type A Behavior and Coronary Disease

Next, Friedman and Rosenman undertook an ambitious longitudinal investigation of the relationship between Type A behavior and heart disease. They identified more than 3500 middle-aged men who had no heart problems initially and obtained health reports for them over the next 8 years. Men displaying Type A behavior at the beginning of the study were several times more likely to have developed heart problems by the time the study was over than were those displaying a more easygoing and relaxed behavior pattern, called **Type B** (Rosenman et al., 1975).

Subsequent research painted a picture of the Type A individual as constitutionally prone to biochemical and physiological overarousal. Biochemically, Type A people were found to produce increased serum cholesterol and catecholamine when under pressure (Glass, 1977). Either substance may contribute, over time, to coronary problems. Type A people were also found to differ from Type B people in certain glandular and metabolic responses that may result in increased risk of coronary difficulties (Williams, Friedman, Glass, Herd, & Schneiderman, 1978).

Physiologically, Type A people appeared to display more arousal (e.g., increased blood pressure) when working on challenging tasks than Type B people (Holmes, McGilley, & Houston, 1984; Houston, 1983). Finally, considerable evidence suggests that Type A people tend to ignore signs of physical distress when working intensely on tasks (Burke, 1988; Matthews & Carra, 1982; Weidner & Matthews, 1978). They may ignore physical warnings from their bodies and literally drive themselves to heart attacks.

Once an individual has had a heart attack, the presence of Type A behavior is the best single predictor of having another. However, before a heart attack occurs, Type A individuals are notorious for denying their behavior patterns (Smith & Anderson, 1986; Wright, 1988).

Refining the Type A Construct: The Two Types of Type A

Initially, individuals who might be called Type A appeared to be a distinct but uniform group. One team of investigators painted the picture of a "tense, driven business executive who struggles for long hours at his desk, tapping his fingers and pencil, gulping down his lunch, and talking rapidly into two telephones at once while grimacing hostilely at his dallying assistant" (Friedman, Hall, & Harris, 1985, p. 1299). Another investigator described Type A people as having "hurry sickness" (Matthews, 1982). But research in the next decade was to show that Type A people are a considerably more diverse lot than was initially assumed (Gray & Jackson, 1990).

Friedman, Hall, and Harris (1985) were among the first to suggest that the so-called Type A personality might encompass more than one type. They pointed out that not all highly vigorous individuals are impatient, hostile, and tense, and not all slow-paced individuals are calm, content, and relaxed. A subsequent study compared various groups of middle-aged men (Friedman &

These people are exhibiting one of the key characteristics of the Type A behavior pattern: a sense of time urgency that includes doing a number of tasks simultaneously. PhotoDisc Inc.

Booth-Kewley, 1987). The results indicated that the men with the poorest emotional adjustment were most likely to have had heart attacks.

Another team of researchers analyzed college students' responses to a questionnaire measure of the Type A behavior pattern and found two relatively independent factors, which they labeled *Achievement Strivings* and *Impatience-Irritability.* Scores on the Achievement Strivings scale were related to students' grade point averages but not to their physical complaints (as measured by a health survey); by contrast, scores on the Impatience-Irritability measure were related to physical complaints but *not* to grades. These and other results suggest that a tendency toward irritability and impatience is the active ingredient in the Type A pattern that leads to health risks (Spence, Helmreich, & Pred, 1987; Helmreich, Spence, & Pred, 1988).

What, then, is the central characteristic of individuals who are at higher risk for heart attacks and other health problems? Some investigators have called it "quality of adjustment"; others have called it "impatience-irritability." But recent research suggests that the characteristic most common to the illness-prone Type A people is that they are plagued by *cynical hostility* (Smith & Frohm, 1985).

The hostility these people experience appears to be more strongly related to health outcomes than any other characteristic of their personalities or behavior patterns (Miller, Smith, Turner, & Guijarro, 1996). Yet, many people experience hostility and apparently are *not* at increased risk of coronary artery or heart disease. What makes the hostility of these type A people different? Some have speculated that this particular brand of hostility, characterized by anger, resentment, bitterness, distrust, and suspiciousness, produces problematic interpersonal relationships. These relationships may, in turn, produce more suspiciousness and resentment, further perpetuating the interpersonal problems (Smith & Frohm, 1985; Williams, Barefoot, & Shekelle, 1985). Williams and colleagues further contend that cynically hostile people, now amid deteriorating interpersonal relationships and because of their generally suspicious nature, must maintain a constant state of intense vigilance to guard against further assaults and insults from others. They suggest the possibility of a biologically mediated mechanism (via increased levels of testosterone and norepinephrine; see Chapter 9) related to this state of heightened arousal that may link cynical hostility to the development of coronary artery disease and heart attack. To date, this remains only a working hypothesis. We consider these issues and their possible assessment and treatment implications further in Chapter 10.

Type A Behavior in Children and Adolescents

Health psychologist Karen Matthews developed the Matthews Youth Test for Health, the MYTH, as a way to assess Type A behaviors in children. The MYTH, a rating scale used by teachers, consists of 17 statements describing children's behaviors (e.g., "gets irritated easily," "does things in a hurry"). Teachers rate the target child for each of the statements on a 5-point scale from extremely characteristic to extremely uncharacteristic. Using the MYTH to identify Type A children, Matthews and her associates found that, independent of ability (IQ scores), Type A children show more early accomplishments than Type B children (Matthews, Stoney, Rakaczky, & Jamison, 1986).

Most significant, research with children from preschool through adolescence then showed, as in adults, Type A children come in two subtypes: those who are competitive and achievement-oriented in a prosocial way and those who are aggressive, hostile, and impatient (Blaney, 1990; Keltikangas-Jarvinen, 1990; Lundberg, Westermark, & Rasch, 1990).

CATTELL'S TRAIT APPROACH

Raymond Cattell introduced the use of factor analysis in the study of personality.
Courtesy of University of Illinois at Urbana-Champagne

Raymond Cattell (1965; 1979; Cattell & Kline, 1977) proposed that three broad sources of data are required for any analysis that aims to uncover all the major dimensions of personality. He labeled the three sources of personality data L-data, Q-data, and T-data. **L-data** are gathered from a person's life records (e.g., school records and work history). **Q-data** are gathered from questionnaires and interviews; the common feature is that people answer direct questions about themselves, based on personal observations and introspection (e.g., "Do you have trouble making and keeping friends?"). **T-data** are obtained from objective testing situations: "The subject is placed in a miniature situation and simply acts [and] does not know on what aspect of his behavior he is really being evaluated" (Cattell, 1965, p. 104).

According to Cattell, the three sources of data must be integrated to capture the full complexity of human personality. Traditionally, psychologists have looked at only one slice at a time. Their research has been *univariate;*—that is, the researchers change one (independent) variable and examine its effects on one other (dependent) variable. In contrast, *multivariate* approaches, which examine many variables simultaneously, have the advantage that "with sufficient analytical subtlety we can tease out the connections from the behavior of the man in his actual life situation—without the false situation of controlling and manipulating" (Cattell, 1965, p. 20).

Factor Analysis as a Tool

Cattell is famous for having quipped that "the trouble with measuring traits is that there are too many of them!" (1965, p. 55). To solve this problem, Cattell introduced the use of **factor analysis,** a statistical tool that takes a highly sophisticated mathematical approach to personality assessment. His intent was to use questionnaire and rating data to discover empirically the natural personality structures that exist in people. Cattell (1965) explained the rationale behind factor analysis using the following analogy:

> The problem which baffled psychologists for many years was to find a method which would tease out these functionally unitary influences in the chaotic jungle of human behavior. But let us ask how, in the literal tropical jungle, the hunter decides whether the dark blobs which he sees are two or three rotting logs or a single alligator? He watches for movement. *If they move together*—come and disappear together—*he infers a single structure* [italics added]. (p. 56)

In the "jungle" of human behavior, however, perfect covariation is rare. Psychological variables do not always "go together." One may get a fleeting glimpse of some strong covariations but never the consistent data generated by Cattell's alligator. How can personality psychologists deal with this situation? Part of the answer lies in the *correlation coefficient* (see Chapter 2), which allows the evaluation of degrees of linear relationship that are less than perfect. The other part of the solution offered by Cattell is factor analysis, which allows analysis of vast numbers of correlation coefficients in search of common elements.

Basically, factor analysis mathematically reduces a large number of relationships (correlations) to a smaller, more manageable, and comprehensible set of relationships. The smaller group is essentially a summary of the entire array of intercorrelations.

Factor analysis was first developed in 1904 by Charles Spearman, a British statistician. (Cattell himself worked under Spearman at the University of London.) Its popularity today results from the availability of high-speed computers; without them, much of the current work using this technique would be virtually impossible.

A Hypothetical Example of a Factor Analysis

Suppose that an investigator wants to analyze college students' patterns of academic performance to discover what underlying skills are involved. Factor analysis could be used in such research. If it were, the investigation would proceed through the five steps summarized in Figure 8.2: collecting data, producing a correlation matrix (i.e., determining the relationship of each variable to every other variable), extracting factors, determining factor loadings, and naming the factors.

Collecting Data

The first step in factor analysis is data collection. In our example, let us say the investigator gathered a large number of students (subjects) and gave them seven different personality tests (measures).

Producing a Correlation Matrix

The next step involves producing a **correlation matrix,** which is a table that shows the exact relationship between each measure and every other measure. Consider the correlation matrix in Table 8.1, which contains the correlations of each of the seven measures with every other measure. This matrix shows a high positive relationship between *a* and *b* (+.70), *a* and *c* (+.80), *a* and *d* (+.80), *b* and *c* (+.90), *b* and *d* (+.70), *c* and *d* (+.80), *e* and *f* (+.80), *e* and

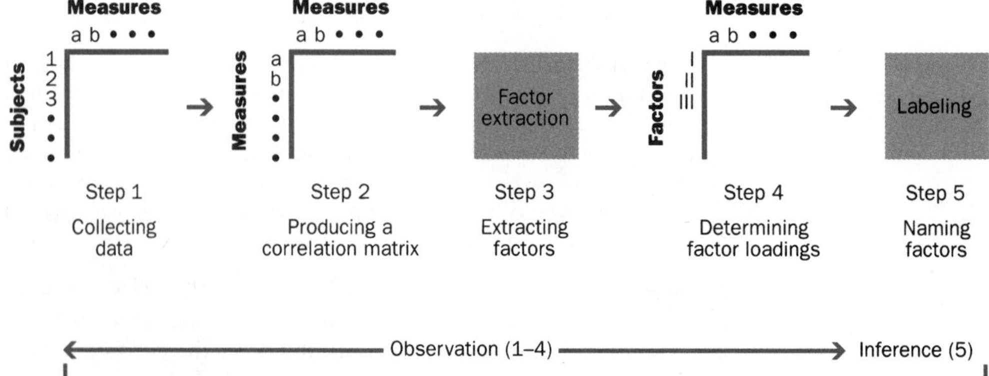

Figure 8.2
The five steps involved in factor analysis. The purpose of the procedure is to reduce the information available about a large number of measures (variables) to manageable size and to interpret the pattern that emerges.

Table 8.1 **Hypothetical correlation matrix**

MEASURE	a	b	c	d	e	f	g
a	+1.00	+.70	+.80	+.80	–.10	.00	.00
b		+1.00	+.90	+.70	+.10	+.10	.00
c			+1.00	+.80	–.10	–.10	–.10
d				+1.00	.00	–.10	.00
e					+1.00	+.80	+.70
f						+1.00	+.70
g							+1.00

g (+.70), and *f* and *g* (+.70). There is virtually no systematic relationship (i.e., correlation coefficients are in the vicinity of zero) between *a* and *e* (.10), *a* and *f* (.00), *a* and *g* (.00), *b* and *e* (+.10), *b* and *f* (+.10), *b* and *g* (.00), *c* and *e* (+.10), *c* and *f* (+.10), *c* and *g* (+.10), *d* and *e* (.00), *d* and *f* (+.10), and *d* and *g* (.00).

Extracting Factors

Our example yielded a correlation matrix from a relatively small number of measures. However, it is not uncommon for 100 or more variables to be correlated in actual factor-analytic studies. Still, the complexities and sheer time needed to summarize and interpret the data should be apparent from the rather laborious enumeration of the results just presented. A major function of factor analysis is to reduce large sets of data to manageable units. By means of complex mathematical formulas, the data are reduced to small numbers of relatively homogeneous dimensions, called **factors.** The factors are said to be *extracted* from the data. (The entire process is, in fact, quite complex and requires the researcher to make a number of subjective decisions along the way. For our purposes you need only know that the mathematics alone does not produce the factors, but rather the mathematics combined with a number of relatively subjective decisions made throughout the process.)

Determining Factor Loadings

Factors extracted in the previous step are the "common denominators" of all relationships between the variables. The factors are like the three primary colors from which all other colors are produced. The next step is determining the relationship between each of the individual measures and each of the factors. (This is akin to deciding if a specific color—for example, aqua—is more closely related to the blue "factor" or the green "factor" in the color spectrum.) The correlation of a measure with a particular factor is its **factor loading.** Thus, a variable is said to "load" onto a particular factor to the extent that it is correlated with that factor.

Naming the Factors

Factor naming is the last step in a factor analysis. It is the point at which inference and subjective judgment most conspicuously enter the process.

Let us return to the correlation matrix in Table 8.1. Suppose that the measures were aptitude tests in academic areas, where *a* = English, *b* = fine arts, *c* = history, *d* = French, *e* = mathematics, *f* = physics, and *g* = engineering. The factor analysis reveals a distinct pattern among these seven measures (*a* through *g*). Specifically, *a, b, c,* and *d* seem to "go together." They are highly correlated with one another but show little or no relationship (i.e., near 0) to the other three measures.

Similarly, *e, f,* and *g* are highly related to one another but not to the other measures. Thus, two units or *factors* emerge from the seven measures. One factor consists of English, fine arts, history, and French; the other factor consists of mathematics, physics, and engineering. These factors might simply be labeled *X* and *Y*. We could also inspect the related measures for common qualities and give the two factors more "meaningful" names. However, the naming itself would be a subjective judgment; it is not a logical consequence of the mathematical process of factor analysis (Tracy, 1990).

Some people might insist that factor *X* represents a "humanities" aptitude and factor *Y* a "quantitative" aptitude; others might say that factor *Y* involves understanding inanimate forces, whereas factor *X* involves understanding people and their products. Still others might label these factors art and nature, emotions and logic, and so on. Overall, "there is nothing in the factor-analytic methods themselves that can demonstrate that one factor solution is more scientifically useful than another," and "the correctness of interpretations based on factor-analytic results must be confirmed by evidence outside the factor analysis itself" (Comrey, 1973, p. 11).

A number of dispositional psychologists rely on factor analysis in their research, but they actively fashion the details of their technique by selecting certain measures and by making various technical decisions along the way. We will discuss three of the more prominent factor analytic research programs, those of Cattell, Eysenck, and McCrae and Costa.

Cattell's 16-Factor Model

In *The Scientific Analysis of Personality*, Cattell (1965) reported that he had scientifically derived 16 personality traits by using factor-analytic and related procedures. He believed that these factors represented the major dimensions of differences in human personality. The 16 traits are listed in Table 8.2.

Three Source Traits Derived from Factor Analysis

Cattell called his 16 personality traits **source traits**—the building blocks of personality. He maintained that source traits can be discovered only through factor analysis. We will take a closer look at Cattell's three most important factors, *A, B,* and *C*.

Consider factor *A*. If it is a source trait, we would expect the same pattern of results to emerge from L-data and Q-data; that is, if the trait is really an underlying dimension of personality, it should be reflected in all measures of personality. Sample L-data and Q-data that load high on factor *A* are shown in Table 8.3. Considering these Q-data, and referring back to the L-data, Cattell (1965) concluded: "The warm sociability at one pole, and the aloofness and unconcern with people at the other are as evident here as in the observers' ratings" (p. 71). (Factor *A* appears similar to a dimension called Introversion-Extraversion, described in detail later.)

Table 8.2 The 16 major factors in Cattell's analysis of personality

LOW-SCORE DESCRIPTION	FACTOR		FACTOR	HIGH-SCORE DESCRIPTION
Reserved	*A–*	vs.	*A+*	Outgoing
Less intelligent	*B–*	vs.	*B+*	More intelligent
Emotional	*C–*	vs.	*C+*	Stable
Humble	*E–*	vs.	*E+*	Assertive
Sober	*F–*	vs.	*F+*	Happy-go-lucky
Expedient	*G–*	vs.	*G+*	Conscientious
Shy	*H–*	vs.	*H+*	Venturesome
Tough-minded	*I–*	vs.	*I+*	Tender-minded
Trusting	*L–*	vs.	*L+*	Suspicious
Practical	*M–*	vs.	*M+*	Imaginative
Forthright	*N–*	vs.	*N+*	Shrewd
Placid	*O–*	vs.	*O+*	Apprehensive
Conservative	Q_1-	vs.	Q_1+	Experimenting
Group-tied	Q_2-	vs.	Q_2+	Self-sufficient
Casual	Q_3-	vs.	Q_3+	Controlled
Relaxed	Q_4-	vs.	Q_4+	Tense

Source: The Scientific Analysis of Personality by R. B. Cattell, 1965, Baltimore: Penguin.

Table 8.3 L-data and Q-data for factor A

Behavior Ratings (L-Data) that Load on Factor A

A+ (Positively Loaded)		*A– (Negatively Loaded)*
Good natured, easygoing	vs.	Critical, grasping
Cooperative	vs.	Obstructive
Attentive to people	vs.	Cool, aloof
Softhearted	vs.	Hard, precise
Trustful	vs.	Suspicious
Adaptable	vs.	Rigid

Factor *A* in Questionnaire Responses (Q-Data)

I would rather work as:
(a) An engineer — (b) ***A social science teacher***

I could stand being a hermit.
(a) True — (b) ***False***

I am careful to turn up when someone expects me.
(a) ***True*** — (b) False

I would prefer to marry someone who:
(a) Is a thoughtful companion — (b) ***Is effective in a social group***

I would prefer to read a book on:
(a) ***National social service*** — (b) New scientific weapons

I trust strangers:
(a) Sometimes — (b) ***Practically always***

Note: A person who selects all the bold italic answers has a highly outgoing personality.
Source: The Scientific Analysis of Personality by R. B. Cattell, 1965, Baltimore: Penguin.

Table 8.4 L-data and Q-data for factor C

Behavior Ratings (L-Data) that Load on Factor C

C+ (Positively Loaded)		*C– (Negatively Loaded)*
Mature	vs.	Unable to tolerate frustration
Steady, persistent	vs.	Changeable
Emotionally calm	vs.	Impulsively emotional
Realistic about problems	vs.	Evasive, avoids necessary decisions
Absence of neurotic fatigue	vs.	Neurotically fatigued (with no real effort)

Factor C in Questionnaire Responses (Q-Data)

Do you find it difficult to take no for an answer even when what you want to do is obviously impossible?
(a) Yes (b) ***No***

If you had your life to live over again, would you:
(a) ***Want it to be essentially the same?*** (b) Plan it very differently?

Do you often have really disturbing dreams?
(a) Yes (b) ***No***

Do your moods sometimes make you seem unreasonable even to yourself?
(a) Yes (b) ***No***

Do you feel tired when you've done nothing to justify it?
(a) ***Rarely*** (b) Often

Can you change old habits, without relapse, when you decide to?
(a) ***Yes*** (b) No

Note: A person who selects all the bold italic answers has high ego strength, whereas selection of all the nonitalicized responses indicates low ego strength.
Source: The Scientific Analysis of Personality by R. B. Cattell, 1965, Baltimore: Penguin.

Using both L-data and Q-data, Cattell concluded that the second largest source trait, factor *B*, "looks like nothing less than general intelligence, and correlates well with actual test results" (1965, p. 72). Cattell labeled the third largest source trait, factor *C*, as *Ego Strength*. The L-data and Q-data in Table 8.4 illustrate the nature of this source trait. Cattell noted the following about factor *C:*

> The essence of factor C appears to be an inability to control one's emotions and impulses, especially by finding for them some satisfactory realistic expression. Looked at from the opposite or positive pole, it sharpens and gives scientific substance to the psychoanalytic concept of "ego strength," which it [factor *C*] has come to be called. (1965, pp. 73–74)

HIERARCHICAL ORGANIZATION AND DEVELOPMENT OF TRAITS

The broad consensus among trait researchers today is that personality traits are hierarchically organized, with broad trait dimensions or ***domains*** at the top, subsuming narrower but more specific traits (Goldberg, 1993) that lie below them in the hierarchy. The practical point is that "the domain level yields a rapid understanding of the individual; interpretation of specific facet scales gives a more detailed assessment" (Costa & McCrae, 1995b, p. 21); that is, there is growing consensus that broad and narrow personality dimensions provide complementary information and that neither is logically more meaningful than the other in isolation (Briggs, 1989; Mathsall et al., 1994). Interestingly, this outlook is consistent with a long tradition of identifying different levels of specificity in personality trait assessment, going back at least to Allport (cf. Goldberg, 1993).

EYSENCK'S P-E-N MODEL

Almost from its original publication, Cattell's model was criticized for having too many traits and for lacking the kind of hierarchical structure we have just introduced (Matthews, 1989). Hans J. Eysenck focused on a considerably smaller number of basic **personality types.** In Eysenck's scheme, types are not categories that a few people fit; rather, types are dimensions on which all persons differ. Types, like traits, tend to be normally distributed; that is, they are continuous dimensions, and most people fall around the middle of the distribution range.

Eysenck's model of personality *is* hierarchical. Types are at the top of the personality structure and, therefore, exert the most commanding influence. Types are composed of traits; traits are composed of habitual responses. At the most specific level, specific responses are the elements from which individuals form habits. This overall view is shown in Figure 8.3.

Using factor analysis, Eysenck and his colleagues performed dozens of studies over more than 50 years. As far back as World War II, Eysenck applied factor analysis to ratings and classifications of approximately 10,000 soldiers. He concluded from all this research that personality can be understood in terms of three basic personality factors: Psychoticism, Extraversion, and Neuroticism. He also acknowledged the importance of the response style factor Social Desirability, which he construed as a validity or *Lie Scale* in his own personality inventory (see Chapter 2).

When measured by Eysenck's inventory, the Eysenck Personality Questionnaire (or EPQ), these same factors appear from data gathered in many different settings and cultures. He therefore contended that they represent universal dimensions of personality (Eysenck & Eysenck, 1985; S. B. G. Eysenck & Haapasalo, 1989; S. B. G. Eysenck & Long, 1986; S. B. G. Eysenck & Tambs, 1990). For example, a recent study using the Dutch version of the EPQ showed that personality structure was quite stable over a 6-year period (Sanderman & Ranchor, 1994). Moreover, the junior version of the EPQ (EPQ-R junior, for school-age children) revealed the same factor structure as found on the adult EPQ and on the EPQ-R in other countries (De Bruyn, Delsing, & Welten, 1995).

Hans J. Eysenck (1916–1997) identified three major factors in personality: Psychoticism, Extraversion, and Neuroticism. Courtesy of H. J. Eysenck/ Photo by Mark Gerson

Extraversion and Neuroticism, as measured by the EPQ and EPQ-R, have received much attention from Eysenck and other investigators (Stelmack, 1991). These factors each represent a continuous, normally distributed range between polar opposites. (Recall Figure 8.1.) In essence, each person can be positioned somewhere along the line between extreme introvert and extreme extravert and between perfect emotional stability and complete emotional chaos. Moreover, most people will be somewhere near the middle. Eysenck repeatedly cautioned that "extremes in either direction are rare, and that most people are somewhere intermediate" (1975, p. 190).

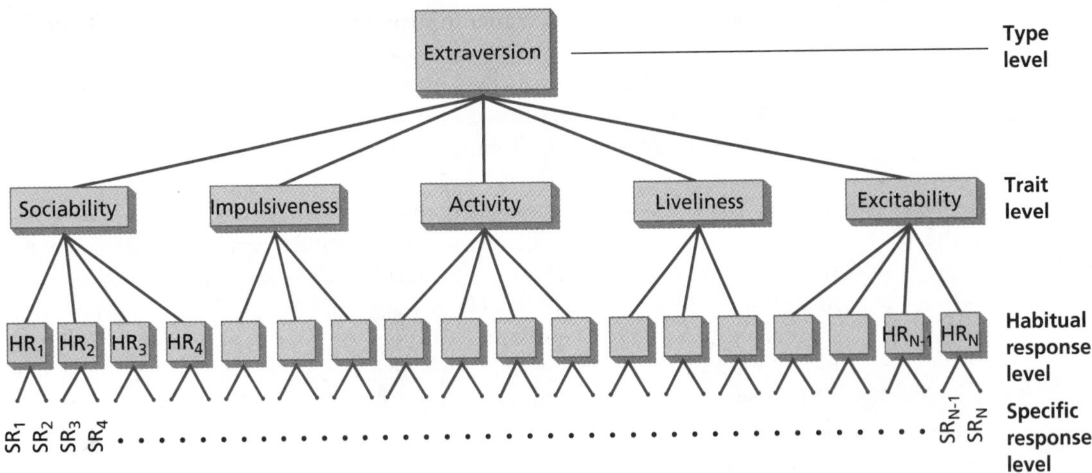

Figure 8.3
Eysenck's hierarchical model of personality.
Source: Adapted from *The Biological Basis of Personality* by H. J. Eysenck, 1967, Springfield, IL: Charles C Thomas.

Eysenck's third underlying aspect of personality is Psychoticism, which is somewhat more controversial. Psychoticism parallels to some extent the psychoses of abnormal psychology, but Eysenck viewed this factor as another broad dimension on which "normal" personality varied. Let's begin by taking a closer look at this construct and recent research findings related to it.

Psychoticism

Psychoticism (P) includes a disposition toward psychosis (a mental disorder characterized by poor contact with reality and inability to effectively perform routine tasks or activities of daily living) and a degree of sociopathy (characterized by an absence of real loyalties to any person, group, or ethical or moral code). Those high on Psychoticism also tend to be quite impulsive (Roger & Morris, 1991). As a general characterization, Psychoticism has been called the opposite of Freudian "superego strength" (McKenzie, 1988).

According to Eysenck, people who score high on Psychoticism are characterized by 11 dispositions. They are typically:

1. Solitary, they tend not to care about others
2. Troublesome, they do not "fit in"
3. Cruel, inhumane
4. Insensitive, lacking empathy or genuine feeling
5. Sensation seeking, underaroused
6. Hostile toward others, aggressive
7. Eccentric, favoring odd, unusual things
8. Foolhardy, disregarding danger
9. Socially rude, enjoy embarrassing or upsetting others
10. Opposed to accepted social customs
11. Avoidant of close personal interaction, preferring "impersonal" sex (1975, p. 197)

Psychoticism is typically higher in men overall than in women, apparently heritable, higher in prisoners than in nonprisoners (and highest in individuals imprisoned for sexual or aggressive offenses), and lower in psychiatric patients who improve with treatment than in those who fail to improve. The higher people are in Psychoticism, the more negative are their attitudes and behavior toward authority (Rigby & Slee, 1987). A recent study using the EPQ among English university students revealed that Psychoticism was associated with poor seminar behavior and academic performance (Furnham & Medhurst, 1995).

In an interesting study, Weaver, Walker, McCord, and Bellamy (1996) gave more than 600 males and females the EPQ and a measure of the way they used TV remote control devices. People high in Psychoticism perceived these devices largely in terms of their *ability to control others;* that is, they apparently used remotes in an offensive, often provocative manner, as a tool to override the will of the other people present. (In contrast, persons high in Neuroticism viewed the remote control as a device that assisted them in *avoiding content to which they did not wish to be exposed.* They apparently used the remotes defensively, to protect themselves against intrusion by noxious stimuli.)

Psychoticism has also been found to correlate (among 18- to 35-year-old men) with engaging in high-risk sexual practices, including intercourse with known intravenous drug users, unprotected anal intercourse, sexual contact with bisexual and promiscuous partners, and indiscriminant sex with multiple partners (Fontaine, 1994).

There is a negative relationship between holding any religious beliefs and Psychoticism (White, Joseph, & Neil, 1993). There are also negative relationships between Psychoticism and both frequency of church attendance and frequency of personal prayer (Lewis & Maltby, 1995; Maltby, 1995).

Psychoticism has also been implicated in illicit drug abuse. First, in a study done in Iceland among drug-dependent and non–drug-dependent prisoners, those with drug dependence showed higher scores on the EPQ Psychoticism scale (Sigurdson & Gudjonsson, 1995). Second, a study done in Saudi Arabia compared drug addicts who were either voluntary or involuntary patients and found that the latter were higher on Psychoticism (Abu & Hashem, 1995).

Thus, Psychoticism is beginning to be explored empirically, and high scores on Psychoticism are apparently related to a number of deviant behaviors and psychological disorders. This relationship is hardly surprising, given that Psychoticism as assessed by the EPQ shares some "symptoms" with psychosis and sociopathy as defined clinically.

Extraversion

Carl Jung (a contemporary of Freud) was the first to offer a description of the Introversion-Extraversion dimension of personality. He believed that **extraverts** focus their psychic energy *outward,* toward the world beyond themselves. In contrast, **introverts** focus their attention and energy *inward,* toward the self and internal private events in the forms of thoughts, feelings, emotions, and fantasy.

The domain described by Eysenck as Extraversion (E) also characterizes people based on their orientation toward external sources of stimulation from the environment (social and physical) versus an orientation inward at the opposite extreme (Introversion). He described the extravert as lively, sociable, outgoing, optimistic, and impulsive. In short, the extravert is an exciting, friendly, and easygoing character, a person who is great fun at parties. The introvert, by contrast, is sober, reserved, passive, thoughtful, and controlled. The introvert is less sociable and quieter. At a large party or gathering, the introvert will likely find a corner to occupy, remaining quiet and inconspicuous.

This distinction has withstood the test of time and continues to stimulate a good deal of interest among personality psychologists today. Modern personality psychologists characterize the dimension in slightly different ways than did Jung, but there is consensus for the most part that extraverts are outward oriented and active, especially in the social domain. We will have more to say about this dimension later, as it is generally accepted as a major personality dimension in most contemporary theories.

Neuroticism

The personality dimension labeled **Neuroticism** (N) in Eysenck's scheme is basically a measure of emotional stability-instability, with high Neuroticism characterized by greater *in*stability. Eysenck described the neurotic pole as characterized by anxiety, moodiness, restlessness, irritability, and aggressiveness. The emotionally stable (low) end is marked by calm, even-temperedness, reliability, and emotional control.

Like Extraversion, Neuroticism has come to be widely accepted as one of the major personality domains of contemporary theorists. It, too, is a topic to which we will return repeatedly throughout the remainder of this strategy. For now, we turn our attention to the other major competing theory of today, the Five-Factor Model (FFM) of personality structure.

PERSONALITY FACTORS OF ADULTS: COSTA AND McCRAE'S FIVE-FACTOR MODEL

More than 30 years ago, psychologist Warren Norman factor-analyzed a large number of adult peer nomination personality ratings. Norman (1963) then extracted five primary factors: Surgency (an exotic term for Extraversion), Agreeableness, Conscientiousness, Emotional Stability (which parallels Eysenck's Neuroticism, low pole), and Culture. Later researchers have repeatedly confirmed that a five-factor model adequately accounts for the domain level of dispositional terms adults use to rate the personalities of others (Digman & Inouye, 1986; Goldberg, 1990; McCrae & Costa, 1987; Noller, Law, & Comrey, 1987).

Paul Costa
Courtesy of Paul Costa

The most significant departure in factor naming of the now popular five-factor model of McCrae and Costa from Norman's earlier five-factor scheme concerns the dimension Norman called *Culture*. McCrae and Costa noted that this factor has only small factor loadings with items referring to being intelligent or cultured, but loads heavily on ratings of originality, creativity, independence, and daring. They therefore labeled this factor **Openness** (O). Although the names are not identical, essentially the same five factors seem to emerge in study after study. (Remember that, in factor analysis, naming of factors is always a subjective process.)

Robert McCrae and Paul Costa expanded the significance of the five-factor model (FFM) for dispositional personality psychology by demonstrating that the same five-factor structure also applies to questionnaires, self-ratings, and observer reports of personality. The fact that the same set of five factors

Robert McCrae
Courtesy of Robert McCrae
McCrae and Costa expanded the five-factor model of personality by showing that it applies across different methods of assessment.

emerges from all these different sources of data provides strong support for the claim that they are the important, underlying dimensions by which individual differences in adult personality can be understood (McCrae & Costa, 1985, 1987). The "big five" have been shown to appear not only in adults but also in children and adolescents, ages 7 to 17 (Digman, 1989). Paunonen and Jackson (1996) analyzed the structure underlying Jackson's own personality inventory (JPI; Jackson, 1976, 1994) and found that it could be understood in terms of the five factors of the FFM.

Recently, McCrae (1996) has written that

> the FFM holds that the common variance among almost all personality trait constructs can be summarized in terms of the five recurrent factors of Neuroticism, Extraversion, Openness to Experience [also called Experiential Openness or, simply, Openness], Agreeableness, and Conscientiousness. . . . The FFM thus offers a powerful conceptual tool for distinguishing between nominally similar constructs and recognizing the similarities among apparently different constructs. (p. 323)

Box 8.1
AVOIDANCE OF EVALUATIVE TERMS IN PERSONALITY INVENTORIES

The items on most personality inventories are self-descriptors. They are questions phrased in such a way that the subject is asked to express how characteristic the descriptor is of them. Subjects respond by stating the degree to which they agree or disagree with each descriptor item.

McCrae and Costa (1995) point out that two different classes of items are possible. One class of items deals with **substantive** descriptions, which could be verified by others in a variety of ways. The other class of items are **evaluative;** they are matters of *approval* and *disapproval.* They involve *value judgments.* As an example, "I am 22 years old" is substantive; "I am youthful" is evaluative.

Personality test items have usually been written to avoid evaluative descriptors. Words of high regard *(great, fabulous, terrific)* or contempt *(sleazy, evil, stupid)* are carefully avoided. But Tellegen (1993) and Benet and Waller (1995) have argued that such evaluative descriptors *should* be included and claim they fall into two general classes: *Positive Valence* (PV) and *Negative Valence* (NV) items.

They assembled a new personality test, purposely including evaluative items as well as nonevaluative, substantive items more typical of existing personality inventories. Factor analysis of this test yielded *seven* factors, encompassing the "big five" and two new factors, called Positive Valence and Negative Valence. The new measure is called the *Inventory of Personality Characteristics 7* (IPC7) and contains 161 items. Tellegen and Waller (1987) believe that PV and NV are "authentic dimensions of personality and appraisal that fall outside of the five factor model" and argue for the replacement of the "big five" by the "big seven."

McCrae and Costa (1995) provided an extensive reply to this suggestion. First, they acknowledge that the domain of "self-evaluation" or "self-esteem" is an important dimension of personality. Second, though, they argue that the relevant information is already captured

Box continued on following page

Box 8.1 *Continued*

AVOIDANCE OF EVALUATIVE TERMS IN PERSONALITY INVENTORIES

in the FFM, as a configural pattern of the big five.

They note that some of the NV items on the IPC7 are *mental* (mentally disturbed, sick, reflecting psychological disturbance or disorder), whereas other items are *moral* (bullying, deceitful, unjust). The mental items tend to be associated with Neuroticism, whereas the moral items are encompassed by the negative pole of Agreeableness—that is, *antagonism*. McCrae and Costa also note that PV items load heavily on Openness and Extraversion; NV is related positively to Neuroticism and negatively to Extraversion, Agreeableness, and Conscientiousness. A somewhat different pattern emerges when we look at descriptions by self and others:

> Individuals who score high on PV are described by themselves *and* by observers who know them well as being Assertive, Open to Ideas, and especially low in Modesty; those who score high on NV are described as being high in Anxiety, Angry Hostility, Depression, and Vulnerability, and low in Warmth, Competence, and Dutifulness. Individuals who score high in PV describe themselves as being high in Competence and Achievement Striving, *but these characterizations are not shared by observers* [emphasis added]. (p. 453)

The conclusion reached by McCrae and Costa (1995) is that PV and NV are best considered as traits that can be subsumed by the big five, rather than as additional general domains in their own right. However, when emotions and emotional reactivity are considered, it *does* appear that people differ in the degree to which they experience and respond to negative versus positive events and experiences. We discuss this distinction and the continuing controversy about the number of factors required to best capture personality as a whole further, as we proceed through the remaining chapters of this strategy.

The NEO Inventories

The NEO Personality Inventory (NEO-PI) and its successors, the NEO-PI-R and the NEO Five-Factor Inventory (NEO-FFI), are personality inventories developed by Costa and McCrae. The NEO inventories are relatively new. They were originally designed for a normal population, and their basis for item selection was not empirical keying but, rather, the lexical approach (see p. 194). The NEO inventories have enjoyed increasing popularity over the last decade; they are fast becoming the most popular personality inventories for research and clinical use. The original NEO-PI was published in 1985. The current versions, the NEO-PI-R and the NEO-FFI, were published in 1992 (Costa & McCrae, 1992a).

Recall that according to the FFM there are five major domains of personality: Neuroticism (N), Extraversion (E), Openness (O), Agreeableness (A), and Conscientiousness (C). The NEO Inventories were developed for the specific purpose of assessing these factors, and the narrow traits (or facets) that comprise them. The NEO scales have proven to be excellent tools for assessing the five factors. Much of the research we will discuss uses these measures for classifying subjects on these personality domains.

Using the NEO-PI, Costa and McCrae (1988) undertook a major longitudinal study in which they followed hundreds of men and women for

6 years, using both self-reports and spousal ratings of personality. The same five factors emerged again, and all five dispositions were remarkably stable over the 6-year period.

FFM Facets

Critical to the evaluation of any testing instrument is the pool of items it contains. When one takes a bottom-up approach, beginning with narrow or specialized traits (e.g., specific mental disorders, which served as a basis for empirically keying the MMPI; see Chapter 2), significant omissions are likely in terms of the instrument's ability to detect unrepresented domains and traits, however important. For example, there appear to be *no* factors on the MMPI related to Conscientiousness (Johnson, Butcher, Null, & Johnson, 1984).

Costa and McCrae (1995a) state that they took the opposite, top-down approach in the development of their theory and the NEO inventories. First the major domains were considered and then more specific facets: "We regarded domains as multifaceted collections of specific cognitive, affective, and behavioral tendencies that might be grouped in many different ways, and we used the term *facet* to designate the lower level traits corresponding to these groupings" (p. 23). Costa and McCrae (1995a) say of facets: "They should represent maximally distinct aspects of the domain, be roughly equivalent in breadth, and be conceptually rooted in the existing psychological literature" (p. 46).

Costa and McCrae (1995) explicitly described the guidelines they used for faceting the domains of the FFM. First, grouping of facets should be mutually exclusive; any given element in the domain is assigned to only a single facet. Second, insofar as possible, facets should be consistent in language and meaning with the already-existing psychological literature. For example, the facets of Neuroticism (anxiety, angry hostility, depression, self-consciousness, impulsiveness, and vulnerability) were all existing psychological constructs before the development of the FFM. Third, facets should be of comparable breadth.

Last but not least, the facets within a domain must show both *discriminant validity* and *convergent validity.* As to discriminant validity, a given facet must be empirically discriminable from other facets in the same domain. Velting and Liebert (1997) demonstrated that *positive emotions* (a facet of E) is a significantly better predictor of mood than is the overall E domain. In their data set, E scores (summed across all six facets) also served to predict mood, but to a lesser extent than positive emotions considered alone. This clear example of the potential utility of discrete facets justifies their continued inclusion and separate consideration in research and applied settings. It also points again to the idea that positive and negative valence items and issues may well be important to consider separately (see Box 8.1).

Then again, the facets within a given domain should show at least moderate correlations with one another. We say "moderate" because

> Some scatter among facets within a domain is the rule; this scatter is not due to unreliability of measurement. . . . Instead, it reflects real differences in standing on different but related traits. If there were no such differences there would be no point in examining facet scales separately. (Costa & McCrae, 1995a, p. 44)

Costa and McCrae (1995a) also argue for including facets in their scheme in terms of selection of appropriate clinical treatment for a particular individual.

> The information facets offer is more specific, more easily tied to the client's problems in living. [Consider a client who] came to therapy because of back and neck pain probably related to her very high Anxiety score. Self-consciousness, however, was not a problem for her, and it is unlikely she would have benefited much from an assertiveness training program. The optimal matching of treatments to persons is likely to be found at the facet level. (Costa & McCrae, 1995a, p. 45)

The five-factor model has become the dominant model in dispositional trait psychology (Goldberg, 1990). The model has held up in replications using other data sets (Peabody & Goldberg, 1989), in other languages and countries (Borkenau, 1988; Digman, 1990), using other methods of self-report (Brand & Egan, 1989), and in studies of children and youth (Digman, 1989). Moreover, the model has been shown to subsume earlier models that presented human trait structure in a different way (Costa & McCrae, 1988a; McCrae & Costa, 1989).

The FFM has been shown to hold up cross-culturally (Paunonen, Jackson, Trzebinski, & Forsterling, 1992; Stumpf, 1993). A study done in Hungary, where, despite its location in central Europe, the native language is Magyar, which is of Finno-Ugric rather than Indo-European derivation, showed the same pattern as the FFM on all dimensions *except* Openness (de-Raad & Szirmak, 1994).

In a recent article, McCrae and Costa (1997) asked, "Are there universals of human nature that transcend cultural differences?" (p. 509). Their interest, of course, is in showing that the FFM represents *the* universal personality structure across all human cultures. As a first step in the process, McCrae and Costa (in collaboration with many researchers from outside the United States) created accurately translated (but otherwise identical) versions of the NEO-PI-R in six different languages (besides the original English-language version). The languages selected were German, Portuguese, Hebrew, Chinese, Korean, and Japanese. After an initial translation was executed (e.g.,

Table 8.5 **Coefficients of factor congruence with the American normative structure**

SAMPLE	N	E	O	A	C
German	.97	.96	.96	.97	.98
Portuguese	.98	.89	.89	.93	.96
Hebrew	.98	.92	.96	.94	.95
Chinese	.97	.93	.92	.93	.97
Korean	.97	.94	.94	.95	.96
Japanese	.94	.78	.92	.68	.92

Note: N = Neuroticism; E = Extraversion; O = Openness to Experience; A = Agreeableness; C = Conscientiousness.

Source: From "Personality Trait Structure as a Human Universal," by R. R. McCrae and P. T. Costa, 1997, *American Psychologist,* Vol 5., 509–516.

translated from English to Chinese) it was *back-translated* to be sure the original English version had been adequately captured in the translation.

The results were striking. All six cultures displayed the same five-factor structure originally described by the FFM. To give you a sense of the uniformity of these data, Table 8.5 presents the *coefficients of congruence* as compared with American-based norms. You do not need a deep understanding of "coefficient of factor congruence" to follow the gist of the data presented. Basically, 1.0 represents complete congruence (the structures are virtually identical). Very high congruence is represented by scores of .90 and above, and high congruence is scores of .80 and above. Note particularly that the coefficients for Neuroticism (N) and Conscientiousness (C) are all above .90.

What are the implications of these findings? McCrae and Costa suggest that human trait structure *is* universal. They close by noting the many fascinating questions that will be dealt with in the years to come and with a final comment on the FFM.

> Is universality due to a common genetic basis for personality? . . . What, if any, is the evolutionary significance of individual differences in traits? . . . Do personality factors influence psychopathology, educational attainment, vocational interests, and political attitudes in similar ways in different cultures?
>
> It took personality psychologists many decades to resolve questions about the number and nature of basic trait dimensions in English-speaking populations. Fortunately, it appears that that long struggle need not be repeated in every other culture. The FFM at least provides a solid beginning for understanding personality everywhere. (McCrae & Costa, 1997, p. 515)

RELATIONSHIP BETWEEN FFM AND P-E-N MODELS

Draycott and Kline (1995) have recently shown that the Neuroticism and Extraversion scales of the EPQ-R and the NEO-PI overlap enough to be considered alternative measures of the same constructs. A similar finding was reported earlier by McCrae and Costa (1985).

Like the NEO scales, the Eysenck scales have been revised over time. The first scale that Eysenck published was the Maudsley Medical Questionnaire (Eysenck, 1952). The most recent personality scale produced by Eysenck is the revised Eysenck Personality Inventory (EPQ-R; Eysenck & Eysenck, 1991). The EPQ-R is distinctly shorter than the NEO-PI-R (106 items versus 240 items) and focuses on three factors—Psychoticism, Extraversion, and Neuroticism—plus a Lie scale (previously referred to as *social desirability;* see also Chapter 2).

From the point of view of the FFM, Psychoticism is a combination of low C and A accompanied by high O. From the point of view of the P-E-N model, Psychoticism is a primary factor. Draycott and Kline (1995) considered the issue of which is the "better" model and recommend that this decision be made empirically. This question must then be resolved through studies that relate the constructs in question to a wide variety of external criteria.

Goldberg and Rosolack (1994) also compared Eysenck's P-E-N model with the FFM. They found that the models are in almost full correspondence regarding the dimensions of N and E and that Eysenck's P was closely related to the negative pole of the A factor, namely, antagonism. Low P strongly overlapped with the FFM factor Conscientiousness (C). Costa and McCrae

(1995b) recently commented on this work that "the recovery of the five-factor model from the [Eysenck] scales is remarkable testimony to its ubiquity" (p. 315). This supports Costa and McCrae's (1992c) earlier claim that Eysenck's P (high pole) is better thought of as a combination of both low A and low C.

DISPOSITIONAL PERSONALITY FACTORS AND MENTAL DISORDERS

One of the most interesting (and potentially informative) questions asked about the FFM and P-E-N models is whether they can tell us something about behaviors considered to be in the abnormal range, or mental disorders (Costa & Widiger, 1994). The underlying assumption of this approach is that mental disorders represent maladaptive extremes of the major dimensions of normal personality.

The American Psychiatric Association has published a series of detailed manuals used to diagnose mental disorders, commonly referred to as the DSM series. Although the current version, DSM-IV (American Psychiatric Association, 1994) appeared several years ago, at the time of this writing, most of the data on the relationship between these models and mental disorders are based on the earlier DSM-III-R because of the obvious time factor and publication lag. In the summary of information in this section, we have described disorders according to the most recent (DSM-IV) guidelines, which, for our purposes, differ little from their DSM-III-R predecessors. For the purpose of our discussion, though, we will refer to the manual only as the DSM. (Direct quotations will, of course, indicate the copyright date and pages of the actual source.)

The DSM distinguishes two classes of mental disorders, which, together with three other dimensions of the patient's life, constitute a complete psychiatric diagnosis. Diagnosis thus involves providing information about the patient on five "Axes" (see Table 8.6).

Personality Disorders

The DSM defines **personality traits** as "enduring patterns of perceiving, relating to, and thinking about the environment and oneself, [which] are exhibited in a wide range of important social and personal contexts" (1987, p. 335). The text continues:

> It is only when *personality traits* are inflexible and maladaptive *and* cause either significant functional impairment or subjective distress that they constitute **personality disorders**. . . . The diagnosis of a personality disorder should be

Table 8.6 Multiaxial diagnosis for mental disorders

Axis I	Clinical Disorders
Axis II	Personality Disorders
Axis III	General Medical Conditions
Axis IV	Psychosocial and Environmental Problems
Axis V	Global Assessment of Functioning

Source: Diagnostic and Statistical Manual of Mental Disorders (DSM-IV) 4th ed., 1994, p. 24. American Psychiatric Association.

Table 8.7 Relationships between the FFM and the personality disorders

PERSONALITY DISORDER	BRIEF DESCRIPTION	FFM CHARACTERISTICS
Cluster A	Exhibits odd or eccentric behavior	Low Extraversion Low Agreeableness
Cluster B	Exhibits dramatic, emotional, or erratic behavior	High Extraversion Low Agreeableness Low Conscientiousness High Neuroticism
Cluster C	Exhibits anxious or fearful behavior	High Agreeableness High Conscientiousness High Neuroticism

Source: Based largely on data reported in Shopshire & Craik, 1994, and Costa & McCrae, 1990.

made only when the characteristic features are typical of the person's long-term functioning and are not limited to discrete periods of illness [emphasis added]. (p. 335)

The current DSM personality disorders are grouped into three clusters. Cluster A includes paranoid, schizoid, and schizotypal personality disorders; Cluster B includes antisocial, borderline, and narcissistic personality disorders; Cluster C includes avoidant, dependent, obsessive compulsive, and passive aggressive personality disorders. (There is also a residual category, personality disorder not otherwise specified [NOS], for mixed conditions.)

The relationship between the FFM and the personality disorders is striking. Of the 11 personality disorders listed in the DSM, 9 have positive and significant correlations with N (Coolidge et al., 1994). Interestingly, a recent study (O'Boyle, 1995) demonstrated that among patients in a drug abuse program, Psychoticism was related to the dramatic personality disorder cluster. Table 8.7 lists some of the other major relationships recently reported.

Clinical Disorders

Perhaps it comes as no surprise that personality as defined with the FFM is meaningfully related to *disorders of personality* (the Axis II disorders of the DSM scheme). Even more impressive evidence for the breadth and versatility of the FFM is that it also relates to the so-called *clinical disorders* of DSM's Axis I (e.g., depression, anxiety disorders, and substance abuse).

Trull and Sher (1994) examined the relationship between NEO-FFI scores and several of the major clinical disorders by comparing diagnosed individuals with otherwise similar control subjects. Figure 8.4 shows their results with lifetime occurrences of drug abuse or dependence, anxiety disorders, major depression, and posttraumatic stress disorder (PTSD).

From a statistical point of view, the following differences are significant, compared to the control subjects: substance abuse disorders were associated with higher Neuroticism, lower Extraversion, higher Openness, and lower Conscientiousness scores; anxiety disorders were associated with higher Neuroticism, lower Extraversion, higher Openness, lower Agreeableness, and lower Conscientiousness scores; PTSD was associated with higher Neuroticism, lower Extraversion, lower Agreeableness, and lower Conscientiousness

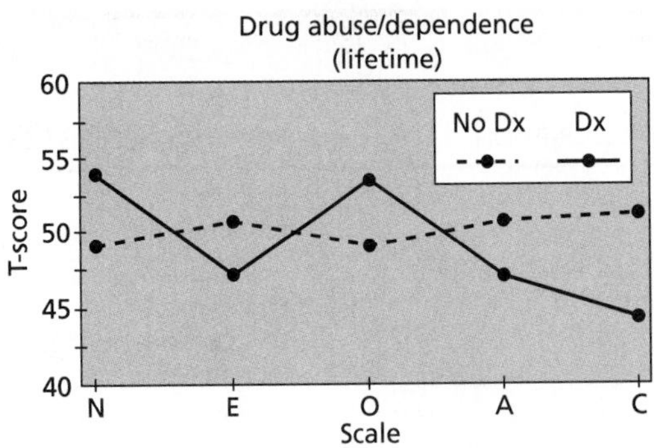

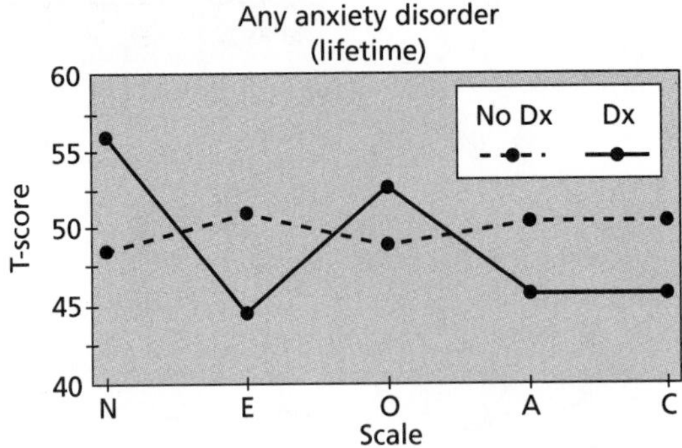

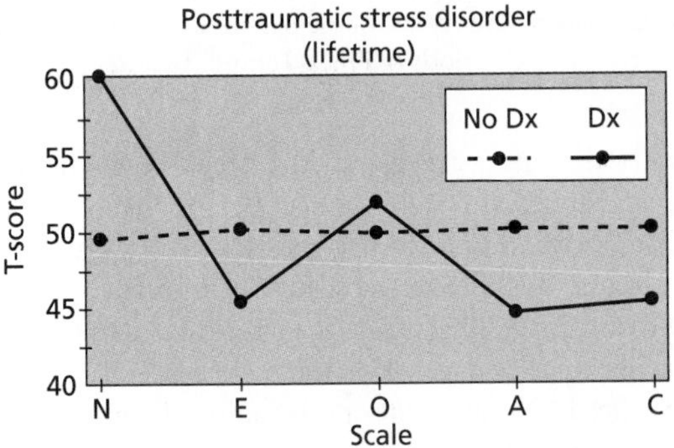

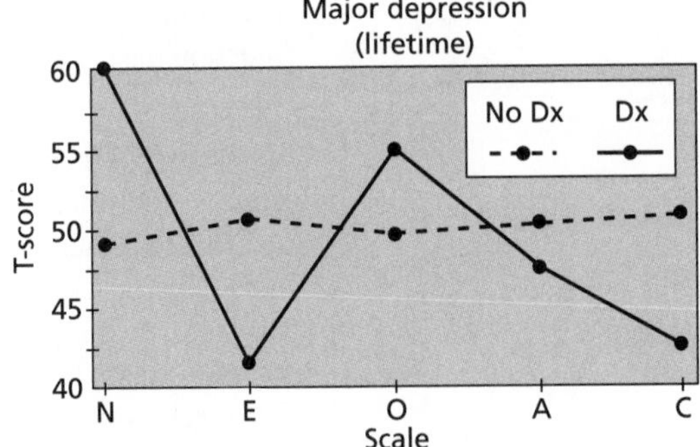

Figure 8.4
Relationship between the five-factor model of personality and Axis I disorders in a nonclinical sample.
Modified from "Relationship Between the Five-Factor Model of Personality and Axis I Disorders in a Nonclinical Sample," by T. J. Trull and K. J. Sher, 1994, *Journal of Abnormal Psychology, 103*(2), 350–360. Copyright © 1994 by the American Psychological Association. Modified by permission of the author.

scores; and major depression was associated with higher Neuroticism, lower Extraversion, higher Openness, and lower Conscientiousness.

We can summarize these patterns in part by saying that the triad of high Neuroticism, low Extraversion, and low Conscientiousness suggest that an individual is at risk of having or developing an Axis I Disorder. Less intuitively obvious, however, is the finding that there is also a relationship between high Openness and increased incidence of clinical disorders. "Relatively higher levels of Openness," write Trull and Sher, "were found to characterize members of any substance use disorder, alcohol abuse or dependence, drug abuse or dependence, nicotine dependence, major depression, and any anxiety disorder diagnostic groups" (p. 358). They go on to (appropriately) caution, though, that clinical disorders may alter Openness (by providing novel states of mind), rather than the other way around. (Zuckerman's construct of sensation seeking may well be related to Openness and does provide one possible explanation for the observed association between high Openness and problems with substances, as well as a number of other high-risk behaviors. We discuss this construct and its relation to the broad personality domains in Chapter 9.)

Among the most prevalent of the clinical disorders is major depression. Recently, Bagby and his colleagues (1995) have shown that N goes up when a person has a major depressive episode and that E is the best predictor of treatment outcome, at least for response to pharmacotherapy.

A number of other associations between personality factors and problem behaviors have been reported. Here is a brief list:

1. Widiger and Trull (1992) found that obsessive compulsive disorder (OCD) is associated with extremely high levels of Conscientiousness.
2. A study done in India revealed that hallucinogen abusers were higher than nonusers on both the Neuroticism and Psychoticism scales (Nishith, Mueser, & Gupta, 1994).
3. Bulimia (gorging and then purging food) has been found to correlate positively with Neuroticism (Geissler & Kelly, 1994). In addition, women with bulimia scored significantly higher on Neuroticism than a comparable control group of women not suffering from bulimia (Wade, Tiggemann, Heath, & Abraham, 1995).
4. In a U.S. study, alcoholics were found to score higher on the Neuroticism and Psychoticism scales than controls (King, Enrico, & Parsons, 1995).

The link between mental and behavioral disorders and the FFM is not strictly limited to adults. A recent study by John, Caspi, Robins, Moffit, & Stouthamer-Loeber (1994) compared the profiles between delinquent and nondelinquent adolescents. The study was based, in part, on a clinical distinction between two broad behavior problem syndromes, referred to as externalizing problems and internalizing problems. **Externalizing problems** include aggression, stealing, lying, and impulsivity; that is, they are problems in relating to the external world. **Internalizing problems** involve anxiety, complaints of physical symptoms with no medical basis, and social withdrawal.

John and colleagues (1994) found that externalizing problems are associated with low Agreeableness and low Conscientiousness; internalizing problems are associated with high Neuroticism and low Extraversion. In the study, boys with externalizing disorders were less Agreeable, less Conscientious, and more Extraverted than nonexternalizing boys; boys with internalizing disorders were characterized by high Neuroticism and low Conscientiousness (Figure 8.5).

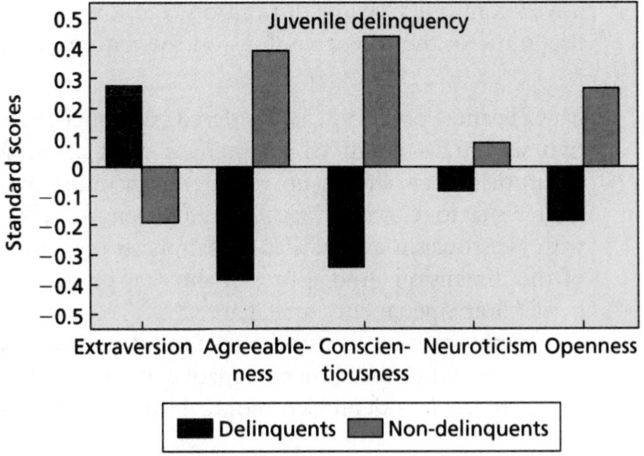

Figure 8.5
The big five personality profiles of delinquent and nondelinquent boys.
From "The 'Little Five': Exploring the Nomological Network of the Five-Factor Model of Personality in Adolescent Boys," by O. P. John, A. Caspi, R. W. Robins, T. E. Moffitt, and M. Stouthamer-Loeber, 1994, *Child Development, 65,* 160–168. Copyright © 1990 Society for Research in Child Development, Inc. Reprinted by permission.

Finally, the FFM may provide "a framework within which to conduct research on the relation of individual differences to treatment outcomes," a suggestion made by Costa and McCrae (1992), who also predicted that those low on E (i.e., extreme introverts) would be more likely to benefit from antidepressant medication than from psychotherapy.

THE SUPERTRAITS: CONVERGING EVIDENCE

The major goals of the Dispositional Strategy are to identify and characterize the important dispositions that underlie personality. In the past 20 years, a true consensus has begun to emerge among dispositional psychologists that there are a small number of "supertraits" and that research is closing in on them rapidly (Digman & Inouye, 1986; Funder, 1991; Goldberg, 1981; McCrae & Costa, 1987; McCrae & Costa, 1997; Noller, Law, & Comrey, 1987).

The number of supertraits acknowledged will depend in part on the definitions chosen and the kind of data relied on. For example, observations of infants in the nursery are more likely to reveal differences in Activity Level than in Conscientiousness (see Chapter 9); similarly, Intelligence can appear as a supertrait only if relevant measures have been included in the research on which the supertrait model is based.

Finally, we will attempt to summarize and integrate the previous discussion. Our reading of the data, taken all together, is that six dispositions appear to be good candidates as supertraits: Extraversion, Neuroticism, Openness, Agreeableness, Conscientiousness, and Intelligence.

Extraversion

Cattell labeled his factor A "Reserved vs. Outgoing," Eysenck concluded that Extraversion is one of the major dimensions of personality, and many other researchers have found Sociability to be one of the three stable, heritable personality temperaments, present from infancy (see Chapter 9). The tendency to be socially inhibited or uninhibited has been observed as a clear individual difference among infants and young children (Kagan & Reznick, 1986; Kagan & Snidman, 1991). Finally, Costa and McCrae (1988; McCrae & Costa, 1987), using ratings and self-report data, found a major factor that they called Extraversion. There seems to be little doubt that Extraversion is a well-confirmed, major disposition (i.e., one of the supertraits). Table 8.8 lists some of the recent findings on the nature of Extraversion.

Neuroticism

McCrae and Costa (1987) considered Neuroticism and Extraversion to be the two supertraits about which there is most agreement. Like Extraversion, Neuroticism has shown up repeatedly in numerous factor-analytic studies. Cattell's factor C, which he called Ego Strength, appears to correspond closely with Neuroticism except that the emphasis is on the nonneurotic, stable end of the dimension. And, Emotionality has consistently appeared as a major, heritable temperament (see Chapter 9).

People high in Neuroticism tend to have few happy thoughts and memories and to recall many negative memories, regardless of whether they are currently in a depressed mood. However, this tendency toward remem-

Table 8.8 Recently reported differences between extraverts and introverts

Extraverts report finding more meaning in life.[1]
Extraverts are happier.[2]
Extraverts are better able to interpret facial expressions and body language.[3]
Extraverts tend to appraise stressful events as challenges.[4]
Extraverts learn faster but less accurately on a maze.[5]
Extraverts respond better to efforts to elevate their mood.[6]
Extraverts are better able to handle time pressure.[7]
Extraverts are better drivers.[8]
Extraverts are less submissive than introverts.[9]
Extraverts are more tolerant toward marginal groups[10] (e.g., the psychiatrically disordered, mentally retarded, the elderly, prostitutes, the incurably ill).
Extraverts participate more in seminars than introverts.[11]
Extraverts smoke more and find it harder to quit (perhaps because nicotine is a stimulant).[12]
Extraverts are less disturbed by music when they are studying than are introverts.[13]

Source: [1]Addad (1987); [2]Argyle and Lu (1990), Furnham and Brewin (1990); [3]Aker and Panter (1988); [4]Gallagher (1990); [5]Howard and McKillen (1990); [6]Larsen and Ketelaar (1989, 1991); [7]Rawlings and Carnie (1989); [8]G. Matthews, Dorn, and Glendon (1991); [9]Gilbert and Allan (1994); [10]Zaleski, Eysenck, and Eysenck (1995); [11]Furnham and Medhurst (1995); [12]Helgason, Fredrikson, and Steineck (1995); [13]Crawford and Strapp (1994).

bering the negative appears to play a key role in the individual's susceptibility to clinical depression (Ruiz-Caballero & Bermudez, 1995). When people high in Neuroticism are in a depressed mood, their tendency to recall more negative than positive events is particularly pronounced (Bradley & Mugg, 1994). In a study done in Canada, Neuroticism was found to be associated with mood fluctuation and with vulnerability to depression, even among a nonclinical sample (Saklofske, Kelly, & Janzen, 1995). High Neuroticism also appears to predispose individuals to seasonal affective disorder (Murray, Hay, & Armstrong, 1995).

In a study conducted in Spain, Neuroticism was found to be associated with fewer happier thoughts and memories and more negative ones (Ruiz-Caballero & Bermudez, 1995). High Neuroticism seems to be associated with lower self-reliance among both males and females (Marusic, Bratko, & Zarevski, 1995).

Openness

Individuals high on Openness (to experience) tend to be original, imaginative, and daring. Their interests tend to be quite broad. Openness may manifest itself in a wide range of fantasy experiences, in creative or unusual ideas or products, or in a high degree of tolerance for what others do, say, and think. Persons who score high on Openness actively seek more educational opportunities and more challenging work experiences than those low on Openness (Barrick & Mount, 1991). Perhaps not surprisingly, open individuals are more susceptible to hypnosis than are "closed-minded" ones (Roche & McConkey, 1990). McCrae described Openness this way:

> We conceive of the open individual as being interested in experience for its own sake, eager for variety, tolerant of uncertainty, leading a richer, more complex, less conventional life. By contrast, the closed person is seen as being impoverished in fantasy, insensitive to art and beauty, restricted in affect, behaviorally rigid, bored by ideas, and ideologically dogmatic. (1990, p. 123)

Openness is a dimension of personality that can be detected only when personality measures are broad enough to ask the right questions. But if the right questions are asked, Openness appears consistently as a personality trait and is quite stable across adulthood (Costa & McCrae, 1988; Digman & Inouye, 1986; McCrae & Costa, 1985, 1987, 1997). Interestingly, McCrae (1976) found that Cattell's 16 personality factors could be meaningfully grouped into three clusters, one of which was Openness. (The other two clusters were Neuroticism and Extraversion.) McCrae argues that Openness subsumes constructs that have arisen more or less independently in several branches of the social sciences and that Openness is a "common dimension of human nature relevant to many different disciplines" (p. 323).

Openness is considered the most controversial of the big five because of its overlap with intelligence and cultural sophistication. However, McCrae (1996) believes that Openness is best understood "as a fundamental way of approaching the world that affects not only internal experience but also interpersonal interactions and social behavior" (p. 323). It is "the personality dimension that most centrally influences social and interpersonal phenomena" (p. 323).

"Open individuals," writes McCrae (1996, p. 328), "prefer more open-ended discussions, more diversity of opinion, and more complexity of thought. . . . What they find intolerable is not dissent but the attempt to stifle dissent by appeal to authority or dogma" (p. 328). In addition, Openness (O) is positively related to Intelligence (as measured by standard intelligence tests), whereas relationships between none of the other four factors of the FFM and Intelligence approach statistical significance (Holland, Dollinger, Holland, & MacDonald, 1995).

Agreeableness

The agreeable person tends to be sympathetic, cooperative, trusting, and interpersonally supportive. In its extreme form, though, Agreeableness becomes unappealing and may be manifested in a dependent, self-effacing manner in dealings with others.

The opposite pole of Agreeableness is antagonism, the tendency to set oneself against others. The antagonistic person tends to be mistrustful, skeptical, unsympathetic, uncooperative, stubborn, and rude. McCrae and Costa also noted the similarity between antagonism and Eysenck's dimension Psychoticism. The hostility associated with certain aspects of Type A behavior also bears a striking similarity to antagonism. Like Openness, Agreeableness is thought to be mainly a product of learning and socialization, rather than biologically based (Costa & McCrae, 1988b).

Agreeableness in its extreme forms affects political sentiments and has been referred to by Costa, McCrae, and Dye (in press) as "tender-minded." It is the style rather than the political content of their beliefs that distinguish the "tender-minded" from the "tough-minded" in the political arena. In this view, fascists and communists are both tough-minded, as both have well-earned reputations for violence as the means to political ends in both foreign and domestic policy matters.

Conscientiousness

Conscientious individuals are hardworking, ambitious, and energetic. They persevere in the face of difficulty and tend to be careful and thorough. Conscientiousness is also associated with physical fitness (Hogan, 1989; Booth-Kewley & Vickers, in press).

Conscientious students tend to earn better grades and to do more extra-credit assignments than those low in Conscientiousness (Digman, 1989; Dollinger & Orf, 1991). The opposite pole of conscientious is "undirected." McCrae and Costa (1987) noted, "In our view, the individual low in Conscientiousness is not so much uncontrolled as undirected, not so much impulse ridden as simply lazy" (p. 88).

Conscientiousness was one of the source traits reported by Cattell (see p. 205). Conscientiousness also appears to bear considerable similarity to what McClelland called achievement motivation (see Chapter 5). Like Openness, Conscientiousness is probably a result of learning and socialization and has a definite evaluative component; in other words, it is commonly considered "better" to be conscientious than to be undirected.

Intelligence

Cattell concluded that his factor B is "nothing less than general intelligence." This factor appears in Cattell's work and not in Eysenck's or McCrae and Costa's work simply because their research did not include measures that could pick up an intelligence factor (Brand & Egan, 1989). Dispositional psychologists are in virtually complete agreement that Intelligence is a supertrait in the sense that it is an important, stable dimension on which people differ. (See Liebert, Wicks-Nelson, & Kail, 1986, for an extensive review.) In addition, studies of twins reared apart show that IQ is largely (but not entirely) attributable to heredity (Bouchard, Lykken, McGue, Segal, & Tellegen, 1990). But there is disagreement on whether Intelligence should be thought of as a true *personality* trait.

Some contend that Intelligence, although broad, enduring, and pervasive, impacts on intellectual and scholarly functioning more so than on interpersonal functioning, as most other "personality" dimensions do. Social Intelligence is a component of Intelligence that is beginning to receive direct attention and study (Cantor, 1990; Cantor & Kihlstrom, 1987) and holds promise as being accepted as a more mainstream personality dimension than general intelligence has to date. We next turn our attention to the many biological phenomena of interest to personality psychology, with a focus on the accumulating evidence for a biological basis for some of these supertraits.

SUMMARY

1. In their search for important dispositions, personality psychologists have used three different approaches. The lexical approach begins with the words that people use to describe others and themselves in everyday conversation. The theoretical approach relies on theory as a guide to identifying important dispositions. The statistical approach feeds large amounts of data about people into complex statistical procedures, especially factor analysis, to identify the most basic personality dimensions on which people differ.
2. Gordon Allport is generally acknowledged as the founder of the modern dispositional strategy. His basic philosophy is heuristic realism, meaning that traits actually exist as part of the person.
3. Allport acknowledged three levels of dispositions that vary in their pervasiveness. The most pervasive traits are cardinal dispositions, which dominate the personalities of those who have them. Central dispositions are the small set of traits that are highly characteristic of the individual. Secondary dispositions operate only in limited settings.
4. Allport spoke of both common traits and patterned individuality. Common traits are the dispositions on which people can be compared; they are usually normally distributed. But Allport also insisted that each of us displays a uniquely patterned individuality that does not lend itself to comparison with other persons.
5. Attempts have been made to categorize people according to a small number of types since ancient times. Typologies of the 20th century include one that categorizes individuals according to their body shape and another that is based on a particular behavior pattern apparently linked to high risk of heart attack.
6. Cattell pioneered the use of factor analysis to determine the underlying dispositions (source traits) on which people differ. Using a combination of questionnaires and interviews (Q-data), observations made in test situations (T-data), and information drawn from people's life records (L-data), Cattell concluded that the three most significant source traits of adults are Introversion-Extraversion, Intelligence, and emotional stability-instability, which he labeled Ego Strength.
7. There is consensus among researchers that personality traits are arranged hierarchically. Broad traits are positioned on the top of the hierarchy and refer to global personality characteristics. Narrower, more specific traits are subsumed by the broad traits and lie below them in the hierarchy.
8. Eysenck used factor analysis to search for underlying dimensions of personality. He also found Introversion-Extraversion and emotional stability-instability (which he called Neuroticism) to be two major dimensions on which people differ. In addition, Eysenck identified a third dimension, Psychoticism, which includes a tendency to be solitary, troublesome, insensitive, sensation-seeking, and aggressive.

Over the years, Eysenck has come to share the geneticists' view that the major dispositions are to a considerable extent heritable.

9. Carl Jung, a contemporary of Freud, was the first to recognize the Introversion-Extraversion dimension of personality. Eysenck adopted these terms as the poles of the dimension Extraversion (E) in his model. This dimension appears in one form or another in virtually all dispositional models of personality.
10. The last dimension in Eysenck's P-E-N model is the N, Neuroticism. The low pole of Neuroticism is emotional stability, so the model presents the person high on Neuroticism as disposed to display emotional *in*stability.
11. Robert McCrae and Paul Costa have found that the same five factors—Neuroticism-Stability, Extraversion-Introversion, Openness, Agreeableness-Antagonism, and Conscientiousness-Undirectedness—appear in self-report inventories and in trait ratings made by peers and spouses. The model that has resulted from their work is commonly called the Five-Factor Model, or FFM.
12. Tellegen and Waller have proposed a seven-factor model, which includes the FFM plus Positive Valence (PV) and Negative Valence (NV). McCrae and Costa have replied that the two "new" factors are already captured in the FFM.
13. The FFM uses the NEO inventories as its principal source of data. These include the NEO-PI-R, and the NEO FFI (a short version).
14. Woven into the NEO-PI-R are the 30 facets in Costa and McCrae's full explication of the FFM. Under each of the five factors are six different facets, making each of the five factors explicitly multifaceted. Costa and McCrae believe facet analysis will prove important in terms of such tasks as matching the right person to the right treatment.
15. The FFM has been studied by using translations of the NEO scales and making cross-cultural comparisons. The same five-factor structure appears in cultures all over the world.
16. Eysenck assessed personality with his Eysenck Personality Questionnaires (EPQ and EPQ-R), rather than with the NEO inventories. Nonetheless, the terms Extraversion and Neuroticism have substantially the same meaning on all of these measures.
17. To explain the phenomenon of Psychoticism within the FFM, Costa and McCrae consider Eysenck's P a reflection of a particular pattern of factors; specifically, a person high in Psychoticism will show up as low on both Agreeableness (low A, or antagonistic) and Conscientiousness (C).
18. The DSM series is the American Psychiatric Association's manual of mental disorders. There is an ongoing effort to relate mental disorders to configurations—that is, personality profiles—from the NEO and the EPQ.
19. Certain personality configurations go with certain personality disorders. Even more impressive is the fact that clinical disorders (depres-

sion, anxiety, and substance abuse) appear to show up with distinctive factor profiles in adulthood and even in adolescence.

20. It is suggested that six supertraits emerge from all the foregoing work, taken together. Specifically, it appears that there are six broad dispositional dimensions: the five factors of the FFM and Intelligence. (Intelligence clearly showed up in Cattell's original factor analysis as the second most important factor in personality.) Subsequently, many personality psychologists have taken the view that although Intelligence is traitlike, it is not an inherent personality dimension. The authors of your textbook disagree.

CHAPTER NINE

The Biological Approach

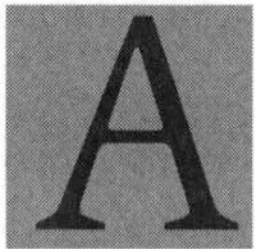

great deal of your behavior is determined not by your "free will," but by your biology. This statement may appear odd or even offensive at first, but it is true not just of you, but of everyone you know. Species-specific behavior patterns exist in all life forms. How you brush your teeth may be unique, but aspects of how you secure resources, seek out a mate, and provide for your offspring are determined to a great extent by your membership in the species *Homo sapiens.*

The goal of this chapter is to introduce you to the means by which some of these behavior patterns have developed, the probable adaptive nature of these behaviors, and the personality domains and dispositions that appear to have some clear biological basis. Toward that end, we touch on issues from evolution, neuroanatomy, neurochemistry, and behavioral genetics. In relating current research to our present state of knowledge in these areas, we draw heavily on the neurochemistry, psychopharmacology, and psychopathology literatures, which are the bases for much of our present understanding. We believe that this information can, and *is beginning to,* inform personality psychologists about the development and functioning of personality in the "normal" range.

EARLIEST SPECULATIONS ABOUT THE RELATIONSHIP BETWEEN BODY AND MIND

Recall from Chapter 7 that speculation about the biological contribution to personality can be traced back to the "body humors" of Hippocrates. Modern personality theorizing is not based on body humors; however, **neurochemistry** (chemical actions in the nervous system) certainly has a prominent role in the theorizing of the biologically based approach to personality. Also of interest are the roles of genetics and inheritance, as well as evolutionary processes that may have served to shape human behavior patterns. As early as 1930, Jennings wrote:

> Temperament, mentality, behavior, personality—These things depend in manifold ways on the genes. It may be safely said that there is no type of characteristic in which individuals may differ that has not been found to depend on genes. (Jennings, 1930, p. 36)

Indeed, Freud himself believed that biological science would ultimately yield answers to questions of human motivation and behavior.

The argument is not that personality is itself inherited but rather that no feature of personality is devoid of hereditary influences, direct or indirect. How these various biological processes operate and interact is the primary focus of this chapter. Our story begins with early speculation and scientific investigation of the relationship between physique and personality characteristics.

Somatypes and Temperaments

In 1921, Ernst Kretschmer (1926), a German psychiatrist, published *Physique and Character.* In it are the earliest roots of the scientific biological approach to personality. Kretschmer began by noting an apparent relationship between physique and specific types of mental disorder among his patients. He set out to systematically study these phenomena and ultimately described a relationship between body types and psychiatric diagnoses.

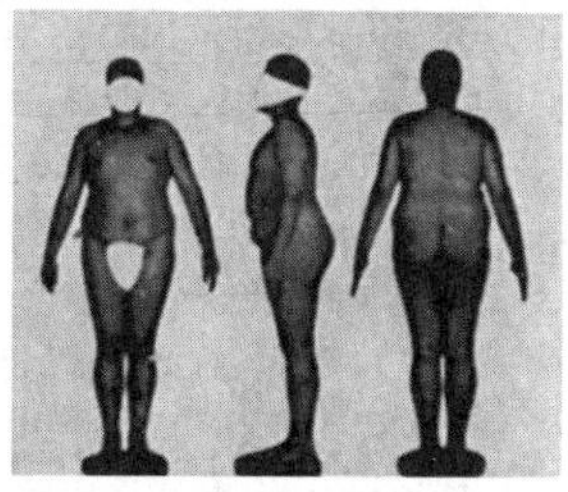
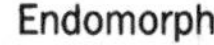
Endomorph

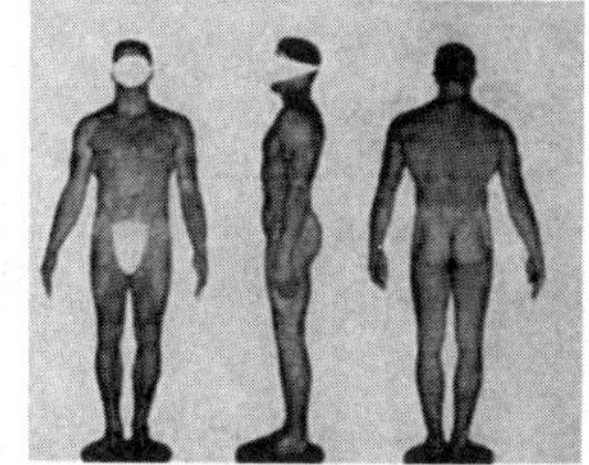
Mesomorph

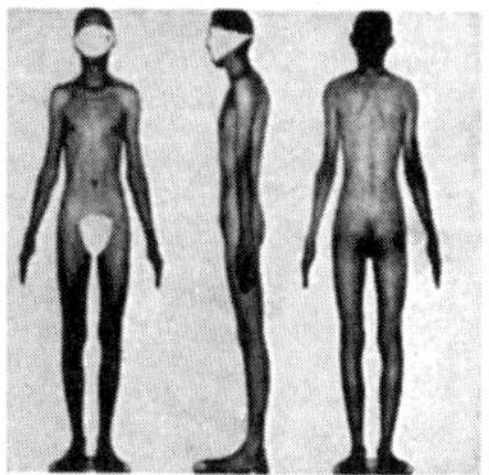
Ectomorph

Figure 9.1
Three views of the extremes of Sheldon's somatypes.
Source: From *Atlas of Men: A Guide for Somatotyping the Adult Male at All Ages* by W. H. Sheldon, 1954. Harper & Row.

Following Kretschmer's lead, the American psychologist William Sheldon (1942) began to try to relate physique to behavior within the "normal" range. He developed taxonomies of both physique and temperament. Sheldon described three basic body types, which he termed **endomorphic** (plump), **mesomorphic** (muscular), and **ectomorphic** (frail). (He labeled anyone not clearly conforming to one of these three types as of "average" build.) However, Sheldon did not simply classify individuals as one type or another; rather, he ranked their appearance on each of these dimensions. The resulting three-point ratings produced individuals who appeared to be predominantly one type or another. See Figure 9.1 for examples of the three possible physiques.

Sheldon then described three basic temperament types, which he labeled **viscerotonia, somatotonia,** and **cerebrotonia.** A sample of the characteristics associated with each of these types appears in Table 9.1.

Table 9.1 A sample of Sheldon's temperament characteristics

I VISCEROTONIA	II SOMATOTONIA	III CEREBROTONIA
Relaxation in posture and movement	Assertiveness of posture and movement	Restraint in posture and movement, tightness
Love of physical comfort	Love of physical adventure	Overly fast reactions
Slow reaction	The energetic characteristic	Love of privacy
Love of polite ceremony	Need for and enjoyment of exercise	Mental overintensity, hyperattentionality, apprehensiveness
Sociophilia	Love of risk and chance	Secretiveness of feeling, emotional restraint
Evenness of emotional flow	Bold directness of manner	Self-conscious motility of the eyes and face
Tolerance	Physical courage for combat	Sociophobia
Complacency	Competitive aggressiveness	Inhibited social address
The untempered characteristic	The unrestrained voice	Vocal restraint and general restraint of noise
Smooth, easy communication of feeling, extraversion	Overmaturity of appearance	Youthful intentness of manner and appearance

Source: Adapted from *The Varieties of Temperament: A Psychology of Constitutional Differences* by W. H. Sheldon, 1942. Harper & Row.

Next Sheldon began the work of seeking relationships between body type and temperament. He studied a sample of 200 white men who were **somatyped** (ranked on his three physique types) and rated for the three components of temperament over a 5-year period. The results were striking; each of the three body types was positively related to one *and only one* of the temperament types and negatively related to the other two. Endomorphy was associated with viscerotonia, mesomorphy with somatotonia, and ectomorphy with cerebrotonia. Sheldon concluded that physique and temperament probably represented different expressions of some basic underlying biological factor or genetic influence.

This early research seeking relationships between physique and personality characteristics was followed by a wave of similar studies. Sheldon himself turned to examination of these issues in women, extending the earlier work on men. In subsequent research, physique was found to be related to school performance, delinquency, occupational choices, and psychopathology, among other things (Damon, 1955; Davidson, McInnes, & Parnell, 1957; Garn & Gertler, 1953; Glueck & Glueck, 1950, 1956; McFarland, 1953; Parnell, 1953, 1957; Sanford, Adkins, Miller & Cobb, 1943; Tanner, 1955).

Ultimately, Sheldon's work was criticized on methodological grounds (Rees, 1961) and lost the appeal it once had for researchers. But the basic idea that *both* physical characteristics and personality are, in part, biologically determined (and therefore related) continues to influence the field of personality psychology. The search for underlying biological mechanisms related to personality has branched in several directions. This chapter explores each of these, beginning with a look at the earliest work to influence contemporary psychologists, the evolutionary theory of Charles Darwin.

THE THEORY OF EVOLUTION AND HUMAN BEHAVIOR

Charles Darwin's *The Origin of Species by Means of Natural Selection* first appeared in 1859. Many of the ideas presented in this text were not actually new. Others had already noted the pronounced effects of selectively breeding plants or livestock over many generations. What Darwin achieved through his careful observation of a wide variety of species (plant and animal) as found in their native environment was to extend these observations to the forces of nature itself operating in the *gradual evolution of species* to optimize their suitability to the circumstances of their environment. In *The Origin of Species by Means of Natural Selection* (1859/1952), Darwin wrote:

> Thus, from the war of nature, from famine and death, the most exalted object which we are capable of conceiving . . . directly follows . . . from so simple a beginning endless forms most beautiful and most wonderful have been, and are being evolved. (1952, p. 243)

Darwin proposed that variations (or mutations) occurring naturally through the course of reproduction in a species might by chance lend an advantage to some members in negotiating the hazards of their environment. In this case, the individual's likelihood of breeding is enhanced (even if only minutely). This slightly greater chance of surviving long enough to breed successfully acts to ensure that the genetic material responsible for the deviation will also survive and be passed into the succeeding generation. This idea, of chance variations that produce adaptive advantages, is the foundation of the **theory of natural selection.**

Obviously, not every chance deviation confers survival advantage. Those that do not will tend to remain constant in the species and those that are *dis*advantageous will tend to disappear over a number of generations. And, importantly, some traits will be more adaptive in *some* environments than others.

Variability in the genetic makeup of a species is itself adaptive. Migration of the species or changes in its native environment may act to favor one or another version of a particular characteristic. Which particular traits are most adaptive is intrinsically linked to features of the external environment. Therefore, a species with great variability among its members will tend to survive in sufficient numbers to endure and reproduce despite radical changes in environment. Versatility of a species is thus enhanced by variability.

So although variability of genetic makeup may not be selected for specifically, it may develop and be maintained as an artifact of a changeable environment. This effect over many generations seems to explain the inter-individual differences observed in the characteristics and behaviors of species, including *Homo sapiens.* This effect has been termed **stabilizing selection** because it serves to enhance survival of the species (Plomin, 1981).

WHAT HAS EVOLVED?

Scientists generally agree with the bulk of Darwin's theory as applied to physical characteristics of species. Just as natural selection operated to favor some physical characteristics, these same forces, or common underlying mechanisms, may have served to favor some psychological and behavioral characteristics.

Indeed, humans seem to possess greater intelligence, linguistic ability, and prolonged neural plasticity than most other living species. These characteristics enabled survival under adverse conditions. They also helped humans endure change. These factors resulted in humans' ability to migrate and ultimately populate virtually the entire planet. Of central importance to our later discussion is the structure and functioning of the human nervous system. We now turn to a brief review of these topics.

The Human Nervous System

The human nervous system regulates all bodily functions. It is the seat of all cognitive activity and no doubt central to human personality. Behavior making up personality derives from brain functions.

The human nervous system is best viewed as a complex network of layered, interwoven, and interacting subsystems. The **central nervous system (CNS)** consists of the brain and spinal cord. The **peripheral nervous system (PNS)** consists of all other nerves extending throughout the body.

The peripheral nervous system is further divided into the autonomic and somatic divisions. The **autonomic nervous system** sends and receives information from the heart, intestines, and other organs. It controls most involuntary behaviors and responses (reflexes and ongoing metabolic functions).

It is composed of two subsystems that operate in more or less complementary fashion. The **sympathetic nervous system** activates the body for "fight or flight." This system increases heart and breathing rates and prepares the individual for action, while slowing the digestive system. Conversely, the **parasympathetic nervous system** decreases heart rate, increases digestive rate, and promotes the conservation (as opposed to the expenditure) of energy.

In contrast to the autonomic system, the **somatic nervous system** conveys information from the sense organs up to the brain and input from the brain down to the muscles and glands of the body. Voluntary behaviors are controlled through the somatic system.

The entire human nervous system is composed of two types of cells, nerve cells called neurons and glial cells. **Glial cells** provide support, structure, and insulation for neurons. At present, they are best understood as playing a "supporting role" in the function of neurons. We focus primarily on the role and function of the **neurons** themselves, which receive and convey information throughout the system (and, to follow through on our analogy, play the "lead role" in the human nervous system).

Neurons do not physically meet or merge into one another; rather, a narrow *gap,* called the **synapse,** separates adjacent neurons. Although the activity *within* neurons is primarily *electrical,* communication *between* neurons is *chemical.* It is through the release and absorption of chemicals at the synapse that neurons communicate with one another. Let's take a closer look at what is understood about this complex system of chemical communication.

Neurochemistry

All subsystems (or networks) of the nervous system communicate within *and* across one another via neurons. Neurons convey electrical impulses down their length **(axons)** and release chemical messengers **(neurotransmitters)** at their end points into the space (synapse) between the communicating neuron and the receiving neuron. We can understand personality and personality differences in part on the basis of the chemistry of neurons, synapses, and receptors.

Neurons synthesize neurotransmitters from **precursor chemicals** provided through the bloodstream. The precursor chemicals are metabolized from various food sources and more complex chemicals. Production of neurotransmitters can sometimes be temporarily increased or decreased by a diet high or low in the relevant precursors for that particular neurotransmitter. Literally dozens of chemicals serve as neurotransmitters and may therefore influence behavior. We have not provided an exhaustive list of these chemicals; rather, we have named the chemicals in the context of the research to which they relate and supplied a reminder of the class (neurotransmitters, hormones, or neuromodulators) to which they belong. A more detailed discussion of the roles and functions of these various chemicals can be found in Kalat (1995).

The **postsynaptic neuron** (messenger recipient) is stimulated by the chemicals via appropriate (and usually quite *specific*) receptors (see Figure 9.2). Chemicals "bind" with (attach their molecules to) appropriate receptor sites and act to either excite or inhibit the postsynaptic neuron. Stimulation

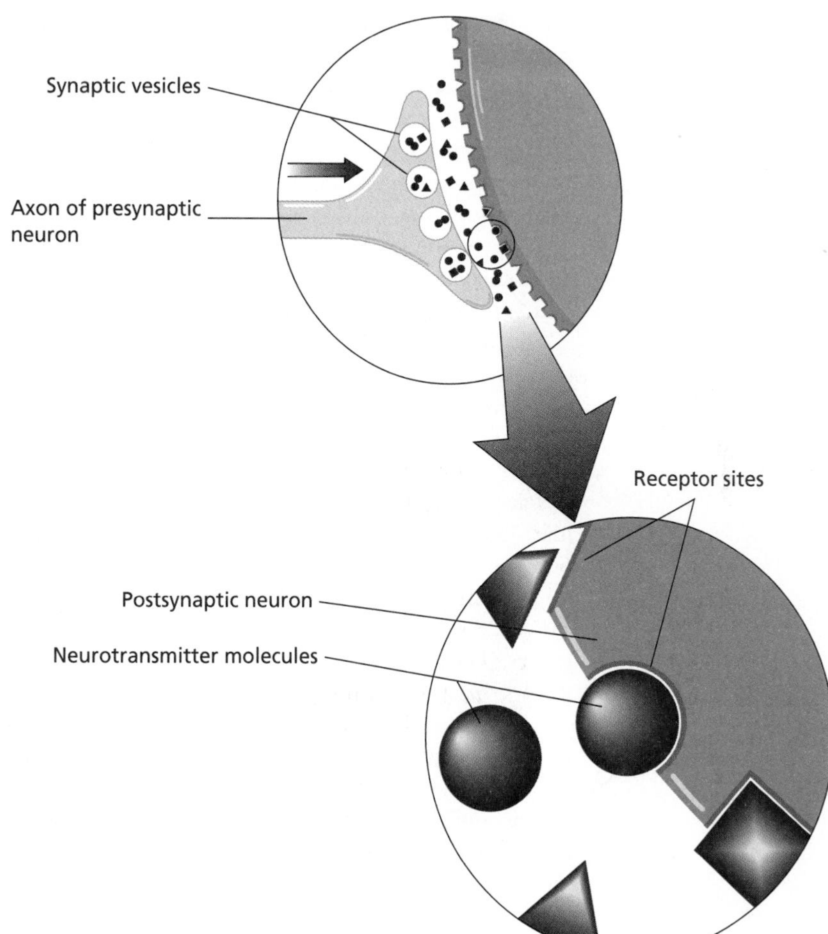

Figure 9.2
Neurotransmitters released into the synapse bind primarily with quite specific receptor sites to stimulate the postsynaptic (receptor) neuron.

in the form of **excitation** increases the likelihood of an **action potential** (the transmission of electrical activity) in the recipient neuron; stimulation in the form of **inhibition** suppresses the triggering of an action potential. Effects of neurotransmitters are often cumulative, amassing over multiple receptor sites or times, to achieve a threshold to stimulate (or actively inhibit) a response from the postsynaptic neuron. Neurotransmitters separate fairly quickly from the receptors and are either metabolized (broken down into component chemicals) or "recycled" (through a process called **reuptake**) by the presynaptic neuron. Reuptake allows the presynaptic neuron to reabsorb and store the neurotransmitter again for future reuse.

Besides neurotransmitters, other chemicals may act to stimulate (or inhibit) neurons. **Hormones** represent a second class of chemical messengers in the nervous system. The primary distinction between neurotransmitters and hormones is their means of transportation about the nervous system. Neurotransmitters are released by neurons at specific end points proximate to the receptor sites of adjacent neurons. Thus, their action is quite specific and restricted. Hormones, by contrast, are circulated through the blood supply and can therefore stimulate many more neurons in a short period. Hormones can spread throughout virtually the entire nervous system and stimulate any neurons with appropriate receptors.

Hormones are secreted by glands, of which the most important is the **pituitary gland,** called the "master gland" because it controls the secretions of other glands throughout the body. The relationship between hormones and behavior is often reciprocal; that is, hormones can influence behavior, which in turn can direct the secretion of hormones.

For understanding personality, the most important class of hormones is steroid or sex hormones; the two types of steroid hormones are **estrogens** (or "*female* hormones") and **androgens** (or "*male* hormones"). Androgens (primarily testosterone) and estrogens occur in both sexes but in different relative amounts. Estrogens activate the genes responsible for breast development; androgens activate the genes responsible for body and facial hair. The sex hormones also play central roles in reproduction and sexual behavior.

Intermediate between the short-range effects of neurotransmitters and the wide-reaching impact of hormones are chemicals called **neuromodulators.** These chemicals spread somewhat further than neurotransmitters but do not have the nearly global range of diffusion of hormones.

A great deal of what is presently understood about the influence of biology on behavior is centered around the *production of, operation of,* and *sensitivity to* these chemical messengers. Both individual differences within the normal range and many psychological problems can be traced to the excess or deficit of neurotransmitters and neuromodulators at the synaptic level. Interventions aimed at the biochemical level are now common and range from dietary restrictions or supplements to the entire field of **psychopharmacology** (drug treatment for the control of psychiatric symptomatology). Applications of the biological approach to personality are discussed in Chapter 10. We turn our attention next to what is understood about the effects of evolutionary processes on complex human behavior patterns (which continue to influence evolution through mating and mate selection, among other things).

SOCIOBIOLOGY

Sociobiology is the study of the evolutionary basis of social behavior (Wilson, 1975). A great deal of research in this area has focused on altruism and its potential adaptive advantage for survival of the group. People are more altruistic toward their own kinship group than toward strangers (Burnstein, Crandall, & Kitayama, 1994). Given that a person's kinship group is likely to resemble that person (both overtly and genetically), it makes sense from an evolutionary standpoint to preserve members of the group, as well as the self, to the extent possible.

This altruistic nature, which results in helping behavior sometimes to the point of self-sacrifice, was sometimes used to argue against the theory of evolution as an explanation for the appearance of human life on earth. Many believed that it was a "moral sense" that distinguished humankind from the animal kingdom. Darwin believed that humans *appeared* moral and might be the only living species capable of "moral" behavior because humans are capable of self-evaluation and cognizant of their past and present behavior, as well as the possibility of a future and of future behavior. Thus, moral behavior is a result of our increased intelligence, and much of what appears to be moral or altruistic is, in fact, good for the survival of the group, the self, and one's own genes (cf. Liebert, 1979). Indeed, humans are extremely social animals and often depend on a division of labor among group members for survival.

Reciprocal altruism refers to the idea that helping others increases the likelihood that they will help you when you need help. It appears that a tendency toward altruism is adaptive and may be a fundamental aspect of human nature (Guisinger & Blatt, 1994).

Another line of theorizing that emerged from sociobiology pertains to human characteristics and their "fit" with the modern social and physical world. Barash (1986) has hypothesized that many of the problems encountered in modern social life result from the fact that **biological evolution** proceeds at a much slower pace than **cultural evolution.** Biological evolution has prepared humans, over several million years, to deal with the demands and rigors of the forests in which humans originally lived.

Cultural evolution has brought about demands and rules for behaving that are often not in tune with biological evolution. For example, using force to overpower and impregnate a mate was probably an adaptive strategy (for ensuring survival of one's genes) in primitive times but today is absolutely prohibited. Similarly, physical aggression may have been extremely adaptive in a hunting-based society. The stress response (fight or flight) that served the survival of the species well thousands of years ago now provides a significant strain on the system because of the changes we ourselves have engineered in our environment. Rarely do we actually need to flee from a predator in modern settings. To survive in modern society, these naturally evolved impulses must be suppressed. This long-term active suppression of instinctive behavior patterns may have wide-ranging consequences for the individual, including health and psychological difficulties. (We discuss some of the implications of this theory and applications in the form of health psychology in Chapter 10.)

Mating Strategies

Although people are usually not subject to selective breeding, multiple forces do influence their choice of mates. Darwin's theory is based, at least in part, on an assumption of *random mating*. However, random mating may be more the exception than the rule for most species. Individuals are attracted, to different degrees, to other members of their species. This is certainly true of people. People in most contemporary cultures choose their mates, and multiple factors influence these decisions.

The idea that people actively choose mates is referred to as **assortative mating.** Many factors have been hypothesized to influence mate selection. According to **genetic similarity theory,** the purpose of assortative mating is to assure the survival of one's own specific genes (Rushton, 1989). Thus, people gravitate toward others with similar genetic makeup for mating. (This is a sort of insurance that your genes will be reproduced: If your mate shares many genes with you, more of these genes will be present in your offspring in greater concentration than would result in pairings with dissimilar others.)

How genetic similarity is determined in these choices remains unanswered, but evidence supports the idea that mates are more genetically similar than would be predicted from the population at large (Rushton, 1988). Physical appearance may play a role in the identification of suitable others, and some have suggested that scent may also provide critical cues. Similarity to self is one common criterion in mate selection that appears to apply across many different cultures (Buss, 1985).

In addition to apparent similarity and sexual attraction, more practical issues guide the selection of mates as well. Trivers (1972) introduced the idea that males and females adopt different *mating strategies* because their roles in reproduction are different. In fact, the bases on which women and men select mates are different, and the criteria are remarkably similar across cultures (Buss, 1989). Women are drawn to men who possess a high degree of material resources, dominance within their society, and high status; men apparently evaluate women in terms of their potential reproductive capacity. They tend to prefer mates who are young, healthy, and appear well suited to reproduction (displaying physical characteristics related to fertility, e.g., narrow waist and full hips; Baker & Bellis, 1995; D. M. Buss, 1989; Feingold, 1992; Singh, 1993).

It *is* adaptive for men and women to value different characteristics in mates. The nature of their investments in the production of viable offspring is very different. To succeed at reproduction, women must give of their physical resources throughout pregnancy, childbirth, feeding, and often protracted childcare. Men generally provide only physical shelter and support (Baker & Bellis, 1995). (These patterns do vary by species, and some general rules have been explicated for determining which parent, if either, will tend offspring after birth or hatching. In general, this follows a pattern based on parental investment of energy, combined with apparent confidence in genetic parentage by gender; see Baker & Bellis [1995] for a complete exposition of this phenomenon.)

There are also realistic constraints on the number of potential offspring each sex is capable of producing. Women are strictly limited based on their physiology, whereas men, given unlimited access to women, are not. From the standpoint of natural selection, both sexes maximize their chances of producing and maintaining viable offspring by using very different mate selection criteria (Baker & Bellis, 1995).

Casual observation of "singles" confirms the truth of these different selection criteria, as well as an awareness of the other sex's selection criteria. Members of each sex aim to impress members of the opposite sex through appropriate *"displays."* Men seeking mates emphasize signs of strength (muscles) and success (expensive homes, cars, clothes, meals); women emphasize their physical appearance, especially attempting to highlight health and youthfulness while deemphasizing signs of aging or unfitness (Buss, 1988).

Even playing "hard to get" appears to have an adaptive basis in that men are more interested in women who appear to be in demand among other men (Buss, 1988; Baker & Bellis, 1995; Kenrick, Sadalla, Groth, & Trost, 1990). In addition, as would be expected from the evolutionary perspective, men tend to mate as widely as possible, whereas women are more selective and seek long-term exclusive relationships (Bailey, Gaulin, Agyei, & Gladue, 1994; Baker & Bellis, 1995; Buss & Schmitt, 1993; Oliver & Hyde, 1993).

"Young Male" Syndrome

Wilson and Daly (1985; Daly & Wilson, 1990) coined the term **young male syndrome** to refer to the fact that human males are most aggressive with one another when they are most likely to be competing for mates. (Similar behavior has been observed in a number of other animal species.) Males commit homicide against unrelated males far more often than females kill

Competition between adolescent males can readily escalate to violent "displays" of strength and dominance.
© Barbara Rios/Photo Researchers, Inc.

other females. These conflicts usually arise between men of similar social status (thus, those who would be in direct competition for the same potential mates). Rates of homicide between males peaks between the late teens and early twenties, when competition for mates is fierce.

Milder forms of conflict between males of this age group are also common. They often result from the need to "save face" or preserve status within the immediate social group (friends or gang). The very high homicide rate probably represents the escalation of these minor clashes, exacerbated by the widespread availability of lethal arms in our society.

This aggression between competitors represents one behavior that is probably biologically influenced. It may be a direct result of our evolution over eons. Those (males) who aggressively sought (and won) fertile mates reproduced at a greater rate than those who did not actively and aggressively seek mating opportunities. Thus, males over time may have come to be genetically "wired" to actively pursue mates, and this behavior peaks as their sexual drive peaks. (Some authors disagree and contend that aggression is socially transmitted and culture bound. The cross-cultural work of Sanday [1981] presents evidence *against* a biological basis for sexual aggression.) Blood levels of the hormone testosterone are highest in males during this same time frame. Testosterone has also been linked to aggressive behavior. (We discuss the role of hormones in behavior in more detail later in this chapter.)

Other behaviors may also arise from evolutionary processes aimed at reproducing one's own genetic endowment. Besides competing to secure access to mates, competition among males apparently continues even after copulation. Recent research suggests that the sperm cells of males compete directly for access to the female ovum. It seems that nature has prepared humans for the possibility of nonmonogamous unions, providing males with one last opportunity to win out over their competitors in the race to procreate (see Box 9.1).

Box 9.1
SPERM WARS—SOCIOBIOLOGY AT THE CELLULAR LEVEL

Do human sperm behave cooperatively, as a group, rather than on an individualistic basis? Are sperm behaving "altruistically" toward their kin? Some recent research suggests this might be so.

Robin Baker and Mark Bellis (1995) present results that suggest that not all sperm simply race to fertilize an ovum. They describe a much more complex process than had been understood until now. They claim that only about one sperm in a hundred is actually actively seeking the ovum after ejaculation.

Of the remaining sperm, about 80% are described as "killers." These sperm chemically attack and disable other "foreign" (contributed by a different male) sperm. Another 20% of sperm are probably somewhat old and tired already (the life cycle of a sperm cell is only a matter of days to weeks). They are more passive, and collect around the cervical opening in an apparent attempt to block the entry of foreign sperm (see Figure 9.3). (They also discriminate between sperm and permit entry of familiar sperm.)

Box continued on following page

Box 9.1 *Continued*

SPERM WARS—SOCIOBIOLOGY AT THE CELLULAR LEVEL

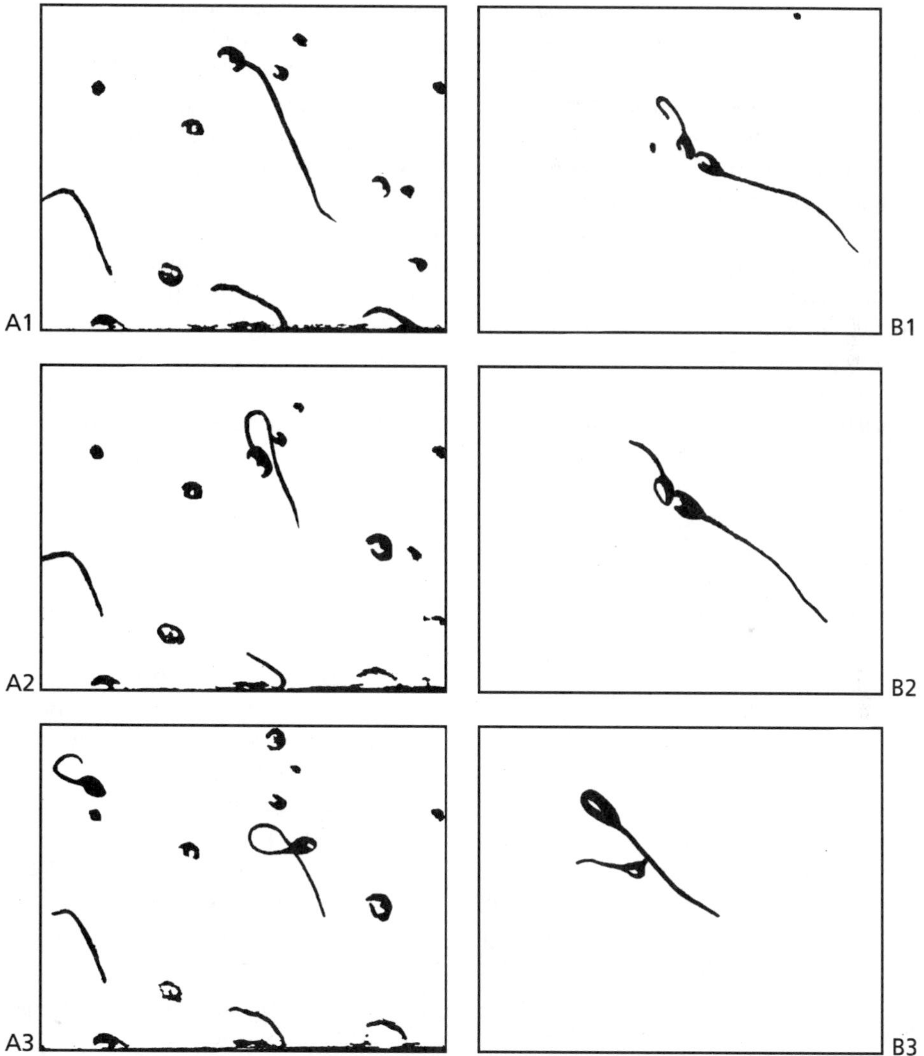

Figure 9.3

The two sequences show previously unfilmed facets of sperm behavior.

(A1–A3) An apparently normal and still alive sperm 'metamorphoses' into a coiled-tail sperm in a single (unmixed) ejaculate. The sequence shown took about 20 seconds. In a further 5 minutes, the sperm was as coiled as the sperm in the top left of A3. Both sperm were still moving.

(B1–3) Possible 'seek-and-destroy' behavior by modal oval-headed sperm in a heterospermic mix of ejaculates from two different males. The pair of sperm (diad) were filmed for 30 minutes attached at the head. Both were active when first seen but by B1 the left-hand sperm was inactive, apparently dead. The surviving sperm, attached at the head tip, spent 15 minutes rotating on its long axis (B1–B2) before eventually breaking free and swimming off (B3).

From *Human Sperm Competition* by Robin Baker, Chapman & Hall Publishing, London, with permission of Robin Baker and the BBC (British Broadcasting Company)

Box continued on following page

Box 9.1 *Continued*

SPERM WARS—SOCIOBIOLOGY AT THE CELLULAR LEVEL

Baker and Bellis's 1995 book, *Human Sperm Competition: Copulation, Masturbation, and Infidelity,* is a scientific examination of the evidence for the operation of evolutionary processes on human mating behavior and their effects. They extend the animal models of the process termed "sperm competition" to humans. Sperm competition implies (in species that rely on internal fertilization, such as humans) multiple matings in close succession, which permit the sperm of multiple males to mix and compete (for the prize of fertilization of the ovum) in the female reproductive tract. An advantage is thus incurred for males who produce many sperm (as human males do) and for differentiated sperm that each perform specific but different functions in the effort to reproduce.

Baker and Bellis's theory can explain the ever-curious overproduction of sperm by males. Only one sperm is needed to fertilize the ovum, but human male ejaculate contains, on average, about 350 million sperm! Their theory does make good evolutionary sense. Each sperm of a given male carries much the same genetic material. Thus, "cooperative" behavior increases the likelihood of successful fertilization by any (familiar) sperm.

Baker and Bellis's research examining characteristics of male ejaculate has produced some interesting results. They examined ejaculate collected under varying conditions. The resulting data suggest that the number of sperm produced by a male partially depends on aspects of the social relationship between himself and his present partner. And beyond simple number of sperm, the ratios of different types of sperm also appears to be subject to some type of "mental" control. More of the killer and blocker type sperm are produced relative to "egg seekers" if the possibility of female infidelity seems plausible than if the male firmly believes his partner to be reliably monogamous.

Baker and Bellis are cautious in extending these phenomena to *conscious* human behavior. They believe that most of these behaviors and effects result from some type of "automatic" unconscious or subconscious processes. But, their data (from an anonymous survey distributed throughout Great Britain and based on more than 3500 responses) suggest that female polyandry (mating with multiple males) is far more common than was previously believed. Their data also suggest that over the course of time and with increasing experience, women become more likely to engage in intercourse with multiple males in increasingly close temporal succession, thereby potentially engaging the process of sperm competition.

Baker and Bellis's theory allows for evolutionary explanations of infidelity (both male and female), mate selection, and even social problems such as rape (or, in their terminology, *forced copulation*), prostitution, and infanticide. If their data are representative, a good many of our most "personal" choices and private behaviors may rely more on instincts and "hard-wired" processes programmed over the course of evolution than we might easily accept. Baker and Bellis (1995) state:

> Human sexuality, in all its anatomical, physiological and behavioral detail, owes more to sperm competition (both in the present and in the immediate and distant evolutionary past) than it does to simple fertilization. (p. 2)

THE QUEST FOR HERITABLE CHARACTERISTICS

Having examined current theories of how we evolved to become the creatures we are, and with a fundamental understanding of the workings of our nervous system, we are prepared to begin the journey into the current field of **behavioral genetics,** the study of the genetic bases of behavior. Let us first briefly review what is presently understood about how characteristics are passed on through generations within a species.

Basic Human Genetics

Gregor Mendel disproved the simple blending theory held earlier to explain the transmission of characteristics from parent to offspring. He demonstrated that inheritance was carried forth by discrete units of material, later named **genes** by biologist Wilhelm Johannsen in 1909 (Lyon & Gorner, 1995). What appeared at one level to be the result of blending was, in fact, the result of the relationships between *pairs* of genes, in which some were dominant, and some recessive.

Dominance refers to the degree to which a particular gene overrides the presence of other genes to produce a given characteristic. **Recessive** genes will exert their influence only when paired with other recessive genes. The resulting overt characteristic is a person's **phenotype.** This is contrasted with their **genotype,** the actual genetic material possessed by the individual. Many human characteristics are, in fact, **polygenic**—that is, influenced by more than a single pair of genes acting in combination.

Literally millions of human genes are located on strands of **deoxyribonucleic acid (DNA)** called **chromosomes.** Humans possess 23 pairs of chromosomes; one of each pair is contributed by each of their parents. Each human set of 46 chromosomes contains about 100,000 individual genes.

Inheritance of particular genes is not a completely random and free process through which any genes of your parents might or might not be passed on to you. Genes are conveyed to offspring in the form of chromosomes so that in many cases groups or sequences of genes are inherited rather than specific individual genes. This point has important implications for behavioral genetics. The presence of one overt characteristic may imply a *predisposition* to one or more other "linked" traits.

Genes appearing on any of the first 22 pairs of human chromosomes are termed **autosomal.** The 23rd pair of chromosomes in humans are the sex chromosomes. Genes on these chromosomes are called **sex-linked.** Very different effects result from these genes in the two sexes, because the sex chromosomes vary by gender. Females carry two X chromosomes, whereas males have a mixed 23rd pair, with one X and one Y chromosome. This gender difference in genetic material also provides clues to a number of inherited characteristics. Let us look at the methods used to decipher inheritance.

How Do We Know? Family Patterns

Today several methods are used to reveal genetic contributions to personality. Examining characteristics (and more and more often now, actual genetic material) shared by related individuals is the foundation of this research. The more closely related people are, the more genetic material they share. Thus, the logic of these techniques lies in examining similarities in an effort to reveal *patterns* that follow the operation of mathematical models of human inheritance. By moving outward from the most closely related individuals (identical or **monozygotic** twins) to less closely related individuals—first-degree relatives (parents, children, and siblings) to second-degree relatives (grandparents, aunts, uncles) and third-degree (cousins)—patterns of similarity are sought. Let us examine more closely the logic and methods of this research.

Pedigree Analysis

The term **pedigree analysis** can be applied to any line of research that tracks the incidence of a characteristic of interest throughout a family line. Most

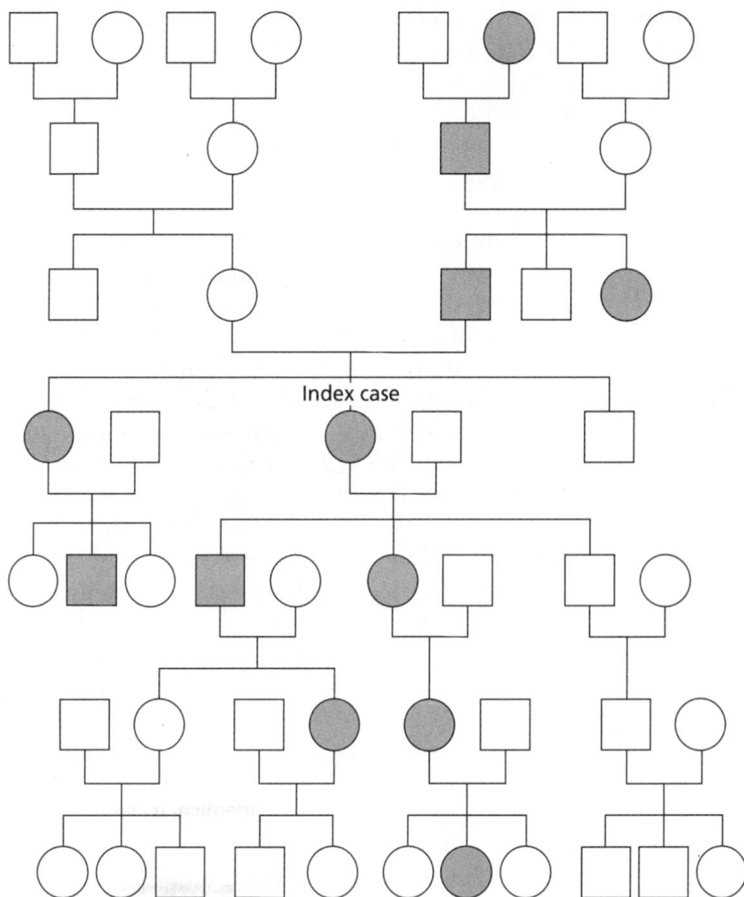

An example of a pedigree; note that occurrence of the trait (indicated by shading) "clusters" around the index case in first-degree relatives and drops off in frequency among more distant relations.

often, an **index case** who displays the characteristic is identified, and then information about all available relatives is gathered to trace the appearance of the characteristic in others. Different rates of occurrence that diminish with movement away from close relations toward more distant ones generally suggest heritability through some mechanism. These types of studies have contributed enormously to the identification of **genetic markers** and ultimately to the discovery of specific genes that predispose to the development of disease or dysfunction.

The Twin Study Method

About one of every 80 births produces twins. Approximately two-thirds of all twins are **fraternal,** or **dizygotic;** that is, they develop from the union of two distinct pairs of ova and sperm. Fraternal twins share only a birthday with their "womb mates." Otherwise, they are no more alike genetically than any other full siblings born separately. The remaining third are **identical,** or **monozygotic** (meaning literally one zygote) twins, who develop from the same ovum and sperm. Shortly after conception, the fertilized egg cell splits into two separate **zygotes** (the fundamental stage of embryonic development), which proceed to develop into separate fetuses. Consequently, they have identical genetic endowments. (Note that monozygotic twins must by definition be of the same sex, whereas dizygotic twins have a 50% chance of sharing the same sex.) See Figure 9.4.

The twin study method capitalizes on these facts by attempting to identify and measure a characteristic or disposition thought to be genetically influenced. Its degree of **concordance**—that is, mutual occurrence—in many pairs of identical and fraternal twins is determined and compared. Greater concordance among the identical twins is taken to be evidence that the characteristic has a heritable component.

Of course, these studies do not rule out possible effects of shared environment. All twin pairs share with each other the intrauterine environment and, when reared together, a common social and physical environment. And because of the effects of the perceived similarity of twins (resulting from physical resemblance in the case of monozygotic twins and, at the very least, similarity of developmental stage in any twin pairs), their parents and others may well treat twins as more alike than other sibling pairs. (Chapter 13 discusses in some detail social influences on the development of personality.) When biological parents rear their own children, they influence them through *both* the genes and the environment they provide.

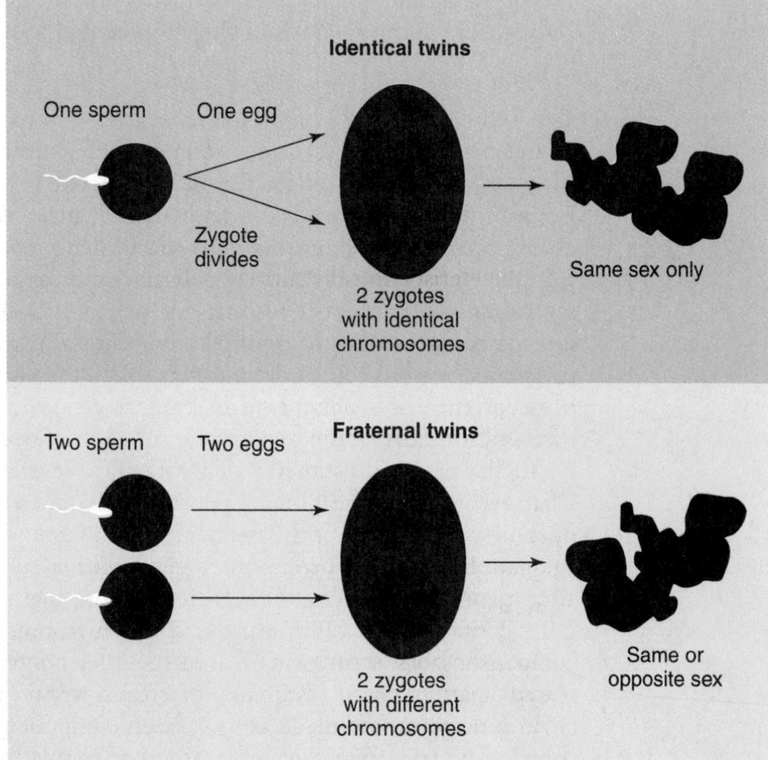

Figure 9.4
Monozygotic (identical) twins result from early splitting of an original ovum-sperm union. Dizygotic (fraternal) twins result from an accident at ovulation yielding two ripe ova, each fertilized by a different sperm.
Source: From *Biological Psychology,* 5th ed., by James Kalat, p. 598. Brooks/Cole Publishing Co.

The Adoptee Method

Adoptee studies address the methodological confound presented by common environment *covarying* with shared genes. Regarding adopted children, the only influence the adoptive parents can have is through the environment, and the only influence the biological parents can have is through heredity. Thus, the two elements are separated, and the contribution of each can be compared more directly. Comparing the personality dispositions of adopted children with those of both adoptive *and* biological parents allows the effects of direct inheritance to be better assessed. Then, too, by noting the similarities among biological and adopted children brought up in the same home (i.e., the same environment), one can get a further sense of the degree of environmental impact.

The power of the adoptee method is further enhanced when monozygotic twins, separated at birth and raised in different adoptive households, can be identified for study. The twins are genetically identical, so observed differences in virtually any characteristic can be logically attributed to environmental influences. Because the children are reared in distinct and separate environments, factors that affect these characteristics might plausibly be identified by comparisons of the two home environments and subjected to further study. These cases are indeed rare, but have yielded some important insights into the separate effects of heredity and environment (Rosen, 1987). Results of sophisticated studies of twins reared together and apart often attempt to produce separate estimates for the influence of *heredity, shared environment,* and *unique environmental factors.* These and similar types of comparisons form the basis of the adoptee method.

The Heritability Index

The ultimate goal of this research is to unravel the effects of genetic endowment from those of environment. **Heritability** refers to the degree to which a particular characteristic is affected by genetic influences. The **heritability index** provides a mathematical measure of heritability. **Heritability scores** can range from zero (no evidence of an effect of heredity) to 1.0 (the characteristic is entirely determined by genetic factors). Heritability scores represent an effort to quantify genetic influences without addressing directly the possibility of multiple gene sites and without any direct access to genetic material. It is determined solely through **incidence** data (rates of occurrence of a phenotype in a select group) and so represents only a theoretical model of the genetic transmission of the characteristic.

In determining estimates of heritability, several factors are important. Characteristics may result from genetic influences, environmental influences, or some combination of the two. Heritability estimates represent an attempt to quantify the genetic component. The residual variance (whatever remains after genetic influences are accounted for, mathematically expressed as 1.0 – heritability) is often attributed to environment. In the case of twin comparisons based on twins reared together contrasted with similar twins reared apart, separate estimates of shared versus nonshared (or unique) environments can be made as well. Each component of these estimates will contain some percentage of error, however, so they must always be construed as merely estimates of the degree of influence of each variable on the characteristic in question.

The importance of the heritability index may diminish as advances in technology allow detection and understanding of the underlying genetic material in the form of specific genes. However, it continues to provide preliminary clues about the existence of genetic factors related to various characteristics and to guide further research.

ACCUMULATING EVIDENCE FOR THE HERITABILITY OF COMPLEX BEHAVIOR

The Human Genome Project is currently under way. It is an attempt to map the entire sequence of genes contained on the full complement of human chromosomes. Many characteristics and complex behaviors are no doubt **polygenic,** and many others **"multifactorial,"** resulting not just from combined effects of multiple genes but also from *critical combinations* of genetic endowment interacting with environmental factors (Lyon & Gorner, 1995). Yet, growing evidence suggests genetic influences in the development of a variety of psychological conditions (bipolar disorder, depression, schizophrenia, and alcoholism), individual differences in behavior within the normal range (dispositions and personality types), and specific disease entities such as diabetes, cancer, and Alzheimer's disease (Edelson, 1990; Lee, 1993; Lyon & Gorner, 1995; Wingerson, 1990).

Our focus is on any possible biological contribution to the development of personality and behavior problems. Thus, we present evidence, often converging from several directions and types of research, to support a role for heredity, neural, or biochemical mechanisms in the behavior of interest. Much of our discussion is based on findings from **psychopathology** (the study of deviant behavior) and psychopharmacology, as these fields are rich sources of information relating biological factors to behavior. Bear in mind the complexity of the behaviors we are about to discuss and that, in all likelihood, no one factor considered will account for the development of any particular behavior in isolation. Rather, multiple influences will sometimes combine, often only in the presence of a critical environmental factor, to produce a given outcome.

Inheritance and Behavior

Are variations in normal personality inherited to any significant degree? A pair of impressive, large-scale heritability studies by John Loehlin and his associates persuasively answer yes.

Loehlin's first study used the twin method. He compared 514 pairs of monozygotic twins with 336 relatively comparable same-sex dizygotic twins. The twin pairs were chosen from the almost 600,000 persons who, in high school, had taken the National Merit Scholarship test in 1962. (This sample is most impressive, in that it was drawn from the *entire* United States, rather than from a single geographic region or ethnic group. The sample also included more than 5% of the entire United States twin population in the age group studied!)

Each subject was given a wide variety of personality, attitude, and interest tests and other questionnaires. The resulting data set demonstrated that monozygotic twins were far more alike than dizygotic twins on a wide range of personality measures (Loehlin & Nichols, 1976).

In the second study, Loehlin and his colleagues used the adoptee method. They followed more than 400 children who were brought up in either biological or adoptive families. Adopted children resembled their biological parents in many personality characteristics, although they had not (since birth) had any direct contact. In contrast, these (adopted) children did not resemble their adoptive parents in personality, even though they had lived with them virtually all of their lives (Loehlin, Willerman, & Horn, 1987). These data certainly suggest that at least some elements of personality may be inherited and biologically (rather than socially or environmentally) determined. Exactly what types of characteristics might be inherited?

Data now accumulating suggest that a wide range of complex behavior patterns, personality domains, and specific dispositions is, in fact, at least partially inherited. Let us begin by looking at the earliest observable differences in infant behavior, which some theorists have concluded remain and influence behavior throughout the life span.

Three Distinct Temperament Types

Three broad temperaments can be identified and measured *very early in life* and *remain relatively consistent* across the life span. Several writers have argued for a distinction between behavioral characteristics observed in infancy and personality domains and dispositions observed and measured in adults (Strelau, 1987; Tarter, 1988). These earliest observable differences in behavior, labeled **temperaments,** include *sociability, emotionality,* and *activity level.* (These are also called *temperament traits* by some authors, but we call them *types* to maintain consistency with our own labeling scheme; see Table 7.2 in Chapter 7.)

Endler suggested that, more than just the earliest overt signs of later personality, "temperament refers to the raw material out of which personality evolves" (1989, p. 151). Temperament types may be more than hints of personality to come; they may, in fact, serve as molds for the formation of later personality characteristics. Evidence has been mounting that these three broad aspects of personality—sociability, emotionality, and activity level—are indeed present at birth, stable across time, and pervasive in their influence (Buss & Plomin, 1984a, b; Goldsmith, 1983; Plomin, Pedersen, McClearn, Nesselroade, & Bergman, 1988; Royce & Powell, 1983).

Sociability

Sociability encompasses a wide range of styles of dealing with the social environment. One extreme is represented by infants who tend to withdraw from all social contacts; they represent the low end of the sociability domain. These infants may actively withdraw from people rather than approach them. Infants at this end of the sociability continuum are termed **"difficult."** In contrast, infants toward the other extreme of sociability (the high end of this dimension) show unusual ease among people, great friendliness, and a marked ability and willingness to interact with just about anyone. These children are sometimes referred to as **"easy." "Slow to warm up"** children fall somewhere between the two extremes. They display initial reluctance to approach new people but gradually adapt and begin to actively interact.

What is the evidence that sociability is innate? Differences in willingness to approach or withdraw can be observed very early in life and tend to remain relatively stable. Friendly infants tend to become friendly adolescents, and unfriendly infants are likely to become unfriendly adolescents (Kagan & Snidman, 1991; Schaefer & Bayley, 1963).

In one interesting study of extremely unsociable children, subjects were followed longitudinally for 30 years. The investigators concluded: "Shy boys were more likely than peers to delay entry into marriage, parenthood, and stable careers [and] to attain less occupational achievement and stability. . . . Shy girls were more likely than peers to follow a conventional pattern of marriage, childbearing, and homemaking" (Caspi, Elder, & Bem, 1988, p. 824).

In addition, monozygotic twins are considerably more alike on sociability measures than dizygotic twins (Buss, Plomin, & Willerman, 1973; Royce & Powell, 1983). One study dealt with almost 13,000 pairs of Swedish twins (Floderus-Myrhed, Pedersen, & Rasmuson, 1980). The sociability measure was correlated +.54 and +.47, respectively, for monozygotic female and male twin pairs; the corresponding correlations for dizygotic twins were only +.21 and +.20.

Similarly, Daniels and Plomin (1984) found that adopted infants tend to be more similar in sociability to their biological mothers, with whom they have had no contact, than to their adoptive mothers. This finding is taken as strong evidence that sociability is largely a genetically (as opposed to environmentally) determined trait (Plomin, 1986).

Sociability seems to overlap with the adult personality of Extraversion, at least to some extent. Recall that extraverts are livelier and more sociable and "outgoing." Extraverts are more likely than introverts to readily engage in approach behaviors. This idea surfaces repeatedly as our discussion continues. For the moment, let us look at the remaining temperament types.

Emotionality

Emotionality is the tendency to become physiologically aroused in response to environmental stimuli. The focus of much of this research is on negative emotions (fear, anger, and distress). (Measured this way, emotionality parallels the negative pole of the adult personality dimension Neuroticism in Chapter 8.) However, emotionality actually encompasses much more.

Buss and Plomin discriminate between the ease of emotional arousal and the intensity of emotional arousal. **Ease of arousal** refers to the degree of stimulation required to elicit signs of arousal, whereas **intensity of arousal** is measured by the vigor of the resulting response. This distinction is important because most research focuses on only one of these aspects or the other.

Considerable evidence suggests that the degree to which a person is emotionally reactive (*ease* dimension) has an innate component and that children differ on this dimension from birth (Birns, 1965; Goldsmith & Campos, 1990; Thomas & Chess, 1977; Thomas, Chess, & Birch, 1970; Worobey, 1986). For example, Thomas and his associates have been following

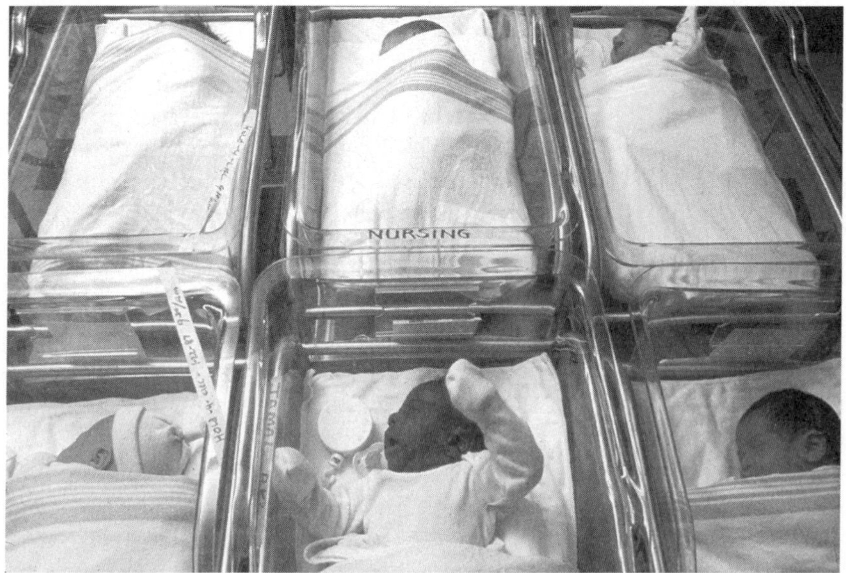

Infants clearly differ in temperament right from birth.
© Herb Snitzer/Stock, Boston

the development of 141 individuals for more than 30 years, since the subjects were infants. The researchers interviewed each youngster's parents every 3 months during the first year, every 6 months until age 5, and every year thereafter. They obtained behavioral data from a variety of sources: teacher interviews; direct classroom observation; personality tests conducted when the children were 3, 6, and 9 years old; and direct interviews with each child between the ages of 16 and 17. These data and other observations reveal that human beings have well-established emotional patterns by the time they are 2 or 3 months old and that the tendency to be highly emotionally reactive or less reactive follows them consistently into their adult lives (Birns, 1965; Fox, 1989; Loehlin, 1989; Schaffer & Emerson, 1964).

An unresolved question is the relationship between the tendency to experience positive emotions and the tendency to experience negative emotions. Tellegen (1985) has argued that the two tendencies are independent of one another. (Recall the distinction between positive and negative valence questionnaire items made in Box 8-1 in Chapter 8.) Thus, one might experience frequent and intense negative emotional reactions but only rarely experience positive emotions. This distinction has been given relatively little attention but may well have serious implications for personality. We can probably all think of people who tend to be brooding and pessimistic in outlook. Other people tend to be upbeat and optimistic, despite serious life circumstances and problems. The tendency to experience positive versus negative emotions may well underlie these differences between people. Some of these issues are discussed further in the section on Neuroticism to follow in this chapter.

Activity Level

Buss and his associates (1973) referred to **activity level** as "the sheer amount of response output" of the individual. Buss and Plomin (1984a, b) further divide activity level into **vigor** (intensity of behavior) and **tempo** (speed of activities).

There seems little doubt that a person's activity level is a temperament type having a substantial heritable component (Eaton & Enns, 1986). During the first 2 years of life, activity level for a given infant is highly stable (Goldsmith & Campos, 1990), but there are marked individual differences among infants (Riese, 1988). Torgersen (1985) found a correlation of .93 for the activity levels of monozygotic twins but only .14 for dizygotic twins.

Numerous studies have also shown that hyperactive children may be as much as 10 times more likely than nonhyperactive children to have had hyperactive parents (Cantwell, 1972; Morrison & Stewart, 1971). In addition, there are significant correlations between the activity levels of normal children and the activity levels of both parents when they were children (Willerman & Plomin, 1973). All this evidence adds up to a strong case that there are innate individual differences in activity level and that activity level qualifies as a major temperament; that is, differences are present very early in life and endure across the life span.

Biology and Broad Domains or Supertraits

The temperament types are the first behavioral differences to emerge from the infant. They seem to serve as the foundation of personality, from which more distinct behavioral patterns evolve and are honed through continuous interactions with the environment. The next most broad class of individual differences can be labeled domains, or supertraits (depending on the language of the particular theorist; see Table 7.2 in Chapter 7). Recall that domains in this sense are patterns of behavior with wide-ranging implications for interactions with others and with the environment. The domains are comprised of narrower traits or facets (see Chapter 8).

Temperament types are described and measured very differently than personality domains. Because of the limited communication capacity of infants, temperaments are measured and inferred from very basic observations, such as reaction time to crying onset, duration of crying, and gross physical movements. Measurement of personality types or domains of adults often takes the form of self-report inventories and more elaborate descriptions of specific behavioral tendencies. Descriptions of personality domains are therefore more specific and detailed than those of temperament types as defined here.

Several broad domains or types have been proposed. Recall the various numbers suggested in Chapter 8: Cattell found 16, Eysenck 3, McCrae and Costa (among others) report 5, and Tellegen and others argue for 7. Many of these show evidence for some degree of biological component in the development and expression of the characteristics involved. Let us begin our discussion with some of the earliest speculations about possible biological mechanisms underlying the expression of the domains of **Psychoticism, Extraversion,** and **Neuroticism.**

Psychoticism

Of the personality domains proposed by Eysenck, Psychoticism (P) has met with the most resistance. McCrae and Costa contend that this domain is captured by combinations of low Agreeableness, low Conscientiousness, and high openness in their five-factor model. According to Eysenck, however, high P is characterized by a tendency toward psychosis. Although this domain has received less direct attention than either N or E, there is considerable evidence that schizophrenia (a clinical disorder characterized by psychosis) has a substantial biological basis.

Schizophrenia may actually represent the far extreme of one end of the "normal" personality domain of Psychoticism. Some theorists have argued that clinical disorders are just that—extreme expressions of the poles of normal personality dimensions. Then, by extension, there is evidence to support the heritability of Psychoticism, as well as considerable evidence for the role of biology in its development and expression. Because this hypothesis remains somewhat speculative, evidence for biological factors in schizophrenia is not detailed here.

Extraversion

Eysenck concluded that major personality types are largely inherited. "However we look at the facts," argued Eysenck in summarizing 35 years of research, "heredity is responsible for a good proportion of the individual differences" (1975, p. 201). In fact, there continues today to be mounting evidence for the heritability of placement on the Introversion-Extraversion dimension.

A massive Finnish twin study (involving more than 14,000 twin pairs) of the heritability of Extraversion and Neuroticism provides strong support for Eysenck's assertion (Rose, Koskenvuo, Kaprio, Sarna, & Langinvainio, 1988). As can be seen in Figure 9.5, for both males and females, Extraversion and Neuroticism were much more closely related among monozygotic twins than among dizygotic twins, suggesting a substantial genetic influence.

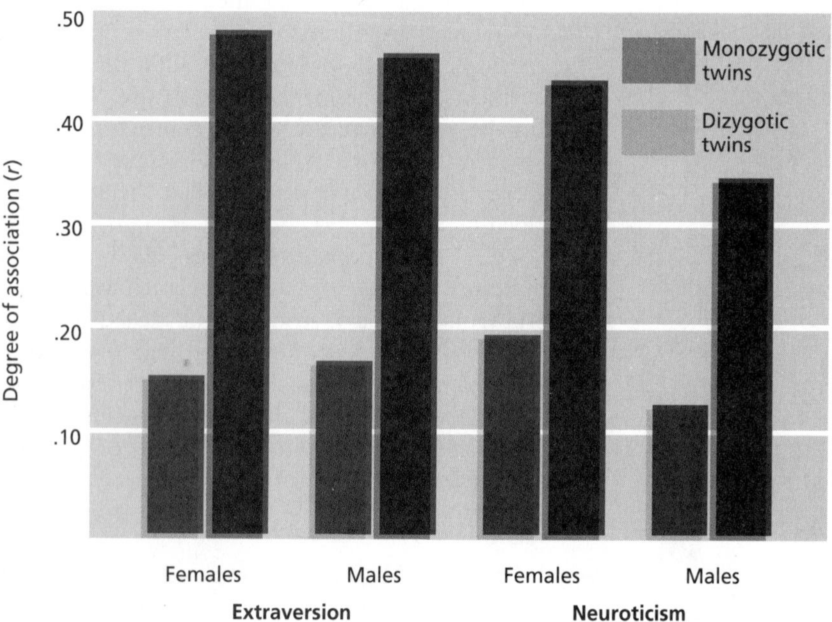

Figure 9.5
The most extensive recent study of the heritability of Extraversion and Neuroticism was done in Finland with more than 14,000 twin pairs. Note that for both males and females Extraversion and Neuroticism were much more closely related among monozygotic than dizygotic twin pairs.
Source: From data reported in "Shared Genes, Shared Experiences, and Similarity of Personality: Data from 14,288 Adult Finnish Co-twins" by R. J. Rose, M. Koskenvuo, J. Kaprio, S. Sama, and H. Langinvainio, 1988, *Journal of Personality and Social Psychology, 54,* p. 164.

The Swedish Adoption/Twin Study of Aging (SATSA) yielded an estimate of heritability of Extraversion of .41 (Pedersen, Plomin, McClearn, & Friberg, 1988). Similar findings have been reported for two other populations, one based on the Virginia twin registry (Heath, Neale, Kessler, Eaves, & Kendler, 1992) and a second based on the Australian twin registry (Heath, Cloninger, & Martin, 1994). These studies reported heritability indexes for Extraversion of +.72 and +.50, respectively.

Several studies of twins reared apart have also reported heritability estimates for this personality domain, ranging from a low of about +.30 to a high of +.60. Although these studies may all be subject to some methodological problems, they combine to suggest substantial evidence for a genetic component in the Introversion-Extraversion dimension of personality.

Based in part on apparent heritability, Eysenck (1967) proposed that differences in the behavior of introverts and extraverts reflect underlying biological processes. He believed these differences might be traced to activity levels in a particular system of the brain, specifically, the **ascending reticular activating system (ARAS).** The ARAS is involved in activating higher brain centers and contributes to the regulation of states of consciousness. When the ARAS is functioning at a high level, a person reports feeling sharp and alert. At low levels of operation, an individual may feel drowsy or sluggish.

According to Eysenck, individuals high in Extraversion have less arousable cortexes and higher sensory thresholds than others. They must seek stimulation to maintain their brain activity levels and avoid boredom. "Extraverts," Eysenck wrote, "tend to have a level of arousal which is too low much of the time, unless their environment can provide excitement and stimulation; hence they tend to be stimulus hungry and sensation seeking" (1975, p. 194). In contrast, extreme introverts (very low in Extraversion) are so easily aroused that they shy away from stimulation. Evidence has been mounting to support this analysis (Bolger & Schilling, 1991; Bullock & Gilliland, 1993; Davis & Cowles, 1988; Ljubin & Ljubin, 1990; Pearson & Freeman, 1991; Stelmack, 1990).

When exposed to the same levels of stimulation, introverts become more physiologically aroused than extraverts. Likewise, when given control to adjust the intensity of stimulation, introverts choose less intense levels (Dornic & Ekhammar, 1990; Green, 1984). In fact, evidence presented by Geen (1984) suggests that not only is the impact of the same level of stimulation different for introverts than for extraverts but also, when allowed to choose for themselves (or exposed to levels chosen by similar others on this dimension), roughly the same level of arousal is attained by both groups. Both introverts and extraverts appear to be operating to optimize their level of arousal by manipulating the intensity of environmental stimulation.

These findings go a long way toward supporting Eysenck's original theory. Thus, introverts and extraverts do, indeed, seem to require different levels of stimulation to achieve the same optimum degree of arousal, and this state appears to be mediated through neural mechanisms.

Introverts are also more likely to be inhibited by punishment than extraverts (Nichols & Newman, 1986; Pearce-McCall & Newman, 1986), perhaps because, for a given level of painful stimulation, introverts actually seem to experience greater pain intensity (Howard, Cunningham, & Rechnitzer, 1987). This finding is also consistent with the previous research in that it appears to represent yet another demonstration of introverts' greater sensitivity to stimulation.

Consistent with these reports is the finding that introverts tend to use stimulant types of substances less than do extraverts. (Recall that their resting, or baseline, level of arousal is higher than that of extraverts.) Stimulant drugs may combine with this baseline level to *exceed* optimum levels of stimulation, bordering on or becoming noxious for the individual. It is also probable that introverts consume more sedating drugs than extraverts, based on the same reasoning. In fact, evidence suggests that introverts are more susceptible to anxiety than extraverts, again probably a reflection of their higher levels of cortical arousal. Extraverts are more susceptible to engaging in activities that endanger themselves or others as a result of their never-ending quest for adequate stimulation. Thus, Eysenck's original theorizing about the biological mechanisms that might account for differences in Extraversion has received some support. However, much of the support is indirect, arising from observation based on related traits or characteristics of extraverts and introverts.

Another related line of theorizing comes from animal models of apparently related behaviors. Jeffrey A. Gray, a neuropsychologist, offers a theory of personality based on brain functions that might also explain the observed differences between introverts and extraverts in terms of basic biological processes. Gray's theory (1981, 1982, 1987) is based on insights gained through animal studies on learning and physiology. He describes two distinct brain systems involved in sensitivity to environmental contingencies surrounding reward and punishment.

According to Gray, the **behavioral activation system (BAS)** acts to motivate animals and (by extension) people to seek out desired goals and rewards. Excessive activity in this system would produce impulsive behavior. The individual pursues vigorously any actions that might result in reward, with little attention to the possibility of negative consequences. Indeed, some evidence suggests that extraverts are more attuned to positive consequences than negative ones and that they vigorously seek out stimulation. Because this same system is hypothesized to control positive emotions, we would expect people with active BAS systems to experience more feelings of happiness as well as more impulsiveness in their behavior, which, in fact, appears to be true. (Note the potential implications of this finding for Tellegen's assertion that positive and negative emotions result from distinct processes and are separable.)

Jeffrey A. Gray described the activity and functions of the complementary behavioral activation and inhibition systems.
Courtesy of Jeffrey A. Gray/ The Maudsley, Institute of Psychiatry

In contrast, the **behavioral inhibition system (BIS)** acts to alert the person to the possibility of danger or punishment, thereby deterring goal-seeking activity. Activity in the BIS is responsible for feelings of anxiety and cues the individual to attend to environmental stimuli that might warn of danger. People differ in the sensitivity and activity level of each of these complementary systems. An overactive BIS will tend to produce excessive anxiety and cause the individual to be especially sensitive to punishment and negative consequences. The BIS system controls negative affect, and so sensitivity to punishment due to a highly active BIS system tends to be accompanied by more anxiety, sadness, fear, and frustration.

According to Gray's model, these two interacting systems in combination produce the observed behavioral differences between introverts and extraverts, as well as on the second major personality domain, Neuroticism. Gray's scheme is distinctly different from that proposed by Eysenck, but the combination of these two independent dimensions can account nicely for the Extraversion and Neuroticism dimensions (see Figure 9.6).

Indeed, evidence suggests that activity of the BAS is associated with the Introversion-Extraversion dimension of personality, and activity of the BIS system appears to be closely related to the concept of anxiety (Carver & White, 1994), which is certainly a central ingredient of the Neuroticism domain.

Neuroticism

Like Extraversion, Neuroticism has shown up repeatedly in factor-analytic studies. In some ways, it resembles the temperament labeled emotionality discussed earlier. However, research over the past few years suggests a more specific picture of the nature of Neuroticism. *Negative emotions* appear to be its hallmark. The individual high on Neuroticism is worry-ridden, insecure, self-conscious, and temperamental. At the opposite pole of this dimension are people who appear to be particularly emotionally stable, contained, and controlled.

Associated with a variety of adjustment and mental health problems, high Neuroticism puts an individual at risk for depression, one of the most common psychiatric problems (Jorm, 1987). Moreover, people high in Neuroticism tend to be anxious, to engage in self-blame and to withdraw quickly from frustrating situations (Parkes, 1986). On the other hand, the lower people are in Neuroticism, the more meaning they find in life (Addad, 1987).

Neuroticism appears to be partially heritable. The SATSA (mentioned previously) placed the heritability of Neuroticism at .31 (Pedersen et al., 1988), which is in close accord with estimates by others and quite similar to heritability estimates for Extraversion.

Like Extraversion, Eysenck believed that Neuroticism reflected individual differences in biological makeup from one person to another. He contended

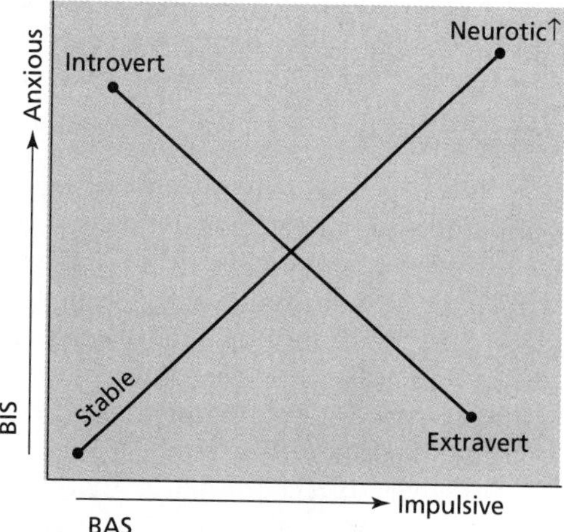

Figure 9.6
Relationship of Eysenck's model of Neuroticism and Extraversion to Gray's model based on operation of BAS and BIS.

that individuals high on Neuroticism have more arousable autonomic nervous systems than more emotionally stable individuals. People very high in Neuroticism can be said to have overreactive or hyperresponsive systems. This biological reactivity leads to the psychological state of instability. (Likewise, people at the opposite pole who are so stable that they seem "steady as a rock" may actually be displaying the *under*reactivity of their emotional systems.)

Consistent with Eysenck's claim, research has shown that individual differences in emotionality among young children are related to individual differences in nervous system functioning (Kagan, Reznick, & Snidman, 1987; Kagan & Snidman, 1991).

Openness, Agreeableness, and Conscientiousness

Of the five factors contained in McCrae and Costa's scheme, Extraversion and Neuroticism have received the most attention. (Note that they are common to most of the current major schemes.) The remaining dimensions are now beginning to draw the attention of researchers. Bergeman and colleagues (1993) have examined measures of Openness, Agreeableness, and Conscientiousness with an abbreviated version of the NEO-PI with subjects from the SATSA. They computed heritability estimates of .40 for Openness, .29 for Conscientiousness, and .12 for Agreeableness.

Heritability estimates for Openness and Conscientiousness are similar to those reported for Extraversion and Neuroticism. According to the findings of this study, neither of these factors evidences much effect for shared environment. For Agreeableness, however, it appears that heritability is less than for the other personality domains, and shared environment *did* exert a significant influence on scores. Thus, from the perspective of heritability, Conscientiousness and Openness conform to the general patterns of Neuroticism and Extraversion, but Agreeableness deviates from this pattern. These conclusions must be considered tentative at this time and await replication in other data sets.

Biology and Specific Dispositions

Beyond the broad domains of personality, a great deal of evidence is beginning to accumulate to support biological contributions to some more specific traits or dispositions. We will look specifically at two dispositions for which ample evidence now supports a role for biological transmission and underlying mechanisms: aggressiveness and sensation seeking.

Aggressiveness

Research on human aggression is accumulating to suggest that it has a biological basis and is (to a greater or lesser extent) a virtually universal human characteristic. Recent research clearly distinguishes between different types (direct and indirect) and different forms of expression (verbal or physical) of aggression. When viewed this way, it is clear that both males *and* females, children *and* adults display relatively consistent rates of aggression over time. Thus, we will review the evidence that aggressiveness constitutes a biologically based personality disposition.

When measured as **direct** (aimed at the target, as opposed to other members of their peer or social group) and **physical** (as opposed to verbal), aggression appears to be a mostly male phenomenon among humans. However, recent research has begun to examine other types (*indirect,* as well as direct) and forms (*verbal* as opposed to physical) of aggression. Results suggest that human females may be just as "aggressive" as males but more likely to express their aggressive impulses indirectly and verbally rather than through direct, physical means (Bjorkqvist, 1994; Bjorkqvist, Lagerspetz, & Kaukiainen, 1992; Burbank, 1994; Rivers & Smith, 1994).

Some of the evidence for a biological influence in aggression (especially direct physical aggression) does suggest mechanisms for greater physical expression of aggression by males. Earlier in this chapter, we discussed competition for mates and male aggression in terms of evolutionary advantages. Let us look more closely at the evidence for a biological contribution to this and other forms of male aggression. Our discussion begins with hormones, specifically, **steroid hormones** (sometimes called *sex hormones*).

Testosterone (an androgen) level in men is highest when males are most readily sexually aroused, roughly between the ages of 15 and 25, which corresponds to the time in life when males are most aggressive, particularly toward their male peers. (Recall our earlier discussion of competition for mates.) A wide range of data now suggests that testosterone plays a substantial role in aggressive behavior.

To deal with certain complications of pregnancy, women are sometimes given synthetic hormones as part of their treatment. These hormones are similar in structure and effects to naturally produced androgens (male hormones). Evidence shows that the children born to these women are more aggressive than other children at middle childhood (Reinisch, 1981).

James Dabbs has studied the relationship between testosterone levels in adult men and found positive correlations with a variety of aggressive and antisocial behaviors. These behaviors range from violent crimes (Dabbs, Frady, Carr, & Besch, 1987) to behavior problems in youth and going AWOL (absent without leave) from military service (Dabbs & Morris, 1990).

Serotonin is a neurotransmitter that may also be involved in aggression or its expression. People with a history of violent behavior, including both homicide and suicide, tend to exhibit low **serotonin turnover** (one measure of serotonin activity in the brain). Similarly, children with low levels of serotonin turnover were more likely than peers to emit problematic aggressive behaviors in the future (Kruesi et al., 1992). Moreover, the homicide rate appears to be highest in countries where the diet is lowest in **tryptophan,** a precursor of serotonin (Mawson & Jacobs, 1978). Spoont (1992) hypothesized that serotonin is related to the *inhibition* of behavioral impulses. Thus, reduced absolute levels or reduced activity of serotonin in the CNS might produce a degree of *dis*inhibition, resulting in less than the usual degree of restraint over destructive or aggressive impulses.

There is also a good deal of evidence for the role of specific brain regions and structures in the development and display of aggression. Rabies is a disease often carried by animals and occasionally transmitted to humans (usually through a bite). It attacks the CNS by targeting especially the temporal lobes, which are home to a structure called the **amygdala.** Rabies produces violent outbursts in its victims (Lentz, Burrage, Smith, Crick, & Tignor, 1982).

Attack behaviors can be produced by electrical stimulation of some brain structures.
Source: From "Neuronal Constellations in Aggressive Behavior," by Jose Delgado, in L. Valzelli & L. Morgese (Eds.), *Aggression and Violence: A Psycho/biological and Clinical Approach,* 1981, pp. 82–98. Edizioni Saint Vincent, Milan.

Stimulation of the amygdala can produce attack behaviors in other species (Siegel & Pott, 1988).

Other evidence suggests that the temporal lobes are one source of human aggressive behavior. Temporal lobe **seizures** (abnormal electrical activity that originates in the temporal lobe) can produce serious violent outbursts (Bear & Fedio, 1977; Mark & Ervin, 1970; Pincus, 1980). Drugs that suppress seizures are sometimes effective in controlling violent temper outbursts, and surgical procedures aimed at destroying temporal lobe structures, including the amygdala, have been reported to reduce violent outbursts as well (Balasubramaniam & Kanaka, 1976; Mark & Ervin, 1970). Aggressiveness (and its expression) clearly has a biological basis in at least some people. We turn our attention next to sensation seeking, which, as it appears now, shares some common mechanisms with aggression.

Sensation Seeking

Eysenck originally described sensation seeking as a specific trait associated with Extraversion. (Recall that Eysenck believed high Extraversion reflected lower baseline levels of cortical arousal. This situation was presumed to lead to impulsive behavior and sensation seeking in a quest to achieve adequate arousal via increased stimulation.)

Marvin Zuckerman (1979; 1994) offers a different interpretation of individual differences in what he terms **sensation seeking.** Zuckerman (1994) defines sensation seeking as "a trait defined by the *seeking* of varied, novel, complex, and *intense* sensations and experiences, and the willingness to take physical, social, *legal,* and *financial* risks for the sake of such experience" (p. 27). He views sensation seeking as related to impulsivity but narrower and more specific still. Zuckerman reports that in his studies both impulsivity and sensation seeking are more closely related to Eysenck's Psychoticism (P)

Marvin Zuckerman is a pioneer in the study of sensation seeking. Courtesy of Marvin Zuckerman/University of Delaware

dimension than to Extraversion (E). (Sensation seeking is one facet of the Extraversion dimension of the FFM as well; see Chapter 8.)

Zuckerman reports that sensation seeking is highly heritable, approaching twice the heritability range of many major personality domains and dispositions. He presents a heritability estimate of nearly .60 for this trait. (For other traits and domains, most reported heritability estimates tend to hover at about .30.)

People high on sensation seeking tend to seek out stimulation in a variety of situations and forms (including but not limited to high-risk situations). They tend to be inclined toward experimenting with drugs, sex, and sports for the sake of the "experience." These activities may include some degree of risk, but it is not for the thrill of risk that the activities are pursued but rather for their novelty and stimulation potential.

Not only do high sensation seekers appear to actively seek out novel forms of stimulation but they are also more responsive to novelty than others. This tendency is evidenced in a more pronounced orienting response to the presentation of stimuli (Neary & Zuckerman, 1976). (The orienting response is a reflexive behavior that allows the organism to perceive and respond quickly to changing circumstances.) People low on measures of sensation seeking tend to display a less distinct orienting response.

People assessed as high on measures of sensation seeking also seem to be more responsive to changes in stimulation over time. They demonstrate an **"augmenting response"** to changing stimuli, such that stimulus changes are enhanced by their nervous system as they are received and processed. Others (low on measures of sensation seeking) show an opposite response; as stimuli change, they tend to suppress these changes through reduced neural responsivity (Zuckerman, 1991). These observations, taken together, suggest one potential biological mechanism underlying differences on measures of sensation seeking. Zuckerman concludes that it is not on *arousal* that high and low sensation seekers differ but rather on *arousability.*

Zuckerman views sensation seeking as one form of expression of a more general class of **approach behavior.** He further describes sensation seeking as the "optimistic tendency to approach novel stimuli and explore the environment" (1994, p. 385). He claims that both impulsivity and sociability are also aspects of the "broader trait" (Zuckerman's own term) he labels **impulsive-sensation seeking (ImpSS).** He goes on to define *impulsivity* as "rapid decision making in deciding to approach" and *sociability* as "the tendency to approach social objects, whether familiar or strangers" (p. 385). He further states that "underlying ImpSS, as well as extraversion, is a mechanism . . . called *approach*" (p. 385). This common mechanism (approach) serves to explain the frequently reported relationship between extraversion and these specific traits.

Zuckerman's model states that the mechanism underlying approach behavior at the biological level is biochemical and based on the activity of the **monoamine** class of neurotransmitters and the sex hormones. Specifically, he claims that dopamine drives approach behavior, and activity of serotonin serves to inhibit approach. (Note the rough parallels with the earlier model presented by Gray of the BIS and BAS operating in a complementary fashion.)

The relationship of this mechanism to the earlier discussion of the roles of testosterone in aggressive behavior and of serotonin in inhibition of impulses are also elaborated later.

Reminiscent of Gray's model, Zuckerman describes dual mechanisms, one a reward-based system and the other a system that warns of impending danger or punishment, thereby inhibiting behavior. Zuckerman notes that sensation seeking peaks in males during the late teens to the early 20s and tapers down steadily thereafter. He goes on to point out that this pattern parallels findings on testosterone levels in males quite precisely, therefore implying a possible link between sensation-seeking behavior and sex hormones. Zuckerman suggests that the observed relationship between testosterone levels and personality traits including aggression, sexual drive, and sensation seeking might all be mediated by the effects of testosterone on the dopamine system of neurotransmitters through an enzyme that regulates dopamine action (B MAO).

Zuckerman also relates a variety of other specific biochemical, physiological, and behavioral differences to observed differences on sensation seeking. He concludes that sensation seeking is a "drive with genetical-biological basis and various learned forms of expression" (p. 387).

The research produced and encompassed by Zuckerman's work is very broad. His work considers evolutionary processes, comparative psychology and animal models, and biochemical, psychophysiological, environmental, and genetic processes. His resulting thesis represents an elaborate, well-articulated theory of the probable biological mechanisms underlying a specific personality trait (Zuckerman, 1994). Despite some minor inconsistencies in the data presented to date, the degree of convergence overall is, indeed, impressive. It appears that sensation seeking (and the proposed general approach mechanism of which it is one component) is an enduring personality trait that differs between individuals and has a heritable biological origin.

Zuckerman (1994) himself, in reflecting on the field of personality and the place of biology within it, recalls Freud's earlier sentiment that biological advances will ultimately serve to inform and illuminate human motivation. He closes his book on an optimistic note, stating:

> Findings in the neurosciences will not negate psychological hypotheses; they will simply place them in a psychobiological context. The genotype and biological phenotypes have been the "ghosts" in the mental structures postulated by personality and cognitive theorists. But they are not ghosts. They are very tangible neurons and chemicals that we share with our animal cousins and our hominid ancestors. A complete theory of any personality trait will have to explore and not exorcise them. (p. 387)

ENVIRONMENTAL INFLUENCES: HOW TEMPERAMENTS ARE TEMPERED!

This chapter has focused on all the many ways that biological factors may combine with or influence personality characteristics. It would be naive, however, to conclude that biology is the sole determinant of any particular characteristic. Each individual is the product of complex and continuous interaction with the environment from the moment of conception on throughout the life span.

Gordon Allport recognized the importance of environmental influences despite growing recognition of the role of inheritance and biological factors in personality. In 1937, he wrote:

> Each human individual so far as heredity is concerned has the possibility of *many* careers, and of *many* personalities, whose realization will depend upon the exigencies of his physical and social environments. (pp. 105–106)

He did have an appreciation of the importance of inheritance, and further stated:

> The more directly a quality is bound to structural inheritance the less modifiable it is. (1937, p. 107)

However, recent commentators have pointed out that the relationship between genetic and environmental factors is actually *reciprocal;* that is, they combine through a dynamic process whereby a person's environment is partly caused by their genetic makeup, as well as the other way around (Bergeman, Plomin, McClearn, Pederson, & Friberg, 1988; Gifford, 1990; Plomin & Bergeman, 1991; Scarr & McCartney, 1983).

Consider the case of **phenylketonuria** (commonly known as **PKU**). The gene responsible for PKU prevents the proper metabolism of phenylalanine, an amino acid found in many types of proteins. Because any phenylalanine ingested cannot be metabolized and disposed of, it is, instead, stored in the body. This storage occurs to a great extent in the fatty tissue of the developing nervous system. Over time, it produces structural and functional abnormalities, ultimately resulting in some degree of mental retardation and behavioral difficulties. However, the adverse effects of PKU are avoidable. If phenylalanine consumption is restricted, there will be no surplus to end up stored in the body.

Newborns in the United States (and most other countries) are now routinely tested for PKU. By maintaining those affected on a strict diet, the adverse consequences of the gene for PKU can be successfully avoided. The child develops normally, effectively preventing the expression of the inherited gene for PKU.

Here the interactions between genes and environment are especially clear. First, the environment (social) produces a situation in which two people develop an interpersonal attraction and mate. (This may well have been due, in part, to some underlying genetic similarity, making the inheritance of the gene responsible for PKU more likely in their offspring than if very different others had instead been chosen as mates.) Now PKU is passed on (genetically) to an offspring. Detection of this inherited disposition compels others to create for the affected child a tightly controlled environment (at least insofar as diet is concerned). Development of the symptoms (phenotype) associated with this genetic endowment now depends at least as much on factors in the environment (diet) as it does on the genes inherited.

If phenylalanine is successfully avoided, no symptoms associated with PKU will emerge. However, consumption of phenylalanine to the point of producing mental impairment may further act to limit the individual's ability to closely monitor his or her own diet. Now a **feedback loop** has been created that will likely further the damage created by initial exposure to the harmful agent in the external environment. Similar relationships between environment and characteristics of the individual operate all around us.

In Part IV, we consider further the means through which the environment can act to influence personality factors. Before proceeding, however, we pause to examine the applications derived from the Dispositional Strategy, as well as the limitations for which it is sometimes criticized.

SUMMARY

1. Much of our personality is biologically influenced through genetics, inheritance, and evolutionary processes.
2. Early scientists who linked biology and personality hypothesized that physique and temperament represented different expressions of a basic, underlying characteristic or genetic influence.
3. Darwin believed that naturally occurring genetic mutations in a species could produce adaptive advantages. Through increased likelihood of survival and reproductive advantage, traits become characteristics of a species. The versatility of a species is enhanced by its variability.
4. According to the process of evolution through natural selection, humans are related to other species but unique as well. Greater intelligence, linguistic ability, and neural plasticity distinguish humans from other species.
5. The human nervous system is a complex network of layered interacting subsystems, including the central nervous system (CNS), and the peripheral nervous system (PNS). Together, they regulate all bodily functions.
6. The peripheral nervous system is comprised of autonomic and somatic divisions. The autonomic division controls most involuntary behavior; it is itself comprised of the sympathetic (activating or "fight or flight") and parasympathetic (energy-conserving) systems. The somatic division is quite important to personality psychology, as it conveys information to and from the brain and is considered the seat of voluntary behavior.
7. The nervous system is comprised of glial cells and neurons, but the glial cells appear to play only a supporting function. It is the transmission of information along and across neurons that is of special interest to us.
8. Neurons do not actually touch but are, instead, separated from adjacent neurons by tiny gaps called synapses. Information is conducted electrically along a neuron, but at the synapse communication is chemical.
9. Neurotransmitters are the chemicals that work at the synapse to bring about this cross-synaptic communication. These chemicals are synthesized by neurons using precursor chemicals taken from the bloodstream, which ordinarily come from food sources. Temporary change in the production of a specific neurotransmitter can sometimes be influenced by diet.

10. The postsynaptic neuron (i.e., the one receiving the message) has specific receptor sites, to which certain neurotransmitters will bind to excite or inhibit the receiving neuron. Neurotransmitters may break down into component chemicals or be subject to reuptake the presynaptic neuron that can reabsorb and store it for future use.
11. Besides neurotransmitters, both neuromodulators and hormones can excite or inhibit synaptic transmission. Hormones are made by the glands and are circulated through the blood supply. The most important hormones for understanding the biology of personality appear to be the sex hormones.
12. Sociobiology is the study of the evolutionary basis of social behavior. Much of the theorizing in sociobiology has focused on how altruism might be fostered by evolution. There is also a good deal of focus on mating strategies. Mating in humans and other animals is assortative rather than random. It appears that we mate with others who are similar to ourselves.
13. According to sociobiology, the two sexes use quite different selection criteria. Women are more selective than men and typically seek long-term relationships and security for themselves and their offspring; this is an adaptive strategy, given the investment a woman must make to have and care for a child. For men, in contrast, it is adaptive (for survival of their genes) to mate as widely as possible.
14. Human males are most aggressive during the age (roughly between 15 and 25) when they are most fiercely competing for mates; this has led to the coining of a term for the phenomenon, the young male syndrome.
15. Human sperm do not all aim for the ovum, as had been long supposed. In addition to "egg-seekers," there appear to be blocker and killer types of sperm that fend off any other male's sperm that are in the vicinity. These non–egg-seekers are not there for nothing. According to one team of researchers, human polyandry (mating with multiple males) may be considerably more common than has often been supposed.
16. Behavioral genetics is the study of the genetic basis of behavior. Inheritance is carried out by discrete units of material called genes, transmitted in groups called chromosomes, which are strands of deoxyribonucleic acid (DNA). Humans have 23 pairs of chromosomes.
17. Children receive a separate set of genes from each parent; this complement of genes is called the person's genotype. However, the genotype itself is not displayed in overt appearance or behavior. The overt characteristics we do display are referred to as our phenotype.
18. The study of family patterns provides a rich source of information about which characteristics are heritable. The three broad types of studies using family patterns are the pedigree analysis method, the twin study method, and the adoptee method.
19. The Human Genome Project is proceeding to map the entire sequence of genes contained on the full complement of human chromosomes.

20. Three basic temperaments, "the raw materials out of which personality evolves," have been identified. These are sociability (whether the infant is easy, difficult, or slow to warm up to others), emotionality (the tendency to become physiologically aroused), and activity level. The evidence is overwhelming that all three have a substantial heritable component.
21. Adult personality domains also appear to be heritable. Introversion-Extraversion (i.e., the dimension E discussed in Chapter 8) has been explained by Eysenck in terms of individual differences in the ascending reticular system, which determines a person's level of arousal. Eysenck's theory is that extraverts have an arousal level that is too low much of the time, while introverts (low E) are so easily aroused that they shy away from stimulation.
22. Gray has a different biological analysis of the basis of E, based on contrasting a behavioral activation system (BAS) and a behavioral inhibition system (BIS), which, respectively, produce or inhibit goal-seeking behavior. From the interaction of these two systems, Gray has been able to derive a model that encompasses both E and Neuroticism (N).
23. Eysenck also has a theory about the biological basis of N, which assumes that people who are very emotional have highly arousable autonomic nervous systems and that those who are steady as a rock (very low N) are actually underreactive.
24. Openness (O) and Conscientiousness (C) appear to be about as heritable as N and E, but the heritability of Agreeableness (A) is quite low. There is relatively less information on O, C, and A than on N or E, so these conclusions must be considered tentative.
25. Two specific dispositions, aggressiveness and sensation seeking, have been studied rather extensively from a biological perspective. Aggressiveness appears to be related to high levels of steroid or sex hormones. At the level of the central nervous system, aggression is associated with activity in the amygdala, located in the temporal lobes of the brain.
26. Sensation seeking is defined by Marvin Zuckerman as seeking varied sensations, often despite risk. Sensation seeking appears to be highly heritable. Zuckerman views sensation seeking as part of the more general class of approach behavior, which he sees as a "drive" with a biological basis.
27. Heritability is only part of the story, and genes, by themselves, are not destiny. Inheritance interacts continuously and reciprocally with the environment.

CHAPTER TEN

Applications and Limitations of the Dispositional Strategy

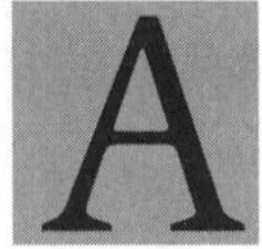

s stated earlier (see Chapter 7), applications derived from the Dispositional Strategy often take the form of matching people (based on their dispositional characteristics) with appropriate environments in educational programs and social and vocational settings. This chapter begins with an examination of the many types of assessment devices arising from this strategy and their current (as well as some potential future) uses.

APPLICATIONS OF DISPOSITIONAL ASSESSMENT DEVICES

A great deal of dispositional assessment is conducted through self-report inventories. These range widely, from extremely broad devices that attempt to measure virtually all major dispositions and characteristics (the MMPI and NEO-PI are two examples; see Chapters 2 and 8, respectively) to much narrower questionnaires aimed at assessing individual traits or dispositions. There are specific paper-and-pencil scales to assess achievement anxiety, argumentativeness, compulsiveness, fear of negative evaluation, fear of fat, interpersonal dependency, irrational values, loneliness, magical ideation, mathematics anxiety, and many other specific dispositions (Corcoran & Fischer, 1987). The choice of appropriate assessment devices and their application is often left to the clinician or researcher.

Personality Inventories and Personnel Selection

No self-report personality inventory is adequate for selecting ideal candidates for important jobs by itself. The accuracy of these tests' predictions simply is *not* sufficient. But what of the opposite approach—using personality inventories to *exclude* individuals who may be *un*suitable for critical roles? Many occupations, such as nuclear power plant operator, surgeon, and air traffic controller, require a strong sense of responsibility and personal stability. Lives often depend on the competent performance of these jobs. The likelihood of accidents or errors in these roles might be reduced by screening out applicants who show any signs of psychopathology or unfitness for the role (Butcher, 1979).

Use of the MMPI (see Chapter 2) for screening out unsuitable job candidates has generated a history of controversy and litigation (Dahlstrom, 1980). In the summer of 1977, five men sued two Jersey City officials and the Laboratory of Psychological Studies, which had conducted psychological screening of aspiring firefighters. This suit was later joined by several civil liberties organizations as well.

The plaintiffs charged that the use of psychological tests (in this case the MMPI) requires applicants to disclose highly personal information and constitutes an invasion of privacy. (Some of the items from the MMPI allude to sexual practices and religious and political beliefs.) The suit further charged that the testing violated fundamental rights of freedom of belief protected by the First and Fourteenth Amendments to the U.S. Constitution.

After a lengthy trial, presiding Judge Coolahan issued his opinion (*McKenna v. Fargo,* 1978). He said that the heart of the case involved the "involuntary disclosure" that accompanied responding to psychological tests. The job applicants did not always know exactly what their responses to specific items were revealing about their personalities. Therefore, privacy was being invaded on some level.

Nevertheless, Judge Coolahan dismissed the allegation that the applicants' constitutional right of freedom of belief had been violated. It did not appear that the applicants were being tested for their beliefs or values. The fire department received only a testing summary; they never received the raw scores of the tests, which would reveal how applicants responded to specific items. Furthermore, the role of firefighter involves life-and-death decisions under the pressure of time and intense danger. The judge therefore recognized the need for the state to protect its interests by hiring only those individuals who were emotionally fit for the role.

Judge Coolahan decided "that the constitutional protection afforded privacy interests is not absolute. State interests may become sufficiently compelling to sustain State regulations or activities which burden the right to privacy." He further determined that psychological evaluation is an acceptable selection procedure, largely because psychological factors play a major role in firefighting. This decision was later upheld by a circuit court of appeals.

The MMPI continues to be used as a screening test for many "sensitive" jobs. The biggest drawback of this practice is that it probably falsely excludes many appropriate candidates. A team of psychologists recently stressed that "organizations must ultimately decide upon the degree to which they are willing to sacrifice candidates who may have been successful in order to screen out those who are unsuitable" (Inwald & Brockwell, 1991, p. 522).

The NEO-PI-R

The NEO-PI-R is the current full FFM inventory (see Chapter 8), having replaced the original NEO-PI in 1992. It consists of 240 items, each answered on a 5-point scale from "strongly agree" to "strongly disagree." Any given item is scored for only one domain, and each domain is covered by 48 items.

The items were selected on their ability to correlate with other measures of the factors (so-called *criterion validity*), as well as the criteria of plausibility and reasonableness *(content validity)*. For most of the items, it is fairly obvious what they are intended to measure. For example, a typical Neuroticism item is "I am easily frightened"; a typical Extraversion item is "I am a warm and friendly person."

An important feature of the NEO-PI-R is that it assesses not only the major domains of personality but also the narrower features, or **facets,** that the Five-Factor Model specifies for each domain. Thus, all together, each respondent is scored for 30 different scales from the NEO-PI-R—six facets within each of the five broad domains. The domains and facets of the NEO-PI-R are listed in Table 10.1.

The NEO inventories were developed for use with normal populations. There are separate norms for males and females, and for college-age (17–20) individuals and older adults. There are also two versions of the NEO-PI-R, one for self-reports and one to be filled out by a rater who knows the person well. The publishers of the NEO-PI-R even provide a service whereby a person completes the inventory on a machine-scorable answer sheet, which is then interpreted by a computer program. These interpretations include a global description of the respondent's personality, a detailed interpretation of

Table 10.1 The personality domains and facets covered by the NEO-PI-R

NEUROTICISM	EXTRAVERSION	OPENNESS	AGREEABLENESS	CONSCIENTIOUSNESS
Anxiety	Warmth	Fantasy	Trust	Competence
Anger-hostility	Gregariousness	Aesthetics	Straightforwardness	Order
Depression	Assertiveness	Feelings	Altruism	Dutifulness
Self-consciousness	Activity	Actions	Compliance	Achievement striving
Impulsiveness	Excitement-seeking	Ideas	Modesty	Self-discipline
Vulnerability	Positive emotions	Values	Tender-mindedness	Deliberation

the facets, and some possible implications of the scores (such as the way the individual would probably cope with daily stress).

The NEO-FFI

For purposes of detailed assessment, full-scale profiles are desirable. Often, though, a concise, global assessment is all that is required. The NEO-FFI (NEO Five-Factor Inventory) was developed for this purpose.

The NEO-FFI contains only 60 items, with 12 items representing each broad domain. It does not provide separate facet scales but has the advantage that most people can complete it within 15 minutes. The NEO-FFI is supplied as a test booklet and answer sheet combined and can be scored in under a minute. (Note, however, that as with most personality tests and measures, interpretation of a NEO-FFI profile is not simple and straightforward. Adequate interpretation may require considerable time and additional information about the person being assessed.)

Like the MMPI scores (see Chapter 2), NEO scores can be plotted graphically to create a "personality profile." The simplest profile is the one derived from the NEO-FFI, an example of which appears as Figure 10.1.

Specific Assessment Devices

For the most part, our discussion has focused on very broad multifactor measures of "global" personality. The MMPI, the NEO-PI, and the NEO-FFI attempt to measure a wide range of characteristics in an effort to produce a description of the individual's entire personality. Dispositional personality assessment is often much more focused than this. Both researchers and clinicians are at times interested in only one or a limited number of personality traits, which may be related to treatment or to specific placement questions.

A range of specific assessment devices are used in industry and education to assess traits perceived as relevant for particular academic or career pursuits. Several standardized intelligence tests (Wechsler Adult Intelligence Scale [WAIS], Wechsler Intelligence Scale for Children [WISC], and Stanford Binet Intelligence Test) have gained wide acceptance and are used routinely for addressing questions regarding academic ability and placement. Although claiming to measure "intelligence," these tests are actually best used to predict academic success. They might be better labeled tests of academic aptitude.

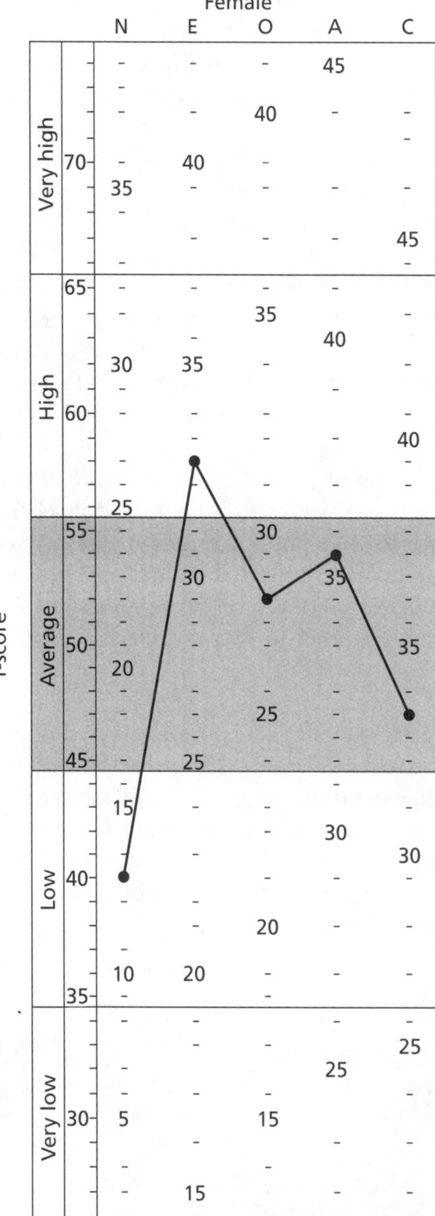

Figure 10.1
Example of a NEO-FFI Profile of a middle-aged woman. The overall profile is in the normal range and reveals a person who is relatively low on Neuroticism and relatively high on Extraversion.

The Myers-Briggs Type Indicator (MBTI; Myers, 1962) classifies individuals as 1 of 16 possible personality types based on combinations of four bipolar scales: extraversion-introversion, thinking-feeling, sensing-intuiting, and perceiving-judging. This instrument has gained wide acceptance in business and industry and is frequently used to identify suitable roles for individuals based on their type. In 1990, approximately 2 million people took some form of this test (Thorne & Gough, 1991). Specific assessment devices are commonly used in all forms of dispositional research as well.

Biologically Based Assessment

Nowhere is the mind-body issue more conspicuous than in the biological approach to personality and its resulting applications. Here the elusive links between mental states, personality characteristics, and health reveal the complex and reciprocal nature of the interface between mind and body. Mental states are not independent of the physical structure, nor is the physical body independent of mental functions. Mental and affective states influence physical functioning and vice versa. Biologically based assessments and interventions arise from this recognition.

Galvanic Skin Response

The **galvanic skin response (GSR)** is one measure of autonomic nervous system activity. (Recall that the sympathetic nervous system—one subsystem of the autonomic nervous system—prepares for energy expenditure, especially in readying the organism for "fight or flight." Digestive processes are slowed while heart rate, respiration, and blood flow to other major organs and muscles are increased.) The GSR is a measure of the electrical conductivity of the skin, which increases with even minuscule changes in perspiration. Thus, the GSR serves as one physical measure of stress, fear, or anxiety. Changes in GSR may indicate the impact of stimuli on a person's cognitive or emotional state. The GSR is used as a response measure for research purposes and in combination with other measures, especially in the polygraph test.

Polygraphs

Polygraphs are measures of multiple physiological responses (the prefix *poly* literally means "many"). Various responses are measured and recorded simultaneously to produce a graphic readout (see Figure 10.2 for an example). Polygraph recordings usually consist of a number of measures of sympathetic nervous system activity (GSR, heart rate, respiration rate, and blood pressure), recorded in conjunction with a series of questions by an examiner and responses provided by the subject.

Figure 10.2
This woman is taking a polygraph test while the examiner looks at the readout as it is generated. Each line of the graph represents one of the physiologic measures being monitored.

Polygraphs are commonly (but incorrectly) called "lie detector tests" because they are most often used to detect deception in the responses of the subject. The reasoning behind the use of polygraphs is as follows: Lying produces stress, which leads to sympathetic nervous system arousal and activation, which would be reflected in changes in the measures recorded. Although this reasoning appears sound, polygraphs clearly are *not* lie detectors.

There are several problems with the interpretation of polygraph results. First, the responses are *generic* and may be triggered by many emotions, including anger, joy, fear, and anxiety. There is no sympathetic nervous system response specific to lying. Another problem with interpretation rests in the nature of the questions themselves. Blatantly accusatory questions may be experienced as provocative or threatening, leading to increased arousal regardless of the content of the response, or its veracity.

Beyond these obvious problems with the technique is the related issue of individual differences in responsivity. Indeed, some personality types are characterized by greater or lesser responsivity at the central nervous system level. (See earlier discussions of Extraversion, sensation seeking, and the BAS and BIS systems in Chapter 9). Little empirical work has been done to relate these personality characteristics to outcome of polygraph tests. It is possible that lowered central nervous system responsivity would color test responses. Also, antisocial personality disorder is characterized by "failure to conform to social norms . . . deceitfulness . . . [and] lack of remorse" (APA, 1994). This being the case, might these individuals not simply fail to respond with arousal to instances of lying? These issues must all be addressed empirically before relying on polygraph data as an objective measure of anything more than autonomic arousal.

Despite their tremendous appeal as an "objective" source of information, polygraphs are usually not admissible as evidence in courts of law because of the extremely subjective nature of their interpretation. It is not difficult to find two polygraph "experts" to offer opposite interpretations of the same polygraph results.

Box 10.1
THE PROMISE OF IMAGING TECHNOLOGIES

Tools for imaging the living brain have advanced tremendously over the last several decades. Not long ago, what was known about human brain structure was based almost entirely on postmortem studies. Current technology allows for increasingly well-defined images of brain structures through the use of **computed tomography (CT)** and **magnetic resonance imaging (MRI).**

Recently, imaging has gone beyond mere structure to begin to display *brain functions* in humans. A variety of techniques (primarily still restricted to research applications) can now assess the functioning of the living human brain under different conditions. These techniques provide images of brain structure, overlaid with images of functional measures of brain activity. These methods are changing the way the brain is studied and promise to reveal new information about what neural processes underlie different types of behavior.

Regional cerebral blood flow (rCBF) is the

Box continued on following page

Box 10.1 *Continued*
THE PROMISE OF IMAGING TECHNOLOGIES

A 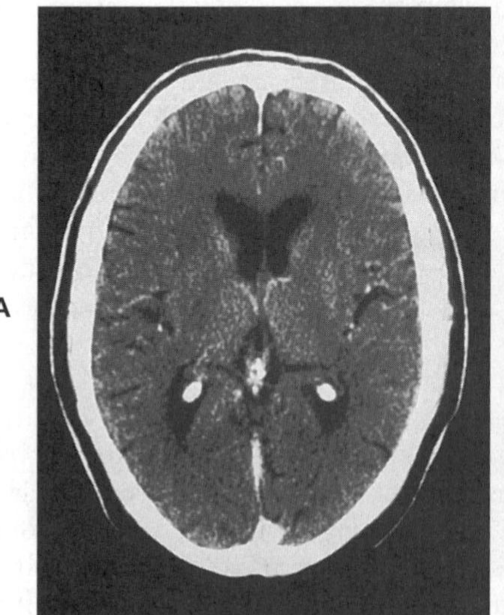

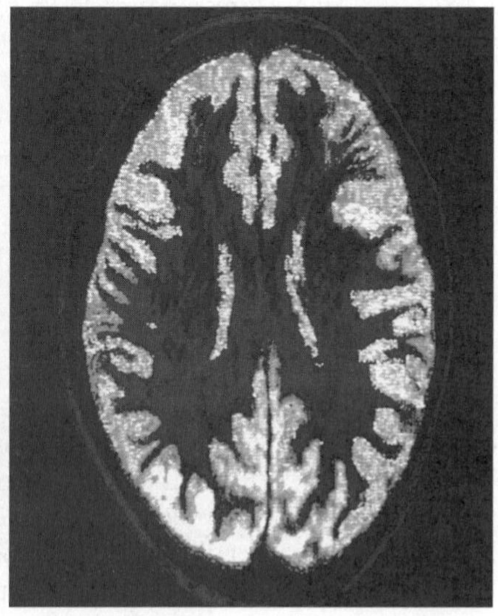 B

A: CT-produced brain image—horizontal section. **B:** MRI-produced image—horizontal section.
A: © Scott Camazine/Photo Researchers, Inc.; **B:** © New York Hospital/Peter Arnold, Inc.

most basic of these techniques. The volume of blood flowing to various regions of the cortex is one measure of metabolic activity in the area. The rCBF serves as a gross measure of blood flow. Detectors are placed in an ordered array over the scalp to measure the level and flow of blood from emissions of an inert gas. (The subject inhales this gas, which is then carried along with oxygen into the bloodstream to serve as "markers" in the blood. Movement of these traceable markers reveals movement of the blood through the brain.) This technique is limited in that it can measure blood flow *only* to the cerebral cortex (outer layer of the brain).

Positron emission tomography (PET) also measures metabolic activity in the brain through the movement and absorption of radioactive markers circulating in the blood, but has the added advantage of being capable of measuring activity in deep structures as well as at the outer surface of the brain.

Single photon emission computerized tomography (SPECT) is similar to PET scanning in most respects but tracks single-photon-emitting isotopes, which have longer half-lives than those used in PET scanning. It results in more prolonged imaging periods than PET and tracks more protracted and complex cognitive activities and their effects on brain activation.

These techniques (rCBF, PET, and SPECT) can be used in conjunction with psychological testing and are beginning to reveal structure-function relationships. They have proven useful in discriminating between possible causes of dementia (Read et al., 1995; Sloan, Fenton, Kennedy, & MacLennan, 1995; Starkstein et al., 1995). These methods are currently being extended to the search for physiological correlates of a variety of psychological disorders.

Although findings remain somewhat mixed, a number of studies have demonstrated reduced metabolic activity in the frontal lobes of patients with schizophrenia (Buchsbaum & Haier, 1987). The "dopamine hypothesis" of schizophrenia is being actively investigated with PET and SPECT, and some data appear to support

Box continued on following page

Box 10.1 *Continued*
THE PROMISE OF IMAGING TECHNOLOGIES

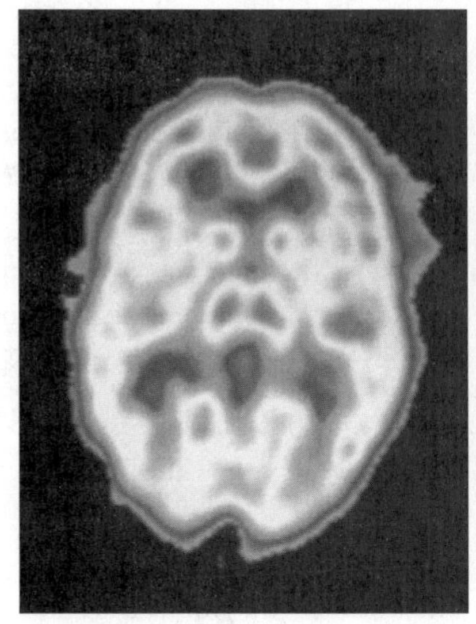

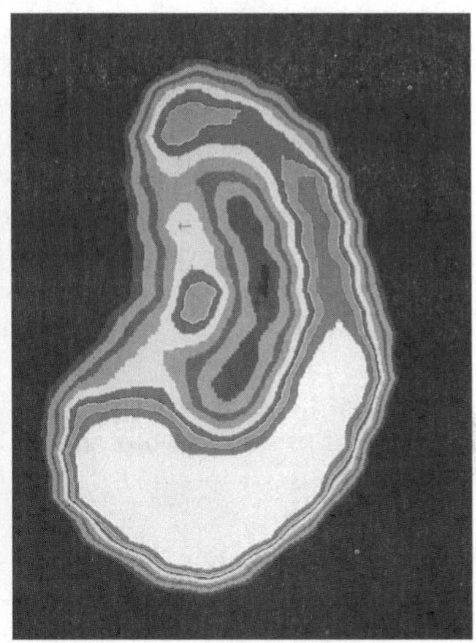

A: The PET scan image is usually color enhanced. **B:** SPECT scan image—horizontal section.
A: Copyright, 1998, Dr. Monte Buchsbaum/Peter Arnold, Inc.; **B:** © CNRI/Phototake

hyperfunctioning of certain dopamine receptors in deep structures of the brain (Waddington, 1989).

A recent PET study examined patterns of glucose metabolism during various sleep stages and found different results for depressed and nondepressed subjects (Ho et al., 1996). The authors conclude that their results support a *hyperarousal* theory of at least some types of depression.

There have been several reports of changes in patterns of brain metabolism associated with distinct personalities of patients with multiple personality disorder (Saxe, Vasile, Hill, Bloomingdale, & van der Kolk, 1992). Preliminary reports of application to other disorders such as alcohol abuse and borderline personality disorder have also appeared (De la Fuente et al., 1994; Mampunza et al., 1995).

PET and SPECT procedures are presently still restricted to research applications, but technology is advancing rapidly. With refinements in technique and continued application to carefully selected patient groups, it is likely that functional relationships that may ultimately be used to diagnose and predict outcomes on a variety of behavioral and psychological measures will be revealed. Personality dispositions may ultimately be assessed not by paper-and-pencil techniques but by brain scans that detect patterns of functioning indicative of traits and behavioral tendencies!

BIOLOGICALLY BASED TREATMENTS

Many interventions arise from the biological approach to personality. Although personality traits and dispositions are assumed to be stable over time, understanding their relationship with health variables can lead to identification of individuals at risk for the development of specific problems. Then, efforts can be made to reduce any unnecessary high-risk behavior.

Many behavior problems are susceptible to pharmacologic treatment. In this section, we consider a number of biologically based treatments, many of which would, in practice, be applied by physicians rather than psychologists.

Psychopharmacology

Perhaps the most obvious of the biologically based treatment strategies is the use of medications for psychological disorders. Three basic terms are used (interchangeably) to refer to pharmacologic agents as used to treat psychological disorders: **psychotherapeutic, psychoactive,** or **psychotropic drugs.** Some of these drugs also have other (nonpsychiatric) uses as well. We will be concerned only with the general classes of drugs and their applications for psychological or behavioral problems. (Note that the classifications are somewhat arbitrary because many drugs can be applied to more than one class of problems and some do not fit neatly into any single category.)

For the most part, psychotropic drugs are commonly used for the control of psychotic symptomatology and schizophrenia (**antipsychotics,** or **neuroleptics**), mood disorders (**antidepressants,** and **antimanics**), and anxiety **(anxiolytics).** Some agents, such as **Antabuse** for alcohol abuse, have very specific applications.

The number of available psychotropic drugs is increasing rapidly with advances in understanding of neurochemistry. New drugs mimic the actions, enhance receptor binding, or inhibit binding or production of neurotransmitters. For the most part, psychotropics exert their effects through the same mechanisms as endogenous (naturally produced) neurotransmitters. However, their actions are not always direct and specific. Predicting medication effects on particular symptoms is often difficult, and arriving at an effective medication and dosage is often a matter of trial and error with any particular individual.

Relationships between personality variables and medication response are just now being explored empirically. A recent study did find a significant relationship between a measure of Extraversion and response to antidepressant medication (Bagby et al., 1995). In this study, those subjects who scored higher on Extraversion responded better to medication. Their symptoms were alleviated more quickly and more effectively than those subjects who scored lower on Extraversion. We believe the near future will provide much more data to relate personality characteristics to biologically based treatments. For now, however, psychotropics are prescribed only by physicians, working independently or in cooperation with psychologists.

Electroconvulsive Therapy and Psychosurgery

Electroconvulsive therapy (ECT) and psychosurgery are also applied to some psychological problems. In ECT, electrical current is delivered to the brain in amounts sufficient to produce a seizure. Its therapeutic effects are apparently due to some form of postsynaptic receptor regulation (specifically down-regulation of the same type of receptors affected by long-term treatment with antidepressant drugs), but the effects throughout the nervous system are multiple and complex. Almost invariably, ECT produces some short-term amnesia and may have other serious adverse effects, including increased hypertension, increased intracranial pressure, breakdown of the blood-brain barrier, and cardiac decompensation in postmyocardial infarction patients (Kaplan & Sadock, 1991). It is most often viewed as a treatment of last resort for intractable cases that have failed to respond to psychotherapy or medication.

Electroconvulsive therapy is an effective treatment for major depression, bipolar disorder, and some cases of schizophrenia (Kaplan & Sadock, 1991). Effectiveness of ECT seems to be greatest for severely depressed patients with many vegetative signs (disturbance of sleep, circadian rhythms, and appetite).

Psychosurgery is a term applied to any surgery aimed at correcting or alleviating psychological problems. For the most part, psychosurgery is brain surgery with the goal of breaking down communication networks that underlie the psychological disturbance. Many early forms of psychosurgery were simply desperate attempts to control the most maladaptive symptoms and consisted of ablating or removing large portions of brain tissue. However, current surgical technology allows for much more discrete lesions than was possible only a decade ago. Psychosurgery continues to be used with reasonable effectiveness to treat extreme and otherwise intractable cases of depression and obsessive-compulsive disorder (OCD).

Kaplan and Sadock (1991) recommend that psychosurgery be considered only when severely debilitating and chronic psychiatric disturbances have proven intractable over a course of at least 5 years. Surgery is most likely to be effective for patients with prominent vegetative symptoms or extreme anxiety. Although psychosurgery applied to uncontrolled anger has been described (see Chapter 9), this application remains questionable and continues to be debated. Psychosurgery, like ECT, fell out of favor because of the immense risk of adverse side effects for the individual, as well as limited public acceptance due to the abuses and misapplications of the past.

Other Biologically Based Therapies

Several other therapies have arisen from the biological approach. **Phototherapy,** or light therapy, is exposure to bright artificial light on a regular daily basis. It has proven useful for some subtypes of depression, especially depression that occurs regularly with a seasonal pattern (Kaplan & Sadock, 1991). Many people lapse into an annual depression beginning in the fall or winter months and remitting in the spring. The DSM-IV (APA, 1994) recognizes that other regular seasonal patterns may also be present among mood disorder patients, but they are apparently much less common than the fall- or winter-onset variety. In fact, daylight hours are more limited during the winter months (in all but tropical regions, which experience very little climate change throughout the year).

The idea behind phototherapy is resetting circadian rhythms, which are shifted out of phase in seasonal depressive episodes. Briefly, the human body exhibits cyclical changes in hormone levels, temperature, and states of consciousness that follow a regular 24-hour pattern. Seasonal depression is associated with a *delayed* circadian rhythm pattern. Exposure to bright light in the early morning seems to *phase advance* the circadian pattern, effectively restoring a normal rhythm for some patients. Although much remains to be

Exposure to bright full-spectrum light on a daily basis elevates mood for some who suffer depression.
© John Griffin/The Image Works

learned in this area, several facts seem clear. Light is most effective when bright, full-spectrum, and administered for at least 2 hours each morning (Kaplan & Sadock, 1991). Briefer durations appear less effective, and the question of when to begin and end exposure remains to be clarified. Phototherapy is generally not effective for treating other types of depression, which suggests that seasonal depression reflects a unique diagnostic entity that may result from different etiologic factors than other types of depression.

Sleep deprivation, or modification of the sleep-wake cycle, has also proven effective in the treatment of some cases of depression. Deprivation of a single night's sleep results in alleviation of depression in about 60% of sufferers (Kaplan & Sadock, 1991). The effectiveness of this treatment is extremely limited, however. Once sleeping is resumed, symptoms return. Thus, after the next night's sleep, or even a brief daytime nap, mood symptoms reappear.

Phase advance of the sleep cycle may have more enduring effects. Specifically, instructing depressed patients to retire earlier (about 2 hours earlier than usual) and rise earlier provides some symptom relief. This relief may last for 1 week or more and seems particularly effective when paired with drug therapy. Much remains to be learned about the relationship between circadian cycles and mood disorders, but these findings suggest that biological rhythms are associated with the development or maintenance of some mood disturbances and may contribute to them.

Box 10.2
GENE THERAPY AND CLONING—THE FUTURE IS HERE!

Gene therapy is a burgeoning new field of biotechnology. Researchers are actively deciphering the human genome and at the same time racing to unravel some of nature's most elusive secrets. The idea of actually replacing defective genetic material in living beings has been considered as a serious possibility only in the past decade. The first major international conference on gene therapy was held on Long Island at the Cold Spring Harbor Laboratory in 1992. Lyon and Gorner (1995), in describing the history of gene therapy, state that it "promises to rewrite not merely the practice of medicine but, in the fullness of time, the evolutionary course of the human race itself" (p. 18).

Indeed, rapid advances in the field of biotechnology suggest that this rewriting may well be under way. Scientists are discovering the genetic material responsible for all types of physical characteristics and disease processes. Because the major domains of personality appear to have a heritable basis, discovery of the responsible gene or linkages with other genes may well follow.

Genetic screening and counseling have come to be accepted features of modern medicine already. Beyond merely screening for the presence of genetic problems and recessive traits, scientists are learning how to replace faulty or undesirable genetic codes with "corrected" ones. Talk of "germ-line gene therapy" (in which the **gametes,** or sex cells, of a mature individual are corrected for genetic problems before offspring are produced) no longer sounds like the ramblings of a dreamer but rather like medical technology that will be perfected over the next few years!

One researcher likens gene therapy to other types of transplants. However, what is transplanted in the process of gene therapy is only microscopic genetic material in the nucleus of one or more cells rather than an entire body organ.

The processes are similar at one level of analysis, yet gene replacement is more profound still. It is the genes that direct all forms of growth and development of the organism. Genes control biological processes from the first cell divisions of the fertilized ovum through the development of the fully mature organism, and everything in between. But gene replacement is here. It has succeeded in some lower organisms and already demonstrated some limited success in humans.

"Biogerontologists" are currently experimenting to not only arrest but actually *reverse* aspects of the aging process, with startling success. Although cloning appeared for many years as a far-fetched fantasy, it has now truly arrived.

Some mammals have been "cloned" by livestock breeders (mostly cows and sheep) by dividing single zygotes at precise stages of development (during the earliest undifferentiated stage at which time the cells are simply dividing rapidly) to produce multiple identical offspring. The resulting fetuses are not clones, in the technical sense, of any existing organism. Rather they are (like identical twins) multiple copies of genetically identical individuals, each of which resulted originally from the pairing of two distinct gametes (from the parent organisms). However, 1997 marked the beginning of a new era in biology.

The February 27 issue of *Nature* described the first viable offspring produced from the cell nucleus (containing the genetic material) of a fully mature organism (Wilmut, Schneike, McWhir, Kind, & Campbell, 1997). The cell nucleus was removed from a mammary cell of a mature sheep and inserted into an **enucleated unfertilized egg** cell from another donor. (The nucleus of the donor egg cell was previously extracted, yielding an egg cell with *everything but* the nucleus, which carries half of the chromosomes and the genes for the organism.) The

Box continued on following page

Box 10.2 *Continued*

GENE THERAPY AND CLONING—THE FUTURE IS HERE!

Dolly—the first ever true clone of an existing mammal.
© Paul Clements/AP/Wide World Photos

donor egg cell now contained not half, but rather the full complement of genes from a single existing mature sheep. The resulting zygote was implanted in the uterus of another ewe, where it matured to term to yield a new sheep, with all the phenotypic characteristics of the nucleus donor sheep!

This is the first demonstration of true cloning of an adult organism of a mammalian species. It represents a breakthrough with enormous practical implications. Whereas earlier replications of animals left some things to chance (the multiples resulted from the pairing of two parent organisms, leaving the ultimate genotype and phenotype of the offsprings to be determined by the usual genetic "lottery"), this form of duplication allows identical replication of fully mature animals. (Of course, it requires the same time investment as normal gestation and development, which varies tremendously from species to species.) Breeders may now exercise much greater control over the composition of herds and therefore the prevalence of characteristics in the larger gene pool of particular species than ever before.

Although the processes used are extremely complex and delicate and outcomes are still limited (only 1 of 29 renucleated cells resulted in a viable pregnancy), refinement will no doubt proceed quickly. However, cloning closes the door to natural selection—the accepted understanding of how species come to benefit over time by gradual changes and improvements to their gene pools.

Box continued on following page

Box 10.2 *Continued*

GENE THERAPY AND CLONING—THE FUTURE IS HERE!

Human cells may be capable of enduring the types of manipulation required for cloning. At the same time, genes responsible for not only physical but also psychological characteristics are being identified. This raises serious practical and ethical questions. Should parents or societies be permitted to choose the characteristics of children before they are even conceived? Should humans use technology to control their own evolutionary course? Advances in technology may be outpacing ethical and practical considerations. The debate is just beginning about the possibilities and implications of human cloning.

HEALTH PSYCHOLOGY AND PERSONALITY

Health psychology is the term applied to any endeavor to elucidate the psychological factors that relate to and maintain health (or disease) status. We have already discussed some of the ways that psychological variables (Type A behavior pattern, emotional reactivity, stress) may influence health-related variables (e.g., blood pressure, cardiovascular disease).

Behavior influences health through a variety of direct and indirect means. Seeking medical attention when necessary is one (indirect) means through which behavior affects health. A more direct effect on health may result from thrill seeking, when, for example, sky diving or bungee jumping results in serious physical injury. Other high-risk behavior, such as smoking, drinking heavily, and illicit drug use, may also have direct adverse effects on health.

Health psychologists attempt to illuminate relationships among psychological variables, behavior patterns, and health consequences. This information often directs interventions, as well as enabling practitioners to identify people at risk for developing particular physical problems. Psychologists are often involved in developing treatments aimed at reducing high-risk behavior, illness behavior, and modification of the individual's environment in an effort to maintain or enhance health status.

For example, many people suffer from chronic and incurable pain. Although pain itself may be debilitating, the social consequences of pain often serve to increase rather than minimize this disability. Chronic pain sufferers may be *reinforced* (see also Chapter 12) for pain and illness behavior. Other people may begin to relieve the sufferer of responsibility for income, domestic chores, and child care. They may also provide reinforcement in the form of increased attention and expressed sympathy. Over time, the activity of the patient may become more restricted, which can actually serve to increase (through inactivity and loss of muscle tone) the intensity of pain experienced.

Health psychologists have found that instructing family members to attend to positive, constructive behavior rather than to pain or illness behavior minimizes the impact of pain on daily activities and independence. Patients often begin to function better and complain less about their pain.

Psychoneuroimmunology

Psychoneuroimmunology is the study of the relationship between the nervous system and immune functioning (O'Leary, 1990; Vollhardt, 1991). The **immune system** is the body's means of defense against invasion by viruses, bacteria, and any other foreign agents that might prove detrimental to physical health and functioning. Its structures control the production and function of leukocytes. **Leukocytes** is the generic term for white blood cells, of which there are several types. They serve as the body's primary defense against infection. Leukocytes identify, attack, and destroy foreign invaders. The path of influence between certain types of stressors and immune functioning is now being delineated.

Certain types of stress, including chronic and acute short-term demands, emotional distress, and physical pain, affect immune functioning. These stressors exert direct effects on a variety of chemical responses in the body. For example, when exposed to protracted painful stimuli, the body produces increased levels of **endorphins** (the body's natural opiates). Endorphins directly suppress pain but also have a secondary effect of lowering blood levels of **natural killer cells,** one class of leukocytes (Mogil, Sternberg, & Liebeskind, 1993). Depressed mood has also been related to diminished immunological responses, as measured by circulating levels of leukocytes (Weisse, 1992).

Although the direct effects of these observed changes remain to be determined, it is likely that suppressed immune activity leaves a person more susceptible to a variety of illnesses. Accumulating research documents the detrimental effects of stress on a variety of chronic illnesses through relapses or general disease progression. Chronic diseases such as acquired immunodeficiency syndrome (AIDS) and multiple sclerosis (MS) may progress more rapidly in the presence of chronic or acute stress, but the exact nature of the relationship remains to be determined.

Coping Styles and Health

Stress has been linked to a variety of health problems and apparently has a direct impact on immune functioning. How people cope with stressors appears to influence their health as well (Aldwin & Revenson, 1987). Some coping styles, especially extreme negativism about outcomes or mismatches between active coping or acceptance and actual degree of control over circumstances, tend to produce adverse effect on health. These variables have been termed **stress moderators** because they may inhibit or exaggerate the health effects of stress on individuals.

Simply being highly reactive to stressful situations (a disposition closely related to emotionality as defined by Buss and Plomin [1984a] and Neuroticism as defined by Eysenck [1967] and more recently by Costa and McCrae) may result in negative health consequences independent of coping response. Manuck, Kaplan, and Clarkson (1983) studied monkeys who were rated as either high or low reactors based on heart rate data. Postmortem studies showed the high reactors to have nearly twice as much blockage of coronary arteries as their low reactive counterparts. These data suggest that *personality variables do affect health outcomes* and that there may be multiple paths of influence.

Neuroticism and Attention to Symptoms

The personality trait of Neuroticism (N in Eysenck and Costa & McCrae's scheme) has been found to be positively correlated with sensitivity to physical sensations. People high on Neuroticism measures are more attuned to their bodily sensations than others. They may reduce their risk of serious illness or injury by seeking medical attention as soon as they become aware of symptoms or unusual sensations that might signal illness. They may therefore prevent progression of minor problems or serious disease by pursuing early treatment. (Then again, they may also seek medical attention for extremely minor and benign ailments as well. Over time this might cause their physicians to take their complaints less seriously than similar complaints by others.) This too could have serious health implications.

Hostility and Heart Attacks

The relationship between Type A behavior pattern and cardiovascular disease was noted many years ago and has received a good deal of attention over the past several decades (see Chapter 8).

Recent work in this area has looked at different components of Type A behavior in an effort to understand this relationship. The *hostility* component of Type A behavior now appears to be most strongly associated with increased risk of cardiovascular disease, as well as other health problems.

Greenglass and Julkunen (1991) used the Cook-Medley hostility scale, derived from the MMPI (see Chapter 7), as a measure of **cynical hostility.** They and other investigators have come up with a remarkably consistent finding. This one ingredient, cynical hostility, seems to predispose an individual to heart attacks and other forms of physical illness (Greenglass & Julkunen, 1989, 1991; Keltikangas-Jarvinen & Raikkonen, 1990; Miller et al., 1996; Smith & Pope, 1990).

What does this kind of hostility encompass? Greenglass and Julkunen developed a 17-item scale to measure it. Here are three of the beliefs endorsed by those who are cynically hostile:

No one cares much what happens to you.
Most people are honest chiefly through fear of being caught.
Most people make friends because friends are likely to be useful to them.

So, there seem to be two types of Type As. One type is engaged in healthy achievement striving; these people are "competitive" only in accepted ways. The other type is poorly adjusted, impatient, irritable, and hostile. In these people, competitiveness takes a destructive, antisocial form. And, back to the original point, it seems clear that only this latter type runs abnormally high health risks. Moreover, research has demonstrated that they are at greater risk than others for a variety of social and psychological problems as well (Barling, Bluen, & Moss, 1991; Volkmer & Feather, 1991).

LIMITATIONS OF THE DISPOSITIONAL STRATEGY

As we did previously with the Psychoanalytic Strategy, we now turn to a critical examination of the major problems facing the Dispositional Strategy.

A number of criticisms have been leveled repeatedly at the Dispositional Strategy. Among them are the strategy lacks its own theoretical concepts, fails to provide adequate explanations, does not predict individual behaviors, pays inadequate attention to personality development and change, overlooks the many subjective decisions involved in factor analysis, and has not adequately confronted the social desirability problem.

Lack of Its Own Theoretical Concepts

Theory plays a central role in all science. However, the Dispositional Strategy has operated without adequate theoretical guidelines. The only theoretical idea common among most trait psychologists seems to be Allport's heuristic realism principle—the idea that traits really exist and that the personality psychologist's job is to find them. This lack of theory has led to confusion and often leaves dispositional researchers talking past one another.

For example, when Cattell encountered a constellation of measures that referred to emotional stability, he provided a meaningless name (factor C) and later borrowed a name from the Psychoanalytic Strategy (ego strength). Meanwhile, other dispositional researchers called the same constellation emotionality, and yet others applied a psychiatric label, Neuroticism.

This same lack of agreement on theoretical concepts has left many dispositional phenomena ambiguous. For example, the Type A behavior pattern involves both a high level of activity and a high level of achievement striving. Yet almost no attention has been given to determining whether standard measures of activity level or standard measures of achievement motivation (such as those used by McClelland) are related to the Type A pattern.

And, although the Five-Factor Model has attracted many trait psychologists, the model has its critics. The most common complaint is that there is no agreed-upon set of terms to name the five factors (Coolidge et al., 1994; Goldberg, 1993), which has been referred to as the "Tower of Babble" problem. Close examination of the model makes no sense if its constructs are not adequately defined and validated.

The nature-nurture issue is another area of confusion for the theoretical concepts used in the Dispositional Strategy. The term *trait* was borrowed from genetics. It is still unclear how much similarity there is between the biological and psychological concepts.

Failure to Provide Adequate Explanations

In discussing the liabilities of the Psychoanalytic Strategy, we noted that psychoanalysts have committed certain logical errors in interpreting their observations. The Dispositional Strategy is also prone to a logical error—namely, confusing description with explanation.

When consistencies or regularities occur in behavior, it is convenient to summarize them with a descriptive label. Thus, Introversion is a label for an observed pattern of behavior or set of relationships. This labeling process is perfectly legitimate if our purpose is *description*, but the label obviously does not *explain* our observations. Yet the logical error of confusing description with explanation is repeatedly made by dispositional personality psychologists.

Skinner (1953) developed a related argument many years ago. Notice how Skinner's argument can be applied to any of the labels (e.g., introversion, intelligence, or anxiety) that have been invented to describe behavior:

> When we say that a man eats because he is hungry, smokes a great deal because he has the tobacco habit, fights because he has the instinct of pugnacity, behaves brilliantly because of his intelligence, or plays the piano well because of his musical ability, we seem to be referring to causes. But on analysis, these phrases prove to be merely redundant descriptions. A single set of facts is described by the two statements: "He eats" and "He is hungry." A single set of facts is described by the statements "He smokes a great deal" and "He has the smoking habit." A single set of facts is described by the two statements: "He plays well" and "He has musical ability." The practice of explaining one statement in terms of the other is dangerous because it suggests that we have found the cause and therefore need search no further. (p. 31)

Finally, dispositional psychologists who claim that dispositions are meant only as descriptions cannot escape this criticism. These dispositions do not provide any explanation of behavior and are therefore little more than common observations.

Inability to Predict Individual Behaviors

Advocates of the Dispositional Strategy have discovered many reliable and intriguing relationships, such as the links between aspects of physical appearance and personality, and no one doubts that there is some consistency in the way people behave. But almost no basis is provided for predicting the behavior of a single individual with any degree of accuracy.

For example, many people with delicate builds love action and adventure, despite the general tendency for this group to be somewhat introverted. Even among those who are introverted, prediction of their behavior in any particular situation is likely to be relatively inaccurate.

To compound the problem even further, analyses by Baumeister and his colleagues suggest that only a small subset of people are generally consistent—that is, behave as if they have some constant amount of a trait that follows them across time and situations. Thus, the proponents of the Dispositional Strategy may be forced to deal with **metatraits,** the trait of having or not having a particular trait (Baumeister, 1991; Baumeister & Tice, 1988).

To illustrate the risks in predicting individual behavior from dispositional self-report measures, let us consider an exaggerated hypothetical example. Suppose that an investigator informally observes that some people seem to be more intrusive than others, and defines *intrusiveness* as "a tendency to provide unsolicited information or advice, to show up uninvited, and to examine and use the belongings of others without asking." Next, the investigator administers a wide array of assessment techniques to measure intrusiveness, including peer ratings, self-report measures, and fantasy measures. The procedure yields reliable intrusiveness scores that show considerable individual differences among people.

At this point, the investigator begins to compare the backgrounds of subjects who are high (above average) and low (below average) in intrusiveness and finds high intrusives tend to report that their parents used to leave the doors to their rooms—and even their homes—unlocked. Apparently they worried little about privacy. In contrast, individuals low on intrusiveness report that their parents locked their doors and emphasized everyone's "right to privacy."

Suppose that given this information, you meet a young woman who mentions that her parents always left their doors unlocked. You would certainly be tempted to think that your new acquaintance is likely to be intrusive. However, that would not necessarily follow. It remains likely that your assumption would be wrong.

Part of the reason can be seen in Figure 10.3, which shows our hypothetical intrusiveness data. We have assumed that intrusiveness is normally distributed. (Modern dispositional psychologists commonly assume normal distributions.) We also show a difference between the "locked-door" and the "unlocked-door" groups that is large enough to be statistically significant. Thus, Figure 10.3 represents the usual magnitude of

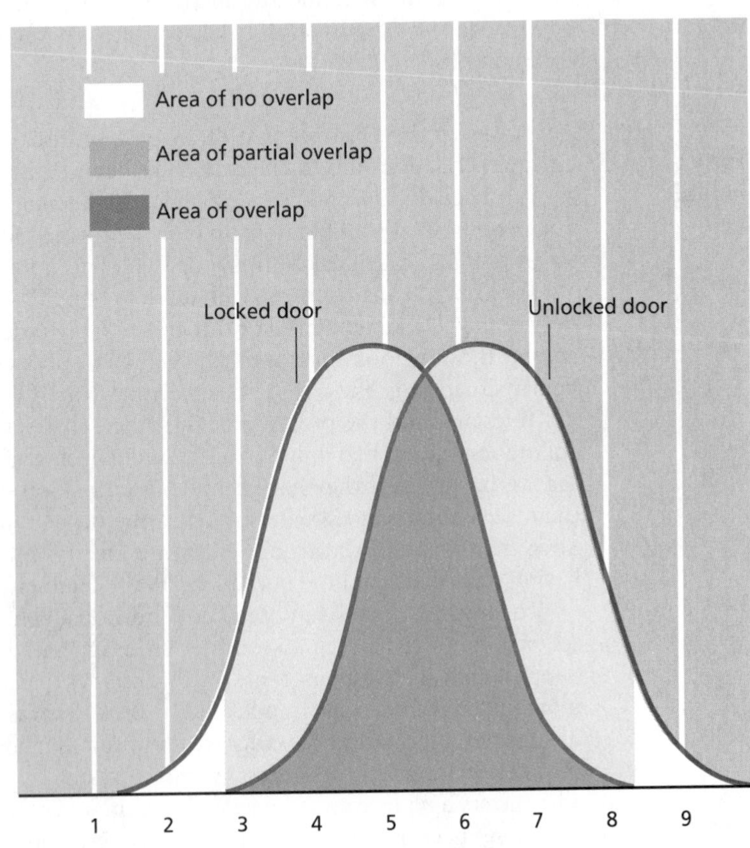

Figure 10.3
Hypothetical distributions of scores for the disposition "intrusiveness," showing that a significant difference between the average trait scores of two groups (here, "locked-door" versus "unlocked-door" backgrounds) does not ordinarily provide the basis for predicting what any specific individual will be like.

difference between "trait-high" and "trait-low" people in typical dispositional research.

Three areas of the figure deserve comment. The dark portion indicates overlap and accounts for more than half of the area under the curves. This overlap shows that most people will tend to get an average intrusiveness score, *regardless of whether the doors in their homes were locked or not.*

The two lighter areas indicate partial overlap. Some members of both groups obtain scores in this range, but one group dominates each area. Notice, for example, that some individuals from each background obtained an intrusiveness score of 4, but most were in the locked-door group.

Finally, the white areas indicate *non*overlap; only one group is represented. In the figure, the only people with scores as low as 2 came from homes where the doors were locked. The only people with scores as high as 9 came from homes where the doors were unlocked. The most important thing to note about the areas of nonoverlap is *how small they are;* only a small percentage of people fall in these extreme ranges.

With this analysis in mind, what conclusion can we draw about an individual's intrusiveness, knowing that she comes from a home where the doors were never locked? We certainly do not want to conclude that the person must be highly intrusive. (Even among people from unlocked-door homes, the majority are only about average in intrusiveness.) As a matter of fact, our new acquaintance could be less intrusive than average—maybe even very *un*intrusive—and still come from a home where the doors were left unlocked. In this case at least, to reach any conclusion about intrusiveness based on door-locking data would be merely to stereotype the person unjustifiably.

This finding does not mean that dispositional assessment is worthless. Rather, it means that the Dispositional Strategy has provided assessment procedures that improve our guessing (above chance) about what other people will be like or what they will do, but it remains *guessing.*

Walter Mischel (1968), in his now-classic critique of the Dispositional Strategy, made the point this way:

> It is important to clearly distinguish between "statistically significant" associations and equivalence. A correlation of .30 easily reaches statistical significance when the sample of subjects is sufficiently large, and suggests an association that is highly unlikely on the basis of chance. However, the same coefficient accounts for less than 10 percent of the relevant variance [i.e., what the variables share in common]. Statistically significant relationships of this magnitude are sufficient to justify personality research on individual and group differences. It is equally plain that their value for making statements about an individual are severely limited. Even when statistically significant behavioral consistencies are found, and even when they replicate reliably, the relationships usually are not large enough to warrant individual assessment and treatment decisions except for certain screening and selection purposes. (p. 38)

Mischel's recent work expands on these ideas and are described at length in Chapter 17.

Underestimation of the Importance of Situational Factors

A related liability is that the Dispositional Strategy underestimates—sometimes overlooks entirely—the influence of the situation and circumstances in determining behavior. For example, for years psychologists sought to determine what traits make a person a leader. Ultimately, however, it was recognized that in most groups, a leader is selected based on how well he or she can facilitate attainment of the group's particular goals.

> What was overlooked . . . in the view that leaders are uniquely endowed . . . was the actual fact of daily life, that is, that persons function as leaders in a particular time and place, and that these are both varying and delimiting conditions; that there are several pathways to leadership, sometimes from higher authority, other times from group consent. . . . Indeed, if any point stands forth in the modern day view of leadership it is that leaders are made by circumstances. . . . The leader's emergence or waning of status is . . . inextricably linked to the prevailing situation. (Hollander, 1964, pp. 4–5, 15)

Failure to Specify When Dispositions Will Be Manifested in Behavior

The last of Allport's eight assumptions about traits is: "Acts, and even habits, that are inconsistent with a trait are not proof of the nonexistence of the trait." The intent of this assumption is clear. People do not always act consistently, and Allport did not want that fact to invalidate a trait approach. At some point, though, the argument is stretched to absurdity. If all of a person's acts are inconsistent with a trait, surely that is proof that the person does not possess the trait. Otherwise, we can describe people in any dispositional way we like, without regard to their actual behavior. An example would be to say that a particular group of people has the trait of dishonesty, even though we have always known its members to behave honestly. How much inconsistency can a dispositional approach endure?

Critics have repeatedly challenged the assumption that human behavior is consistent enough across situations to justify a dispositional view of personality (e.g., Bandura & Walters, 1963; Mischel, 1968; Rotter, 1954). They have gathered empirical evidence from psychological investigations and compelling everyday examples to support their argument. For instance, an individual who is aggressive at the office may be timid at home, completely dominated by his or her family.

Overstated, the criticism becomes unfair. Allport's point was that a person with the trait of hostility will not be hostile in every conceivable situation. But if a person is not hostile in every situation, it is essential to know *when* the characteristic will and will not appear. The Dispositional Strategy fails to provide useful ways of describing or predicting when a person's disposition will show up in behavior, and this is a fundamental flaw.

Pays Inadequate Attention to Personality Development and Change

As much as any other strategy, the dispositional view has examined longitudinal data. The characteristics of people have been measured at various times (e.g., in childhood and again in adulthood), and similarities and differences have been noted. These data certainly indicate some consistency in personality over time. But *changes* over time are also apparent for most people. The Dispositional Strategy has paid little attention to these changes and has hardly been concerned with the processes underlying development or with changing a person's traits, types, or needs over time. When and how do source traits develop? Why does one behavior pattern emerge and not another? The Dispositional Strategy has just recently begun to address some of these questions.

In sum, the Dispositional Strategy tries to capture and describe a *static* person. The strategy ignores the dynamics of development, growth, and change, although they are obviously important aspects of personality.

Factor Analysis Involves Many Subjective Decisions

Factor analysis, the favored research tool of the Dispositional Strategy, entails many subjective decisions. Because these decisions can greatly influence the apparent structure of personality, it is incorrect to say that "the structure of personality can be objectively discovered by factor analysis."

Because factor analysis involves sophisticated mathematical procedures, it has an aura of precision and objectivity. However, naming factors is *invariably* a subjective decision. In addition, the number and kinds of factors extracted will depend on the mathematical procedure chosen—another subjective decision. Thus, Eysenck finds 3 factors, Costa and McCrae find 5, Tellegen finds 7, and Cattell finds 16. In part, this is due to the specific statistical analysis selected by the researchers. Obviously, then, Eysenck did not *discover* 3 factors, and Cattell did not *discover* 16 personality traits. These investigators actually just divided up their particular data sets in such a way that particular patterns emerged.

The preconceptions of raters and of researchers can influence factor analyses. There is evidence that Norman's original "discovery" of five supertraits was largely determined by the preconceptions and stereotypes regarding personality organization that his raters held. Norman (1963) used factor analysis to look at peer ratings across a number of diverse groups of people. He consistently found a stable set of the same five factors. Later, however, Passini and Norman (1966) showed that very similar factors emerged when students rated classmates with whom they were unacquainted. Passini and Norman concluded that ratings do not reflect the "true" organization of traits in the rated persons. Instead, they reflect the ideas raters have about personality (e.g., the belief that some behaviors ought to go together).

The fact remains, though, that some dispositional psychologists may confuse subjectively based impression with objective discovery. This problem is by no means limited to factor analysis or its results. There are endless arguments about the definition of specific traits. Multiple definitions exist for intelligence, achievement, power, aggression, and other traits in the dispositional literature.

Premature Acceptance of the Five-Factor Model

The widespread acceptance of the Five-Factor Model of personality has been criticized as naive and premature (Block, 1995; Briggs, 1989). The five-factor solution originally emerged from a lexical approach to a taxonomy of traits (Goldberg, 1982; John, Angleiter, & Ostendorf, 1988). This approach makes the fundamental assumption that those aspects of people most salient in a given setting will come to be labeled in the language. Although this approach makes good intuitive sense and has obviously produced a workable solution to the taxonomy issue, its inherent limitations must be recognized and acknowledged.

Perhaps the most outspoken critic of the rush to embrace the FFM has been Jack Block, a well-known researcher from the University of California at Berkeley. Block (1995) has raised a series of related questions:

> How does one conclude that a description is "reasonably sufficient" or "comprehensive" or "fully adequate"? How compelling and indisputable were the procedures by which the five factors were discovered and settled upon? What is the role of concept and theory in personality psychology?" (p.187)

Jack Block has challenged the uncritical acceptance of the Fiver-Factor Model. Courtesy of Jack Block/University of California, Berkeley

Block points out that the development of the FFM was *not* theoretically based; that is, no prespecified or clearly stated theory led to the five factors. Rather, they were "discovered" empirically, on the basis of a single tool, factor analysis. He argues: "I maintain that the task of evolving the theoretical constructs necessary for the scientific study of personality cannot be entrusted solely to the pervasively useful method of factor analysis" and adds that "the problems or arbitrariness of the method have not been given sufficient attention" (pp. 188–189).

Beyond a critique of factor analysis, Block has reservations about whether the use of the correlation coefficient (the heart of factor analysis and of most dispositional work) is the correct way of examining personality functioning. The problem, simply put, is that correlation coefficients assume a symmetrical relationship between the variables being correlated. Block points out that many important psychological relationships are not symmetrical. For example, "wittiness" and "intelligence" are positively correlated. Moreover, it seems clear that to be witty (except by accident) relies in part on intelligence. But the relationship is *not* symmetrical. Wittiness implies intelligence, but intelligence does not imply wittiness. Some highly intelligent people are not witty at all; we have known some who are outright bores. The correlation coefficient does not deal with such asymmetries and thus may lead to groupings that are misleading.

Another major issue raised by Block is that the dimensions of the FFM are expressed in single words (*agreeableness, conscientiousness,* and so on). He writes:

> For example, how does one convey with a single adjective or a number of separate, unlinked adjectives what might be called the "pecking order personality," the kind of person who is affable with peers, deferent to superiors and nasty to individuals of lower rank? How does one convey the kind of individual who is so disorganized or capturable by a compelling social surround as to be negligent in fulfilling responsibility but who is racked by guilt? How does one convey with suitable one-word descriptors the person who, confronted with an anxiety-inducing situation, is quickly decisive, not with the confidence that rapid decision is so often interpreted to imply but only to get past the stress of the situation? . . . My own belief is that [single word descriptors] cannot do the scientific job the field of personality psychology requires. (p. 196)

Block raises an equally serious problem when we move from the factors of the FFM to the facets. "The facet distinctions," notes Block, "were *not* rooted in factor analysis, formal theorizing, or . . . empirical findings. Rather, the facets derived from [Costa and McCrae's] personal thinking . . . " (p. 201, italics in original). Thus, uncritical acceptance of the FFM is, at least, premature. The five factors are not empirical facts, such as the fact that there are seven continents on planet Earth or that there have been eight U.S. presidents from Virginia.

Dispositional Assessment Has Not Adequately Confronted the Social Desirability Problem in Self-Reports

Most people try to put their best foot forward and make a good impression whenever they can. We are speaking of the general phenomenon of social desirability, which has been extensively studied by dispositional psychologists. For the most part, however, the Dispositional Strategy has not adequately confronted the social desirability problem in personality assessment. This is especially unfortunate because social desirability is a major threat to the validity of self-report inventories.

The Psychoanalytic Strategy takes into account the fact that people will present themselves in a favorable light when asked about psychological or personal matters. The intense, in-depth nature of the psychoanalytic session and the subtlety of interpretation of the responses to projective techniques are intended to penetrate a person's superficial veneer.

In contrast, the Dispositional Strategy relies heavily on arm's-length assessment; that is, subjects or their friends and relatives fill out a questionnaire and hand it in or mail it. The absence of a professional observer makes the evaluation impersonal and distant. Respondents need not fear, for example, that facial expressions or other signs of nervousness will give them away. Instead, the inaccurate or misleading response is made by simply checking a category or circling a number.

Numerous studies have shown that faking can be quite successful under these conditions (e.g., Anastasi, 1988b). Self-reports often do not correspond with objective ratings of the relevant behavior (Hessing, Elffers, & Weigel, 1988; Lowman & Williams, 1987). Thus, it appears that the problem of social desirability in dispositional assessment has not been adequately handled.

SUMMARY

1. Dispositions, including both broad personality dimensions and narrow individual traits, are most commonly assessed by self-report inventories.
2. Personality inventories such as the MMPI are often used to screen job candidates.
3. Two biologically based assessments of personality are galvanic skin response (GSR) and polygraph measures, which are both measures of sympathetic nervous system arousal.
4. Psychotropic drugs are used to treat psychological disorders influenced by genetic factors, particularly psychotic and schizophrenic symptoms, mood disorders, and anxiety.
5. A variety of imaging techniques now allow us to see the brain in action and begin to map physical functions onto mental processes.

6. Electroconvulsive therapy (ECT), which is the administration of electrical current to the brain, and psychosurgery on the brain are used to treat extreme cases of depression, schizophrenia, and OCD that are unresponsive to more traditional treatments. Phototherapy and sleep deprivation have also been used successfully to treat depression.
7. The most dramatic possible application of biology to personality psychology is the potential ability to change inherent personality characteristics through gene therapy, the practice of replacing genetic material. Although this approach is still in its infancy, the ability to alter and then clone (exactly copy) genes may make for a rewriting of all of medicine.
8. It is now possible to imagine copying a real person by transplanting genetic material from the cells of a mature adult and then growing a new organism genetically identical to the nucleus donor.
9. Health psychologists study the relationship between psychological variables and health-related behavior. They design and implement interventions that target high-risk behavior in order to maintain or improve health status.
10. A variety of stressors can negatively affect the immune system and potentially make the body more susceptible to illness.
11. Personality variables related to coping styles, such as neuroticism and cynical hostility, influence how people react to stress, which directly affects health outcomes. An individual's negativism about health outcomes appears to make its own contribution to illness.
12. Interestingly, because of their heightened emotional sensitivity, persons high on N (Neuroticism) may seek medical help for life-threatening illnesses sooner than other individuals. So, in some cases, Neuroticism makes a positive contribution to physical health through the mechanism of early detection.
13. Type A behavior, discussed in Chapter 8, turns out to be mainly of interest when it includes cynical hostility. As a part of a person's belief system, cynical hostility unquestionably has a negative effect on health. This may be due to the suppression of immune functions by stress, as well as or combined with increased risk of stress resulting from problematic interpersonal relations.
14. The Dispositional Strategy lacks its own theoretical concepts; they must be borrowed from the other strategies.
15. The Dispositional Strategy fails to provide adequate explanations for the causes of behavior. To explain a behavior by saying that it is caused by a disposition and then claim that the presence of the disposition is proved by the occurrence of the behavior is a circular argument.
16. The Dispositional Strategy has been criticized for its inability to predict individual behaviors.
17. The Dispositional Strategy has been criticized for underestimating the importance of situational variables.
18. The Dispositional Strategy cannot accurately predict the behavior of individuals or specify when dispositions will or will not be manifested in behavior. One reason for this inability is that situational factors often

exert considerable influence over people's behavior. Dispositional psychologists tend to minimize or completely ignore the influence of situational factors. They are also inattentive to the possibility that only some people behave in a traitlike way across time and situations.

19. The Dispositional Strategy has paid relatively little attention to the processes by which personality change occurs over time, although it is recognized that longitudinal change does occur.
20. Dispositional psychologists make many subjective decisions while using factor analysis, so factor analysis can hardly be described as a completely objective procedure.
21. The Five-Factor Model (FFM) has been widely accepted relative to competing models with greater or fewer factors. Some critics think that acknowledging a consensus is premature, partly because factor analyses involve subjective decisions that will influence the number of factors that emerge as candidates for study.
22. The Dispositional Strategy is based mainly on self-report data but (with the exception of Eysenck) has tended to ignore the problem of social desirability, which has long been known to have a large potential effect on how much respondents consciously or unconsciously reveal on personality tests.

PART FOUR

THE ENVIRONMENTAL STRATEGY

It's All Out There

CHAPTER ELEVEN

Introduction to the Environmental Strategy

he theories and research described within the Environmental Strategy share a common theme. They all focus attention on forces in the individual's external environment that influence behavior. Personality is viewed as the constellation of behaviors displayed by an individual. These behaviors are assumed to arise primarily in response to external conditions. In their desire to study relationships between environmental conditions and behavior, these theorists seek out **overt** (directly observable) events. They typically avoid speculating about **covert** (private, internal) processes within the organism.

Psychologists within this strategy are interested in both the processes of learning that shape behavior and the content of what is learned and evidenced in subsequent behavior. Although most environmental theorists do not deny the operation of internal forces, they look *first* to the environment and learning history over time to determine how and what behaviors are molded and maintained.

This emphasis contrasts sharply with the focus of the previous strategies. Psychoanalytic theorists focus on *drives,* forces within the individual that produce personality characteristics and behavior. Similarly, the focus of the Dispositional Strategy is on characteristics *intrinsic* to the individual. The Representational Strategy (discussed in Part V) focuses almost exclusively on private events (mental representations and operations).

Thus, the Environmental Strategy presents a unique perspective on human personality. A great many of the theories discussed within this strategy are based on basic laboratory research. This, too, distinguishes the Environmental Strategy from the other three. Yet, interests within the Environmental Strategy range from the most basic learned relationships to an examination of the intricate interplay between individuals and the social and cultural forces that shape their world. Each person is viewed as the product of continuous complex interactions between the individual and an ever-changing environment.

BEHAVIORISM: THE ROOTS OF THE ENVIRONMENTAL STRATEGY

The Environmental Strategy grew out of **behaviorism,** a school of thought within psychology that can be traced back to the writings of John Broadus Watson (1878–1958). Watson (1924) wrote:

> Give me a dozen infants, well formed, and my own specific world to bring them up in, and I'll guarantee to take any one at random and train him to become any type of specialist I might select, doctor, lawyer, artist, merchant-chief, and yes, even beggar-man and thief, regardless of his talents, penchants, tendencies, abilities, vocations, and race of his ancestors. (reprinted 1970, p. 104)

Watson (1914, 1919) believed that psychology should be a natural science, in the tradition of physics and biology. He made no distinction between human and nonhuman behavior. He believed that there was no need to study subjective phenomena, such as thoughts and feelings. Instead, Watson's "stimulus-response" psychology was concerned only with predicting overt behaviors by knowing the external stimuli that influence them and vice versa. In 1914, he wrote:

John Watson (1878–1958) the father of radical behaviorism, believed that psychology should deal only with observable stimuli and responses.
Archives of the History of American Psychology—University of Akron

> Psychology as the behaviorist views it is a purely objective experimental branch of natural science. Its theoretical goal is the prediction and control of behavior. . . . The behaviorist attempts to get a unitary scheme of animal response. He recognizes no dividing line between man and brute. The behavior of man, with all of its refinements and complexity, forms only a part of his total field of investigation. . . . It is possible to write a psychology, to define it as . . . the "science of behavior" . . . and never go back upon the definition: never to use the terms consciousness, mental states, mind, content, will, imagery, and the like. . . . Certain stimuli lead . . . organisms to make . . . responses. In a system of psychology completely worked out, given the responses the stimuli can be predicted; given the stimuli the responses can be predicted. (pp. 1, 9, 10)

The philosophical approach Watson prescribed is now known as **radical behaviorism.** It takes the extreme position that *only* overt behaviors and external stimuli should be studied. Besides dictating the subject matter of psychology, radical behaviorism specifies the methods used to study them—namely, direct observation of behavior, objectivity, precise definitions, and controlled experimentation. Behaviorism as a philosophy and method applied to personality is the subject of Chapter 12.

In contrast, **methodological behaviorism** prescribes that the same scientific methods be used but does not specify what can be studied. In fact, the term *methodological behaviorism* has dropped out of current usage, but its essence is retained in the philosophical approach of much of contemporary psychology. The social learning approach discussed in Chapter 13 falls under this heading. So, too, do most of the approaches discussed in Part V, the Representational Strategy. In founding behaviorism, Watson hoped to provide a model for the entire field of psychology. Although radical behaviorism has provided a sound framework for the study of some aspects of behavior, it never realized Watson's ultimate goal (Lee, 1988; Staats, 1989b, 1991, 1993b). However, the *philosophy* advanced by Watson of tough-minded empiricism, characterized by rigorous scientific methods and direct observation, has been embraced by psychologists from the radical behavioral approach through to modern-day cognitive psychologists. It remains his greatest contribution to the field.

THE KEY ROLE OF LEARNING AND EXPERIENCE

In the Environmental Strategy, personality is presumed to develop and be modified through learning (usually defined as changes in overt behavior) and experience with the environment, rather than as an inevitable result of hereditary and biological factors. This is a basic assumption of the Environmental Strategy. Three different learning processes are emphasized: classical conditioning, operant conditioning, and observational learning (or modeling).

In **classical conditioning,** behavior is acquired (learned) through associations between stimulus and response. **Operant conditioning** focuses on how behavior is acquired and modified primarily in response to the consequences (i.e., reinforcement and punishment) of actions. **Observational learning** deals with the role of others **(models)** in learning.

Consider, for example, some of your own experiences in the classroom. In virtually every group of students, one or two participate actively in all group discussions. These same students may volunteer answers for every question posed by the instructor. Meanwhile, other students take a back seat and rarely contribute spontaneously. They may even actively avoid eye contact with the instructor when questions are addressed to the group. What accounts for these enormous differences in classroom outspokenness? Are the differences due to some innate forces within the individuals? Environmental psychologists would say no. The differences, they contend, reflect different learning histories. Let us examine how the three core learning processes might play their roles.

Several events might have encouraged an outspoken classmate. Perhaps this person's first experience with speaking up in class brought a surge of positive feelings of confidence and competence related to knowing the appropriate answer or having something important to contribute. The behavior (speaking up in class) was paired with another experience (enjoying feelings of competence), which increased the likelihood of speaking up again at other times. This is the process of classical conditioning at work. The critical point is the *pairing* of behaviors and stimuli (internal or external) associated with them. (Note that although the positive feelings in this example were internal and private, they are not the focus of environmental psychologists. The focus here remains on the environmental events that produced these feelings and the *changes in behavior* that can be observed as a result.)

There are other possibilities. Perhaps a particularly insightful answer evoked praise from an earlier teacher; that is, similar behavior was *reinforced*, and so behavior resembling it (speaking out) is more likely to recur. This is operant conditioning at work. Operant conditioning relies on the consequences of behavior for influencing the likelihood of the behavior's recurrence at subsequent times.

A third possibility is that this student observed that other students were lavished with praise and attention for participating in class. This is modeling, the third learning process of interest to environmental psychologists. Social learning through modeling is involved whenever the behavior exhibited by others and the consequences they receive influence the observer's subsequent behavior. You and others might describe your classmate with "personality adjectives" such as outspoken, assertive, self-confident, or dominant; environmental psychologists would focus specifically on descriptions of the person's *overt behavior* and the particular context in which it occurs. To explain any given behavior, environmental psychologists will look to the learning history and environmental forces that may have served to shape that particular behavior over time.

Note that one, two, or all three processes might have influenced your classmate's outspoken behavior. The three processes of learning—classical conditioning, operant conditioning, and observational learning (modeling)—reflect different but *not* incompatible processes. Environmental theories assume that most human behavior is acquired and sustained by some *combination* of these three learning processes. In fact, there is increasing recognition within this strategy of the *complex* nature of the environmental forces that influence an individual at any point. It is fine to study the behavior of laboratory-bred rats in tightly controlled experiments to explore the most fundamental learning mechanisms. However, because people are not bred and reared in similar circumstances, no such control (or direct generalization from the rats) is possible. People are products of the *interacting* and *ever-changing* physical, social, and cultural environment of their immediate world.

THE ENVIRONMENT OF COMPLEX SOCIAL FORCES

The Environmental Strategy emphasizes the role of external forces acting on individuals to "shape" their behavior and styles of interacting with the world around them. This is most clear in the social learning theories presented in Chapter 13. In this context, examination of more complexly determined behaviors begins. This approach recognizes that environmental forces may operate concurrently at a number of levels. These multiple forces are particularly evident in the social realm. Here, individuals must learn to conform to the rules of behavior (often *implicit* rules) of their immediate family, local community, and broader social and cultural surroundings. How these behaviors are learned and maintained is of interest to psychologists of the Environmental Strategy.

Social Roles and Behavior

Social roles can be defined as all of the behaviors and attitudes appropriate to a particular socially defined group, or status. Within any cultural context, a range of behaviors is associated with particular roles, such as mother, father, son, daughter, teacher, and law enforcement officer. These roles (and their labels) are all defined by socially prescribed relationships as dictated by the family and cultural environment.

Note that one person can simultaneously occupy multiple roles, as in the case of the mother who is *also* a teacher, a daughter to her own mother, *and* a spouse to her husband. You, too, fill multiple concurrent social roles. You are a student, a son or daughter, and probably a roommate (or partner) to someone you live with, and you may also be a sibling to someone, a parent, and an employee. Thus, social roles are generally not exclusive, and most individuals fill multiple social roles throughout their lives.

Gender as a social role has received a great deal of attention over the past 30 years from psychologists and sociologists. Gender is particularly interesting because it is (at least in part) defined by biology (one's apparent sex at birth). However, the full implications of gender are far from realized at birth and encompass a wide range of purely social phenomena. In fact, much of what we (in contemporary Western cultures) consider masculine and feminine derive almost entirely from social forces, sometimes termed **social constructions.**

Social constructions of appropriate role behavior result from demands of the environment in which they occur. Finchilescu (1995), in speaking of social constructions, states that "behaviours are seen as arising from the demands of the social situation in which [they] occur" (p. 136). She further states that "gender is socially constructed, and the behaviour and beliefs patterned by any number of discourses and social demands" (p. 137).

Social constructions tend to be accepted and perpetuated over time. However, there may be no biological basis for many of these stereotypes, as will be seen in Chapter 13 when we examine the evolution of gender roles within Western societies and cross-culturally.

The shift in emphasis from very basic learned relationships toward more complex, multiply determined behavior patterns will be clear as we move from presentation of the behavioral approach in the next chapter to the social learning approach of Chapter 13. Even in studying these complex social factors, though, commonalities with the earlier approaches will be apparent. The focus will continue to be on *external* factors and *overt behaviors. Internal* factors are either discounted or deemphasized. We now turn our attention to the Environmental Strategy with an emphasis on these shared elements.

BEHAVIOR IS SITUATION SPECIFIC

Accounting for the apparent consistency of people's behaviors is a fundamental task for all personality theories. Psychoanalytic theories posit that lifelong patterns of behavior are established in the first years of life. Dispositional approaches speak of relatively stable and enduring personality characteristics that result in consistent behaviors. Representational theories (discussed at length in Part V) attribute behavioral consistency to how people think about and understand themselves, others, and events in their lives.

Environmental personality theories hold that the apparent consistency of the person depends on features of the immediate environment. *Situational cues* indicate which behaviors are expected, which are likely to meet with approval, and which will be adaptive in a particular circumstance. Thus, environmental theories assume that people's behaviors are consistent in the same or similar situations but *vary* across different situations. In other words, behavior is *situation specific.*

For example, Greg sits quietly in classes, is mildly animated in casual conversation at the cafeteria, and vigorously expresses his support for his college athletic teams. In each case, Greg's behavior is influenced by the requirements and restrictions of the immediate situation. How Greg acts will be consistent within similar situations. He will tend to say little in each of his classes, for example. But Greg's behavior will vary across different situations (environments). He may cheer enthusiastically at basketball games despite saying virtually nothing in classes. This situation-specific viewpoint contrasts with the generality-consistency assumptions of the Dispositional Strategy, which would categorize Greg as disposed to be either a passive *or* an active type of person.

ENVIRONMENTAL PERSONALITY RESEARCH

In the tradition of methodological behaviorism, environmental research emphasizes studying personality phenomena through *systematic,* highly *controlled* research, especially true experiments. The research frequently is carried out in psychology laboratories, where strict control of conditions is possible. The dependent variables are samples of the behavior under investigation. For example, in studying aggression, the measures are direct samples of aggressive responses, such as delivering an electric shock or physically or verbally attacking another person.

Environmental research is predominantly ***nomothetic***. Samples of subjects are studied with the aim of making generalizations to a larger population of interest. Idiographic, single-subject studies are typically reserved for evaluating the effectiveness of personality-change (therapy) techniques. (There are exceptions to this general rule, and Skinner's argument in favor of an idiographic approach is discussed in Chapter 12.)

ENVIRONMENTAL PERSONALITY THEORY

Environmental approaches vary in the amount and kind of theorizing they spawn. Considerably more theorizing occurs in the social learning approach than in the behavioral approach (e.g., Schlinger, 1992). However, three characteristics are common to all of these theories. They (1) are relatively parsimonious, (2) make minimal use of theoretical constructs, and (3) attempt to minimize inferences.

Parsimonious Explanations

Environmental theories tend to be parsimonious, or simple, in the sense of being based on few assumptions. Often a single set of principles is used to explain a variety of phenomena.

Take the common experience of forgetting the name of a person you know well. This is an example of *unexpressed* behavior, which refers to an act that a person can perform (the behavior is in the behavioral repertoire) but is not performing at the moment. The explanation is simple and straightforward: You do not remember the person's name because the stimuli that would elicit it are absent. Later, some relevant cue immediately brings the name to mind. (You may have experienced this yourself when you have encountered a familiar person outside the usual context. You might realize that you know the person but in the absence of the environmental cues associated with this individual—clothing, uniform, the specific location—you are unable to recall the name or even remember *where* you know this person from.) Remembering and forgetting are thus explained by the same principle: the presence of appropriate stimuli or environmental cues to facilitate recall.

In contrast, the psychoanalytic explanation of the same phenomenon makes several assumptions. First, multiple levels of consciousness exist. Second, conscious responses are made unconscious by a defensive process, such as repression. Third, because you cannot recall the name of this particular person at this particular time, there must be something extremely threatening about the individual that causes you to repress the name. Clearly, this psychoanalytic explanation is considerably more complicated and makes more assumptions than the parallel environmental explanation.

Minimal Use of Theoretical Constructs

Compared with the other three personality strategies, environmental theories use relatively few theoretical constructs. These theories are not free of theoretical constructs, but they typically avoid explanations that involve speculation about covert processes within the person. For example, these theories do not posit any kind of unifying force or structure for personality. There are no equivalents of ego, id, or self-concept.

Theoretical constructs often serve as shorthand summaries of personality phenomena. Because environmental psychologists use theoretical constructs sparingly, descriptions of personality phenomena tend to be lengthy but *precise* and *specific* (e.g., Addis, 1993).

Minimizing Inference

Personality psychologists make inferences whenever they assume something about one event based on information derived from another event. Inferences always provide *indirect* information, but how indirect an inference is depends on how far removed the two events are. Consider two very different kinds of inferences. A psychoanalyst posits the existence of an Oedipus complex from observing 5-year-old Calvin's affection toward his mother and avoidance of his father. A high degree of inference is involved because the analyst must make a series of inferential steps. They begin with observation of overt behavior, from which internal causal mechanisms are inferred (the boy *dislikes* his father and *therefore* avoids him). But the ultimate explanation of the behavior goes well beyond this and culminates in recourse to a broad, general, theoretical construct (existence and operation of the Oedipus complex).

In contrast, an environmental psychologist might predict that Calvin would go to his mother when he had a problem, based on the recent observation that Calvin invariably seeks out his mother when hurt. Calvin has a history of past learning experiences with his mother and will tend to repeat the same behaviors (seeking out his mother) in similar circumstances (times of distress or discomfort). In this case, there are no complex inferences. Only a single prediction is made, from one *overt* behavior to another similar behavior. No covert processes are proposed, and thus no unnecessary inferences about their roles or operation are required. The organism can be construed as a "black box," the inner workings of which are not available for scientific study because of their covert, subjective nature.

ENVIRONMENTAL PERSONALITY ASSESSMENT

Environmental personality assessment can be characterized as (1) *direct*, (2) *present-oriented*, and (3) *highly focused*. The behavioral model of assessment, especially as used by classical and operant theorists, requires *rejecting* any type of subjective report (by self or others). Instead, they would observe directly the behaviors and actions of the person and attempt not to make any inferences at all. These observations will be described, but they will not lead to inferences about internal states or events, as they might for psychologists of the other three strategies.

Direct

The difference between indirect and direct approaches to personality is illustrated by the following example. Consider two therapists—one psychoanalytically oriented and one environmentally oriented—presented with a child described by parents as having "difficulty at school." The psychoanalytically oriented therapist is likely to begin some form of interpretation through play therapy and other indirect clues to the child's school difficulties. The environmentally oriented therapist, by contrast, is likely to simply go to the school to unobtrusively observe the child interacting with teachers and peers in the actual environment of interest.

The methods of assessment themselves do not distinguish environmental personality assessment. Rather, it is the *way* the methods are used and the

Direct observation of overt behavior provides an important source of data about personality for behavioral psychologists. It is often carried out in naturalistic settings, where subjects are engaged in their normal activities.
Photo Source, Inc./St. Louis

results are construed. For example, environmental psychologists use some self-reports and some reports by other observers. Most often, though, these reports deal only with *overt behavior;* they are not used to infer any private mental states or events. A teacher asked to observe and monitor the child with "school difficulties" will most likely be provided with some type of behavior checklist to report instances of particular behaviors and their frequency of occurrence.

In obtaining self-reports, environmental psychologists often devise a method of sampling the behavior of interest over time. For example, the client might be asked to wear a special wristwatch and record current behavior and the environmental context whenever the alarm of the watch sounds. The watch might sound its alarm at regular intervals or randomly throughout the day. Such procedures allow the environmental psychologist to estimate the frequency of occurrence of any problem behaviors and to note any environmental conditions that may trigger these behaviors.

Present-Oriented

To predict future behaviors, the contemporary environmental psychologist looks to the individual's *present,* learning history, and family and cultural background. This is consistent with the concept of situational specificity. There is little reason to explore an adult's remote childhood experiences to assess present functioning. This emphasis on the present has two rational justifications.

First, it does not deny that past events may have been responsible for a person's originally developing a problematic behavior. However, these past events cannot be changed and cannot directly influence the continuation (maintenance) of the behavior. Quite simply, the factors that existed in the past are past. They cannot be altered from the present. Only present circumstances can be changed to influence the troublesome behavior that has already been established.

For instance, crying to elicit attention from others may have been acquired through a variety of mechanisms. You may have learned it by observing your mother's reacting this way and eliciting sympathy from your father. It might also have arisen spontaneously and been directly reinforced by the environment in some way (your mother or father might have offered comfort directly to you). But the habit will persist in adulthood only if it continues to be reinforced in the present, such as through attention from your spouse or friends.

Second, *trustworthy* information about the past is not likely to be available. Accurately assessing what occurred in a person's early childhood is usually not possible, at least not without a time machine! At best, correlations between past and present behavior can be obtained, but such relationships rarely yield clear-cut information about causation. For example, a man who is compulsively neat in his daily life may also have been severely toilet-trained. This correlation does not necessarily imply that the man's early toilet-training history contributed to his current compulsive habits. Even if it did, it would not be particularly helpful in formulating a plan to change his current behavior.

Highly Focused

Environmental personality assessment examines particular *aspects* of an individual's behavior rather than a whole personality. Features of personality are assumed to be semiautonomous. The situational specificity of behavior holds even for different types of the same class of behaviors. Take the example of Pam, who regularly refuses unreasonable requests. Can we infer from this behavior pattern that she will also make her personal desires known to others? Both can be labeled "assertive" behaviors, but they must be assessed independently. The assumption that a person's behaviors are semiautonomous also has implications for research and personality change (therapy). In research, specific phenomena are studied in depth. In psychotherapy, particular behaviors, rather than the client's total personality, are the targets of change.

ENVIRONMENTAL PERSONALITY CHANGE

Environmental personality-change procedures are commonly known as **behavior therapy.** Behavior therapy is not a single method of personality change. Like psychodynamic therapy, behavior therapy refers to a class of treatments, of which there are many. Particular therapies are associated with each of the approaches in the Environmental Strategy. The common theme of these therapies is that they alter maintaining conditions in the environment in an effort to modify specific target behaviors. These therapies are typically action-oriented; that is, the focus of assessment and treatment is on *behavior* rather than on thoughts, feelings, or mental processes.

Changing Behavior by Changing the Environment

Clients typically enter therapy with multiple problems that are described vaguely (e.g., "I'm uptight most of the time, and I am lonely"). Behavior therapy begins by narrowing the client's complaints to one or two specific problems. Then a precisely defined, measurable aspect of the problem, known as a **target behavior,** is specified as the first focus of change.

The definition of the target behavior must allow for direct observation and measurement (quantification) of the behavior at the assessment phase, as well as during and after treatment for comparison. Consider, for example, a client who presents with a problem described only as "binge eating." Before proceeding further, the therapist must formulate a more precise definition of the target behavior. It might be eating more than one serving of a predetermined amount of any particular food within a 1-hour period.

Only one or two distinct target behaviors are treated at a time. When the initial target behaviors have been successfully treated, therapy turns to other target behaviors. Thus, multiple problems are treated *sequentially* rather than simultaneously.

Successful therapy now involves two major tasks. First, the factors that are currently maintaining (causing) the target behavior—known as **maintaining conditions**—must be identified. Second, the maintaining conditions must be modified to change the target behavior. Behavior therapists look for the maintaining conditions of a target behavior in the current antecedents and consequences of the behavior.

Antecedents are the stimuli present *before* the target behavior occurs. They include **situational cues** (where the target behavior occurs), **temporal cues** (time of day), and **interpersonal cues** (who is present). These cues serve as **discriminative stimuli** that trigger the individual's performance of the target behavior. Antecedents can also include the **setting events** that increase the likelihood of the behavior's occurrence.

For example, consider again the target behavior of binge eating. A critical setting event for this behavior might be skipping an earlier meal. (This may predispose the person to binge eating by producing extreme hunger, which increases the likelihood of overeating when time permits.) Careful observation might reveal that binge eating *always* occurs after a skipped meal. (Note that this does not imply that binging *only* occurs after a meal has been skipped; binging may also occur in response to other environmental cues.)

Specific discriminative stimuli may also play a role in the problem behavior. The presence of favorite foods (ice cream or potato chips) in large quantities may signal that it is possible to overindulge. Antecedents are critical because they often constitute the conditions that allow, as well as maintain, problem behaviors.

Consequences are events that occur *after* and as a result of performing the target behavior. Consequences can include immediate and long-range outcomes—for the person, for other people, and for the physical environment. Consequences can maintain or extinguish behaviors. Typically, favorable consequences make it more likely and unfavorable consequences make it less likely that the person will perform a particular behavior again in the future.

In the last example, the individual may experience a variety of consequences for binge eating. There may be immediate aversive (punishing) consequences, such as stomach upset. There may also be long-term and chronic aversive consequences, in the form of excessive weight gain and hypertension. These factors will combine to reduce the likelihood of engaging in the behavior subsequently.

Table 11.1 Antecedents and consequences of a client's "binge eating junk food"

ANTECEDENTS	CONSEQUENCES
At home	Provides an activity
Alone	Lowers anxiety
Evening, weekend	Enjoys the junk food
Nothing to do	Gets a stomachache
Feels anxious	Gains weight
Has bought junk food	Clothes do not fit
Junk food in house	Gets tired when exercising

However, most problem behaviors *become* problem behaviors because they are *intrinsically* rewarding (reinforcing). The rewarding consequences are either more immediate (and therefore more powerfully associated with the target behavior) or greater in perceived magnitude than the aversive consequences. Thus, in our example, the food is enjoyed tremendously when it is consumed, and the activity itself might also distract the person from daily problems and concerns. These rewarding consequences of eating cause the binging to continue to the point of producing serious problems for the individual.

Table 11.1 lists the antecedents and consequences of one client's target behavior, "binge eating junk food." This behavior was specifically defined as eating more than one item of junk food per hour.

Environmental therapists intervene primarily by modifying the environmental conditions in the form of antecedents and consequences of the target behavior. At times, other adaptive behaviors may be introduced and reinforced to supplant the maladaptive target behavior. This usually requires the client's active cooperation. Clients are expected to do things to alleviate their problems, rather than merely talk about them. Clients are often given homework assignments to be performed outside therapy sessions. They may be asked to observe and record their target behaviors. They may also be instructed to practice adaptive behaviors they have learned in therapy. Ultimately, clients will need to participate in arranging conditions in their lives to elicit and reinforce specific adaptive behaviors, while identifying means to prevent the occurrence of the target behavior. This will ensure that problem behaviors will no longer be reinforced.

In our example, efforts might first be focused on preventing the person from skipping regular meals in the future. The client may also be instructed to empty the pantry and refrigerator of the junk foods, to weigh in daily in an effort to increase the salience of this issue, and so on.

BEYOND ENVIRONMENT

Although the primary focus of all environmental psychology is the external environment, the relative emphasis placed on learning differs among the various approaches. Learning is a common theme, but the specific approaches vary both (1) in terms of the accepted definitions of *learning* (radical behaviorists do *not* include private events in their definition because learning is simply shorthand for behavior change contingent on environmental conditions) and (2) in the overall focus on learning in theoretical accounts of behavior. The behavioral approach deals only with classical and operant conditioning. These forms of learning are restricted to relationships between observable environmental stimuli and overt responses. In the social learning approach, the importance of classical and operant conditioning is acknowledged, but observational learning is added. Thus, models in the environment and the consequences they experience enter their formulations. For models to affect the behavior of observers, some private, internal processing of information *must* occur. First, models must be accepted as sources of vicarious information. Then, the receiver must attend to the modeled behavior and choose to demonstrate acquisition of it. These covert events are understood as serving at times as the critical antecedents and consequences of overt behaviors. However, the fact that the existence of covert phenomena is *inherent* in their theories distinguishes the social learning theorists from the behaviorists.

SUMMARY

1. The Environmental Strategy focuses on forces in the individual's external environment that shape personality. Personality is assumed to develop in response to external conditions.
2. The Environmental Strategy is concerned with both the learning processes that shape behavior and the content of what is learned from the individual's particular social environment.
3. The Environmental Strategy focuses on overt behavior and avoids speculation about unobservable processes inside the individual.
4. The Environmental Strategy grew out of behaviorism, a school of thought that can be traced to John B. Watson. Watson viewed psychology as a natural science, concerned with the relationship between observable environmental stimuli and the overt responses of the organism, animal or human. Watson's view is now referred to as radical behaviorism because it takes the extreme position that psychologists should study only overt behavior.
5. Methodological behaviorism prescribes objective, scientific methods but does not specify or limit what can be studied. Today, most psychologists subscribe to methodological behaviorism, although the term itself is not frequently used.
6. Learning plays a key role in the Environmental Strategy. The three types of learning that have been identified and studied are classical conditioning, operant conditioning, and observational learning (or modeling).
7. Classical conditioning refers to the pairing of a stimulus that is known to elicit a given response with a stimulus that does not initially produce the response. The effect of such pairing of stimuli ultimately causes the initially neutral stimulus to elicit the response.
8. Operant conditioning refers to increasing or decreasing the likelihood of a given response by manipulating the consequences of the response.

9. Modeling involves learning through exposure to the behavior of one or more other individuals (models) and observing the consequences they receive.
10. Within the Environmental Strategy, personality is assumed to develop and change through a combination of the three types of learning.
11. The Environmental Strategy assumes that individuals learn the various roles they are expected to play, as prescribed by the social group(s) of which they are members. Individuals learn to fulfill multiple roles. Such roles are social constructions.
12. The Environmental Strategy assumes that behavior is situation specific; the fact that an individual behaves in a particular way in one situation does not necessarily mean that the individual will behave the same way in different situations.
13. Environmental personality research emphasizes systematic, controlled research, most often involves the experimental method, and is primarily nomothetic.
14. Environmental personality theories tend to be parsimonious, use a minimum of theoretical constructs, and avoid speculative inferences.
15. Environmental personality assessment is direct, present-oriented, and highly focused.
16. Environmental personality-change procedures are commonly called behavior therapy. Behavior therapy refers to a class of treatments; the common themes of behavior therapies are their focus on maintaining conditions in the environment and their effort to modify specific target behaviors. These therapies are action-oriented, in that they focus on a person's actions (behaviors) rather than on thoughts, feelings, or mental processes.
17. Behavior therapies focus on antecedents and consequences of target behaviors. Antecedents are the stimuli present before a target behavior occurs; they include situational, temporal, and interpersonal cues, as well as critical setting events.
18. Clients in behavior therapy are often asked to do homework outside therapy sessions. Ultimately, clients are taught to control their own environments to maintain desirable behavior and to prevent undesirable behavior from occurring.
19. Unlike behaviorists, social learning theorists attend to covert as well as overt events and concern themselves with individuals' internal processing of information gathered from the environment.

CHAPTER TWELVE

The Behavioral Approach

The behavioral approach emphasizes the study of overt (observable) behaviors and the environmental conditions that influence them. In studying how behaviors are learned and maintained, behavioral psychologists usually focus on the processes of classical conditioning or operant conditioning.

CLASSICAL CONDITIONING

Classical conditioning involves pairing stimuli such that an automatic, reflexive response evoked by one of the stimuli comes over time to also be evoked by the paired (previously neutral) stimulus. The original discovery of this process was accidental.

Early Animal Models of Classical Conditioning

In the late 19th century, Russian physiologist Ivan Pavlov (1849–1936) was studying the digestive processes of dogs (see Figure 12.1). To induce salivation, meat powder was placed on the dogs' tongues. One day, Pavlov noticed that dogs that had been involved in the study for some time salivated even before the presentation of food. Pavlov recognized the potential importance of his accidental discovery. He spent much of the rest of his career studying this phenomenon, which came to be known as the process of classical conditioning.

Ivan Pavlov (1849–1936) was the first to note and describe the process of classical conditioning in animals.

Pavlov's first approach to understanding the process was through **introspection**—trying to imagine the situation from the dog's point of view. This method proved unproductive. He and his assistants could not agree on what the dog would or ought to think or feel. Pavlov subsequently banned introspection from his laboratory and turned to a more objective, verifiable approach (Hyman, 1964). He reasoned that the animal's natural, or reflexive, tendency to respond to the food in its mouth with salivation had somehow also come to be evoked by the mere *sight* of food. This latter reaction was not innate. Dogs that had not been involved in the study did not display this response initially. It had to be conditioned (learned) by experience with environmental events, which meant that it could be studied experimentally.

The order of events in a traditional classical conditioning experiment is illustrated in Figure 12.2. First, a **conditioned stimulus (CS),** such as a light,

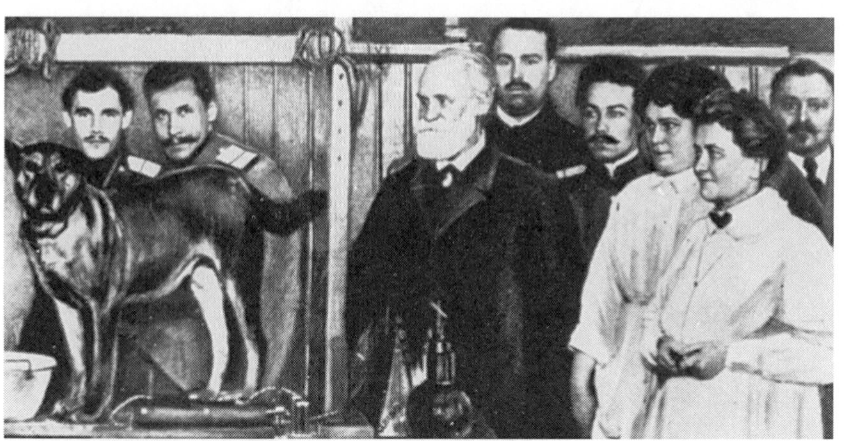

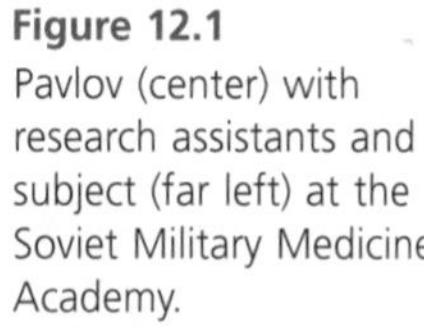

Figure 12.1
Pavlov (center) with research assistants and subject (far left) at the Soviet Military Medicine Academy.

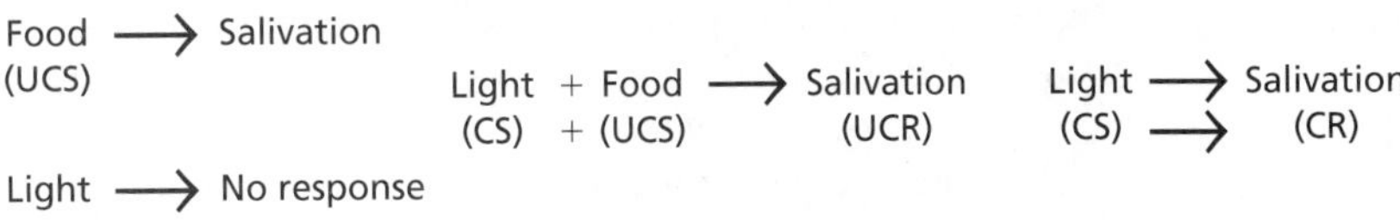

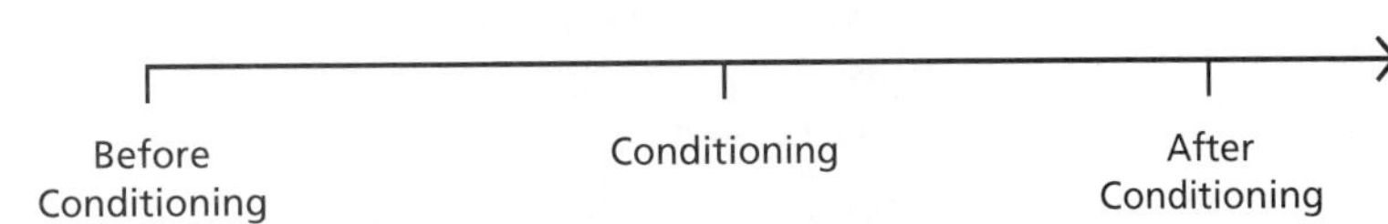

Figure 12.2 Schematic diagram of one of Pavlov's classical conditioning experiments.

is presented; the CS does not initially produce the relevant response (salivation in Pavlov's work). Very shortly thereafter (a fraction of a second to no more than a few seconds), a stimulus that reflexively produces the desired response is introduced; this is the **unconditioned stimulus (UCS).** The (automatic, reflexive) response that it produces is the **unconditioned response (UCR).** In Pavlov's studies, the food was the UCS, and salivation was the UCR. After the CS and UCS were presented together a number of times, the CS (light) came to produce salivation even before the UCS (food) was presented. The behavior, now elicited by the CS alone, is called the **conditioned response (CR).** (Salivation was the CR in Pavlov's experiments.)

Pavlov continued to study the process of classical conditioning throughout his career. He defined elements of the process and described their operation and limits. Four basic phenomena were identified during early studies of classical conditioning: acquisition, discrimination, generalization, and extinction.

Acquisition refers to the process by which a conditioned response comes to exist in the first place. Research demonstrated that it often takes repeated pairings of the CS and the UCS, over which time a response to the CS alone (on "test" trials when no UCS is presented) gradually becomes stronger and more reliable.

Discrimination and generalization refer to the question of what happens when a response that has been conditioned to one specific stimulus is then tested with similar stimuli. For example, if a person is conditioned to experience fear of a tone because the tone has been repeatedly paired with an electric shock, how will that person respond to a tone of a different pitch? If the person responds to the original CS but not to a similar one, we say that **discrimination** has occurred; the person has discriminated between the two stimuli. If the person responds to the new tone with fear (though conditioned to only a slightly different tone), then we say **generalization** has occurred; the response has generalized from one stimulus (tone) to a different but similar stimulus.

Discrimination and generalization form a **gradient;** that is, the more similar the original stimulus is to the test stimulus, the more likely it is for generalization to occur. The less alike the original and new stimuli (e.g., tones of very different pitches) are, the more likely discrimination is to occur. After a particular CR is established, it requires additional pairings with the UCS to be maintained. Without these additional pairings, **extinction** will gradually occur over repeated tests until the once conditioned response has vanished. Finally, after extinction has occurred (responding to the CS alone has ceased), the presentation of the CS at a later time may again produce some conditioned responding. This last phenomenon is called **spontaneous recovery;** that is, even after extinction (the CR no longer occurs), the response may reappear. This seems to be most likely after a period of time elapses, during which no further presentation of the CS occurs.

A famous psychologist came to one of our classes a number of years ago and gave the following demonstration to make vivid the various processes associated with classical conditioning.

> The psychologist entered the large lecture hall dressed as a cowboy, complete with hat, scarf, boots, jeans, and a 45-caliber revolver strapped to his hip. (The revolver was, as it turned out, loaded with blanks, which produced an incredibly loud noise in the closed lecture hall.) First, the psychologist yelled out the letters "CS." No one evidenced a distinct reaction. (This was expected, as the CS in this demonstration was yelling "CS" and the actual conditioning process had not yet begun.)
>
> Then the psychologist wandered about the aisles, yelling "CS" and almost simultaneously firing his gun. The loud "bang" of the gunshot produced an obvious response (a startle reaction) at first; this response became stronger as the psychologist repeatedly paired his yelling "CS" with the firing of his gun. This constituted the *acquisition* phase of the demonstration.
>
> Next, the psychologist continued walking up and down the aisles yelling "CS" but *without* firing the gun. On the first several occasions, most people now evidenced a startle response to the "CS" alone. He then continued to repeat the process of simply yelling "CS" without firing the gun. These were the extinction trials, and the reaction to "CS" alone diminished and finally disappeared.
>
> The psychologist then came to the podium and gave a short lecture on the classical conditioning process. He was thanked for the demonstration and walked to the door of the lecture hall. As he was about to depart, he turned back, faced the class, and yelled "CS." All present were startled again. This was a clear demonstration of the existence of *spontaneous recovery.*

Classical Conditioning in Humans

John Watson was inspired by Pavlov's conditioning experiments. Watson believed that classical conditioning might have vast implications for understanding and managing human behavior. In his classic case study of "little Albert," he and Rosalie Rayner demonstrated that fear could be classically conditioned (Watson & Rayner, 1920). (Note that this research would not be permitted today because of ethical considerations; see Chapter 2.)

Albert, an 11-month-old boy, appeared to be afraid of nothing except very loud sounds and sudden loss of support. (Both fears are apparently innate and universal in human infants; that is, both typically evoke a startle response and crying or other signs of distress.) Watson and Rayner sought to classically condition a new fear in Albert. They placed a white rat (CS) in front of the child and simultaneously made a very loud sound (UCS). Albert had experienced no fear of white rats previously. After seven paired presentations of the rat and the loud sound, the rat alone aroused a definite fear reaction (CR), including Albert's crying and trying to escape from the situation (see Figure 12.3).

Watson and some of his followers considered the case of little Albert clear evidence that emotional reactions could be conditioned in humans. Later, critics found methodological flaws in the study (Harris, 1979; Marks, 1981; Paul & Blumenthal, 1989). But Watson's basic idea inspired many psychologists to study the role of classical conditioning in developing emotional reactions (cf. Eysenck, 1985).

Geer (1968), for example, showed graphic, close-up color photographs of victims of violent and sudden death (UCS) to college students. The photos elicited strong emotional reactions, as measured by **galvanic skin responses** (changes in skin conductivity). The students saw the photos 5 seconds after the presentation of a tone (CS) that initially elicited no emotional response. After 20 such pairings, the previously neutral tone produced galvanic skin responses.

Positive emotional reactions can also be classically conditioned. In the latter years of his career, Watson applied classical conditioning to marketing techniques. A new product (CS) was associated with a positive UCS (e.g., an extremely attractive model) to make it more appealing. Today's marketing and advertising firms continue to use classical conditioning in this way with great success (e.g., Shimp, Stuart, & Engle, 1991; Stuart, Shimp, & Engle, 1987).

Neoclassical Conditioning

Pavlov's basic model can be summarized as follows: A previously neutral stimulus (CS) comes to evoke the response (UCR) originally evoked by a different stimulus (UCS). This occurs as a result of the two stimuli being paired through nearly simultaneous presentation. Since the time of Pavlov's initial discovery, the study and understanding of the classical conditioning process has expanded greatly (Kimmel, 1989; Rescorla & Wagner, 1972; Turkkan, 1989a, 1989b).

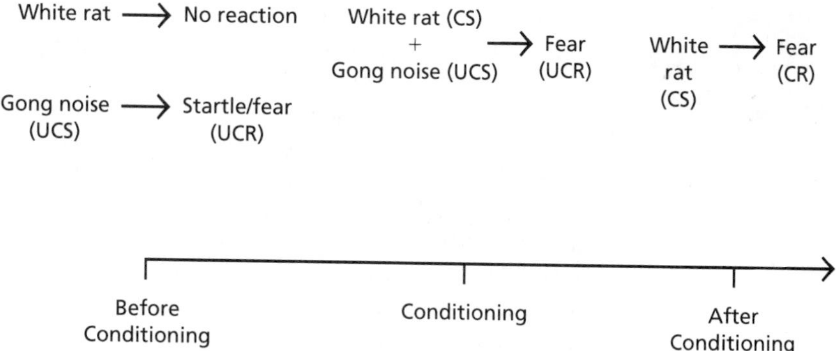

Figure 12.3
Schematic representation of the classical conditioning of fear in little Albert.
Source: From "Relationship of Cue to Consequence in Avoidance Learning," by J. Garcia and R. A. Koelling, 1966, Psychonomic Science, Vol. 4, pp. 123–124.

Today, many psychologists have come to believe that classical conditioning is more accurately described as "the learning of relations among events so as to allow the organism to represent its environment" (Rescorla, 1988, p. 151). For these psychologists, classical conditioning is no longer viewed as an "automatic" association of any two stimuli that happen to occur together (e.g., Gardner & Gardner, 1989; Huertas-Rodriguez, 1991). The *information* that the CS provides about the UCS is critical, not the simple CS-UCS pairing.

Aspects of the relationship between stimuli influence the effect obtained. For example, whether or not the CS is *invariably* paired with the UCS will certainly influence the effect produced. Only if the two appear coincident over numerous trials will the response generalize to the CS in other situations.

The Garcia Effect

It was obvious to several classical conditioning researchers that some associations could be learned very readily and that others were considerably more difficult. Rats were quickly taught to associate taste with subsequent illness but did not seem capable of associating visual or auditory cues with later illness. John Garcia and his colleagues began to investigate further to determine the limits of classical conditioning and what constraints might exist to restrict it.

Garcia and Koelling (1966) first noted that earlier research failed to distinguish adequately between two possible explanations for rats' failure to learn auditory and visual associations. First, organisms might be more *prepared* to form associations based on taste than on sight or sound. Second, taste might be especially salient to the animal because it remains constant and is always recognized. Other stimuli, such as noises and lights, might also remain constant, but the animal might fail to "notice" them. Garcia and Koelling devised an experiment to tease apart these two possibilities.

John Garcia carefully delineated the range and limitations of classical conditioning. Courtesy of John Garcia

The results obtained clearly demonstrated that for an illness reaction, rats were *more prepared* to acquire an association based on taste than on other characteristics of the stimuli. For an external stimulus (electric shock), however, environmental cues (lights and sounds) were more salient for learning. Thus, rats learned to avoid sweetened water when it was associated with later illness. They did *not* learn to avoid tasteless water paired with lights and noise, which also later produced illness. In the case of an association with subsequent shock, rats readily learned to avoid the "bright noisy" water but did *not* learn to avoid the sweetened water in the same situation. Thus, the rats of earlier research were not simply failing to attend to other features of the environment (noises and lights); rather, they were not biologically "prepared" to form an association between noise or light and subsequent illness. (This seems to make some adaptive sense. Animals that formed associations between illness and irrelevant environmental cues might well starve in their natural environment or simply continue to consume poisonous food on a regular basis.) The actual design of Garcia and Koelling's ingenious experiment is depicted in Figure 12.4.

Garcia and Koelling also found that the timing of presentation of the UCS did not conform to the principles accepted earlier. They were able to condition avoidance even with delays of up to 1 hour between presentation of the CS and UCS in the case of taste and illness. They and others have concluded that, in fact, organisms are *prepared* to acquire certain types of associations and may not acquire others, despite repeated pairings (Garcia & Koelling, 1966; Garcia, McGowan, & Green, 1972; Seligman, 1971). Similar findings have now been reported throughout the animal literature. Most of these studies focused on fear and avoidance reactions. It appears that many organisms are born (or hatched) prepared to fear or flee from specific types of stimuli. Intense reactions are often observed, even with the first presentation of a relevant stimulus. Critical characteristics of the stimuli often include shape, size, and movement (Marks, 1969, 1977; Rachlin, 1976).

What *is* learned in classical conditioning is that (given appropriate circumstances) the CS will predict the occurrence of the UCS (e.g., Power, 1991; Van den Hout & Merckelbach, 1991). Thus, the contemporary perspective on classical conditioning holds that the organism is "an information seeker using *logical and perceptual* relations among events, along with its own preconceptions, to form a sophisticated representation of its world" (Rescorla, 1988, p. 154).

Anxiety as a Classically Conditioned Response

Anxiety may be learned through classical conditioning (e.g., Levis, 1985; Öst & Hugdahl, 1985; Sandin, Chorot, & Fernández-Trespalacios, 1989; Wolpe & Rowan, 1988, 1989). Take fear of going to the dentist as an example. A person's initial visit to the dentist, often as a child, usually elicits no anxiety (unless the person has heard that dental work is painful). However, if the person experiences pain or discomfort while at the dentist's, the previously neutral cues in the dental office may come to elicit discomfort.

Pavlov's traditional model of classical conditioning—based on CS-UCS pairing—encounters difficulties in explaining how anxiety develops. For

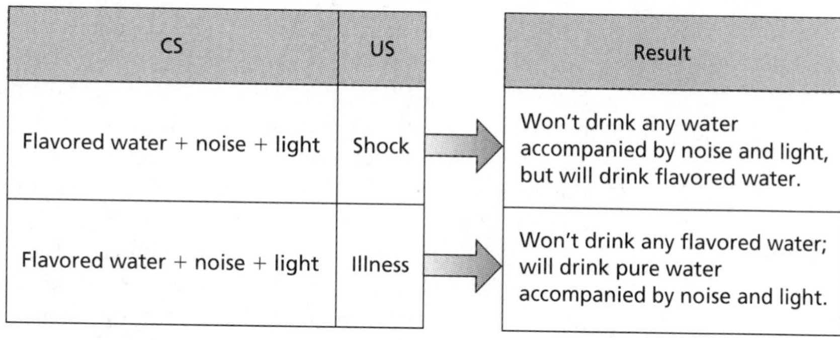

Figure 12.4
Schematic diagram of the results of Garcia and Koelling's conditioning study of different classes of stimuli.
Source: From "Relationship of Cue to Consequence in Avoidance Learning," by J. Garcia and R. A. Koelling, 1966, *Psychonomic Science, Vol. 4,* pp. 123–124.

instance, why is it that all people who are exposed to painful experiences during dental treatment do not develop dental phobias? This important question can be handled by contemporary models of classical conditioning that stress evaluation of the UCS (Davey, 1989b).

First, people should be less likely to develop dental anxiety following a painful experience at the dentist's if they had experienced previous *painless visits*. This phenomenon—in which the CS is less likely to predict the UCS if the CS has been previously presented without the UCS—is known as **latent inhibition.** In fact, people who have had painful dental visits and do not develop dental anxiety tend to have had their first painful experience after a number of benign dental visits. In contrast, people who *do* develop dental anxiety tend to have their initial painful experience after fewer visits (Davey, 1989a).

Second, people may fail to develop dental anxiety because factors other than the pain are more important in evaluating the dental situation (UCS). Some may focus on the beneficial effects of regular dental treatment. Others may believe that pain is a necessary evil of dental treatment. Still other individuals may have a higher tolerance for pain. Each of these factors results in evaluations that render the UCS less aversive and therefore less likely to lead to the development of dental anxiety (cf. Davey, 1989a).

Complex Behaviors Acquired Through Classical Conditioning

Traditional classical conditioning theory has been primarily used to explain learning simple reflexive (e.g., salivation, eye blink) and emotional (e.g., galvanic skin) responses. Consistent with broadened theoretical explanations of classical conditioning, the areas to which classical conditioning is being applied have also been expanded (e.g., Turkkan, 1989a, 1989b). We will consider two such areas: placebo effects and the effects of psychoactive drugs.

Placebo Effects

A placebo effect occurs when a patient is given an inert substance or treatment—a **placebo**—that results in a healing or therapeutic effect (White, Tursky, & Schwartz, 1985). Placebo effects have been demonstrated for a wide array of physical disorders ranging from the common cold, cough, and headache to insomnia, rheumatoid arthritis, hypertension, and angina (Evans, 1985).

Classical conditioning provides a parsimonious explanation of placebo effects (Turkkan & Brady, 1985). The placebo is a neutral (inert) event (CS), such as a "sugar pill." It is administered in a medical context (UCS)—visiting a physician in a white coat, who prescribes medication—that has a history of resulting in a patient's feeling better or getting well (CR). The patient easily associates the placebo (CS) with stimuli (UCS) that typically lead to therapeutic benefits (UCR). Thus, the placebo comes to elicit therapeutic benefits (CR).

Interestingly, voodoo may be explained as the opposite of the placebo effect, what has been called a **nocebo effect** (Wickramasekera, 1985). Voodoo rituals (CS) become associated with common stimuli related to illness and death (UCS) and hence result in the ultimate demise of the victim.

Effects of Psychoactive Drugs

Consider the following scenario. College students are recruited for a study of the effects of alcohol. In groups, they are provided with pitchers of beer and left to drink as much as they wish and to socialize with each other. The researcher returns about 30 minutes later and asks how they are doing. One student volunteers that she has become giddy. Another observes that the group is now more talkative. A third student reports tingling sensations in his arms, which, he explains, he typically experiences after a few beers. What accounts for the students' behaviors?

The effects of psychoactive drugs—substances that act on the brain to create psychological changes—are determined by two factors: the biochemical action of the drugs *and* learned responses to the drugs. The study we just described illustrates the powerful effects of learned responses, because the students were drinking (unbeknownst to them) *non*alcoholic beer! The potency of these learned responses is clear from this example.

As with the placebo effect, cues (CS) associated with drinking alcoholic beverages (UCS)—pitchers of beer, liquid that smells and tastes like beer, socializing—predict the psychological and physiological effects of alcohol. This effect has been observed in a number of controlled studies paralleling this scenario (e.g., Lang, Goeckner, Adesso, & Marlatt, 1975; Marlatt & Rohsenow, 1980; Rohsenow & Marlatt, 1981). The cues are received and *interpreted*, rather than just passively accepted by the organism. The drinking cues in these studies have come to be strongly associated with alcohol consumption and its effects, to the extent that the cues alone not only *predict* the effects but can also *elicit* them independent of alcohol.

The finding that stimuli associated with drug use (alcoholic beverages are, indeed, mind-altering drugs) can create drug-like effects provides an explanation for the development of tolerance. **Tolerance,** which is one indication of physical dependence on a drug, refers to a person's needing larger and larger doses of the substance over time to experience the same effect. Like other drug effects, tolerance has both biochemical and learned components.

The learned aspects of drug tolerance could arise from associating stimuli related to taking the drug—such as the syringe and needle—with the physiological response to the drug. In fact, people addicted to heroin have been known to inject themselves with water when they do not have access to heroin to produce heroin-like effects (McKim, 1986). This association between stimuli results in the contextual stimuli (CSs) alone coming to elicit one of two types of responses (CRs): drug-mimicking or drug-mirroring effects (Siegel, 1985).

A **drug-mimicking** effect produces an experience similar (albeit usually less intense) to consumption of the actual drug. This is the case with the heroin addict shooting up with water and the students who reported alcohol effects from nonalcoholic beer.

Drug-mirroring is a response that is *opposite* to that produced by the drug. Consider the use of morphine for pain management. In this case, contextual stimuli (e.g., being hospitalized after an injury) make the person more sensitive to pain. (In fact, the novelty of the context—the hospital—

likely maximizes the salience of all illness-related cues.) To deal with the heightened sensitivity to pain, the person requires greater and greater doses of morphine to alleviate it. This need for increasingly large doses of a drug to achieve the same effect over time is exactly what tolerance is (Siegel & Ellsworth, 1986).

OPERANT CONDITIONING

Classical conditioning acts by pairing stimuli to create associations between them. In contrast, **operant conditioning** deals primarily with associations between actions (behavior) and their *consequences.* When the consequences of a particular behavior are pleasant, the behavior is likely to be repeated; when they are aversive, the behavior is not likely to be repeated. Many of our everyday behaviors are learned and maintained by operant conditioning. The term *operant conditioning* was introduced in the writings of B. F. Skinner about 60 years ago.

The Skinnerian Tradition

B. F. Skinner's name is synonymous with the operant tradition. He set the ground rules for the operant approach, which, combined with classical conditioning, he considered the totality of the "scientific study of behavior." Skinner believed that behavior is primarily determined by external environmental influences, particularly by the consequences of one's actions (e.g., Skinner, 1989). He challenged the notion that humans are autonomous beings whose behaviors are influenced by internal factors, such as unconscious impulses, traits, or self-actualizing tendencies.

Skinner (1953) rejected explanations of behavior in terms of theoretical constructs, which he viewed as convenient but redundant fictions.

> The practice of looking inside the organism for an explanation of behavior has tended to obscure the variables which are immediately available for a scientific analysis. These variables lie outside the organism, in its immediate *environment* and in its *environmental history*. . . . The objection to inner states is not that they do not exist, but that they are not relevant. (pp. 31, 35, italics added)

B. F. Skinner (1904–1990) believed that behavior is primarily determined by external environmental influences, particularly the consequences of one's actions.
Courtesy of B. F. Skinner

In place of theoretical constructs, Skinner advocated discovering empirical relationships between behaviors and the conditions that influence them. As a radical behaviorist in the tradition of John Watson, he was concerned only with observable characteristics of the environment (stimuli) that influence overt behaviors (responses) (Delprato & Midgley, 1992; Hineline, 1992).

In a sense, Skinnerian psychology deals with an "empty organism." Variables that come between, or mediate, stimulus and response and that cannot be explained in terms of stimulus and response are beyond the domain of the operant approach. Like Watson, Skinner believed that there were only two goals of psychology: *prediction* and *control* (Biglan, 1993; Delprato & Midgley, 1992).

Skinner (1974) did not deny the existence of private events, such as thoughts and emotions. Instead, he was interested in identifying and studying the environmental conditions that influence them and that are reflected in the organism's overt behavior (Delprato & Midgley, 1992; Hayes & Brownstein, 1986; Holland, 1992; Place, 1993; Throne, 1992).

Functional Analysis of Behavior

Skinner believed (and contended throughout his nearly 60-year career) that psychology was not yet at a stage where elaborate formalized theorizing was justifiable. Skinner felt that, as a science, psychology was still in its infancy and that speculations about complex phenomena like human personality were premature. Accordingly, Skinner's own research remained directed toward complete and detailed descriptions of discrete behaviors. He termed these descriptions **functional analyses** of behavior. Their aim was to reveal empirical relationships between behaviors and the conditions that influence and control them. Skinner's (1956) maxim was: "Control your conditions and you will see order."

Like Watson before him, Skinner focused his attention on overt, observable events. These observables took the form of both behaviors emitted by the organism as responses and the external environmental stimuli that prompted them.

Skinner's Idiographic Orientation

Skinner stressed the importance of detailed and thorough analysis of the behavior of individual subjects. The typical experiment is not concerned with the average subject; rather, the aim is to establish control of a particular subject's behavior. Skinner (1956) explained his focus on the behavior of individuals as follows:

> In essence, I suddenly found myself face to face with the engineering problem of the animal trainer. When you have the responsibility of making absolutely sure that a given organism will engage in a given sort of behavior at a given time, you quickly grow impatient with theories of learning. Principles, hypotheses, theorems, satisfactory proof at the .05 level of significance . . . nothing could be more irrelevant. No one goes to the circus to see the average dog jump through a hoop significantly oftener than untrained dogs raised under the same circumstances, or to see an elephant demonstrate a principle of behavior. (p. 288)

Operant researchers still use the idiographic approach to research (in the form of single-subject designs, to be discussed later) for both basic research (often focused on animal models) and applied research (examining the effectiveness of operant based treatments on people).

THE NATURE OF OPERANT AND RESPONDENT BEHAVIOR

Skinner (1938) was the first to distinguish between two distinct types of behavior: operant and respondent. **Operant** behaviors are those that an organism *emits* in such a way as to "operate" on the environment. These behaviors are controlled by the consequences they produce. Operant behavior is also known as instrumental behavior because the subject is *instrumental* in producing a desired effect.

In contrast, **respondent** behavior is *elicited* by some identifiable stimulus in the environment; the subject is responding to something already present in the external environment. The purest examples of respondents are reflexes, such as the constriction of the pupil in response to a bright light or blinking in response to an object approaching the eye. Respondents can also be acquired through the process of classical conditioning described earlier.

Many behaviors originally acquired as operants may eventually come to function as respondents. They are "overlearned" behaviors—that is, behaviors that are practiced repeatedly. Stopping in response to a red light is an example. Originally learning to bring your car to a stop at traffic lights was probably the result of direct instruction or of observing others. This behavior probably produced a rewarding consequence during the acquisition phase (perhaps your driving instructor offered praise for stopping in appropriate circumstances). Over time and many trials, though, the response of stopping for a red light becomes almost automatic and occurs whenever a red light is present. Note that now the presentation of the external stimulus (red traffic light) evokes the response (stopping). This behavior is, in part, maintained by its consequences (avoidance of traffic accidents) but is heavily dependent on environmental cues (red lights). Red lights now serve as a discriminative stimulus for stopping. **Discriminative stimuli** cue the individual that a particular behavior is appropriate, or likely to be reinforced. The behavior itself has now come under **stimulus control**—that is, its execution is cued by environmental conditions.

Measurement of Operant Behaviors

The most commonly used measure of operant behavior is its *rate of occurrence*. It is an elegantly simple measure because it involves merely counting behavior in specified time intervals; the result is expressed in terms of the number of responses per unit of time (e.g., number of words typed per minute, distractions per hour, or cookies consumed per day).

Operant data are often presented graphically, depicting either the number of responses in each time period *or* the *cumulative number* of responses over time periods. **Cumulative records** are useful for portraying an individual's rate of responding and the changes in this rate. The steeper the slope of the cumulative record, the greater the rate of responding on which it is based. A cumulative record that depicts a line approaching vertical represents a very high rate of responding, whereas a line approaching horizontal represents a very low rate of responding. **Acquisition** (or learning) **curves** rise at an increasing (approaching vertical) slope. **Extinction curves** (dropping off toward horizontal) level off or drop away from vertical direction. They represent a decrease in the rate of responding over time. Figure 12.5 depicts a record of one student's studying behavior graphed both cumulatively and noncumulatively. Note the contrast in clarity and ease of interpretation of the two presentations.

The choice between the two methods of presentation depends a great deal on the intended purpose of the record. If one is primarily interested in progress—or changes in rate of responding—cumulative records are most appropriate. These behavior changes can be recognized immediately from changes in the *slope* of the resulting line. If, however, one is interested in examining responding during particular time periods (perhaps corresponding to changes in some external conditions), then noncumulative presentation is more appropriate. The number of responses emitted in any given period can be easily compared to any other time period.

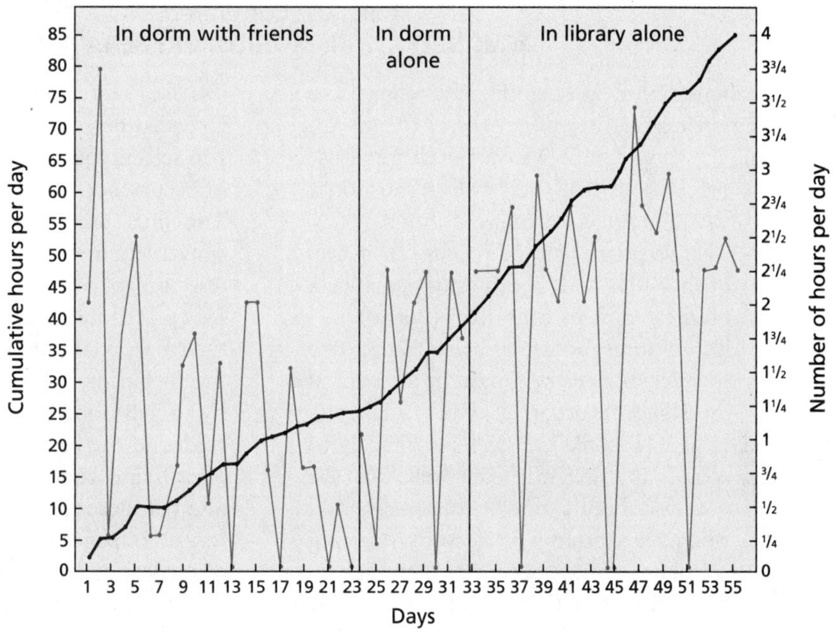

Figure 12.5
Cumulative record of daily studying (shown in black) and noncumulative record of daily studying (shown in color)

Box 12.1
DEMONSTRATION: MONITORING BEHAVIOR

Direct observation and recording of behaviors are important behavioral procedures for assessment in both research and applied settings. In this Demonstration, you will observe and record one of your own behaviors. (The instructions can easily be adapted to observing and recording another person's behaviors.)

1. First, choose a response to observe and record. For clarity's sake, the response should be defined in such a way that it is *overt and discrete* (has a clear beginning and ending). For example, consider the behavior "reading." Defined as simply reading, its measurement and quantification are very difficult. But, when reading is **operationally defined** (for the exclusive purpose of direct study) as number of pages read in a specified unit of time (per hour), measurement becomes straightforward and objective.

   Table 12.1 contains examples of responses you might select but you can pick any

Table 12.1 Examples of target behaviors to observe and record

BEHAVIOR	UNIT OF BEHAVIOR	TIME PERIOD
Reading	Pages	Day or hour
Writing	Lines or pages	Day or hour
Swimming	Laps in pool	Day
Studying	Minutes spent	Day
Drinking (coffee, beer, etc.)	Cups or ounces	Day
Smoking	Number of cigarettes	Day

Box continued on following page

Box 12.1 *Continued*
DEMONSTRATION: MONITORING BEHAVIOR

response that meets the following two requirements:

A. You should be able to define the response precisely so that there will be no doubt whether you have engaged in it.

B. The response should occur at a frequency that makes recording possible. A practical unit of time for observation—like minutes, hours, or days (as opposed to weeks or years)—must be chosen. If the response occurs at a very high rate (e.g., eye blinks), it will be difficult to count and record accurately. If the response occurs only occasionally, you will have nothing to record. (Getting married does not occur often enough to be used in this Demonstration—at least for most people!)

2. Now, select a *unit of behavior* and an *observation time period* that are appropriate for your chosen response. Table 12.1 contains examples of adequate operational definitions, as well as observation periods for the behaviors suggested. (A behavior that you engage in many times a day would most likely be recorded in hours or minutes, whereas a less frequent behavior would probably be recorded per day.) No matter what response you select, you will be counting the number of occurrences in each specified time period.

3. The final preparatory step is to devise a convenient means of recording how often the response occurs. For example, mark off a 3- × 5-inch index card in time intervals, and then make a tally mark each time you perform the behavior, as shown in Figure 12.6. (Materials for this Demonstration are included at the back of this book.) At the end of each time period, total the tally marks. This number becomes your rate for the period (e.g., "26 pages read on day 1"). Other ways of recording responses include making tally marks on a piece of masking tape on your watchband or purse. An inexpensive golf or knitting counter might also be used.

The recording procedure should be convenient and available whenever you are observing the behavior. You should also make brief notes whenever possible about special events or circumstances that may have influenced the frequency of the response (see Figure 12.6).

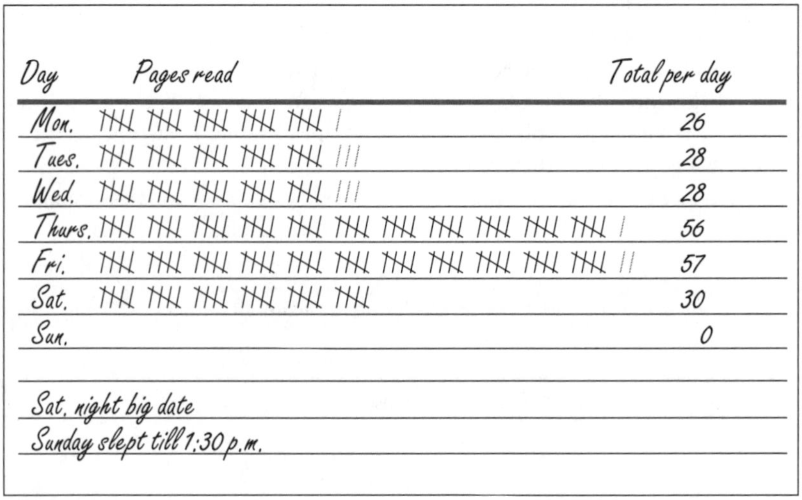

Day	Pages read	Total per day
Mon.	卌 卌 卌 卌 卌 /	26
Tues.	卌 卌 卌 卌 卌 ///	28
Wed.	卌 卌 卌 卌 卌 ///	28
Thurs.	卌 卌 卌 卌 卌 卌 卌 卌 卌 卌 卌 /	56
Fri.	卌 卌 卌 卌 卌 卌 卌 卌 卌 卌 卌 //	57
Sat.	卌 卌 卌 卌 卌 卌	30
Sun.		0

Sat. night big date
Sunday slept till 1:30 p.m.

Figure 12.6
Example of an index-card record of pages read in a week.

Box continued on following page

Box 12.1 *Continued*
DEMONSTRATION: MONITORING BEHAVIOR

4. Now you are ready to record the behavior whenever it occurs. You should record for a minimum of 6 time units (e.g., days or hours).
5. To help you inspect and interpret the data you've collected, graph your observations. The horizontal axis should be marked off in time intervals, such as days or hours. The vertical axis should represent the number of responses per unit of time.

As an example, the data recorded in Figure 12.6 have been graphed in Figure 12.7. Notice that the person read approximately the same number of pages for the first 3 days. On Thursday, the number of pages nearly doubled and continued at this same high rate on Friday. On Saturday, the number of pages dropped back to approximately the Monday-through-Wednesday rate, perhaps because the Saturday night date was more compelling than reading. On the seventh day, no pages were read (perhaps the person rested).

Note that this graph is noncumulative. Your responses can also be graphed cumulatively by simply adding the number of responses for each of the previous time units to the total for the current time unit and then plotting this number on the vertical axis. The resulting graph will look very different from the first and will be more

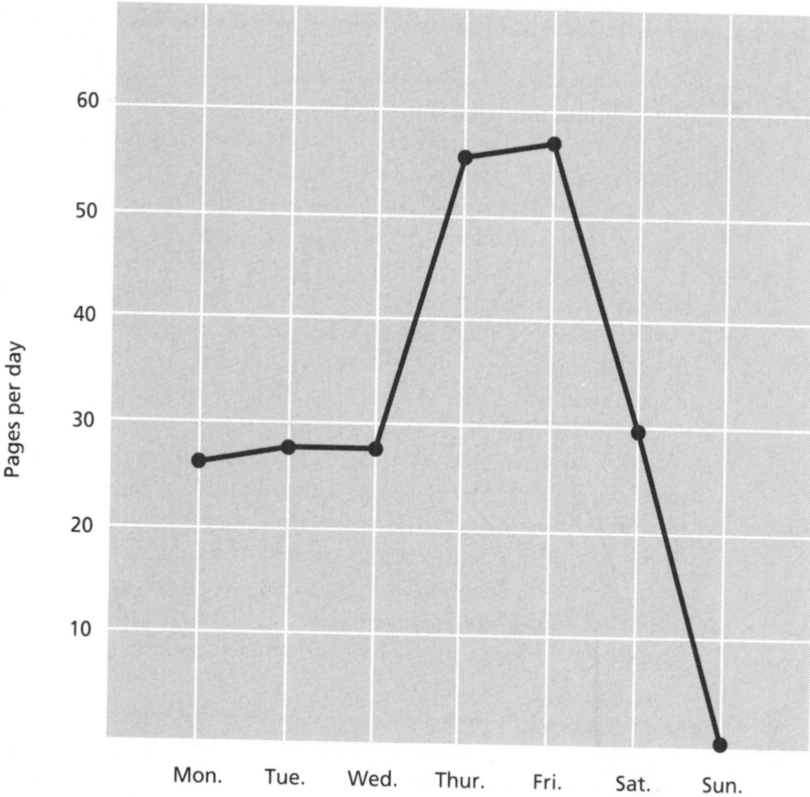

Figure 12.7
Graph of a week's reading behavior.

Box continued on following page

Box 12.1 *Continued*
DEMONSTRATION: MONITORING BEHAVIOR

useful for identifying trends in your rate of responding. (Note that the first graph invited speculation about the events that might have corresponded to changes in responding on particular days.)

In doing this Demonstration, you may have encountered some of the common problems associated with self-recording behaviors. First, you may have been unsure at times whether you performed the behavior, probably because you did not define the behavior specifically enough.

Second, you may have forgotten to record the behavior or found recording a burden. These problems can be minimized by making the recording procedures as simple and convenient as possible.

Third, you may have the impression that the frequency of your behavior changed simply because you were observing and recording it. This common problem, known as **reactivity,** is more likely to occur if you specifically want to increase or decrease how often you engaged in the behavior.

You may also have learned something new about the particular behavior you were observing. The data may provide information about how often and when (time of day or day of the week) you are most likely to perform the behavior. This information may even suggest simple environment-based means to influence the behavior, if you are interested in doing so. You may perform these same procedures on another person (or animal) for comparison.

PUNISHMENT

Punishment as defined in operant theory is any consequence that reduces the likelihood of recurrence of the behavior that precipitated it. Like other types of operants, punishment can take several forms.

Punishments can include the presentation of a noxious stimulus contingent on a specific behavior (operant). Electric shock delivered in response to a bar press by a rat serves as a punisher, for example. A dramatic scowl in response to a statement you make also serves as a punisher. For example, your current partner may display a hostile reaction to comparisons you make between him or her and your previous partner(s). You may therefore stop drawing explicit contrasts between them in the future.

Punishment can also include removal of access to a reinforcer, which is fairly common in everyday life. For example, children are often told that they will lose recess privileges if they fail to complete their classwork. The procedure, commonly known as **time out,** is, in fact, technically termed "time out from positive reinforcement" and denies (for a brief time) access to a number of potential reinforcers. We will have more to say about punishment and time out procedures in Chapter 14, where we examine the applications derived from environmental theories.

REINFORCEMENT

At the heart of operant conditioning is the concept of **reinforcement**—the process by which the consequences of a behavior increase the chances that the behavior will be performed again. This is an **empirical definition** because the occurrence of reinforcement depends on an observed effect—namely, an increased likelihood of the behavior occurring—and *not* on subjective desirability. In most cases, however, **reinforcers**—the consequences that increase behaviors—*are* pleasurable or desirable events. (However, note that what serves well as a reinforcer for one person might not reinforce another, and might even be a punisher. For example, avid gardeners might work hard in other realms to earn the opportunity to go out and work in the garden. This same reinforcer might be a punisher for another person, who might go to great lengths to avoid pulling weeds.)

Positive and Negative Reinforcement

Two broad categories of reinforcement have been distinguished: positive and negative. **Positive reinforcement** occurs when a reinforcing stimulus is presented (added) after a behavior. For example, a father praises his son for cleaning his room. **Negative reinforcement,** by contrast, involves the removal of a noxious stimulus contingent on a behavior. For instance, a father stops criticizing his son after the boy has cleaned his room. In both cases, the *reinforcing consequences* increase the likelihood of the behavior being repeated. Reinforcement always refers to *increasing* the likelihood of occurrence (strengthening) of a target behavior. The designation *positive* indicates only the presentation or addition of a stimulus, and *negative* the removal of a stimulus.

Negative reinforcement should not be confused with punishment. Recall that punishment is defined empirically as the process by which the consequence of a behavior decreases the likelihood of the behavior's recurrence. In fact, technically speaking, punishment, too, comes in both positive and negative forms. The removal of a stimulus (presumably a rewarding stimulus) is negative punishment, and the addition of a stimulus (noxious) is positive punishment. Any form of punishment, by definition, has the *opposite* effect of any form of reinforcement.

The role of reinforcement in operant conditioning is illustrated in the therapy procedures used to increase a boy's studying. The treatment was evaluated with a **single-subject reversal design.** This research design compares a subject's behavior during periods in which a treatment is present to periods in which it is not. (These later periods are called *reversals* because conditions are returned, or reversed, to those that prevailed before the introduction of treatment.)

The Case of Robbie

Robbie, an elementary school boy, frequently disrupted class activities and spent little time studying (Hall, Lund, & Jackson, 1968). Initially, Robbie was observed during seven 30-minute **baseline** (pretreatment) periods in his classroom. The naturalistic observations were carried out when pupils were supposed to be working in their seats.

Figure 12.8 shows a record of Robbie's study behavior, defined as "having his pencil on paper for at least half of a 10-second observation period." As you can see from the graph, during the baseline period, Robbie engaged in study behavior an average of only 25% of the time. He spent the remaining time engaged in such behaviors as "snapping rubber bands, playing with toys from his pocket, talking and laughing with peers, slowly drinking the half pint of milk served earlier in the morning, and subsequently playing with the empty carton" (Hall et al., 1968, p. 3).

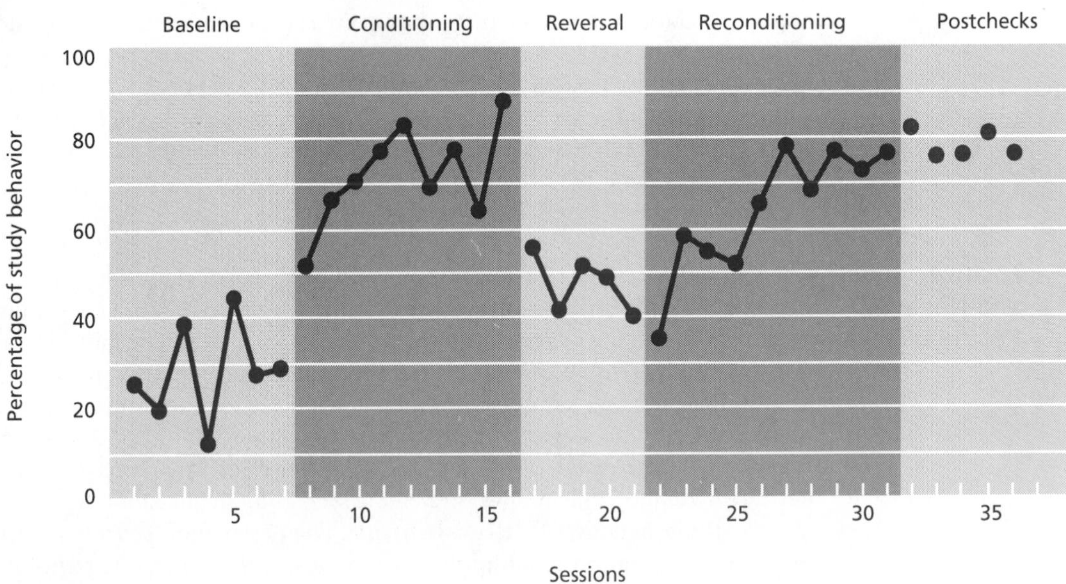

Figure 12.8
A record of Robbie's study behavior. *Note:* Postcheck observations were made during the 4th, 6th, 7th, 12th, and 14th weeks after the completion of reinforcement conditioning.
Source: Adapted from "Effects of Teacher Attention on Study Behavior," by R. V. Hall, D. Lund, and D. Jackson, 1968, *Journal of Applied Behavior Analysis, 1,* pp. 1–12.

In the course of the naturalistic observation, it was noted that Robbie's teacher frequently paid attention to Robbie's nonstudy behaviors, such as by urging him to work or reminding him to put away his toys.

Following the baseline period, the conditioning (experimental) phase of the study was begun. Now, every time Robbie engaged in 1 minute of continuous studying, an observer signaled the teacher, who promptly reinforced the behavior with attention. The teacher ignored Robbie at all other times. The results were striking. As Robbie received attention only when he studied, his studying increased markedly in the first session and continued to rise in subsequent sessions (see Figure 12.8). Robbie spent an average of 71% of his time studying during the conditioning phase, compared to 25% during baseline.

Reinforcement appeared to be responsible for Robbie's increased rate of studying because studying increased from the baseline period, when reinforcement for studying had not been given. Still, some other factor that occurred in the conditioning phase but not in the baseline period could have increased Robbie's studying. For example, Robbie's parents might have begun to reward him when he said he studied at school.

To provide additional evidence that the reinforcement rather than some other factor had increased Robbie's study behavior, a reversal phase was instituted. The teacher stopped reinforcing Robbie's studying, which reinstated (reversed back to) the circumstances that prevailed before the conditioning phase. This period constituted an extinction phase. (In this case **extinction** refers to the withdrawal of reinforcement.) If Robbie's studying was controlled by reinforcement, his study behavior should decrease with the withdrawal of reinforcement. Robbie's studying declined to a mean of 50% during the reversal period (see Figure 12.8).

The researchers could have ended the procedures at this point if the only goal had been to demonstrate that reinforcement was maintaining Robbie's study behavior. However, the major objective of the investigation was to increase Robbie's studying. Therefore, a reconditioning phase was instituted. Specifically, teacher attention was reinstated as a reinforcer for studying. Robbie's study rate increased, stabilizing between 70% and 80% (see Figure 12.8).

Periodic checks made during the remainder of the school year showed that Robbie's studying was maintained at an average rate of 79% (see Figure 12.8). Furthermore, Robbie's teacher reported that the quality of his studying had also improved. He was now completing written assignments and missing fewer words on spelling tests.

Eliciting Behaviors

For a behavior to be reinforced, it must first occur, When a target behavior occurs at least occasionally, such as Robbie's studying, it can be reinforced (although one may have to spend some time waiting first). But suppose the baseline level for a particular behavior is at or near zero. Some means must be devised to elicit the target behavior. The techniques of prompting and shaping are used for this purpose.

Prompting Behavior

Prompting involves telling or reminding someone to perform a behavior. Prompting cues may be verbal (as when a parent reminds a child, "Say thank you") or physical (as when a coach moves a student's arms to produce a swimming stroke). Once the behavior occurs often enough to be reinforced, the prompts are gradually withdrawn—a procedure called **fading.**

Prompting and subsequent fading often are used to teach language to children with severe disabilities. For instance, to teach the name of an object, the teacher points to it and says, "What is this?—Cup." As the child begins to say "cup," the teacher fades the prompt by saying "cup" at successively lower volumes, then silently mouthing the word, and finally withdrawing all prompts (so the teacher only asks, "What is this?").

Shaping Behavior

Another way to elicit a particular behavior is to shape it. **Shaping** involves reinforcing progressively closer approximations of the behavior. First, the desired behavior is broken down into its component parts. Then each component is reinforced until the entire behavior emerges. The logic of shaping is illustrated schematically in Figure 12.9.

The children's game of "hot and cold" is similar to the process of shaping a behavior. One child has to find an object in a room. A playmate directs the child by saying "hot" when the child gets closer to the object and "cold" when the child moves farther away. Using these "clues," the seeking child eventually zeros in on the target object.

Schedules of Reinforcement

A **schedule of reinforcement** refers to the sequence or pattern in which reinforcement is received. In a **continuous reinforcement schedule,** the individual is reinforced for every performance of the target behavior. Continuous reinforcement is often used initially to establish a desired response.

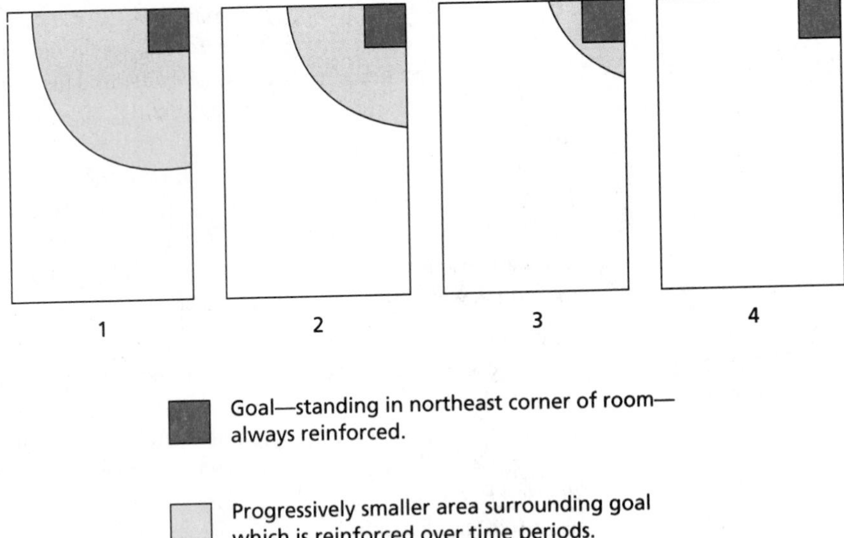

Figure 12.9
Behavior is shaped by reinforcing successive approximations to the desired behavior; that is, behaviors that "approach" the goal behavior.

Once a behavior has been adequately established, an **intermittent reinforcement schedule** can be used to increase or maintain it. On intermittent or partial schedules, only some instances of the desired behavior are reinforced. Behaviors that have been reinforced intermittently will be maintained longer, even without reinforcement, than behaviors that have been reinforced continuously (Pittenger & Pavlik, 1988, 1989; Pittenger, Pavlik, Flora, & Kontos, 1988). In fact, continuous schedules of reinforcement serve to highlight changes in contingencies or the withdrawal of reinforcement entirely. Individuals usually recognize changes as soon as they occur, which is often reflected in their behavior (which changes in response). Similar changes are not as readily detectable in intermittent schedules. Most of our habitual everyday behaviors are actually reinforced on intermittent schedules.

Four basic schedules of intermittent reinforcement are produced by the combination of two dimensions: (1) the number of responses or period of time since the last reinforcement and (2) fixed versus variable reinforcement rate (see Figure 12.10).

In **ratio schedules,** reinforcement occurs only after a certain number of responses have been made. That number can be **fixed** (e.g., after every fifth response) or **variable** (e.g., after the third response, then after the seventh response, and so on). With **interval schedules,** reinforcement occurs if the person performs the behavior (at least once) after a specified period since the last reinforcement. The time interval can also be **fixed** (e.g., after 5 minutes) or **variable** (e.g., 3 minutes, then 7 minutes, and so on). The four schedules of intermittent reinforcement are compared in Figure 12.11.

Fixed-Interval Schedules

In a **fixed-interval schedule,** a reinforcer is given for the first response made after a set time has elapsed, such as every 2 minutes (see Figure 12.11). Studying for college examinations and working for a salary are common

	Interval (time since last reinforcement)	**Ratio** (number of responses)
Fixed (set time period or number)	**Fixed-interval**	**Fixed-ratio**
Variable (changing time period or number)	**Variable-interval**	**Variable-ratio**

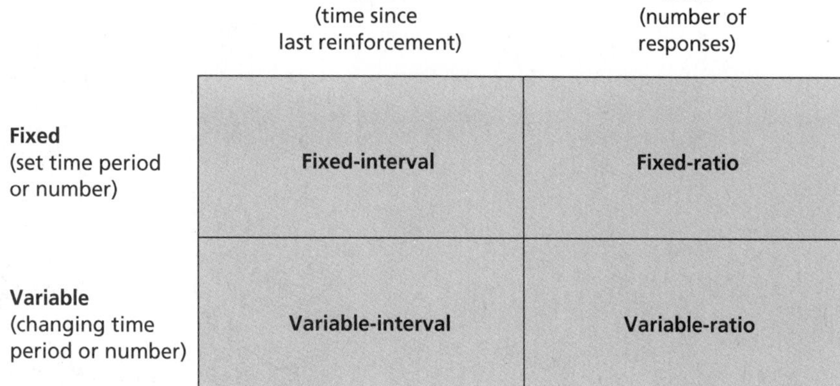

Figure 12.10
The four basic schedules of intermittent reinforcement.

examples of behaviors maintained by fixed-interval schedules. Fixed-interval schedules produce a reliable pattern of responding that looks "scalloped" when graphed cumulatively (Figure 12.12). The person makes few responses immediately after reinforcement, and then the rate of responding accelerates as the time for the next reinforcer nears.

Think about your own study habits. You are not likely to study much right after a test in a class, but your studying increases dramatically as the time of the next exam approaches. You are in distinguished company. Even members of the U.S. Congress behave on a fixed-interval schedule (Weisberg & Waldrop, 1972). They pass bills at a very low rate in the first few months of each session. As adjournment draws closer, the number of bills passed increases sharply, which produces the "scalloped" cumulative record in Figure 12.13.

Fixed-Ratio Schedules

On **fixed-ratio schedules,** reinforcers are administered after a set number of responses. For example, a 4 : 1 fixed ratio means that every fourth response is

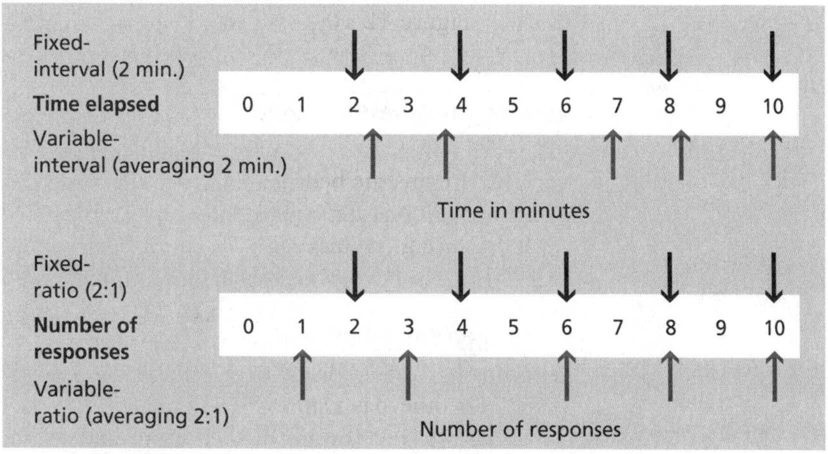

Figure 12.11
Comparison of fixed- versus variable-interval and ratio schedules of reinforcement (arrows indicate reinforcement delivery).

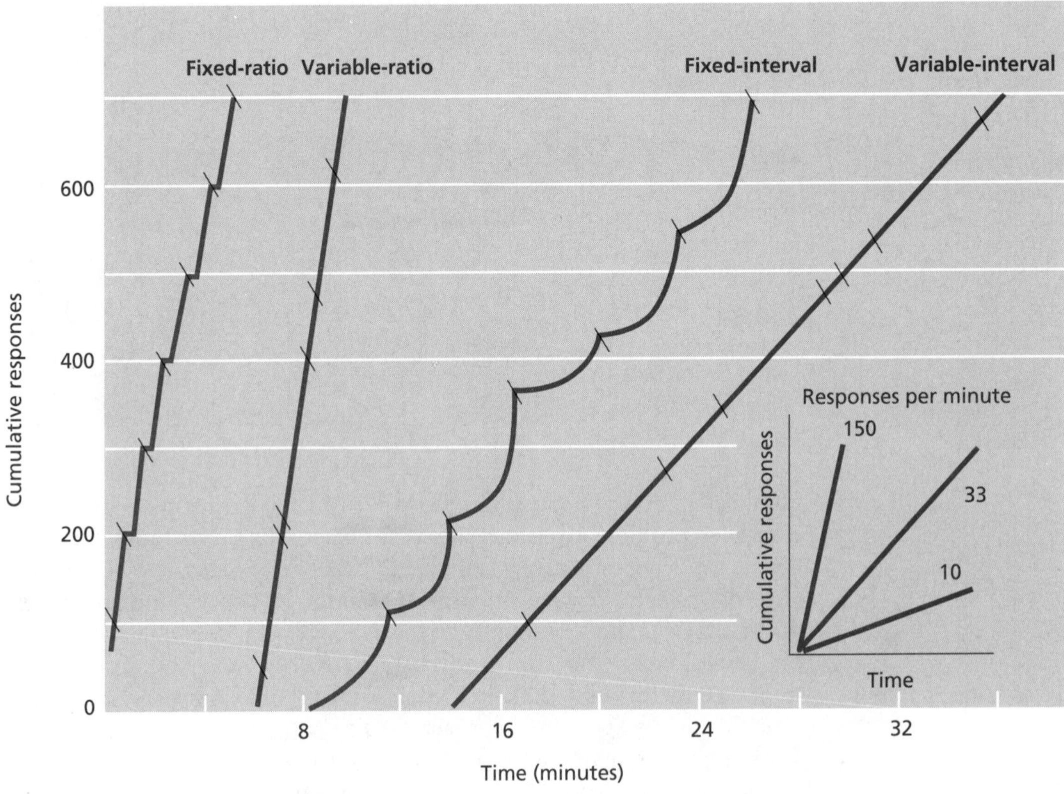

Figure 12.12
Stylized records of responding under basic schedules of reinforcement.
Source: Adapted from "The Analysis of Human Operant Behavior" by E. P. Reese, 1966, in J. A. Vernon (Ed.), *Introduction to Psychology: A Self-Selection Textbook,* Dubuque, Iowa: Brown.

reinforced. A salesperson who is earning a commission and a student who gets a grade for solving a specified number of problems are both being reinforced on fixed-ratio schedules.

Fixed-ratio schedules generally produce considerably higher rates of responding than either continuous reinforcement or fixed-interval schedules. As Figure 12.12 illustrates, the cumulative curve for a fixed-ratio schedule is steeper than for a fixed-interval schedule, indicating a higher rate of responding. If the number of responses required for reinforcement is gradually increased, people will tend to continue responding. People have occasionally been reported to respond on even extremely "lean" schedules, where the ratio of nonreinforced to reinforced responses is very high (e.g., 1000 : 1).

Variable-Interval Schedules

In everyday life, there is often variability in the reinforcement we receive. **Variable-interval schedules** reinforce the target behavior based on time, in which the interval between reinforcers is randomly varied around a specific amount of time. For instance, *on average,* an individual might be reinforced every 2 minutes, with some behavior reinforced at 1.75 minutes, some at 2.25 minutes, and so on (see Figure 12.11).

Dialing a telephone number that has been busy is an example of a common behavior that is reinforced on a variable-interval schedule (Shaver & Tarpy, 1993). The amount of time for a connection to occur (reinforcement) varies from one attempt to another. Hunting and fishing are examples of other

Many workers are paid on an hourly basis. This is an example of a fixed-interval schedule of reinforcement.
Photo Source Inc./St. Louis

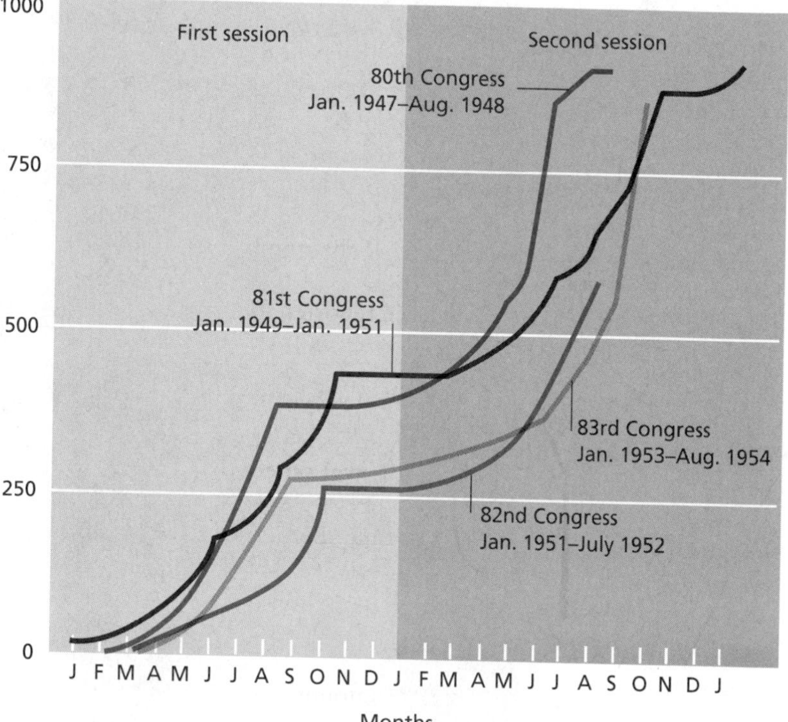

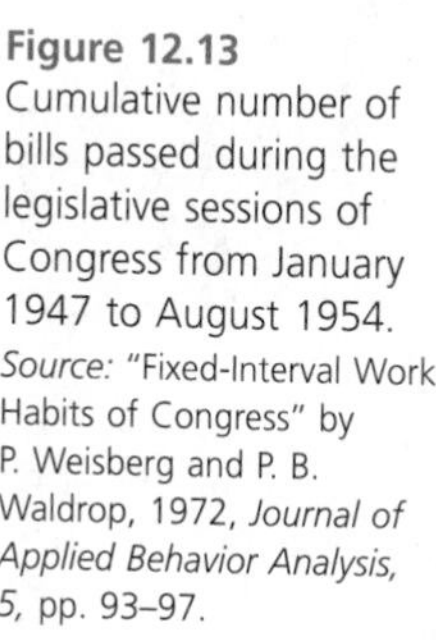

Figure 12.13
Cumulative number of bills passed during the legislative sessions of Congress from January 1947 to August 1954.
Source: "Fixed-Interval Work Habits of Congress" by P. Weisberg and P. B. Waldrop, 1972, *Journal of Applied Behavior Analysis, 5,* pp. 93–97.

behaviors reinforced on variable-interval schedules. Even though both endeavors involve skill, the availability of reinforcers—that is, the presence of game or fish—is unknown, and varying amounts of time will elapse between "payoffs" (Lundin, 1961). Variable-interval schedules produce steady but relatively low response rates.

Piecework is an example of reinforcement based on a fixed-ratio schedule.
© Michael Melford/Image Bank

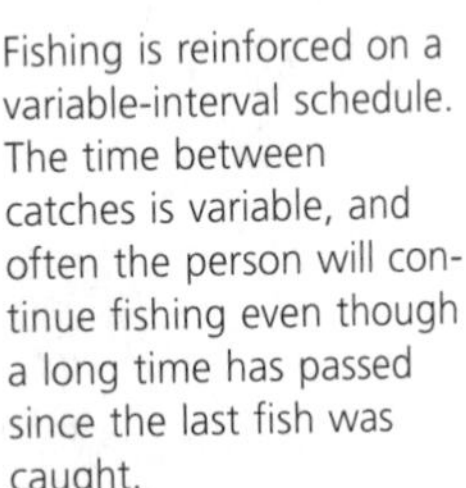

Fishing is reinforced on a variable-interval schedule. The time between catches is variable, and often the person will continue fishing even though a long time has passed since the last fish was caught.
© Jim Grace/Photo Researchers

Variable-Ratio Schedules

On a **variable-ratio schedule,** the number of responses required for reinforcement is varied randomly around a given ratio, such that the target ratio represents the average number of required responses (see Figure 12.11). Variable-ratio schedules are among the most potent for inducing very high, steady rates of responding (see Figure 12.12). Compulsive gambling illustrates the potentially powerful effect of variable-ratio schedules.

> Even though the returns are very slim, . . . [the gambler] never gives up. Families are ruined and fortunes lost; still the high rates of behavior are maintained, often to the exclusion of all alternate forms of activity. Witness the "all night" crap games in which a single person will remain until all . . . funds and resources are gone. (Lundin, 1961, p. 91)

As we have seen, there are distinct differences in the various schedules and in some of their effects. You may wonder, then, which one is the best or about the advantages and disadvantages of each schedule. In practice, ratio schedules are generally more effective than interval schedules. The necessary ratio to begin to establish a particular response may be 1:1. However, this ratio can often be thinned out over the course of conditioning. Thus, although a "thin" variable ratio schedule is often the best way to *maintain* a response, continuous reinforcement is often required to establish the response in the first place.

Matching Theory

How often a behavior is performed depends on more than the schedule on which it is being reinforced. Response rate is also influenced by the amount of reinforcement available for *all other* possible responses (Herrnstein, 1970). Specifically, Richard Herrnstein's **matching theory** predicts that if there are a number of alternative behaviors you can perform, your frequency of

Gambling pays off on a variable-ratio schedule. The number of bets between wins is quite variable, and gamblers continue to bet even though many preceding bets have not paid off. This is one explanation of the lure of and even the addiction to gambling.
© Dave Bellak/Jeroboam

engaging in each will be *directly proportional* to the amount of reinforcement you receive for each.

One of the practical implications of matching theory is that the response rate of a given behavior can be affected by the amount of reinforcement provided for other behaviors (e.g., Martens, 1990, 1992; Martens & Houk, 1989; Martens, Lochner, & Kelly, 1992; McDowell, 1988). As an example, matching theory was used to design a treatment to reduce a mildly retarded 22-year-old man's "oppositional behaviors," which included failure to comply with requests, arguing, and displaying temper tantrums (McDowell, 1982).

The treatment involved increasing the reinforcement available for behaviors unrelated to the man's oppositional behaviors, such as shaving, helping prepare dinner, and reading. By the eighth week of treatment, the frequency of oppositional behaviors had decreased by about 80%. Note that nothing was done to directly decrease the reinforcement for the oppositional behaviors; the treatment involved only *increasing the reinforcement for other behaviors.*

Stimulus Control

Learning involves knowing (1) how to perform a behavior and (2) the conditions under which the behavior is likely to be reinforced. Recall that **discriminative stimuli** are environmental cues that indicate when a response is likely to be reinforced. They cue the individual that the time is ripe for reinforcement.

Discriminative stimuli should not be confused with setting events. **Setting events** "set the stage" for the performance of a given behavior by preparing the individual in some way. For example, thirst might be a setting event for drinking, and drinking will occur if conditions are conducive. Discriminative stimuli for drinking, by contrast, might be anything in the environment that signals to the individual that water is present and available. Drinking behavior, therefore, is *made more likely* by the setting event (thirst) but *made possible* by the presence of a discriminative stimulus (water). Behaviors that are cued (triggered) by discriminative stimuli are said to be under **stimulus control.**

Many of our everyday behaviors are under stimulus control. The ringing telephone signals you to pick up the receiver and say hello. (Note that you may raise the receiver at other times, but you are not likely to say hello or expect to be reinforced by a response from the other end.) You are more likely to smile at someone who smiles rather than frowns at you. A police car up ahead may be a discriminative stimulus for *slowing down.* (In this example, *speeding* might be considered a setting event for the subsequent deceleration.)

Different discriminative stimuli may control the same response for different people. For example, in countries where food is scarce, people eat when their stomachs "tell" them they are hungry. In more affluent societies, people tend to eat when the clock "tells" them to.

The right amount of stimulus control is necessary for efficient functioning. Too much or inappropriate stimulus control leads to rigidity. For example, parents of young children sometimes discover that bedtime is likely to be observed only when they are home and not when the children are left with babysitters. The parents have become the discriminative stimuli for observing bedtime; the children have not learned to generalize the behavior to other discriminative stimuli such as time of day, sunset, or the after-dinner winding-down period.

More often, problems arise from insufficient stimulus control. Insomnia, for instance, may occur because sleeping is not under appropriate stimulus control. The relevant cues of nighttime and being in bed are, for one reason or another, insufficient to initiate or maintain adequate sleep for some people. In Chapter 14, we discuss therapies based on behavioral principles.

SUMMARY

1. The behavioral approach emphasizes the study of overt (observable) behaviors and the environmental conditions that influence them. Behaviorists focus on two learning processes: classical conditioning and operant conditioning.
2. Classical conditioning involves pairing a stimulus that produces an automatic, reflexive response with an initially neutral stimulus. Over repeated pairings, the neutral stimulus also comes to elicit the response.
3. Ivan Pavlov accidentally discovered classical conditioning and then devoted the remainder of his career to elaborating the process through systematic research.
4. A stimulus that reflexively produces a response is called an unconditioned stimulus (UCS), whereas the neutral stimulus with which it is paired is called the conditioned stimulus (CS). The reflexive response is called the unconditioned response (UCR) and the response made to the initially neutral stimulus is called the conditioned response (CR).
5. The process by which the conditioned response comes to be displayed is called acquisition. Generalization is said to occur when a subject makes a conditioned response to stimuli similar but not identical to the conditioned stimulus; discrimination is said to occur when the subject distinguishes between the conditioned stimulus and a similar stimulus and does not display the conditioned response when the similar stimulus is presented.
6. The greater the similarity between the conditioned stimulus and another stimulus, the more likely is generalization to occur; less similar stimuli are less likely to elicit the conditioned response. Behaviorists thus speak of a generalization gradient.
7. Repeated presentation of the conditioned stimulus without the unconditioned stimulus leads to extinction, the gradual disappearance of the conditioned response. However, if a conditioned stimulus is again presented some time after extinction has occurred, the conditioned response may briefly reappear. This phenomenon is known as spontaneous recovery.
8. John Watson and Rosalie Rayner demonstrated human classical conditioning with an 11-month-old boy, little Albert. Subsequent research has shown that both negative and positive emotional reactions can be classically conditioned in children and adults. Watson

himself applied the principle of classical conditioning to develop marketing techniques that are still used today.

9. Classical conditioning has come to be viewed by some contemporary psychologists as the learning of information about relationships.
10. Garcia and Koelling demonstrated that organisms are more likely to be classically conditioned to stimulus associations for which they are biologically prepared. This phenomenon has been referred to as the Garcia effect.
11. Research shows that anxiety can be classically conditioned; however, conditioning is less likely to occur if the conditioned stimulus has previously been presented without the unconditioned stimulus. This phenomenon is known as latent inhibition.
12. Classical conditioning can explain placebo effects, in which a neutral substance (such as a sugar pill) produces a therapeutic effect. There is also evidence for a nocebo effect, as in the case of voodoo rituals that actually produce illness and death in cultures where these associations have been learned.
13. Drinking cues are conditioned to alcohol effects, so that beverages such as nonalcoholic beer may produce effects similar to those produced by alcohol.
14. In connection with drugs, two types of conditioned responses have been observed. Drug-mimicking effects are those in which a stimulus associated with a drug produces effects similar to those produced by the drug itself (as in the case of nonalcoholic beer). Drug-mirroring effects are those in which cues associated with receiving drugs produce effects opposite to those produced by the drug; for example, the contextual cues of being a patient in a hospital may actually increase the experience of pain or illness.
15. Operant conditioning deals with associations between actions (behaviors) and their consequences. Pleasant consequences tend to increase the likelihood of a behavior, whereas unpleasant consequences tend to reduce the likelihood of a behavior recurring.
16. B. F. Skinner is the psychologist who founded the operant tradition. Skinner, like Watson, eschewed all efforts to look "inside" the person and looked to a person's environment and environmental history as the primary explanations of behavior. He termed his detailed observational assessments the functional analysis of behavior.
17. Skinner believed that psychology must explain the behavior of individual subjects and rejected group designs and the practice of averaging scores across individuals; instead, he championed single-subject research designs.
18. Skinner distinguished between operant behavior, which is emitted by the individual and operates on the environment, and respondent behavior, which is elicited (often reflexively) by the presence of specific environmental stimuli.
19. A discriminative stimulus cues a particular behavior; for example, a red traffic light is a discriminative stimulus for stopping. Behavior cued by discriminative stimuli is said to be under stimulus control.

20. The most common measure of operant behavior is its rate of occurrence, usually displayed as a cumulative record. Such records allow us to depict both acquisition and extinction curves.
21. Punishment is defined as any consequence that reduces the likelihood of recurrence of the behavior that preceded it. One type of punishment is removal of an individual's access to pleasant stimuli, which is referred to as time out from positive reinforcement or simply time out.
22. Reinforcers are consequences that increase the likelihood of recurrence of behaviors they follow. Positive reinforcement occurs when a reinforcing stimulus is presented following a behavior. Negative reinforcement occurs when a noxious stimulus is removed following the occurrence of a behavior. Negative reinforcement is not the same as punishment.
23. To demonstrate the effect of reinforcement on behavior, operant conditioners often use a single-subject reversal design. These designs begin with a baseline period, followed by a treatment period. Next there is a return to baseline (no reinforcement), or extinction period. The final step in the design is reinstatement of the reinforcement treatment.
24. Prompting, fading, and shaping are three techniques used in operant conditioning. Prompting involves telling or showing someone how to perform a desired behavior. Fading is the gradual withdrawal of prompts. Shaping involves reinforcing progressively closer approximations of the desired behavior.
25. A schedule of reinforcement is the sequence or pattern in which reinforcement is administered. A continuous reinforcement schedule is one in which every desired response is reinforced. An intermittent or partial schedule of reinforcement is one in which only some instances of the desired behavior are reinforced.
26. Partial schedules may be based either on ratios (e.g., reinforcing every fourth desired response) or on intervals (e.g., reinforcing a response after a period of time has passed). Schedules can also be either fixed or variable. Each of the four types of schedules (fixed ratio, fixed interval, variable ratio, and variable interval) produces its own distinctive pattern of responding.
27. Matching theory states that if more than one behavior can lead to reinforcement, the frequency of each of the behaviors will be proportional to the frequency with which each is reinforced. Thus, the frequency of a given behavior can be modified by altering the frequency with which other behaviors are reinforced.
28. Setting events set the stage for a behavior by preparing the individual in some way to make the behavior more likely (e.g., thirst is a setting event for drinking). They are not the same as discriminative stimuli (such as the presence of water), which make a behavior (drinking) possible.

CHAPTER THIRTEEN

The Social Learning Approach

he social learning approach to personality begins where the earlier behavioral approaches left off. Earlier approaches stressed the importance of learning—classical and operant conditioning—and situational factors in the genesis and evolution of personality. **Social learning** theory goes an important step further. It emphasizes the *social* aspects of the situation that influence personality, including the important influence of learning and changing oneself by observing how others behave. This third form of learning is called *observational learning, modeling,* or *vicarious conditioning.*

LEARNING FROM THE SOCIAL ENVIRONMENT

Some behavior related to personality is, indeed, shaped and acquired through reinforcement and punishment delivered by the environment. However, much of what people know about how to navigate their social world was learned without direct instruction or planned training. The rules of appropriate behavior are occasionally made explicit (as when a child is prompted and reminded of the necessity for saying "thank you" for a gift), but more often they remain unspoken, to be gleaned from the behavior and reactions of others.

Consider, for example, how young children acquire the language of their family and surrounding culture. For most children, language is learned with little or no formal instruction. Children mimic the utterances of others, and their verbal behavior is shaped over time by interactions (rewarding and punishing) with the environment in the natural course of development. Adult human language is consistent with an extremely complex system of unstated rules—syntax and semantics—not to mention a substantial vocabulary of words and their often multiple meanings. If most people learn a system this complex without any formal instruction, then a good deal of other learning must also take place through unplanned, naturally occurring interactions. Indeed, most social behavior is acquired this way, including knowledge of rules of appropriate and adaptive behavior within the context of the individual's social environment. The forces that combine to "teach" behavior through the more or less spontaneous operation of social environmental influences is the focus of this chapter. The consistent point made in the pages that follow is that much of what we call personality in ourselves and others is a product of social learning.

Psychologists pursuing the social learning approach have been interested in three complementary questions: By what processes does social learning occur? Who are the principal players in the process of social learning? and What specific personality characteristics are acquired through social learning?

This chapter is divided into three broad sections, corresponding to these three questions. The first section deals with the processes of social learning, with particular emphasis on learning that takes place "naturally," through the observation of others.

The second section is devoted to what is currently perhaps the most widely discussed and debated topic in social learning, namely, the centrality of social learning in gender-related personality characteristics, which differ widely from one culture to another. Many sex differences in personality are socially learned rather than biologically based.

Our final section addresses broad cultural factors as we examine the role of the family, culture, and subculture as agents of social learning. Here our focus is the role of culture in what is taught and learned, as we describe some of the differences between the behaviors and personality characteristics transmitted by various cultural environments.

EARLY SOCIAL LEARNING THEORY

The phrase "social learning theory" has been in the psychology literature since the mid-20th century. The first social learning theory was introduced more than 50 years ago by Neal Miller and John Dollard following years of experimentation. Their argument that **social models** are central factors in determining how people behave is the major legacy of Miller and Dollard's (1941) social learning theory.

In this chapter, we discuss social learning as it was defined more recently by Bandura and Walters (1963), that is, as an approach that views personality as acquired through the mechanisms of classical conditioning, operant conditioning, and modeling and through the agencies of family and cultural environments.

Observational Learning

Bandura and Walters believed that a comprehensive account of personality required more than classical and operant conditioning. Therefore, they introduced a third mechanism, observational learning.

Observational learning is the process through which the behavior of one person, an *observer*, changes as a result of being exposed to the behavior of another, a *model*. Specific components of a model's behavior are called **modeling cues,** which can be live or symbolic. **Live modeling** refers to observing models "in the flesh," that is, models who are physically present. **Symbolic modeling** involves indirect exposure to models, such as through movies, television, reading, and verbal accounts of a person's behavior. Symbolic modeling accounts for a high percentage of exposure to modeling cues in our culture because of the impact and availability of television and movies.

Three Stages of Observational Learning

Observational learning can be viewed as a three-stage process: (1) exposure to modeling cues, (2) acquisition in the form of retention and recall of the cues, and (3) subsequently accepting the cues as a guide for behavior (Liebert, 1973).

Exposure to (observation of) modeling cues is the obvious first stage. A person must witness and attend to the behavior of a model. **Acquisition** of (learning and remembering) modeling cues is the second stage. Acquisition does not follow automatically from exposure; it requires that a person pay adequate attention to the modeling cues and retain them. Acquisition is, in the terms of early social learning theory, a **covert** behavior. However, it is generally demonstrated as an overt behavior: the observer's verbal account or physical reenactment of the model's behavior. Thus, acquisition is objectively verifiable.

After exposure and acquisition have occurred, the third and final stage in observational learning becomes relevant. **Acceptance** refers to whether observers actually use the modeling cues as a guide for their own actions. To measure acceptance, subjects are observed in a situation in which they are free to mimic the model's behavior or not.

Acceptance can take either of two forms of behavior: imitation or counterimitation. **Imitation** is simply behaving as the model did. **Counterimitation** is behaving in a different, nearly opposite way. Modeling cues may also indirectly influence observers by suggesting the effectiveness of a general class of behaviors. **Indirect imitation** involves behavior similar to the model's that does not duplicate the model's behavior precisely; often, it is a display of the modeled behavior in a new situation. Indirect imitation is thus akin to generalization in classical or operant conditioning. **Indirect counterimitation** uses modeling cues as a basis for engaging in an opposing class of behaviors. For example, seeing others punished for being selfish may lead an observer to be generous. Table 13.1 provides examples of each of the four possible types of acceptance of modeling cues.

The three-stage process of observational learning makes it clear that exposure and acquisition are necessary but *not sufficient* conditions for acceptance (imitation or counterimitation). Simply stated, there is a distinction between what a person sees and remembers and what the person eventually *does*. The importance of what Bandura originally called the *acquisition-performance distinction* was first demonstrated in Bandura's (1965) classic "Bobo doll study."

Bandura's "Bobo Doll Study"

Bandura's "Bobo doll study" is one of the most famous in the entire psychological literature. In this experiment, nursery school children participated as the observers. Modeling cues were provided symbolically through presentation of a brief film. The film depicted a woman interacting with a 3½-foot-tall, inflated plastic Bobo doll that looked like a clown. The woman (model) approached the doll and ordered it out of the way. When the doll failed to move, the model performed a series of four aggressive acts.

Table 13.1 Forms of acceptance of modeling cues

Situation: Five-year-old Doug often sees his parents donate money to charities.

TYPE OF ACCEPTANCE	EXAMPLES
Direct imitation	Doug puts a coin in the collection box at church.
Indirect imitation	Doug shares his toys with his friends.
Direct counterimitation	Doug walks past the collection box at church without donating.
Indirect counterimitation	Doug does not allow his friends to play with his toys.
Nonimitation	Doug's behavior is unaffected by observing his parents' behavior.

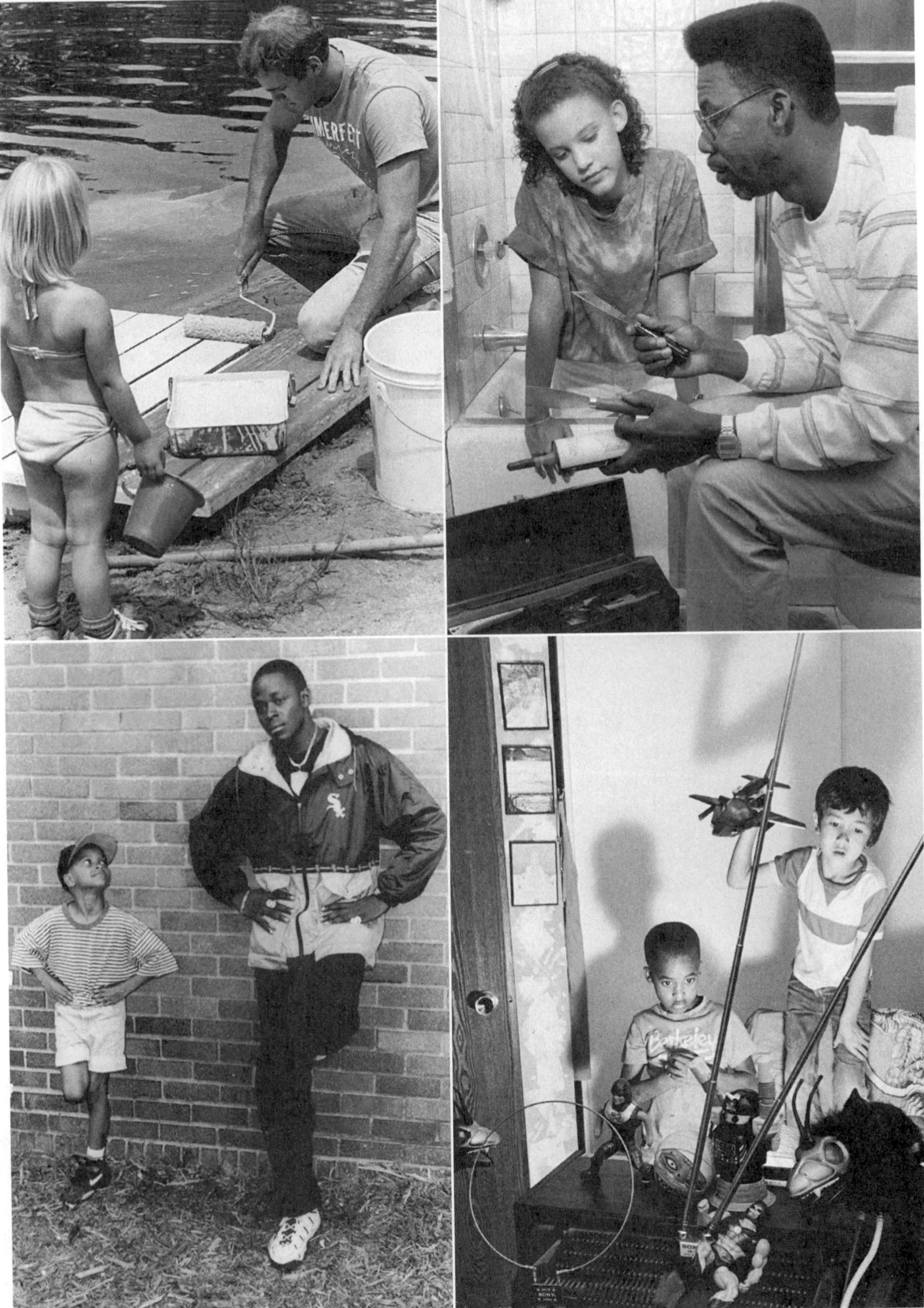

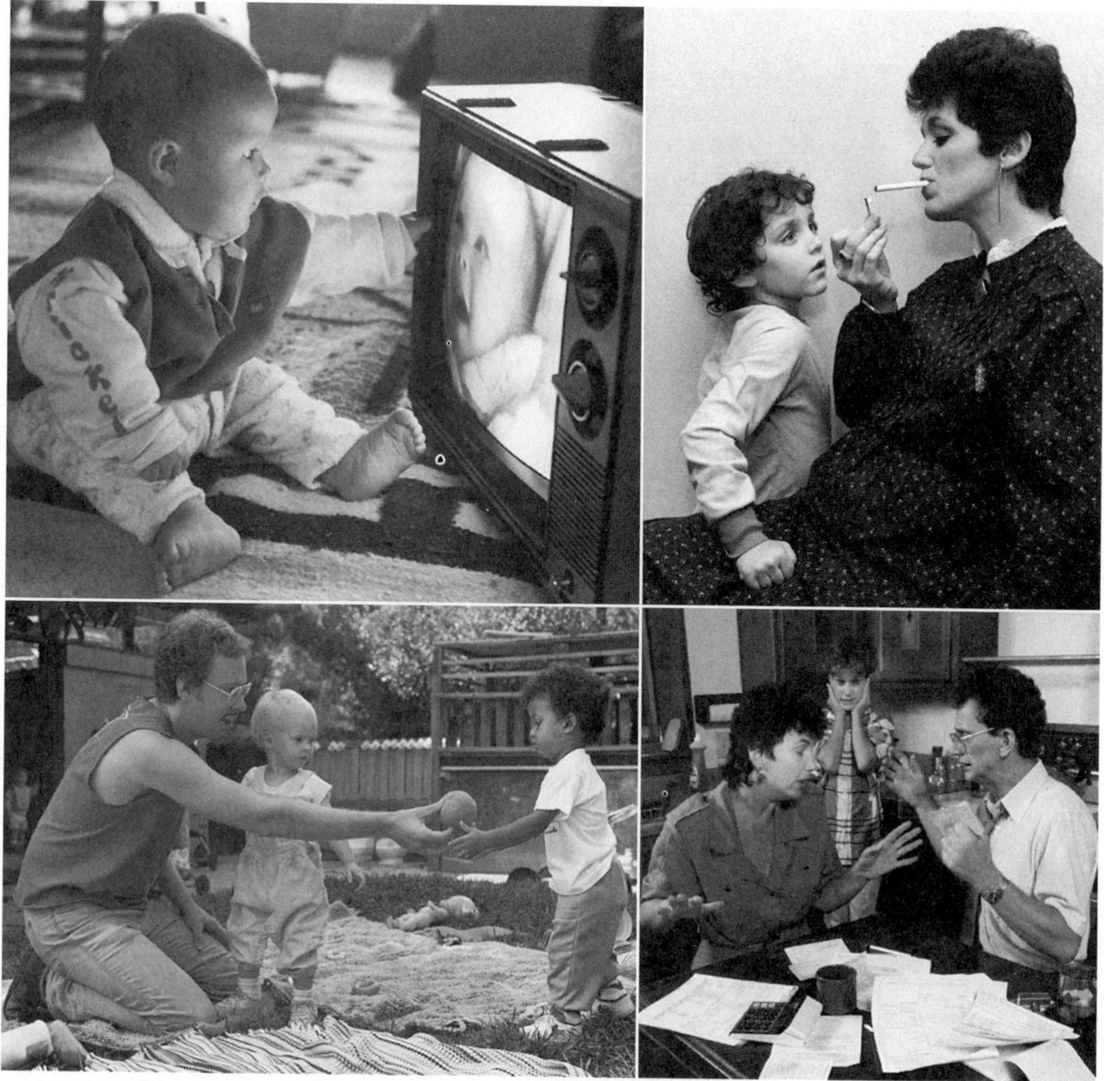

For better or worse, a great deal of learning occurs through modeling and begins at a very young age.
Page 340: top left: © Bob Kalman/The Image Works; top right: © Laima Druskis/Stock, Boston; bottom left: © CLEO Photography/Jeroboam, Inc.; bottom right: © Jane Scherr/Jeroboam, Inc. Page 341: top left: © Dennis Budd Gray/Jeroboam, Inc.; top right: © Jim Anderson/Stock, Boston; bottom left: © Suzanne Arms/Jeroboam, Inc.; bottom right: © Billy E. Barnes/Jeroboam, Inc.

> First, the model laid the Bobo doll on its side, sat on it, and punched it in the nose while remarking, "Pow, right in the nose, boom, boom."
>
> The model then raised the doll and pommeled it on the head with a mallet while saying, "Sockeroo . . . stay down."
>
> Next, the model kicked the doll about the room and said, "Fly away."
>
> Finally, the model threw rubber balls at the Bobo doll, each strike punctuated with "Bang." (Bandura, 1965, pp. 590–591)

The children were assigned to three experimental conditions, each of which differed in terms of the consequences they observed for the model. Children in the *no consequence* condition merely watched the film of the four aggressive acts.

Children in the ***model-rewarded*** condition saw the same film with the addition of a final scene in which the model was rewarded for the aggressive responses by a second adult. For example, the other adult said that the model was a "strong champion" and gave the model food treats in the form of soda and candies. As the model consumed the treats, the other adult recounted the model's "praiseworthy" aggressive acts.

Children in the ***model-punished*** condition also saw the same basic film, but with a different final scene in which the model was punished for her aggressive behavior. For example, the second adult shook a finger menacingly at the model and said, "Hey there, you big bully. You quit picking on that clown. I won't tolerate it" (Bandura, 1965, p. 591). The second adult then spanked the model with a rolled-up magazine while recounting her many transgressions against the doll.

After seeing the film, each child was taken to a room containing a plastic Bobo doll, balls, a mallet, a pegboard, plastic farm animals, and other toys. Each child was left alone with the toys for 10 minutes. From behind a one-way mirror, judges observed the children to assess their spontaneous performance (i.e., acceptance) of the model's behaviors (as evidenced by reproductions in the form of imitation).

Then, the children's acquisition was assessed by determining the degree to which they could reproduce the modeled behaviors when encouraged to do so. The experimenter gave each child a small treat of fruit juice and then promised the child would receive more juice and a sticker for each of the model's behaviors that were reproduced. (These incentives were provided to

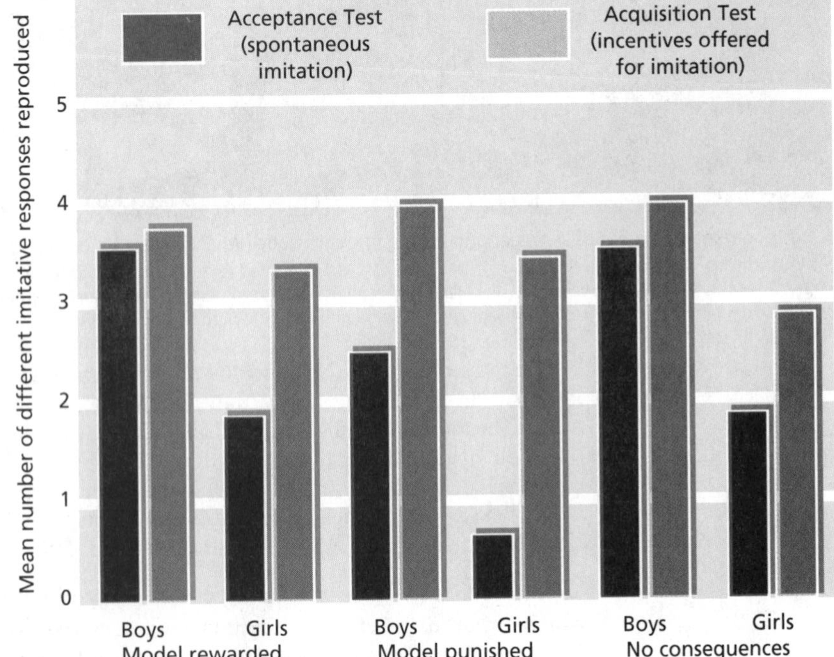

Figure 13.1
Results of Bandura's Bobo doll study demonstrating the importance of the acquisition-acceptance distinction in observational learning. Children acquired more of the model's responses than they accepted (spontaneously performed).
Source: Adapted from *Social Learning and Personality Development,* by A. Bandura and R. H. Walters, 1963, Holt, Rinehart & Winston.

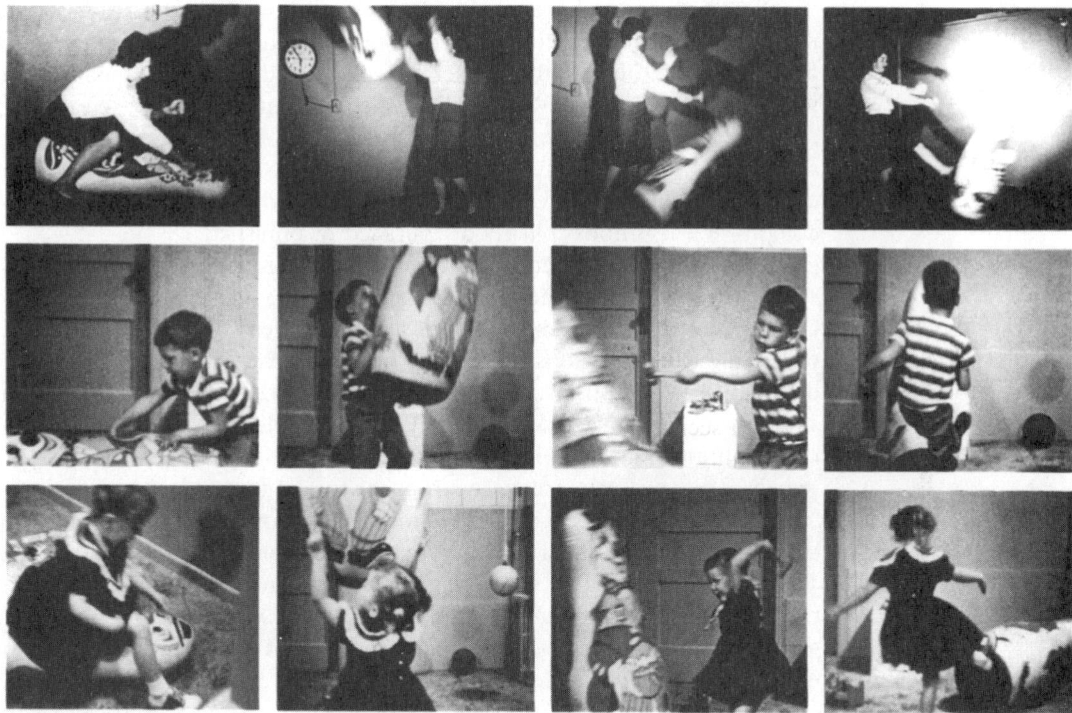

Figure 13.2
Examples of the model's aggressive acts (top row) and children's imitation of the model's acts (middle and bottom rows) in Bandura's Bobo doll study.
Source: From "Imitation of Film-Mediated Aggressive Models," by A. Bandura, D. Ross, and S. A. Ross, 1963. *Journal of Abnormal and Social Psychology,* pp. 3–11. Copyright 1963 by the American Psychological Association. Reprinted by permission.

minimize possible reluctance to demonstrate the model's aggressive acts. Such reluctance was expected among children in the model-punished condition.)

The results clearly support the view that *acquisition* and *acceptance* (spontaneous performance) must be distinguished. The children clearly acquired more aggressive behaviors through observational learning than they accepted (spontaneously performed); see Figure 13.1. This result was especially true of children in the model-punished condition.

One of the most remarkable findings of this study was how precisely children imitated the model's aggressive acts when they were given incentives for reproducing them. Compare the model's acts and the children's acts in Figure 13.2. This finding demonstrates the power of modeling for teaching behaviors.

Vicarious Consequences

Observing a model usually provides information about (1) what the model did and (2) the effects of the model's actions. **Vicarious consequences** are the observed outcomes of a model's behavior. From vicarious consequences, observers can infer the outcomes they are likely to receive for similar actions. Thus, vicarious consequences are indirect consequences for the observer.

Vicarious reinforcement refers to a consequence for the model that an observer views as desirable; vicarious reinforcement increases the chances that the observer will imitate the model. **Vicarious punishment** is a consequence that the observer considers undesirable, and it reduces the likelihood that the observer will imitate the model (e.g., Schnake & Dumler, 1990).

Vicarious consequences almost invariably influence an observer's spontaneous performance (acceptance) of a modeled behavior. In Bandura's Bobo doll study, children in the model-punished condition spontaneously imitated fewer of the model's actions than children in the model-rewarded or no-consequence conditions (see Figure 13.1). (Note that in the case of socially prohibited behaviors such as aggression, observers are likely to conclude that the modeled behavior is deemed appropriate or at least acceptable if it is not explicitly discouraged or punished.)

In everyday life, we benefit from vicarious consequences. We often "check out" what happens to other people when they engage in a behavior we might consider engaging in ourselves. For example, students learn how a professor will respond to questions in class by observing the professor's reaction to other students' questions. And professors clearly acquire a reputation among students as receptive or unreceptive to questions (e.g., about upcoming examinations or grading policies) based on the experiences of other students (which serve as vicarious consequences for the students who learn of them).

Vicarious consequences serve another function besides informing the observer of the type of reaction a particular behavior will probably elicit. They also indicate that the model's behavior is important enough to warrant a reaction, either punishing or reinforcing. This *attention-focusing function* of vicarious consequences increases the likelihood that the observer will attend to and remember what the model did. Thus, children who see a model either reinforced *or* punished for some behavior show better acquisition of the behavior than those who see the same behavior performed without any apparent consequences (e.g., Cheyne, 1971; Liebert & Fernandez, 1969; Spiegler & Weiland, 1976).

An early study of college students clearly demonstrated this effect. The students were all given a brief story to read about a high school student's response to program cuts in extracurricular activities at her school. What differed between groups was the reaction this symbolic model's behavior elicited from her school principal. In one version, she was commended for her outspoken response, in a second version she was harshly reprimanded, and in a third she was simply told her position would be taken into consideration.

When measures of separate aspects of recall were examined, an interesting finding emerged, as shown in Figure 13.3. Whereas subjects who observed the model receive punishing consequences had high recall of the details of the situation and the modeled behavior, they had the lowest recall of the consequences themselves. In terms of recalling vicarious consequences (but not the model's acts or the details of the situation), the valence of the consequences—whether they are reinforcing or punishing—appears to be critical.

Looking at both acquisition and acceptance data, we can conclude that reinforcing consequences enhance both of these aspects of observational learning. In contrast, observing a model experience punishing consequences *decreases* the likelihood that the observer will immediately imitate the model but *increases* the chances that the observer will remember the model's actions and the related details. At the same time, the observer is apt to forget the punishing consequences that befell the model. The net result suggests that punishing vicarious consequences inhibit immediate imitation but not

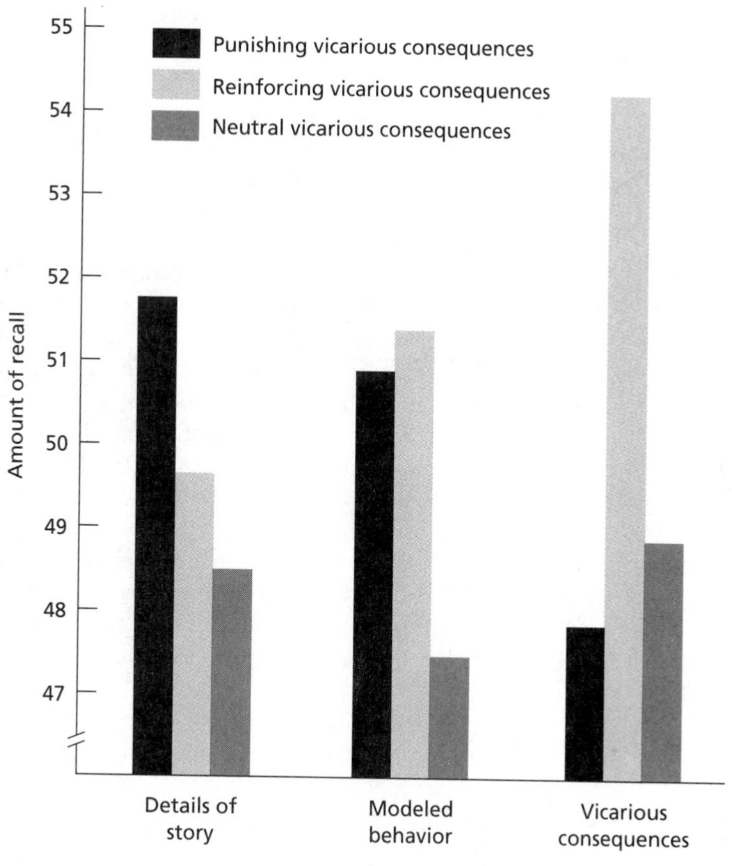

Figure 13.3
The relative amount of recall of details of the modeling story, of the modeled behavior, and of the vicarious consequences by subjects exposed to punishing, reinforcing, and neutral vicarious consequences in Spiegler and Weiland's (1976) study. Note that for the negative vicarious consequences condition, recall of story details and of the modeled behavior is high but recall of vicarious consequences in this group is lower than in the other two groups.
Source: Data from "The Effects of Written Vicarious Consequences on Observers' Willingness to Imitate and Ability to Recall Modeling Cues," by M. D. Spiegler and A. Weiland, 1976, *Journal of Personality 44,* 260–273.

necessarily future imitation because the observer is likely to remember the model's actions and associated details but forget that they were punished (Spiegler & Weiland, 1976).

These results have several important implications. First, people may learn much more than they spontaneously demonstrate from observing others. Second, vicarious consequences of any sort (reinforcing or punishing) serve to enhance acquisition of the modeled behaviors. Third, because punishing consequences may not be recalled as well as reinforcing ones, observers may tend to avoid mimicking a punished model's behavior in the very short term but, having acquired the behavior, may later accept it (and use it in the future when recall of the punishing consequences has faded).

Relevant Observer and Model Characteristics

In everyday life, we are exposed to many different people and a wide range of behaviors. We are often exposed symbolically (through TV, movies, and other media) to many more. We are frequently aware of the consequences of other people's actions. How do we go about choosing which actions to imitate, which to ignore, and which to actively avoid? The consequences (reinforcing or punishing) provides one answer, but we do not attempt to copy every behavior we are exposed to, even when we see models clearly rewarded for their performance.

As an extreme example, consider bank robbers as models. Robbing banks clearly does pay (in the quite literal sense) when it succeeds, and some people actually *do* succeed at robbing banks. This fact is often made public via news media. Yet, even when bank robbers escape apprehension, few people elect to imitate their felonious behavior. Why are there not outbreaks of holdups subsequent to one successful robbery? The factors that determine whether a particular behavior will be imitated are many and complex, ranging far beyond immediate consequences alone.

Research has revealed a number of characteristics of the observer, model, and surrounding circumstances that serve to influence the degree of acceptance of modeled behavior. From the late 1960s to the mid-1970s, Liebert and his associates (e.g., Allen & Liebert, 1969a, 1969b; Liebert, 1973; Liebert & Fernandez, 1969; Liebert & Ora, 1968; Liebert & Poulos, 1975; McMains & Liebert, 1968) examined these issues. Here is a brief summary of the conclusions of that work.

A prime determinant of whether modeling cues will be accepted, all other things being equal, is whether the behavior is exhibited by a model who is *similar* to the observer. Perceived similarity informs observers about the likelihood that a behavior is appropriate and possible for them, in their own situation.

A second determinant of whether modeling cues will be accepted is the number and consistency of the models to whom the observer has been exposed. Multiple consistent models, who successively or simultaneously display the same behavior in a given situation, are more effective than single models, even when the total amount of exposure to modeling cues is held constant. When multiple modeling cues are discrepant, the observer will choose to either imitate the model whose behavior was least demanding or ignore the modeling cues altogether. This determinant is one reason that consistent models (e.g., similar models within the individual's culture or subculture who display the same behaviors and values) have such a powerful effect. We discuss cultural influences later in this chapter.

Third, single models who display consistent reactions to a situation are more effective than those who are inconsistent or those who do not "practice what they preach." Parents who urge their children not to smoke or drink but who are observed to smoke or drink themselves behaviorally undermine their own advice and admonitions.

Fourth, with respect to tasks involving skill or judgment, models who are perceived to be competent are more likely to be emulated than are those who are less competent. (We have already mentioned Bandura's early work, demonstrating that vicarious reinforcement facilitates performance of modeled behavior.) Engaging in behaviors that yield rewards suggests competence, as does seniority in age or experience.

One way to integrate these various findings is through the theoretical construct of **information value,** the apparent pertinence of the model's behavior to the circumstances and capabilities of the observer. The more similar the model appears to be to the observer, and the more similar their circumstances, the more likely the behavior displayed will result in similar consequences if performed by the observer. Characteristics of the model such as gender, age, and skill level provide pertinent information to observers. If the model and observer are similar in relevant characteristics and the situations in which they find themselves, the likelihood of direct or indirect imitation or counterimitation is increased. All of this research, conducted during the early days of social learning theory, focused on delineating model characteristics associated with acceptance. Many of these findings have since been replicated in different cultures and social contexts and across age groups ranging from very young children to adults (Liebert, Kail, & Wicks-Nelson, 1986).

How the full array of environmental forces combine to determine the behavior of any particular person at any specific time requires understanding a great many factors. Recently, interest has focused on identifying the multiple forces within the natural environments of home, school, and community that act to influence various aspects of personality. Our discussion turns now to an aspect of personality that has received considerable attention in the past two decades, namely, gender roles and the means through which they are acquired.

GENDER ROLES AND THE SOCIAL ENVIRONMENT

Some "masculine" and "feminine" roles are determined by our biology; that is, males and females *are* fundamentally different in several ways. The most apparent differences are related to reproduction. (It is, after all, presumably for purposes of reproduction that males and females are differentiated biologically in the first place; see Chapter 9.) The rest of gender differentiation in personality may be environmentally rather than biologically determined. Our attention now turns to evidence related to this contemporary hypothesis.

The Birth of Gender as a Concept

The term **gender** came into use to refer to the socially (as opposed to biologically) determined differences between the sexes about 30 years ago (Deaux, 1985; Nicholson, 1994; Unger, 1979). With the introduction of this concept has come an increasingly full appreciation of the *social* determination of aspects of gender (Bullough & Ruan, 1994; Crawford, 1994; Finchilescu, 1995).

Most personality characteristics that are widely accepted as "masculine" (dominance, independence, competitiveness) and "feminine" (nurturance, cooperation, empathy) in Western culture rest on long-held stereotypes of "appropriate" behavior for males and females. These different traits were once taken for granted to represent two opposite ends of a *single* continuum—from extremely feminine to extremely masculine (Figure 13.4*A*). In contrast, more contemporary theorists contend that masculinity and femininity represent two distinct and independent personality dimensions (Bem, 1972; Constantinople, 1973; Nicholson, 1994; Spence, Helmrich, & Stapp, 1974). These theorists further contend that the link between genetic sex and gender roles is, at most, far more limited than was previously supposed. The contemporary bidimensional view of gender-related personality characteristics states that every person, regardless of genetic sex, may express traits previously considered masculine, as well as traits previously considered feminine.

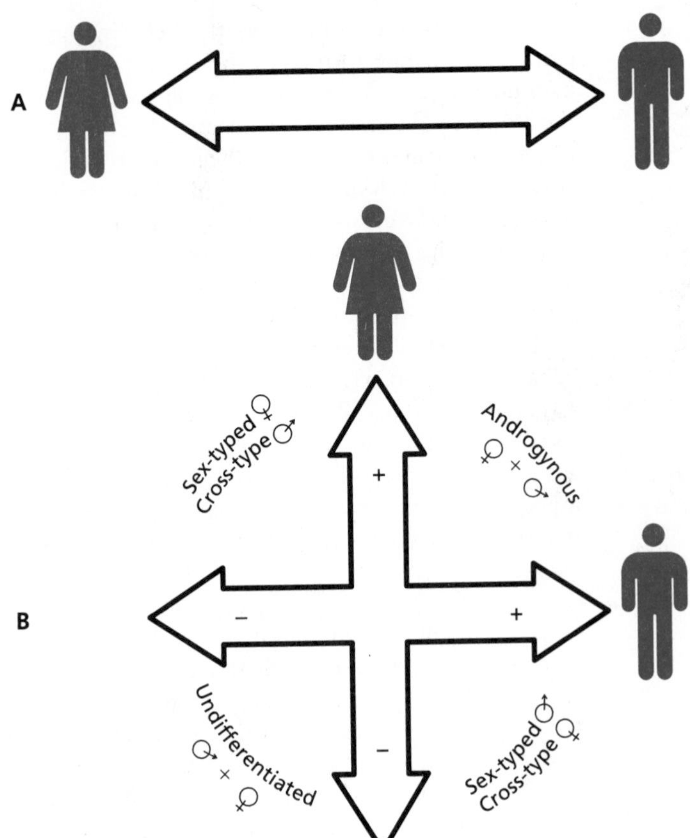

Figure 13.4
A: The traditional unidimensional view of masculinity-femininity (and sex); **B:** The contemporary bidimensional view of masculinity and femininity, which allows for four resulting gender role "types."

Sex Role Types

It is now known that individuals can possess many stereotypically masculine traits and simultaneously possess many stereotypically feminine traits. The bidimensional view of masculinity and femininity, when combined with knowledge of biological sex, allows for the identification of the following four possible categories of "sex-role types": (1) **Sex-typed** individuals who conform closely to stereotypic roles for their own genetic sex, (2) **cross-sex types** lean more toward traits associated with the *opposite* genetic sex and display relatively few traits associated with their own sex, (3) **sex-type undifferentiated** people display few traits strongly associated with either sex, and (4) **androgynous** individuals display many traits associated with *both* male and female role stereotypes. Figure 13.4*B* is a graphic representation of this bidimensional model and the resulting four personality types.

Researchers have begun to reexamine masculine and feminine behavior patterns and attitudes with this new bidimensional conception of gender and gender roles. Zeldow, Daugherty, and Clark (1987) used a longitudinal design to assess masculine and feminine traits in first-year medical students and subsequently evaluated the effects of these differences on later performance. In both males and females, higher masculinity scores were positively related to self-esteem, confidence in future success, and extraversion. Higher femininity scores were related to later interpersonal satisfaction, extent and quality of social networks, and a humanistic attitude toward patient care. (The humanistic view is discussed in Chapter 15.)

O'Heron and Orlofsky (1990) examined sex-typing as it relates to psychological well-being. Of the males in the study, those who were categorized as androgynous were best adjusted; males with few typically male characteristics were least well adjusted. Females also seemed to benefit from male traits, so that androgynous females *and* cross-sex-typed females appeared better adjusted than females with fewer male characteristics.

Other researchers have also found that stereotypically masculine traits tend to contribute to overall self-esteem for both males and females (Marsh, 1987; Taylor & Hall, 1982; Whitley, 1983). However, these findings must be understood in light of both the measures used to assess self-esteem and Western conceptions of successful adjustment. The self-esteem measures used in these studies may be indirectly tapping the very same traits traditionally identified with the male role in our society. Males who succeed have high self-esteem, but their success may itself be based on the effects of masculine traits that emphasize active and often aggressive competition. When interpersonal issues such as relationship satisfaction are the focus of comparisons, it appears that those who possess the most stereotypically feminine traits come out ahead (Antill, 1993; Kurdek & Schmitt, 1986). This pattern holds across a variety of relationship types (e.g., heterosexual, gay, and lesbian; cohabitating as well as married).

Stereotypic feminine and masculine traits both appear to offer adaptive advantages that are specific to the domain of functioning assessed, corresponding closely to society's conception of the differences between the sexes. Thus, feminine traits enhance interpersonal functioning and coping, and masculine traits confer an advantage in competitive arenas. As Box 13.1 reveals, a combination of both types of behaviors within a person's repertoire is the most adaptive personality of all.

Box 13.1
ANDROGYNY—THE BEST OF BOTH WORLDS

Androgyny was originally introduced into the psychological literature to identify individuals who possessed both masculine and feminine characteristics (Bem, 1972, 1974). It is commonly used now to refer exclusively to those high in both masculine and feminine traits. (Recall that those who are low in both stereotypic masculine and feminine characteristics are now referred to as *undifferentiated.*) This usage is consistent with the model of sex-types proposed by Spence, Helmreich, and Stapp (1974), and with our presentation of the four sex-role types.

People who are sex-typed may respond too rigidly in situations that require an approach stereotypically associated with the opposite sex. Bem and Lenny (1976) found that sex-typed individuals had more difficulty performing

Box continued on following page

Box 13.1 *Continued*
ANDROGYNY—THE BEST OF BOTH WORLDS

behaviors typically associated with the opposite sex than did less sex-typed individuals. This same conclusion has been reached by a number of other studies (Bem, 1974; Ellis & Range, 1988; Spence & Helmreich, 1978). Bohan (1993) suggests that different environmental situations "bring out" different behaviors by signaling what contingencies are operative. Thus, some situations are best responded to with behaviors consistent with masculine traits, while others are best responded to with feminine-type behaviors. The type of behavior most likely to be reinforced at any given time varies with the circumstance, so being able to discriminate between environmental circumstances and having an androgynous behavioral repertoire enable a person to perform most effectively across many situations. It makes sense that those individuals with the greatest range of potential behaviors are best able to deal with changing circumstances or multiple settings. Of the various sex-types described, in fact, androgynous types *are* the most adaptable. Possessing both a large number of characteristically feminine traits and a large number of characteristically masculine traits enables people to adjust their behavior to maximum advantage, regardless of circumstances.

Given the growing consensus that an androgynous personality is adaptive, we might examine the factors that may produce androgyny. Research suggests that development of androgyny in children is related to parental androgyny (Orlofsky, 1979; Spence & Helmreich, 1978). For example, a recent study found that working mothers had more androgynous children than did mothers not working outside the home (Ellis, 1994), which is consistent with earlier findings reported by Hansson, Chernovetz, and Jones (1977). Although both studies were correlational (and thus firm conclusions about causation cannot be drawn from them), they do suggest some interesting possibilities.

A mother employed outside her home may serve as a model of nonstereotypic sex-role behavior that, in turn, contributes to her children's embracing an androgynous style. In addition, these mothers may themselves be androgynous. Finally, lacking a more conventional stay-at-home mother leaves children less protected, thereby encouraging the development of a wide range of adaptive behaviors, specifically including both masculine and feminine traits. Ellis (1994) concludes that this evidence supports a social learning model of the development of androgyny and, by extension, other sex roles and complex behavior patterns.

Social Learning of Gender Roles

How do people learn their gender role behavior? Virtually all of the learning principles examined earlier seem to come into play. From the first moments of life, boys and girls are handled differently (Bandura, 1969). Parents of both sexes perceive male and female children differently from birth and handle them accordingly (Rubin, Provenzano, & Luria, 1974).

Male and female children are differentially reinforced for various behaviors. Girls may be positively reinforced for imitating traditionally feminine behaviors such as dressing up, wearing makeup, and tending the needs of their dolls. These same behaviors exhibited by a boy tend to be punished. In fact, several studies have demonstrated that girls who exhibit masculine behaviors ("tomboys") are better tolerated than boys who exhibit feminine behavior ("sissies") (Langlois & Downs, 1980; Martin, 1990; Tauber, 1979).

Although fathers may be willing to provide masculine toys (trucks) for their daughters, they are much less willing to allow their sons to play with dolls (Snow, Jacklin, & Maccoby, 1983). Overall, girls are encouraged to remain dependent and display positive emotions and interpersonal sensitivity, while boys are encouraged to be independent and engage in competitive, physical activity (Block, 1983).

Children also learn a great deal about "appropriate" behavior through modeling. All of the characteristics of models act to influence a child's acceptance or rejection of the behaviors they display. Of particular importance to this discussion is the fact that children recognize their membership within a particular sex at a very young age and tend to emulate the behavior of same-sex adults more than opposite-sex adults (Bandura, 1969). Thus, gender role behavior is readily transmitted from parents to their same-sex offspring. Parents serve as role models for all of their children, but where the roles of fathers and mothers diverge, children tend to mimic the behaviors of the same-sex parent rather than crossing the gender line.

Recall the earlier discussion of relevant model characteristics. Similarity is an important consideration in evaluating the personal relevance of modeled behavior. When confronted with models of different sexes performing distinctly different behaviors, the tendency is to follow the example of the model seen as most relevant (or similar) to the self. Thus, if both parents enjoy cooking and skiing, the child is likely to attempt these activities. If only one parent ever repairs the car and the other is the only available model for gardening and yard work, however, the children are likely to follow the example of the parent of their own sex.

Similarly, children learn from the examples modeled by siblings, although the patterns are very complex and appear to be influenced by number of children and the sex ratio among them (McGuire & McGuire, 1988). Symbolic models presented in the media may also display and vicariously reinforce stereotypic gender role behavior. Content analyses of children's television programs reveal stereotype-consistent behaviors depicted not only in actual program content but also in TV advertisements (Liebert & Sprafkin, 1988). Baby dolls are almost invariably depicted with girls; trucks, action figures, and construction sets are almost invariably portrayed as boys' toys (Courtney & Whipple, 1983).

Acquisition and acceptance of gender roles are thus influenced through both social learning mechanisms and ongoing interactions with all the agencies of the social environment. The effects of conditioning and observational learning are not limited to gender role behavior. These same influences extend to all types of social behavior and are inculcated by the combined force of media, family, social groups and institutions, and the broad cultural environment. How these various forces combine and interact may well vary from person to person. We are not yet able to fully characterize these interactions because of their complex and interrelated nature. But we can describe these influences to some extent and explain how they vary across settings to produce differences in personality between individuals and between social and cultural groups.

AGENTS, AGENCIES, AND LESSONS OF SOCIAL LEARNING

The two agencies that have received the most attention within the environmental strategy are (1) the family and (2) the culture and subculture in which the person grows up. A child in the United States, for example, is influenced by many overlapping environmental forces: a national culture, one or more ethnic cultures, an immediate local culture, and a family environment. This section describes some of what we have learned about family and cultural influences.

First, in studying family and culture, we find both *universal* and *culture-specific* forms of behavior. In the language of anthropology, an **etic** is universal, that is, a behavior or behavior pattern that is common to all members of a particular species. An **emic,** in contrast, refers to a behavior or behavior pattern that varies from setting to setting (or culture to culture) within a species. In other words, an emic is culture specific. Our discussion centers around emic behaviors, which are more informative as to which aspects of a particular environment might be directly involved in shaping and maintaining individual differences in personality.

We begin with an examination of some important family influences on personality development. The family provides the primary context in which children learn the basic attitudes, beliefs, and behaviors expected of them, but families differ in form (configuration) as well as in how they go about socializing their children. We will next look at some of the interesting findings concerning both the form and style of the family environment.

Family Configuration

Family configuration refers to the number of adults and children in a family who reside in the same household. The traditional (intact) **nuclear family** consisted of the father, mother, and all of the dependent children of the union. Today, there are also a significant number of **single-parent** families with only one adult (most often the mother) and **remarried families** (or **stepfamilies**), which include previously married adults (or involved partners) and the children from one or more previous unions. When both partners bring children to a new union, the resulting combination is referred to as a **blended family.**

Because the number of possible combinations is huge, we do not try to even begin to cover them all. (Consider that both parents can be present, just the mother, or just the father; each child may have no siblings, just one, or a dozen or more; the siblings may be all boys, all girls, or an assortment; the siblings may also be separated by age differences as small as 11 months—or 11 minutes, in the case of twins and stepsiblings—or as wide as 30 years.) Children's birth order also figures into a complete portrait of the family configuration in which they grew up. The fundamental point is that family configuration plays a very important role in personality development, as the following sampling of topics and findings attests.

Family Size and Birth Order

In general, the larger a person's immediate family, the worse off the person is in terms of verbal intelligence and certain other cognitive and social skills. In what is commonly called the **dilution effect,** as family size increases, the amount of time and attention that can be given to any one child decreases (Blake, 1989; Zajonc, 1976; Figure 13.5). Additional children dilute the amount of capital (as discussed later) a family has to devote to any given child (Parcel & Menaghan, 1993).

Once, being an only child was thought to be a disadvantage because only children missed the socializing effects of having other children present in the home environment. This belief turns out to be false. Only children fare quite well overall and, in some important ways, may actually be more advantaged than those with siblings. In adulthood, only children (considered as a group) outperform every other family configurational group on such measures as achievement, intelligence, sociability, character, and adjustment (Falbo & Polit, 1986; Polit, Nuttall, & Nuttall, 1980; Veenhoven & Verkuyten, 1989).

Because of the additional attention they get or for other as-yet unexplained reasons, firstborn children are generally more successful than later-born children. (Note that they share a common environmental situation with only children in that for at least some period they are the only child present in the family home. Parental attention is likely to be, in part, responsible for their success.) Firstborns speak at an earlier age, perform better on intelligence tests, and are more likely to be achievement-oriented than children born with siblings already on the scene (Zajonc & Markus, 1975). There is also some evidence to suggest that children born into households in which the next-oldest child is at least 5 years older may look more like firstborn and only children in terms of their abilities and achievement, which again points to the availability of parental attention as causal in determining later success.

Many of the differences we see as a result of sibling configuration make sense in terms of observational learning. For example, boys of preschool age exhibit more feminine behavior when they have older sisters and more

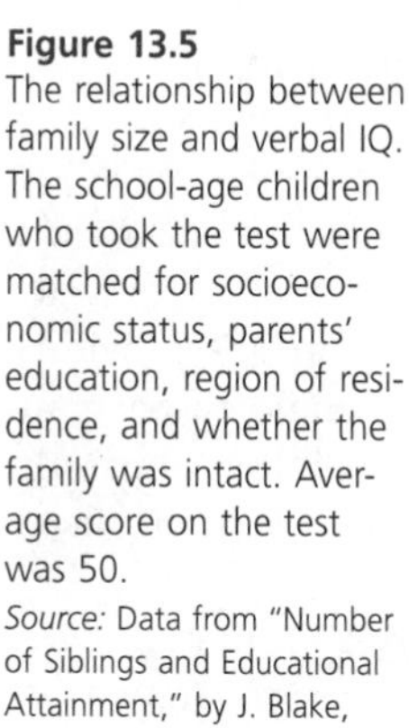

Figure 13.5
The relationship between family size and verbal IQ. The school-age children who took the test were matched for socioeconomic status, parents' education, region of residence, and whether the family was intact. Average score on the test was 50.
Source: Data from "Number of Siblings and Educational Attainment," by J. Blake, 1989, *Science, 245,* pp. 32–36.

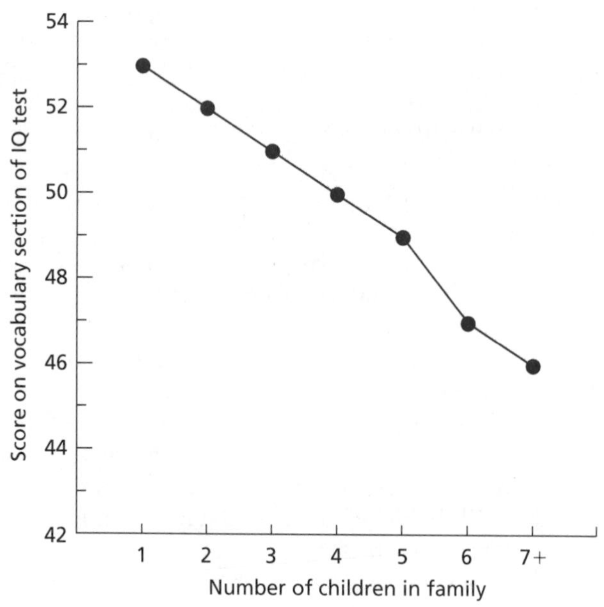

masculine behavior when they have older brothers. Boys with older sisters are also more likely to play with "feminine" toys (e.g., dollhouses) than boys who do not have older sisters (Stoneman, Brody, & MacKinnor, 1986; Sutton-Smith & Rosenberg, 1970). Similarly, girls with older brothers are more aggressive than girls who have only older sisters (Dunn & Kendrick, 1981).

Parent Variables

Until 20 to 30 years ago, the traditional nuclear family was taken for granted as the norm in the United States. Most research on children and families focused on these intact family units. A dramatic rise in the divorce rate and unprecedented numbers of births to single women have now overshadowed the old standard American family. Bluntly, the intact nuclear family is no longer the norm for American children. Research attention is currently focused on varying family configurations and the impact they may have on children who live in them.

Most single-parent homes are headed by women, and children who lack a male role model suffer for the loss. Male children appear particularly vulnerable, especially when they have no appropriate same-sex role model in their immediate environment. (Recall again the importance of similarity of the model to self and that being of the same sex is a major hallmark of similarity.) Accumulating evidence suggests that boys lacking an appropriate male model experience a variety of behavior and adjustment problems, especially during adolescence (Phelps, Huntley, Valdes, & Thompson, 1987).

The effects of father absence are not restricted to male children. Girls from mother-only households have noticeably greater sexual interest than girls from intact homes and are also more likely to be involved in delinquent behavior (Hetherington, 1972). (There is much less information available on father-only households.)

Another serious question for American society today is the fate of children reared in stepfamilies. These children are more likely than those who live in intact homes to have problems with aggression, school dropout, and drug abuse. Parental remarriage often leads to a further decline in adjustment for girls. Girls of stepfamilies tend to become sexually active at an earlier age than girls from intact families. Interestingly, younger children appear to adjust better to their parents' remarriage than older children (Lawton & Sanders, 1994).

Divorce and remarriage must ultimately be viewed on an individual basis, however. Children who live in a well-functioning single-parent family or stepfamily have fewer problems than children whose biological parents both live with them but remain in a constant state of conflict (Hetherington, Stanley-Hagan, & Anderson, 1989).

Marital disruption and remarriage may affect the parents' functioning as well. Parents whose personal relationship with a spouse is threatened are likely to be distracted and less involved with their children. Similarly, parents may be less available to their children during the early stages of courtship and marriage than they would in the context of a long-established, stable relationship.

Remarried families with children from previous relationships are also at high risk for a variety of problems. Different households have different rules and expectations for behavior. Therefore, it should not be surprising that conflict over household rules is a problem when a child is expected to move to (or shuffle back and forth between) different households (Hobart, 1991). In addition, second marriages often break up because of problems between stepparents and stepchildren (Bray, 1988; Hetherington, 1989). Moreover, second marriages are more likely to end in divorce (and to do so more quickly) than first marriages. As a result, growing up in a single-parent home is the lot of a great many American children (Guisinger, Cowan, & Schuldberg, 1989). Research on the children of these families will no doubt continue and shed further light on the effects of family configuration on personality development.

Parenting Styles

Diana Baumrind (1967, 1971) examined differences in **parenting styles** and described three types. This early work has been extended, and contemporary research describes four basic parenting styles (Rothbaum & Weisz, 1994).

Parenting styles are now understood to vary along two dimensions: *acceptance-involvement* and *strictness-supervision*. Table 13.2 shows how these dimensions give rise to four basic styles of parenting: authoritative, authoritarian, indulgent, and neglectful (Steinberg, Lamborn, Darling, Mounts, & Dornbusch, 1994).

Authoritarian parents are restrictive and rejecting. This parenting style has been found to be related to children who are insecure, apprehensive, socially withdrawn, and low in both self-reliance and self-control. Adolescents from authoritarian homes score reasonably well on measures of school achievement and deviance but relatively poorly on measures of self-reliance and self-concept.

Authoritative parenting is characterized by parental warmth, an inductive and nonpunitive style of discipline (e.g., use of reasoning and explanation), nonpunitive discipline, and consistency in child-rearing. This type of parenting is associated with children who are socially assertive, competent, and responsible. They score higher than their peers from authoritarian, indulgent, or neglectful homes on a wide variety of measures of competence, achievement, social development, self-perceptions, and overall mental health.

Neglectful parenting lacks both adequate involvement with the children and adequate supervision. It is associated with children who score poorly on the same measures on which authoritative parenting styles get high marks

Table 13.2 The four parenting styles in terms of the dimensions of acceptance-involvement and strictness-supervision

	ACCEPTANCE-INVOLVEMENT	
STRICTNESS-SUPERVISION	HIGH	LOW
HIGH	Authoritative	Authoritarian
LOW	Indulgent	Neglectful

(e.g., assertiveness, competence). Neglectful parenting leads to children who are perceived as irresponsible about a number of matters, including those that affect their own physical health and well-being.

Indulgent parenting characterizes those parents who fail to adequately enforce rules (some may not even formulate household rules) and who readily give in to their children's coercive demands. This style of parenting is linked to children's drug and alcohol use and school misconduct. Interestingly, however, these same youngsters do relatively well on measures of social competence and self-confidence.

In general, the patterns just described do not vary as a function of adolescent age, gender, ethnicity, or family background (Baumrind, 1967, 1971; Bronstein, 1994; Maccoby & Martin, 1983; Steinberg et al., 1994). Rothbaum and Weisz (1994) summarize the overall pattern as follows:

> Parents who are accepting and responsive to their children's needs will have children who are more motivated to and better understand how to seek control in appropriate ways. Perhaps most important, the children gain experience in sustaining noncoercive joint activity. . . . The experimental studies on parent effects strongly support this interpretation. (p. 66)

Family Capital

Besides differences in style of parenting, families display other stylistic differences in the form of "capital." Three kinds of environmental capital have been distinguished in the literature.

Financial capital is a measure of the amount of economic or monetary resources made available for the benefit of the child. Children from economically advantaged and poor families typically lead very different lives (Kagitcibasi & Berry, 1989). Impoverished family environments are associated with increased likelihood of delinquency, criminality, lower academic achievement, and drug abuse (Denton & Kampfe, 1994).

Human capital "refers specifically to individuals' training and educational attainment, generally embodied in diplomas, credentials, and certifications" (Valenzuela & Dornbusch, 1994). Human capital, like financial capital, is important, but "if the human capital possessed by parents is not complemented by social capital embodied in family relations, it is irrelevant to the child's educational growth that the parent has a great deal, or a small amount, of human capital" (Coleman, 1988, p. 110). Thus, human capital can have an impact on children, but can do so only if the parties are directly involved with the children in question.

Social capital is defined as the family relations and community organizations (formal and informal) "that are useful for the cognitive or social development of the child or young person" (Coleman, 1990, p. 300). It refers to supportive relationships involving bonds of trust; the more supportive relationships a person has, the more social capital one has (Coleman, 1988). Social capital specifically includes the positive attention a person receives from parents, relatives, and others. "Whereas human capital refers to characteristics of individuals, social capital refers to characteristics of relationships" (Parcel & Menaghan, 1993, p. 121).

In a study of the grades attained by more than 400 university undergraduates, parental social support and reassurance of worth were associated with higher grades, even when controlling for academic aptitude, family education, and family conflict (Cutrona, Cole, Colangelo, Assouline, & Russell, 1994).

Familism is closely related to the idea of social capital. It refers to the degree to which individuals are actively and regularly involved with their extended families. Familism includes a sense of family identification, obligation, and support. Valenzuela and Dornbusch (1994) found that familism has no relationship to academic achievement among Anglo adolescents; however, familism is positively related to academic achievement among Mexican American youth, provided their parents have attained at least 12 years of schooling themselves. This point is consistent with the finding that American university students attach less importance to family than do Mexican or Chinese students (Chia et al., 1994).

Familism consists of three factors: contact, structure, and attitudes. In this context, *contact* refers to sharing time with relatives beyond a person's immediate residence. It is measured by asking how often a person sees or communicates with relatives who do not live in the same home. *Structure* refers to the number of adult relatives who live in close proximity. *Attitudes* are measured by rating items that reflect family commitment and the importance of family in a person's life (Valenzuela & Dornbusch, 1994).

Familism interacts with socioeconomic status (SES) to produce higher academic achievement in both Anglo American and Mexican American students, but is especially important for Mexican American students. As Coleman had predicted, there is an interaction between social and human capital. It is the combination of familism and human capital that appears to have a positive effect on students' academic achievement.

So, we may conclude that in a strong family environment children are provided with physical safety, cognitive stimulation, and social involvement and support. Children need all three kinds of capital to develop optimally. We now turn our attention to the still broader concept of culture and different cultural environments.

Culture and Enculturation

Culture refers to the set of attitudes, values, beliefs, and behaviors shared by a group of people and communicated from one generation to the next. Cultures vary on many different values and expectations for behavior. Individualism-collectivism is one factor that distinguishes among cultures. Many Asian and Hispanic cultures value the welfare of the group over that of the individual, whereas North American and European cultures are individualistic. Where collectivism is the rule, a greater degree of obedience and compliance is necessary and required than is typically found among members of individualistic cultures (Doi, 1985; Stropes-Roe & Cochrane, 1990).

Within any given culture, however, individuals differ according to how completely they embrace and comply with the values and behaviors of the cultural group to which they belong (Matsumoto, 1997). Within any broad cultural group, moreover, there are likely to be major subcultural differences.

Enculturation is the process by which the values, beliefs, and behaviors of a culture are transmitted to its members. Observational learning and interactions with the social environment are central to the enculturation process. Members of a given culture convey the culture's values to others directly and indirectly, through nonverbal as well as verbal communication.

As a result of enculturation, we can interact successfully with people from our own culture because we share the same verbal and nonverbal language. Behaviors that within our own culture we readily understand and use in day-to-day commerce can be decidedly inappropriate for communicating with members of other cultures.

Nonverbal Aspects of Communication

Over the past few decades, more and more social scientists have come to appreciate the role of *non*verbal behavior in both the way children are socialized and the way they learn to interact with other people. Nonverbal behaviors convey a great deal. They allow us to remain "silent" and yet be coy, flirtatious, disapproving, or even annoying. But people from other cultures may attach a different meaning than we do to our nonverbal behavior. These wrong interpretations, in turn, may lead to misunderstanding and even severe (and unnecessary) conflict. Often interpretation of the subtle meaning of another person's gestures and behavior, especially their nonverbal behavior, occurs almost reflexively, without full awareness. These interpretations depend to a great extent on understandings common to a person's own local culture.

"Body Language": Gestures and Emblems

Gestures are body movements intended to convey meaning. They are particularly subject to misunderstanding across cultures because similar gestures may be used to convey very different messages. For example, although head nodding (up and down) means yes and head shaking (side to side) means no in many cultures, they are not universal. In some cultures, these two gestures have meanings that are exactly the opposite (Ekman, Friesen, & Bear, 1984; Kendon, 1987).

The overall amount of gesturing that is common in conversation also differentiates one culture from another. Jewish and Italian Americans encourage expressiveness in gestures and mannerisms when speaking. There is

Even within a shared culture, distinct subcultures exist (e.g., the "on-line" subculture), which can produce gross misunderstandings.
Cartoon by Alex Liebert

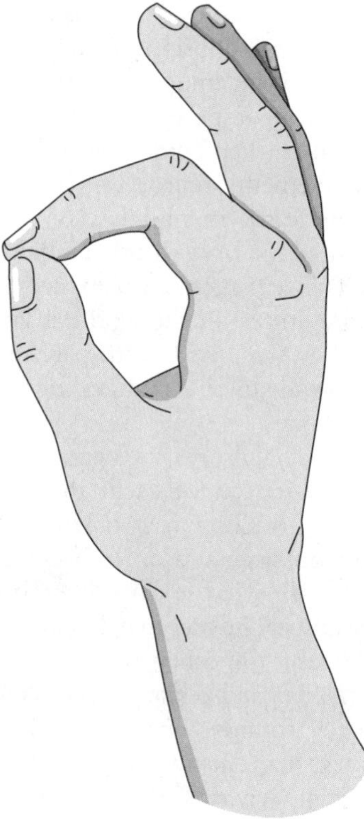

Figure 13.6
One of the many emblems that may meet with a surprising reaction if directed toward someone of another cultural background.

less gesturing among other Americans, and Asians use still less gesturing (Kendon, 1987).

Emblems are physical "signs" that have specific meanings that vary across cultures. The A-OK sign in the United States is almost never misunderstood. However, the same emblem in some European cultures is considered a vulgar invitation to have sex (see Figure 13.6). The common American thumbs-up sign will meet with a hostile reception from people of the Middle East. Similarly, the V-for-victory emblem (making a **V** with the index and middle fingers) is commonly used in the United States, regardless of whether the palm is facing outward or inward. In Britain, however, when this "same" emblem is displayed with the palm facing inward, it means "up yours" (Matsumoto, 1997).

Personal and Interpersonal Space

The amount of **personal space** required by, or afforded to, people is another example of culture-specific nonverbal behavior. In most cultures, personal space is a nonverbal cue to status, power, and dominance. The higher a person is in the social hierarchy, the more physical space others allow. Where particular areas are identified with individuals (e.g., office space), people of higher status are given the better locations, and members of high status are afforded space that is more distinct, more private, and less accessible to other group members.

The **interpersonal space** we give others is orderly and to a great extent predictable, based on social relationships. Although these rules hold for most cultures, cultures vary as to the amount of space considered appropriate, as well as what type and location of space are most desirable. Americans generally require more personal space than people of most other cultures.

Even sleeping arrangements reflect the relatively large personal space "requirements" of Americans. In middle-class America, children typically sleep in a separate room alone or with other siblings. Parents almost invariably sleep elsewhere. This arrangement is exceedingly rare among contemporary and past world cultures; in the world at large, sleeping in the same room (and sometimes the same bed) with parents is the norm (Crawford, 1994). Table 13.3 shows the distance ranges for four different types of relationship in the United States.

In many Middle Eastern cultures, two people customarily stand so close together to converse that they can feel each other's breath (Hall, 1963, 1966; Watson & Graves, 1966). An American talking with an Arab may find the conversational partner too close and move back; in all likelihood, the Arab will move closer, to restore what is (in the Arab's mind and culture) the appropriate space proximity. The pair may begin moving back and forth as if dancing, with each thinking the other is impolite.

People from Latin American backgrounds interact at closer distances than those of European backgrounds (Forston & Larson, 1968). Indonesians interact at closer distances than Australians (Noesjirwan, 1977, 1978). Italians interact more closely than Germans or Americans (Shuter, 1977).

When people of different cultures meet, the situation is ripe for misunderstanding and for misperceptions of the other's personality. Because personal space is linked with social status, attempts to invade a person's comfortable range may be viewed as offensive, insulting, or disrespectful. Attempts to "move in" on another's personal space may also be interpreted as aggressive. This misunderstanding could result in hostile verbal behavior or even overt physical aggression if the intent is not clarified.

All of the cultural differences described can fuel serious misunderstandings between people who do not share common cultural backgrounds. Behaviors of individual people that in the context of their own native culture would be innocuous may be interpreted as offensive or hostile to others. They may turn people off because they are interpreted as negative reflections of the person

Table 13.3 Level of interpersonal space in the United States as a function of psychological closeness of the relationship

TYPE OF RELATIONSHIP	DISTANCE
Intimate	0–1.5 feet
Personal	1.5–4 feet
Consultative	4–8 feet
Public	9 feet or more

Source: Data from "Gender Effects in Decoding Nonverbal Cues," by J. A. Hall, 1978, *Psychological Bulletin, 85,* 845–857.

who displays them (in total innocence). Most of these gestures and nonverbal behaviors are learned in childhood by observing the behaviors of others and then adopting and accepting them as proper and appropriate. Yet, taken out of context, they may be interpreted as peculiar or offensive and a reflection of some deviant aspect of the individual's personality.

Activity Settings

Social learning and enculturation are mediated through so-called activity settings (O'Donnell, Tharp, & Wilson, 1993). **Activity settings** are the specific environmental contexts in which cultural values are transmitted to others. Gallimore, Goldenberg, and Weisner (1993) define *activity settings* as follows: "activity settings are the architecture of everyday life, not a deliberate curriculum; they are homely and familiar parts of a family's day: preparing meals, eating dinner, cleaning up, mowing the lawn, repairing cars, watching television, getting ready for school."

Activity settings pervade daily life. The personality of every individual is influenced through a combination of direct and indirect, subtle and overt forces that operate continuously in each person's environment. How these forces combine and interact determines to a great extent the **behavioral repertoire** acquired by any particular individual, as well as the range of behaviors that person accepts (displays overtly) in the normal course of her or his life.

This chapter has examined both the processes and agents of social learning. None of the factors or mechanisms discussed operates in isolation. Rather, all these influences combine in complex ways to produce the particular characteristics and behavior that constitute human personality. Most of these factors continue to influence the individual throughout the entire life span. Social forces that operate in childhood to shape and reinforce particular behaviors continue to operate and thereby ensure consistency in behavior over time. Environmental forces, especially the examples of others around us, clearly exert a powerful influence on many of the characteristics we commonly think of as reflecting personality.

SUMMARY

1. The social learning approach focuses on social factors that shape personality. This approach is concerned with three related issues: the processes by which individuals learn from social models, the actual models to which all persons are exposed (family members, teachers, and numerous individuals in the surrounding culture), and the content of social learning (the various behaviors, beliefs, and attitudes the individual has learned).
2. According to Bandura and Walters's social learning theory, articulated in the 1960s, the mechanisms through which personality is shaped are classical conditioning, operant conditioning, and modeling. The theory states that the "vehicles" or agencies through which social learning occurs are the person's family and other members of the cultural environment.
3. Observational learning is the process by which the behavior of one person, the observer, is altered through exposure to the behavior of

one or more other persons (models). The specific behaviors exhibited by the model are referred to as modeling cues, which may be live or symbolic (e.g., models presented through movies and television, models read about in stories and legends, and verbal accounts of other people's behavior).

4. Observational learning is a three-stage process: exposure to modeling cues, learning from these cues (acquisition), and accepting these cues as a guide for the observer's own actions (manifested in spontaneous performance).
5. Acceptance may be demonstrated by imitation or counterimitation (e.g., behaving in a fashion opposite to those displayed by a model) and may be direct (as in direct copying of specific behaviors) or indirect (in which the observer generalizes from the model's actions so that behaviors similar but not identical to the model's behavior are displayed).
6. Bandura's famous Bobo doll study demonstrated the effects of vicarious consequences (consequences received by the model) upon observers' behavior. Vicarious reinforcement tends to increase the likelihood that a model will be emulated, whereas vicarious punishment tends to decrease the (immediate) likelihood that a model will be emulated.
7. Vicarious consequences also have an attention-focusing effect. The behavior of models who are observed to receive clear consequences for their behavior is more likely to be remembered than is the behavior of models who receive no consequences for their observed actions; however, vicarious punishment is more likely to be forgotten than is vicarious reinforcement.
8. All models are not received the same. Acceptance of modeling cues is enhanced when the model is similar to the observer, when consistent multiple models are observed, when models practice what they preach, and when models appear competent. Thus, the information value of modeling cues appears to determine their acceptance.
9. Although some aspects of "masculine" and "feminine" behavior are determined by biology, many are influenced by social learning.
10. Among the most important roles to which the individual is socialized are gender roles, which differ from one culture or subculture to another. The concept of gender refers to differences between females and males that are socially (as opposed to biologically) determined. Gender roles and the meaning of "feminine" and "masculine" have changed dramatically over the course of the 20th century in most Western cultures.
11. Today gender is viewed as bidimensional rather than unidimensional; that is, any given individual (irrespective of the person's biological sex) may be high or low on masculinity and high or low on femininity. Thus, with respect to gender, there are essentially four more-or-less distinct personality types.

12. Western stereotypic masculine traits include assertiveness, independence, and an active, instrumental approach to situations. Stereotypic feminine traits include understanding, warmth, and sympathy.
13. The best-adjusted females appear to be those who display both stereotypic feminine and stereotypic masculine attitudes and behaviors. Relationship satisfaction and interpersonal success are associated with the presence of feminine traits in both females and males.
14. Androgyny, for members of either sex, refers to being high on both masculine and feminine traits. Androgynous individuals are able to behave in either "masculine" or "feminine" ways, depending upon the requirements of the situation. They therefore enjoy high self-esteem (a "masculine" trait) and high interpersonal success and relationship satisfaction (stereotypic "feminine" traits).
15. Children with mothers who work outside their home tend to be more androgynous than those whose mothers are exclusively homemakers.
16. Evidence suggests that parents perceive male and female children differently from birth and handle their children accordingly. For example, girls are likely to be rewarded for playing with dolls and makeup, whereas boys are likely to be punished for these same behaviors.
17. In general, girls are encouraged to be dependent and to display positive emotions, whereas boys are encouraged to be independent and to engage in competitive physical activity.
18. Family configuration has been shown to play a significant role in personality development. In general, the larger a person's immediate family, the worse off the individual is in terms of verbal intelligence and cognitive and social skills. According to the dilution effect, as family size increases, the amount of time and attention parents can give to any one child decreases.
19. In general, firstborn children and only children are more successful than those born later. The sex of the children in the family also has a significant effect; boys exhibit more feminine behavior if they have older sisters, and girls are more aggressive if they have older brothers.
20. Being reared in a home in which the father is absent has adverse effects on children of both sexes. Father-absent boys tend to exhibit more adjustment problems (especially during adolescence), and father-absent girls are more likely to be sexually promiscuous and delinquent.
21. Children reared in remarried families, especially blended families (in which some children have different fathers and different mothers) suffer from the possibility of conflicting rules from the parents; second marriages are more likely to end in divorce than first marriages, and one of the reasons appears to be conflict between stepparents and stepchildren.
22. Families also differ in their styles of parenting. These styles vary along two dimensions: acceptance-involvement and strictness-supervision. These dimensions give rise to four basic parenting styles: authoritarian, authoritative, indulgent, and neglectful.

23. Authoritarian parenting is characterized by restrictive and rejecting behavior, authoritative parenting is characterized by warmth and the use of reasoning and nonpunitive punishment, neglectful parenting lacks adequate involvement or supervision, and indulgent parenting is characterized by a failure to adequately enforce rules and a tendency to give in to the children's coercive demands. Children exposed to authoritative parenting fare better than others.
24. Families differ in the amount of family capital available to their children. There are three kinds of family capital: financial, human, and social. Financial capital is economic or monetary resources; human capital is the training and educational level of the adults; social capital refers to family and community relations. Children require all three kinds of capital for their optimal psychological development.
25. Familism is the degree to which children are involved in their extended families; it is a form of social capital. Familism includes three factors: family contact, family structure, and family attitudes.
26. Culture is comprised of the entire set of beliefs, values, and language common to a group of people. Within any given culture, there are also subcultural differences.
27. One dimension on which cultures differ is the degree to which they value and foster individualism and independence or collectivism and interdependence among group members.
28. Enculturation is the process by which the values, beliefs, and behaviors of a culture are transmitted to new members. It includes verbal and nonverbal communication, gestures and emblems, and the use of personal and interpersonal space. A person reared in one culture is not prepared to deal with people and problems that arise in other cultures.
29. Activity settings are the environmental contexts in which cultural values are transmitted. They pervade and are the architecture of our daily lives, including such mundane activities as eating dinner, cleaning up, and having fun.

CHAPTER FOURTEEN

Applications and Limitations of the Environmental Strategy

he major applied contributions of the Environmental Strategy have been *specific therapeutic techniques* for behavior (personality) change. As noted earlier, environmentally oriented psychologists make use of the same *range* of assessment techniques that are used in the other strategies. What distinguishes environmental assessment is not so much the specific techniques as the interpretations of the data they provide. Behaviorally oriented psychologists are less likely than others to draw *inferences* from the responses they collect than to accept them at face value. Questioning tends to be direct, specific, and present-oriented. Whenever possible, clients are observed directly in the context of the problematic situations. Their *overt behavior*, in the form of verbal responses and direct actions, is addressed in treatment; underlying intrapsychic causes of the symptomatic behavior are ignored.

The Environmental Strategy has produced a wide range of applied techniques aimed at behavior change. Therapies derived from this strategy are usually aimed at *discrete* problem behaviors, ranging from mutism to phobias. We present specific techniques derived from environmental theories and then conclude this chapter with a discussion of the limitations of this strategy.

CLASSICAL CONDITIONING THERAPIES

A variety of behavior therapies use classical conditioning techniques. The goal of these techniques is to substitute an adaptive behavior for a maladaptive one by changing the CS-UCS pairings that have produced the problem. We examine three examples: the urine alarm method for treating nocturnal enuresis, systematic desensitization for treating anxiety, and aversion therapy for treating maladaptive behaviors.

The Urine Alarm Method

Nocturnal enuresis is defined as the inability of people older than 4 to suppress urination while sleeping. The normal developmental sequence begins with a child achieving daytime continence; nighttime continence follows shortly after. Bladder tension (UCS) has to become a sufficient stimulus to provoke awakening before urination (UCR) occurs. More than 50 years ago, Mowrer and Mowrer (1938) developed a simple procedure that teaches people to awaken in response to bladder tension. It became the *prototype* of the urine alarm method used today. Mowrer and Mowrer viewed the sensations of bladder fullness as a conditioned stimulus (CS) that, when paired repeatedly with an alarm (UCS), came to evoke the unconditioned response (UCR) of awakening, allowing the person the opportunity to void in the toilet instead of the bed.

Mowrer and Mowrer's original procedure was called the *bell-and-pad* method. The child slept on a specially prepared pad, consisting of two pieces of screening separated by heavy cotton (see Figure 14.1). When urination began, (1) the urine would seep through the cloth, (2) closing an electric circuit and (3) setting off an alarm. After a number of these pairings (bladder tension with alarm), bladder tension (CS) alone would come to wake (CR) the child before urination began. (A modern version of the urine alarm attaches directly to the child's undergarments but operates on the same principles.) Treatment requires using the alarm on a nightly basis for 8 to 12 weeks.

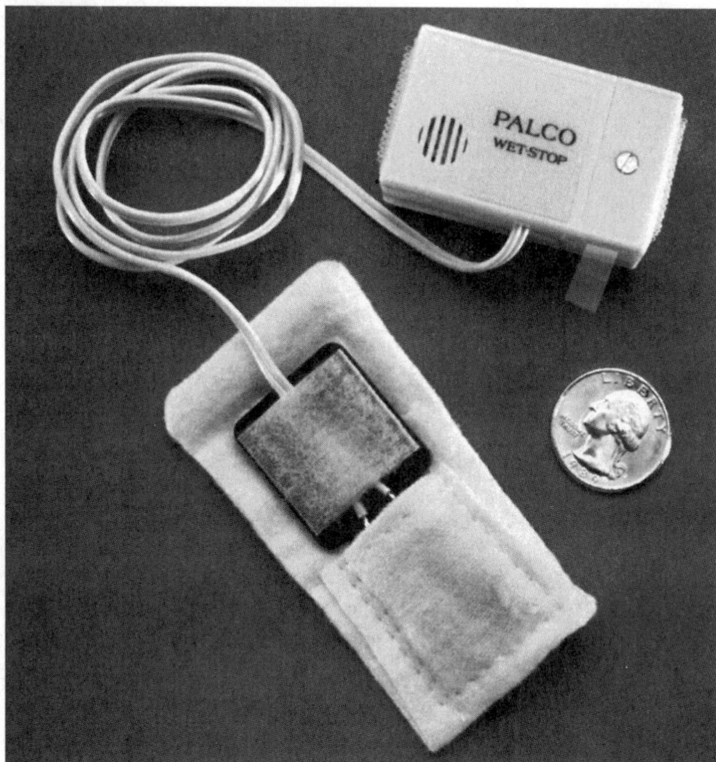

Figure 14.1
The essential elements of the modern urine alarm used to treat nocturnal enuresis.
Courtesy of PALCO Laboratories

In fact, although Mowrer and Mowrer invoked classical conditioning to explain their procedure, they may have been wrong. Bladder tension builds gradually over time, depending on a number of factors (e.g., how much and over what period of time fluids were consumed). Varying degrees of bladder tension can precede the onset of urination (which also depends on many factors, including availability of a toilet). Thus, the alarm onset is probably not being associated with bladder tension as originally supposed, but rather with onset of urination. From this perspective, onset of somnolent urination is being *punished* (reducing the likelihood of future occurrences) by a noxious stimulus (the alarm that produces abrupt awakening). This interpretation is actually based on *operant* principles, as it is the consequences of an act (urination) that is being punished, rather than an association between paired stimuli that is being learned.

Despite these theoretical disputes, the urine alarm method has been used for more than 50 years and is effective in 70% to 80% of cases (e.g., Abramson, Houts, & Berman, 1990; Doleys, 1977; Houts, 1991; Johnson, 1980; Walker, Milling, & Bonner, 1988). Although more rapid procedures have been developed (and are discussed later in this chapter), none is as simple to implement as the urine alarm method (e.g., Azrin, Sneed, & Foxx, 1973; Houts & Liebert, 1984; Houts, Peterson, & Whelan, 1986; Liebert & Fischel, 1990), which continues to be the preferred first approach to treatment. We continue our discussion with classical conditioning therapies that clearly do conform to the model of learned associations between stimuli.

Systematic Desensitization

Systematic desensitization, developed by Joseph Wolpe (1958), is a behavior therapy for alleviating anxiety. The client is gradually exposed to increasingly more anxiety-provoking stimuli while engaging in a behavior that *competes* directly with symptoms of anxiety. Muscle tension signals the onset of anxiety for most people, so muscle relaxation is the competing response most commonly employed.

In classical conditioning terms, the goal is to substitute an adaptive response (CR) for the anxiety (UCR) elicited by particular stimuli (CSs). Before therapy, the stimuli that lead to anxiety are UCSs; after therapy, the same stimuli become CSs that lead to the adaptive response (CR).

Competing Response: Deep-Muscle Relaxation

Deep-muscle relaxation is most often used as the competing response to anxiety. Other possible competing responses include thinking pleasant thoughts, laughing, and eating.

Deep-muscle relaxation training proceeds systematically, covering major skeletal muscle groups (arms, head, neck, shoulders, and so on). Clients first learn to differentiate between relaxation and tension by tensing and relaxing each set of muscles. Then, clients practice just relaxing their muscles, both in the therapy sessions and at home. The following excerpt from a therapist's relaxation instructions illustrates the beginning phases of relaxation training.

> Close your eyes. Settle back comfortably. We'll begin with your right hand. Clench your right hand into a fist. Clench it tightly and study the tensions you feel. Hold that tension . . . (5-second pause) and now relax. Relax your hand and let it rest comfortably. Just let it relax, let the muscles smooth out (15-second pause). Now, once again, clench your right hand . . . clench it tightly and study the tension . . . (5-second pause) and now relax. Relax your hand and note the pleasant contrast between tension and relaxation.

Joseph Wolpe developed systematic desensitization, a widely used behavior therapy for treating anxiety, fear, and other negative emotions.
Courtesy of Joseph Wolpe

Anxiety Hierarchies

A careful assessment of the specific stimuli that make a client anxious is undertaken. Using this information, the client and therapist construct one or more lists of the anxiety-evoking stimuli, which the client rank-orders in terms of the amount of anxiety they evoke. The resulting list is called an **anxiety hierarchy.** Often there is a common theme among the stimuli in an anxiety hierarchy, as the examples in Table 14.1 illustrate.

Desensitization: Exposure to Anxiety-Evoking Stimuli

The final step in systematic desensitization is gradually exposing the client to anxiety-evoking stimuli—that is, the actual desensitization process. The aim is to associate the stimuli that provoked anxiety with relaxation, which will "break" the maladaptive link between the stimuli and anxiety.

A desensitization session begins with the client becoming deeply relaxed, using the relaxation skills previously learned. Then, the client is asked to

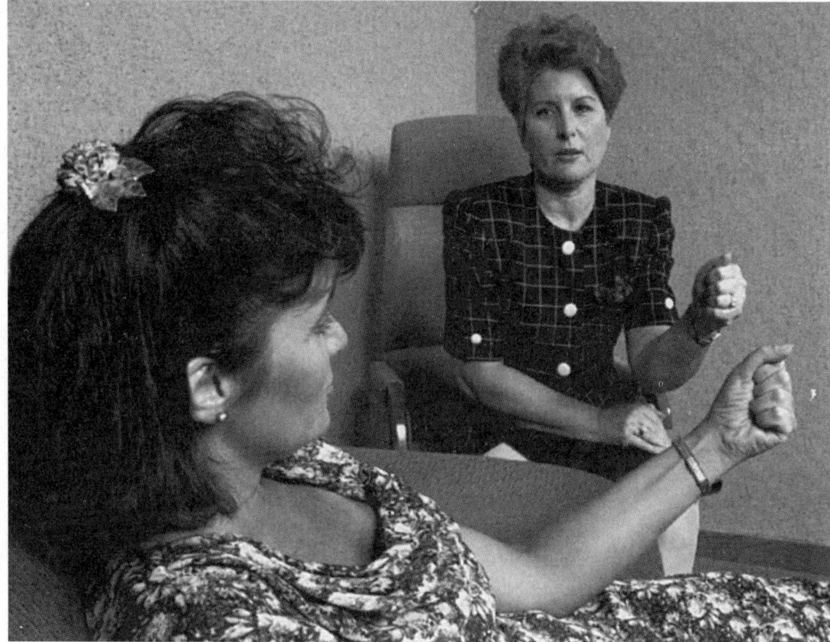

Deep-muscle relaxation is the most commonly used response to counter anxiety in systematic desensitization. Clients learn deep-muscle relaxation by first tensing and then relaxing various muscle groups. The aim is to learn to discriminate between tension and relaxation, which helps the client achieve the latter.
Photo Source Inc./St. Louis

Table 14.1 Examples of two anxiety hierarchies. The higher an item is on the list, the more anxiety it produces.

Examination Series

1. In the process of answering an examination paper.
2. The examination paper lies face down before her.
3. Awaiting the distribution of examination papers.
4. Before the unopened doors of the examination room.
5. On the way to the university on the day of an examination.
6. The night before an examination.
7. One day before an examination.
8. Two days before an examination.
9. Three days before an examination.
10. Four days before an examination.
11. Five days before an examination.
12. A week before an examination.
13. Two weeks before an examination.
14. A month before an examination.

Discord Between Other People

1. Her mother shouts at her sister.
2. Her sister engages in a dispute with her father.
3. Her young sister whines to her mother.
4. Her mother shouts at a waiter.
5. She sees two strangers quarrel.

Source: Modified from *Behavior Therapy Techniques: A Guide to the Treatment of Neurosis* by J. Wolpe and A. A. Lazarus, 1966, Pergamon Press.

imagine the scenes or items in the anxiety hierarchy, beginning with the least anxiety-evoking scene and working toward the most anxiety-evoking item. Each scene is repeated until the client reports virtually no disturbance while visualizing it. Only then does therapy proceed to the next scene on the hierarchy.

Variations on Systematic Desensitization

Variations on Wolpe's basic technique have been developed for use with groups of clients (Deffenbacher & Suinn, 1988) and for treating problems other than anxiety, such as anger (e.g., Schloss, Smith, Santora, & Bryant, 1989; Smith, 1973) and insomnia (e.g., Steinmark & Borkovec, 1974).

Clients can also be exposed to the actual anxiety-evoking stimuli, a procedure known as **in vivo desensitization** or **in vivo exposure,** sometimes contrasted with the conventional (or **imaginal**) exposure (e.g., G.J. Hill, 1989; Marks, 1987). In vivo exposure can be more effective than imaginal exposure, and it allows clients to carry out the exposure independently and in a familiar environment. (e.g., Marks, 1978).

Aversion Therapy

Systematic desensitization substitutes positive responses to specific stimuli for negative responses, such as anxiety. In some situations, just the opposite effect is required. **Aversion therapy** creates a negative emotional reaction to a maladaptive behavior that the subject currently experiences as pleasurable. The target behaviors are most often addictive or sexually deviant behaviors.

A UCS that normally produces an unpleasant, distasteful, or otherwise negative reaction (UCR) is paired with a CS associated with the pleasurable, maladaptive behavior. This conditioning continues until the CS elicits a similar negative reaction as a CR.

A classic example is the use of Antabuse (disulfiram) to treat alcoholism. This drug is sometimes prescribed to aid in alcohol withdrawal and abstention. Antabuse alone has no clinical effect on the body, but when combined with even small doses of alcohol, it creates noxious body sensations ranging from flushing and hot flashes to nausea and malaise, which can last more than an hour (Kaplan & Saddock, 1991).

Clearly, the positive feelings (UCR) previously associated with the consumption of alcohol are replaced by strongly negative ones. Use of Antabuse or of any other aversive technique in therapy is considered a last resort. These forms of treatment are generally used only after more benign methods have failed.

Aversion therapy has stirred some real controversy. The 1971 film *A Clockwork Orange* featured a graphic depiction of aversion therapy as applied to criminal reform. The use of aversion therapy as a form of treatment always raises serious ethical issues. Should psychologists, even in an effort to help or cure, be permitted to use aversive and potentially harmful methods? The issue has not been satisfactorily resolved, but for the present, aversion therapy has fallen out of favor with most practitioners. Its contemplated use must, at the very least, first prompt a therapist to consider very carefully the availability and effectiveness of less noxious techniques, and to fully inform clients of all the possible risks and discomforts associated with the treatment.

OPERANT CONDITIONING THERAPIES

The principles of operant conditioning have been applied extensively to personality change. Operant therapy procedures primarily involve *changing the consequences* of behaviors to modify them. You have already read about one specific application in Chapter 12, the case of Robbie.

Operant-based treatment procedures have three possible goals: (1) to increase desirable or adaptive target behaviors, (2) to decrease undesirable or maladaptive target behaviors, or (3) to simultaneously decrease undesirable target behaviors and increase desirable target behaviors.

Increasing Adaptive Behaviors

Reinforcement therapies are used to increase adaptive behaviors (already present in the client's behavioral repertoire) that are being used too infrequently. Examples are encouraging appropriate social interaction in clients suffering from schizophrenia and assertive behaviors in clients who are passive to the point of being perpetually victimized. Unlike many verbal, insight-oriented psychotherapies (e.g., psychoanalysis), reinforcement therapies can be used with almost any client, including young children, clients with limited intellectual capacity, and clients who are nonverbal (Spiegler & Guevremont, 1993). We will examine several variations of reinforcement therapy to illustrate its versatility. (Note that these principles can be easily extended to everyday life. Reinforcement is the principle behind, for example, parental praise for positive behavior and pay for work.)

The Premack Principle

Activities people frequently engage in can serve as powerful reinforcers. David Premack (1965) discovered that high-probability behaviors can serve as reinforcers for low-probability behaviors. This finding has come to be called the **Premack principle.** Any lower-frequency behavior will increase if it is made contingent on the higher-frequency behavior—even if the higher-frequency behavior is *not* considered pleasurable.

David Premack described what has come to be known as the "Premack principle." Any high frequency behavior can be used to reinforce a lower frequency behavior.
Courtesy of David Premack

For example, suppose you decided that you wanted to make your bed each morning, which you now almost never do. You realize, though, that you brush your teeth without fail, first thing each morning. If you allow yourself to brush your teeth only after you make your bed, you will definitely make your bed more often. Note that although you regularly brush your teeth, it is probably not something you would say you particularly enjoy doing. Yet it is, despite this, a high-probability behavior.

The Premack principle is especially useful with clients for whom it is difficult to identify reinforcers. Consider the case of B. H., a 44-year-old woman in a psychiatric hospital who rarely interacted with other people (Spiegler & Guevremont, 1993). She spent virtually all her waking hours sitting in one particular chair. The hospital staff was able to shape the time B. H. spent in social interactions by permitting her to sit in her chair only after spending a specified amount of time with others.

Token Economies

A **token economy** is a reinforcement system designed to motivate clients to perform adaptive behaviors. Clients are reinforced with tokens, such as stickers, poker chips, or points, for adaptive behaviors. The tokens can be exchanged for various **backup reinforcers,** such as desired items (e.g., candy) and activities (e.g., watching TV).

Token economies often are used with groups of clients, in classrooms, and in institutional settings. A list of desirable behaviors, the number of tokens earned for performing each, and a list of backup reinforcers and their "prices" in tokens are posted (see Table 14.2). Clients know ahead of time exactly what they have to do to earn tokens and how they can spend them (Spiegler & Agigian, 1977).

Token economies have been used successfully in treatment programs for psychiatric patients, predelinquent adolescents, and "normal" children (Glynn, 1990; Spiegler & Guevremont, 1993). Token economies for individual clients have also been developed, usually aimed at children but occasionally for adults as well.

An example of the latter is found in a token program designed for an 82-year-old man who had a massive heart attack (Dapcich-Miura & Hovell, 1979). The token program effectively motivated the client to engage in critical

Table 14.2 Example of a list posted in a foster home token economy of (1) desirable behaviors and the number of tokens earned for performing each and (2) backup reinforcers and their costs

HOW YOU CAN EARN TOKENS

BEHAVIOR	TOKENS EARNED
Reading the newpaper for 15 minutes	15
Watching TV news program	15
Pleasure reading for 20 minutes	15
Washing dishes	10
Making bed	5
Washing hands before meals	5
Having room considered neat at daily inspection	10
Finishing homework before dinner	10
Being on time for school	5
Doing chores	10–30

HOW YOU CAN SPEND TOKENS

REWARD	TOKEN COST
Riding bike for 1 hour	10
Watching TV for ½ hour	20
Listening to music for ½ hour	10
Playing games for ½ hour	10
Having a snack	15
Going out to dinner	35
Going to movies	25
Taking an all-day excursion	60

aftercare behaviors such as walking regularly and taking medication as prescribed.

Decreasing Maladaptive Behaviors

Increasing adaptive behaviors to supplant maladaptive ones is the optimal way to reduce or eliminate maladaptive behavior. For example, when Robbie's studying behavior increased, his disruptive behaviors naturally decreased. Time formerly spent disrupting class was now filled instead with "on task" (studying) behavior.

Sometimes it is still necessary to decrease undesirable behaviors directly. The basic process involves changing the consequences of the undesirable behavior by (1) *eliminating direct reinforcement* (often in the form of attention, even if the attention appears punitive to those providing it, such as the case of Robbie, whose teacher was reprimanding him and encouraging him to work when he was originally observed to be "off task") or (2) *making the consequences aversive*—for instance, by disallowing access to a favorite reinforcer. (This is just what teachers are doing when they deny a child playground privileges for having done "X.") Both procedures make it *less* likely that the client will repeat the maladaptive behavior in the future.

Eliminating Reinforcement

Extinction, as a therapy procedure, involves withdrawing or withholding the reinforcers that have been maintaining a behavior. Extinction is often used when the reinforcer is social attention. For example, it appeared that 4-year-old Cindy's severe temper tantrums were maintained by her mother's attention (Piacentini, Schaughency, & Lahey, 1985). Accordingly, the therapist instructed Cindy's mother to ignore the tantrums.

To deal with Cindy's verbal and physical aggression, **time out from positive reinforcement** (**time out,** for short) was instituted. Time out involves withdrawing a client's access to positive reinforcers for a brief, preset period immediately after the client engages in the maladaptive behavior. (Time out has the secondary benefit of allowing *both* parties a brief cooling off period once a bad situation has escalated to the point where both are feeling angry or upset.) Whenever Cindy behaved aggressively, she was put in her room for 5 minutes, thereby removing her access to the many potential reinforcers beyond her room.

Extinction and time out were supplemented with **positive reinforcement for appropriate behavior.** Cindy's mother was instructed to take note of and comment on Cindy's behavior when she was engaged in approved-of activities such as reading to herself or playing appropriately with her toys. The combined treatments successfully eliminated Cindy's temper tantrums.

Establishing Aversive Consequences

Punishment is the term applied to any consequence that decreases the likelihood of recurrence of the behavior that precipitated it. (Recall that the alarm sounding contingent on somnolent urination was reconceptualized as a punishment.) Like other types of operant treatments, punishment can take several forms.

Response cost decreases maladaptive behaviors by removing a valued item or privilege whenever the maladaptive behavior is performed. This is an example of *negative* punishment—that is, removal of a reinforcer to *decrease* the likelihood of the behavior's recurrence. For example, Ellen, a college senior, used a response cost procedure to decrease her habit of failing to put her clothes away after she wore them (Spiegler, 1989). Each morning Ellen collected all articles of clothing she found lying around her room and put them in a large box. She did not allow herself to remove any of the clothes until the end of the week, which meant that she frequently had to do without favorite items. This relatively simple procedure substantially reduced her long-standing habit of failing to put her clothes away as she disrobed.

Often the threat of response cost is a powerful incentive that, once imposed, may even prevent the client from ever engaging in the undesirable behavior. For example, a client addicted to amphetamines gave her therapist ten $50 checks (Boudin, 1972). The therapist was to forward the checks as a donation to the Ku Klux Klan if the client (who was African American) used amphetamines. During 3 months of treatment, the response cost contingency had to be used only once. The client was drug free at a 15-month follow-up. Note that this client was, at the start of treatment, actually *addicted* to the drugs.

Overcorrection reduces undesirable behaviors by first having the client correct the negative effects of the maladaptive behavior and then having the client intensively and repeatedly practice an alternative, adaptive behavior. Overcorrection simultaneously (1) decreases the undesirable behavior by introducing aversive consequences and (2) increases (through required practice) an alternative, desirable behavior.

Overcorrection is the major component of dry bed training for bedwetting (Azrin, Sneed, & Foxx, 1973, 1974). Whenever the child wets the bed, the child is awakened to change the wet sheets and nightclothes and then practice going to the toilet 20 times before returning to bed. Used in conjunction with a urine alarm, dry bed training can take less than a week to eradicate bedwetting (Azrin, Thienes-Hontos, & Besalel-Azrin, 1979).

Prompting and Shaping Behavior

Prompting and shaping (see Chapter 12) are often used in combination to elicit behavior. Consider the case of a 40-year-old man with schizophrenia who had been completely mute during 19 years of hospitalization. To elicit the word *gum,* the experimenter first reinforced eye movement indicating attention, then lip movements, next vocalizations, and finally successive approximations of the word *gum.*

> The subject [S] was brought to a group therapy session with other . . . [patients] (who were verbal), but he sat in the position in which he was placed and continued the withdrawn behaviors that characterized him. He remained impassive and stared ahead even when cigarettes, which other members accepted, were offered to him and waved before his face. At one session, when the experimenter [E] removed cigarettes from his pocket, a package of chewing gum accidentally fell out. S's eyes moved toward the gum and then returned to their usual position. This response was chosen by E as one with which he would start.

S met individually with E three times a week. The following sequence of procedures was introduced in the private sessions.

Weeks 1, 2. A stick of gum was held before S's face, and E waited until S's eyes moved toward it. When this response occurred, E as a consequence gave him the gum. By the end of the second week, response probability in the presence of the gum was increased to such an extent that S's eyes moved toward the gum as soon as it was held up.

Weeks 3, 4. The E now held the gum before S, waiting until he noticed movement in S's lips before giving it to him. Toward the end of the first session of the third week, a lip movement spontaneously occurred, which E promptly reinforced. By the end of this week, both lip movement and eye movement occurred when the gum was held up. The E then withheld giving S the gum until S spontaneously made a vocalization, at which time E gave S the gum. By the end of this week, holding up the gum readily occasioned eye movement toward it, lip movement, and a vocalization resembling a croak.

Weeks 5, 6. The E held up the gum, and said, "Say gum, gum," repeating these words each time S vocalized. Giving S the gum was made contingent upon vocalizations increasingly approximating gum. At the sixth session (at the end of Week 6), when E said, "Say gum, gum," S suddenly said, "Gum, please." (Isaacs, Thomas, & Goldiamond, 1960, pp. 9–10)

Box 14.1
DEMONSTRATION: SHAPING A BEHAVIOR

To do this Demonstration, you will need the help of a friend for about 20 minutes. First, select a behavior to shape. Choose a relatively simple behavior, like those suggested in Table 14.3. The behavior should be brief (requiring less than a minute to complete) and should have easily definable components.

Write down the major components of the behavior—see the examples in Table 14.4. Keep these in mind as possible components to reinforce. However, your friend may not perform each of the specific components you have identified. You may have to break down the components you have identified into smaller components. Remember, reinforce only *closer approximations* to the final behavior. Now you are ready for your friend's help. Read the following instructions to your friend.

> I am going to try to get you to perform a simple behavior by saying "good" each time you get closer to doing it. I can't tell you anything about the behavior I want you to perform, but it is something simple that you will have no trouble doing. I'll let you know that you are approaching the actual final behavior by saying "good" each time you do something that resembles it more closely.

Table 14.3 Example of behaviors to be shaped

BEHAVIOR	UNIT OF BEHAVIOR	UNIT OF TIME
Stating own name	Name (first or full)	Minutes elapsed (to execution of complete sequence)
Opening and closing a book	One complete sequence	Minutes elapsed to completion
Sitting in a particular chair	Moving to target chair and sitting	Minutes elapsed to completion

Box continued on following page

Box 14.1 *Continued*
DEMONSTRATION: SHAPING A BEHAVIOR

Table 14.4 Major components of two simple responses

Opening and Closing a Book

1. Movement of either hand
2. Movement of either hand in the direction of the book
3. Touch the book with the hand
4. Opening the book partially
5. Opening the book fully
6. Closing the book partially
7. Closing the book fully

Stating Own Full Name

1. Any verbal utterance
2. Any word
3. Any part of name

At this point, your friend may ask you, "What do you want me to do?" Your answer should be "Just get me to say 'good'."

1. To begin, *reinforce*—by saying "good"—the first movement (or utterance, for a verbal behavior) that your friend makes (as was done with the man who had been mute for 19 years).
2. Now that your friend is active, continue by *selectively reinforcing* only behaviors that constitute steps approaching the desired behavior. Be sure to say "good" as quickly as possible after each progressive behavior has occurred; otherwise, your friend may associate the reinforcement with some extraneous behavior and be led in the *wrong* direction.
3. Continue this process of reinforcing *successively closer approximations* of the behavior until the final behavior is performed. At that point, explain the purpose of the exercise and the procedures you used to achieve the final outcome of overt performance of the specific behavior. Invite feedback, and note your friend's views on the experience.

Stimulus Control Procedures

Stimulus control procedures are also part of operant-based therapies. One therapy based on stimulus control is for the treatment of chronic insomnia. The treatment involves establishing appropriate *setting events* and *discriminative stimuli,* in an effort to bring sleeping behavior back under stimulus control (e.g., Bootzin, 1985; Spielman, Saskin, & Thorpy, 1987). The client is asked to follow a basic set of rules, like those in Table 14.5. Being sleepy becomes a setting event for going to sleep (and in this case going to *bed*). Being in bed becomes a discriminative stimulus for *sleeping* and *no other activities,* such as reading, talking on the telephone, and especially, staying awake at night.

Table 14.5 Rules clients follow in stimulus-control treatment of insomnia

RULE	RATIONALE
1. Go to sleep only when sleepy.	Establish feeling sleepy as setting event for sleeping.
2. Use bed only for sleeping.	Establish bed as a discriminative stimulus for sleeping and not for any other behavior (e.g., reading, watching TV, eating). (Sex is the one exception.)
3. If unable to fall asleep (within 10 minutes) get out of bed.	Establish bed as discriminative stimulus for falling asleep quickly.
4. If unable to fall asleep after returning to bed, repeat rule 3.	Same as above.
5. Get up at same time every morning.	Helps establish consistent sleep rhythm.
6. Do not nap.	Disrupts sleep rhythm and decreases chances of being sleepy at bed time.

Source: Based on "Behavioral Treatments for Insomnia," by R. R. Boorzin and P. M. Nicassio, 1978. In R. M. Eisler and P. M. Miller (Eds.), *Progress in Behavior Modification, Vol. 6.* Academic Press.

SOCIAL LEARNING THERAPIES

Social learning therapies capitalize on the efficiency by which people learn from others' experiences. Modeling is often combined with other behavior therapy procedures, including prompting, shaping, reinforcement, in vivo exposure, and behavior rehearsal. In **behavior rehearsal,** the client practices adaptive behaviors learned in therapy. Modeling therapies have been used to treat two broad classes of psychological problems: skill deficits and fear.

Skill Deficits Treated by Modeling

Clients' problems often result from **skill deficits;** in other words, the clients do not know how to perform certain appropriate or adaptive behaviors. Modeling is an important component in skill training; direct instruction may not adequately convey the subtleties of performing complex skills, and prompting and shaping alone may not be sufficient to acquire new skills (e.g. Charlop & Milstein, 1989). Live modeling typically is used with severe skill deficits, such as teaching language to clients with autism (e.g., Celiberti, Alessandri, Fong, & Weiss, 1993; Lovaas, 1977, 1987), mental retardation (e.g., Goldstein & Mousetis, 1989), learning disabilities (e.g., Rivera & Smith, 1988), and head injuries (e.g., Foxx, Martella, & Marchand-Martella, 1989). The therapist models the response, then prompts the client to imitate, and finally reinforces imitation.

> ***Therapist:*** This is a table.
> ***Therapist:*** What is this?
> ***Client:*** Table.
> ***Therapist:*** That's right! Table.

Symbolic modeling is more efficient (although somewhat less effective) than live modeling and can be used to treat less severe social skill deficits.

Modeling films have been demonstrated to be effective for increasing interaction among socially withdrawn children (e.g., O'Connor, 1969; Rao, Moely, & Lockman, 1987). These films portray children interacting with other children and receiving positive consequences for their actions (an example of vicarious reinforcement).

Self-modeling is another form of symbolic modeling in which clients serve as their own models (e.g., Dowrick, 1991; Kahn, Kehle, Jenson, & Clark, 1990; Kehle, Owen, & Cressy, 1990; Pigott & Gonzales, 1987). A videotape is made of the client performing the target behavior. The client then watches the self-modeling tape. Various cinematic techniques are used so that in the final videotape the client appears to be performing the target behavior *competently* (Dowrick, 1991).

For example, Jamal, an 8-year-old boy, was unable to maintain his attention on schoolwork for more than 30 seconds. Jamal was videotaped solving math problems for a number of 20-second segments. The segments were then combined and edited so that the resulting video showed Jamal working on the math problems for 5 minutes straight!

Fear Treated Through Modeling

Clients who experience intense fear or anxiety revolving around social situations often do not have a skill deficit. Rather, they are afraid of (often only imagined) aversive consequences for performing specific behaviors, such as speaking in public or being in crowded places. *Vicarious consequences* are essential for modeling therapies that deal with fear or anxiety. Clients are exposed to models (live or symbolic) who deal with fear-evoking situations *without* experiencing aversive consequences. Thus, clients vicariously learn that it is "safe" to perform the dreaded behavior. This process is known as **vicarious extinction.** Note that what is extinguished in this example is the reaction of *fearfulness,* as displayed or reported by the client.

Participant modeling is an especially potent treatment for fear (e.g., Downs, Rosenthal, & Lichstein, 1988; Ritter, 1969; Williams & Zane, 1989). It combines the therapist's live modeling of the feared behavior with closely supervised practice of the behavior by the client. (Live modeling is generally more effective, although less efficient, than symbolic modeling in treating fears.) Participant modeling involves three basic steps.

1. The therapist models the fear-evoking behavior.
2. The client performs the same behavior along with the therapist's verbal and, if necessary, physical prompts. For example, the therapist holds the client's arm and accompanies the client up an escalator (the feared behavior).
3. Gradually, the therapist fades the prompts, so that eventually the client is performing the feared behavior alone.

The behaviors are modeled and practiced as listed in an anxiety hierarchy. Therapy proceeds from the least to the most feared behavior (much like the systematic desensitization procedure).

Participant modeling is a potent behavior therapy for fears. A model demonstrates the feared behavior and then physically prompts the fearful person to imitate the behavior.
Photo Source Inc./St. Louis

Modeling Medical Procedures

Reducing fear of medical procedures is important for two reasons. First, it minimizes patients' emotional upset both before and after the procedures (e.g., Peterson, Schultheis, Ridley-Johnson, Miller, & Tracy, 1984; Pinto & Hollandsworth, 1989). Second, it increases the probability that people will seek regular checkups and obtain necessary treatment. Many pediatric hospitals use modeling films to prepare children for hospitalization and surgery on a regular basis (Peterson & Ridley-Johnson, 1980).

The first and most widely used of these is *Ethan Has an Operation* (Melamed & Siegel, 1975; Peterson et al., 1984). The 16-minute modeling film shows the experiences of a 7-year-old boy who has been hospitalized for a hernia operation. The scenes depict various events that most children encounter when they are hospitalized for surgery, such as meeting hospital staff, having blood tests, being separated from their parents, and being in the recovery room. In the film, Ethan describes his feelings and concerns about the events.

Ethan serves as a **coping model** in that he is initially somewhat anxious but gradually overcomes his fear. Coping models, who enhance perceived-model similarity, are usually more effective for treating fears. In contrast, a

mastery model is an exemplar who is fearless and competent from the beginning. Mastery models are more effective for teaching skills (e.g., Ozer & Bandura, 1990).

Modeling films similar to *Ethan* have been made to reduce fear of receiving injections (Vernon, 1974), painful treatments (Jay, Elliot, Ozolins, Olson, & Pruitt, 1985) and dental work (e.g., Kleinknecht & Bernstein, 1979; Melamed, 1979).

LIMITATIONS OF THE ENVIRONMENTAL STRATEGY

We conclude our presentation of the Environmental Strategy, as we have concluded our discussions of the previous strategies, by critically examining its limitations. A number of criticisms have been leveled at the strategy in general. These include lack of comprehensive theory, logical errors, overdependence on laboratory experiments, and excessive reliance on situational tests. Moreover, the behavioral approach in particular has acceptability problems for both psychologists and laypeople. Finally, there is the issue that behavioral approaches have lost their coherence and identity over time. (Recall that what began as complete reliance on the external environment and overt behavior has evolved to allow for more internal, covert processes.)

Lack of Comprehensive Theory

As we have observed, critics have faulted the Psychoanalytic and Dispositional Strategies for their theoretical *in*adequacy. The Environmental Strategy, too, has a major theoretical limitation; namely, it does not even attempt to provide a comprehensive account of personality. In fact, some critics have said that the strategy does not try to explain personality at all.

By its very nature, each strategy emphasizes some aspects of personality and devotes little or no attention to other features. Like each of the other three strategies, the Environmental Strategy has "blind spots." Behavioral approaches have the most glaring limitation because they focus on public, overt behaviors and ignore all private, covert behavior. The social learning perspective does allow for study of broader phenomena, including overlapping cultural forces, but also ignores covert events even when clearly implied.

Finally, environmental personality theories largely ignore the effects of biological and hereditary factors on personality (cf. Staats, 1993a, 1993b). Environmental psychologists do not deny these influences. (Recall the Garcia effect discussed in Chapter 12.) Even early behaviorists such as Skinner (1974) acknowledged their existence. But environmental psychologists choose to focus on other factors—namely, those present in the external environment. In doing so, they can present only a partial conceptualization of personality.

The Relation of Theory to Behavior Therapy

Regarding personality change, critics have argued that no specific theory or theories underlie environment-based therapies (Spiegler, 1983). Rather, these therapists may use only a "nontheoretical amalgamation of pragmatic principles," from which their procedures derive strength (Weitzman, 1967, p. 303). For example, the effectiveness of systematic desensitization can be explained in terms of a variety of nonbehavioral as well as behavioral theories, *including* psychoanalysis (Spiegler & Guevremont, 1993; Weitzman, 1967).

Moreover, most behavioral change techniques were in common use long before environmental theories were formulated (Breger & McGaugh, 1966; Wilson, 1986). Thus, these theories have not generated the change techniques with which they are associated.

Logical Errors

We have seen that the psychoanalytic and dispositional psychologists commit logical errors in their reasoning. Environmental psychologists also have been guilty of thinking illogically in certain respects. They have been accused of one logical error in particular: committing the error of affirming the consequent.

The Error of Affirming the Consequent

Environmental psychologists take great pride in the success of their therapy techniques. They often claim or imply that these successes demonstrate the validity of their personality theories. The logic of such an assertion is faulty.

As an example, environmental psychologists theorize that many fears are acquired through classical conditioning. One source of evidence they cite for this assertion is that fears can be eliminated by counterconditioning procedures, such as systematic desensitization. However, this does not prove that the fear was acquired through conditioning in the first place.

The logical fallacy at issue here is the **error of affirming the consequent.** It involves assuming that "because behavior is generated under one set of circumstances, every time this or similar behavior occurs in nature, it had developed because of the same set of controlling conditions" (Davison & Neale, 1974, p. 28). A common analogous experience illustrates the erroneous reasoning. You take aspirin for a headache. Often, the medicine relieves your pain and "cures" your ailment. Still, the fact that taking aspirin eliminated the pain hardly means that your headache was caused initially by a lack of aspirin in your bloodstream. In general, demonstrating that a therapy procedure eliminates a psychological problem through a particular process does *not* imply that the same process accounted for development of the problem. In fact, logically, the success of the treatment by itself reveals nothing about the processes that originally produced the problem.

Overdependence on Laboratory Experiments

Controlled laboratory experiments are the favored method of research in the environmental strategy. The advantage of controlled experiments is that conclusions regarding cause-and-effect relationships can be drawn with confidence. The strength of the experimental method notwithstanding, experiments in the field of personality have limitations.

Failure to Study Multivariate Phenomena

To achieve precision, experimental situations often are narrow and simplified. Experiments generally involve the effect of one or two independent variables on no more than a few dependent variables. However, real-life experiences tend to be much more complex. Behavior is almost always multiply determined.

Inadequacy of Experimental Analogs

Experiments are limited by the conditions that can be arranged in the laboratory. Many factors that influence human behavior and personality cannot be studied because of both practical and ethical limitations. For instance, it would be impossible to set up a real emergency, such as a fire, to investigate stress, Instead, psychologists are restricted to experimental analogs, such as creating mild stress by having subjects fail at solving puzzles.

The dependent variables that can be researched also are restricted by conducting experiments in the artificial confines of the psychological laboratory. In studying interpersonal aggression, for example, it would be unethical to encourage one person to inflict actual physical pain on another person. Instead, an experimental analog must be used, such as having subjects ostensibly administer shock to another subject.

Laboratory situations often restrict the form and content of the subjects' responses, which differ from the free-responding characteristic of natural situations. For instance, angry experimental subjects are provided with only one option for expressing aggression, such as "administering shocks" to another person in a contrived situation.

The motivation of subjects in laboratory experiments and of people in actual situations is also different. Often, experimental subjects are asked to perform tasks in which they have no particular personal interest or investment.

Consider a consistent finding of laboratory studies of "delay of gratification": Most children and adolescents can tolerate long delays while waiting for a promised reward (e.g., Funder & Block, 1989; Mischel, Shoda, & Peake, 1988; Mischel, Shoda, & Rodriguez, 1989; Rodriguez, Mischel, & Shoda, 1989). Do these findings mean that most children and adolescents have an easy time delaying gratification in their everyday lives? Probably not. More likely, the experimental conditions in delay-of-gratification studies have not duplicated real-life conditions.

> The ordinary situations in life in which adaptive delay is so important typically involve both immediate and delayed rewards that are vastly larger, more powerfully motivating, and more conflicting than anything that can be ethically administered in a brief, experimental situation. (Funder & Block, 1989, p. 1049)

For example, it is difficult to equate forgoing a small, immediately available snack and forgoing the temptation of powerful and immediately available real-life gratifications such as sex or recreational drugs. Despite the rigor of controlled analog experiments, therefore, the results may have low external validity (e.g., LeShan, 1991; Wilson, 1982, 1984). The bottom line is that the experiments may reveal little about the phenomena as they occur in everyday life.

Excessive Reliance on Situational Tests

Environmental psychologists often use situational tests to assess personality. For instance, to learn how people respond to frustration, subjects might be placed in a situation in which they are kept from reaching a goal, and their reactions are observed and recorded.

Situational tests make sense "intuitively." Measuring a person's overt behaviors today is an "obvious" way of determining what the person will do tomorrow. Situational tests typically have high face validity; that is, they look like they measure what is being tested. This high face validity is, in part, the reason that there has been little systematic evaluation of such personality assessment techniques.

A classic application of situational tests occurred during World War II. American and British armed forces had to rapidly select suitable officer candidates and individuals for military intelligence assignments (Morris, 1949; OSS Assessment Staff, 1948). Extensive situational tests were developed for this purpose. One test, for example, required subjects to assemble a small wooden building. They were "helped" by two other people who, unknown to the subjects, were instructed to impede progress. Observers rated candidates' performance and emotional reactions to the situation.

In general, the reliability of these tests was not high. Predictive validity—the ability to identify candidates who subsequently performed well on assignments—was also quite low (Anastasi, 1976). This disappointing performance of situational tests is, no doubt, partially attributable to factors that were independent of the assessment methods. Wartime conditions necessitated the rapid development of mass assessment procedures, which provided less-than-ideal circumstances. Still, some of the failure appears to be due to the general problems of situational tests.

Merely being observed alters subjects' behaviors to an unknown degree. As a consequence of having to "perform," people may behave differently than they normally do. Some people become anxious, which causes them to "flub" their performance, even when they are normally competent in the behavior being assessed. Others rise to the occasion and perform better than they usually do, perhaps because they have an audience to perform for.

A related problem occurs with situational tests that involve role playing in simulated situations. The tests may tap somewhat different abilities than those called for in real life. For example, a soldier may be able to pretend to be a strong leader under test conditions but not be an effective leader in the field against real enemies.

Finally, situational tests may not be lifelike enough for adequate predictive validity. A person who can pick up a harmless snake in the laboratory may still show considerable fear of a small snake unexpectedly encountered in the woods. Indeed, assuming that behavior is always situation specific, as most environmental psychologists do, people would be expected to act differently in the laboratory than in the woods!

Recently, the reliance on situational tests has decreased in the environmental strategy (e.g., Jacobson, 1985), although they remain an important source of data (e.g., Foster & Cone, 1986). This change is partly in response to the problems with situational tests that we have just described.

Limited Acceptability of the Behavioral Approach

Acceptability is one criterion by which theories are judged (see Chapter 1). To the extent that both psychologists and laypeople have difficulty accepting the behavioral approach, the approach has an added burden to prove itself. The acceptability of the behavioral approach is limited by (1) its seemingly simplistic view of personality and (2) its deterministic stance.

Simplistic View of Personality

The behavioral view of personality is simplistic. Stimulus and response are the two essential variables. People are reluctant to view their own behaviors and those of others in such simple terms. We like to think of ourselves as highly complex.

Moreover, there is nothing ennobling about being governed by the same psychological principles as Skinner's pigeons and rats. We are human beings—thinking beings—who are capable of reflecting on what we do. Yet, since Watson's (1914) insistence that there is "no dividing line between man and brute," some behaviorists have derived their learning principles almost exclusively from the study of laboratory animals (e.g., LeShan, 1991).

Deterministic Stance

Free will and self-determination are considered essential human values. However, the behavioral approach is highly deterministic. How we act, feel, and think is presumed to be determined solely by external factors.

Humans may not have free will, as behavioral psychologists argue, but people seem to have a need to think they do, which appears to be beneficial. For example, research on locus of control (see Chapter 17) indicates that individuals who believe they control their own fate generally are healthier and more successful than those who believe they are the pawns of external circumstances.

There is a way in which the highly deterministic stances of the Psychoanalytic and Dispositional Strategies may be more palatable than the determinism of the behavioral approach. With psychoanalytic and dispositional determinism, the factors affecting our behavior are located within us rather than external to us. Our unconscious desires and traits are our own, an intrinsic part of each of us.

Thus, the seemingly simplistic view of human personality and the emphasis on environmental determinism make the behavioral approach a hard product to sell. Indeed, experience has shown that many people will not buy it.

Loss of Identity

The Environmental Strategy changed significantly in the latter half of the 20th century (cf. Liebert & Spiegler, 1970). The prominent role once played by the behavioral approach has diminished greatly in academic circles. The social learning approach, although originally focused on *overt* behavior, made implicit assumptions about covert processes. Thus, for the behavior of a model to be imitated in overt behavior, that model's actions must first have been recognized (attended to), remembered (retained and recalled accurately), and accepted as appropriate by the observer. All of these processes are now considered to be within the "cognitive" domain. Thus, many early social learning theorists ultimately crossed the line between the Environmental and the Representational Strategies. This, too, will be obvious when we encounter their later work, which often considers private mental processes explicitly. Thus, we now turn our attention to the final strategy for the study of personality, the Representational Strategy.

SUMMARY

1. The major applied contributions of the Environmental Strategy have been specific therapeutic techniques for behavior (personality) change. These techniques focus on altering overt, specifically targeted problem behaviors.
2. Classical conditioning behavior therapies involve changing CS-UCS pairings to substitute adaptive responses for maladaptive ones.
3. Systematic desensitization, developed by Joseph Wolpe, is a behavior therapy for anxiety based on classical conditioning. The procedure is designed to replace anxiety with an adaptive response to what were initially anxiety-eliciting situations. The most common substitute response is deep-muscle relaxation, which involves tensing and then relaxing major muscle groups.
4. Systematic desensitization begins with the creation of an anxiety hierarchy, tailored to the individual client. The individual learns to relax in the face of progressively more anxiety-provoking situations. The anxiety-provoking stimuli may be presented imaginally or in direct experience; the latter method is referred to as in vivo desensitization.
5. Aversion therapy is a classical conditioning technique used to eliminate an undesirable response that the client experiences as pleasurable. It is accomplished by pairing the stimulus that produces the maladaptive response with an unpleasant stimulus. This treatment is successful but controversial because it purposely induces a noxious experience.
6. Operant conditioning therapies change the consequences for a given behavior. Reinforcement therapy involves reinforcing adaptive behaviors; it is highly effective and enjoys widespread application today.
7. The Premack principle refers to the findings of David Premack in 1965 that any high-probability behavior can be used as a reinforcer for any lower-probability behavior. For example, to increase the probability that a client will exercise in the morning, the act of brushing one's teeth (a high probability but not particularly pleasant behavior) is made contingent on first exercising.
8. A token economy is a reinforcement system based on operant conditioning. Clients are rewarded with tokens (e.g., stickers, poker chips, or simply points) for performing any of a prescribed list of desirable behaviors. The tokens, in turn, can be exchanged for tangible backup reinforcers, such as candy, the opportunity to watch television, or an outing. Token economies have been successfully used in institutional settings and in classrooms.
9. Operant conditioning offers two ways of decreasing maladaptive behaviors: eliminating reinforcement for the undesirable behavior (extinction) and administering an aversive consequence (punishment) when a maladaptive or undesirable behavior is emitted. Often, these procedures are combined with concurrent administration of positive reinforcement for desirable alternative behaviors.
10. Several types of punishment have been successfully used to decrease the likelihood of maladaptive behavior. One is response cost (or

negative punishment), in which performance of a maladaptive behavior leads to the removal of a valued item or privilege. Time out is an example of the response cost technique.

11. Prompting and shaping (discussed in Chapter 12) are often used in combination to establish adaptive behavior that has a low or zero probability of initial occurrence.
12. Stimulus control is also an effective behavior therapy based on operant conditioning. An example is behavioral treatment of insomnia by limiting time spent in bed to sleeping; that is, the client may not read, watch television, or talk on the telephone while in bed, and thus bed becomes a discriminative stimulus for sleep. (Note that in this case becoming sleepy is used as the setting event for going to bed.)
13. Modeling has been widely used to treat skill deficits. This treatment may involve live or symbolic modeling, or self-modeling may be used (e.g., by preparing a videotape in which the client can see herself or himself engaging in the desired behavior).
14. Vicarious extinction is a modeling therapy for fear or anxiety, in which the client is exposed to models who deal with the situations that provoke the client but do not become afraid or fearful.
15. Participant modeling involves three steps. First, the therapist models the fear-evoking behavior. Second, the client performs the same behavior, while being verbally or physically prompted as necessary by the therapist. Third, the therapist fades out the prompts until the client can engage in the previously fear-provoking behavior alone.
16. Modeling medical procedures through specially prepared modeling films, in which an individual similar to the client is observed to undergo the procedure successfully and without undue discomfort, is highly effective in reducing fear. For this purpose, it has been shown that coping models (who are seen as initially fearful but gradually overcome their fear) are more effective than mastery models (who are competent from the outset). In contrast, mastery models are more effective when modeling is used to teach skills.
17. The Environmental Strategy is limited by the lack of a comprehensive theory because it ignores private events and largely disregards biological and hereditary factors known to play an important role in personality.
18. Most behavior therapies were not initially derived from theory; similar principles have been used for centuries. Moreover, many behavior therapy techniques can be explained on the basis of nonbehavioral principles or theories.
19. The Environmental Strategy suffers from the logical error of affirming the consequent. For example, the fact that counterconditioning can reduce or eliminate problems such as anxiety does not logically imply that the fear was caused by adverse conditioning in the first place. The fact that aspirin relieves pain does not imply that the pain arose from a lack of aspirin in the bloodstream.
20. The Environmental Strategy is said by critics to be overdependent on laboratory experiments that may not necessarily be generalized to

real-life conditions outside the laboratory. Specifically, laboratory experiments fail to deal with the fact that most behavior is multiply determined and often use artificial procedures that are at best loosely analogous to the real-life counterparts they are intended to represent.

21. Environmental psychologists rely heavily on situational tests, but research shows that such tests are often unreliable and have questionable predictive validity.
22. The behavioral approach that underlies much of the Environmental Strategy has limited acceptability because it is seen as overly simplistic and pessimistic in its thoroughgoing determinism. Free will and self-determination are considered by most laypeople and many psychologists as inherent to human existence.
23. Finally, the strict behavioral approach that characterized the Environmental Strategy during its heyday in the 1950s and 1960s has gradually given way to consideration of private cognitive events and processes. The strategy has therefore lost much of its original identity.

PART FIVE

THE REPRESENTATIONAL STRATEGY

Eye of the Beholder

CHAPTER FIFTEEN

Introduction to the Representational Strategy

I had just bought a brand new car, and I was very protective of it. My son, age 7, had a sleep-over at the home of a friend, and I had driven over to retrieve him the next morning. I noticed the driveway was quite steep, so I decided to park at the bottom and walk up to the door. Suddenly, the younger brother of my son's host (age 4) came careening out of the garage toward my new car on a small tricycle. The impact was hard, putting a large dent in my car door, and a rather small dent on the bike's front fender. The boy himself was not hurt. He got up, brushed himself off, surveyed the situation, and reassured me gently, "Don't worry. It was my *old* bike."

This unit is about the Representational Strategy for studying and understanding human personality. The core premise of the Representational Strategy is that personality reflects how people represent their environments and experiences mentally (or cognitively) and that their thoughts, feelings, and actions toward self and others are based on these *perceptions* and *representations.* Thus, abstract representations (and not actual events or objects) guide our actions. Often, as in this vignette, two different people may experience and construe the same event in very different ways. These different perceptions will yield different reactions and responses. (The 4-year-old calmly returned his "old" bike to the garage while I hurried off to the body shop and to place a call to my insurance agent!)

A further assumption is that our perceptions and representation of events are actively *constructed;* that is, rather than being passively "given" by external objects and events, they come to exist through an *active process* of sorting, assembling, and piecing together into a coherent whole all that we have experienced.

Up to a point, people sharing a common culture share perceptions of events; these people live in largely the same reality with one another. But even people within a single culture or family do not fully share their interpretations and perceptions of events. In the last analysis, our representational systems are idiosyncratic; we all have our own distinct, individual understanding of ourselves and the world we inhabit.

EYE OF THE BEHOLDER

The idea that the reality of phenomena lies solely in the way they are perceived is central to the Representational Strategy and the basis for its conceptualization of personality. What is real to an individual is what is in the person's **internal frame of reference**—or subjective world—which includes everything the person is aware of at a particular point in time.

For centuries, the representational view was in disrepute among philosophers of science because it seemed to deny the possibility of establishing "objective facts." The whole thrust of Watson's philosophy, radical behaviorism (see Chapter 12), was to rid psychology of subjectivism and mentalism.

But modern philosophers and contemporary scientists have begun to respect the idea that all experience—and thus all knowledge—depends on subjective interpretation (Heelan, 1983; Manicas & Secord, 1983; Rock, 1983; Watzlawick, 1984). At the heart of this new acceptance is the growing recognition that perception is an interpretive act. To prove this for yourself, take 5 minutes to do the demonstration in Box 15.1 now, before reading further.

Box 15.1
DEMONSTRATION: PERCEIVED REALITY IS AN ILLUSION

Look at Figure 15.1. Notice particularly the two horizontal line segments, labeled *P* and *Q* in this figure. Then decide which of these statements best describes what you see.

1. *P* is shorter than *Q*.
2. *Q* is shorter than *P*.
3. *P* and *Q* are the same or very nearly the same length.

Most people see *P* as shorter, and this is the answer given by about half of the students to whom we have shown the figure. The remaining students answer that *P* and *Q* are the same length. (Some of these confess that they believe they've encountered this illusion before.)

Now we are going to make a claim that may surprise you. *P* is actually *longer* than *Q*! Don't believe us? Suppose we use a ruler—*any* ruler—to see who's right. Go ahead and do the measurement now. (For your convenience, a ruler is provided at the end of this book.)

We have had a lot of fun with this figure, and we encourage you to show it to your friends and family. But it is introduced here to make a basic point: When people "just look with their eyes" and report what they see, there can be major differences in their perceptions based on factors other than the "objective stimulus." Moreover, note how people split on this figure. The half who report that *P* is shorter are responding to some innate perceptual mechanism that "makes" *P* look shorter because of the contextual cues provided by the arrowheads. Those who say the two are equal in length are responding neither to what they see nor to what they know they are "expected to see." They believe they have reasoned through the answer. But virtually no one gives the objectively "right" answer (using the ruler as the criterion); they are all led into error by mental processes of one type or another.

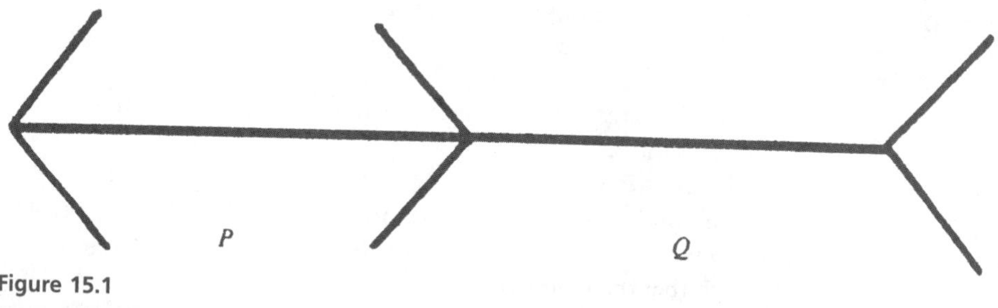

Figure 15.1

The common phrase "only in your mind" does not mean that subjective reality is trivial. In fact, just the opposite is true. Subjective phenomena—such as the perception of line length—are as important as so-called objective phenomena. The columns of some ancient buildings were purposely built *crooked* so they would *appear straight* from the perspective from which they would most commonly be viewed. So, too, we want our social and personal roles to look "straight," even when they are, by someone's else's test, flawed or all wrong. And psychologically, subjective reality often takes precedence over objective reality. How we interpret events—that is, our subjective reality—influences how we behave. This position has important practical implications. For instance, taking into account people's subjective realities has been applied to city planning.

> In a sense, social scientists find, the city does not exist. There is no such single entity, but rather many cities, as many as there are people to experience them. And researchers now believe that the subjective reality is every bit as important to understanding and fostering successful urban life as the concrete and asphalt of objective measurement.
>
> Although most earlier approaches to assessing the quality of city life led researchers to consider such factors as noise levels and density, the new work shows that how people actually perceive their environments is as important as the environments themselves. (Goleman, 1985, p. C1)

From the representational perspective, reality is only *reality as perceived.* Two people observing the same event may experience two very different occurrences. What we see is, in part, a function of what we already know and understand about the world. Perception, like all else, is *relative.* The reports of eyewitnesses demonstrate this. Retrospective accounts of any sort tend to be highly inaccurate when compared with objective information about the incident in question. A great deal of data attests to the inaccuracy of retrospective accounts, even under oath. People's descriptions of events—even those witnessed directly—often conflict with known facts to the point that they bear little resemblance across witnesses and often appear to refer to entirely separate incidents (e.g., Kohnken & Maass, 1988; Loftus, 1997). We will have more to say about this topic later.

The importance of how events are perceived and interpreted subjectively is illustrated by an experiment on stress (Geer, Davison, & Gatchel, 1970). The investigators hypothesized that the stress people experience is influenced by whether they believe that they can control what is happening. In the experiment, all the subjects received a series of identical electric shocks. None of the subjects had any control over the shocks. However, some of the subjects *believed* that they could control the shocks because of what they were told by the experimenter, whereas others believed that they had no personal control in the situation.

The experiment was presented to the subjects as a study of reaction time and was conducted in two phases. In Phase 1, all of the subjects were treated alike. They were given painful electric shocks, each lasting 6 seconds. To measure their reaction time, the subjects were told to press a switch as soon as the shock began. During this period, the subjects' degree of physiological arousal were recorded as a measure of stress.

During Phase 2, half the subjects were assigned to a perceived control condition; they were told that they could cut the duration of the next 10 shocks in half if they pressed the switch "quickly enough" (although the necessary speed was not specified). The remaining subjects were assigned to a *no* perceived control condition; they were told that the next 10 shocks would be shorter. Actually, all of the subjects received shocks lasting 3 seconds, during which time their physiological arousal was again measured.

If a degree of perceived control reduces the experience of stress, perceived control subjects should have experienced *less* arousal during Phase 2 than no control subjects. This is what occurred, as you can see from Figure 15.2. The two groups evidenced similar levels of arousal in Phase 1, but the perceived control subjects displayed significantly lower levels of arousal than

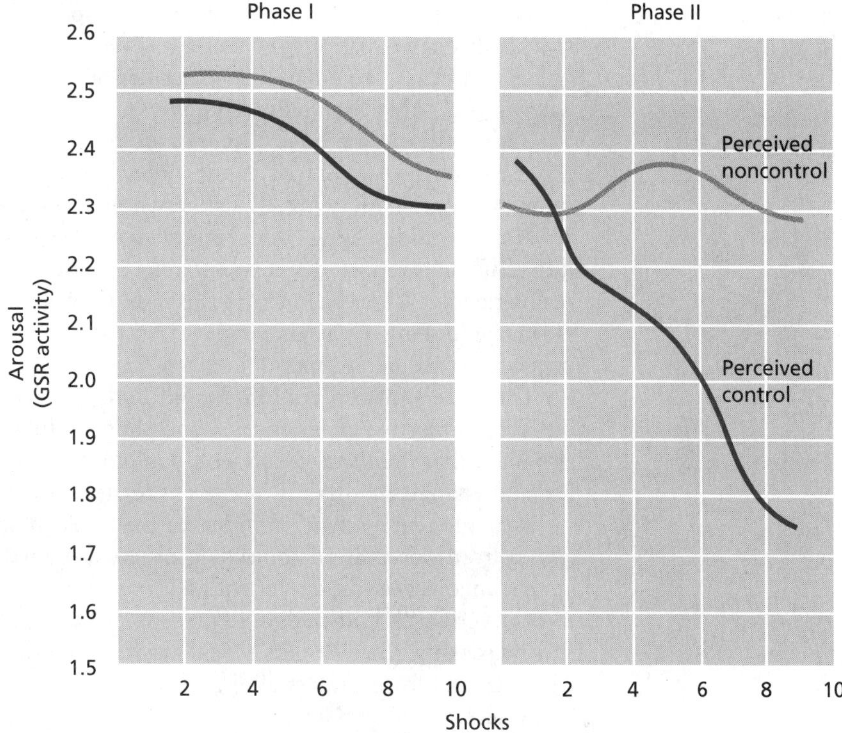

Figure 15.2
The effects of perceived control on the amount of arousal subjects experienced while awaiting electric shocks in Geer et al.'s experiment. During Phase 1, all subjects received shocks of 6 seconds' duration. During Phase 2, all subjects received shocks of 3 seconds' duration.
Source: Adapted from "Reduction of Stress in Humans Through Nonveridical Perceived Control of Aversive Stimulation" by J. H. Geer, G. C. Davison, and R. I. Gatchel, 1970, *Journal of Personality and Social Psychology, 16,* pp. 731–738.

the no control subjects in Phase 2. These results support the idea that humans create their own "reality"

> to fill gaps in . . . knowledge about a sometimes terrifying environment, creating at least an illusion of control which is presumably comforting. Perhaps the next best thing to being master of one's fate is being deluded into thinking one is. (Geer et al., 1970, pp. 737–738)

So, one person's subjective experience or interpretation of a situation may or may not coincide with "objective" reality. (Recall our discussion of cultural differences in Chapter 13.) The same kind of misunderstanding can arise even between people within the same culture. Consider the following somewhat whimsical example taken from Kelly (1955).

> A man construes [views] his neighbor's behavior as hostile. By that he means that his neighbor, given the proper opportunity, will do him harm. He tries out his construction [view] of his neighbor's attitude by throwing rocks at his neighbor's dog. His neighbor responds with an angry rebuke. The man may then believe that he has validated his construction of his neighbor as a hostile person.
>
> The man's [perception] of his neighbor as a hostile person may appear to be "validated" by another kind of fallacy. The man reasons, "If my neighbor is hostile, he will be eager to know when I get into trouble, when I am ill, or when I am in any way vulnerable. I will watch to see if this isn't so." The next morning the man meets his neighbor and is greeted with the conventional, "How are you?" Sure enough, the neighbor is doing just what was predicted of a hostile person. (pp. 12–13)

What a person perceives—subjective experience—determines the ultimate reality of a situation for that person. Consider 8-year-old Beth. Her family has just moved to a new city. After her first day at the new school, Beth's parents ask, "How was school today?"

Beth replies: "I hated it. The kids are really unfriendly. When I came into the class, all the kids stared at me. They were grinning and thought I was funny looking. Only two kids in the whole class talked to me at lunch."

Now consider how Beth might have perceived the same situation differently and reported a very different experience. "I liked it. The kids are really friendly. When I came into the class, they were all interested in me. The kids were looking at me and smiling. And two kids I didn't even know came over to talk to me at lunch!"

The same situation could have led Beth to have either of these two very different subjective experiences, depending on how she interpreted it. (It is also likely that Beth's reactions would influence how her classmates reacted to her and change the nature of the entire situation for all later interactions.)

Psychology is a scientific endeavor that seeks objective knowledge, which comes from observations on which others can agree. Subjective knowledge always involves a single individual's personal experience; others cannot directly verify this knowledge. Representational psychologists solve this problem by seeking what Rogers (1964) called **phenomenological knowledge,** which comes from understanding a person from the person's own internal frame of reference.

The importance of subjective experience, interpretation, and meaning is acknowledged in everyday psychology with expressions such as "Beauty is in the eye of the beholder," "One person's meat is another person's poison," and "Try walking in the other person's shoes." In fact, we often create problems by failing to take others' subjective experiences into account. For example, if David teases Ann when she is anxious about being 5 minutes late for dinner at a friend's, Ann gets angry. From Ann's perspective, being punctual is very important. David obviously considers her concern amusing. He feels social obligations are less serious than other types of appointments.

We will examine several somewhat different representational approaches to personality. The phenomenological approaches of Carl Rogers and Abraham Maslow consider personality to be reflected in each person's unique inclinations to develop and change in particular directions. This perspective constitutes an important element of **humanistic psychology,** sometimes called the *third force* in psychology. Humanism was founded in the 1960s as a reaction to psychoanalysis and behaviorism, the two competing orientations at that time (DeCarvalho, 1990b, 1991a, 1991b; Smith, 1990). We will have more to say about this important approach later in this chapter.

George Kelly was also sympathetic to the humanist movement. His **personal construct** approach and the **cognitive approach** that subsequently developed in academic psychology deal with how people interpret and anticipate the events in their lives and thereby develop unique personalities. The **social cognitive approach,** detailed in Chapter 17, focuses on the actual mental (cognitive) representations and processes that give rise to conscious thought, experience, affect, perception, and behavior.

The cognitive approach to personality has had an interesting history. Speculations about subjective (private) experiences and processes led theorists into interminable disputes during the late 19th and early 20th centuries. (You may recall that Pavlov banned introspection from his laboratory.) From the 1930s through the early 1960s, *cognitive* was considered a dirty word among many academic psychologists. Nonetheless, two important books focusing almost entirely on cognitive processes were published during this period: George Kelly's (1955) two-volume *The Psychology of Personal Constructs* and Leon Festinger's (1957) *A Theory of Cognitive Dissonance.*

By the early 1970s, experimental psychologists began to demonstrate that mental processes could be studied *rigorously*—that is, in a methodologically sound way. Thus began "the cognitive revolution." *Cognitive* was no longer a dirty word, and cognitive psychology became an active, and ultimately the dominant, approach within most branches of academic psychology.

In the wake of the revolution, personality psychologists turned their attention to cognitive processes. Cognitive issues suggested new ways of thinking about many of the traditional questions in personality psychology, such as the "real" nature of underlying personality differences between people.

REPRESENTATIONAL PERSONALITY THEORY

The theories we describe in this part differ among themselves in at least two basic respects. First, there are differences in the breadth of their coverage. Rogers's and Kelly's theories of personality are comprehensive, attempting to account for the full range of human behaviors. In contrast, Maslow's theory is narrower, as are most of the social cognitive theories. And contemporary cognitive theorists often focus on still narrower topics. Second, many specific concepts and terms are unique to individual theories. (The cognitive approach suffers from some of the same language problems as the Dispositional Strategy; that is, a rapid proliferation of research has been accompanied by an expanding vocabulary of terms, which are often partially or entirely redundant and overlapping. This problem is, in good part, due to the newness of the field, and some researchers are now attempting to equate terms and offer suggestions for a common language for research.)

Despite these differences, all representational personality theories share broad, underlying theoretical assumptions about the nature of personality. In turn, these common assumptions have important implications for how personality is to be studied.

Focus on Higher Functions

Representational personality theories deal with "higher" (cognitive or mental) functions. Although representational theories acknowledge the importance of basic biological needs, they are not the focus of attention. Rather, the theorizing concentrates on the nature of human personality after one's basic needs have been satisfied. Specifically, Rogers and Maslow were concerned with **self-actualization** (striving to reach one's full potential). Kelly and the social cognitive theorists focus on how people *interpret* their experiences and *predict* future outcomes. They are also interested in such practical day-to-day matters as goal setting, planning, and self-control.

Representational theories assume that people are rational. Each person's actions represent "sensible" responses to the world as that person perceives it. This assumption implies that people are aware of many of their own psychological processes. Thus, the Representational Strategy emphasizes conscious experience. (In fact, people are admittedly not aware of all of the mental processes of interest to these researchers; thus, a number of creative methods for accessing "nonconscious" material via related conscious material or resulting behavior have been devised.)

The Active Nature of Human Beings

All personality theories deal with the basic issue of motivation: what "moves" people to act. Motivation involves factors that compel behavior—what gets us "moving"—as well as factors that determine the direction, intensity, and persistence of behavior (Evans, 1989).

Within this strategy, most efforts to evaluate motivation deal exclusively with factors that account for the *direction* of movement—that is, what interpretations people arrive at and how these interpretations direct behavior. (This is a good example of the focus on "higher" human functions.) To explain the direction that an individual's behavior takes, each of the broad theories advances a general principle. Rogers posited that behavior is directed by each person's unique self-actualizing tendency. Maslow proposed that behavior is determined by a person's unique hierarchy of needs. Kelly theorized that people act to maximize their ability to accurately anticipate events in their lives—that is, to develop an understanding of their worlds. Modern cognitive psychologists often implicitly adopt this latter assumption, however; the idea of goals and agendas has become a central topic for cognitive psychologists today. These researchers view goals and motivation as reflecting a variety of cognitive processes, with potential to account for a wide range of observed differences between people. This area is addressed further in Chapter 17.

Being active involves more than just being in motion. People are assumed to be in a more or less constantly evolving state. As Rogers (1961) put it: "Life, at its best, is a flowing, changing process in which nothing is fixed" (p. 27). Accordingly, representational theories give little attention to stable, enduring personality characteristics (the focus of the Dispositional Strategy). Stability, when present, is explained by the *consistency of underlying mental representations* of the important elements of the immediate context (psychological or physical).

Salience of Present and Future

The Representational Strategy is most concerned with the present (e.g., Bohart, 1991a). Moreover, the focus is often on the time frame that is considered most salient for people—namely, the momentary experience, or the **here-and-now.** In contrast to the present, which may mean this hour or day or even the current year, here-and-now refers to what is at this very moment. For example, your here-and-now is reading these words (and perhaps some other concurrent experiences—the chair you sit on, ambient noise, and room temperature).

Although it is acknowledged that past experiences influence present behavior, the past is important only in terms of how it affects here-and-now perceptions. For example, there is ordinarily little attention paid to a person's experiences in early childhood (the central focus of the Psychoanalytic Strategy).

The future, too, has a role in representational theories because each person is considered to be constantly changing and evolving. Further, Rogers's and Maslow's theories are concerned with individuals who are striving to fulfill their potentials, which is a future-oriented process. Kelly's theory specifically deals with people *anticipating* future events. Other cognitive theories deal with how goals are set and then pursued, achieved, or abandoned.

"Idiothetic" Approach

Appreciation of individuality is central to the Representational Strategy. Phenomenological theories use a fundamentally **idiographic** approach to studying personality. They focus on the uniqueness of each person and minimize comparisons across people. Rogers and Maslow held that all behavior is governed by a self-actualizing tendency, although the specific nature of the tendency is idiosyncratic to the individual. Kelly and most later cognitivists believe that all human behavior is determined by the subjective *worldview* of each individual.

The theories of the cognitive approach are less idiographic, however, than those of the phenomenological approach. These theories are often focused on identifying cognitive mechanisms and styles that influence people generally. Cognitive research has typically used a nomothetic between-groups approach. However, like the theories and theorists of the phenomenological approach, cognitive and social cognitive theorists recognize the importance of individual differences in cognitive styles and processes on behavior.

In response to their somewhat conflicting interests and concerns, researchers of the Representational Strategy have begun to combine and blend the idiographic and nomothetic approaches. This blended approach, which has come to be termed **idiothetic** to reflect the elements of each approach, has been endorsed and adopted by many contemporary researchers (Austin & Vancouver, 1996; Klinger, 1995; Pervin, 1983; Roberson, 1989; Shoda, Mischel & Wright, 1994; Winell, 1987). The idiothetic approach holds great promise for the future of personality research. By seeking out patterns of behavior in individuals, which may then be related to groups of people characterized by some common characteristics, this approach allows researchers to maintain an individual-centered orientation while still investigating and comparing multiple subjects in an effort to identify common mechanisms. The combined approach "allows potentially generalizable findings of broad relevance while still retaining an essentially idiographic, person-centered focus" (Shoda, Mischel, & Wright, 1994).

Existential Psychology, Humanism, and the Representational Strategy

The Representational Strategy encompasses what is termed *existential psychology,* as well as humanism (e.g., DeCarvalho, 1990a, 1990b, 1991a). Rollo May (1967) described **existential psychology** as

> an attitude, an approach to human beings, rather than a special school or group . . . it is not a system of therapy but an attitude toward therapy, not a set of new techniques but a concern with the understanding of the structure of the human being and his experience. (p. 245)

Rollo May was one of the founders of the existential movement in psychology.
© Peter Vandermark/Stock, Boston

This existential attitude requires an intimate understanding of a person's experiences. Thus, psychologists should try to *know* persons rather than merely *know about* them. Rogers (1965, 1973) was especially adamant on this point in his approach to both therapy and research. His approach to the person served as the foundation for the movement termed **humanism,** or **humanistic psychology.** The humanistic approach is characterized by an optimistic view of human nature and emphasis on the individual's intrinsic tendency to develop in positive and self-enhancing ways. Like the existential approach, the humanistic approach requires achieving a thorough understanding of individuals and their own personal perspective on themselves and their life circumstances.

Three themes in existential and humanistic psychology are central to the phenomenological approach: free will, choice, and "being there." We will repeatedly see the related themes of free will, choice, and decision making in representational personality theories. Both Rogers and Maslow assumed that individuals are capable of directing their own lives. Rogers's formula for personality change involves establishing conditions conducive to self-growth. Kelly's personality theory is based on the assumption that people can choose to view events in their lives in an almost limitless variety of ways. Modern cognitive therapies are designed to change clients' perceptions of issues that are important to them personally, rather than issues judged important by some artificial, external standard.

Consistent with the existential notions of free will and choice, representationalists assume that people can freely choose how they will behave. People are not viewed as victims of their past, as in the Psychoanalytic Strategy; of enduring personality characteristics, as in the Dispositional Strategy; or of the environment, as in the Environmental Strategy. Thus, the Representational Strategy is *non*deterministic.

The third common theme in existential and phenomenological psychology is the emphasis on the present, and particularly momentary experiences. Existentialists focus on *Dasein* (German for "being there"), which emphasizes immediate experience. Cognitive theorists and therapists also focus on the here-and-now.

REPRESENTATIONAL PERSONALITY ASSESSMENT

A basic dilemma for the Representational Strategy arises in personality assessment. How can person A know how person B is perceiving the world when all that person A can actually know is what person B describes? Ignoring issues of trust and accuracy, how can one be sure that the experience another person describes is even remotely like the one that he or she has in mind? Think of all the possible meanings of a simple statement such as "I'm tired," "I'm scared," or "I love you."

Representational personality assessment involves gaining knowledge of private mental events. Recall that this is also the essential task of psychoanalytic personality assessment. In both strategies, behavior is neither the basic unit of personality nor the exclusive means of understanding personality.

Consider the student who does not speak up in class. What can be inferred from this behavior? Is it that the student has not done the assigned reading and is not prepared to participate? Is the student thoroughly familiar with the reading but afraid of being considered a show-off? The student's behavior will not answer these questions because the same overt behavior can result from vastly different motivations.

Within broad limits, behavior can yield information about an individual's personality, but for more specific information one must find the meaning of the behavior *for that person*. Representational personality assessment is aimed at discovering personal meaning. The meaning and interpretation of experiences constitute personality and direct behavior.

Often people confuse their own view of events with someone else's described experiences. Consider the case of Jim, a college sophomore, who told his parents that he wanted to drop out of school because he was not learning anything. Jim's father told him, "I understand exactly how you feel. When I was in college there were times that I felt tired and depressed and wanted to quit." Jim's mother endorsed similar sentiments of loneliness, boredom, and tediousness. What Jim's parents "understood" was how they had felt in a superficially similar situation. They did *not* actually know how their son was feeling. While they described feelings of fatigue and boredom, Jim might actually be feeling frustrated and understimulated by his very basic course material. Or Jim may have been trying to convey his inability to grasp complex concepts and his resulting poor academic performance and repeated failures.

Representational psychologists seek understanding of what the experience means for the person, not what the experience means for the assessor or for people in general. Representational personality assessment requires **empathy**—understanding a person's experiences in terms of what they mean for that particular person. To empathize with another, one must abandon one's connotations of the words and phrases of the other, one's own interpretation of the experiences, and one's preconceived notions about such experiences. Instead, one attempts to grasp the idiosyncratic personal meaning of the other's verbal descriptions of the experience. (We have more to say about empathy in Chapter 18.)

Representational assessment focuses on the present, usually the here-and-now. An individual's past experiences are important only insofar as they clarify present perceptions. For example, in a Rogerian interview, if a person talked about past experiences, the interviewer would not consider them significant unless they specifically related to present feelings and experiences.

Representational personality assessment is relatively straightforward, which contrasts with the largely inferential tack of the Psychoanalytic Strategy. Many representational personality assessment techniques involve simple self-report measures. Descriptions of subjective experiences are accepted more or less at face value (Jankowicz, 1987). They are not considered signs or indications of some inferred psychological state, such as an intrapsychic conflict, or used to indicate some underlying personality disposition.

Conscious experiences are often taken as direct evidence of important personality functions. They are not viewed as signs of underlying unconscious processes. A basic assumption of the Representational Strategy is that people are usually aware of or have direct access to their own subjective experiences.

In fact, this awareness is presumed to guide most behavior. Although not denying the existence of experiences outside awareness, these psychologists generally believe that unconscious processes have little influence on most "normal" behavior. (Unconscious processes *are* assumed to play a role in abnormal behavior, and behavior is sometimes used to assess the operation of nonconscious mental operations by cognitive researchers.)

REPRESENTATIONAL PERSONALITY RESEARCH

Much of the early research in the Representational Strategy used correlational and case study methods. These two methods are optimal for studying people as they are. Rogers's perspective on research is consistent with the existential approach, which is to gain knowledge *of* people rather than *from* them. Rogers (1973) advocated a research approach that did not view the person as an object (of study) and did not "push the individual into some contrived situation to investigate some hypothesis we have imposed" (p. 380). Instead, he suggested that psychologists study personality by learning from people and by being open to "hearing" what they are "saying." (Walter Mischel actually *listened* to what elementary school children had to say about the process of *planning* and thus learned a great deal about the cognitive processes and strategies children spontaneously employ; see Chapter 17.)

Representational research is often idiographic, using the case study method. A prime example is Maslow's large-scale investigation of self-actualizing people. The data were detailed, qualitative descriptions of subjective, intensely personal experiences. They yielded rich, in-depth portraits of single personalities. By studying subjects with a particular characteristic, such as self-actualization, the researcher can combine data to produce a composite of that personality characteristic. What begins as a series of idiographic investigations can also yield nomothetic information applicable to many people. This goal is now being realized by researchers who employ the idiothetic approach.

Some research on mental representations has been related to and conducted in conjunction with psychotherapy, much like psychoanalytic research. As clinical psychologists, Rogers and Kelly developed their theories and approaches to personality while actively practicing psychotherapy. Representational approaches also emphasize application of theory to other practical human problems. For example, Rogers's and Kelly's theories have been applied to a vast array of human endeavors besides psychotherapy, including education, politics, health, and environmental planning. Cognitive theories are also beginning to find application in wide-ranging settings.

REPRESENTATIONAL PERSONALITY CHANGE

Because personality is considered a product of perceptions and subjective evaluations, representational personality change involves modifying these private experiences. Among other things, it means helping people become more aware of their subjective experiences and the influence of these experiences on their behaviors.

Self-determination is a major theme of representational personality-change procedures. It is assumed that people can change their own personalities. Furthermore, clients (as the "patients" of these therapists are called) know themselves and their own subjective experiences far better than anyone else can know them. Therefore, the client, rather than the therapist, must assume ultimate responsibility for the change process.

The therapist's major role is to facilitate the client's change, which requires the therapist to understand the client's experiences from the client's perspective (e.g., Chambers, 1985). The therapist does not judge the client and his or her problems. Nonevaluative support is assumed to facilitate clients' abilities to develop new perspectives and bring about constructive changes in their lives. (Contemporary cognitive therapists are somewhat more active and offer more explicit guidance and interpretations or "reconstructions" to clients.) The humanistic approach to therapy emphasizes empathic understanding of clients and respect for them and their feelings and experiences. This attitude has influenced the practice of psychotherapy *across* strategies and approaches.

In contrast to psychoanalysis, representational personality change devotes little attention to the past. Instead, it is primarily present-oriented. Typically, the focus of attention is the here-and-now—in other words, what is going on in the therapy session—including all of a client's thoughts and feelings during the therapy hour, as well as the interactions between the client and the therapist.

SUMMARY

1. The core premise of the Representational Strategy is that personality reflects how people perceive and mentally represent their environments and experiences.
2. The Representational Strategy also assumes that our perceptions and representations are actively constructed; they come to exist through an active process of piecing together our experiences into a coherent whole.
3. Each person's representational system is idiosyncratic, based on the internal frame of reference or subjective world in which that person lives.
4. Modern philosophers and contemporary scientists have come to respect the idea that all perception—and thus all knowledge—is subjective. In an important sense, perceived reality is a mentally constructed illusion.
5. The belief that one has control over the environment can influence our behavior, even when that sense of control is an illusion.
6. To understand another person, we must get into that person's internal frame of reference; this is called having phenomenological knowledge of the person.
7. Phenomenological approaches arose in part from the humanistic approach, sometimes called the "third force" (after psychoanalysis and behaviorism) in psychology.
8. Kelly's personal construct approach deals with how people interpret and anticipate events in their lives and thus develop unique personalities.

9. The social cognitive approach focuses on the actual mental (cognitive) representations that give rise to our perceptions, experiences, and behavior.
10. Until the 1960s, "cognitive" was considered a dirty word by many academic psychologists. Nonetheless, two important books taking a cognitive approach were published in the 1950s: George Kelly's *The Psychology of Personal Constructs* and Leon Festinger's *A Theory of Cognitive Dissonance.*
11. The theories of Kelly and Rogers are quite broad, whereas the theory of Abraham Maslow and contemporary social cognitive theories have a much narrower focus.
12. Representational personality psychology deals with "higher" mental functions such as self-actualization, goal setting, and self-control.
13. Representational theorists view people as inherently active and as constantly evolving, but they also assume that people seek stability in the form of consistency in their underlying mental representations.
14. The past is paid relatively little attention by representational personality psychologists; instead, they focus on the present and the future.
15. Whereas the phenomenological approach is idiographic, the social cognitive approach may be said to be idiothetic, combining the idiographic and nomothetic approaches.
16. The Representational Strategy is concerned with understanding the nature of the human experience, thus reflecting aspects of the philosophies of existentialism and humanism. Consistent with the ideology of humanism, this strategy tends to take an optimistic view of human nature and views people as having free will and choice. Thus, the strategy takes a nondeterministic stance.
17. Representational personality assessment is concerned with the meaning particular experiences have for particular persons and requires an empathic attitude. Assessment is direct and takes the person's conscious experiences at face value.
18. Representational research is idiothetic and frequently concerned with practical implications or applications.
19. Representational personality change attempts to modify a person's interpretations and private experiences. Consistent with the ideology of humanism, representational therapists attempt to facilitate self-determination; they do not manipulate, control, or dictate appropriate behaviors.

CHAPTER SIXTEEN

The Phenomenological Approach

he phenomenological approach is characterized by an emphasis on the idiosyncratic perspective of the individual. To understand a person, phenomenological theorists believe that you must first understand how that person construes his or her experiences. Phenomenological theories are *holistic:* They view and explain specific acts in terms of an individual's entire personality, the full range of a person's mental processes and interpretations. The holistic view implies that there is **congruence** in personality—the parts fit together in an organized whole. The idea of personality congruence (absence of stark inconsistencies or contradictions) pervades the theories of the phenomenologists. For instance, Rogers stressed the importance of agreement between how people see themselves and how they hope to be seen by others. He is often credited with beginning the humanistic movement in psychology. We begin our discussion of the phenomenological approach with the work of this central theorist.

CARL ROGERS'S THEORY

When Rogers began his work in 1927, what existed of personality psychology was essentially psychoanalytic. Rogers proposed the first major theory to serve as an alternative to Freud's. In contrast to the deterministic and pessimistic perspective of psychoanalysis, Rogers's theory offered an optimistic outlook on humans' ability to develop and enhance themselves in positive and healthy ways.

Although many differences between the theories of Rogers and Freud exist, some interesting parallels can also be drawn. Like Freud, Rogers began as a psychotherapist. Rogers used his experiences in therapy both as a source of ideas about personality and as a setting for testing, refining, and revising them. Rogers developed a new form of personality change that became a significant alternative to psychoanalytic psychotherapy. Rogers's theory was comprehensive and innovative, as was Freud's. Finally, Rogers's ideas, like Freud's, have been widely adopted and applied to diverse human problems, including interpersonal relations, education, and the development and survival of cultures.

NORMAL PERSONALITY DEVELOPMENT AND FUNCTIONING

Rogers's personality theory is based on two major assumptions: (1) Behavior is guided by each person's unique actualizing tendency, and (2) all humans have a need for positive regard. We will first examine these concepts in terms of normal personality development and functioning.

The Actualizing Tendency

Rogers believed that personality is governed by an inborn **actualizing tendency:** "the inherent tendency of the organism to develop all its capacities in ways which serve to maintain or enhance the organism" (Rogers, 1959, p. 196). The actualizing tendency affects both biological and psychological functions. It maintains an individual by meeting fundamental biological needs (e.g., for oxygen and food); it also governs physical maturation and regeneration. Psychologically, the actualizing tendency guides people toward increased autonomy and self-sufficiency, expands their experiences, and fosters personal growth. Thus, the actualizing tendency guides us toward

Carl Rogers (1902–1987) believed that people have unique, innate self-actualizing tendencies that guide their behaviors in positive directions.
Courtesy of Carl Rogers

positive, constructive, and adaptive behavior rather than toward destructive or maladaptive behavior (e.g., Bozarth & Brodley, 1991). In Rogers's (1980) words,

> the organism does not tend toward developing its capacity for nausea, . . . for self-destruction, nor to bear pain. Only under unusual or perverse circumstances do these potentialities become actualized. It is clear that *the actualizing tendency is selective and directional—a constructive tendency* [italics added]. (p. 121)

How does the actualizing tendency lead people to act in positive ways? According to Rogers, people evaluate each experience they have in terms of how well it maintains or enhances them, a process he called the **organismic valuing process.** *Experiences* include all events and stimuli that the person can be aware of (Rogers, 1959). Experiences perceived as maintaining or enhancing the individual are evaluated positively; they result in feelings of satisfaction, and people actively seek them. In contrast, experiences perceived as opposing maintenance or enhancement are evaluated negatively; they result in dissatisfaction, and people actively avoid them.

The actualizing tendency can be thought of as having two aspects. One aspect consists of shared (mostly biological) tendencies, inclinations that protect and maintain us physically. The other aspect involves each individual's unique (psychological) tendencies toward increased autonomy, self-sufficiency, and personal growth (cf. DeCarvalho, 1990a). The unique (psychological) aspect is what is meant by self-actualization because it involves maintenance and enhancement of *the self,* a cognitive concept central to Rogers's theory, to which we will return later (cf. Ford, 1991b).

Positive Regard: A Basic Need

The second major assumption in Rogers's theory is that all people have a need for positive regard. **Positive regard** can be defined simply as positive social feedback. It can take the form of acceptance, respect, sympathy, warmth, and love. Rogers believed that positive regard is essential for the healthy development of the self (e.g., Raskin, Novacek, & Hogan, 1991) and for successful interpersonal relations (e.g., Lutfiyya, 1991). For example, children raised by parents with significant psychological problems, such as alcoholism, are likely to receive less positive regard from their parents than other children do (Jones & Houts, 1992). This inadequate positive regard may result in problems with assertive behavior and intimacy-trust issues later in life (Black, Bucky, & Wilder-Padilla, 1986).

For infants and young children, positive regard comes exclusively from external sources—parents, older children, and other adults. As children develop more autonomy and a sense of self, they are able to provide their own (internal) positive regard. This **positive self-regard** is, in large part, modeled after the positive regard previously received from others (see Figure 16.1).

Most often, one receives and gives positive regard for specific behaviors, which is called **conditional positive regard.** It is contingent on a person's behavior. You receive conditional positive regard whenever you are praised for *doing something.*

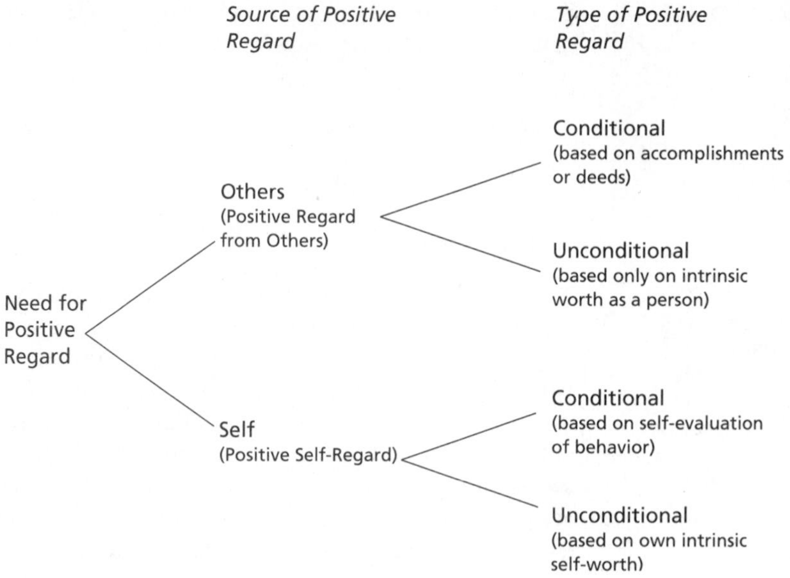

Figure 16.1
The need for positive regard can be met by others or by oneself. Both sources of positive regard can be conditional or unconditional.

Unconditional Positive Regard

Positive regard need not be conditional. **Unconditional positive regard** is provided independent of the behavior of a person. The person is valued simply for being. Unconditional positive regard is believed to provide the optimal conditions for being guided by one's own intrinsic actualizing tendency.

One retrospective study in Sweden found that men and women's self-esteem in adulthood was positively related to perceived unconditional positive regard as children, especially from their fathers (Forsman, 1989). In contrast, conditional positive regard, which involves value judgments, is believed to interfere with the innate actualizing tendency.

Unconditional positive regard can come from either internal or external sources. Unconditional positive self-regard is considered an ideal because people need rely on only themselves for overall feelings of worth and esteem.

The prototype of unconditional positive regard is a parent's love for a child. Parents accept their own child "because it is . . . their child, not because the child has fulfilled any specific condition, or lived up to any specific expectation." Offering unconditional positive regard requires viewing another's actions from the other person's perspective. The parent who disapproves of a child's misbehavior can still give the child positive regard. In effect, the parent is saying, "I do not approve of what you did, but I still approve of you."

How prevalent is unconditional positive regard? In your own life, how often are you regarded positively by others regardless of how you behave? How often do you give other people unconditional positive regard? Unconditional positive regard is the exception rather than the rule (e.g., Culp, Culp, Osofsky, & Osofsky, 1991). It may be that we receive unconditional positive regard only from our parents and ourselves. Of course, most parents rarely, if ever, provide this to their children (e.g., Gaylin, 1987), and few people provide it for themselves. Of equal concern to us then (given the continuing need for positive regard) is conditional positive regard.

Conditions of Worth

In our everyday lives, the conditional positive regard we receive is based on external standards and expectations for behavior. This contrasts—and often competes directly with—the behaviors guided by the individual's unique (internal) actualizing tendency. Because of this conflict and competition, conditional positive regard is less likely to maintain and enhance the individual than unconditional positive regard. Nonetheless, our need for positive regard is great, and we will take it in any form available. (Think about how important it is for you to feel that others consider you worthy.)

We are also influenced by the opposite of conditional positive regard: criticism, scorn, and punishment. These evaluations might be called "conditional negative regard" (although Rogers never used this term). We tend to avoid acting in ways that result in "negative regard," just as we actively pursue behaviors that result in positive regard. (Note the obvious parallel with behavioral constructs of reinforcement and punishment here.) The external value placed on a person's specific behaviors is called **conditions of worth.** Conditions of worth are evidenced by conditional positive and negative regard.

Conditions of worth result in a person feeling prized in some respects and not in others (Rogers, 1959). Conditions of worth often substitute for and compete with the organismic valuing process. Thus, conditions of worth, which are based on external standards, often preclude "optimal" functioning, which in this theory is defined by pursuit of self-enhancement via actualization.

Self-Determination versus External Control

Deci (1975) and colleagues have focused on a construct that they term **self-determination,** which is closely related to the conditions of worth of Rogers's original theory. Deci contends that self-determination of activities and pursuits enhances interest and dedication to the activities; that is, an individual who chooses to pursue an activity for its intrinsic value is likely to pursue it more vigorously, intently, and diligently than one who feels somehow compelled to perform the same activity. Deci and Ryan (1980, 1987, 1991, 1995) refer to activities engaged in because of external demands as "controlled." It is the external origin of the pressure that parallels the conditions of worth in Rogers's scheme. The actualizing tendency, in contrast, motivates from within and is based on intrinsic preferences and desires.

A good deal of empirical support has been gathered to support the idea that rewards and incentives may actually decrease motivation (Deci & Rogers, 1980). In fact, though, it is not simply the presence of an incentive that undermines motivation. Exactly how the incentive is construed seems to be the determining factor. An incentive might be offered and construed by the person as reflecting appreciation for their particular talents or abilities. In this case, the effect of the incentive may well be to increase motivation (Koestner,

Zuckerman, & Koestner, 1987). If, however, the incentive is construed as the source of motivation (in other words, the task is now being pursued for the sake of obtaining the reward), motivation is often diminished (Flink, Boggiano & Barrett, 1990; Grolnick & Ryan, 1989). Internally motivated tasks appear to produce the greatest motivation and, ultimately, maximum personal satisfaction. However, determining exactly what motivates particular activities or pursuits is not a simple matter. Idiosyncratic interpretations and intrinsic values may combine differently for different people.

THE SELF-CONCEPT

The self is an important concept, and focus on the self pervades the entire Representational Strategy. Rogers wrote a great deal about the self and self-concept. The self or self-concept (the terms are often used synonymously) is a theoretical construct that refers to the way people see themselves (Rogers, 1959). The perceptions that comprise the **self** (1) are *organized* in a coherent, unified fashion; (2) are *compatible* (free of inconsistencies and contradictions); and (3) are *integrated*, making up a whole rather than merely being a set of unrelated aspects (e.g., Jensen, Huber, Cundick, & Carlson, 1991).

Because the self is made up of many interrelated aspects of self-knowledge, it would be more accurate to refer to a person's selves or self-concepts, although the singular is more common (e.g., Neisser, 1988, 1991). Among the dimensions of the self that have been suggested are self-esteem, self-regard, moral self-concept, self-confidence, self-reliance, self-control, selfishness, self-disclosure, self-as-agent, self-critical, self-identity, and self-reflection (Jensen et al., 1991).

Rogers divided the self into two basic aspects: The **actual self** (sometimes called the *real self*) refers to the way people actually see themselves. The **ideal self** refers to how people would like to see themselves.

Life Satisfaction and the Self-Concept

Not surprisingly, people with psychological problems see themselves (actual self) differently than the way they would like to see themselves (ideal self), especially in terms of satisfaction with life or happiness (cf. Csikszentmihalyi, 1990). In Western societies, life satisfaction is commonly evaluated in terms of the degree to which one achieves personal goals and ideals. (Western societies are characterized by an individualistic philosophy not typical of many Eastern cultures.) Traditionally, the similarity between a person's actual self-concept and ideal self-concept has been used as an index of life satisfaction. (Methods of assessing these different aspects of self-concept are addressed in Chapter 18, which examines applications and limitations of the Representational Strategy.) The more similar the actual and ideal selves, the more satisfied people feel about themselves.

Another measure of personal satisfaction has been proposed. Ogilvie (1987, 1988) suggested looking at the discrepancy between one's actual self-concept—how one sees oneself—and one's *undesirable self-concept*—the personality characteristics and behaviors that one considers undesirable in oneself (see also Paprota, 1988). The greater the difference between the actual and undesirable self-concepts, the more satisfied people feel about themselves.

In a study with college students, Ogilvie (1987) found that life satisfaction can be predicted better by the discrepancy between actual and undesired self-concepts than by the similarity between actual and ideal self-concepts. Ogilvie suggested that this finding may indicate that "the implicit standard individuals use to assess their well-being is how close (or how distant) they are from subjectively being like their most negative images of themselves" (p. 383). The reason that life satisfaction may not be predicted as well from comparing actual and ideal self-concepts (as was thought) may become apparent by using a reconceptualized concept of actual self. We address this topic further in Chapter 17.

IMPEDIMENTS TO SELF-ACTUALIZATION

Psychological adjustment depends on the extent to which the actualizing tendency, rather than conditions of worth, govern a person's behavior. Psychological disorders develop when conditions of worth dominate and direct behavior. Conflict and competition between these two standards for behavior interfere with the optimal development and functioning of the self.

Threat

In the course of personality development, conflict arises because experiences are evaluated by two divergent sets of rules. One set of rules is based on the organismic valuing process. The other set comes from conditions of worth now embraced by the individual as an aspect of the self-concept.

Rogers (1959) defined **threat** as the perception—conscious or unconscious—of incongruity within the self-concept. The conflict is threatening because the individual's personality may become fragmented and disorganized if the conflict is not adequately resolved.

Threat is experienced as a vague uneasiness or tension—in other words, as *anxiety*. Anxiety serves as a warning that the unified self-concept is imperiled. The anxiety, in turn, leads to defensive processes that reduce the incongruity within one's self.

Defensive Processes

Defensive processes maintain consistency within one's self-concept. Rogers (1959) divided defensive processes into two categories: perceptual distortion and denial. Through **perceptual distortion,** we modify threatening experiences to make them compatible with our self-concepts. For example, 15-year-old Grace considered herself popular, but she complained that no one invited her to do things on weekends. Grace explained this apparent inconsistency by telling herself that her peers do not invite her out because they think she must be busy on weekends (because she is so popular). This explanation became Grace's perception of the situation—that is, her reality. From the representational perspective, an experience is only the person's perception of it. Perceptual distortion alters the experience as it is received.

Denial prevents awareness of the existence of experiences that are incongruent with our self-concepts. In one way or another, the self is "convinced" that the experience does not exist. Grace could deny her threatening experiences—not being invited to join activities with her friends—by simply believing that she *is* too busy to join them and not "noticing" the lack of invitations she receives.

Table 16.1 Examples of defensive processes resulting from perceptual distortion and denial and their parallel with ego defense mechanisms (as noted in parentheses)

Situation: A wealthy man who spends 12 to 14 hours every day working at his job views himself as being a devoted husband and father.

Perceptual Distortion

"I have to work so hard to provide for my family's needs." *(Rationalization)*

"I am always doing things with my family." *(Reaction formation)*

Perceptual Distortion and Denial

"I spend so much time with my family that I am neglecting my work." *(Reaction formation)*

"I think it is horrible that some men work so hard that they have no time for their families." *(Projection)*

Denial

"I spend as much time with my family as I do at work." (*Denial*)

The man is totally unaware of how little time he spends with his family. *(Repression)*

Examples of the defensive processes that result from perceptual distortion and denial, singly and in combination, are presented in Table 16.1, which also indicates parallel psychoanalytic ego defense mechanisms. The two theoretical perspectives posit quite different sources of threat and anxiety: sexual and aggressive impulses in psychoanalysis versus experiences that are incompatible with one's self-concept in Rogers's theory. Still, the basic means of defense appear similar (cf. Zhurbin, 1991). Recent research suggests that these processes do indeed operate and are adaptive for most people (see also Chapter 17).

Breakdown and Disorganization

Even the most psychologically well-adjusted individuals are occasionally threatened by experiences that are inconsistent with their self-concepts. When this happens, their defensive processes often protect them from becoming aware of the inconsistency. However, when the inconsistency between self and experience becomes too great, defenses may be inadequate to shield them from awareness. The person becomes consciously aware of the threatening experience, and the self-concept may become fragmented and disorganized.

The behaviors of those whose self-concept is so shattered often seem strange to others because they are "not like themselves." However, the seemingly out-of-character behaviors may actually be completely congruent with elements of the individual that they were simply unaware of. The behaviors are odd only insofar as they are incongruent with how the person was previously seen by others.

Personality disorganization can occur because the person, behaving in "uncharacteristic" ways, feels that he or she is not understood. There is no consensual validation (affirmation from other people) for the person's view of the world. Rogers (1980) explains that when a person tries

> to share something that is very personal with another individual and it is not received and not understood, this is a very deflating and a very lonely experience. I have come to believe that such an experience makes some individuals psychotic. It causes them to give up hoping that anyone can understand them. Once they have lost that hope, then their own inner world, which becomes more and more bizarre, is the only place where they can live. They can no longer live in any shared human experience. (p. 14)

Reintegration

We all know people whom we would describe as "uptight" or "always on the defensive." Such colloquial descriptions usually refer to individuals who seem to perpetually distort or deny their experiences. Their behaviors illustrate the potentially disastrous consequences of excessive reliance on defensive processes. For example, Joan questions the meaning and sincerity of even the most innocent comments others make. She is quick to respond as if the comments were hostile or critical. From her internal frame of reference, innocent remarks are received as negative because she perceives them in a distorted form.

People who inaccurately perceive experiences cannot function optimally. They are closed to (defended against) many experiences because they must avoid potentially threatening information and insights. Consider the case of a college senior, Jeff, whose self-concept included only the perception of

Edvard Munch's "The Scream" (1895) depicts the utter despair that occurs when, according to Rogers, total personality disorganization occurs.
Art Resource/Archive Foto Marburg

himself as successful. He was threatened by any situation in which he might fail. Jeff distorted his view of such situations from ones that could lead to failure to ones that were undesirable. He thereby successfully avoided potential failures. Rather than apply to graduate school, Jeff "decided" he did not want to continue his formal education. He "reasoned" that he might as well be making money while his friends in graduate school were still borrowing.

Discrepancies between one's self-concept and one's experiences can be reduced or eliminated through the process of reintegration. **Reintegration** restores consistency to the self-concept by reversing the process of defense. Reintegration requires the individual to become aware of previously distorted or denied experiences. For example, reintegration for Jeff could mean recognizing that he might, in fact, not be offered admission to graduate school. Jeff could make this possibility tolerable by accepting and integrating it into his self-concept. He might simply embrace the philosophy: "It is not necessary for me to succeed at everything I try." This reintegration would reduce the threat of potential failure in a variety of endeavors, thus freeing Jeff to enjoy broader experiences without discomfort or anxiety.

Rogers believed that we can face minor, inconsistent experiences and successfully restructure our self-concepts. He maintained, however, that reintegration on one's own is possible only when their consistency between the self and experience is minor and produces minimal threat. When the inconsistency is large, anxiety (threat) is greater; thus, reintegration is more difficult. These situations require a secure relationship with another person who provides acceptance in the form of unconditional positive regard.

THE PERSON-CENTERED APPROACH

Carl Rogers's career as a psychologist spanned more than half a century; he was still professionally active when he died suddenly at the age of 85 following surgery for a broken hip (Gendlin, 1988). In the last two decades of his life, Rogers broadened his interests and professional endeavors considerably. He became involved in issues ranging from international and race relations to group decision-making processes. Still, his basic views about personality remained unchanged (e.g., Bozarth, 1990; Kirschenbaum, 1991).

Rogers found that empathic understanding, unconditional positive regard, and genuineness were essential for effective psychotherapy. Moreover, he later came to realize that these factors are not restricted to the therapeutic relationship (e.g., Horton & Brown, 1990; Walsh, 1991). Rogers (1980) believed they

> apply whether we are speaking of the relationship between therapist and client, parent and child, leader and group, teacher and student, or administrator and staff. The conditions apply, in fact, in any situation in which the development of the person is a goal. (p. 115)

Rogers (1979) used the term **person-centered approach** when principles of his approach are extended beyond the boundaries of psychotherapy. A person-centered approach has been applied by Rogers and his followers to discover and create psychological climates that facilitate growth and enhancement in diverse human endeavors, including learning, medical treatment, research, and promoting interracial and intercultural harmony (e.g., Barnard, 1984; Bell & Schniedewind, 1989; DeCarvalho, 1991c; Hayashi, Kuno, Osawa, Shimizu, & Suetake, 1992; Mearns & McLeod, 1984; Patton, 1990; Rogers, 1980; 1983; Thomas, 1988; cf. Meuris, 1988).

MASLOW'S THEORY OF HUMAN MOTIVATION

Abraham Maslow was a leading spokesperson for the psychology of *health* and *strength*. He shared Carl Rogers's distinctly optimistic view of human nature and played a central role in the humanist movement. Maslow believed that people are inherently good and that they are fully capable of developing in healthy ways if circumstances allow them to express their innate potential.

Maslow's focus was narrower then Rogers's. His theory and research dealt primarily with the factors that motivate behavior. In particular, Maslow explored in depth the role of self-actualization motives, including how such motives are manifested at the highest levels of human functioning.

Although Maslow focused on "needs" similar in some ways to those theorists discussed in the psychoanalytic strategy, his emphasis and approach were distinct. Maslow does not speak of unconscious processes, nor does his theory propose internal conflict as a source of motivation. Maslow instead emphasizes the individual, idiosyncratic nature of human motivation and a systematic progression through a hierarchically organized system of needs.

Maslow's Hierarchical Theory of Motivation

For Maslow, the source of human motivation resides in needs that are common to all human beings. We will discuss the specific nature of these needs and examine how needs are prioritized and fulfilled in hierarchical order.

Abraham Maslow (1908–1970) emphasized the healthy side of personality, proposed a hierarchy of needs that motivate human behavior, and extensively studied the highest level of needs, self-actualization.
Courtesy of Abraham Maslow/photo by William Carter

The Need Hierarchy

Maslow postulated five levels of fundamental human needs. Listed from strongest to weakest, these needs are *basic physiological* (e.g., food), *safety* (e.g., shelter), *belongingness and love* (e.g., companionship), *esteem* (e.g., feeling competent), and *self-actualization* (e.g., creativity). The hierarchy is shown pictorially in Figure 16.2.

The lower the need in the hierarchy, the more basic it is in terms of survival. Lower needs exert a more pervasive influence on behavior. The higher the need in the hierarchy, the less basic it is and thus the weaker is its potential influence. Also, the higher the need in the hierarchy, the more distinctly human it is. Humans definitely share physiological and safety needs with all other animals, and humans may share belongingness and love needs with higher animal species, but it is assumed that humans alone have esteem and self-actualization needs.

Progression through the Need Hierarchy

As people satisfy their needs at one level in the hierarchy, they progress (up) to the next level (cf. Neher, 1991). Needs at a particular level do not have to be totally satisfied before people can begin to fulfill needs at a higher level. Usually, though, we are not concerned with meeting higher needs until our more basic needs are met.

At various times in our lives, some of our basic needs are inevitably frustrated. Then we must temporarily suspend pursuit of higher needs until

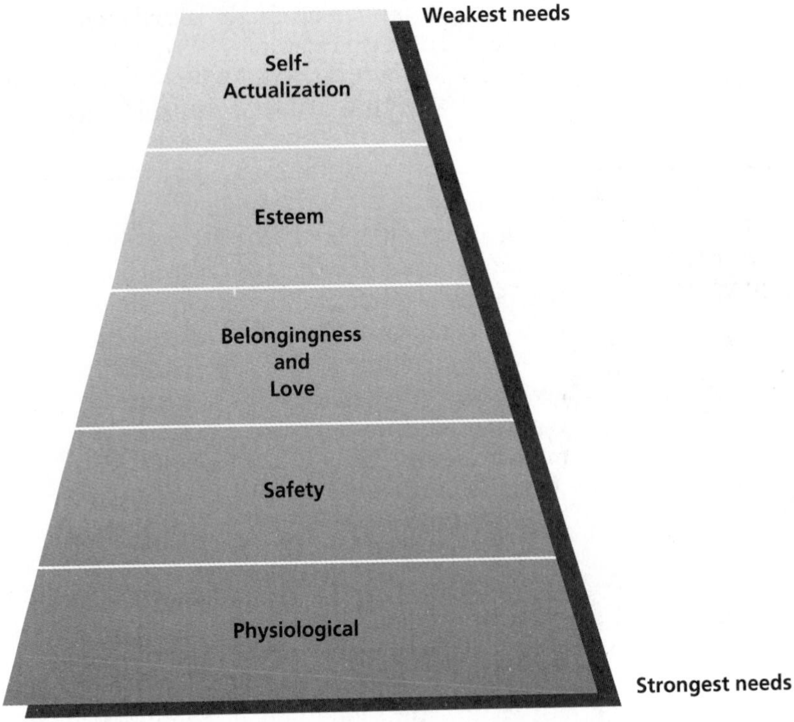

Weakest needs

Self-Actualization

Esteem

Belongingness and Love

Safety

Physiological

Strongest needs

Figure 16.2
Schematic representation of Maslow's hierarchy of needs. The higher the need in the hierarchy, the weaker the need in terms of motivating behavior.

the frustration is resolved. A common example is when we are too physically ill to perform normal daily functions, including work and social obligations. Until we recover, life revolves around physiological needs. Higher social and esteem needs and even some safety needs are, of necessity, pushed to a back burner.

Need Categories

The need hierarchy is comprised of different classes of needs. Each class consists of a variety of specific needs. We will address these needs by beginning at the bottom of the hierarchy and working up through it, as individuals are presumed to do.

Physiological Needs

Our most basic survival needs are **physiological,** including food, water, oxygen, elimination, and rest. Because physiological needs are directly related to survival, they are the most powerful human needs. When a basic need is not met, it consumes a person's full attention. Food becomes the central focus of the hungry person's life; it pervades actions, thoughts, and fantasies. (Maslow used the term **instinctoid** to label human biologically based needs because he believed that they drive human behavior less directly than that of lower species.)

Because you, and most of the people you know, probably do not experience deprivation of food or other physiological requirements on a regular basis, physiological needs usually exert only minimal influence over your behavior. Unfortunately, this is not the case for an alarming number of people in the world. These less fortunate others rarely move beyond the physiological level.

Safety Needs

Safety needs include physical well-being as well as psychological security. Safety needs include basic necessities such as shelter and warmth, as well as psychological security derived from stability, predictability, and structure in our daily routines. Most safety needs are met through social institutions, such as the legal system, police and fire departments, and insurance policies. In Western cultures, safety needs generally do not motivate much adult behavior.

In contrast, safety needs are dominant in children, especially infants who "will react in a total fashion and as if they were endangered, if they are disturbed or dropped suddenly, startled by loud noises [or] by loss of support in the mother's arms" (Maslow, 1970, p. 39). The urgency of safety needs becomes obvious when a child suffers even a minor injury.

> At such a moment of pain . . . for the child, the whole world suddenly changes from sunniness to darkness . . . and becomes a place in which anything at all might happen, in which previously stable things have suddenly become unstable. (Maslow, 1970, p. 40)

Abnormal adult behavior often parallels the child's quest for safety. The adult may see the world as hostile, threatening, and overwhelming. The person may behave "as if a great catastrophe were almost always impending . . . usually responding as if to an emergency" (Maslow, 1970, p. 42). For

Even minor incidents or injuries can totally threaten a child's sense of safety and security.
© Robert Pleban

example, people with obsessive compulsive disorder (OCD; see Chapter 8) "try frantically to order and stabilize the world so that no unmanageable, unexpected, or unfamiliar dangers will ever appear" (Maslow, 1970, p. 42).

Belongingness and Love Needs

When physiological and safety needs are substantially gratified, **belongingness needs,** those related to affiliation and affection, press to be met. Many people experience deep feelings of loneliness in the absence of a social network of friends and family. They long for affectionate relationships and a secure place in a primary group, like a nuclear family. When belongingness and love needs predominate, people are keenly aware of and upset by feelings of rejection and social isolation. Maslow and others (e.g., Fromm, 1963) believed that unsatisfied belongingness needs represent a significant problem in Western cultures, probably because of increased mobility and erosion of the traditional extended family. Note that some of these issues were also addressed in the Psychoanalytic and Environmental Strategies.

Esteem Needs

If needs in the first three levels of the hierarchy are adequately satisfied, the person becomes concerned with meeting esteem needs. Maslow (1970) distinguished two types of esteem needs.

Esteem from others includes desires for recognition, appreciation, attention, prestige, reputation, status, and fame. In short, individuals need to feel respected and valued by others for their accomplishments and contributions.

Self-esteem involves a personal desire for feelings of competency, mastery, achievement, confidence, and independence. When these needs are met, people feel worthwhile, confident, capable, useful, and necessary. If these needs are frustrated, they feel inferior, weak, and helpless. Enduring and healthy self-esteem is based on the earned respect of self and others—that is, recognition earned through a person's efforts, rather than on mere status or fame.

Self-Actualization Needs

Most people spend their lives trying to fulfill physiological, safety, belongingness, and esteem needs. They never satisfactorily accomplish these goals. A few individuals, however, substantially gratify their needs in the first four levels of the hierarchy and are motivated by self-actualization needs. Maslow (1970) defined **self-actualization** as "the desire to become more and more what one idiosyncratically is, to become everything that one is capable of becoming" (p. 46). Note that his definition is essentially the same as Rogers's.

Self-actualization is a process, rather than a state. Movement in the direction of self-actualization is neither automatic nor easy. Maslow believed that people are intimidated by and resist the self-knowledge necessary for pursuit of self-actualization. Insights of the sort that produce growth can be extremely threatening. Although conducive to self-actualization, these clear insights may alter or fragment one's existing self-concept. And self-actualization requires tremendous freedom of expression. A person must feel comfortable following unconventional paths. Few environments are conducive to this type of growth. Most modern cultures, through established social customs about the "proper" expression of feelings, inhibit the genuine spontaneity that tends to characterize self-actualizing people.

The specific nature of self-actualization needs varies considerably from person to person. By contrast, lower needs are relatively uniform. Self-actualization itself (recall that it is a *process* and *not* an end or product) does not require special talent or ability. Self-actualization may be manifested through any human endeavor.

Growth Motivation

Maslow placed self-actualization needs at the top of the hierarchy of human motives. But, in a sense, these needs do not fit within the hierarchy; they are fundamentally different from the needs of the preceding four levels. Maslow (1955) theorized that the first four levels of needs motivate people by *deficit,* whereas self-actualization needs are motivated by growth (cf. Neher, 1991).

Deficit motivation involves reducing tension or filling a void. We drink because we are thirsty. We seek company when we are lonely. Deficit motivation is goal-oriented, with the goal of reducing or eliminating the immediate need. Being hypervigilant while driving home on icy roads is motivated by safety needs. Once safely home, what we do is likely to be determined by other needs, so we might eat or engage in shared activities with family.

Growth motivation, in contrast, is process-oriented. Growth motives are self-actualization motives, which revolve around "intrinsic values" such as beauty, truth, and justice rather than externally (socially) determined values. Examples of typical growth motives are listed in Table 16.2.

Satisfying growth motives often results in increased tension, whereas satisfying deficit motives produces tension reduction. For example, satisfying the growth motive for beauty by hiking through the mountains may produce increased wonder and awe inspired by nature. In contrast, the deficit motive for safety can be satisfied by simply staying home.

When people are motivated by growth needs, even routine work takes on a "higher" meaning. It becomes broader and more universal and less narrow and self-centered. For example, "The law is apt to be more a way of seeking justice, truth, goodness . . . than financial security, admiration, status, prestige, [and] dominance" (Maslow, 1971, p. 310).

Table 16.2 Examples of growth motives identified by Maslow

Truth	Justice
Goodness	Order
Beauty	Simplicity
Unity, wholeness	Richness, comprehensiveness
Uniqueness	Playfulness
Perfection	Self-sufficiency
Completion	Meaningfulness

MASLOW'S STUDY OF SELF-ACTUALIZING PEOPLE

Theories of normal personality have usually been based primarily on observation of abnormal behaviors, which inevitably leads to a pessimistic and distorted image of human nature (e.g., DeCarvalho, 1991a). Relatively little theorizing and research have been based on optimal functioning of psychologically healthy people (cf. Seeman, 1984). Rogers (1963) did speculate that fully functioning people are guided by their organismic valuing processes; they are open to all experiences (cf. Mittelman, 1991); their self-concepts are whole and consistent with their experiences; they are free of threat and anxiety and therefore have no defenses. In short, the **fully functioning person** epitomizes psychological health and successful adjustment. Actually, the type of person Rogers described is an ideal. Such a person has yet to be found (cf. Coan, 1991; Landsman & Landsman, 1991; Miller, 1991). However, some individuals approximate the ideal of being fully functioning or self-actualizing. Maslow (in an ambitious undertaking) set out to identify and study these people.

Maslow selected his subjects by using both negative and positive criteria. The negative criterion was absence of psychological disorders. The positive criterion was evidence of some degree of self-actualization, which Maslow (1970) defined as "the full use and exploitation of talents, capacities, potentialities" (p. 150).

Using the case study method, Maslow gathered data from interviews with a relatively small, select group of subjects and from the written accounts of historical figures. He selected 60 subjects in all. Ethical considerations preclude naming his living subjects, but the historical figures are known and featured in Figure 16.3.

Characteristics of Self-Actualizing People

Through extensive analysis of the accumulated biographical material, Maslow created detailed descriptions of his subjects. With such qualitative data, the investigator's ability to accurately capture and summarize impressions is paramount. Fortunately, Maslow had a distinct talent for this task.

Maslow identified 15 key characteristics of self-actualizing people. These characteristics are listed in Table 16.3. Three important points should be kept in mind, though. First, self-actualization is a process, not an end state. No one is ever self-actualiz*ed* (i.e., finished with the process). Second, the characteristics often overlap. Third, none of Maslow's subjects exhibited every characteristic described. However, self-actualizing people do tend to display a number of them over time or concurrently.

For the most part, Maslow's study was significant as a serious attempt to study "healthy" and well-functioning people. It has been criticized (legitimately) for being tautological or circular. Maslow described self-actualizing people as displaying certain characteristics, identified people who appeared to display these characteristics, and then went on to describe the characteristics they displayed. However, his idea of peak experiences was a new contribution that continues to stimulate research today. We will therefore take a closer look at this idea.

Table 16.3 Maslow's 15 characteristics of self-actualizing people

Efficient perception of reality
Acceptance (of self, others, and nature)
Freshness of appreciation
Spontaneity, simplicity, and naturalness
"Direction" focused
Discrimination of means from ends and right from wrong
Detachment
Independence from culture and environment
Resistance to encultration
Creativeness
Deep desire to help humankind
Democratic philosophy
Deep interpersonal relations
Philosophical sense of humor
Peak experiences

"Freshness of appreciation" is one of the characteristics that Maslow found typified self-actualizing individuals. It involves repeatedly experiencing the wonder of the world *as if* it were being experienced for the first time.
G & J Images/Image Bank

Figure 16.3
Some of the historical figures whom Maslow identified as self-actualizing. **A:** Martin Buber (1878–1965), theologian; **B:** William James (1842–1910), psychologist; **C:** Harriet Tubman (1821–1913), abolitionist; **D:** Thomas Jefferson (1743–1826), political philosopher; **E:** George Washington Carver (1864–1943), agricultural chemist; **F:** Abraham Lincoln (1809–1865), politician; **G:** Albert Einstein (1879–1955), physicist; **H:** Jane Addams (1860–1935), peace activist; **I:** Sholom Aleichem (1858–1916), author; **J:** Ralph Waldo Emerson (1803–1882), writer; **K:** Albert Schweitzer (1875–1965), medical missionary; **L:** Benjamin Franklin (1706–1790), inventor.

All photos from The Bettmann Archive except **A:** UPI/ Bettmann Newsphotos, **C:** Library of Congress; **I:** The Sperus College of Judiaca, Chicago.

G
H
I
J
K
L

Peak Experiences

A **peak experience** refers to a brief, intense feeling that may include a sense of limitless horizons, of being simultaneously more powerful and more helpless than ever before, of ecstasy, appreciation, and awe. The conventional sense of time and space may disappear (this experience is related to "flow"; see Box 16.1). The peak experience often leaves people feeling that something very significant and precious has occurred (Thomas & Cooper, 1980). Peak experiences sometimes result in dramatic alterations of one's day-to-day existence thereafter.

Peak experiences may occur in conjunction with any activity or event. The experience itself consists of feelings that are more or less independent of the circumstances. Peak experiences are usually brief and fleeting, lasting a few seconds to a few minutes, but the effects of the peak experience can be enduring. These experiences transcend immediate, concrete circumstances. However, many people cite particular events as triggers for peak experiences, including appreciation of nature, music, quiet reflection, and prayer (Keutzer, 1978).

Maslow believed that peak experiences are all growth enhancing; they have some effect on the individual beyond the experience itself. However, for a peak experience to maximally enhance the person, it must be recognized as significant. Maslow (1966) conjectured that people may reject peak experiences or their significance to defend themselves "against being flooded by emotion, especially the emotions of humility, reverence, mystery, wonder, and awe" (p. 139).

Maslow believed peak experiences to be *spontaneous;* they cannot be created or anticipated. An individual may expect an event to be special, but that is no guarantee that it will result in a peak experience. However, recent research suggests some means of creating conditions conducive to peak experiences (see Box 16.1).

Maslow (1962) believed—and subsequent empirical studies seem to indicate—that most people probably have occasional peak experiences (Davis, Lockwood, & Wright, 1991; Greeley, 1974; Thomas & Cooper, 1980). Definitive assessment of peak experiences, as with dreams, depends on self-reports, and people may be reluctant to report peak experiences. A survey of 246 college students found that the major reasons given for not telling others about peak experiences are that (1) the peak experience is too intimate to share, (2) they fear that the experience will be devalued by others, and (3) they are unable to adequately describe the experience (Davis et al., 1991).

Having frequent peak experiences is a characteristic of self-actualizing people; Maslow (1963) found they tend to have more peak experiences than most people (see also Thomas & Cooper, 1980; cf. Daniels, 1988). In addition, self-actualizers' openness to and acceptance of all experiences make it more likely that they will (1) recognize peak experiences and (2) be able to use them to enhance personal growth. The concept of flow and optimal experiences as defined by Csikszentmihalyi (1990) parallels the peak experiences described by Maslow in many ways.

Box 16.1
GOING WITH THE *FLOW*

In his efforts to understand and define what constitutes an "optimal experience," Mihaly Csikszentmihalyi (cheek - sent - mē - high - yē) began by interviewing "experts" in a variety of fields such as art, athletics, music, chess, and medicine. From their reports, Csikszentmihalyi developed a theory of **flow,** a condition in which people become so involved in an activity that nothing else seems to matter to them. Further research revealed that this type of experience was not unique to "experts" but was described in much the same way by men and women of various ages and occupations across cultures.

Mihaly Csikszentmihalyi introduced the concept of "flow," which is a mental state characterized by total absorption in a task. Courtesy of HarperCollins/ Mark Tuschman Photography

These people described experiences in which they sensed that their skills were adequate for coping with challenges in a goal-directed and rule-bound system that provided them with clear cues about how well they were performing. Their concentration was so intense that they had no irrelevant thoughts or outside worries. Their self-consciousness disappeared, and their sense of time became distorted. Activities that create this type of experience are so intrinsically rewarding that people are willing to engage in them for their own sake. They are not concerned with what they will get out of the activity, external standards, or contingencies. (Note the parallels with the findings of Deci discussed earlier.)

Csikszentmihalyi used a research method called the **experience sampling method** to gain more information about people's daily flow experiences. In this method, subjects wear electronic pagers and write down what they are thinking and feeling when the pager signals them randomly (about eight times a day). An advantage to this technique is that subjects do not have to recall how they felt retrospectively during a certain day or week. If they were having a flow experience when they were paged, the subjects could describe it for the researchers at that moment.

Csikszentmihalyi found that all types of flow activities are rewarding because they provide a sense of discovery and a creative feeling of being transported into a new reality. They push the people engaged in the activities to higher levels of performance and new states of consciousness. In this way, the self is enhanced and made more complex.

For flow to occur, the challenges a person is facing must balance with his or her skill for meeting the challenges. If challenges are greater than the person's present skill level, the person will experience anxiety or frustration rather than flow. If challenges are too limited, the person will feel boredom. Because neither anxiety nor boredom is as rewarding as the flow experience, people will be motivated to return to the flow state by modifying the challenge or their skill level.

One recent study showed that students in basketball classes who were in flow experienced more enjoyment, satisfaction, concentration, and control than those students who were in

Box continued on following page

Box 16.1 *Continued*
GOING WITH THE *FLOW*

anxiety or boredom states (Stein, Kimiecik, Daniels, & Jackson, 1995). As people practice a flow activity and improve their skills at the activity, they will want to gradually increase the challenges they are facing in order to avoid boredom and maintain flow. This dynamic feature explains why flow activities lead to growth and discovery.

Flow experiences often occur during physical activities such as yoga, rock climbing, or dance, but can also occur during mental activities such as problem solving, reading, or chess. Many people experience flow in their jobs or their interactions with others. To facilitate having flow experiences, one might follow four steps: setting clear goals, becoming immersed in activities, paying attention to what is happening, and learning to enjoy immediate experiences even if they are objectively unpleasant. Being in control of one's mind means that anything can become a source of flow and, therefore, growth and joy.

Psychological or mental involvement appears to be one of the key elements of the flow experience. A study of college students using the experience sampling method found that optimal experience in flow was characterized by feelings of intense involvement (Clarke & Haworth, 1994). In the same study, students who experienced flow as a highly enjoyable "optimal experience" scored significantly higher on measures of psychological well-being than students who did not experience flow as highly enjoyable. A longitudinal study by Rathunde and Csikszentmihalyi (1993) looked at the "undivided interest" component of flow in talented high school students and found that (after adjusting for effects of family background, scholastic aptitude, and other individual differences) undivided interest when engaged in activities related to their talents was positively correlated with the students' levels of performance in their talent areas 3 years later. Thus, flow appears to be closely related to the peak experiences described by Maslow, and research supports many of his earlier conclusions about the state. However, it does appear to be experienced at least infrequently by most people and can be cultivated by selecting conducive activities and appropriate challenges.

KELLY'S THEORY OF PERSONAL CONSTRUCTS

George A. Kelly wrote a complete, systematic theory of personality. Like Rogers and Maslow, though, he conducted relatively little direct research. Rather, he spelled out a theory that stimulated others to investigate his ideas.

Kelly's theory is "formal," with a fundamental postulate, a systematic series of corollaries to the postulate, explicit definitions of every term, and a breadth potentially capable of dealing with an enormous range of issues.

Kelly articulated a philosophical position he called **constructive alternativism,** which states that there are always multiple ways for any person to view her or his world. Nothing is *fixed* or given. All people have the potential to view events as they choose. In other words, what *is* is a construction of the mind. One implication of this position is that no one need be a victim of circumstances or history.

Early in his career, Kelly, like Rogers and many other personality theorists, was a practicing clinician, which, in 1931, meant a psychoanalyst. The more he interpreted his clients' behaviors, the more he began to realize that the accuracy of his interpretations was not critical. What *was* important in helping

George Kelly (1905–1967) theorized that personality consists of a unique, organized set of personal constructs—ways of viewing experiences that people create to anticipate events in their lives. Courtesy of National Library of Medicine

clients change was that the interpretations enabled clients to see themselves and their problems in new ways. Kelly (1969) performed an informal experiment, which he described as follows:

> I began fabricating "insights." I deliberately offered "preposterous interpretations" to my clients. Some of them were about as unFreudian as I could make them. . . . My only criteria were that the explanation account for the crucial facts as the client saw them, and that it carry implications for approaching the future in a different way. (p. 52)

Eventually, Kelly concluded that clients had their own interpretations of events in their lives, which were ultimately responsible for their behavior (and problems). He came to believe that clients would change if he could help them *reinterpret* themselves and events in their lives. Kelly used the term **event** to refer to anything going on in a person's life that might have a corresponding mental representation, including people, things, and occurrences (Horley, 1988).

In 1955, Kelly published *The Psychology of Personal Constructs.* In it, he laid out what may be the most organized presentation of a comprehensive theory of personality ever written (e.g., Harris, 1990; John & Soyland, 1990). However, his theory received little recognition at the time. One reason was that Kelly's theory was viewed as cognitive, which was counter to the then current approaches. Kelly's ideas were, indeed, ahead of their time, antedating the emergence of modern cognitive personality psychology by almost 20 years (Adams-Webber, 1990; Anastasi, 1988a; Jankowicz, 1987; Mischel, 1980).

Interestingly, Kelly (1966) himself did not think of personal construct theory as a "cognitive" theory (Mascolo & Mancuso, 1990; Rychlak, 1990; Warren, 1990, 1991). He treated cognition, actions, and feelings in the same psychological terms, rather than as separate processes, which is consistent with the holistic emphasis characteristic of the phenomenological approach.

People as Scientists

Kelly (1955) recognized a paradox in the way personality psychologists studied people.

> It is customary to say that the scientist's ultimate aim is to predict and control. . . . Yet curiously enough, psychologists rarely credit the human subjects in their experiments with having similar aspirations. It is as though the psychologist were saying . . . "I, being a scientist, am performing this experiment in order to improve the prediction and control of certain human phenomena; but my subject, being merely a human organism, is obviously propelled by inexorable drives welling up within." (p. 5)

This elitist position erroneously assumes that scientists are the only beings interested in prediction and control.

Many times every day, we make predictions about events. Most of the time, we are unaware of this implicit predictive process (Berzonsky, 1990). We usually become aware of it only when our predictions fail. For example, rushing to brush your teeth before going to class, you might be rudely surprised by the unpleasant taste of your "toothpaste," if, in fact, it turns out instead to be your roommate's styling gel! Only now may you even realize that you made an assumption (prediction) that the tube on the vanity held toothpaste.

People are constantly predicting and attempting to control events in their lives. This observation led Kelly to view all people as practicing "scientists" who hold implicit theories that they test to guide their actions in dealing with their environment.

Personal Constructs: The Basic Units of Personality

Kelly (1955) suggested that each of us views the world through patterned forms or templates. We create these templates and then attempt to fit them over the realities that constitute the external world (see Figure 16.4). **Constructs,** as Kelly called the templates, are mental representations or interpretations of events—ways of viewing something. In other words, constructs are imposed on events as they are perceived and processed (Kirkland & Anderson, 1990).

No event is inextricably tied to any particular construct. An event can *always* be viewed from different perspectives. As people change the constructs they use to construe an event, their behavior changes. Consider the case of a psychiatric patient we will call Kay (Neale, 1968). Kay's behavior was among the most deviant on the ward. Her speech was unintelligible. She had extremely poor personal habits. She babbled and made strange gestures in the presence of other patients and visitors.

One day, a nurse took Kay to the beauty parlor to have her hair done and then dressed her in an attractive outfit, including stockings, high heels, and lipstick. When Kay returned to the ward several hours later, she no longer behaved in the bizarre manner that had been her trademark. Yet, she was still a patient in a psychiatric hospital. In every other respect, her circumstances were the same. It seemed, however, that she had changed *the way she construed herself,* and her new constructs resulted in new behaviors.

Kellian constructs always take the form of one characteristic opposed to another. Kelly believed that through a complex system of carefully ordered

Figure 16.4
Kelly likened constructs to templates that people fit over events to make sense of them. In this representation, a template of a house is being placed over an unconventional dwelling place. In other words, the construct of house is being used to interpret the unusual dwelling.

constructs, any event could effectively be construed by the observer. (We discuss the binary nature of constructs and the organization and structure of construct systems later.) Examples of Kellian constructs might be:

just vs. unjust
stable vs. fixed
flexible vs. dogmatic
warm vs. aloof

Specific constructs are unique to each individual; Kelly therefore called them *personal.* But the labels we use to describe our constructs are usually not unique. For instance, virtually everyone makes occasional use of the labels *bright* and *dull,* but each person's meaning for these labels is different. Verbal labels are not constructs; they are merely symbols representing constructs. Two constructs with the same label do not necessarily have the same meaning. Thus, to understand an individual's personal constructs, one must explore how that person uses them to construe experiences (Delmonte, 1989).

Constructs are used to **construe,** or interpret, events. In construing an event, a person generates a hypothesis based on a construct to predict things about the event. Then the person tests the hypothesis by acting as the construct dictates.

The validity of a construct is measured by its success in anticipating events, its **predictive efficiency.** People hold on to constructs that predict events and discard or revise those that fail to predict events accurately.

The Fundamental Postulate and Corollaries

Kelly's theory of personal constructs is organized around a fundamental postulate and 11 corollaries (see Table 16.4). Kelly's words are sometimes difficult to understand, perhaps because his language reaches toward alternative ways of saying things that have become "lost in too much familiarity" (Mair, 1990, p. 129). Once "translated," his words are rich in meaning, as you will see.

The Fundamental Postulate and the Construction and Choice Corollaries deal with how people predict events, which is the ultimate role of personal constructs. Kelly's Fundamental Postulate indicates that the purpose of all psychological processes is to accurately predict events, which is why Kelly referred to people as "scientists" (Walker, 1992). Kelly, like Carl Rogers, saw humans as active organisms who do not need to be pushed by needs or drives or pulled by incentives (Castorina & Mancini, 1992; Walker, 1990). Instead, people are intrinsically motivated to actively anticipate events simply because that is their "reason for being" (Delmonte, 1990).

People make predictions about events by viewing them in terms of *recurrent themes.* In other words, we search for characteristics of events that are relatively stable over time and in different circumstances. This is necessary because no two events are ever exactly the same. For example, each class a student attends is different. Yet there are enough similarities (recurrent themes)—the roles played by students and teachers, lectures, examinations—that students can predict much of what will happen in each new class and thus anticipate appropriate behaviors.

Table 16.4 Kelly's fundamental postulate and corollaries

Fundamental Postulate	A person's processes are psychologically channelized by the ways in which the person anticipates events.
Construction Corollary	A person anticipates events by construing their replications.
Choice Corollary	A person chooses that alternative in a dichotomized construct through which he or she anticipates the greater possibility for extension and definition of his or her system.
Dichotomy Corollary	A person's construct system is composed of a finite number of dichotomous constructs.
Range Corollary	A construct is convenient for the anticipation of a finite range of events only.
Organization Corollary	Each person characteristically evolves, for convenience in anticipating events, a construct system embracing ordinal relationships between constructs.
Experience Corollary	A person's construct system varies as the person successively construes the replications of events.
Modulation Corollary	The variation in a person's construction system is limited by the permeability of the constructs within whose range of convenience the variants lie.
Fragmentation Corollary	A person may successively employ a variety of construction subsystems that are inferentially incompatible with each other.
Individuality Corollary	Persons differ from each other in their construction of events.
Commonality Corollary	To the extent that one person employs a construction of experience that is similar to that employed by another, his or her processes are psychologically similar to those of the other person.
Sociality Corollary	To the extent that one person construes the construction processes of another, he or she may play a role in a social process involving the other person.

Source: From *The Psychology of Personal Constructs, and a Theory of Personality* by G. A. Kelly, 1955. W. W. Norton.

To construe events effectively, we must identify themes that are both *similar* and *different*. Differences provide *contrasts* that are presumed necessary to comprehend any concept. Without knowledge of a contrast or opposite, concepts have no meaning. "Delicious meal," "dry wine," and "stimulating companion" mean something to us only because we can refer to potential contrasts: "tasteless meal," "sweet wine," and "boring company."

In the course of a day, we encounter hundreds of events about which we must make predictions. In each instance, we choose (1) one of our personal constructs and (2) *one of the two poles* of that construct to interpret the event. The criterion we use to make these choices is predictive efficiency. We enhance the predictive efficiency of a construct either by *defining* it more precisely or by *extending its range of convenience to encompass new events.* (The **range of convenience** is the entire set of events to which a construct is reasonably applicable.)

Definition involves applying a construct similarly to how it has been applied on past occasions. If the present prediction is accurate, the construct becomes more refined and precise (defined) because it has successfully predicted yet another novel event.

Extension involves choices that are most likely to expand the usefulness of the construct by increasing its range of convenience. One way to extend a construct is to use it to anticipate a familiar event in a novel way. For example, Dave had always used the pole "plain" of his construct *attractive versus plain* to characterize women with short hair. When he fell in love with Kristina, who wore her hair short, he was "forced" to extend the attractive pole of his construct to encompass this new experience and thus expand the construct overall.

Definition can be thought of as a relatively safe wager with a modest payoff; if the prediction is correct, the construct becomes slightly more precise. Extension, by comparison, is a riskier bet with a larger payoff; if the prediction is correct, the construct becomes substantially more comprehensive. Kelly (1955) spoke of the difference between definition and extension as being between security and adventure. "One may anticipate events by trying to become more and more certain about fewer and fewer things [definition] or by trying to become vaguely aware of more and more things on the misty horizon [extension]" (p. 67).

Kelly conceived of constructs as having two dichotomous poles. A construct must have two poles so that both similarity and difference can be recognized. Consider the example of Ernie, who dives into a swimming pool and screams, "It's *cold!*" To construe the water as *cold,* Ernie must *contrast* it with water he previously experienced (and construed) as *warm.* His concept of cold has no meaning without the inherent (implicit) contrast.

A construct's range of convenience is limited, and we possess a finite number of constructs. Thus, we sometimes encounter events that we cannot adequately construe. Either we have no applicable construct to interpret the event, or our existing relevant constructs are too limited to encompass it adequately. Consider what happens when we visit a foreign culture very different from our own. We are likely to encounter "strange" customs that we cannot decipher or comprehend in any meaningful way. Our constructs have proven inadequate to process the behavior we have witnessed.

Even in our everyday lives, we encounter events we cannot make sense of because we do not have adequate constructs to interpret them. When this happens, we experience anxiety. Anxiety signals us that our existing construct system is in some way inadequate for the present situation. Kelly stipulated other emotional reactions based on his construct theory, which are discussed later.

Construct Systems: The Structure of Personality

A **construct system** consists of all of an individual's constructs, arranged in a meaningful hierarchical order. Whereas constructs are the units of personality, the relation of constructs to one another—the construct system—makes up the *structure* of personality. The Organization, Experience, Modulation, and Fragmentation Corollaries explain the nature of a construct system.

Constructs are arranged in a hierarchical order that facilitates their application to events. People differ not only because they use different constructs but also because their constructs are organized in different ways. Two people can have similar personal constructs yet have vastly different personalities because their constructs are ordered differently (e.g., Chiari, Mancini, Nicolo, & Nuzzo, 1990).

Most constructs are subordinate to some and superordinate to other constructs. This organization allows a person to move from one construct to another in an orderly fashion and to resolve conflicts and inconsistencies among constructs by moving up and down *between levels,* rather than simply across parallel constructs. A person's construct system changes as the person continuously recognizes and appreciates similarities and *dis*similarities among events. As we construe and reconstrue events, inevitable failures in prediction occur; that is, our assumptions of similarity between previous events and new events do not always hold. When this happens, the construct used must be modified or discarded. Modifying any construct inevitably results in changes in the construct system. Minor shifts and modifications of our personal construct systems occur constantly (e.g., Castorina & Mancini, 1992).

Our construct systems evolve with increased experience. Kelly (1955) defined **experience** as construing novel events. Experience is an active process. To gain experience, people must interpret events differently than they have before; in short, they must reconstrue events. Kelly (1980) believed that events do not change people; rather, people change themselves by reconstruing events—that is, through experience.

Emotion: Awareness of Construct Change

In personal construct theory, **emotion** is defined as the awareness of change or the need for change in one's construct system. The degree and nature of the change varies with different emotions (McCoy, 1981). The change can be:

Major or *minor:* involving many constructs or a few
Validating or *invalidating:* involving successful or unsuccessful prediction of events
Core or *peripheral:* involving constructs that are comprehensive, relatively impermeable, and essential to one's identity or constructs that are narrower, more permeable, and not critical to one's identity.

Table 16.5 contains examples of common emotions defined according to personal construct theory.

Individual Differences and Similarities

One's personality is what makes one both distinct from and similar to others. The Individuality, Commonality, and Sociality Corollaries explain the basis of the unique and shared aspects of personality.

Each person has a unique set of personal constructs, which means that people differ in the way they construe events. No two people ever have exactly the same interpretation of an event (see Figure 16.5). All qualities, not just beauty, are in the eye of the beholder. Construing events differently from other people can lead to disagreements about "the way things are."

The Commonality Corollary (the flip side of the Individuality Corollary) states that similarities between people are due to similarities in construing events. Two people are likely to behave similarly if they construe events in similar ways.

Table 16.5 Emotions as defined by personal construct theory

Threat*	Awareness of imminent major change in one's core constructs
Fear*	Awareness of imminent minor change in one's core constructs
Bewilderment	Awareness of imminent major change in one's peripheral constructs
Doubt	Awareness of imminent minor change in one's peripheral constructs
Love	Awareness of validation of one's core constructs
Happiness	Awareness of validation of part of one's core constructs
Satisfaction	Awareness of validation of part of one's peripheral constructs
Complacency	Awareness of validation of a small part of one's peripheral constructs
Anger	Awareness of invalidation of one's constructs, which leads to hostility
Sadness	Awareness of invalidation of implications of a part or all of one's core constructs
Guilt*	Awareness of deviating from one's core role constructs
Self-Confidence	Awareness of one's self-concept fitting with one's core role constructs
Shame	Awareness of one's self-concept deviating from another person's construal of one's role
Contempt (Disgust)	Awareness that core constructs of another person are different in a major way from one's own and/or do not meet norms of social expectation
Surprise	Sudden awareness of a need to construe an event
Anxiety*	Awareness that events lie outside the range of convenience of one's constructs
Contentment	Awareness that events lie within the range of convenience of one's constructs

*These definitions are Kelly's (1955); the others are derived from his theory (McCoy, 1977).
Source: Adapted from "A Reconstruction of Emotion," by M. M. McCoy, 1977. In D. Bannister (Ed.), *New Perpectives in Personal Construct Theory.* Academic Press.

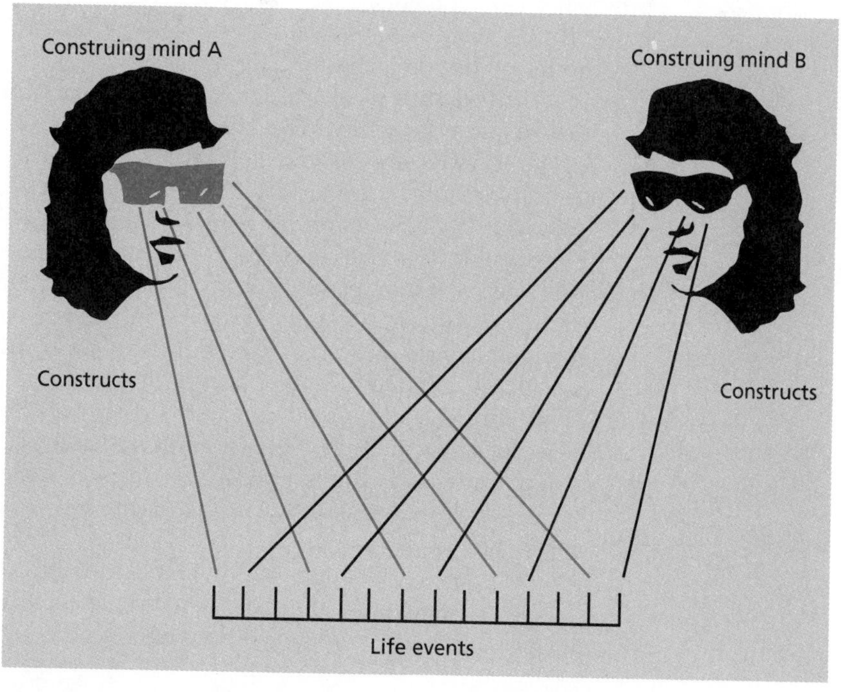

Figure 16.5
The same life events are viewed somewhat differently by different people because they are perceived through unique individual constructs, which are analogous to different colored glasses.
Source: Adapted from "The Psychology of Personal Constructs" by George A. Kelly, 1973. In J. Rychlak (Ed.), *Introduction to Personality and Psychotherapy.* Houghton Mifflin Company.

Recall from Chapter 13 that *culture* generally refers to a group of people who exhibit similar behaviors because they share similar environments and experiences. From the perspective of personal construct theory, it is not the similar experiences themselves that define a cultural group but the similarities in how people construe their experiences.

The basic requirement for an interpersonal relationship is that one person play a particular *role* (see Chapter 13) in relation to another person. To do this, the role player must effectively construe how the other person views the role being played.

Accurately construing another person's constructs is important in interpersonal interactions. Moreover, the ability of person A to play a role with respect to person B increases as A construes constructs that are more personally meaningful to B (Benesch & Page, 1989). The most personally meaningful constructs are **core constructs;** they define us, form the basis of our identity, and have the greatest value for us (Horley, 1991). Thus, playing roles effectively requires an understanding of the other and their expectations for that role.

Guilt

We play many roles in the course of our daily lives: student, child, friend, team member, listener, helper, and so on. Most of the roles we play are **noncore** (or peripheral). They are not particularly important to us; they are not essential to our basic identity. We can shift easily in and out of these peripheral roles. For instance, we often assume the role of customer; how well we play that role generally makes little difference in our overall functioning.

In contrast, each of us has some core roles that are critical to our lives. **Core roles** are essential to one's personal identity. How well one fills them has important consequences. Core roles vary from individual to individual. "Parent" may be a core role for one person, "breadwinner" for another, and both may be core roles for a third.

When we stray from a core role, we experience **guilt.** Think about times that you have felt guilty. What made you feel that way? Your answer is apt to be that you were doing something wrong. But "wrong" in this context means contrary to some expectations (your own or others'). Thus, we experience guilt when we deviate from expectations for a core role (e.g., Green, 1988). For example, Tammy considers herself a "good mother." She experiences guilt when she loses patience or openly expresses anger toward her children.

Kelly's definition of guilt as a deviation from a core role is *value free*. It is different than traditional definitions that are value-laden with moralistic judgments about evil (e.g., Mascolo & Mancuso, 1990). Kelly does not decide for others what their core roles should be, or how they should seek to fill them. These judgments are entirely internal and based on the individual's own priorities and expectations. In fact, many of Kelly's unique definitions of key personality concepts, such as anxiety, are marked by the absence of value judgments.

This chapter has discussed a number of broad theories and specific theoretical constructs. Many of the ideas presented by these early representational theorists have served to fuel research by later representational psychologists right up to the present. In Chapter 17, we take a closer look at some related ideas and research, particularly how the mental representations of self and others influence the interpretation of experiences and, ultimately, human behavior.

SUMMARY

1. The phenomenological approach rests on the assumption that to understand someone's personality one must know how that individual construes his or her experiences.
2. Phenomenological theories are holistic; they view and explain specific acts in terms of the individual's overall mental representations and interpretations.
3. Carl Rogers proposed the first major alternative to psychoanalytic theory; Rogers's view, unlike Freud's, takes an optimistic view—namely, that humans have an inborn, natural tendency to develop and enhance themselves in positive ways.
4. Rogers makes two fundamental assumptions: that all behavior is guided by the person's unique actualizing tendency and that all humans have a need for positive regard. According to Rogers, people evaluate each of their experiences in terms of the degree to which the experience maintains or enhances them; this is the so-called organismic valuing process.
5. Positive regard refers to positive social feedback, taking the form of acceptance, respect, sympathy, warmth, and love. Rogers viewed positive regard as essential for the healthy development of the self.
6. Infants and young children obtain positive regard from others; however, as autonomy and the sense of self develop, we are able to provide positive self-regard to ourselves.
7. Positive regard may be conditional or unconditional; conditional positive regard is contingent upon our actions, whereas unconditional positive regard does not depend on acting in specific ways to gain approval. Unconditional positive regard is based on valuing the worth of the individual as a person. Each individual is presumed worthy and valuable irrespective of his or her abilities and behavior.
8. Conditions of worth are external values placed on a person's behavior; they compete with the organismic valuing process and stand in the way of optimal development.
9. Deci contends that self-determination increases motivation, whereas being controlled by external demands decreases motivation. Self-determination requires that individuals construe their actions and goals as self-chosen.
10. The way people see themselves is represented by the theoretical construct of self or self-concept. Perceptions of the self are organized, compatible with one another (i.e., free of contradictions), and integrated into a coherent whole.
11. Rogers divided the self into two aspects: the actual self and the ideal self. He believed that life satisfaction depends upon similarity between these two aspects of self.

12. Ogilvie's research suggests that it is the discrepancy between one's actual self-concept and one's undesirable self-concept that is the major determinant of life satisfaction.
13. Rogers defined threat as the perception of incongruity within the self-concept. Threat is experienced as anxiety and leads to two defensive processes: perceptual distortion and denial. These processes parallel the ego defense mechanisms posited by psychoanalytic theory.
14. When the inconsistency between self and experience becomes too great, individuals experience breakdown and disorganization. The process of reducing this inconsistency is reintegration.
15. In his later career, Rogers adopted a person-centered approach to a wide range of social issues, from international and race relations to group decision making.
16. Abraham Maslow's phenomenological theory is primarily concerned with motivation and the nature of human needs. Maslow posited the existence of a need hierarchy in all humans. From strongest to weakest, these needs are for physiological requirements (such as food and water), safety, belongingness and love, esteem, and self-actualization. Usually we are not concerned with higher needs until our lower needs are met.
17. Maslow distinguished two types of esteem needs: esteem from others and self-esteem. Healthy self-esteem is earned through a person's efforts and not merely as a result of status or fame.
18. Self-actualization needs refer to the desire to become everything one is capable of becoming. Such needs differ considerably from person to person and are based on growth motivation rather than deficit motivation. Satisfying growth needs increases tension, whereas satisfying deficit needs reduces tension.
19. Maslow undertook an effort to identify self-actualizing (or fully functioning) people, emphasizing that self-actualization is a process rather than a state. His subjects, both historical and contemporary people, were characterized by an absence of psychological disorders and by the full use and exploitation of their talents, capacities, and potentials.
20. Maslow identified 15 related characteristics of self-actualizing people. Among the most important of them is the tendency to have peak experiences, which are brief, intense periods in which one experiences limitless horizons, a feeling of being both more powerful and more helpless than ever before, and a sense of ecstasy, appreciation, and awe. Mihaly Csikszentmihalyi's concept of flow (or optimal experience) is similar to the peak experience as described by Maslow. Csikszentmihalyi empirically studied flow by using the experience sampling method.
21. George Kelly's phenomenological theory is formal, based on a fundamental postulate and a systematic set of 11 corollaries. The theory is rooted in a philosophical position called constructive alternativism, which states that there are always multiple ways for people to view their worlds.

22. Kelly viewed all people as scientists who make predictions based on their personal constructs and then test and modify their theories through experience. Personal constructs are mental representations that we impose on our experiences.
23. Kelly's Fundamental Postulate states that the purpose of all psychological processes is to accurately predict events, based on recurrent themes we note in our experiences.
24. All personal constructs are bipolar and evaluated on the basis of their predictive efficiency. Predictive efficiency may be enhanced by either definition (applying a construct much as it has been applied in the past) or by extension (applying a construct in a new way and thus potentially increasing its range of convenience). When we encounter events that we do not have adequate constructs to interpret, we experience anxiety.
25. A person's constructs are arranged in a meaningful hierarchical order, which Kelly called a "construct system." Construct systems evolve with experience; people change themselves by changing their construct systems and thus reconstruing their experiences.
26. Kelly defined "emotion" as awareness that our construct systems require modification. The specific emotion experienced depends on the nature of the change that is perceived to be needed.
27. The Individuality, Commonality, and Sociality Corollaries explain both the unique and the shared aspects of personality. Similarities between people result from similarities in their construct systems. Interpersonal relationships require us to play particular roles in relation to other people, which require the role player to effectively construe how the other person views the requirements of the role.
28. Roles may be either core or noncore (peripheral). When we stray from a core role, we experience guilt. This definition of guilt—and, in fact, all of Kelly's theorizing—is nonjudgmental and value free.

CHAPTER SEVENTEEN

The Social Cognitive Approach

n this chapter we explore the broad range of social cognitive theories of personality, with a special emphasis on the person variables related to both the structure and function of personality. Specifically, we discuss the schemas (or *knowledge structures*) of the person and the self-regulatory processes that guide—and are guided by—personal goals. The discussion encompasses behavior planning and self-evaluations of the individual person, as well as the means by which goals are prioritized and pursued. These elements and their interplay combine to constitute the essence of personality as described by contemporary social cognitive personality theorists and researchers.

The theories of Rogers, Maslow, and Kelly (discussed in Chapter 16) were rooted in speculation and clinical observations. Although these phenomenological theorists all clearly emphasized mental representations of the self and world, none pursued a vigorous empirical approach to substantiating their claims. These early theoretical writings did, however, set the stage for the researchers to come. The phenomenological emphasis on mental representations, constructs, and the self-concept inspired those who followed to begin to formulate research programs designed to examine and measure the role of these and other mental phenomena through systematic research.

Central to all of this research is the concept of the self and how various aspects of self are mentally represented and serve to influence the behavior of individuals. Although the self is the central common theme, contemporary researchers have approached the construct of self from different perspectives. Some have explored the broadest self-representations (the overall self-concept), while others have examined much narrower features of the self-concept. We begin with a look at the first social cognitive theories and theorists. Then we proceed to describe the most current and active research areas within the contemporary Representational Strategy.

Many who have contributed to research in the social cognitive approach "converted" from other strategies (primarily from the environmental and particularly the social learning approach). Others' contributions derive from basic experimental studies of learning, neuropsychology, or modern cognitive psychology. Findings from these various origins are beginning to coalesce into a distinct view of humans as active, thinking beings who mentally process environmental input and adjust their beliefs and behavior in response to this information. We begin by taking a brief look at the forces that converged to create this new view of the person.

THE COGNITIVE REVOLUTION

The history of cognitive personality psychology is, in fact, surprisingly long. Although the dominance of cognitive thinking within academic psychology dates back only about 20 years, the roots of this thinking first appeared in the 1930s, in the writings and experimental studies of Edward Chase Tolman. Tolman argued that animals can learn without reinforcement, forming "cognitive maps" of their environments.

But academic psychology in Tolman's time, particularly the behavioral approach, had rejected efforts to explore internal events as too inherently subjective for serious scientific study. The behaviorists' view led most researchers to focus on "clearly observable" phenomena—namely, overt behavior. Many were skeptical of any attempts to look inside "the black box" of the mind. They therefore simply discounted the work of Tolman and his immediate followers.

But a new force, which was ultimately to serve as a working model for human cognitive processes, was the advent and rapid growth of computer technology in the middle and late 20th century. The recognition that elements of what were viewed as private (internal) mental events could be duplicated by the workings of human-made machines led many younger psychologists to see that although mental events themselves could not be accessed directly, they could be assessed and observed through sophisticated analysis of *resulting* behavior. Computer programs, based on binary (i.e., yes-no, on-off) logic demonstrated conclusively that complex decisions can be arrived at through a straightforward stepwise process. Moreover, because computers have memory ("mental capacity") sufficient to store large and highly complex programs (decision trees) of simple yes-no decisions structured in multiple layers, it became clear that vast information can be processed efficiently and rapidly, leading to sophisticated decisions. Like humans, computers receive input (information) from the environment, which is processed to yield *decisions;* changes in behavior (selection of algorithms or decisions *yet to be* made) can therefore be predicted. Today the most advanced types of computer programs allow the devices to "learn" from previous experience (outcomes produced through processing environmental input) and revise their own algorithms (decision tree structures) over time, thus actually modifying their own behavior in response to accumulating experience with the environment. The introduction of *parallel* (as opposed to serial or sequential) *processing* has added further to the speed and efficiency of modern computers and suggests that the human mind might work in much the same way.

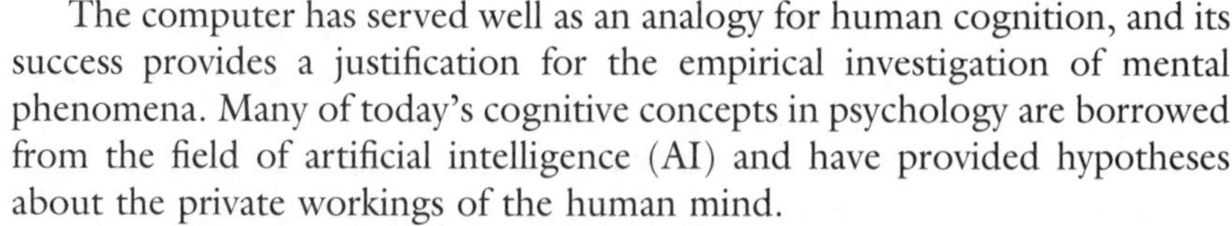

Julian Rotter developed a social learning theory that emphasizes cognitive factors, such as values and expectations, that mediate the effects of environmental factors on behavior. Courtesy of the University of Connecticut

The computer has served well as an analogy for human cognition, and its success provides a justification for the empirical investigation of mental phenomena. Many of today's cognitive concepts in psychology are borrowed from the field of artificial intelligence (AI) and have provided hypotheses about the private workings of the human mind.

One of the first psychologists to begin to discuss the role of cognition in personality was Julian Rotter. Rotter (1954) published a comprehensive personality theory with a major cognitive emphasis almost concurrently with Kelly's book. Rotter, like Kelly, is more often cited now (especially for his work on *locus of control*) than he was in the 1950s.

ROTTER'S EXPECTANCY-EVALUATION THEORY

Rotter's (1954) theory acknowledged the importance of situational factors and reinforcement as determinants of behavior. (Like some of the other theorists who contributed to this approach, Rotter fancied himself a "behaviorist" initially.) He even called his approach a "social learning theory." However, Rotter believed that the external situation and reinforcers have only an *indirect* influence on behavior. His theory actually deals with the cognitive factors that mediate the effects of the situation and environmental reinforcers on behavior. Specifically, Rotter claimed that personal values and expectancies ultimately determine how one behaves.

Rotter's theory is based on four basic constructs: the psychological situation, reinforcement value, expectancy, and behavior potential. These four factors operate as follows: Within a given psychological situation, the likelihood that a person will engage in a particular behavior **(behavior potential)** is determined by (1) the **reinforcement value** (intrinsic reward associated with the desired outcome) and (2) the person's **expectancy** that the reinforcer will actually be obtained.

Reinforcement Value

Generally, people act to bring about their most preferred outcomes. Reinforcement value refers to a person's individual preference for a particular outcome or reinforcer relative to other possible outcomes or reinforcers. Assuming that you could spend an evening (1) going to a movie, (2) attending a concert, or (3) having dinner at a local restaurant, which would you prefer? Obviously, people differ in the value they place on these activities.

Now suppose you had a fourth choice: flying to Paris on the Concorde for dinner. Which of the four would you choose? Unless you are afraid of flying or have an aversion to French cuisine, you are likely to choose the evening in Paris. Thus, reinforcement value is not only a matter of personal taste but is also relative to the range of potential reinforcers available.

Expectancy

Besides preferences for various reinforcers, each person has an expectancy about the likelihood that a particular outcome will be obtained. Expectancy is independent of reinforcement value. You may relish the idea of an evening in Paris, but you may also doubt that you will actually be offered it. In contrast, going to the movies may be your least desired option, but it may be the one you feel is most likely to really be available to you.

Expectancy, like reinforcement value, is subjective. What matters is how the person assesses the likelihood of a particular outcome, rather than some "objective" probability. Maggie may believe that she is more likely to be invited to spend an evening in Paris than an evening at a local movie theater. Even though most people would say the opposite, it is *her* personal expectancy that will determine her actions.

Rotter (1982) distinguished between two types of expectancies: specific and generalized. A **specific expectancy** is a person's subjective estimate of the chances of obtaining a particular outcome by performing a particular behavior. An example is the probability that asking a *particular friend* for a loan will get you the money you need *today.*

Some expectancies, however, come to be applied to a variety of related experiences. A **generalized expectancy** is a person's subjective prediction of the odds of obtaining a particular class (category) of outcomes by engaging in a given class of behavior. An example is your overall estimate of the probability that asking for favors will meet with success. We use generalized expectancies when we perceive an important psychological similarity across a range of situations. (This is a lot like Kelly's idea of extending the range of a given construct.) Thus, people come to respond to similar situations in similar ways. Later, we discuss *locus of control,* a generalized expectancy that has been studied extensively.

The Psychological Situation

All behavior occurs in a context of both *external* and *internal* stimuli. Rotter (1981) recognized that people differ in how they perceive and respond to specific stimuli. Thus, the context of behavior is the **psychological situation**—the existing circumstances from each individual's personal (subjective) perspective. For example, earning $50 is likely to be more reinforcing if you have been laid off from work than if you have just won a sweepstakes. Similarly, the threats of a fellow prisoner may be a much more serious concern for a prison inmate than the reprimands of a prison guard, even though for most people the reprimand of an authority figure would be more serious than similar feedback from a peer.

Behavior Potential

In most situations, a person can behave a number of ways. Behavior potential is the likelihood that a person will engage in a particular behavior to obtain a desired outcome. Behavior potential depends on two factors: reinforcement value and expectancy. Because reinforcement value and expectancy are *independent* factors, behavior potential must be predicted by taking both into account. It is convenient to state the relationship as a formula:

$$\text{Behavior potential} = \text{Reinforcement value} \times \text{Expectancy}$$

The multiplication sign has important implications. When *either* reinforcement value or expectancy is low, the likelihood of engaging in the behavior is also low. Moreover, when either reinforcement value or expectancy is zero, the behavior will *not* be performed because the behavior potential (as predicted by the formula) is zero. Thus, the most valued reinforcer will not motivate us to perform a behavior when we believe it is *unobtainable*. Likewise, an easily obtainable but personally *undesirable* reinforcer will not motivate behavior.

Similarly, if either reinforcement value or expectancy is extremely high (and the other is greater than zero), behavior potential will be relatively high. Thus, a student who places great value on the pursuit of a particular profession (reinforcement value) may study long hours every day in an effort to attain this goal, despite awareness of intense competition for the required graduate-level training (relatively low expectancy of success).

Locus of Control: A Generalized Expectancy

When you receive an "A" on an examination or a bonus at work, to what factors do you attribute this outcome? When you receive a poor grade or a pink slip, what do you construe as the cause? One possible answer to these questions is that the outcome resulted from your own (internal) effort, ability, or skill. Another answer is that the outcome was due to (external) factors beyond your personal control, including chance or fate.

Some outcomes are clearly the result of one's own efforts, such as earning a 4.0 grade point average three semesters in a row; other outcomes are clearly the result of chance; for example, being dealt a royal flush in poker. However, in many situations, whether an outcome is due more to internal or external factors is ambiguous and open to subjective interpretation.

Locus of control refers to each person's view of the source of his or her outcomes (Rotter, 1966). **Internal locus of control** is the belief that outcomes are the result of our own personal efforts and resources. **External**

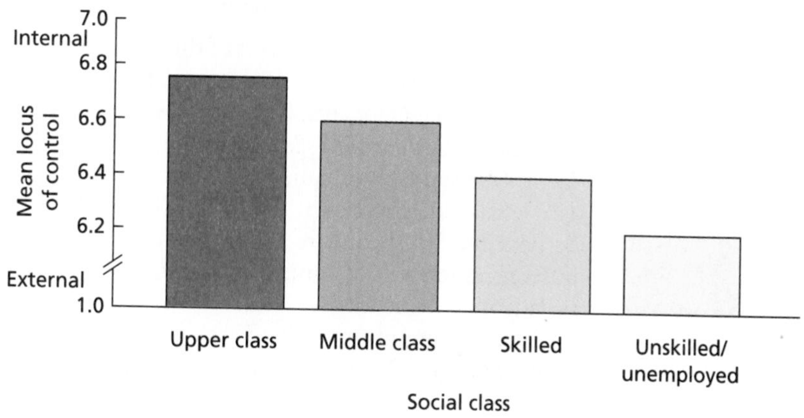

Figure 17.1
Mean differences in locus of control (higher score is more internal) by social class among residents of nine European countries.
Source: Adapted from "Association of Country, Sex, Social Class, and Life Cycle to Locus of Control in Western European Countries," by L. Jensen, J. Olsen, & C. Hughes, 1990, *Psychological Reports, 67,* 199–205.

locus of control is the belief that outcomes are due to outside forces over which we have no control. Locus of control is always subjective. Even when the source of an outcome is "objectively" internal or external, the way the person perceives the source is what determines the individual's locus of control.

Our perceptions of locus of control develop as a result of life experiences, such as the child-rearing practices to which we have been exposed. For example, parental approval and attention to positive behaviors are associated with a child's developing *internal control;* parental reinforcement based on social comparisons of the child's behaviors and devaluing the child without attention to the child's specific behaviors are both associated with *external control* (Krampen, 1989).

On a broader scale, demographic variables such as social class and the immediate culture are likely to influence our perception of locus of control (e.g., Tyler, Dhawan, & Sinha, 1989). For instance, a comparison of large samples of residents of nine European countries found that degree of internal control was positively correlated with social class (Figure 17.1). Furthermore, there were wide differences in locus of control according to country of residence (Figure 17.2), suggesting potent cultural factors impacting on locus of control (Jensen, Olsen, & Hughes, 1990).

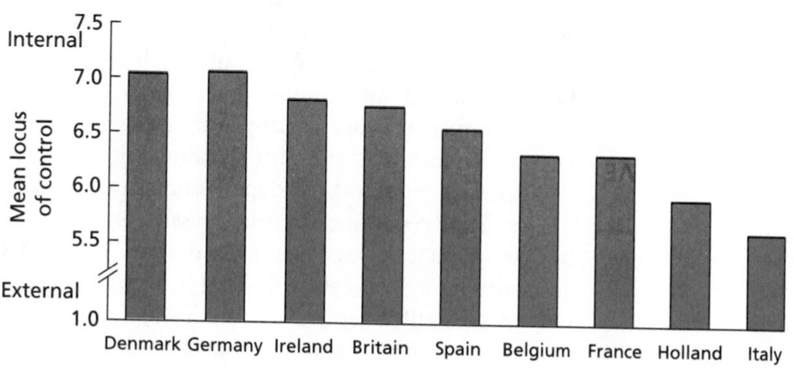

Figure 17.2
Mean differences in locus of control (higher score is more internal) of residents in nine European countries.
Source: Adapted from "Association of Country, Sex, Social Class, and Life Cycle to Locus of Control in Western European Countries," by L. Jensen, J. Olsen, & C. Hughes, 1990, *Psychological Reports, 67,* 199–205.

Correlates of Locus of Control

Clearly, people *do* differ in terms of the degree to which they believe outcomes are controlled by internal or external factors. This has been demonstrated cross-culturally (Doganis, Theodorakis, & Bagiatis, 1991; Engstrom, 1991; Heaven, 1990; Hoffart & Martinsen, 1991; Lester, Castromayor, & Icli, 1991; Maqsud & Rouhani, 1991; Ormel & Schaufeli, 1991; Singh & Verma, 1990; Strassburger, Rosen, Miller, & Chavez, 1990; Thurman, Jones-Saumty, & Parsons, 1990) and in many different regions of the world. Individual differences in locus of control appear to be related to a variety of adaptive and maladaptive behaviors.

Internals are more likely to seek information than externals (e.g., Ingold, 1989; Phares, 1984). Because internals consider themselves responsible for their outcomes, they want information that improves their chances of obtaining positive results and helps them avoid undesirable ones. One early study demonstrated that internal students consulted with their instructor *before* a classroom examination more than external students (Prociuk & Breen, 1977). Another study showed that internals were more likely to seek information about the negative side of careers *before* committing to them (Friedrich, 1988).

Internals also seem to have the advantage over externals when it comes to physical health (e.g., Marshall, 1991; Rosolack & Hampson, 1991). They seek more general information about health maintenance, have more knowledge of healthful behaviors, engage in more precautionary health practices, have more positive attitudes about exercise, and are less likely to have cardiac problems (e.g., Quadrel & Lau, 1989; Strickland, 1978, 1979; Tinsley & Holtgrave, 1989; Waller & Bates, 1992).

An internal locus of control is also associated with less severe physical illness (e.g., Brandon & Loftin, 1991; Engstrom, 1991). Moreover, internals tend to be more responsive to treatment (e.g., Johnson, Magnani, Chan, & Ferrante, 1989). They are more successful in quitting harmful habits such as smoking (Segall & Wynd, 1990). Internals also are less likely to become substance abusers (Haynes & Ayliffe, 1991). These studies suggest that if you believe that you control your circumstances, you may feel less need to *escape* them and more pressure to *actively cope* with them.

Generally, internals are higher achievers than externals (e.g., Ashkanasy & Gallois, 1987; Bigoness, Keef, & Du Bose, 1988; Wildstein & Thompson, 1989). From elementary school to college, internal students tend to excel academically, outperforming their external peers (e.g., Boss & Taylor, 1989; Pani, 1991; cf. Wilhite, 1990). Internal locus of control also is associated with higher achievement motivation (Volkmer & Feather, 1991; see also Chapter 5), as well as more daydreaming about achievement and less preoccupation with the threat of failure (Brannigan, Hauk, & Guay, 1991).

Internals tend to be independent but cooperative in their dealings with others. They resist undue social pressure more than externals (Phares, 1978) but are generally less hostile and have more favorable attitudes toward authority figures (Heaven, 1988). Internals' coping skills in social situations tend to be highly adaptive (Parkes, 1984). Their methods of achieving marital happiness are direct and active and tend to be successful (Miller, Lefcourt,

Holmes, Ware, & Saleh, 1986). An investigation of seventh-grade children who were faced with frustration found that internals were more likely to react with positive assertive responses and externals with negative aggressive responses (Romi & Itskowitz, 1990).

Internals tend to have better overall psychological adjustment than externals (e.g., Hoffart & Martinsen, 1990, 1991; Katerndahl, 1991; Lester et al., 1991; Ormel & Schaufeli, 1991). Internals cope with stress better than externals (e.g., Cummins, 1988; Jennings, 1990; Lefcourt, Martin, & Saleh, 1984; Lunenburg & Cadavid, 1992). For example, internals in the process of divorce experience less stress after the divorce than externals (Brown, Perry, & Harburg, 1977; Pais, 1979). However, internals experience more stress before the divorce; the reason may be that internals, consistent with their accepting control of their lives, try to solve problems sooner than externals (Barnet, 1990). Moreover, internals are more likely to benefit from psychotherapy (e.g., Trice, 1990) and less likely to relapse after therapy (e.g., Hoffart & Martinsen, 1991). Again, people who assume personal responsibility for their circumstances are more likely to adopt an *active approach* to problems.

Internal locus of control is positively correlated with such healthy psychological characteristics as self-esteem and self-efficacy (e.g., Doganis et al., 1991; Ormel & Schaufeli, 1991; Rokke, al-Absi, Lall, & Oswald, 1991), which are discussed later. Internals also report more job satisfaction than externals (e.g., Achamamba & Kumar, 1989; Bein, Anderson, & Maes, 1990).

From our discussion so far, it would seem that it is always better to have an internal locus of control, which is generally true. But there is one major exception. When limited personal control is *actually available*, external locus of control can be more adaptive. One study dealt with elderly people who were institutionalized and therefore had little control over their circumstances. External locus of control was associated with better adjustment and feelings of satisfaction in the institutional setting (Felton & Kahana, 1974). Thus, externals can probably accept the condition of limited personal control, whereas internals resist such conditions. The opposite effect for locus of control was found in a group of *non*institutionalized elderly—in other words, those who presumably did have greater control over their immediate circumstances (Wolk & Kurtz, 1975). Overall, it appears that locus of control represents one aspect of self that differs from person to person and has a significant impact on many areas of functioning.

Given that different beliefs about locus of control are more adaptive in different circumstances (internal in situations in which active coping is most effective and external in circumstances that allow for very limited personal control), can locus of control change? Locus of control can vary with the specific situation. Although general locus of control is fairly stable, it may shift or alter as life circumstances change. One study found that shortly after divorce many women became *less* internal. However, they tended to return to predivorce locus of control as they learned to adjust and deal effectively with their new circumstances (Doherty, 1983). Similarly, beginning college students who were externals became more internal at the end of a semester-long course that emphasized taking personal responsibility for success in college (Cone & Owens, 1991).

BANDURA'S SOCIAL COGNITIVE THEORY

We introduced Albert Bandura in our discussion of the Environmental Strategy (see Chapter 13). Bandura began his career as a behaviorist who wished to extend the bounds of behaviorism (classical and operant conditioning) to include modeling as a third form of environmental learning. Bandura, in keeping with trends occurring in academic psychology, ultimately shifted his emphasis to social cognitive factors as determinants of personality.

Triadic Reciprocal Determinism

According to Bandura's (1986a, 1986b) social cognitive theory, our behavior is influenced by both environmental factors and **person variables,** including thoughts and feelings. Moreover, each of the three factors—behavior, environment, and person variables—can influence and be influenced by the other two factors (Figure 17.3). Bandura calls this process **triadic reciprocal determinism.**

The potential of three-way bidirectional influences of behavior (B), environment (E), and person variables (P) can be illustrated with a simple example. Heather is learning to ski (B) because her school offers weekly skiing lessons at a nominal cost (E) and she *believes* that she can learn to ski (P). Encouragement from her instructor (E) and improved skill (B) increase Heather's confidence in her ability (P). When Heather is skiing poorly on a particular day (B) and her confidence begins to wane (P), she finds easier ski trails (E) so that she can practice her basic skills and restore her confidence (P).

Perceived Self-Efficacy: An Important Person Variable

In the children's book *The Little Engine That Could,* the Little Engine successfully pulls the stranded train over the mountain while chanting, "I think I can." The Little Engine succeeds, the story tell us, because she believes that she can. Like the Little Engine, our daily functioning is enhanced by belief in our own ability to solve problems and overcome difficulties.

One aspect of Bandura's social cognitive theory that has received a good deal of attention is the more specific **theory of perceived self-efficacy.** This theory states that whether a person undertakes a task depends, in part, on his or her perceived level of efficacy regarding that task. This estimate of one's own ability to perform a specific behavior is called **self-efficacy.** Self-efficacy is more than telling ourselves that we can succeed. Self-efficacy is a strong

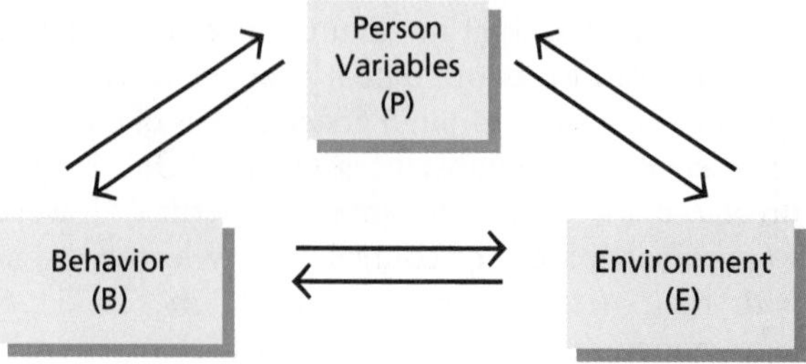

Figure 17.3
Schematic diagram of Bandura's principle of triadic reciprocal determinism. Each of the three factors influences and is influenced by the other two factors.

Albert Bandura developed a social cognitive theory that views personality as an interaction of behavior, environment, and personal variables and stresses the role of observational learning and self-efficacy. Photo by Chuck Painter, News and Publications Service, Sanford University

conviction of competence that is based on our evaluation of various sources of information about our abilities (Bandura, 1989a, 1989b).

Perceived self-efficacy is at least partially independent of one's actual abilities. People who are highly competent at a particular task but have little faith in their ability are unlikely to attempt the task. (Note the parallel with the earlier work of Rotter on expectancies.) Research supports the independence of actual ability and self-efficacy (e.g., Bouffard-Bouchard, Parent, & Larivee, 1991).

Efficacy expectations must be distinguished from outcome expectations (e.g., Bandura, 1986a; Shell, Murphy, & Bruning, 1989; Skinner, 1992). **Outcome expectations** refer to one's estimate that a given action will result in a particular outcome (these parallel Rotter's outcome expectancies); they are beliefs about the *responsiveness* of one's environment (Gecas, 1989). In contrast, **efficacy expectations** are beliefs about one's own competence. Optimal performance usually requires both efficacy and outcome expectations to be high (e.g., Lent, Lopez, & Bieschke, 1991).

Bandura's (1986a) theory also predicts that once a task is undertaken, the amount of energy we expend and how long we persevere are influenced by our perceived self-efficacy. The stronger our self-efficacy, the more vigorous and persistent are our efforts in the face of obstacles and setbacks (e.g., Cervone, 1989; Schwarzer, 1992b).

Although high self-efficacy (like internal locus of control) is desirable in most circumstances, there may be situations in which high self-efficacy produces dangerous complacency. For example, "reformed" smokers are notorious for their high relapse rate. Recidivism (relapsing back to smoking) is higher for high self-efficacy ex-smokers than for those with modest perceived self-efficacy (Haaga & Stewart, 1992, 1993). The explanation is simple. Resisting the urge to smoke requires sufficient control (perceived self-efficacy)

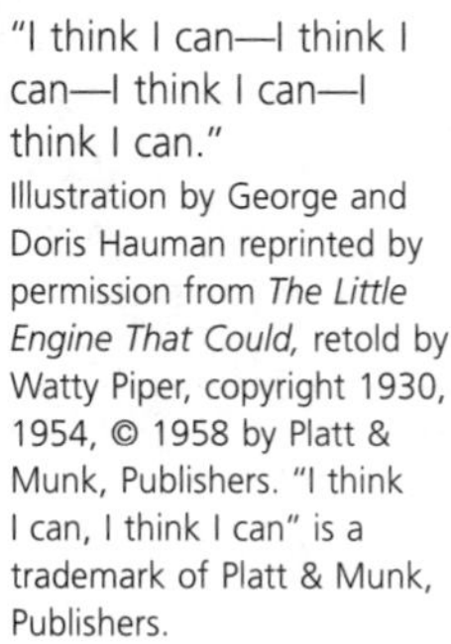

"I think I can—I think I can—I think I can—I think I can."
Illustration by George and Doris Hauman reprinted by permission from *The Little Engine That Could,* retold by Watty Piper, copyright 1930, 1954, © 1958 by Platt & Munk, Publishers. "I think I can, I think I can" is a trademark of Platt & Munk, Publishers.

not to indulge. However, excessive sense of control (perceived self-efficacy) might convince ex-smokers that they could resist future temptation despite the one cigarette they allow themselves now. But this behavior actually increases the likelihood that they will ultimately relapse.

Sources of Efficacy Expectations

Our efficacy expectations stem from four major sources of information. The first is **performance accomplishments.** When we perform a task well, our efficacy expectations are enhanced. Also, the threat of potential failure is likely to be reduced, which may increase persistence on subsequent tasks. Performance accomplishments are a powerful source of efficacy information because they provide direct experiences of personal ability.

Vicarious experience can also contribute to efficacy expectations. By observing others succeed at a task, we develop the expectation that we can do it too. Thus, modeling cues remain an important determinant of behavior, as they were in Bandura's original social learning theory (see pp. 338–347).

Verbal persuasion is another source of efficacy expectations. Being told that we can succeed increases our efficacy expectations. Verbal persuasion is probably the most common source of self-efficacy expectations because it is easily provided and often readily available.

Emotional arousal also informs a person about their efficacy for a particular task. People often rely on their state of physiological arousal (e.g., heart rate and breathing) to judge their level of fear or anxiety. Feeling calm and relaxed (or even moderately aroused, if some arousal is necessary for effective performance) may serve as feedback that influences efficacy expectations.

Information from each of these sources will influence self-efficacy only if we interpret it as indicative of our own abilities (reflective of internal factors, as in internal locus of control; see earlier discussion). When people attribute their successes to external factors, the effects of performance accomplishments on self-efficacy are minimized (Toshima, Kaplan, & Ries, 1992).

The Reciprocal Determinism of Self-Efficacy

Self-efficacy influences how we think and feel as well as what we do. Cognitive abilities, such as analytic thinking and academic performance, are enhanced by a strong sense of competence (e.g., Bandura, 1992a, 1992b; Bandura & Wood, 1989; Bouffard-Bouchard et al., 1991; Multon, Brown, & Lent, 1991; Wood & Bandura, 1989). Low self-efficacy is associated with anxiety, depression, helplessness, and feeling shy (e.g., G. J. Hill, 1989; Jerusalem & Schwarzer, 1992; Kavanagh, 1992; Williams, 1992).

Consistent with Bandura's principle of triadic reciprocal determinism, there is an ongoing interaction between self-efficacy and actions, emotions, and cognitive processes. This interaction is *multidirectional* and *multiply determined* (Bandura, 1992a), as depicted in Figure 17.4.

Consider just two of many possible paths of influence. A happy mood can heighten self-efficacy, which may lead people to accept more challenges and perform more competently (e.g., McAuley & Courneya, 1992). Thinking about factors that would enhance one's performance may increase self-

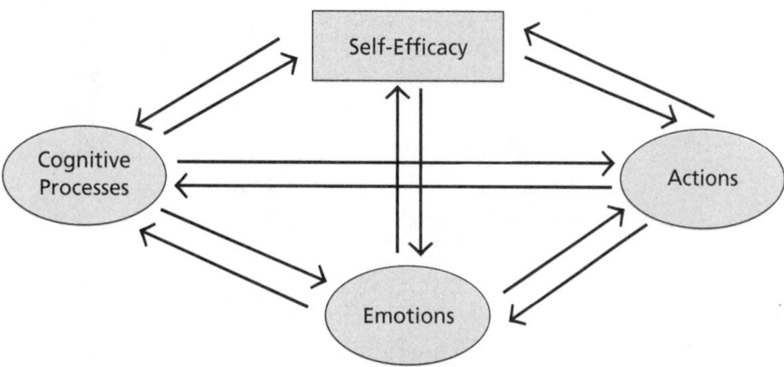

Figure 17.4
The relationship between self-efficacy and actions, cognitive processes, and emotions is reciprocal and multiply determined, involving two or more of the components.

efficacy, which may result in greater persistence and, ultimately, success at a task (e.g., Cervone, 1989).

The preceding two examples illustrate how self-efficacy serves as a *mediator* (an intermediary) between two other variables. In those examples, emotion and thinking did not directly influence behavior. Their effects on behavior were mediated by their influence on self-efficacy, which affected behavior.

The Situational Specificity of Self-Efficacy

No one feels equally competent to succeed at all times or all tasks. One study of high school students found that males had higher self-efficacy in athletics and females had higher self-efficacy in leadership (Peters & Brown, 1991). Thus, perceived self-efficacy usually is considered to be situation specific rather than a global personality trait that influences diverse behaviors. To appreciate just how situation specific self-efficacy can be, consider a sample of the range of specific behaviors for which self-efficacy has been assessed empirically: maternal behavior (Teti & Gelfand, 1991), infant care (Froman & Owen, 1989), sexual behavior (Rosenthal, Moore, & Flynn, 1991), condom use (Brafford & Beck, 1991), diabetes (Padgett, 1991), breast self-examination (Gonzalez & Gonzalez, 1990), dieting (Stotland, Zuroff, & Roy, 1991), and resistance to drug use (Hays & Ellickson, 1990) among others.

Some researchers have examined self-efficacy as a global concept, the composite of important successes and failures that people attribute to themselves (e.g., Eden & Kinnar, 1991; Jerusalem & Schwarzer, 1992; Shelton, 1990; Waller & Bates, 1992). However, task-specific self-efficacy scales are better predictors of actual behavior (e.g., Wang & Richarde, 1988).

The Generality of Self-Efficacy Theory

The generality of self-efficacy theory has been demonstrated across many domains. Consider just two: career development and health-related behavior. Occupational preferences and success are related to an individual's perceived self-efficacy (e.g., Landino & Owen, 1988; Lent & Hackett, 1987; Lent et al., 1991; Poidevant, Loesch, & Wittmer, 1991; Post, Stewart, & Smith, 1991). Specifically,

> the stronger people's belief in their efficacy, the more career options they consider possible, the greater the interest they show in them, the better they

> prepare themselves educationally for different occupations and the greater their staying power and success in different occupational pursuits. (Bandura, 1992b, p. 11)

Self-efficacy influences a variety of health-related behaviors as well (e.g., Ewart, 1991; Holden, 1991; Kok, De Vries, Mudde, & Strecher, 1991). For example, higher self-efficacy is associated with effective weight loss (e.g., Clark, Abrams, Niaura, Eaton, & Rossi, 1991; Slater, 1989; Stotland & Zuroff, 1991; Stotland et al., 1991), decreased alcohol consumption (e.g., Sitharthan & Kavanagh, 1991; Solomon & Annis, 1990), smoking cessation (e.g., DiClemente et al., 1991; Garcia, Schmitz, & Doerfler, 1990; Kok et al., 1992; Pedersen, Strickland, & DesLauriers, 1991), positive adaptation to illness (e.g., Cunningham, Lockwood, & Cunningham, 1991; Holman & Lorig, 1992; Schiaffino, Revenson, & Gibofsky, 1991), coping with medical procedures (e.g., Gattuso, Litt, & Fitzgerald, 1992), complying with medical regimens such as aftercare procedures and rehabilitative exercise (e.g., Heller & Krauss, 1991; Schwarzer, 1992a), and eliminating high-risk behaviors such as unprotected sex and use of unsterile hypodermics (e.g., Bandura, 1990, 1991; Kok et al., 1991; McKusick, Coates, Morin, Pollack, & Hoff, 1990).

High self-efficacy can promote health through diverse means (O'Leary, 1992). One path of influence is through adoption of healthy behaviors, regular exercise, and balanced diet (e.g., Ewart, 1992; Kok et al., 1992; Schwarzer, 1992a). Another path is to alter components of the physiological stress response, which affects immune functioning (e.g., Bandura, 1992c; Dienstbier, 1989; Wiedenfeld et al., 1990; see also Chapter 10). Perceived self-efficacy has become one of the most extensively studied theoretical constructs in personality. Clearly, it reflects one aspect of the self-concept that influences a wide range of behaviors. We have more to say about this subject when we address the applications of this theory in Chapter 18. For now, we turn to another major theorist in the social cognitive realm, Walter Mischel.

THE CONTRIBUTIONS OF WALTER MISCHEL

Walter Mischel is considered by many psychologists as the most prominent cognitive personality psychologist of the late 20th century. He has integrated many streams of thought within both the Representational and Environmental Strategies and has demonstrated full appreciation of the strictures of methodological behaviorism. The breadth of Mischel's theorizing and research is remarkable. Mischel has written on many topics critical to personality theory and research. Most of his early writings reveal the concerns that are captured in his subsequent social cognitive theory of personality. We begin by examining several of his early contributions and then proceed with a review of his own social cognitive theory (although his ideas and name will continue to crop up throughout our later discussions).

Mischel's Critique of Traditional Personality Assessment

In his 1968 book, *Personality and Assessment,* Mischel identified and challenged the assumptions underlying dispositional and psychodynamic personality assessment. Both approaches, according to Mischel, assume that a subject's responses on a personality test are a *sign* of his or her true underlying personality. For example, a person's score on the NEO-PI-R Extraversion scale is assumed to show how introverted or extraverted the person "really is." Someone who scores low on this scale would be expected to be modest, shy, and self-effacing in a wide range of situations. However, the average correlation between Extraversion scale scores and actual behavior in various situations is quite modest—typically about +.30. Correlations between test scores and actual behavior are no higher for most dispositional dimensions.

Walter Mischel has advanced our understanding of person variables, important situational variables, the use of plans, and the interaction of emotion and cognition.
University Photographer, Joe Pineiro, Columbia University

Mischel (1968) coined the phrase **personality coefficient** to refer to correlations between +.20 and +.30, the range typically found when a self-report inventory measure of a personality dimension is correlated with another type (usually behavioral) of measure of the "same" dimension. Personality coefficients of this magnitude do not allow for prediction of one variable from the other at an individual level because two variables whose correlation is between .20 and .30 share only 4% to 9% of the observed variance within the dimension of interest.

Nonetheless, in the 1960s, personality test scores were commonly used to make important decisions about a person's life and future. Attacking such practices, Mischel (1968) argued that personality assessment should be based on *samples of behavior* (rather than signs). The samples should be taken in situations as similar as possible to actual performance circumstances. For example, suppose an employer wanted the best candidates to do telephone interviews. Observing the candidates doing mock telephone interviews would be a better assessment procedure than using their NEO-PI-R Extraversion scores. (Recall that this theme, the importance of situational factors on determining behavior, is also clear in the writings of Rotter and Bandura.)

Mischel believed that situational variables were more important than personality dispositions in determining how people behave. However, like a growing number of personality psychologists, he acknowledged that behavior is not completely situation specific (e.g., Carson, 1989; Haynes & Uchigakiuchi, 1993; Kendrick & Funder, 1988; Russo, 1990).

> We do not have to relearn everything in every new situation. We have memories, and our past predisposes our present behavior in critically important and complex ways. Obviously people have characteristics, and overall "average" differences in behavior between individuals can be abstracted on many dimensions and used to discriminate among persons for many purposes. Obviously knowing how a person behaved before can help predict how [the person] will behave again in similar contexts. Obviously the impact of any stimulus depends on the organism that experiences it. No one suggests that the organism approaches every new situation with an empty head. (Mischel, 1973, pp. 261–262).

Thus, Mischel also emphasized the importance of **person variables,** the relatively enduring cognitive and behavioral attributes of the individual.

He and many others use person variables instead of the dispositions and traits of the Dispositional Strategy, as we will see as our discussion of Mischel's work continues.

The Consistency Paradox

A good deal of Mischel's research has been aimed at clarifying what he calls the **consistency paradox.** Most people construe themselves and others in terms of stable dispositions, and relatively consistent behavior. However, behavioral research generally *fails* to demonstrate a high degree of behavioral consistency in individuals. This marked difference between our impressions of individual consistency and the actual observed behavioral *in*consistency is what Mischel meant by the consistency Paradox. How can the paradox be explained? Mischel's answer revolves around the distinction between cross-situational and temporal consistency.

Cross-Situational versus Temporal Consistency

Cross-situational consistency refers to the extent that a person behaves the same way in different circumstances; it is consistency across situations and time (Figure 17.5). Consider 9-year-old Herbie. If we found him to be aggressive with virtually every child he meets, we would say that he shows substantial cross-situational consistency. In contrast, **temporal consistency** refers to an individual's behaving the same way in the same basic situation but at different times; it is consistency within similar situations across time (see Figure 17.5). Herbie's aggressiveness would be considered temporally consistent if he were aggressive exclusively with younger children on the playground—today, tomorrow, next week, and next month.

Mischel (1984) argued that there is little reason to expect broad cross-situational consistency, but temporal consistency is likely. Both claims are based on real-life contingencies. Herbie's aggression with younger children on the playground probably pays off. Younger children are likely to be intimidated by a bigger playground bully. His aggression is reinforced because it gets him what he wants, immediate access to the playground equipment. If Herbie's aggression is successful with younger or weaker children today, it

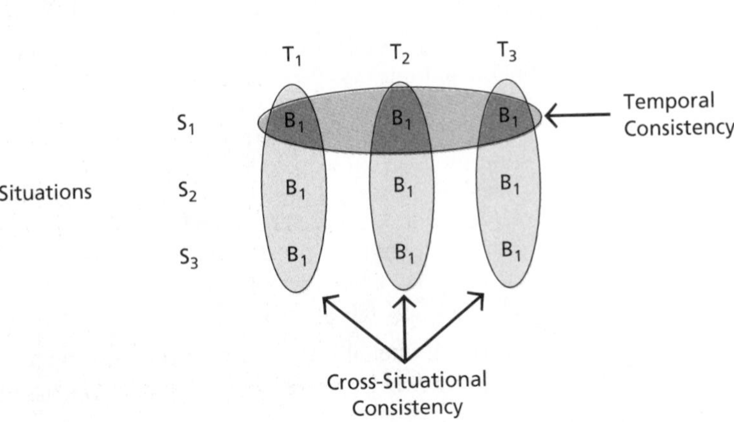

Figure 17.5
Temporal consistency refers to a person's engaging in the same behavior (B) across time (T) and within a given situation (S). Cross-situational consistency refers to a person's engaging in the same behavior in different situations and at any point in time.

will likely be successful tomorrow and the following week as well. Thus, aggression becomes a stable mode of responding *in this specific situation*.

Now suppose Herbie meets a group of older boys on the street. Here the contingencies are quite different. Older children are able to respond to Herbie's aggression with counteraggression. Aggression in the first situation (with smaller children in the playground) would not predict aggression in the second situation (with older children in the street)—at least not if our bully could effectively distinguish one situation from the other. Thus, Herbie's behavior should have temporal consistency but *not* cross-situational consistency (unless, for some reason, Herbie is incapable of discriminating between the different situations).

Mischel's Social Cognitive Personality Theory

Mischel's social cognitive theory owes a debt to several earlier personality psychologists. While working toward his doctorate at Ohio State University, Mischel studied with both George Kelly and Julian Rotter, whose cognitive ideas clearly influenced him. Later, Henry Murray, one of his colleagues at Harvard, made Mischel aware of the importance of taking both person and environmental variables into account in predicting behavior (see pp. 116–118). You may also recognize parallels between Mischel's and Bandura's conceptualizations; they were colleagues at Stanford University for more than 20 years and collaborated on a number of research projects.

Person Variables

Mischel (1973) considers five broad person variables as central to the study of personality: competencies, encoding strategies and personal constructs, expectancies, personal values, and self-regulatory systems and plans.

Each person has a set of behavioral and cognitive skills or **competencies**—overt and covert behaviors that the person is capable of engaging in when the circumstances call for them. **Encoding strategies** and **personal constructs** are the specific ways of sorting and categorizing, respectively, the interpersonal and physical events we encounter. These parallel the personal constructs that Kelly considered the basis of personality.

Like Rotter, Mischel described **expectancies** as probability estimates about the outcomes of particular courses of action in specific situations. For instance, the amount of studying a student will do in preparation for a test partially depends on the student's estimate of the chances that increased studying will result in a higher grade.

People place a specific **personal value** or worth on each possible outcome of courses of action. Two people with identical expectancies about the outcome of a particular behavior will behave differently if they value the outcome differently. This idea closely parallels Rotter's concept of reinforcement value.

Self-regulatory systems and **plans** are self-imposed rewards and personal goals of an individual. They provide motivation and direction for behavior. We address these ideas later in this chapter.

Person Variables versus Dispositions

What is the difference between Mischel's person variables and traditional personality dispositions? Person variables *interact and vary with the specific situation*. For instance, one's competencies are likely to vary in different circumstances. The professor who is highly articulate when she lectures or talks with students in her office may have difficulty speaking on topics other than her area of specialization or in intimate contexts. In contrast, traditional personality dispositions are assumed to remain constant across situations. They are characteristic inclinations to behave in particular ways that are considered independent of the situation. Thus, we would (naively) expect an "articulate" professor to converse well during her lectures, while talking with students, and in all other contexts as well.

Interaction of Person Variables and Situational Variables

According to Mischel's theory, behavior is determined by three factors, as depicted in Figure 17.6: (1) the demands and restrictions of the situation, (2) the individual's person variables, and (3) the interaction of situational and person variables (as indicated by the multiplication sign in the figure; Shoda, Mischel, & Wright, 1989).

The situation provides cues about appropriate or adaptive behavior. These cues are *mediated* by person variables. How you view a situation will influence the course of action you take. Suppose you are walking down a road and a passing motorist stops to offer you a ride. Situational factors will clearly influence your response. There are several possible variations on the situation to be considered. You might know that you will need to walk several miles to get to the nearest telephone, or you might be only one block from your home; similarly, you might be personally acquainted with the driver of the vehicle or the driver might be a large, sinister-looking stranger. Whether you perceive the driver's question as a friendly gesture or a threat will influence your response. To actually emit a response, though, you must also have the relevant capability to respond—that is, be capable of accepting graciously (or running fast).

When Are People Consistent?

Mischel concluded that people are generally consistent in their behavior in the same situation across time; that is, they show temporal consistency. But under normal circumstances, behavior does not show cross-situational consistency

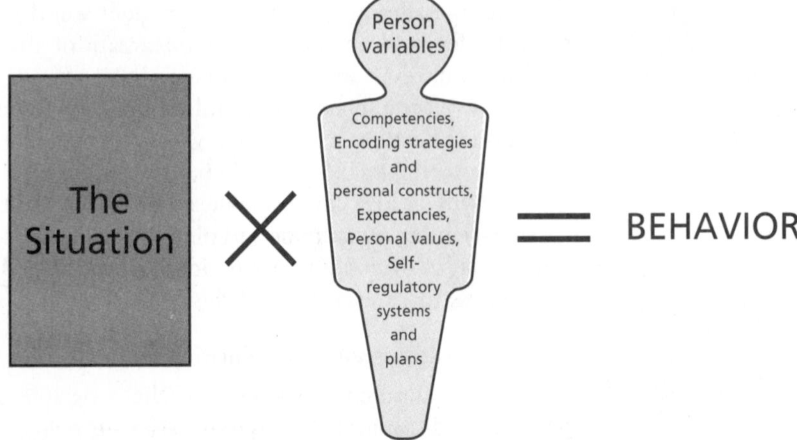

Figure 17.6
According to Mischel, characteristics of the situation interact with person variables to determine behavior.

because people recognize that different behaviors are called for in different situations, and they change their behaviors accordingly.

Mischel (1991; Shoda, Mischel & Wright, 1994) proposes that the consistency of personality can be seen in the distinct patterns of behavior observed *within* individuals over time and across situations. He focuses on the *psychologically meaningful* elements of the situation rather than merely the physical or social setting.

Mischel and colleagues studied the behavior of a large number of children over time and across different settings and determined that the valence (positive or negative) and social source (adult or peer) of experiences constituted the psychologically meaningful and salient characteristics of the events for the children involved. By equating these two dimensions across different activities and settings, a high degree of consistency in the patterns of responding to psychological situations was demonstrated for the vast majority of the children studied (Shoda, Mischel, & Wright, 1994). These authors describe responding to particular psychologically meaningful events in a consistent *if . . . then . . .* pattern as **"behavioral signatures of personality."** They conclude that it is these stable patterns of responding to psychologically meaningful situations that reveal consistency within individuals and highlight differences (in person variables) between people.

By contrasting situations that shared many or few psychological characteristics, Mischel and his associates also demonstrated that behavioral responding can be predicted quite well by common elements of the psychological situation. Although the behavior of any individual might seem unstable and inconsistent if examined across settings and time, when the psychological similarity of the situations is considered, clear patterns of responding emerged. These patterns differed from person to person but remained relatively predictable within persons across time.

These data combine to make a strong case for the idea that behavior is determined by an interaction between person variables and characteristics of the situation, especially the psychologically meaningful elements of the situation (which, no doubt, influence expectancies). However, there also appear to be times when cross-situational consistency is high, despite differences in the psychological characteristics of the situations. Specifically, cross-situational consistency may be expected in *abnormal circumstances,* characterized by high stress and the need to behave beyond one's competency (Cantor, 1990; Wright & Mischel, 1987). In such extreme situations, it appears that people tend to react in a rigid fashion. They use tried-and-true means of responding, even though the responses may be poorly suited to the current situation.

Evidence for this idea comes from a study of the behavior of emotionally disturbed children at a summer camp (Wright & Mischel, 1986). The camp staff observed the children engaged in 21 distinct activities (e.g., music, athletics, and group cabin meetings) over a 40-day period. The staff rated each child's aggressive and withdrawn behaviors.

The cognitive and self-regulatory requirements of each situation were categorized according to the demand they placed on the child. Low-demand situations were within the children's capacities; high-demand situations were

Table 17.1 Mean cross-situational consistency coefficients as a function of a situation's cognitive and self-regulatory requirements. When the situation's requirements were high (and thus exceed the children's competencies), consistency was high; when the situations were less demanding, there was considerably less cross-situational consistency.

	SITUATION COMPETENCY REQUIREMENTS	
BEHAVIOR CATEGORY	LOW	HIGH
1981		
Aggression	.37	.73
Withdrawal	.27	.69
1982		
Aggression	.32	.61
Withdrawal	.06	.37

Source: From data reported in "Convergences and Challenges in the Search for Consistency," by W. Mischel, 1984, *American Psychologist, 39,* 351–364.

tasks beyond their capabilities. The cross-situational consistency of the children's behavior in low-demand and high-demand situations was compared. Some of the results are shown in Table 17.1. As predicted, the children showed much more cross-situational consistency in situations requiring a high degree of competency.

Thus, cross-situational consistency occurs under certain predictable conditions—namely, mentally taxing, high-demand situations that elicit rigid responding. In contrast, good adjustment and competence require that the person choose the specific responses that are likely to produce desirable results in the situation at hand. When people are sensitive to the context, their behaviors vary considerably from situation to situation.

To summarize, most often the consistency in a person's behavior is temporal and *not* cross-situational. People have learned particular ways of behaving successfully in specific situations, and they tend to respond in the same situation-specific ways time after time.

Mischel's work illustrates the importance of considering both person variables *and* the psychologically important characteristics of the context in evaluating personality. A good deal of recent research has focused on a number of person variables, particularly aspects of the self-concept, and the structure of mental representations of the self. We turn our attention now to these more restricted "mini theories" and some of their implications. First, though, we must examine some important cognitive concepts that will inform much of our later discussion.

CONTEMPORARY SCHEMA THEORY

Jean Piaget, the renowned Swiss psychologist, introduced the idea that even young children display organized thought. Piaget's core idea was that similar experiences are stored together to form *memory organizations,* which he called schemata, but are now more commonly called schemas. **Schemas** are "knowledge structures" or mental categories that control the way we recognize and store experiences. They loosely parallel what Kelly termed personal constructs (see Chapter 16). A great deal of the research of contemporary cognitive psychologists focuses on the types, structure, and functions of schemas.

Schemas and Prototypes

Although schemas are abstract, the ease and speed with which a particular experience, stimulus, or event is processed and categorized appear to be based on its "fit" to an idealized or typical representation of the schema. These typical examples of the schema category are called **prototypes.** Schema categories are often represented by prototypical exemplars of the most critical and salient features of the category at hand.

Take, for example, the abstract category "bird," for which most English language speakers have a schema. A blue jay is a bird but so are some very different-looking creatures, such as penguins, ostriches, and chickens. If you ask people to name a type of bird, however, they are much more likely to mention a more typically birdlike (pigeon, sparrow, or crow) rather than a less birdlike (penguin or flamingo) variety. If you show people pictures of various animals and ask them to say whether each *is* or *is not* a bird, they will respond more quickly to a picture of a blue jay than to a picture of an ostrich or penguin. Human beings are presumed to develop an enormous array of interrelated schemas that allow them to process and categorize incoming information efficiently.

The Importance of Schemas

The existence and content of schemas have repeatedly been shown to influence the processing and categorizing of information. People process information for which they have a relevant schema more quickly and efficiently than information not related to a personal schema. This rule holds for

Both are birds, but the songbird will be recognized as a bird much more quickly than the ostrich by most people. PhotoDisc, Inc.

Nancy Cantor emphasizes the importance of schemas in how people receive, process, store, and recall information.

Courtesy of Nancy Cantor, Provost and Executive Vice President for Academic Affairs/The University of Michigan

information related to the external world, personal skills, abilities and performance, and characteristics of other people.

Schemas seem to enhance information processing by providing a context for evaluation of incoming information. These comparisons are often made against the prototypic exemplar of the particular schema that appears most relevant to the information or situation at hand. Although this does enhance processing speed, categorization of information, and later recall and retrieval of the information acquired, there is a price to be paid. Because schemas offer up prototypical examples of information categories, some bias is introduced in the processing of new information relevant to an existing schema.

Information is compared with prototypes, leading the observer to focus intently on those features of the new stimulus that are most relevant for the operative schema and its exemplary prototype. Often, later recall of the stimulus is somewhat distorted. Because attributes most relevant for the particular schema receive the most attention and are most likely to be actively processed, inconsistent or less relevant information may be ignored or forgotten. The result is that, on recall, the new information appears *more consistent with* (or, where contrast is particularly attended to, *more distinct from*) the existing prototype, and details of the specific stimulus are often deemphasized or completely lost. This effect appears to account for a good deal of the distortion found in retrospective recall of past events, people, and experiences. Thus, experiences are processed and stored *relative to* the schema operative at the time of processing and *not* simply on the basis of objective stimulus characteristics. Nancy Cantor (1990) summarized the functions of schemas in processing and recalling information. She states that schemas "provide each person with unique cognitive filters that color the perception of events, determining the very ways in which events are 'seen' and remembered" (p. 736).

THE SELF: THE STRUCTURE OF PERSONALITY

We have discussed how particular aspects of self-knowledge differ from person to person and influence behavior. Locus of control, perceived self-efficacy, expectancies, and reinforcement value are all "person variables" in the language of Bandura and Mischel's social cognitive theories. These variables all reflect, at some level, aspects of an individual's self-concept or *personality structure*. They combine and *interact* with aspects of the environment and the process of personality as represented by the goals, aspirations, and means of the person.

Interest in the self and in how it is represented mentally has emerged as an important research area within cognitive and personality psychology. Sedikides and Skowronski (1995) defined the **self** as "the cognitive representation of the kind of person we think we are" (pp. 244–245).

Although the theorists of the phenomenological approach speculated about mental representations of the self, contemporary researchers are now actively defining and delineating the actual roles and functions of self-knowledge. It appears that the self influences how information is received, processed, and stored *not just about the self* but about the external world and others in it as well (Markus & Zajonc, 1985; Von Hippel, Jonides, Hilton, &

Narayan, 1993). The self often guides future goal formation, as well as behaviors aimed at attaining these goals. Finally, emotional responses have been related to the self-concept and how it is assessed by the individual relative to personal standards (Higgins, 1987; Sedikides & Skowronski, 1995). We will examine a number of these theories, their interrelations, and then some implications derived from their integration.

Markus's Self-Schemas

Hazel Markus (1977; Markus & Kitayama, 1991; Markus & Nurius, 1986; Markus & Wurf, 1987) is a major contributor to cognitive theories of the self. She refers to the cognitive structure of one's self-concept as the **self-schema.** More specifically, Markus (1977) writes that the "self-schemata, or cognitive generalizations about the self, . . . organize, summarize, and explain behavior along a particular dimension" (p. 75). Thus, self-schemas serve to capture and summarize a person's abilities, thoughts, feelings, and experiences in a particular life domain (Cantor, 1990). According to Markus, our self-schemas are comprised of specific self-attributions regarding our own personal characteristics.

Cantor (1990) goes one step further in suggesting that these schemas may be construed "as the cognitive carriers of dispositions" (p. 737). Thus, self-schemas parallel the person variables of other theorists *and* influence individuals' understanding of themselves and their world in all the ways suggested by recent research on schemas.

Markus distinguishes people as **schematic** or **aschematic** with respect to various traits or characteristics. A person may be schematic on one trait and aschematic on another. For example, when Michael is asked about his *intelligence,* he quickly recites his many intellectual accomplishments and gives numerous examples of situations in which he feels he has acted intelligently. Asked about his athletic ability, however, Michael is slow to answer and does not seem very involved with the question. According to Markus, Michael is *schematic* for intelligence and *aschematic* for athletic ability; that is, he has a concept of self based on intelligence but does not usually "think of himself" in terms of athletic ability. For another person, the reverse might be true; Tommy might be schematic for athletic ability but not for intelligence.

Hazel Markus has studied and delineated the roles and functions of self-schemas.
Courtesy of Hazel Rose Markus/Stanford University

The dimensions on which a person is schematic or aschematic depend, in part, on the particular strengths and weaknesses of the individual. People tend to be schematic for areas in which they have a clear talent or deficit or areas that for personal reasons are particularly important to them. Thus, people tend to be schematic for issues of high salience in their personal experiences (Markus & Nurius, 1986).

On the basis of their self-schemas, people make plans and set goals for themselves and evaluate themselves and their experiences. Schemas in general and self-schemas in particular serve a clear *information-processing* role for understanding our experiences and relationships with others. They are composed of discrete "chunks" of information derived from our life experiences and cause us to *selectively* process information. Some information is highlighted, whereas other information is downplayed or ignored. This has important implications for personality.

Self-Consistency

One widely held view of the concept of self is as the product of an innate organizing function that provides a sense of unity, wholeness, and consistency to the person. Gordon Allport, most famous in psychology for his early trait theory (see Chapter 8), believed in such a selflike central organizing mechanism, which he called the **proprium.**

More than 40 years ago, Leon Festinger (1957) argued that all people have a motive to think *and* behave consistently. When a person is forced to behave in a fashion inconsistent with prior behavior or beliefs, an uncomfortable state, which Festinger termed **cognitive dissonance,** is produced. Cognitive dissonance results from inconsistency between two or more of a person's beliefs or perceptions about himself or herself. People work to reduce or eliminate dissonance in a variety of ways. At the most general level, efforts to maintain consistency and coherence influence not only our present and future thoughts and actions but also our representations of the past. Several writers have emphasized the importance for each person of developing a **personal life story,** which, like any satisfying *narrative tale,* is written to be consistent and coherent (Bruhn, 1990; McAdams, 1985; McAdams et al., 1988). This task is especially important as people come to face their mortality (either in seniority or with catastrophic illness). It seems more important to create a *coherent* story than an *accurate* story, which again reflects the primacy of mental representations over "objective" facts.

Different Aspects of Self

William James (1890) speculated in his *Principles of Psychology* that there are three important "selves": a **material self,** composed of representation of one's body, abilities, family composition, and the like; a **social self,** containing one's beliefs about others' perceptions; and a **spiritual self,** which consists of one's deepest emotions and desires. Therefore, the self has many interrelated but separable facets. (Although similar, the self is *not* identical to Freud's concept of *ego.* Unlike the Freudian ego, the cognitive self thinks about itself.)

The idea of multiple selves continues to pervade contemporary personality psychology. Showers (1992b), in noting this trend toward multiple self aspects, describes contemporary models of the self as multidimensional and multifaceted. Current research commonly distinguishes between aspects of the self related to specific social settings or life contexts. Other important distinctions are drawn between actual and potential selves. We will now examine a number of these current distinctions and related research.

Multiple Selves

Carl Rogers drew a distinction earlier between the *actual* self and the *ideal* self (see p. 410). Most contemporary writers agree that the global self-concept is more accurately described as comprised of a number of narrower and more distinct selves. Some selves may be specific to particular social relationships (the "self when with significant other" concept, for example). Beyond these specific selves are other "potential" selves. E. Tory Higgins (1987; Higgins, Roney, Crowe, & Hymmes, 1994) has developed a theory that incorporates several ideas from Rogers's self-actualization approach (see pp. 406–415).

E. Tory Higgins described the emotions resulting from disparities between different aspects of the self-concept.
Courtesy of E. Tory Higgins/ Columbia University

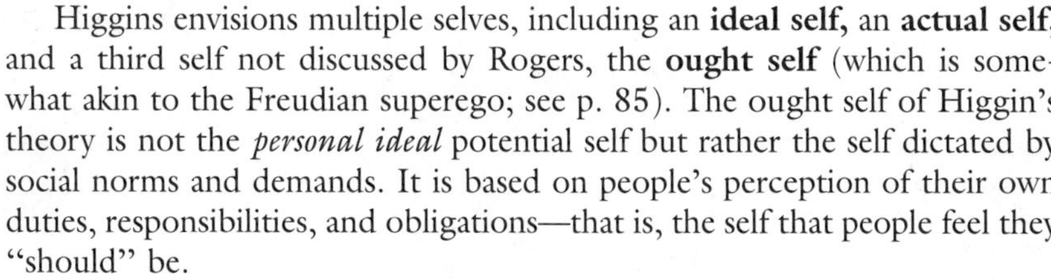

Higgins envisions multiple selves, including an **ideal self,** an **actual self,** and a third self not discussed by Rogers, the **ought self** (which is somewhat akin to the Freudian superego; see p. 85). The ought self of Higgin's theory is not the *personal ideal* potential self but rather the self dictated by social norms and demands. It is based on people's perception of their own duties, responsibilities, and obligations—that is, the self that people feel they "should" be.

Like Rogers, Higgins believes these multiple selves must be reasonably consistent for the individual to function as a healthy being. He reports that disparities between the actual and ideal selves produce sadness, disappointments, and depression, whereas disparities between the actual and ought selves produce anxiety, fear, and guilt. In fact, a good deal of empirical support has been generated for this distinction and the emotions resulting from the different types of disparities (Higgins, 1987; Higgins, Bond, Klein, & Strauman, 1986; Strauman & Higgins, 1987). Thus, how we think about and represent our selves *to ourselves* plays a major role in personality and in our day-to-day emotions.

Another theory of potential selves has been presented by Markus and Nurius (1986), who write of possible selves as models for guiding and planning and behavior. They define **possible selves** as "individual's ideas of what they might become, what they would like to become, and what they are afraid of becoming" (p. 954). Markus and Nurius emphasize the social nature of the possible selves. They are based on the needs and tastes of the individual but often formulated and refined in response to social models and interactions.

These authors conclude that representations of potential selves serve as models to motivate behavior (toward or away from specific outcomes) and provide a context for evaluating the present self. These processes enable people to make plans, formulate goals, and direct behavior toward desired outcomes. (We discuss goals and the self again later in this chapter.) Another feature of the self-concept on which people appear to differ is complexity.

Self-Complexity

Patricia Linville described the protective function of self-complexity.
Courtesy of Patricia Linville/ Duke University/Photo by Les Todd

People differ on the *complexity* of their overall self-schemas. Patricia Linville (1985, 1987) has argued for the importance of the dimension of **self-complexity**—that is, the number of different self-concepts a person has and their distinctness or the degree to which the self-concept in one domain "spills over" into a person's self-concept in other domains (Figure 17.7). Linville argues that high self-complexity protects the individual from negative "spillover."

According to this theory, aspects of the self are *compartmentalized,* so shortcomings in one specific domain need not reflect negatively on other domains of functioning or on the person in general. For a person with an overly simple self-concept, even trivial failures may be intensely threatening. For them, failure at one particular task may well suggest *global inadequacy,* which obviously has implications for the person's overall feelings of worth and competence.

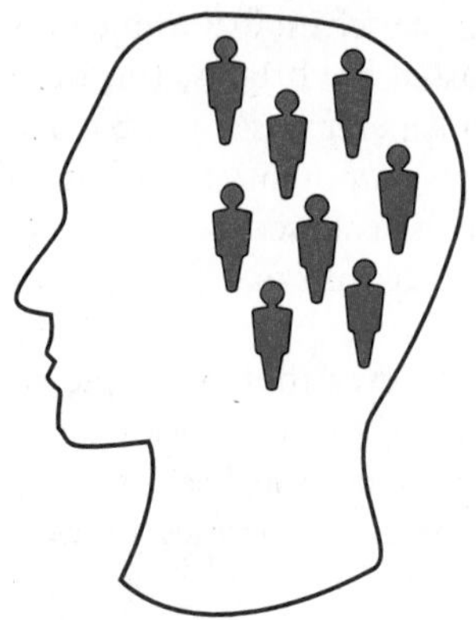
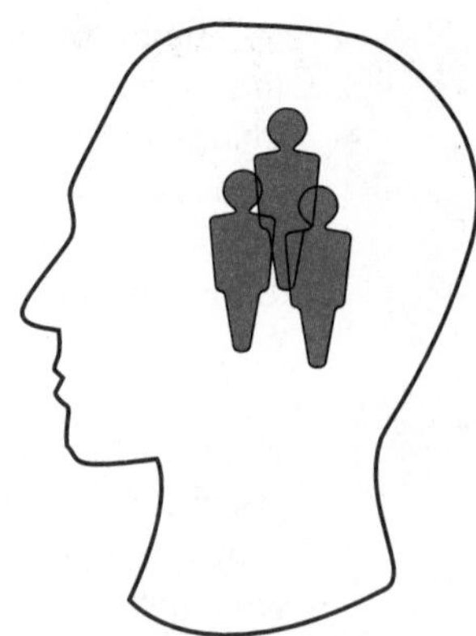

Figure 17.7
According to Linville, both number and distinctness of self representations influence the impact of self-relevant feedback.

Self-complexity is usually measured by the number of categories an individual requires to adequately represent their own self-knowledge. Linville assesses this dimensions with a card-sorting task in which subjects arrange descriptors into as many or as few groups as they feel necessary to adequately describe themselves. Subjects are permitted to reuse descriptors in multiple categories, allowing for additional measurement of the *relatedness* or *independence* of the categories they generate.

Using this method, Linville has found that "emotional spillover" is greater for less complex subjects than for those with greater self-complexity; that is, given negative feedback, those with limited self-complexity experience greater distress and a greater negative impact on measures of self-esteem and mood. In relating naturally occurring mood fluctuations to self-complexity, Linville found the less complex subjects to have greater mood swings. It appears that self-complexity may serve to buffer the impact of negative events.

Linville (1987) extended these early findings to an examination of stress and health outcomes. She reasoned that if self-complexity serves to buffer the negative impact of life events, then more complex subjects should evidence fewer negative health or mood outcomes in response to stress than less complex subjects. In fact, what she found was that in the presence of relatively high stress, those who measured higher on self-complexity reported fewer physical symptoms and negative emotions than those lower on self-complexity. However, among subjects who reported *few* stressful life events, it appeared that the less complex subjects had an advantage. They reported experiencing less stress and fewer physical symptoms than the more complex subjects. This outcome seems to make good sense intuitively. If emotional spillover accounts for observed differences in emotions and health, then self-complexity serves a *protective* function in the face of negative experiences. However, the same limiting effect would also presumably operate relative to positive emotions and experiences. The less complex person may benefit most from positive experiences in the sense that they spread and create global positive feelings.

Others have suggested that the *structure* of self-knowledge may be *as or more* important than the content of that knowledge. Carolin Showers (1992a) argues that the degree to which positive and negative elements of the

Carolin Showers emphasizes the importance of the valence of self-knowledge and how positive and negative self-knowledge is distributed among aspects of the self.

Courtesy of Carolin Showers/ University of Wisconsin, Madison

self-concept are either compartmentalized or intermingled within different aspects of the self may be an important determinant of feelings of worth, competence, and emotions. Showers's work suggests that an interaction occurs between the valence (positive or negative) of self-knowledge and the importance placed on the specific domain of self (Figure 17.8).

For people who place great importance on aspects of self in which they feel capable, it is adaptive to keep negative self-descriptors at bay, secluded in narrow and relatively unimportant domains of functioning that need not be accessed frequently. However, for people who feel less capable in areas they themselves deem important, it appears best to include some positive features in these domains to buffer against the harsh reality of their deficiencies. Including such features allows for people to readily access positive aspects of self, even in a context that would ordinarily invoke a relatively negative or deficient self-concept. This relates to the idea of **working self-concept,** which is defined as those features of self that are relevant to the task at hand and most accessible in memory. (The idea of a working self-concept is akin to the idea of *working memory,* defined as that part of memory that is presently active and from which material can be readily retrieved.)

By defining less important aspects of self, which carry negatively valenced self-knowledge very narrowly, this negative information can be "filed away" and encountered only when absolutely necessary. More important domains of functioning will necessarily be accessed more regularly. Thus, if significant deficiencies exist in some important (and therefore frequently accessed) domains, it is best to pad these self-concepts with a modicum of favorable self-knowledge, lest the person become bogged down in negativity.

Consistent with Linville's earlier work, which suggested that self-complexity was most beneficial in the face of negative experiences and emotions, Showers contends that compartmentalization also appears most useful as a *protective device* against negative self-knowledge. Negative self-knowledge is best stored far from frequently accessed self-concepts *unless* the aspects of self to which it is related are so central that they cannot usually be avoided. In the latter case, negative self-knowledge should be diluted to the extent possible with positively valenced self-knowledge applicable to the same domain. The frequency of accessing negative self-knowledge and its per-

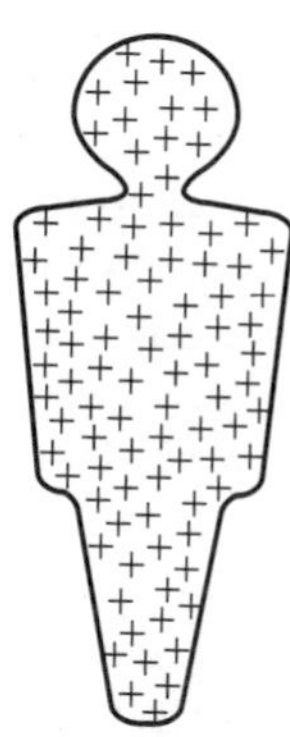

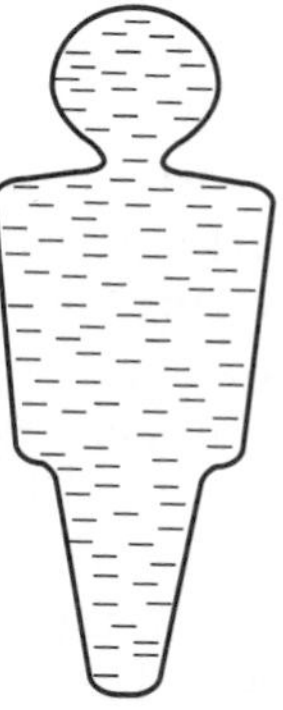

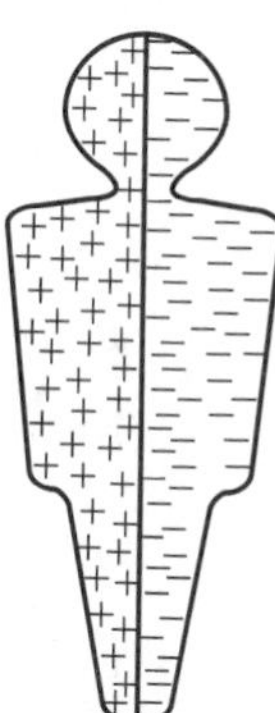

Figure 17.8
Each particular self-concept may be all positive, all negative, or a mixture of positive and negative elements. What is most adaptive depends on the importance of the particular domain.

vasiveness within the self-concept, will affect the individual's overall self-evaluations and functioning. Self-esteem serves as one measure of an individual's self-evaluations.

Self-Esteem

Self-esteem refers to feelings of satisfaction and pride in one's self. High self-esteem serves as a buffer against anxiety when we are threatened or challenged (e.g., Solomon, Greenberg, & Pyszczynski, 1991a, 1991b). Thus, self-esteem refers to the degree of positive worth a person feels. More than a century ago, William James (1890) wrote an equation for self-esteem:

$$\text{Self-esteem} = \frac{\text{Success}}{\text{Aspirations}}$$

This formula actually reveals tremendous insight. It illustrates how an "objectively successful" person may have miserably low self-esteem by simply having extremely high aspirations and goals for the self. Similarly, a person of only modest accomplishment may have very high self-esteem because success is always *relative to* aspirations.

The person operates to maintain and enhance self-esteem; in this sense, self-esteem is a concept very similar to Rogers's notion of positive self-regard (see Chapter 16). People engage in a variety of activities and behavior patterns to bolster and protect their self-esteem. Of the many techniques, perhaps the most interesting is self-handicapping.

Self-handicapping is acting in such a way as to increase the likelihood of failure at a task. It can be done by inadequate preparation or by choosing tasks that are obviously too difficult. Although self-handicapping may at first appear to be a highly dysfunctional strategy, it actually operates to *protect* self-esteem. In the face of failure, the self-handicapper can blame the lack of preparation or task difficulty and thus avoid making negative self-evaluations (Rhodewalt, Morf, Hazlett, & Fairfield, 1991; Snyder, 1990).

Another way to maintain self-esteem is through **self-enhancement.** People generally favor information that puts them in a good light and misinterpret "ambiguous" information to their best advantage (Markus & Wurf, 1987; Taylor & Brown, 1988.) (Note the parallel between self-enhancement and feedback distortion, discussed in the preceding chapter.) Another factor that influences self-evaluations is the degree to which different people attend to self-relevant information and feedback, that is, monitor themselves.

Self-Monitoring

Snyder (1974) introduced the concept of **self-monitoring** to describe the degree and ways in which people objectively observe their own behavior and purposely "posture" in their self-presentation. Self-monitoring is assessed from a true-false scale, a number of which have been developed over the years (Gangestad & Snyder, 1985; Lennox & Wolfe, 1984; Shuptrine, Bearden, & Teale, 1990; Snyder, 1974).

Those who score high on self-monitoring scales are more effective than those low on these scales when it comes to their attempts to deceive others (DePaulo, 1992). Larkin (1991) goes as far as to say that high self-monitors are often cunning in the way they manage self-representation, in contrast to low self-monitors, who relate to others in a consistent, straightforward manner without an eye toward seeking advantage. High self-monitors are particularly attuned to the reactions of others and work hard to ensure that these reactions will be favorable.

Self-Concept: A Reconceptualization

The idea that healthy psychological adjustment depends on accurate self-perception is hardly new. "Know thyself" has been recommended for centuries by philosophers, sages, and theologians (Brown, 1991). More recently, personality theorists, including Freud (1957b; Sackeim, 1983), Erikson (1950), Fromm (1955), and Allport (1943), as well as Rogers (1951) and Maslow (1950), have also endorsed the importance of undistorted self-knowledge.

Much of the recent research cited here, though, taken together, suggests that this quest for accurate self-knowledge may well be misguided. It appears that most people have a pervasive tendency to evaluate their selves and their world more favorably than is actually justified by objective circumstances and the opinions of observers (e.g., Brown, 1991; Dunning, Meyerowitz, & Holzberg, 1989; Taylor & Brown, 1988). A good deal of empirical evidence has accumulated to suggest that this style is both common and *very adaptive.*

Debilitating negative thoughts about one's performance (irrespective of actual performance) are linked to anxiety (e.g., Beck & Emery, 1985; Ellis, 1989; Luccock & Salkovskis, 1988; Sarason, Sarason, & Pierce, 1990). Maladaptive (not self-serving) cognitive distortions, such as over generalizations and arbitrary inferences about causality, are associated with depression (e.g., Beck & Weishaar, 1989; Dykman & Abramson, 1990; Stiles & Götestam, 1989; Stiles, Schröder, & Johansen, 1993). The most psychologically adaptive strategy seems to be capitalizing on every opportunity for self-enhancement, attributing all success experiences to oneself (rather than external factors), and avoiding, at all costs, negative feedback, while managing to distort, discard, or "file away" any absolutely unavoidable negative reflections on the self. Research generally supports these conclusions.

Mischel has investigated and theorized about how our mood affects the way we evaluate situations. In one experiment, Wright and Mischel (1982) had college students imagine scenes that induced a positive (happy) or negative (sad) mood. Then the students performed a perception task that was set up so that they either succeeded or failed. To assess the effects of mood and success experience, the subjects were asked a series of questions about their performance on the perception task.

A positive mood resulted in higher estimates of past performance, higher expectations about future success, and higher overall self-evaluation of ability on the task. These results held both for subjects who had succeeded and for those who had failed.

A negative mood had little effect on the self-evaluations of the success group, but subjects in the failure group were much less satisfied with their performance if they were in a negative mood. When subjects were asked to set goals for future trials on the task, the combination of failure and a negative mood was particularly devastating. Subjects in this group were the only ones to set minimal goals that they did *not* expect to meet.

What is the process by which mood influences thought? Wright and Mischel (1982) suggested that people have a **mood-congruent bias.** We process information about past experience selectively, in a way that is consistent with our current mood. This suggestion is completely consistent with findings on schemas. Induction of a negative mood may encourage access of related schemas—that is, schemas containing negative information, especially negative information about the self and past failure experiences.

The same mechanism appears to operate in depression. In one study, the social competence of depressed and nondepressed individuals was rated by observers and by the individuals themselves (Lewinsohn, Mischel, Chaplin, & Barton, 1980). Contrary to expectations, depressed subjects rated themselves as they were seen by others and were actually quite accurate. In contrast, the nondepressed subjects rated themselves more positively than they were seen by others. As the depressed subjects' mood became more positive, their self-perceptions began to change.

> In the course of treatment, the depressed not only rated themselves more positively [but] began to increase the discrepancy between how they rated themselves and how they were rated . . . their self-perceptions became more unrealistic in the sense that they began to see themselves more positively than the observers rated them. It is tempting to conjecture that a key to avoiding depression is to see oneself less stringently and more favorably than others see one. If so, the beliefs that unrealistic appraisals are a basic ingredient of depression and that realism is the crux of appropriate affect may have to be seriously questioned. To feel good about ourselves we may have to judge ourselves more kindly than we are judged. (Lewinsohn et al., 1980, pp. 211–212)

From all of these data, we conclude that people's portraits of the self are generally "brighter, more colorful, and more beautiful" than "objective" reality (Brown, 1991, p. 173). However, rather than reflecting a deviant or problematic perceptual process, the evidence indicates that people's self-enhancing illusions are "associated with, and may contribute to, psychological adjustment and superior functioning" (Brown, 1991, p. 173). Thus, people's self-distortions serve a positive function.

There are limits to the extent of distortion that can be tolerated and continue to enhance functioning, however. Self-enhancing illusions are most effective when they are moderate—that is, *only slightly* more positive than can be reasonably justified (Baumeister, 1989). Estimates of one's abilities or attributes that are either overly grandiose or excessively modest are likely to result in poor psychological adjustment and functioning. Grossly inaccurate estimates may produce repeated failure experiences (if excessively grandiose) or limit functioning and growth by deterring active pursuit of personal goals.

Another theme common to many personality theories is the need for self-consistency. Here again, the recent data argue *against* consistency as an ideal. It appears that a large number of selves *that are mostly independent* of one another serves a protective function. These clearly distinct self-concepts allow people to avoid or deemphasize negative self-knowledge and thereby enhance their day-to-day functioning and overall self-concept.

The Perceived Self as Primary

The findings on self-evaluation call into question the earlier distinction between one's actual self and ideal self. One's "actual" self-concept may, in fact, *lean toward* the ideal rather than accurately reflecting some "objective" reality. A better term for the actual self, then, would be the *perceived self.* This term captures the inherent subjectivity of this and all other mental representations.

The high prevalence of self-enhancing illusions means that we engage in considerable self-deception—albeit with apparently healthy consequences. Yet, few people are consciously aware of their self-deception. (They certainly would be reluctant to acknowledge it if they were!) How do we maintain self-enhancing illusions? The answer lies in the host of strategies we use to avoid, cope with, and deal with feedback, many of which were mentioned throughout this discussion (Brown, 1991).

As a first line of defense, we engage in behavioral strategies to maximize our exposure to positive feedback while minimizing exposure to negative feedback. For example, consider the implications of the finding that teenagers are more likely to seek out the opinions of peers than adults on issues related to the appropriateness of their dress, grooming, or music preferences. People tend to actively seek out approval and positive feedback while they shy away from criticism.

When we cannot avoid negative feedback, we use cognitive strategies to actively cope with it, such as selectively attending to, remembering, interpreting, and explaining the negative feedback. A student whose term paper evokes more criticism than praise may (1) glance over the negative comments quickly but read the positive comments several times, (2) remember only the positive comments, (3) interpret any negative comments that are ambiguous as "backward compliments," and (4) attribute the negative comments to the professor's critical nature (external) while gladly taking personal credit for successes (internal).

Finally, when negative feedback is unavoidable and too blatant to be ignored or easily distorted, we resort to strategies that minimize the damage to our overall sense of worth. We belittle the value of a skill that we know we lack (e.g., "I don't need to be good at math to be a musician") or dilute this negative self-knowledge by surrounding it with positive self-knowledge.

All of these processes influence the resulting self-concept, which, through selective processing, influences how we view, experience, and represent our world. These "person variables" then serve to set the stage for our behavior relative to (1) the existing environment, (2) our expectations of various outcomes, and (3) the goals we set for ourselves and our preferred means for pursuing them. Let us now take a closer look at the other side of this coin, the process side of personality in the form of "life tasks," or goals.

GOALS AND SELF-REGULATION: THE PROCESS OF PERSONALITY

The related concepts of goals, aspirations, and plans have been touched on several times earlier in this chapter. We have seen that self-esteem can be thought of as based on evaluation of success relative to aspirations. Rotter spoke of the reinforcement value of desired outcomes. Bandura writes of expectancies and self-efficacy, which are specific to particular tasks or endeavors. Mischel wrote of plans and goals. Clearly, all of these theorists acknowledged (explicitly or implicitly) mental processes of goal setting, planning, and evaluation of progress toward desired ends.

The idea that people actively set agendas for themselves and then evaluate their progress against these goals and aspirations has become a focus of recent personality research. Nancy Cantor (1990) refers to this as the "doing" part of personality, or the *process* (as opposed to the structure and content) of personality. This idea is not new to psychology. William James (1890) wrote: "The pursuance of future ends and the choice of means for their attainment are the mark and criterion of the presence of mentality in a phenomenon" (p. 8).

In fact, goals and their function in guiding and driving behavior have come to be central to the study of cognition in personality. Austin and Vancouver (1996) define **goals** as "internal representations of desired states" (p. 338). They construe goals as organizing constructs that can make sense of otherwise inexplicable behavioral inconsistency. Austin and Vancouver also contend that the demands of the immediate situation may pull for different types of behavior from the individual. But when the behavior is viewed from the perspective of the goals the individual is pursuing, it appears more rational and predictable. This thinking is reminiscent of Mischel's and Rotter's insistence on the importance of situational factors and the *psychologically meaningful* aspects of the environment as determinants of behavior. The goal may remain the same across time, but the best means for pursuing the goal may well shift with changes of context.

Goals clearly differ from person to person and situation to situation. The literature on goals is wide ranging and plagued by language problems reminiscent of the Tower of Babel problem of the Dispositional Strategy because researchers from diverse areas are concurrently examining related issues. Like the earlier discussion of research on the self-concept, research on goals has exploded over the past decade or so. Our discussion attempts to capture the essence of recent theorizing and empirical findings, while emphasizing their importance for the study of the self and personality.

Organization of Goals

People clearly pursue multiple goals both over time and concurrently. Goals can be examined at many levels of abstraction, and they vary in personal importance from person to person. For example, all people share some basic physical needs (food, water, sleep), and meeting these needs on an ongoing basis might be considered a universal goal. However, because these goals are common to all, they reveal little about the individual. Goals at very high levels of abstraction (e.g., to be a "good" person) also tend to reveal little that is specific to a particular individual; they are also difficult to measure and assess.

Most researchers examine a middle level of goals, with enough specificity for meaningful individual differences and empirical evaluation.

Like schemas and other mental representations, goals are organized, and connections between levels clearly exist. Some lower-level goals subserve goals at a higher level of abstraction. A lower-level goal may also serve multiple higher-order goals, and higher-order goals may be met through many different paths. These relationships between goals may also explain behavioral inconsistencies in differing circumstances.

Consider the relatively abstract goal of being "responsible." This goal might be served by multiple lower-level goals such as paying bills on time, attending all classes, doing class assignments, and calling home regularly. Many of these lower-level goals also serve the goal of performing well academically. Thus, pursuing some goals may automatically advance other goals, and individual goals can be pursued through multiple paths. How a particular goal is best served varies over time and circumstances.

In fact, individuals may focus their attention on particular goals or levels of abstraction at any point in time. Movement between goals and levels can be in any direction—within or across levels (as contexts change or priorities shift). This potential for multidirectional movement has led some to label the goal system structure as a "heterarchy" (Hyland, 1988).

Planning and Strategies

Once a particular goal is formulated or adopted by an individual (many goals are supplied by groups or institutions), they must plan a means to the desired end state. Such planning involves developing a strategy to meet the goal. Strategies may consist of a series of specific subgoals reduced to the level of minor discrete steps. They may also include multiple possible routes and means, providing the potential for behavioral flexibility in response to obstructions. If one route to a particular goal is blocked, another may be pursued.

For example, a student whose goal is to become a lawyer must first complete law school. Before completing law school, a student must be offered admission, which requires completing college and passing the LSAT. Each of these goals can be further reduced to lower and lower sets of subgoals, many of which must first be met (e.g., doing well in college by attending classes regularly and studying for examinations) to enable pursuit of goals at the next level.

Planning also enables people to test out strategies and subgoals mentally, in an effort to avoid wasting time and energy in fruitless pursuits. Even young children recognize the value of planning and display clear recognition of some personal goals.

The Purpose of Plans

As early as 1979, Mischel used structured interviews to study the development of personal plans in children. He found that children as young as 8 years old can discuss plans explicitly and provide concrete examples of how they use plans to structure and organize their actions.

By age 11, children have a surprisingly good grasp of the nature, organization, and function of plans in their lives. They appreciate that plans have a purpose or goal. For example, "I'm going to clean up my room tomorrow because I want to have a friend over." Some children interviewed could tell the researchers that a plan helps people move toward a goal and guides progress toward its attainment.

Evaluating Progress

Once particular goals are set, progress must be evaluated periodically. If movement is not in the direction of goal attainment, the goal, or strategies for obtaining it, will be reevaluated.

Goals have been described as having the property of *equifinality* (Austin & Vancouver, 1996); that is, the goal can be satisfied through any available means. Reaching lower-level goals may move one toward or enable one to reach other goals as well. Any goal, once met, may be satisfied forever or only until the same need arises again. Once a particular goal is met, new goals may be established, or attention may be shifted to other existing goals.

Consider the goal of being a good student. Earning A's on several examinations contributes to achieving this goal. Earning a 4.0 semester average also contributes. These achievements may have constituted subgoals themselves. The higher-order goal (being a good student) might not be fully satisfied until graduation day arrives, and then only if the individual's own personal standards for being a "good student" have been met. Now new goals are set. They may be related (e.g., be a good *graduate* student) or independent of the previous goal.

Evaluation of progress typically requires feedback from the environment. Often movement toward or away from a goal and movement between goals form a *feedback loop;* input about the status of one factor leads to adjustments and ultimately feedback from the other in a reciprocal fashion. When feedback about progress is not obvious or forthcoming, individuals often try to obtain the required feedback by asking others to evaluate their performances or proximity to goal states. (Ed Koch, former mayor of New York City, became recognized by his trademark question, "How am I doing?") This feedback often guides goal revision, rejection, or energy expenditure.

Goal Content

Goal content—that is, the specific goals set within the goal system of an individual—largely depends on the individual's self-concept. A person for whom intelligence is central may choose goals related to this image, such as high academic achievement, a scholarly profession, or simply recognition as a very bright person.

Successful goal attainment often informs the self-concept as well (recall the earlier feedback loop). A student who views herself as intelligent may set the goal of earning an A in calculus. Meeting this goal enhances her view of herself as intelligent. Self-efficacy for mathematics and self-esteem may also benefit from this achievement, as well as any related self-concepts.

As stated earlier, the self-concept guides goal selection. Goal progress and attainment then affect the self-concept. Goals differ in the level of abstraction they represent. Some authors have speculated that the highest-order goals are directly related to self-concept development (Hattie, 1991; Markus & Wurf,

1987; Steele, 1988). This being the case and given that people apparently use every available means to enhance the self and avoid negative feedback, it seems plausible that the highest-order goals (and, by extension, all related subgoals) may ultimately serve to create, enhance, and maintain a positive, adaptive, and healthy (if somewhat optimistically distorted) self-image.

The social cognitive perspective emphasizes the central role of representations of the self in personality. These representations influence our perceptions of, interpretations of, and interactions with the external world. If positive distortion actually enhances adaptive functioning, then working to build and maintain a positive self-image is a worthwhile effort. And one concise way to summarize all of this work would be to view these cognitive processes and representations as the self in service of self.

SUMMARY

1. Social cognitive theories focus on both the structure of personality, in the form of schemas or knowledge structures, and the process of personality, in the form of self-regulatory processes, plans, and goals.
2. Although phenomenological approaches emphasized mental representations, they were based on speculation and clinical observations. In contrast, social cognitive theories are rooted in systematic research.
3. The concept of self is central to social cognitive theories. However, various social cognitive theories have considered the self from a variety of perspectives.
4. Julian Rotter was one of the first psychologists to discuss the role of cognition in personality. Rotter's theory is based on four basic constructs: the psychological situation, reinforcement value, expectancy, and behavior potential. Reinforcement value refers to a person's individual preference for certain outcomes (reinforcers) and is always relative to the range of potential reinforcers available. Expectancy refers to the perceived likelihood that a particular outcome will be obtained in a particular situation. The psychological situation is the existing circumstances people perceive themselves to be in at any given time.
5. Behavior potential is the likelihood that a person will engage in a particular behavior. It is equal to reinforcement value multiplied by expectancy. If either reinforcement value or expectancy is zero, the behavior will not occur.
6. Locus of control refers to a person's perception of the source of outcomes. Internal locus of control is the belief that one's outcomes are determined by one's personal efforts and resources, whereas external control is the belief that outcomes are due to outside forces. Locus of control develops as a function of life experiences.
7. Bandura's theory of triadic reciprocal determinism refers to the three-way bidirectional influences of behavior (B), environment (E), and person variables (P).
8. Perceived self-efficacy, the most important theoretical construct in Bandura's social cognitive theory, refers to a person's estimate of his or her own ability to perform a particular behavior. It is at least par-

tially independent of a person's actual abilities. Whereas outcome expectancies refer to one's estimate that a given action will result in a particular outcome, efficacy expectations are beliefs about one's own competence. High self-efficacy generally leads to favorable outcomes, but excessive self-efficacy can lead to dangerous complacency.

9. Walter Mischel is one of the most prominent social cognitive theorists of the late 20th century. His 1968 book, *Personality and Assessment,* offered a devastating critique of dispositional and psychoanalytic personality assessment. In it, he coined the term personality coefficient to refer to the fact that traditional measures of personality are only weak predictors of behavior and thus not suitable for making predictions about individuals. He argued that assessment should rely on samples of actual behavior rather than indirect signs gleaned from paper-and-pencil inventories or projective tests.
10. Mischel's social cognitive theory, like Bandura's, emphasized the importance of person variables, the relatively enduring cognitive and behavioral attributes of the individual.
11. Mischel has identified and explained the consistency paradox, that people perceive more consistency in their own and others' behavior than actually exists according to direct behavioral measures. His argument is that persons show temporal consistency (i.e., consistency in the same or similar situations over time) but that they ordinarily do not display cross-situational consistency.
12. Mischel's social cognitive theory considers five broad person variables: competencies (i.e., behavioral and cognitive skills), encoding strategies and personal constructs, expectancies, personal values, and self-regulatory systems and plans. Person variables are unlike traditional dispositions in that they interact and vary with the specific situation.
13. Cross-situational consistency is likely to occur only in abnormal circumstances, such as those characterized by a high degree of stress or by the need to perform beyond one's competencies.
14. Contemporary schema theory is rooted in the early writings of Jean Piaget. Schemas are knowledge structures or mental categories that direct the recognition and storage of experiences.
15. Schemas are abstract, and particular events are categorized in terms of how well they fit an ideal or typical representation, called a prototype. The more similar an object or event is to a given prototype, the more readily it will be categorized.
16. The self is the cognitive representation of the kind of person we think we are. The self influences how we process information about others as well as ourselves, and it guides goal formation and attainment.
17. Hazel Markus refers to the cognitive structure of one's self-concept as the self-schema. She distinguishes people as schematic or aschematic with respect to various traits or characteristics. Self-schemas cause us to process information selectively.
18. The idea of multiple selves can be traced back to William James, who distinguished among the material, social, and spiritual selves in 1890.

Many distinctions among aspects of the self have been proposed by modern writers.

19. E. Tory Higgins envisions three selves: an ideal self, an actual self, and an ought self. Disparities between one's actual and ideal selves produces sadness, disappointment, and depression, whereas disparities between the actual and ought selves produces anxiety, fear, and guilt.
20. Markus and Nurius define possible selves as individuals' ideas of what they might become, what they would like to become, and what they are afraid of becoming. These representations motivate behavior, provide a context for evaluating the present self, and guide the formulation of plans and goals.
21. Linville has written about self-complexity, which refers to the number of distinct and different self-concepts a person has. These different self-concepts may "spill over" to one another, and high self-complexity helps to protect the person from negative spillover.
22. Showers argues that the degree to which positive and negative aspects of the self are compartmentalized is an important determinant of feelings of competence and worth. Negative information that can be filed away from the working self-concept is less likely to bog us down with negativity. Thus, compartmentalization is another protective device against negative self-knowledge.
23. Self-esteem refers to feelings of satisfaction and pride with oneself. James defined self-esteem as success divided by aspirations. People who are objectively successful may have very low esteem because they are still not meeting their own extremely high standards; by the same token, people with modest objective accomplishments may have high self-esteem because their aspirations are minimal.
24. One technique for bolstering self-esteem is self-handicapping, which refers to acting to increase the likelihood of failure at a task. Self-handicapping allows us to blame failure on task difficulty or lack of preparation, thereby avoiding the need to make negative self-evaluations.
25. There appears to be a pervasive tendency for people to evaluate their selves more favorably than is actually justified, which turns out to be a very adaptive strategy.
26. Mood appears to play a significant role in self-evaluation. Wright and Mischel have suggested that people have a mood-congruent bias, meaning that we selectively process information about past experiences so that they are consistent with our current mood. Interestingly, depressed people (who are perpetually in a negative mood) are quite accurate in their estimates of how they are seen by others, whereas nondepressed people believe they are seen more favorably than they actually are.
27. Self-enhancing illusions are most effective when they are moderate rather than extreme because, in the latter case, we set ourselves up for repeated failure experiences.
28. Goals are internal representations of desired states. Most people pursue multiple goals. Like other mental representations, goals are

organized into levels, such that meeting lower goals may assist us in reaching higher goals and vice versa. The goal system has thus been called a "heterarchy."

29. Planning and evaluating progress are essential to reaching goals; even young children recognize this fact. Goals have been described as having the property of equifinality, which means that a goal can be satisfied through a variety of means.
30. Goal content refers to the specific content of the goals people have set for themselves. The self-concept exerts an enormous influence on goal selection. Meeting our highest goals serves to create and enhance a positive, adaptive, and healthy self-image, which, ironically, appears to require a degree of optimistic distortion.

CHAPTER EIGHTEEN

Applications and Limitations of the Representational Strategy

s with each of the earlier strategies, we conclude our look at the Representational Strategy with an examination of the applications derived form its theories and then turn to its limitations. We begin with a discussion of assessment as it is practiced by the theorists operating from a representational orientation.

REPRESENTATIONAL ASSESSMENT STRATEGIES

Consistent with the overall philosophy of this strategy—emphasizing an understanding of idiosyncratic meaning and private mental processes—representational assessment relies heavily on self-report measures. Many standardized measures (questionnaires and personality inventories) are used, along with more open-ended techniques. Some of the techniques specific to this strategy are somewhat unstructured, like the projective techniques of the Psychoanalytic Strategy. These measures may not be substantiated by group norms; rather, they represent an effort to allow subjects to express their own feelings, thought processes, and beliefs. However, the results of these processes are not subjected to extensive interpretation, as projective data would be. Rather, the examiner uses them to gain *empathic understanding* of the client. The primary goal of these methods is to gain insight into the clients' own frame of reference and idiosyncratic understanding of themselves and their experiences. These techniques are used most often by phenomenologically oriented psychologists.

Cognitively oriented psychologists' assessment techniques tend to be much more focused on specific cognitive processes, sets, or representations. Several theorists have devised assessment strategies for critical aspects of their own theories. We examine both types of assessment devices in the Representational Strategy.

The Q-Sort Technique

The Q-sort is a standardized procedure for assessing the self-concept. It entails making comparative judgments of statements about one's self (e.g., "I am lazy"; "I don't like to be with others"). The statements are printed on cards, and people arrange the cards in piles according to how characteristic each statement is of themselves (i.e., based on the degree to which the statements fit their self-concepts). Usually, the number of statements per pile is specified (Figure 18.1). Both a person's actual self-concept and ideal self-concept can be assessed by the Q-sort. To assess actual self, the instructions are to "sort the statements in terms of how you actually see yourself." To assess ideal self, the instructions are to "sort the statements in terms of how you would like to see yourself."

Repeated Q-sorts can be used to assess how the self-concept changes over time and the relationship between a person's actual self and ideal self. To assess the effectiveness of psychotherapy, Rogers (1961; Rogers & Dymond, 1954) had clients do actual-self and ideal-self sorts before, during, and after therapy to measure changes.

Generating Descriptors

An even more open-ended method of determining features of self-concept(s) is to ask subjects to generate a list of adjectives they would use to describe themselves. With this technique, the assessment is neither clearly defined nor

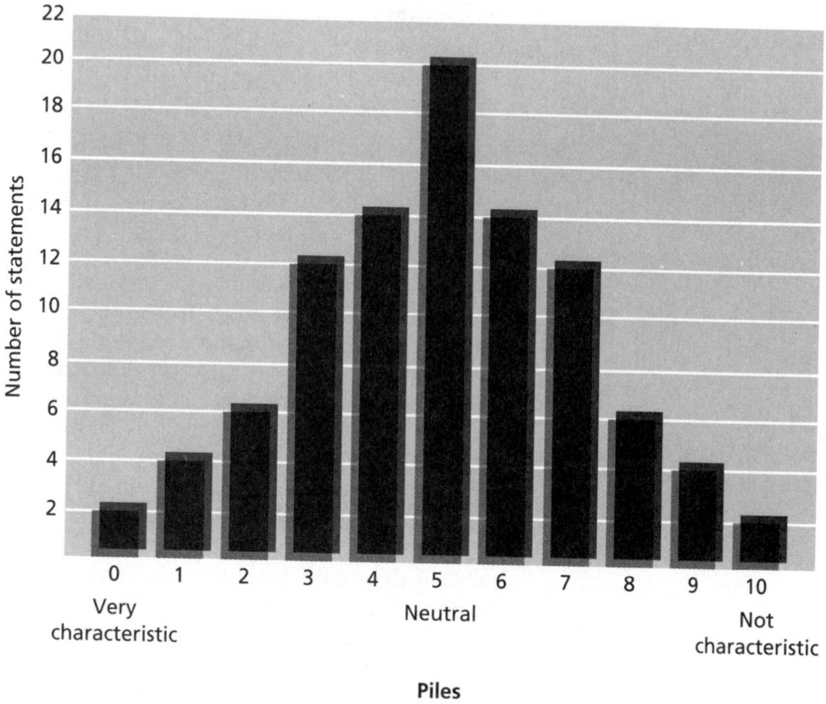

Figure 18.1
Example of the distribution of self-referent statements in a Q-sort. Subjects must sort the statements so that the specified number is put in each pile.

constrained by descriptors provided by the examiner. Subjects are entirely free to use terms *they* find most comfortable.

This technique, like the Q-sort, allows for separate assessment of different aspects of the subject's self-concepts. Subjects might be asked to repeat this process for their actual, ideal, and ought selves. They might also be asked to list characteristics they feel *others* would use to describe them. This allows the examiner to glimpse their concept of how others view them and compare it for consistency with how subjects view themselves.

Subjects may also be asked to "rank" the features they list from most to least typical, pervasive, desirable, undesirable, and so on. The result will be an idiosyncratic and highly personalized view of the self that allows the examiner to more readily adopt the frame of reference of the other (client or subject).

The Assessment of Personal Constructs

Identifying an individual's personal constructs is not easy because personal constructs are not directly observable. An individual's overt behaviors are, at best, suggestive of how a person construes events. Two people may behave quite similarly, although they construe events in very different ways.

People may also be unable to provide adequate answers to direct questioning about their own construct system. Constructs are generally unarticulated abstractions, of which a person may be genuinely unaware. Personal constructs are best detected through an evaluation of the categories people use in processing information.

Kelly devised a procedure for assessing these personal constructs through a process of categorization. The **Role Construct Repertory Test (Rep Test)** elicits constructs used to construe other people or events. Subjects compare and contrast important people (or events) in their lives. Similarities and differences between the events or people filling the various categories yield indirect information about the construct system underlying the judgments.

The Rep Test uses a grid to organize and sort information provided by the subject. Significant people in the subject's life are listed across the top of the grid. Descriptors used to "construe" the people are recorded on the side of the grid. Referring to the abbreviated Rep Test grid in Figure 18.2, we will outline the steps for completing the grid.

> First, the subject writes the name of a person to fit each of the role descriptions provided at the top of the grid.
>
> Next, the subject considers the three people designated by the circles in the boxes under the names in the first sort (Terry, Stephen, and Harry in Figure 18.2). (The selection of which names to begin comparing is relatively arbitrary at first but becomes more systematic as similarities and differences emerge through the process.) The subject decides in what important way two of the people are alike and different from the third. The subject places an *X* under the names of the two people who are alike (Stephen and Harry), and the characteristic that makes them alike becomes the emergent pole of the construct (organized). The characteristic that makes the third person (Terry) different becomes the implicit pole of the construct (spontaneous).
>
> Next, the subject considers the figures not compared and contrasted in the initial sort (Al, Anne, Martin, and Barbara) and places an *X* under the names of those people who also would be described by the emergent pole (Anne and Martin).

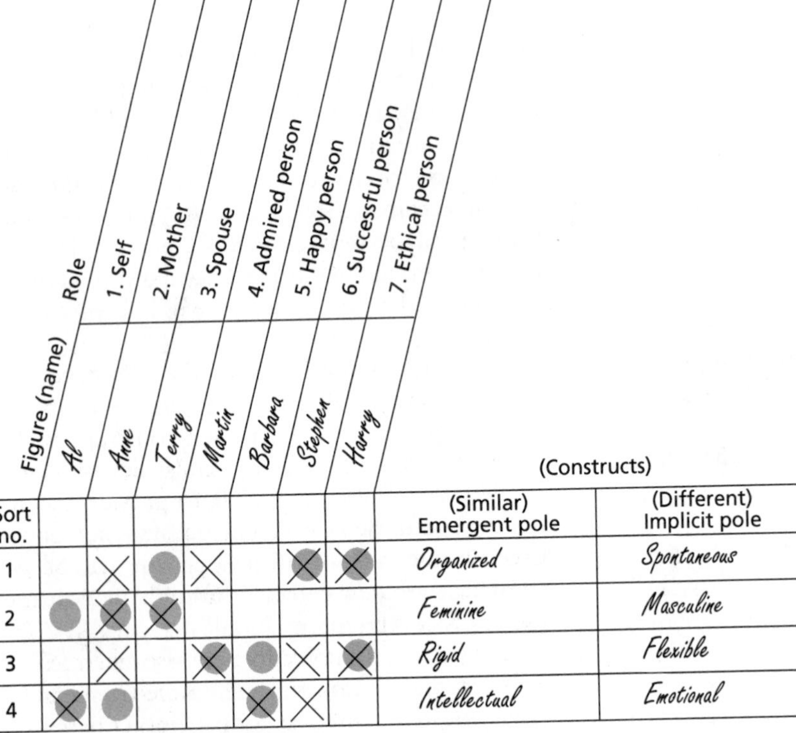

Figure 18.2
Example of part of a completed grid form of the Rep Test.

The subject repeats steps 2 and 3 for each of the successive sorts, gradually revealing relevant attributes within their own personal construct system in the process.

The pattern of *X*s in the Rep Test grid indicates the similarity of the constructs employed by the subject. Constructs with identical patterns of *X*s are assumed to be equivalent, *even if the verbal labels assigned to them by the subject are different.* In Figure 18.2, for example, organized versus spontaneous is functionally equivalent to rigid versus flexible in this person's construct system. (Despite applying different labels, no significant differences in the classification of significant others emerged in the sorting process between the two constructs; therefore, the different labels are actually inconsequential.)

We have just described how the Rep Test is used to elicit constructs about other people. The basic idea of sorting figures in terms of their similarities and differences to yield constructs can be employed to identify a person's constructs about any type of event (e.g., Adams-Webber, 1989; Metzler & Neimeyer, 1988; Watson, Doster, & Michaelsen, 1990). In market research, for example, the Rep Test has been used to identify the basis of consumers' judgments in evaluating products (Stewart & Stewart, 1982). Products are simply substituted for people. A sample of consumers compare and contrast various combinations of products and label the constructs they used to compare them. Another illustration of the versatility of the Rep Test is in assessing changes in cognitive conflicts, which has even been used as a measure of success of psychoanalytic therapy (Bassler, Krauthauser, & Hoffmann, 1992).

The Rep Test has proved to be a highly useful and versatile means of assessing personal constructs (e.g., Beail, 1985; Landfield & Epting, 1987). The analysis of increasingly complex grids has been made possible by computer technology (e.g., Mancuso & Shaw, 1988; Sewell, Adams-Webber, Mitterer, & Cromwell, 1992). The Rep Test is, by far, the most frequently used assessment procedure in research related to personal construct theory (Neimeyer, Baker, & Neimeyer, 1990).

Variations on the test can be used to rate the organization and relative importance of the constructs used. The hierarchical order of constructs can be assessed through "implications grids," created by asking subjects such questions as "If construct Y changed, what other constructs would also change?" (Caputi, Breiger, & Pattison, 1990).

Assessing Locus of Control

Locus of control is a construct of considerable interest to contemporary cognitive psychologists. Locus of control is typically assessed by brief self-report inventories. For example, Rotter (1966) devised a scale to assess this construct. His **I-E Scale** consists of 29 forced-choice items: 23 items that tap locus of control and 6 filler items that partially disguise the purpose of the test. Respondents are asked to choose the alternative that better describes them in each case. See if you can identify the alternative in the following two items that suggests an *internal* locus of control.

a. In the long run, people get the respect they deserve in this world.
b. Unfortunately, an individual's worth often passes unrecognized no matter how hard one tries.

a. Many times I feel that I have little influence over the things that happen to me.
b. It is impossible for me to believe that chance or luck plays an important role in my life.

Individuals who choose a majority of internal alternatives are labeled *internals,* and those who choose a majority of external alternatives are called *externals.*

Rotter's I-E Scale is the most widely used measure of general locus of control in adults. Other scales have been developed for children (e.g., Nowicki & Strickland, 1973; Richaud de Minzi, 1991), including a cartoon version for preschool children (Nowicki & Duke, 1974). A series of life-span I-E scales that allow comparison of locus of control from preschool through elderly populations also exists (Nowicki & Duke, 1983), as well as a variety of *domain-specific* scales (cf. Bunch & Schneider, 1991; Georgiou & Bradley, 1992; Heaven, 1989; Johnson, Nora, Tan, & Bustos, 1991; Mooney, Sherman, & lo Presto, 1991; Orpen, 1991; Spector, 1988; Trice & Hackburt, 1989).

PERSONALITY CHANGE: THERAPEUTIC APPROACHES OF THE REPRESENTATIONAL STRATEGY

The Representational Strategy has given birth to a wealth of ideas about personality change, especially in psychotherapy. We examine a number of the best-known and most widely used representational therapies, all of which are outgrowths of the theories discussed in the preceding chapters.

ROGERS'S PERSON-CENTERED THERAPY

Carl Rogers's theory of personality was both a reaction to and a radical departure from psychoanalysis. The same is true for Rogers's (1942, 1965) innovative approach to psychotherapy. Rogers originally termed his approach *client-centered therapy,* but later renamed it *person-centered.* His was among the first major alternatives to psychoanalytic psychotherapy, and it is the contribution for which Rogers is best known (e.g., Gendlin, 1988).

The name **person-centered therapy** is consistent with the representational perspective. The therapy is focused (centered) on the person seeking help, the client. Therapy deals with the person's unique problems, feelings, perceptions, attitudes, and goals. In short, person-centered therapy proceeds from the client's internal frame of reference. Although one person can never *fully* understand another person's subjective experiences, the therapist tries to learn as much as possible about how the client views his or her particular experiences (Bozarth, 1990).

The essence of person-centered therapy can be seen in Rogers's (1965) choice of the term *client,* which "seems to come closest to conveying the picture of [someone] . . . who comes actively and voluntarily to gain help on a problem, but without any notion of surrendering . . . responsibility for the situation" (p. 7). Note that Rogers assumed that clients were responsible for their behaviors, including solving their own problems (albeit with the help of a therapist). Rogers (1942) originally called his psychotherapy *non-directive* therapy to emphasize that the therapist did not direct the course of therapy (see also Grant, 1990; Hayashi, Kuno, Osawa, Shimizu, & Suetake, 1992).

Basic Ingredients of Person-Centered Therapy

In a nutshell, person-centered therapy establishes conditions in which the person is able to assume responsibility for making the changes required to deal with the problems that brought the client to therapy (e.g., Bozarth & Brodley, 1991; Bozarth & Shanks, 1989). Rogers believed that the therapist must provide three ingredients for such growth-enhancing conditions to exist.

Empathic Understanding

In person-centered therapy, the therapist attempts to see the person from the client's internal frame of reference, and the person experiences that he or she is being perceived accurately (understood) by the therapist. This is **empathic understanding.** Rogers (1975) considered empathy to be the single most potent factor in fostering personality change. Indeed, he felt that empathy is a prerequisite for genuine unconditional positive regard.

Empathy also is important in other types of psychotherapy, although its specific role is different (Bohart, 1991a). For example, psychoanalysts use empathy primarily to understand the person's unconscious dynamics. In contrast, person-centered therapists use empathy to create a "safe" psychological climate that is conducive to reintegration and personal growth (e.g., Bohart, 1991a; Bozarth & Brodley, 1991).

Unconditional Positive Regard

The therapist provides the client with a nonpossessive acceptance and respect, no matter what the client is doing or feeling at the time (e.g., Cain, 1990b). Rogers believed this set the stage for personal growth, even in the therapy process.

Genuineness or Congruence

The therapist is open or transparent, totally being who she or he is, with no holding back and no façades. Such a self-presentation serves as a model of openness for the client (e.g., Boy, 1990).

The Process of Person-Centered Therapy

Person-centered therapy creates a nonthreatening situation in which clients feel understood (empathy) and accepted as a whole person (unconditional positive regard). By minimizing or eliminating the effects of conditions of worth, clients' behaviors can be guided solely by their organismic valuing processes. Under these special circumstances, clients can safely become aware of and examine experiences that are inconsistent with their self-concepts.

How does the therapist create these basic conditions for effective person-centered therapy?

Person-centered therapy involves a verbal interchange between the client and the therapist, focusing on the here-and-now (the person's experiences during the session). The therapist listens to the client and accepts equally and without evaluation all of the client's feelings and behaviors (unconditional positive regard). This process is especially important for the host of "negative" feelings and behaviors that clients bring to therapy. The therapist models what the client should be doing—namely, removing the conditions of worth associated with undesirable aspects of the self and replacing them with unconditional positive self-regard.

The therapist conveys empathy and unconditional positive regard by reflecting back to the client what the therapist believes the client is feeling and thinking. To do this, person-centered therapists use two basic responses (e.g., Essig & Russell, 1990; Mahrer, Nadler, Stalikas, Schachter, & Sterner, 1988). One is **clarification of feelings,** in which the therapist synthesizes or reorganizes the feelings that the client has expressed, directly or indirectly. The other is **restatement of content,** in which the therapist rephrases the cognitive or intellectual aspects of what the client has expressed, explicitly or implicitly.

The major difference between these two basic responses is whether the focus is on the client's *emotions* (clarification of feelings) or *thoughts* (restatement of content). Because the emphasis in person-centered therapy is on the client's feelings, clarification of feelings is considered more important than restatement of content. For either type of response to be empathic, the therapist must experience what the client is relating from the client's internal frame of reference.

Clarification of feelings and restatement of content serve three functions: First, the client learns how she or he is being viewed by the therapist; the client is then able to confirm or correct these views. Second, when the therapist's reflections are accurate, they show that the therapist is empathizing with the client. Third, the reflections provide the client with a slightly different perspective on the problems at hand—a "stepping back from oneself" phenomenon. (In our daily lives, we often gain insight about our thoughts and feelings when people reflect back to us what we are telling them.)

KELLY'S FIXED-ROLE THERAPY

In **fixed-role therapy,** the client plays the role of a fictitious person whose behavior is consistent with a construct system that would be beneficial for the client. By playing this fixed role, the client behaves in ways that will modify his or her existing construct system.

Based on extensive personality assessment and evaluation of the client's problem, the therapist writes a **fixed-role sketch.** The sketch describes the fixed role the client will play. The fixed-role character is assigned a name to make the role more credible and to distinguish the fixed role from the client's customary role. The following fixed-role sketch was written for a male client who was having difficulties with his sex-role identity. He characterized himself as passive, self-conscious, shy, and occasionally boring.

> Dick Benton is probably the only one of his kind in the world. People are always just a little puzzled as to how to take him. About the time they decide

> that he is a conventional person with the usual lines of thinking in religion, politics, school . . . they discover that there is a new side to his personality that they have overlooked. At times, they think that he has a brand-new way of looking at life, a really fresh point of view. Some people go through an hour of conversation with him without being particularly impressed, while others find that afterwards they cannot get some of his unusual ideas out of their minds. Every once in a while he throws an idea into a discussion like a bomb with a very slow fuse attached. People don't get it until later.
>
> At times he deliberately makes himself socially inconspicuous. Those are the times when he wishes to listen and learn, rather than to stimulate other people's thinking. He is kindly and gentle with people, even on those occasions when he is challenging their thoughts with utterly new ideas. Because of this, people do not feel hurt by his ideas, even when they seem outrageous.
>
> He is devoted to his wife, and she is the only person who always seems to understand what is going on in his mind.
>
> His work in college is somewhat spotted and the courses are interesting to him only to the extent that they give him a new outlook.
>
> All in all, Dick Benton is a combination of gentleness and intellectual unpredictability. He likes to take people as they are but he likes to surprise them with new ideas. (Kelly, 1955, p. 421)

Clients are not asked to *be* the person described in the fixed-role sketch or even to adopt the role as their own. They are told merely to play the role for a week or two. However, clients often stop thinking of their new behaviors as a prescribed role. They begin to consider the role as their own "natural" way of behaving. They adjust the fixed role so that it is more consistent with their other behaviors and styles. Clients who can get into the fixed role begin to adopt the constructs that underlie the fixed-role behaviors.

Fixed-role therapy is aimed at creating minor personality changes. The fixed role deals with only a few of the client's constructs, often including some of the client's positive attributes or strengths, which bolsters the client's most efficient constructs and makes the role easier to enact. Although originally designed as an individual therapy (Kelly, 1955), fixed-role therapy has been adapted to marital therapy (Kremsdorf, 1985) and group therapy (Beail & Parker, 1991).

Personality change ultimately involves changing one's constructs. However, the process involves directly changing overt behavior, which results in a new perspective for viewing events. In fixed-role therapy, the client temporarily plays the role of a fictitious person who uses constructs that the client might benefit from adopting.

SELF-EFFICACY AND BEHAVIOR CHANGE

Why do people benefit from psychotherapy? Bandura (1984) has hypothesized that all forms of personality change are effective because they create and strengthen a client's perceived self-efficacy. Table 18.1 provides examples of the primary source of efficacy expectations postulated to occur in various therapeutic procedures. Much of the research examining the role of self-efficacy in psychotherapy has focused on treating anxiety and fear (e.g., Williams, 1992).

If perceived self-efficacy accounts for changes in therapy, then the more effective a treatment, the more it will enhance clients' efficacy expectations.

Table 18.1 Examples of therapy procedures that are postulated to provide clients with each of the four primary sources of self-efficacy

SELF-EFFICACY SOURCE	THERAPY PROCEDURE
Performance Accomplishments	Fixed-role therapy Reinforcement therapy In vivo exposure Participant modeling Problem-solving therapy Behavior rehearsal
Vicarious Experience	Modeling therapies
Verbal Persuasion	Interpretations Rational-emotive therapy Cognitive therapy Self-instructional training
Emotional Arousal	Systematic desensitization Relaxation training Biofeedback

To test this hypothesis, Bandura, Adams, and Beyer (1977) recruited adults whose fear of snakes restricted their lives in some significant way. Before and after treatment, these subjects were given a behavioral avoidance test.

In a **behavioral avoidance test,** people are asked to perform a series of tasks requiring increasingly more threatening interactions with a feared object or situation. In this experiment, there were 29 tasks. The first was looking at a boa constrictor in a glass cage; the last was allowing the snake to crawl freely on the subject. To assess changes in self-efficacy, subjects rated their expectations for performing each of the steps in the behavioral avoidance test on a 100-point probability scale.

The subjects were assigned to one of three conditions. Subjects in the *modeling condition* observed a female therapist perform a series of tasks that involved increasingly more threatening interactions with the snake. After observing the model, subjects in the *participant modeling conditioning* practiced the same behaviors with the therapist's assistance. A third group of subjects, who served as *untreated controls,* were just given the assessment procedures.

Participant modeling provides two sources of efficacy information—namely, vicarious experience and performance accomplishments. Because modeling alone provides only one source of efficacy information—vicarious experience—participant modeling should lead to higher efficacy expectations and consequently to more effective treatment than modeling alone.

The results were consistent with these predictions. Subjects' efficacy expectations were *markedly enhanced* by participant modeling, *moderately increased* by modeling alone, and unchanged in the control condition. The changes in self-efficacy were reflected in the subjects' overt behaviors. Participant modeling produced somewhat more approach behavior in the behavioral avoidance test than did modeling alone. Both treatments improved approach over the control condition.

Self-Efficacy and Pain Tolerance

Another area to which self-efficacy theory has been applied is the tolerance of pain. Pain is patients' most common complaint to physicians and the most frequently cited cause of disability. Indeed, pain can be disabling and enduring. Our beliefs about pain and its treatment can affect how we experience pain, however. For example, patients who are given a placebo drug, which they believe is an actual painkiller, report less pain than patients who receive nothing. Placebo subjects, in fact, sometimes seem to experience as much pain relief as those who take real painkillers (Evans, 1974).

Self-efficacy regarding the ability to tolerate pain is one type of belief that can influence pain tolerance (e.g., Bandura, 1991, 1992c; Holman & Lorig, 1992; Kores, Murphy, Rosenthal, Elias, & North, 1990; Williams & Kinney, 1991). This was demonstrated in an experiment in which subjects were exposed to intense pain stimulation (holding their hands in ice water) to assess their tolerance for pain (Bandura, O'Leary, Taylor, Gauthier, & Gossard, 1987).

Subjects were assigned to one of three conditions. Those in the *cognitive coping skills condition* received training in such techniques as diverting attention away from pain and imagining pain sensations to be nonpainful sensations. These cognitive coping skills were chosen to produce changes in subjects' self-efficacy regarding both their ability to withstand pain and their ability to reduce it. A second group of subjects was given a *placebo.* A third group served as *no-treatment control* subjects.

Overall, self-efficacy for pain tolerance and actual pain tolerance were strongly related (average correlation of +.75). Relative to the no-treatment control group, both the coping skills and placebo groups increased their self-efficacy for withstanding pain. However, only the coping skills group showed an increase in their self-efficacy for actually reducing pain once it was experienced. Thus, the coping skills had a broader effect on self-efficacy for pain tolerance than did the placebo.

These findings regarding self-efficacy paralleled the results for increasing pain tolerance. The coping skills subjects showed the greatest gains in actual pain tolerance. The placebo group showed a small gain, whereas the control group showed almost no gain in ability to tolerate painful stimulation.

To identify the mechanisms that led to increased pain tolerance, the researchers used a clever procedure. Half the subjects in each pain treatment group were given an injection of weak saltwater; the remaining subjects received an injection of *naloxone.* Weak saltwater has virtually no physiological effect. Naloxone blocks the action of *endorphins,* which are naturally occurring opioids that reduce pain. Thus, for several hours after subjects are given naloxone, they cannot benefit from the body's "natural painkillers." The influence of endorphins in reducing pain could be determined by comparing the naloxone and saltwater subjects in each treatment group.

Subjects in the cognitive coping skills and placebo groups given naloxone showed less improvement in pain tolerance than those who had received saltwater. This finding was expected because the naloxone subjects could not have benefited from endorphins.

However, even with endorphin action blocked (i.e., in the naloxone group), subjects using cognitive coping skills that created high self-efficacy exhibited the most tolerance for pain. In the critical pain tests (20 and 60

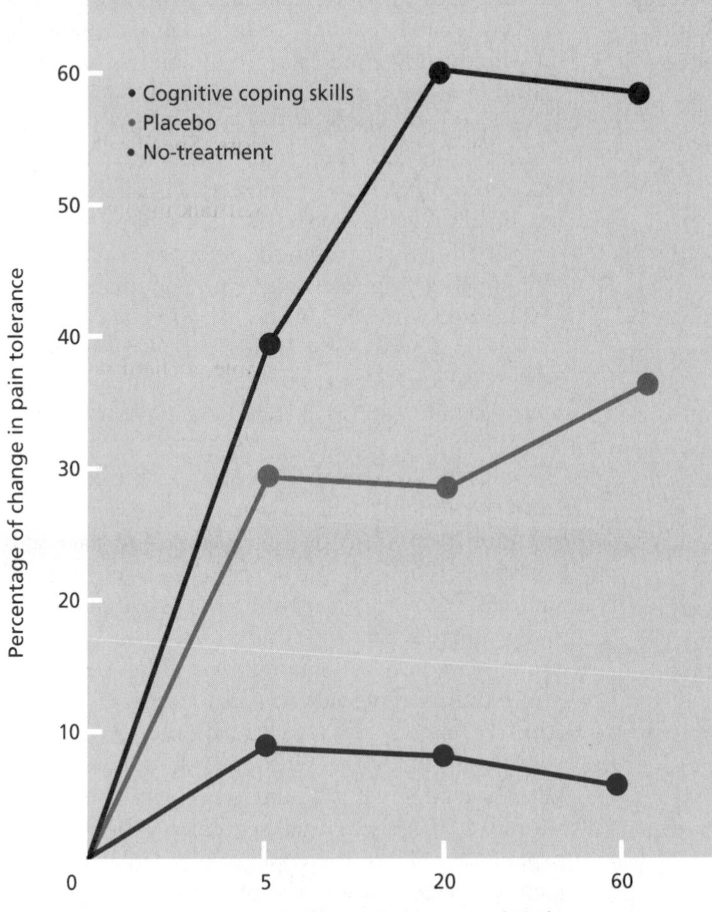

Figure 18-3
Average percentage change in pain tolerance achieved by cognitive coping skills, placebo, and no-treatment control subjects when the opioid action of endorphins was blocked by naloxone. In the critical pain tests (20 and 60 minutes postinjection), the coping skills group showed greater improvement in pain tolerance than the placebo group who, in turn, did better than the no-treatment controls.

minutes after their injections), the coping skills group showed greater improvement in pain tolerance than the placebo group, who, in turn, did better than the no-treatment controls (see Figure 18.3). Thus, procedures that heighten self-efficacy lead to changes in pain tolerance beyond those produced by the action of endorphins.

COGNITIVE THERAPY

According to the cognitive approach, *maladaptive cognitions* play a central role in the development and maintenance of psychological disorders. These cognitions may take the form of self-deprecating thoughts, illogical ideas, or irrational beliefs. **Cognitive therapies** modify the maladaptive cognitions (1) by directly altering the cognitions or (2) by changing overt behaviors to indirectly modify the cognitions. Most cognitive therapies involve a combination of both tactics. *Cognitive-behavioral* interventions, as these combined treatments are often called, are the most frequently used representational treatments and are applicable to a wide array of disorders (Cottraux,

1990; Craighead 1990b; Goldfried, Greenberg, & Marmar, 1990; Mahoney, 1993b).

Cognitive Restructuring

Cognitive restructuring, the basic procedure used in many cognitive therapies, involves modifying the thoughts, ideas, and beliefs that maintain the client's abnormal behaviors. Specifically, cognitive restructuring modifies **self-statements** or **self-talk,** what clients say to themselves (e.g., Dush, Hirt, & Schroeder, 1989). Self-talk involves the "soundless, mental speech, arising at the instant that we think about something, plan or solve problems in our mind. . . . We think and remember with the aid of words which we articulate to ourselves" (Sokolov, 1972, p. 1).

The client learns to recognize maladaptive cognitions and replace them with adaptive ones. For example, a client who lost her job believed that she would never get another job. This belief was maladaptive because it reduced her motivation to do anything constructive about the situation. The client learned to restructure her beliefs by thinking such thoughts as "Many people lose jobs and find others" or "Maybe my next job will be better than the last one."

Beck's Cognitive Therapy

Cognitive therapy was developed by University of Pennsylvania psychiatrist Aaron Beck. The therapist and client collaborate to (1) identify the client's dysfunctional beliefs, (2) challenge their validity, and (3) provide the client with the skills and experiences that will result in more adaptive thinking (Beck & Weishaar, 1989). Specifically, the irrational beliefs are posed as hypotheses that the client then gathers evidence to refute. For example, clients who believe that they are worthless might be asked to make a list of their accomplishments, both small and large.

Beck's cognitive therapy originally was designed to treat depression, and today it is considered one of the most effective treatments for that disorder (e.g., Beckham & Watkins, 1989; Dobson, 1989; Hollon, Shelton, & Davis, 1993; Thase, Bowler, & Harden, 1991; Thase, Simons, Cahalane, & McGeary, 1991). More recently, cognitive therapy has been expanded to treat other disorders (Beck, 1993), including anxiety (e.g., Beck & Emery, 1985; Butler, Fennell, Robson, & Gelder, 1991; Chambless & Gillis, 1993), personality disorders (Beck & Freeman, 1989), and marital discord (e.g., Baucom & Epstein, 1990; Dattilio & Padesky, 1990).

Aaron Beck developed cognitive therapy, in which clients gather empirical evidence to refute the validity of the illogical beliefs that are maintaining their abnormal behaviors.
Courtesy of Aaron Beck, Beck Institute for Cognitive Therapy

In analyzing the thoughts of depressed patients, Beck (1976, 1984) identified three common themes: (1) negative interpretation of external events, (2) pessimistic view of the future, and (3) self-dislike. Beck argued that these distorted views are all due to a common set of overlapping logical errors (Table 18.2).

Beck's cognitive therapy has behavioral as well as cognitive components (DeRubeis & Beck, 1988). Variations of cognitive restructuring comprise the cognitive component. An example of a behaviorally based intervention is **graded task assignments.** Clients engage in a series of brief, simple behaviors that gradually become lengthier and more complex. The aim is to counter patients' views that they cannot competently perform specific behaviors. The shaping procedure allows patients to succeed and thus prove to themselves that they can perform the behaviors competently.

Table 18.2 The six cognitive errors associated with depression

Arbitrary inference: Drawing negative conclusions not warranted by evidence.

Selective abstraction: Focusing on one negative aspect of a situation, while ignoring other (positive) aspects.

Overgeneralization: Drawing an across-the-board negative conclusion from one or a few negative instances.

Magnification and minimization: Greatly overestimating or underestimating the importance of an event, making it grossly out of proportion.

Personalization: Relating negative events to oneself without a reasonable basis.

Dichotomous thinking: Thinking only in terms of black or white, "wonderful or terrible," instead of in gradations.

Source: Based on "Cognitive Therapy" by R. J. DeRubeis and A. T. Beck, 1988. In K. S. Dobson (Ed.), *Issues and Approaches in Personal Construct Theory.* Academic Press.

For example, a hospitalized patient who was depressed believed that he could not walk. First, Beck (1976) persuaded the man to walk 5 yards, then 10 yards, and so on. Each time the man protested that he could not walk the requested distance. However, when he succeeded each time, he was forced to revise his beliefs. Research suggests that the combination of cognitive restructuring and behavior rehearsal, as practiced in Beck's therapy, is more effective than either component alone (Zettle & Hayes, 1987).

Meichenbaum's Self-Instructional Training

Donald Meichenbaum (1986, 1991) is one of the architects of cognitive-behavioral therapy. He developed a procedure to capitalize on our inclination to coach ourselves when we are in difficult situations. For instance, when we lose our car keys, we may say to ourselves: "Don't panic. Just stop and think. Where did I put them when I came in?" **Self-instructional training** teaches clients to instruct themselves about how to act, feel, and think (Meichenbaum, 1985). We will illustrate self-instructional training by describing its initial use to decrease children's impulsive behaviors (Meichenbaum & Goodman, 1971).

Donald Meichenbaum is a leading spokesperson for cognitive-behavioral therapy and has developed a number of therapeutic interventions, including self-instructional training.
Courtesy of Donald Meichenbaum

Children who act impulsively do not think before they act, which often has undesirable consequences for themselves and others. The general goal of self-instructional training for impulsive behavior is to teach children to think and plan before they act—to "stop, look, and listen" (Figure 18.4). Five steps are involved.

Progression of Self-Instructional Training

The first step in training, **cognitive modeling,** is having a model perform a task while verbalizing an adaptive, counterimpulsive strategy. For example, while copying line patterns, an adult model might say, "Okay, what is it I have to do? You want me to copy the picture with the different lines. I have to go slowly and carefully. Okay, draw the line down, down, good" (Meichenbaum & Goodman, 1971, p. 117).

The next step is often **cognitive participant modeling.** At this stage, the child performs the task as the model verbalizes the instructions. Now the child is prepared to assume an active role in self-instruction. This next phase is called **overt self-instruction.** Here the child performs the task while verbalizing the instructions out loud.

Figure 18.4
Cue cards used to prompt children to use self-instructions in solving problems.
From *Think Aloud: Increasing Social and Cognitive Skills–A Problem-Solving Program for Children (Primary Level),* by B. W. Camp and M. A. S. Bash, 1981. Copyright © 1981 by Research Press. Reprinted by permission of the author.

Now that self-instruction has been established, a process of **fading** begins. The child next performs the task while whispering the instructions. The process continues until the child can succeed by using **covert self-instruction.** The child no longer states instructions audibly but is, instead, directed to self-instruct silently (mentally).

The child first practices with brief and simple perceptual motor tasks, such as coloring figures within boundaries. Gradually, the length and complexity of the tasks are increased as the child demonstrates increasing success with the technique.

Thomas D'Zurilla
Courtesy of Thomas D'Zurilla

Applications of Self-Instructional Training

Self-instructional training has been used successfully to treat a variety of problems in a number of different populations, including anxiety (Meichenbaum, Gilmore, & Fedoravicius, 1971), lack of creativity in college students (Meichenbaum, 1975), deficits in problem solving among children (e.g., Camp & Bash, 1981) and the elderly (Labouvie-Vief & Gonda, 1976); academic skills in children (e.g., Guevremont, Osnes, & Stokes, 1988); pain in adults (Turk, Meichenbaum, & Genest, 1983); and "schizophrenic" (disorganized) speech (e.g., Meyers, Mercatoris, & Sirota, 1976).

Problem-Solving Therapy

Thomas D'Zurilla and Marvin Goldfried (1971), in a now classic article, argued that the *ability to solve problems* is related to competence and adjustment. They outlined a therapeutic approach called *problem-solving therapy.* Problem-solving skills have subsequently been shown to be involved in an enormous range of activities. For example, the more consistently children generate effective solutions to social problems, the more socially competent they appear to be (Hopper & Kirschenbaum, 1985). Conversely, difficulty in problem solving is associated with interpersonal problems and psychological disorders such as depression (e.g., Asarnow & Callan, 1985; Lochman & Curry, 1986b; Nezu & D'Zurilla, 1989).

Marvin Goldfried
the originators of problem-solving therapy.
© Marvin Goldfried

Problem-solving therapy teaches general problem-solving skills to clients with two aims: (1) to alleviate the particular personal problems for which clients have sought therapy (e.g., D'Zurilla & Nezu, 1982; Wasik, 1984) and (2) to provide clients with a general coping strategy for personal problems (e.g., Heppner, Neal, & Larsen, 1984). In problem-solving therapy, clients learn and practice a series of basic steps for solving problems: (1) defining the problem, (2) selecting a goal, (3) generating alternative solutions, (4) choosing one of the alternative solutions, (5) implementing the solution, and (6) evaluating the success of the solution.

Problem-solving therapies have been used to treat a variety of personal and interpersonal difficulties (D'Zurilla, 1986), including depression (e.g., Nezu, Nezu, & Perri, 1989), aggressive behaviors (e.g., Guevremont & Foster, 1993; Lochman, 1992), anger (e.g., Lochman & Curry, 1986a), marital conflicts (e.g., Jacobson, 1989, 1991, 1992), harmony among family members (e.g., Robin & Foster, 1989), and child abuse (e.g., MacMillan, Guevremont, & Hansen, 1989).

Box 18.1
DEMONSTRATION: BRAINSTORMING

Successful problem solving often depends on generating a number of solutions from which to choose. The greater the number and range of possible solutions imagined, the greater the likelihood of identifying a successful approach to the problem. According to Spiegler and Guevremont (1993) a form of *brainstorming exercise* can be used to do this. First, list *any* and *all* potential solutions to the problem, without regard to practicality. Even if a solution cannot possibly be implemented, it should be included on the initial list.

Wild ideas may lead to more realistic solutions that might not have been formulated otherwise. For instance, suppose you are having difficulty with one of your professors. While brainstorming, you might come up with a possible solution: "Stop going to class." Although the solution itself has its flaws, its goal—no longer having to deal with the professor—may elicit more adaptive means of resolving the problem, such as switching to another section of the course.

Generating novel solutions to problems is a skill. It may be improved with practice. To practice generating solutions by brainstorming, formulate a minimum of 20 different solutions for each of the problems described here. You might want to compete with a friend to see who comes up with the most (or the most novel) solutions. Remember, the solution must solve the problem, but it need not be entirely feasible.

Situation 1. You are visiting a large city. While you are taking a shower in your hotel room, someone steals all of your clothes. The room has no phone. What might you do?

Situation 2. You have somehow made dates for a romantic dinner with two different people on the same evening. You have told both of them to meet you in front of the same restaurant at 7:00 P.M. What could you do?

Situation 3. Telephone access to the city in which your parents live (200 miles from your home) will be out of service for the next 24 hours. It is imperative that you get a message to your parents in the next 2 hours. What can you do?

Now select the single best alternative you listed to solve each problem. Try to imagine how well the solution serves your immediate needs and how successful it might prove to be as a solution. You will probably recognize that your first idea, or even your first few ideas, for each problem was not the one you ultimately selected as "best." Chances are the best solution reflects either a combined strategy based on earlier ideas or an unusual approach arrived at through an originally absurd one.

Cognitive-Behavioral Marital Therapy

Marital problems tend to be complex. Consequently, treatment typically involves multiple interventions. Cognitive-behavioral marital therapies involve (1) communication and problem-solving training, (2) increasing positive behavior exchanges, and (3) cognitive restructuring (Spiegler & Guevremont, 1993).

Distressed couples generally have difficulties with effective communication and problem solving in the relationship (e.g., Geiss & O'Leary, 1981). Couples learn communications skills such as listening, restating what the other person has said, and providing constructive feedback. The skills are taught through modeling, prompting, shaping, role playing, and direct feedback.

Couples experiencing marital discord usually do not act positively or lovingly toward one another. The **caring-days technique** increases the number of positive behavior exchanges between the pair (Stuart, 1980). First, the partners each make a list of specific positive behaviors that the other partner could do to show that he or she loves the other. Then, each partner is asked to perform a set number of behaviors from the list each day.

Marital problems are often maintained by distorted views partners have of each other or their intentions (Baucom & Epstein, 1990; Beck, 1989). For example, one spouse may erroneously attribute the other's silence to anger when it is actually due to fatigue. Couples are encouraged to verify the validity of their beliefs and to modify erroneous beliefs through cognitive restructuring. Cognitive-behavioral marital interventions have been shown to be effective not only in alleviating marital distress but also in *preventing* it through premarital training (Hahlweg & Markman, 1988; Jacobson, 1989).

LIMITATIONS OF THE REPRESENTATIONAL STRATEGY

So far, we have examined the Representational Strategy from the viewpoint of its proponents and examined its strengths and successful applications. Now it is time, as we did with the three preceding strategies, to cast a critical eye on the strategy. Many of the criticisms are germane to the strategy as a whole. However, as was true of the preceding strategies, some criticisms apply directly to only a subset of the approaches covered. In these instances, we will point out which approach is targeted.

The Representational Strategy (or its component approaches) has been subject to several major criticisms. The strategy is limited in scope, presents a simplistic view of personality, pays inadequate attention to nomothetic concerns, uses circular reasoning, provides inadequate coverage of personality development, places excessive reliance on self-report measures, and presents a romanticized view of personality.

Limited in Scope

Psychoanalytic personality theory has been called a "rubber sheet theory" because it can be stretched to fit (explain) any observations. The Dispositional Strategy has been accused of a different, but equally serious, theoretical problem: The strategy has no theoretical concepts of its own and uses those concepts that it has borrowed inconsistently or sloppily. Not surprisingly, representational personality theories also have their problems. Specifically, the theories are restricted by assuming that virtually everything we need to know about a person can be gleaned from the person's conscious, momentary experiences. Clearly, many objective features of a person's real-life situation *are* important.

To make the point, consider the extreme example of a person who enters therapy complaining of chronic loneliness. Attempting to change this person's thoughts and feelings about loneliness may miss the point if the person's job requires working the graveyard shift and guarding an empty, isolated warehouse. This person's sleep-wake cycle and particular job might well be producing extreme social isolation. This distress, then, would better be dealt with by changing jobs or, at least, work shifts.

Unconscious Experience Is Ignored

By focusing on conscious experience, the Representational Strategy comes close to dealing with aspects of existence that laypeople most often think should be the focus of psychological investigations—namely, their conscious thoughts and feelings about themselves, others, and events in their lives. Thus, the Representational Strategy makes sense intuitively and is consistent with commonsense notions of personality.

This focus virtually excludes from study events of which a person is not immediately or fully aware. (Kelly's REP measure is a creative way to tap mental phenomena of which people may, indeed, be "consciously" unaware, as do some of the assessment methods of the cognitive approach.) Can behavior be predicted accurately if we know only what is in the person's immediate awareness? Many personality psychologists would say no. Psychoanalysts, for example, argue that events that are unconscious, even permanently unconscious, form the core of personality and play a crucial role in determining behavior.

The Past Is Ignored

Can present actions be explained without reference to past experiences? Again, many personality psychologists would say no. They believe that knowledge of past experiences is essential for predicting and understanding present behaviors and personality. The Representational Strategy often ignores the influence of the past (with some notable exceptions, for example, Bandura's claim that present efficacy expectations are based primarily on past behavior), focusing instead on immediate, subjective experiences.

Representational personality psychologists do acknowledge that the past can affect a person's immediate experiences, but they do not usually try to account for its influence. Neither do they explain the nature and extent of the influence. Furthermore, they do not attempt to examine an individual's past experiences, even when they might directly relate to present experiences. The strategy assumes that a past experience that is important in the present will be manifested in the person's present experiences. This assumption implies that there is no need to look at the past.

Moreover, representational psychologists believe that the form the past experience assumes in the present is all that is relevant to an understanding of current personality functioning. All these assumptions are largely unsubstantiated.

Gaps in Coverage

Representational approaches have large gaps in coverage that result from the particular emphasis of the theories. This point is particularly true of the phenomenological theories, which tend to appear broad and comprehensive at first inspection. (Note that the cognitive approaches tend to be much more circumscribed, most having the status of only "mini-theories" at this time.)

Rogers's approach focuses on the emotional aspects of our self-representations and largely ignores the intellectual, thinking aspects. Kelly's bias is exactly opposite; the theory of personal constructs emphasizes cognitive processes but pays relatively little attention to emotions. Bruner (1956) remarked that Kelly was so perturbed by psychoanalytic, dispositional, and radical behavioral psychologists who regard humans as irrational (emotional) animals that he overreacted and turned *Homo sapiens* into a species of super-rational college professors.

As another example of theory-generated tunnel vision, consider Maslow's assertion that most adult behaviors are motivated by needs beyond the physiological and safety level. No doubt this is true for the college students Maslow taught, for his acquaintances, and even for the majority of people in the United States. But what of the millions of people in the world for whom hunger is a primary source of motivation? (In fairness to Maslow, virtually all Western personality psychologists have theorized about and studied an unrepresentative sample of the world's population and then have overgeneralized to all humankind.)

The source of Maslow's tunnel vision seems to be his focus on healthy and optimal personality functioning. That bias also may have accounted for Maslow's belief that safety needs are largely met in adults. Even if we remain within the restricted sample of humans to which his theory is most applicable, Maslow may have overestimated the extent to which people's safety needs are satisfied.

Consider psychological safety or security. Uncertainties—about one's grades, job, relationships, and future—are a pervasive part of most people's lives. Many people have personal insecurities, for example, about their abilities or physical attractiveness. An estimated one-third of the people in the United States suffer from a serious psychological disorder during their lifetimes (Holmes, 1991; Wilson, O'Leary, & Nathan, 1992). Indeed, safety needs appear to play more of a role in adult motivation than Maslow assumed, and some substantial minority of people in the United States, such as those who live in our large inner cities, are concerned about their physical safety on an enduring, daily basis.

Vacuous Nature of Representational Theory

Representational personality theories, especially Kelly's, provide the structure of personality with little attention to the content. It is analogous to trying to learn human anatomy from just a skeleton.

Kelly presented an elaborate description of the nature of personality or, in his terms, a personal construct system. The system is composed of a finite number of personal constructs that are bipolar and dichotomous, and they are arranged in a hierarchical order. As sturdy as this skeleton is, it contains no flesh.

The theories of Rogers, Maslow, Bandura, and Mischel do put more meat on the bones of their basic structures. A variety of substantive personality processes are theorized to be operative in all people. For example, Rogers proposed that all people have a basic need for positive regard, and he spelled out the nature and functions of this universal need. The same is true for Maslow's hierarchy of needs, the content of which is described in some detail.

Still, self-actualization, which is at the heart of Rogers's and Maslow's theoretical approaches, remains a unique process in each person. The nature of self-actualization—the inherent potentialities of each individual—remains almost completely unspecified (Ford, 1991a; Maddi, 1989). As one critic noted:

> Having appreciated the view that the inherent potentialities function to maintain and enhance life, we are in a position to inquire further as to their precise content. Extraordinary though it is, Rogers is almost completely mute on this matter! About the most insight one can gain through careful reading of Rogers is that he is thinking in terms of some sort of genetic blueprint to which substance is added as life progresses. But the precise outlines of the blueprint are a mystery. (Maddi, 1989, p. 102)

Simplistic View of Personality

Representational theorists often criticize other personality theories as being oversimplified. Yet, in many ways, these theories have also been simplistic.

As an alternative to the positions they consider limited, representational personality psychologists offer various inborn tendencies—to actualize one's potentialities, to construe events, or to characterize and evaluate oneself—as "explanations" of the causes of behavior. However, representational psychologists do not specify the origins of these tendencies; they are simply said to exist. For example, Rogers (1965) categorically stated: "The organism has one basic tendency and striving—to actualize, maintain, and enhance the experiencing organism" (p. 487). (Although the specific drive is new, the underlying premise sounds suspiciously like Freud's theory.) And Kelly (1955) said in his Fundamental Postulate that a person's processes are psychologically channelized by the ways in which he or she anticipates events. Having stated that these natural, inborn tendencies exist, Rogers and Kelly then applied them as all-purpose explanations of behavior. The problem with this tack, according to one critic, is that it "provides too few parameters to account for complex behaviors. Some ad hoc way must be found to stuff many diverse observations into one or two pigeonholes, yielding serious distortions and omissions" (Wylie, 1968, pp. 731–732).

The fundamental premises of the representational approaches that we have examined can be easily stated in a sentence or two. Each approach has a single core idea about the nature of personality and builds a theory of personality on it. This simplicity may make understanding the positions easier and also yield theories with internal consistency. But such simplification is probably inappropriate for the study of a topic as complex as human personality. As Albert Einstein put it, "Everything should be made as simple as possible, *but no simpler.*"

Another facet of this oversimplification is easily illustrated by the phenomenologists' naive vision of human social life (e.g., Neher, 1991). For example, Millon (1967) criticized phenomenological psychologists' simplistic conception of human nature as follows:

> The notion that man would be a constructive, rational, and socially conscious being, were he free of the malevolent distortions of society, seems not only sentimental but invalid. There is something grossly naive in exhorting man to live life to the fullest and then expecting socially beneficial consequences to follow. What evidence is there that one's inherent self-interest would not clash with the self-interests of others? There is something as banal as the proverbs of a fortune cookie in the suggestion "be thyself." Conceiving man's emotional disorders as a failure to "be thyself" seems equally naive and banal. (p. 307)

In fact, though, recent social cognitive conceptions of person variables that interact with characteristics of the situation are beginning to reveal a much more complex and realistic view of human nature and behavior. This approach, relying heavily on the combination of idiographic and nomothetic concerns, appears to hold real promise for the future of personality psychology and may yield a more accurate picture of the interface between the person and their world.

Inadequate Attention to Nomothetic Concerns

A major criticism of the phenomenological approach to personality is that it is highly idiographic, and therefore its findings cannot be generalized to form scientific laws.

A hallmark of the Representational Strategy is its appreciation of the uniqueness of each human personality. Although appreciation of individual differences characterizes cognitive theorists, they generally adopt a nomothetic approach in identifying and delineating cognitive styles and mechanisms that influence people generally. This is certainly not true of earlier phenomenological theorists. One basic assumption of the phenomenological approach is that each person is directed by psychological processes whose content is unique to the individual. The nature of the self-actualizing tendency varies from individual to individual, and each person has a different set of personal constructs, competencies, beliefs, and values. To understand a given individual's personality, it is therefore necessary to have knowledge of the unique processes as they occur in that person.

An idiographic model is most applicable when a single individual is the focus of interest, such as in psychotherapy. However, a heavy emphasis on an idiographic approach to personality creates a dilemma. Personality psychology is predominantly a basic science. Its goals are to develop theories and collect data that will allow prediction, control, and understanding of the behaviors of people in general rather than individuals. The phenomenological approach is severely limited in its ability to generalize its theory and findings to people in general. This problem stems largely from the fact that most of the theorists of the phenomenological approach were primarily interested in psychotherapy and conducted research based on ideas generated by their applied experiences.

The interest expressed by social cognitive theorists in the "idiothetic" approach, which permits some between-group analyses of idiographically focused data, holds much promise for reducing this problem over time. Data are emerging that suggest the utility and advantages of this approach. The idiothetic approach has been endorsed by many contemporary researchers and may well become the dominant outlook of this strategy in the future.

Use of Circular Reasoning

Some representational explanations involve circular reasoning and thereby confuse description and explanation. Consider the following line of reasoning.

1. You observe that Vivian reads a great deal. She always has a book or magazine with her. The first thing she does each morning is read the newspaper, and she reads each night before going to sleep.
2. Curious about her extensive reading, you inquire: "Why does Vivian read so much?"
3. Her husband, Stan, a phenomenological psychologist, answers: "Vivian reads because reading is consistent with her self-actualizing tendency."
4. You might inquire further: "How do you know that reading is consistent with her self-actualizing tendency?"
5. Stan replies: "Just look at how much time Vivian spends reading."

This reasoning is tautological: A = A, Vivian is who she is. It provides only a pseudoexplanation because it concludes exactly where it began. Such a journey is not enlightening, as travel is supposed to be. The danger is that pseudoexplanations of this sort may appear convincing at first and thus pass as genuine explanations. In fact, they provide no more information than we had originally and do not help us to predict other behaviors.

Circular reasoning is standard in the phenomenological approach. Kelly uses personal constructs and the hierarchical order in construct systems to "explain" a person's behaviors (e.g., Vivian is a prolific reader because she construes reading as worthwhile or enjoyable). In studying self-actualizing individuals, Maslow ran headlong into this problem (Coan, 1991). A priori, he defined certain individuals as self-actualizing; then he studied such people; finally, from what he learned about them, he further described the characteristics of self-actualizers. This approach is completely circular.

Representational psychologists are not the only ones to fall into the alluring trap of circular reasoning. Psychoanalysts, at times, confuse observation and inference (see Chapter 6), and dispositionalists apparently mistake description for explanation (see Chapter 10). The question then arises as to whether circular reasoning is endemic to personality psychology. Although a widespread problem, not all research in this area proves tautalogical on close inspection.

Inadequate Coverage of Personality Development

None of the representational positions to date provides adequate coverage of personality development.

Kelly certainly did not believe that people are born with personal constructs. In fact, he stated that constructs develop to predict events in one's life. But little in Kelly's theory specifically outlines how constructs develop (Jankowicz, 1987; Katz, 1984; Solas, 1992; Warren, 1989). The psychology of personal constructs describes the nature of constructs, how they operate, and how they change. But this information is applicable only to an already construing person—someone who has (magically?) developed a set of constructs through which experiences are viewed.

The needs in Maslow's hierarchy are inborn. However, they develop and change as the individual attempts to meet them. Maslow's theory does not specify what factors result in changes in either the needs themselves or how a person satisfies them. Presumably, how people satisfy their needs becomes more sophisticated and complex as they grow older and have more experience. However, Maslow's theory says little about such developmental issues.

Maslow's theorizing about self-actualizing individuals fails to address how a person develops into a self-actualizer. Does every person have the potential to become self-actualizing? What is different in the biological endowment or life experiences of the small number of people who are self-actualizers? These obvious and tantalizing questions remain unanswered in Maslow's theory.

Rogers's theory does include discussion of the development of personality, particularly in relation to the self-concept and conditions of worth. However, he does not make the developmental process explicit. For instance, Rogers indicates that the self-concept develops as part of the actualizing tendency's process of differentiation—that is, as one learns what is "me" and "not me." But how does 2-month-old Laura distinguish between herself and her mother, with whom she is so close? Rogers provides few details of how the process operates. A more serious problem with Rogers's concepts of personality development is that little empirical support for them exists, which is related to the criticism of ignoring nomothetic concerns discussed earlier (cf. Cartwright, DeBruin, & Berg, 1991; Cartwright & Mori, 1988).

Social cognitive theorists recognize that individuals learn and change based on experiences with the environment, and Mischel has focused attention on children in some of his research. None of these theorists, though, has tried to delineate or describe the developmental processes that may impact on functioning or how they change over the course of maturation.

Excessive Reliance on Self-Report Measures

The major liability of representational personality assessment is its excessive reliance on self-report measures. Reliance on self-report stems directly from the underlying philosophy of this strategy.

The goal of representational personality assessment is to learn about a person's subjective, private experiences in order to understand the world from that person's internal frame of reference. Only the individual has direct knowledge of subjective experiences. Thus, representational personality assessment relies almost entirely on self-reports. These often take the form of questionnaires that are relatively arbitrary operationalizations of the constructs of the theory. Even when more open-ended measures allow the subject free expression, it is not at all clear that they will report openly and honestly about their experiences. Indeed, they are at times apparently unable to do so even if they are willing. (Recall Kelly's indirect method of inferring personal constructs and the fact that many schemas, although operative, appear beyond the range of conscious awareness or recognition.)

And, if subjects do provide candid self-reports, how can assessors be confident that their interpretation reflects the subject's own? Even where vocabulary is shared, subtle shades of meaning can be misunderstood or fail to be conveyed at all.

Thus, two basic assumptions are made in representational personality assessment: (1) People are willing to describe their private experiences, and (2) they are able to do so accurately. How valid are these assumptions?

People are not always willing to share their personal experiences, particularly when private experiences are intimate or reveal unfavorable aspects of personality. People may disclose highly personal information only if they trust the examiner, which usually requires time to develop. However, personality assessment is often a one-shot deal (in both research and clinical practice).

Both psychological research and everyday observations suggest that self-reports are often intentionally distorted. People tend to report what they want others to know about them. Usually, they will distort their personality picture in a favorable light (e.g., Brown, 1991). Occasionally, individuals distort their responses so that they are seen unfavorably, as when someone wants to be dismissed from a job. People may also distort their self-reports in ways they are not fully aware of, such as answering questions with a response set (see Chapter 2).

Both psychoanalytic and dispositional assessment involve self-reports and thus share all of the problems we just have outlined. Psychoanalysts and dispositionalists deal with the problems by using indirect methods of assessment, such as projective techniques and empirically keyed personality inventories, so that the respondent is not fully aware of what is being assessed. Social cognitive researchers, too, are beginning to use and advocate indirect methods. Recently, some have even called for the use of projective devices for assessment of "nonconscious" cognitive material. Again, it appears that some researchers are moving in a direction to address this criticism, but whether they will be successful remains to be seen.

Even if people are willing to report their experiences honestly, there is still the problem of whether they *can* report them accurately. Representational personality assessment assumes that people are, for the most part, aware of the private experiences that directly influence their behavior. Psychoanalysts, in contrast, argue forcefully that people are often unaware of the determinants of their behavior.

Memory also determines the accuracy of self-reports. When memories are vague or lacking, people construct the memories they report (e.g., Ross, 1989; Shapiro, 1991). Moreover, in this process, "must be" becomes "is so," which is similar to making up a story and then later believing it yourself. For example, when David failed to make his high school swimming team, he told his friends that he had injured himself. Years later, when asked about his high school activities, he reports what he believes to be true—namely, that an injury kept him from being on the swim team. A good deal of research has accumulated to suggest memories are often distorted, enhanced, or created entirely through simple suggestion (Loftus, 1997).

Finally, can people describe their subjective experiences in a way that is both meaningful and useful to others? We have all experienced frustration in trying to tell someone else how we feel. Our inability to describe feelings to others or even specify them for ourselves is partly due to the limitations of language. It may also occur because Western societies place a higher value on thought and rationality than on emotion.

Moreover, for language to convey information to another person, the meanings of words and phrases must be commonly agreed upon and understood. It is often difficult to translate private experiences into words that fully describe them and, at the same time, communicate them to others. When language is imprecise, observers can base their understanding of the words on only their *own* experiences and perspectives, not necessarily shared by the person being assessed. Thus, although at some basic level the words were understood, the meaning was lost. Simple agreement on terms does not imply thorough understanding of meaning. Much of what was said in earlier chapters about the interpretive nature of perception can be applied to speech and language as well. And because our primary means of communicating subjective experiences is via language, we cannot be completely confident of our interpretations of what others say or write.

In sum, numerous factors raise doubts about the general assumptions that people are able and willing to accurately relate their subjective experiences. At present, the Representational Strategy may rely too heavily on self-report measures.

Romantic Vision

Both Rogers and Maslow and, to some extent, Kelly, Bandura, Rotter, and Mischel offer an optimistic and life-affirming view of human personality. Their theories emphasize positive, creative aspects of human nature. On the one hand, this is to their credit because many other views of personality are overly pessimistic. The Psychoanalytic Strategy, to which representational approaches were at least partly a reaction, is a prime example (DeCarvalho, 1990b, 1991b). Freud's theory focused on the seedy side of human nature, viewing people as victims of unconscious urges that offend society's sensibilities and are difficult to manage. The Dispositional Strategy also relegates us to the fate of largely immutable traits. In such company, the rosy picture of human nature painted by representational psychologists is refreshing.

On the other hand, in their zeal to emphasize the positive, many representational psychologists adopt an overly idealistic view of human nature. They assume that people are intrinsically good and that they have the potential to enhance themselves and grow independently. Some of their writings about personality sound more like fairy tales than scientific description. Landsman and Landsman (1991), for example, have referred to Maslow's self-actualizer as a "beautiful and noble person" (cf. Rule, 1991). Phenomenological theories may say more about how humans *should be* than about how they actually are (e.g., Walker, 1992). It has been suggested that self-representations function as a "myth of human development" (Daniels, 1988, p. 13). Even the emerging view of people seeking to enhance self through all available means can appear too optimistic. In fact, it appears that for people who are unable to imagine positive possible selves, their self-enhancement may take a very negative, antisocial form. This seems to be the case with some criminals and delinquents, who, seeing no other possibility for themselves, seek to be the best criminal they can be (Oyserman & Markus,

1990). Few would consider this attempt at self-enhancement a direction of positive growth.

SUMMARY

1. The Representational Strategy relies heavily on self-report measures, including both questionnaire and personality inventories. It also uses several unstructured procedures that are, in some ways, similar to projective techniques. The aim of all these efforts, though, is to gain insight into clients' internal frame of reference and idiosyncratic understanding of themselves and their experiences.
2. The Q-sort is a standardized procedure for assessing the self-concept. It entails making comparative judgments about statements printed on cards, which are then sorted by clients in terms of the degree to which each statement applies to them.
3. A common open-ended assessment procedure is to ask clients to generate a list of descriptors to describe either themselves or how they believe others see them. Clients may also be asked to rank the descriptors they have generated according to various criteria.
4. Kelly devised the Role Construct Repertory Test (Rep Test), which uses a grid to elicit clients' personal constructs. Clients may also be asked to generate implications grids to determine the hierarchical order of constructs by asking such questions as: "If construct Y changed, what other constructs would also change?"
5. Rotter assessed locus of control with his I-E Scale, consisting of 29 forced-choice items between internal and external responses. Similar measures (including a cartoon version for preschoolers) have been devised for a variety of populations and purposes, including domain-specific scales.
6. Rogers developed person-centered therapy as an alternative to psychoanalysis. This nondirective verbal interchange with a therapist who provides unconditional positive regard is intended to assist clients in assuming personal responsibility for themselves and their actions. Empathic understanding from the therapist is considered the most potent factor in producing therapeutic change through this form of therapy; the two specific methods used are clarification of feelings and restatement of content.
7. In Kelly's fixed-role therapy, clients play the role of a fictitious person whose behavior is consistent with a construct system that would be beneficial for the client. Originally intended for individual clients, fixed-role therapy has been adapted to marital and group therapy.
8. Bandura has argued that all forms of personality change are effective because they foster the client's perceived self-efficacy. One of the most potent ways to enhance perceived self-efficacy is through participant modeling, which involves observing a model engage in the desired behavior and then performing the behavior oneself with the therapist's assistance.
9. In one experiment, Bandura and his associates taught subjects to increase their pain tolerance through cognitive coping skills; this

treatment was successful in bolstering both self-efficacy for pain tolerance and actual pain tolerance.

10. Cognitive therapies are aimed at modifying maladaptive cognitions, by a combination of directly altering relevant cognitions and altering behavior. These treatments are often called "cognitive-behavioral therapies."
11. Cognitive restructuring identifies a client's maladaptive cognitions and then modifies what clients privately say to themselves (self-statements) in difficult or trying situations. In Aaron Beck's version of cognitive therapy, irrational beliefs are proposed to clients as hypotheses that clients are asked to refute. Originally designed to treat depression, Beck's cognitive therapy has now also been used to treat anxiety, personality disorders, and marital discord. Interestingly, this therapy also uses behavioral components (such as graded task assignments) as well as verbal interventions.
12. Meichenbaum's self-instructional training teaches clients to instruct themselves about how to act, feel, and think in various situations. It typically involves cognitive modeling, cognitive participant modeling, overt self-instruction, and covert self-instruction. This therapy has been used successfully to treat anxiety, deficits in academic skills, and even schizophrenic speech.
13. D'Zurilla and Goldfried developed problem-solving therapy, which was perhaps the first cognitively oriented intervention to become widely known. This therapy teaches clients general problem-solving skills (such as brainstorming, demonstrated in the text) and provides not only treatment for a particular problem but also a general coping strategy that can be used for almost any problem they subsequently encounter. Problem-solving therapy has been used successfully to treat depression, aggression, marital and family conflicts, and child abuse.
14. Cognitive-behavioral marital therapy includes communication and problem-solving training, increasing positive behavior exchanges between mates (e.g., through the caring-days technique), and cognitive restructuring. It has been shown effective not only in relieving marital distress but also in preventing it through premarital training.
15. The Representational Strategy is limited in scope because it assumes that everything of importance about a person can be gleaned from the person's conscious experience and memory. Unconscious experience is largely ignored.
16. This strategy is also limited by discounting the past, thus potentially overlooking the actual causes of present difficulties and failing to provide the person with real understanding.
17. There are large gaps in the coverage provided by the Representational Strategy, which largely ignores biological factors. The phenomenological approach also ignores environmental factors, despite clear evidence of their impact on the person.
18. Much of representational theory is vacuous, in the sense that it says little about the actual content of personality. The strategy is also

simplistic, using all-purpose explanations and proposing tendencies that are assumed to be "given," but which are never really accounted for or explained.

19. The idiographic viewpoint that lies at the heart of the phenomenological approach precludes the identification of (nomothetic) scientific propositions and laws, although the recent emergence of an "idiothetic" approach within the social cognitive approach holds considerable promise for the Representational Strategy in general.
20. Some of the reasoning used in the Representational Strategy is tautological, yielding pseudoexplanations that amount to no more than "Vivian is who she is."
21. The Representational Strategy provides inadequate coverage of personality development, relies excessively on self-report measures, and provides a romantic vision of the person that appears overly optimistic in view of the persistent problems and troubles that plague individuals, nations, and the entire planet as much or more so than they did 2000 years ago.

PART SIX

EPILOGUE

The Path Ahead

CHAPTER NINETEEN

Commonalities and Continuing Controversies

n this epilogue, we examine briefly how the findings, theories, and viewpoints you have read about in the past 18 chapters add up to a meaningful picture. We do this by examining how the theoretical constructs used by different theorists and researchers discussed in this book relate to one another and to the field of personality psychology as it exists today. We begin with a quick review of the journey we've made.

HOW FAR WE HAVE TRAVELED!

We have covered a great deal of ground in the last 18 chapters. We have examined more than two dozen theories or mini-theories that pertain to personality psychology from within four different and relatively distinct "strategies." It is important for you as the reader to know that a great many personality psychologists would not choose to identify their own work as being merely the manifestation of a single strategy. Nor would they see their work as an ardent demonstration or argument for some grand theory. Then again, many other theorists *do* identify themselves as psychoanalytic, behavioral, social cognitive, or dispositional, and some describe themselves with more complex or broader phrases such as "cognitive-behavioral," "psychodynamic," or even "eclectic" (i.e., operating without a *single* firm theoretical base).

Thus, the strategy labels we have used are themselves largely *constructs* rather than existing realities. But, we feel the strategy approach allowed us to organize the presentation of material related to personality in a coherent and meaningful way. Our four strategies, like all good theoretical constructs, served the purpose of organizing and consolidating a vast range of observations into comprehensible "chunks."

Because the labels individual writers use are also *constructions* (constructs), the ideas we have discussed may seem at first so diverse as to be unfathomable. The strategy labels are intended to capture some shared features of the theories they encompass, as well as some of the distinctions between related assumptions and trains of thought.

We hope the "strategy" approach served our purpose well for you. As you have probably realized by now, some theories do not fall neatly within the bounds of any one strategy, and some theorists have been discussed in more than one strategy (e.g., Albert Bandura was discussed in both the Environmental and the Representational Strategies).

In fact, the scope of some theorists' work is very broad, while the writings of others are quite narrow and circumscribed. Some researcher-theorists, like Albert Bandura and Walter Mischel, actually span the division between two or more strategies.

The field of personality psychology is growing and changing constantly. We believe that it is growing *toward unification* rather than toward greater divergence. Of the several reasons why this is so, the most important is that the findings and ideas are themselves beginning to converge and coalesce into an image of "the person."

COMMON CONSTRUCTS, DIFFERENT LANGUAGE

Close examination of the various strategies reveals a number of common themes, as well as shared constructs, although the specific terms used may differ. Our aim in this section is to highlight some of these commonalities. The discussion is intended to be neither comprehensive nor exhaustive. Your own personal review of the material covered will reveal many other shared elements, and you may have already noticed several as you read the preceding chapters.

Let us begin from the very foundation of personality psychology. Sigmund Freud remains the most influential psychologist of all time; it is almost impossible to find an introductory psychology, personality, or psychopathology textbook that does not list his name in the index. He devised a comprehensive theory of personality beginning from its earliest developmental roots, and he must be credited with fathering the wide acceptance of psychotherapy. The appearance of clinical psychology as an applied profession can be traced directly to him. Freud's ideas—or *reactions and comparisons to them*—continue to pervade contemporary thinking. Many psychoanalytic concepts reappear in contemporary theories (most often with new names and somewhat modified connotations).

Decades before the "cognitive revolution" in psychology, Freud wrote of the importance of object representations. These ideas were carried forward by his followers in the object relations theories but were virtually disregarded in academic psychology for 50 years. Recognition of the power and importance of mental images and operations is now at the heart of contemporary cognitive psychology.

Freud wrote about the ironies of mental life, such as the fact that we often consciously intend to act in a particular way and end up behaving in ways directly opposite to our conscious intentions. Wegner (1994) gives the following examples of these counter-intentional outcomes:

> It is not just that we cannot sleep, for instance, or that we cannot stop thinking about food when on a diet; the problem is that the more we want to sleep or banish food thoughts the more we fail. We stay awake worrying that we cannot sleep, and we spend all day mentally in the refrigerator when we are hoping to diet. The agony of mental control is this oppositional quality that always seems to haunt attempts to direct our minds. (1994, p. 34)

How can these phenomena be explained? Wegner, like Freud, suggests these are not mere accidents but are a logical (although ironic) effect of the effort to exercise mental control. He postulates that any attempt to control the mind involves two opposing processes: (a) an *operating process* that promotes the intended mental state and (b) a *monitoring process* that searches for mental contents inconsistent with the desired state. Wegner further suggests that the operating process requires greater cognitive capacity (cf. Freud's concept of psychic energy) than the monitoring process. Thus, when we are mentally taxed, the monitoring process may supersede the operating process and bring into play the very conditions and behaviors we intended to avoid. Phenomena such as Freudian slips (see p. 77) may be understood and anticipated through a modern theory of the nature and limitations of intentional cognitive control.

Freud's primary process as a means of gratification is the conjuring of mental images to fulfill a wish or drive. Cognitive psychologists now acknowledge the potence of mental imagery and recognize that visualizing is often the first step in attaining a goal. (In fact, mental practice can even improve performance of motor skills and is now used by many professional athletes and endorsed by their coaches.)

Freud also spoke of delay of gratification and the potential role of *mental imagery* in this skill. Representational psychologists have examined this issue, and while imagining the desired object may not always enhance a person's ability to wait for it, other mental operations may well do so. Mischel and Baker (1975), approaching this problem from a cognitive perspective, found that thinking about a desired object in ways that minimize its appeal could enhance ability to endure delay.

The defense mechanisms of Freud parallel the cognitive filters, distortions, and response biases discussed by modern psychologists. Repression and the defensive process of denial described by Carl Rogers both disallow from awareness material that would be threatening to the self and result in overwhelming anxiety. (Other examples of parallels between Freud's defense mechanisms and Roger's defensive processes were presented in Chapter 16, in Table 16.1, p. 412.)

Freud's belief that intrapsychic conflict produces anxiety parallels the process of cognitive dissonance described by Leon Festinger. Kelly also spoke of the emotional distress experienced in reaction to perceived threat to an internally coherent construct system. Each of these ideas was proposed to account for the discomfort (anxiety) produced by *internal inconsistency.* (Freud's conflict is between different mental structures—id versus ego, and so on—and Festinger's and Kelly's are between conflicting information that threatens an integrated and coherent image of the self.) The processes are quite similar, though.

The links between psychoanalytic theories and others extend beyond the realm of the Representational Strategy and can be found in *all* of the other strategies as well. Freud's ideas of incorporation and identification, used to explain the process of internalizing the values of an important other, clearly parallel the acquisition of behavior via social modeling.

Freud's reality principle addresses the impact of the external environment, which acts to constrain behavior and the quest for drive reduction in much the same way that environmental contingencies and learning history do. Thus, beyond innate drives and internal forces, Freud acknowledged features of the *external environment* as significant in molding behavior and, ultimately, personality. (Note that the social cognitive theorists also acknowledge the interplay between external situational factors and internal person variables.)

Freud was deeply influenced by the theory of natural selection as it was proposed by Darwin. He believed that the existence of the mental structures he identified (id, ego, and superego) may have been favored through evolution. In fact, because people are *social* and *inter*dependent, development of the a moral sense or superego may well have been favored by evolution and natural selection.

Specifically, for survival of the group, a degree of altruism (putting the needs of the group and its members before the self) may well be necessary. Thus, the conscience (one aspect of the superego) may help to ensure personal survival through continued membership in a protective social group. (Freud's conscience also seems very like Higgins's idea of the ought self.)

Darwin himself embraced some of these ideas and felt that the "moral sense" attributed to humans in an effort to discredit his theory might actually serve to support it. (Humans developed a "moral sense" because they are interdependent [social] and also have the memory capacity and linguistic ability to express these ideas in a way other animals could not; see Chapter 9 for details.) Thus, altruism may be necessary for long-term survival (which ensures successful breeding and transmission of genetic material and characteristics). The development of a conscience (and, by extension, superego) may well have been favored through natural selection (Nesse, 1990).

To extend the role of the superego, let us examine its second aspect, the ego ideal. Freud spoke of the ego ideal as that part of the self that promotes the *quest for the ideal and the perfect* rather than the necessary or desired. Examination of this part of the self reveals some close parallels with the concepts of self-actualization, openness, and ideal self of other strategies. Rogers and Maslow spoke of the actualizing tendency as the drive to develop all capacities of the individual. The FFM supertrait of "Openness" is characterized by willingness to try new experiences, creativity, tolerance, daring, and originality. Both of these concepts seem closely related to the "ideal seeking" aspect of the superego. And clearly, the quest for the greatest possible similarity between the perceived self and the most ideal possible self parallels Freud's earlier theory.

In fact, the innate drives that Freud deemed central to personality development and functioning appear to be quite like the traits and temperaments of the Dispositional Strategy. Traits are assumed to be innate, broad in their influence, and enduring over the lifespan of the individual. So, too, are the drives of Freud. More and more, the biological basis of personality traits is being acknowledged. Freud also believed that the two universal drives (Eros and Thanatos) emanated from basic biological forces that evolved with the human species over time, and contemporary social cognitive psychologists acknowledge the important influence of stable person variables as they interact with important elements of the situation.

Although our discussion so far has focused on parallels between Freudian theories and the other approaches to personality, many parallels exist between the other strategies as well. We spoke earlier of the overlap between the behavioral and social cognitive approaches, and the term *cognitive-behavioral* is quite common today, especially as applied to personality change (therapy) techniques. Many other areas of overlap exist, and a good deal of cross-fertilization and sharing of ideas occurs in all areas of psychology today. Easier access to information, through computers searching large data sets and on-line material, will increase this sharing over time.

Divisions between approaches and the broad strategies will tend to shrink with this increased communication. The tendency to naively repeat the work of previous theorists will diminish. It appears to us, now, that the germs of most modern-day personality theories can be traced back to the original writings of Sigmund Freud. Keep in mind, though, that many of Freud's specific beliefs and many of the ideas of theorists from all strategies have also been (for all practical purposes) cast aside or discarded. One common reason is failure to meet the scientific standards of explicit definitions and empirical verification (largely ignored by Freud). These are now requirements of the overwhelming majority of personality psychologists, professional societies, and scholarly journals.

CONVERGING METHODS OF PERSONALITY CHANGE

One area where the sharing of information and perspectives has had a tremendous impact has been in the application of techniques for change. The entire field of psychotherapy is moving toward *integration* of techniques from diverse origins. Twenty years ago, most psychotherapists would have chosen to label themselves as adherents of one type of therapy or another. Thus, there were psychoanalysts, behavior therapists, humanists, cognitive therapists, Jungians, Rogerians, and so on. It became fashionable at some point to claim to be "eclectic," which meant choosing at various times from among a broad range of techniques derived from different approaches.

Today, most psychologists defer to strict scientific tests and agree on the need for empirical validation and logical rigor in basic personality psychology *and* the practice of psychotherapy. The field is now beginning to reflect these changes. Therapists no longer choose one approach or another based on personal inclination or conviction, but rather on the available efficacy data. Psychotherapy is now moving *beyond eclecticism* to a point where specific combinations of techniques are being identified as most effective for particular types of problems or clients. The use of medication as an adjunct to psychotherapy is now commonplace, as is the combined use of techniques that originated within different strategies. Common elements from different approaches, such as empathy, are also being identified. And, more and more, practicing clinical psychologists can look to treatment handbooks that detail the empirical findings and most effective approaches for the treatment of specific types of psychological disorders. We expect that these rigorous standards and intense research efforts will continue and guide the second century of personality psychology.

EVOLUTION IS ONGOING

Darwin believed that the evolution of life on Earth is an ongoing process; the field of personality psychology is also evolving continuously. The migration and integration of ideas across different approaches have been startling in the past three decades (i.e., since the first edition of this book published in 1970). Everywhere there is evidence of increasing sophistication and greater appreciation of the complexity of forces that combine and interact to produce behavior and human personality.

The recent trend within the social cognitive approach of blending and combining elements of the idiographic and nomothetic approaches holds great promise. This "idiothetic" approach to research allows for attention to individuals and description of their behavior while still permitting some group comparisons and generalizable conclusions. This approach allows researchers to *appreciate the uniqueness* of individuals and still address the scientific requirement of delineating general principles of human behavior.

In their review of the recent literature on goals, Austin and Vancouver (1996) call for "informed methodological pluralism," which would include "striking a balance among experimental, observational-correlational, simulation, and other methods" (p. 363). They also suggest studying theoretical issues in applied settings, which may prove more productive than either purely theoretical *or* purely applied research in isolation.

This increasing methodological sophistication will surely increase the efficiency of research. It may also continue to break down existing barriers between theoretical positions. For researchers who held firmly that individual differences were more than "noise" in their data, research that combines an individual focus with nomothetic concerns is likely to be more palatable and better appreciated than pure between-groups designs. And, it is *amply* clear that the behavior of humans is complexly determined. It will likely require a very complex and sophisticated approach to research to actually illuminate the most important individual characteristics and the ways they combine with the environment to produce the many features of the person we attribute to "personality." As of now, no one approach or strategy has all the answers—or even addresses all the questions that remain about psychology, personality, and the human condition.

WHERE WILL THE JOURNEY END?

Each of the strategies discussed offers some evidence that converges with those of other approaches. Each strategy also offers a unique view of the person. Yet it appears that the paths that earlier seemed so divergent are now moving toward convergence. Each strategy offers some pieces to the puzzle of personality, and by combining them we will ultimately understand human nature as we have come to understand much about our physical world.

Even now, the effects of cross-fertilization are evident. Not only can parallels between different theories be found but also researchers have begun the task of *translation* across different theoretical orientations. Psychoanalytic constructs are being defined and operationalized in contemporary cognitive terms (Anderson & Cole, 1990; Singer, 1988; Wegner, 1994; Westen, 1988). These "redefined" constructs are then being empirically investigated following the strictures of methodological behaviorism. A recent psychoanalytic study focused on the "working self-concept" in transference and described the "mental representations of significant others [as] crucial in transference" (Hinkley & Anderson, 1996, p. 1279) These authors clearly embrace the mental representations as captured by the self-schema construct and fit the process of transference to a cognitive model of self. The results are impressive indeed; their data support the operation of transference *and* enable cognitively oriented researchers to understand and appreciate the process in familiar terms.

Recall that Freud felt that empirical research of his ideas was unnecessary but could do no harm. In fact, though, as it looks today, empirical research of Freud's ideas may well continue to boost his status in contemporary academic circles beyond what it currently is. This same type of translation process can be seen elsewhere as researchers from different orientations begin to recognize the contributions of other approaches and how they interface with their own.

PERSISTING CONTROVERSIES

Despite increasing sophistication about the complexity of personality, stark differences continue to exist between some strategies and approaches. Many from the environmental camp still contend that internal factors are not subject to direct observation or intervention and insist that they should be excluded from scientific study. Most dispositional psychologists attend only to factors that can be observed directly and resist drawing inferences about "deeper" meaning. Some psychoanalytically oriented psychologists believe that the most significant factors influencing the person are inaccessible to direct study because they are unknown even to the self; that is, they remain in the unconscious. These unconscious phenomena are most often only suggested by vague inference. Cognitive psychologists also choose to study private mental events; however, they study them by identifying relatively objective measures that reflect the operation of internal, private processes.

Clearly, other divisions exist between the four broad strategies and often even between approaches within strategies. We contend, though, that the human mind *is* amenable to study through scientific means. The challenge facing contemporary psychology is to continue to create and refine techniques that allow for psychological investigation through scientifically sound, humane, and ethical procedures.

THE JOURNEY IS THE END

Watching the field of personality grow and evolve has been very exciting for us. Changes have occurred in the field that seemed unimaginable only a few years ago. The dominance of behaviorism at one time seemed to suggest the end of the quest for mental phenomena. It certainly directed most research efforts toward the external environment and away from internal factors and events. The tide has surely turned. Researchers are now rediscovering the importance of mental events and also discovering the genetic bases of all types of characteristics, including personality differences. Moreover, *agreement*, rather than disagreement, is more and more apparent as we review the most recent scientific journals.

Like so many human endeavors, the pendulum of opinion swings from extreme to extreme before settling on an intermediate position. This "natural" phenomenon tempers the radical views on either end of the spectrum of ideas. Personality psychology has experienced many such swings over its history. We believe that the pendulum is beginning to slow and the field is gradually becoming more moderate overall, with greater and greater appreciation for the contributions emerging from different approaches. No one strategy discussed in this book can by itself capture the essence of personality. It will be through the gradual blending of ideas that understanding will increase. We believe the journey will continue for many years to come.

The journey itself has been filled with many exciting advances and transitions. We have often found ourselves drawn from topic to topic as exciting new research results appeared. Even as we write now, we realize that theoretical positions are shifting and changing. In some areas, this book will be somewhat dated by the time it is printed. We have enjoyed following the recent progress and eagerly look forward to writing the next edition of *Personality,* which will reflect the many changes that accumulate over the coming years. For us, though, the journey is, and has been, extremely gratifying. Like the state of flow described by Csikszentmihalyi (see Box 16.1, p. 425), we have often been so absorbed as to lose track of time and place while pursuing a fascinating new idea or unique application of an old one. We hope you have found the trip as fascinating and stimulating as we have.

We would like to close this chapter, and the book, with an analogy you may find useful. Each individual is like a kaleidoscope. Each unique personality is composed of minute elements, all interrelated, and to some extent interdependent. Over the course of development, personality, like the view through a kaleidoscope as it rotates slowly, is ever shifting and evolving in response to minor perturbations. Gradual changes in the resulting image may be almost imperceptible and even escape notice. Then again, sudden dramatic movements or shocks to the system may alter the entire design. These shifts, like a kaleidoscope shaken, have profound effects that reverberate throughout the entire pattern and color scheme.

Changes in context (external or social), like moving the kaleidoscope's aim from a dark wall toward a bright window, are reflected in subtle changes of hue. For example, a normally reserved, quiet person may in fact become bright and animated in the company of a few close friends.

Despite multiple forces and constant subtle shifting over time, the elements of design seen in a kaleidoscope continually fall into place to portray a coherent, unified whole. So, too, with the person. Each maintains a unique pattern of features and characteristics that, while colored by different social roles and contexts, remains coherent and recognizable to the self and others.

Only the most dramatic life events or traumas will alter the person profoundly enough to produce major discontinuity in an individual's overall personality structure. Such events are generally quite rare. Their profound impact is usually clearly evident to the self and observers alike. Most "normal" personality development is actually slow and gradual, its transitions often slipping by unnoticed.

Individual pattern elements, like the many possible person variables or traits, are relatively small and intricately interwoven. The resulting pattern is *unique* and *astonishingly complex.* Thus, complete understanding of personality—or even the personality of a specific individual—eludes us still. Each strategy offers some truths, some elements of the picture, yet none captures the entirety of human personality. We are making great strides in understanding, but the task is such that the journey will continue for a long time to come.

For most of you, the ideas presented here may help to inform your day-to-day interactions with others and the world around you. You may even have gained new insight into *your* self. Perhaps a few of you are intrigued enough to continue to follow the field of personality psychology or, better yet, to join it, and even help to light the way.

Glossary

Note: Italics in the definitions indicate terms that are defined elsewhere in the Glossary.

accept (Maslow) Observe human nature without criticizing or demanding that it be otherwise.

acceptability The degree to which a theory is palatable to the scientific and general community.

acceptance In *observational learning,* the stage at which the model's behavior is accepted as a guide for one's own actions.

acquisition In *observational learning,* the stage at which the model's behavior is recognized and stored in memory.

acquisition curve Graphic plot of the frequency of a target behavior as it accelerates over time—the line rises at an increasingly sharp angle upward toward the right.

action potential Transmission of an electrical impulse throughout a *neuron.*

activity level The intensity and speed of a behavioral response.

activity setting Any environmental context in which cultural values are transmitted to others.

actualizing tendency (Maslow and Rogers) Inborn tendency of people to develop all of their capacities in a particular direction that maintains or enhances them.

actual-self The way people actually see themselves.

actual-self sort *Q-sort* in which subjects sort self-referent statements in terms of how they actually see themselves.

adoptee/family method A procedure used to assess the degree to which a disposition is heritable by contrasting biological and adopted children brought up in the same home.

Agreeableness (Costa and McCrae) One of the "big five" personality factors characterized by willing cooperation with others, contrasted with antagonism.

aggressive drive (Freud) *Thanatos* the motivational force that accounts for destructive aspects of human behavior.

ambivalent attachment (Ainsworth) One form of *insecure attachment* characterized by resistance to separation by the child and rejection and aloofness on the return of the parent.

amygdala Structure in the temporal lobe of the brain that, when stimulated, may produce aggressive behavior.

anal character (psychoanalysis) Adult behavior pattern that presumably results from *fixation* at the *anal stage,* characterized by orderliness, stinginess, and stubbornness.

anal eroticism (anal retentive) In the *anal stage,* pleasure from retaining feces; in later life, pleasure from being orderly and stingy.

anal erotic phase Portion of the *anal stage* during which pleasure is obtained by retaining feces.

anal expulsive character Individual fixated at the *anal sadistic phase.*

anal retentive character Individual fixated at the *anal erotic phase.*

anal sadism (anal expulsive) In the *anal stage,* pleasure from expelling feces; in later life, pleasure from being messy and disorderly.

anal sadistic phase Portion of the *anal stage* during which pleasure is obtained from expelling feces.

anal stage Freud's second *psychosexual stage* of development (age 2 to 3 years), when the *libido* is centered in the anal area.

androcentric Male-centered perspective that characterizes Freudian psychoanalysis.

androgen Male *hormone.*

androgynous Label applied to people who possess many stereotypic masculine *and* feminine characteristics.

androgyny Term for the combination of many traits typical of *each* gender and their associated roles.

Anima (Jung) Archetype of the feminine aspects of men responsible for mood swings.

Animus (Jung) Archetype of the masculine aspects of women responsible for solid convictions. Parallel of Freud's bisexual nature of personality.

Antabuse Drug used specifically to deter alcohol abuse.

antecedents In *operant conditioning,* the stimuli (including situational, temporal, and interpersonal cues) present before the *target behavior* occurs.

antidepressants *Psychotropic drugs* used to control mood disorders (specifically, *depressive symptoms*).

antimanics *Psychotropic drugs* used to control mood disorders (specifically, *manic symptoms*).

antipsychotics *Psychotropic drugs* used to control *psychotic* symptoms and schizophrenia.

anxiety Generally, the emotional experience of threat or danger; the precise definition varies with the personality theory.

anxiety disorders Anxiety symptoms that are pervasive, enduring, or interfere with daily functioning.

anxiety hierarchy List of situations that make a person anxious, ordered in terms of the amount of anxiety engendered; used in *systematic desensitization.*

anxiolytics Psychotropic drugs used to control *anxiety.*

approach behavior (Zuckerman) Tendency to orient or move toward novel stimuli.

ARAS (ascending reticular activating system) Part of the brain involved in activating higher brain centers and contributing to the regulation of states of consciousness.

archetypal dreams (Jung) Unusual dreams with mythical symbolism.

archetype (Jung) Predisposition to form a common idea that may direct behavior; part of the *collective unconscious.*

artificiality A problem that can occur in research experiments conducted in controlled laboratory settings that greatly differ from real-life or natural environments.

asceticism (Anna Freud) Coping strategy whereby adolescents abstain from physical pleasure to gain a sense of control over their lives.

aschematic (Markus) The state of lacking a *schema* for a particular class of information or personal characteristic.

assortative mating People actively choose their mates, as opposed to mating randomly with other members of the species.

asthenic (Kretschner) Narrow and frail body type with general personality correlates.

athletic (Kretschner) Muscular body type with general personality correlates.

atrophy Tissue shrinkage.

attachment (Bowlby) Tie between child and parent that serves the protective and survival needs of the child but which is experienced subjectively as an intense emotional commitment to the other.

attachment style (Ainsworth) Refers to differences in the type and quality of the parent-child bond in infancy.

attachment theory (Bowlby) Focuses on the qualitative differences in the bond between children and their parents.

attention hierarchies A phenomenon in which the higher one's status is in the group, the more likely one is to receive attention from others.

attributive projection (psychoanalysis) Projecting a characteristic that one is aware of personally possessing (see also *projection*) onto others.

augmenting response Tendency of the nervous system to enhance the perception of novel environmental inputs.

authoritarian parenting A parenting style marked by restrictive and rejecting behavior toward the child.

authoritative parenting A parenting style marked by parental warmth, inductive style of discipline, nonpunitive punishment practices, and consistency in child rearing.

autonomic nervous system Controls most internal body systems and involuntary (reflexive) behaviors.

autosomal Genetic material contained on any of the first 22 pairs of human *chromosomes.*

aversion therapy *Classical conditioning* therapy that creates a negative emotional reaction to a maladaptive behavior.

avoidant attachment One form of *insecure attachment* characterized by a lack of distress on parent's departure and rejection and active avoidance upon the parent's return.

axons Long branching "arms" of *neurons.*

back-translation A procedure used by cross-cultural researchers in which one's materials are translated into the second language and then translated back into the original language by another translator. If the back-translation matches the original, the transaction is taken to be reasonably accurate.

backup reinforcers In a *token economy,* tangible rewards, such as food, gum, or cigarettes, that clients get by trading tokens they have earned for adaptive behaviors.

baseline Pretreatment period of a study.

base rate The existing rate of occurrence of a phenomenon within the population of interest.

basic behavioral repertoires Complex sets of learned skills: language-cognitive, emotional-motivational, and sensory-motor.

behavioral activation system (BAS) Motivates people to seek desired goals and rewards.

behavioral avoidance test A series of tasks requiring increasingly more threatening interactions with a feared object or situation (e.g., from looking at a snake in a container to letting it crawl on one's lap).

behavioral genetics A field of study concerned with the genetic basis of personality differences.

behavioral inhibition system (BIS) Deters goal-seeking behavior by alerting a person to possible danger or punishment.

behavioral repertoire The range of behaviors acquired and accepted by a child, largely influenced by forces operating in a child's environment.

behavioral signatures of personality (Mischel) Particular "if . . . then . . ." relationships between environmental circumstances and behavior that distinguish personalities.

behaviorism An approach within the Environmental Strategy that focuses on external, directly observable factors as determinants of *personality.*

behavior modification *Behavior therapy* that uses the principles of *operant conditioning.*

behavior potential (Rotter) The likelihood that a given behavior will occur in a particular situation.

behavior rehearsal Therapy procedure in which the client practices adaptive behaviors.

behavior therapy Any psychotherapy technique or combination of techniques derived from the behavioral approach.

bell-and-pad method *Urine alarm method* of treating enuresis in which a child sleeps on a special pad that sounds an alarm to awaken the child when the pad becomes wet from urine.

belongingness (Baumeister and Leary) A basic need of humans to feel membership in one or more stable social groups.

belongingness needs Needs pertaining to affiliation and affection.

benzodiazapines Drugs used to treat anxiety. They work by enhancing the binding of the neurotransmitter GABA to receptor sites.

biofeedback Technique that provides individuals with physiological information about their bodies, so they can learn to regulate otherwise automatic processes.

biogerontologists Scientists who study arresting and reversing the aging process through genetic manipulation and cloning.

biological evolution How species characteristics develop over time.

bipolar I disorder Depressed mood with episodes of elevated, expansive, or irritable mood (mania).

birth trauma (Rank) The initial biological separation of child and mother, which is the prototype for all separation, loss, and anxiety in later life.

blended families Families that include previously married adults (or involved partners) and the children from both partners' previous unions.

brainstorming exercise In problem-solving therapy, a list of any and all solutions to a problem is generated, maximizing the range of solutions from which to choose.

capital Resources of the family that include financial, social, and human capital.

cardinal disposition (Allport) A trait that dominates a person's entire existence; very few people have cardinal dispositions.

caring-days technique (Stuart) Method used in cognitive-behavioral marital therapy to increase a couple's positive behavior exchanges.

case study Research method involving detailed qualitative descriptions of the behavior of a single individual.

castration anxiety (Freud) Male's fear of loss of his penis, usually considered the probable retaliation for unacceptable sexual desires (e.g., incest with mother). It is the impetus for resolving the *Oedipus complex.*

catharthis An intense emotional release after the recollection of a traumatic event.

cathect (psychoanalysis) To invest *psychic energy* in the mental representation of a person, behavior, or idea.

cathexis The investment of *psychic energy* in the mental image of an activity or person. *Cathect* is the verb form.

causal attribution Interpretations about the causes of our observations, which influence how we act and react to our environment and experiences.

central disposition (Allport) A trait that manifests itself in many aspects of personality; most individuals have between 3 and 10 central dispositions.

central nervous system (CNS) The brain and spinal cord.

cerebral cortex The outermost layer of the human brain.

cerebrotonia (Sheldon) One of three basic temperaments associated with a particular physique.

chance control (Rotter) Belief that personal outcomes are due to chance factors beyond ones own control.

character type (psychoanalysis) Adult personality characteristics resulting from *fixation* at a childhood psychosexual stage.

chromosome Units of genetic material consisting of tightly packed and compartmentalized *deoxyribonucleic acid* (DNA).

clarification of feelings (Rogers) *Client-centered therapy* technique in which the therapist reflects back the emotions that the client is expressing (cf. *restatement of content*).

classical conditioning Learning process in which a stimulus comes to elicit a response because the stimulus is now associated with another stimulus that already elicits the response.

classical projection (psychoanalysis) Projecting a characteristic that one is unaware of onto another (see *projection*).

client (Rogers) The term used for the person seeking therapy, which connotes someone actively seeking help with a problem.

client-centered therapy (Rogers) Therapy in which the client assumes responsibility for working out the solutions to problems, and the therapist assumes a non-directive role, primarily restating the content of what the client has said and clarifying the client's feelings.

cognitive approach A perspective that deals with the mental representations and processes that give rise to conscious thought and experience.

cognitive behavior therapy *Behavior therapy* that focuses on changing people's thoughts and perceptions to modify their behavior.

cognitive dissonance (Festinger) An uncomfortable state caused by an inconsistency between existing attitudes and behavior.

cognitive distortions Inaccuracies in thinking and beliefs.

cognitive factors (Rotter) Personal values and expectancies that directly determine behavior.

cognitive filters Past experiences, information, and biases through which new information is filtered and encoded.

cognitive modeling (Meichenbaum) A *model* performs a behavior while stating aloud the steps and strategy used.

cognitive participant modeling (Meichenbaum) Subject performs a behavior while a model recites steps and strategies to be used.

cognitive prototypes (Mischel) The "best examples" of a trait concept, from which people draw inferences about the degree to which a trait is generally present in themselves or another person.

cognitive restructuring In *cognitive behavior therapy*, teaching clients to think about themselves in positive and adaptive ways.

cognitive therapy (Beck) Techniques for helping patients think about themselves in more positive ways.

coherence Absence of stark inconsistencies or contradictions.

collective unconscious (Jung) Level of awareness or division of the mind that is the product of the combined experiences of humans through their evolution.

common traits (Allport) *Dispositions* that allow direct trait comparisons across people.

competence (White) A person's fitness or ability to carry out those transactions with the environment that will result in maintaining, growing, and flourishing as an individual.

complete penetrance The presence of a gene means the *phenotype* will appear.

comprehensiveness The breadth of the phenomena that a theory can encompass.

compulsions Ritualistic repetitive behavior.

computed tomography (CT) Brain imaging technique.

concordance The term given to describe similarity or agreement in diagnosis between pairs.

condensation (Freud) The *dream work* process in which separate thoughts are combined or compressed.

conditional dispositional construct (Mischel) A rule that provides a meaningful "if-then" link between clusters of situations and clusters of behaviors.

conditional positive regard (Rogers) Esteem *(positive regard)* from others based on how the person behaves (cf. *unconditional positive regard*).

conditioned response (CR) A response acquired through pairing an initially neutral stimulus with a stimulus that already elicits the response in question.

conditioned stimulus (CS) An initially neutral stimulus that acquires the ability to elicit a response after it has been paired with an *unconditioned stimulus.*

conditioning Learning that occurs through processes of *reinforcement* and *punishment.*

conditions of worth (Rogers) Differential values that other people place on particular behaviors. Counterforce to the *self-actualization tendency.*

confidentiality of subjects Ethical guidelines by the American Psychological Association stipulate that the privacy of research subjects be rigorously protected.

conflicts Early developmental issues that manifest themselves as *neuroses* in adulthood if left unresolved.

confounding variable Any factor that may have been permitted to covary with the variable of interest (or *dependent variable*) and thereby jeopardizes the validity of interpretation of results.

confrontation In *object relations* therapy, the third stage of therapy, during which the therapist confronts the patient's pathology directly.

congruence Agreement or lack of inconsistency between multiple measures or personality characteristics.

congruent externals Persons whose life experiences are consistent with their belief that most outcomes are out of their hands (cf. *defensive externals*).

conscience (Freud) The sphere of the *superego* concerned with morally right behavior.

Conscientiousness (McCrae and Costa) One of the "big five" personality factors characterized by the tendency to be goal-oriented and hard working, contrasted with undirected.

conscious (Freud) The part of the mind containing all that human beings are immediately aware of.

conscious ego (Jung) Level of the mind that involves conscious perceptions, thoughts, feelings, and memories.

consequences In *operant conditioning,* the events or outcomes that occur as a result of *target behaviors* being performed.

consistency paradox (Mischel) The fact that people tend to see others' behavior as quite consistent across situations when, in fact, there is much cross-situational inconsistency.

construct (Kelly) A concept used to interpret events.

constructive alternativism (Kelly) Philosophical position that any event can be viewed in a variety of ways.

construct system (Kelly) The hierarchical order of an individual's *constructs.*

construe (Kelly) To place an interpretation on an event.

container function of women A primary criticism of Freud's psychoanalytic theory, that women are portrayed as the receptacle of all that is negative, undesirable, or not embraced by the male character. This allows women to be characterized as merely the opposite of masculinity and subsequently cast aside.

content validity The adequacy with which a test samples the domain it is intended to measure.

continuous reinforcement schedule A *schedule of reinforcement* in which the individual is reinforced every time the behavior to be strengthened is emitted.

control In psychological research, systematically varying, randomizing, or holding constant the conditions under which observations are made.

control group In an *experiment,* the group that does not receive the treatment being examined but is like the treated group in every other respect (cf. *experimental group*).

controlled activities (Deci) Those pursuits engaged in to comply with externally imposed expectations or demands. These activities are experienced as less rewarding and enjoyable than *self-determined* activities.

convergent validity The degree to which measures of presumably the same disposition in different forms (e.g., paper-and-pencil versus projective measures) correlate or agree with one another.

coping model *Model* who is initially somewhat fearful and incompetent and then gradually overcomes the fear and becomes more competent.

core constructs (Kelly) Constructs that define us and form the basis of our identity.

core role (Kelly) A role a person plays that is central to his or her life.

correlation The co- or joint relationship between variables. Variables that are correlated "go together."

correlational study Research method that examines quantitative relationships between two or more variables for a group of people observed under the same conditions.

correlation coefficient A statistical index of the strength of a relationship, most often expressed as the Pearson product-moment correlation *(r)*.

correlation matrix The array of correlations between each variable and every other variable in a data set.

counterimitation Behaving in a way opposite to the way a *model* has behaved.

countertransference Feelings a psychoanalyst has for a patient that are *displacements* from the analyst's past.

covert Private, not observable by others, often applied to mental operations that can only be described subjectively.

covert behavior Behavior that occurs inside the person and thus is not directly observable by others (cf. *overt behavior*).

covert self-instruction Private (silent) speech providing step-by-step directions and strategies for success.

covert self-instruction (Meichenbaum) A client performs a *target behavior* while stating privately (in *self-talk*, or mental speech) the required steps and strategy for success.

cross-sex typed In reference to gender roles, people who conform more closely to the traits characteristic of the other sex than to their own.

cross-situational consistency The degree to which a person behaves in a consistent fashion from one situation to another.

cultural evolution How cultures develop.

culture The set of attitudes, values, beliefs, and behaviors shared by a group of people and communicated from one generation to the next.

culture-bound Constructs and behaviors that must be examined within the context of the culture of interest because their meanings vary across cultures.

cumulative records Graphically displayed data that represent the participant's rate of response and response rate changes over time.

cynical hostility That aspect of *Type A behavior* that is most strongly associated with health problems. It is characterized by a lack of interpersonal trust, pessimism, and general negativity of affect.

day residues Elements of actual external events in waking life that appear in dreams.

death drive Another term for *aggressive drive*.

death instinct Another term for *aggressive drive*, or *thanatos*.

debriefing The systematic explanation of the purpose and methods of research, given to a subject after his or her participation is completed.

deception A research technique by which subjects are deliberately misinformed about the nature and purpose of a study. Ethical considerations demand that deception be avoided whenever possible or, when used, expediently corrected.

decision tree Hierarchical structure of constructs with broader constructs flowing down to increasingly narrower ones.

deep muscle relaxation A component of *systematic desensitization* used to teach clients a competing response to anxiety. This procedure involves instructing the client to tense and then relax each major muscle group to facilitate the identification and reduction of tension in anxiety-evoking situations.

default information The attribution of features to people or events based on information from mental prototypes rather than from direct evidence.

defense mechanisms *Unconscious* ego processes for reducing *anxiety;* primarily a psychoanalytic term.

defensive externals Persons who claim that most outcomes are out of their hands only when it suits them to make this claim (cf. *congruent externals*).

defensive identification A defense process that involves becoming like a threatening person; follows the *unconscious* "reasoning": "If I cannot beat the person, I'll join the person."

defensive processes (Rogers) Mechanisms for reducing perceived incongruities within the self.

defensive projection The *defense mechanism* whereby the individual unconsciously attributes his or her own unacceptable impulses or wishes to someone or something else.

deficit motivation (Maslow) Energizing and directing behavior to satisfy an unmet *need* (cf. *growth motivation*).

definition (Kelly) Choosing the pole of a construct that previously has been more successful at predicting events (cf. *extension*).

delay of gratification The ability to forgo a small immediate reward for a large reward to be obtained later.

delusion of unique individuality Concept introduced by Sullivan to describe the phenomenon of each person's need to claim a "specialness" of one sort or another to contain the anxiety that would otherwise be generated by the threat of losing relationships with significant others.

democratic (Maslow) Free of prejudice regarding characteristics such as race or ethnicity; having respect for all people as individuals.

denial Defensive process in which the person does not acknowledge a threatening experience.

deoxyribonucleic acid (DNA) Biological molecule that carries genetic material.

dependent variable In an *experiment,* the subject's behavior that is measured; it is expected to be influenced by (depend on) the *independent variable.*

depressive symptoms Behaviors and problems associated with *major depressive disorder.*

depth psychology Another name for *psychoanalysis* that refers to the process by which thoughts and feelings previously buried in the unconscious are recovered.

description Effectively measuring and communicating about important personality dimensions.

desensitization Gradually exposing the client to anxiety-evoking stimuli while the client employs relaxation. It is intended to reduce the association between the stimuli and feelings of anxiety.

detachment (Maslow) The ability to be relatively unaffected by external events or surroundings.

determinism (Freud) All behavior is caused by innate drives.

differentiation (Mahler) Process whereby the child breaks away from the mother.

difficult As pertains to the *temperament type* labeled *sociability,* it is characterized by general unwillingness to approach or interact with new people.

dilution effect When family size increases, the amount of time and attention that can be given to any one child decreases.

direct aggression Social manipulation aimed at a specific target person rather than other members of a social group.

direct correlation A *positive correlation* (high scores on one variable tend to be accompanied by high scores on the second variable).

direct counterimitation Avoiding the specific behavior that one has seen a *model* perform.

direct imitation Copying the specific behavior that one has seen a *model* perform.

direction (Maslow) A sense of mission or purpose in life.

directionality problem In correlational research, the fact that a *correlation* does not, by itself, indicate if, or which variable is causing the other (cf. *third-variable problem*).

direct observation Research involving the observation of a subject in either a natural environment or a contrived environment.

discrete Refers to a response that has a clear beginning and ending.

discriminant validity The degree to which measures of presumably different *dispositions* assessed by the same form of assessment diverge (i.e., are not highly correlated).

discriminate (Maslow) Distinguishing between two separate concepts (i.e., means and ends, right and wrong).

discrimination Failure of a stimulus similar in some characteristics to the *conditioned stimulus* to evoke the *conditioned response.*

discrimination gradient The less similar a new stimulus is to the original *conditioned stimulus,* the less likely it is to evoke the *conditioned response.*

discriminative stimulus A stimulus that signals that a response is now appropriate and likely to be reinforced.

disorganized attachment One form of *insecure attachment* characterized by inconsistent and sometimes conflicting behavior in response to separation and return of the parent.

displacement As a *defense mechanism,* shifting an impulse from a threatening or unacceptable event or person to something less threatening or unacceptable. In a *dream,* shifting the emphasis from an important element to a seemingly trivial element.

disposition A tendency to behave in a particular way over time and across situations (e.g., a trait).

dizygotic Twins that develop from the union of two distinct ovum-and-sperm pairs.

domain Broad personality *factor.*

dominance Degree to which a particular gene overrides the presence of other genes to produce a given characteristic.

dopamine *Neurotransmitter* implicated in schizophrenic symptoms.

dopamine hypothesis Theory that the *neurotransmitter dopamine* is the biological mechanism that causes *schizophrenia.*

dream A mental experience during sleep that involves mainly vivid visual images.

dream work (Freud) Process of transforming *latent content* into *manifest content.*

drive (psychoanalysis) An inborn, intrapsychic force that, when operative, produces a state of excitation or tension.

drug mimicking Contextual stimuli that become associated with a particular substance, so that environmental cues alone can elicit a conditioned response like that to the drug.

drug mirroring When individuals become more sensitized to contextual cues, they often need more and more of a drug in order to experience the same intensity of response.

DSM series (American Psychiatric Association) Diagnostic and statistical manuals used to diagnose mental disorders.

DSM-III-R (American Psychiatric Association) Revised third edition of the *DSM.*

DSM-IV (American Psychiatric Association) Current version of the *DSM.*

dual theory of drives (Freud) Theory that human motivation is based on the operation of two independent drives: the *sexual drive* and the *aggressive drive.*

dynamic (Freud) The flow of psychic energy among the personality structures.

dysphoric Depressed mood.

dysplastic (Kretschner) Body type that is not frail, muscular, or plump.

ease of emotional arousal Degree of stimulation required to elicit signs of arousal.

easy As pertains to the *temperament type* labeled *sociability,* it is characterized by an eagerness to interact with others, including new people.

ectomorphic (Sheldon) Frail body type with specific personality correlates.

effect size A measure of the magnitude of a reported effect independent of statistical significance.

efficacy expectations (Bandura) The belief that one can perform the behaviors necessary to achieve a desired outcome.

ego (Freud) The reality-oriented aspect of personality; also mediates the demands of the other aspects of personality (*id* and *superego*).

ego defense mechanism Unconscious ego processes that keep disturbing thoughts from surfacing in consciousness.

ego ideal (Freud) The sphere of the *superego* concerned with urging the individual toward idealistic and perfectionistic goals.

ego psychologists Those who practice or subscribe to *ego psychology.*

ego psychology *Post-Freudian psychoanalysis* emphasizing ego and conscious aspects of personality.

Electra complex The female parallel of the *Oedipus complex.*

electroconvulsive therapy (ECT) Electrical current administered to the brain sufficient to produce *seizure* activity. Used to treat psychological disorders that are resistant to psychotherapy or medication.

electroencephalogram Tracings of brain waves made by an electroencephalograph.

electroencephalograph Device to measure brain electrical activity.

electromyogram (EMG) Used to measure and provide feedback about degree of muscle tension.

emblems Physical gestures that have specific meanings that vary across cultures.

emergent pole (Kelly) Pole of a *construct* used to directly interpret an event by noting its similarity to other events (cf. *implicit pole*).

emic A behavior or behavior pattern that varies from setting to setting (or culture to culture) within a species.

emotionality Tendency to become physiologically aroused in response to environmental stimuli.

emotions (Kelly) Feelings that result from an awareness of change or a need for change in one's *construct system.*

empathic understanding (Rogers) When the therapist conveys an ability to perceive the client from the client's internal frame of reference.

empathy Experiencing how another person is feeling from the other person's viewpoint.

empirical Relating to or obtained by objective methods so that observations and results can be independently confirmed.

empirical approach Research characterized by direct observation and objective means.

empirical keying A method of test construction in which items are selected on the basis of their demonstrated predictive power rather than their content.

empirical relationships Associations between behaviors (responses) and environmental conditions (stimuli) determined by *systematic observations.*

empirical research Systematic attempts to gather evidence through observations and procedures that can be repeated and verified by others.

empirical validity The degree to which a theory is supported by evidence derived from observations.

encoding strategies (Mischel) Specific ways of sorting the interpersonal and physical events people encounter.

enculturation The process by which the values, beliefs, and behaviors of a culture are transmitted to new members.

endomorphic (Sheldon) Plump body type with specific personality correlates.

endorphins The body's natural opiates that act directly to suppress pain.

enduring dispositions Permanent inherent elements of personality.

engagement In *object relations* therapy, the first stage of therapy, when the therapist must become a significant person for the patient.

enucleated unfertilized egg Donor egg cell (ovum) from which the nucleus has been extracted.

environmental stimuli Situational cues that prompt specific behaviors.

Environmental Strategy An approach to the study of personality that emphasizes the study of external forces that act on individuals and shape their behavior.

EPQ (Eysenck) A personality questionnaire measuring Extraversion, Neuroticism, Psychoticism, and social desirability.

erogenous zone Area of the body especially sensitive to erotic stimulation (e.g., mouth, anus, genitals).

eros (Freud) The life instinct or *sexual drive.*

error of affirming the consequent Assuming that "because a behavior is generated under one set of circumstances, every time this or similar behavior occurs in nature, it had developed because of the same set of controlling conditions" (Davison & Neale, 1974, p. 28).

esteem from others (Maslow) Desire for recognition and appreciation from other people and the accompanying feelings of worthwhileness and competence (cf. *self-esteem*).

estrogens Female *hormones.*

etic A behavior or behavior pattern that is common to all members of a particular species.

evaluative Based on value judgments or subjective worth.

evolutionary process How species develop over time.

excitation Stimulation of a *neuron,* which increases the likelihood of an *action potential.*

existential psychology A perspective that emphasizes free will, choice, and "being there."

expectancy (Rotter) The subjective probability that a given behavior will result in a given reinforcer.

experience (Kelly) Interpreting an event in new ways (not just repeated exposure to the event).

experience sampling method A research method for data collection in which the subject reports on current activities, thoughts, and/or feelings immediately when prompted by the researcher. The prompts are usually delivered remotely (e.g., via a pager, wristwatch) and may occur at regular intervals or randomly throughout the day.

experiment Research method that examines the quantitative cause-and-effect relationship between one or more *independent variables* and one or more *dependent variables.*

experimental group In an *experiment,* subjects who are exposed to the *independent variable* (cf. *control group*).

experimental hypothesis A prediction, which is operationally defined, about the effect of the *independent variable* on the *dependent variable.*

experimental method Research method used when performing an *experiment.* The method involves some direct manipulation and control over extraneous variables.

explicit pole (Kelly) Pole of a *construct* used to directly interpret an event (cf. *implicit pole*).

exploitative character (Fromm) Adult behavior pattern that develops from being raised in an environment that fostered the attitude of having to take in order to receive (cf. *receptive character*).

exposure Observation of *modeling cues;* the first stage in *observational learning.*

extension (Kelly) Choosing the pole of a construct that is more likely to expand the construct's ability to view new events (cf. *definition*).

extensiveness The breadth of the phenomena that a theory can deal with.

externalizing problems Behavior problems involving "acting out" behaviors (e.g., aggression, stealing, lying, and impulsivity).

external locus of control (Rotter) The belief that the reinforcements one gets in life are due to chance factors or factors that are out of one's control.

extinction Cessation of responding when a learned response is no longer reinforced; also, cessation of *reinforcement* for a previously reinforced response.

extinction curve Graphical line dropping off toward the horizontal that represents a drop in rate of responding over time.

Extraversion (Eysenck) The personality dimension that differentiates people according to their tendency to be socially outgoing.

extravert A person who tends to be outgoing with people (cf. *introvert*).

facet Narrow, specific feature of personality of which *traits* or *dispositions* are composed.

face validity The superficial appearance of actually testing for a personality characteristic (cf. *content validity*).

factor analysis A family of mathematical procedures for sorting personality measures and other variables into groupings such as factors or clusters.

factor loading In *factor analysis,* the correlation of a particular measure with a particular factor.

factors Relatively homogeneous dimensions extracted from data by *factor analysis.*

fading In operant *behavior therapy,* the gradual removal of prompts so that the person finally performs the response without cues.

familism The degree to which individuals are actively involved with their extended families.

familism attitudes Beliefs about the importance of keeping in contact with relatives.

familism contact Contact between relatives who do not live together.

family configuration The number of adults and children in a family who reside in the same household.

fear of power (Winter) That portion of the power motive that seeks to avoid giving others *power* over oneself (cf. *hope of power*).

feedback loop Term often associated with artificial intelligence, a system wherein changes in the value of one feature or *variable* inform and influence changes in another, which in turn informs and influences the first. Reciprocal influences between variables.

feminist movement Group led by Karen Horney that criticized and challenged Freudian theory. In particular, they protested that Freud's ideas about the Oedipal complex and penis envy were distorted because he exclusively studied neurotic women.

file drawer problem Studies that fail to produce statistically significant results are usually not published, therefore biasing the literature toward "successful" outcomes and inflating the apparent likelihood of achieving certain results.

financial capital The amount of economic or monetary resources made available for the benefit of a child.

Five-Factor Model (FFM) (McCrae and Costa) A model demonstrating that the same five-factor structure emerges from various methods of measuring personality.

fixation Leaving a portion of *libido* permanently invested in an early *psychosexual* stage. The more difficult it is for a person to resolve the conflict, the more libido will remain fixated at the stage.

fixed Not subject to variation or ranging values.

fixed-interval schedule A *schedule of reinforcement* in which the individual is reinforced for the first response made after a set amount of time has elapsed.

fixed-ratio schedule A *schedule of reinforcement* in which the individual is reinforced after a set number of responses.

fixed role (Kelly) A role of a fictitious person whose behavior is consistent with a *construct system* that would be beneficial for a client to adopt (in *fixed-role therapy*).

fixed-role sketch (Kelly) A detailed description of a *fixed role.*

fixed-role therapy (Kelly) Therapy in which a client temporarily adopts the behavior of someone whose behavior is consistent with *constructs* that would be helpful for the client to adopt.

flow (Csikszentmihalyi) A mental state characterized by pure concentration, absorption, and focus on the immediate task, often growth enhancing and experienced as enjoyable and effortless.

forced-choice inventory A questionnaire structured such that subjects must select between two descriptors for each item.

focus of convenience (Kelly) The events that a particular construct is best able to predict.

fraternal twins Another term for *dizygotic* twins.

free association In psychoanalytic psychotherapy, the patient's saying whatever comes to mind without any censoring.

Freudian Theories and practices that follow Freud's theory and practices (cf. *post-Freudian*).

Freudian slips Generic lay term for mistakes that Freud believed had definite *unconscious* causes and meanings.

frustration (Freud) Feelings evoked by an individual's unmet needs in a specific stage of personality development.

fully functioning person (Rogers) Person who is guided by *organismic valuing processes,* is free of threat, and in short, epitomizes psychological health.

functional analysis Term used by Skinner to describe his complete, detailed descriptions of discrete behaviors, including their antecedents and consequences.

GABA (gamma amino butyric acid) *Neurotransmitter* that, in excess, causes *anxiety* symptoms.

galvanic skin response (GSR) Measure of the electrical conductivity of the skin, which is influenced by stress, fear, or anxiety.

gamete Reproductive or sex cell (sperm or ovum) of an organism that carries the genetic material of the donor parent.

gender Socially (as opposed to biologically) determined differences between the sexes.

gender roles A set of traits and behaviors stereotypically associated with a particular sex.

gene mapping Locating the actual position on a *chromosome* of the *genes* responsible for a particular characteristic.

generalization The "spread" of a *conditioned response* to a stimulus similar, but not identical, to the *conditioned stimulus.*

generalized expectancies (Rotter) Expectations that apply across a range of situations.

generalization gradient The more similar a new stimulus is to the original *conditioned stimulus,* the more likely is *generalization* of the *conditioned response* to the new stimulus.

general locus of control Person's usual perception across situations of the degree to which they determine outcomes.

generativity (Erikson) Involvement in guiding the next generation.

genes Units that guide inheritance across generations.

gene therapy Replacing defective genetic material.

genetic marker Particular genetic material or gene sequences that are associated with the occurrence of a particular characteristic or predisposition.

genetics Branch of science concerned with the mechanisms and forces of inheritance.

genetic similarity theory People actively choose their mates based on genetic similarity in order to ensure the survival of their own specific *genes.*

genital stage Freud's fourth and final *psychosexual* stage of development (puberty through adulthood), in which *libido* is centered in the genital region.

genome Full set of *genes* on all *chromosomes* present in a *species.*

genotype Specific genetic material possessed by an organism.

gestures Bodily movements that convey specific meanings within a particular culture or subculture.

glial cells Fatty cells of the nervous system that provide support and insulation for *neurons.*

goal content Specific aspirations of the individual.

goals Personal aspirations of the individual, desired end states.

good enough mother In object relations, the idea that mothering is never perfect and that what is required for normal development is that the child's needs be met adequately, most of the time.

graded task assignments A *shaping* exercise in which clients engage in a series of brief, simple behaviors that gradually become lengthier and more complex.

growth motivation (Maslow) Energizing and directing behavior by following one's *self-actualization tendency.*

guilt (Kelly) Awareness of playing an important role in one's life inadequately.

health psychology Study of the psychological factors that relate to maintenance of health or disease status.

here-and-now Immediate experience; what is going on for the person at the moment.

heritability Degree to which a particular characteristic is influenced by genetics.

heritability index Mathematical measure of the amount of variance of a characteristic that is accounted for by genetic factors.

heritability score Quantification of the genetic influence of a characteristic, ranging from 0 (no heritability) to 1.0 (entirely determined by genetics).

heterozygous Describing an organism that possesses two different *genes* for a particular trait.

heuristic realism (Allport) The belief that people really have *traits.*

hierarchically organized The assumption that personality traits are organized so that broad dimensions are at the top, subsuming the narrow, specific *traits* below.

history Chronological account of events.

history records Research data that can be objectively obtained or confirmed (e.g., educational, employment, or marital history).

holistic Belief that all aspects of personality are related and must be viewed together as a whole; an important position of the phenomenological approach.

homozygous Describing an organism that possesses two identical *genes* for a particular trait.

hope of power (Winter) That portion of the power motive that seeks to gain *power* (cf. *fear of power*).

hormones Any chemical secreted by glands that travels via the bloodstream to other organs or systems on which it exerts an influence.

human capital The parents' formal education and training, which has the potential for having an impact on children.

humanism A "third force" in psychology founded in the 1960s as a reaction to psychoanalysis and behaviorism. *Self-actualization* is an important element of humanism, as is a focus on the individual.

humanistic psychology Orientation within psychology based on the philosophical positions of *humanism*.

hypotheses Plural of *hypothesis*.

hypothesis Any specific prediction derived from a theory.

id (Freud) Biological, instinctual, pleasure-oriented aspect of personality (cf. *ego, superego*).

ideal self (Rogers) How people would like to see themselves.

ideal-self sort *Q-sort* in which subjects sort self-referent statements in terms of how they would like to see themselves.

identical twins Another term for *monozygotic* twins.

identification (psychoanalysis) Taking on other people's characteristics to reduce *anxiety*, envy, or other negative emotions.

identity As used by Erikson, the confidence that others see a person as the person sees himself or herself.

idiographic Pertaining only to a specific individual (cf. *nomothetic*).

idiographic approach Research philosophy that emphasizes examination of individuals over between group comparisons.

idiothetic Research that combines elements of *idiographic* and *nomothetic* perspectives.

I-E Scale (Rotter) A paper-and-pencil measure of the degree to which an individual has an *internal* or *external locus of control* (as a *generalized expectancy*).

illness-related cues Environmental stimuli that relate to the illness experience (hospitals, medical staff, medical equipment).

imaginal desensitization The process of directing the client to mentally picture the items or events from an *anxiety hierarchy* while practicing a competing response (cf. *in vivo desensitization*).

imitation Making one's own behavior similar in some way to that of a *model*.

immune system The body's means of defense against invasion by viruses, bacteria, and any other foreign agents.

implicit motives (McClelland) Primitive, unconscious motives, said to be more like animal drives than like conscious goals.

implicit pole (Kelly) Pole of a construct used to indirectly interpret an event by acting as a contrast (cf. *explicit pole*).

implicit theory of personality A set of informal ideas that an individual has about the nature of personality.

impulsive sensation seeking (impSS, Zuckerman) A personality *factor* that includes the *facets* of impulsivity and sociability.

incidence Rate of occurrence of an event, behavior, or phenotype in a select group.

incorporation (psychoanalysis) The "taking in" of others' values in a manner analogous to the way one takes in food.

independent variable In an *experiment*, the variable that is systematically varied by the experimenter and is expected to influence the *dependent variable*.

index case In pedigree analysis, family member who expresses a particular genetic characteristic and around whom *incidence* is tracked.

indirect aggression Behavior directed toward others in an effort to harm the targeted person.

indirect counterimitation Avoiding the general type or class of behavior that one has seen a *model* perform.

indirect imitation Performing the general type or class of behavior that one has seen a *model* perform.

individuality and emotional object constancy In Mahler's object relations theory, the last subphase of development in which the person achieves a defined lifelong individuality and a sense of permanence regarding the people in one's life.

individual traits (Allport) Those important characteristics of the individual that do not lend themselves to comparison across persons.

individuation (Mahler) The earliest stage of identity, in which the individual discovers "that I am." Only later is there recognition of "who I am."

indulgent parenting A parenting style in which the parents fail to adequately enforce rules and readily give in to their children's coercive demands.

infantile amnesia Most people are unable to recall events before 3 to 4 years of age.

inferences Assumptions made about an event based on information from a different event.

inferiority complex (Adler) Exaggerated, neurotic reaction to one's weaknesses.

information processing The way the mind organizes new information.

information value Credibility and representativeness of *modeling cues* as perceived by an observer.

informed consent Subjects in a research study must be told about the nature of the research, as well as their rights and responsibilities as a subject before beginning their participation.

inheritance The process by which traits are passed from parent to offspring.

inhibition Stimulation of a *neuron* that serves to suppress or decrease the likelihood of an *action potential.*

insight (psychoanalysis) Emotional experiencing and accepting of parts of one's *unconscious;* necessary for cure in *psychoanalysis.*

instinctoid needs (Maslow) Biologically based human needs.

instrumental conditioning A term used interchangeably with *operant conditioning.*

intact family Another term for *nuclear family;* consisting of both parents and their offspring.

intellectualization (Anna Freud) Coping strategy whereby adolescents develop theories about love and life in general to gain a sense of control over their lives.

intensity of arousal Refers to the vigor of an elicited emotional response.

intermittent (partial) schedule of reinforcement A pattern of *reinforcement* in which only some instances of the desired response are reinforced.

internal consistency The degree to which the propositions and assumptions of a theory are consistent and fit together into a coherent, larger explanation.

internal frame of reference A person's subjective view of the world.

internality-externality A dimension on which causal attributions vary, referring to whether the event or experience is caused by something within ourselves (internal) or outside ourselves (external).

internalizing problems Problems focused inward, such as anxiety, social withdrawal, and physical symptoms with no medical basis.

internal locus of control (Rotter) The belief that the reinforcements one gets in life are due to one's own effort and ability.

internal reliability The degree to which the items on a test measure the same thing.

interpersonal cues The presence of, or specific behaviors of, another that serve to trigger a *target behavior.*

interpersonal psychoanalysis Another term for *interpersonal therapy.*

interpersonal space The amount of space given to others that is predictable based on social relationships but varies across cultures.

interpersonal therapy (IPT, Sullivan) An alternative to psychoanalytic psychotherapy that emphasizes examination of interpersonal functioning and intervenes directly to increase and enhance adaptive social behavior. IPT has been empirically demonstrated to be effective in the treatment of depression.

interpersonal trust (Rotter) A *generalized expectancy* that the words or promises of others can be relied on.

interpretation (psychoanalysis) Pointing out unconscious meanings to a patient.

interrater reliability Agreement among raters or judges.

interval schedule of reinforcement A pattern of reinforcement in which a reinforcer is received if the desired response occurs (at least once) after a specified length of time has elapsed since the last *reinforcement.*

intimacy (Erikson) The capacity to commit to a relationship without losing one's own identity.

intrapsychic conflict (psychoanalysis) Discord within the personality occurring when the aims of *id, ego,* and *superego* are at odds.

intrapsychic events Processes occurring in the mind (usually in the *unconscious*), such as thoughts, images, and wishes.

introspection Process of looking inward and examining one's own thoughts and feelings.

introvert A person who tends to be shy and anxious in social situations (cf. *extravert*).

inverse correlation A *negative correlation* (high scores on one variable tend to go with low scores on the other).

in vivo desensitization The process of exposing a client to the actual stimuli in an *anxiety hierarchy,* instead of having the client imagine them.

in vivo exposure Another term for *in vivo desensitization.*

ironic processes (Wegner) Mental operations function such that actively trying to avoid thinking about or doing something increases the likelihood that the avoided outcome will result under certain (taxing) conditions.

latency In Freud's developmental sequence, the period between the *phallic* and *genital stages.*

latent content Underlying meaning of a dream (cf. *manifest content*).

latent inhibition Refers to the situation in which the expected effect of pairing of stimuli (CS with UCS) does not result in the CS producing the CR. It may occur because the pairing of stimuli was inconsistent, or the CS preceded the UCS or was temporally separated from it.

L-data (Cattell) Information that can be gathered from the life records of the individual.

learned responses Behaviors that have been *classically* or *operantly conditioned.*

learning In *observational learning,* the process in which the person pays attention to the *modeling cues* and remembers them.

leukocytes The generic term for white blood cells, which are the body's primary defense against infection by foreign agents.

lexical approach Determining the importance of a *disposition* based on the frequency with which it appears in ordinary language.

libido (Freud) *Psychic energy* of the *sexual drive.*

life history An account of past experiences provided by a subject. A complete life history should provide reasonable continuity over time and circumstances.

life records Another term for *history records.*

line of perfect correlation In the case of a perfect correlation, the hypothetical line on a graph on which all points would fall.

live modeling The observation of the behavior of *models* "in the flesh"—that is, models who are physically present.

locus of control (Rotter) The generalized way that the person perceives the source of his or her outcomes (see *external* and *internal locus of control*).

longitudinal study Research method that tracks subjects prospectively over time collecting data as events occur rather than retrospectively.

magnetic resonance imaging (MRI) Technique used to image brain structures.

maintaining conditions In *behavior therapy,* the factors that are currently *reinforcing* the *target behavior.*

major depressive disorder Distinct periods of depressed *(dysphoric)* mood and impaired social or occupational functioning.

mania Expansive or irritable mood.

manic symptoms Irritability, euphoria, impulsivity, and impaired judgment characteristic of periods of *mania.*

manifest content What a person remembers and reports of a dream (cf. *latent content*).

mastery model A *model* who is fearless and competent from the beginning.

matched random assignment Subjects are assessed and paired based on similarity on a relevant characteristic, then *randomly assigned* to treatment groups for study.

matching Assigning subjects to treatment groups after forming pairs based on their ranking on some variable assumed to be related to the variable of interest, and then assigning one member of each pair to each treatment group so as to ensure rough equivalence of groups at the outset.

matching theory Theory predicting that the frequency of engaging in each of a number of alternative behaviors will be directly proportional to the amount of *reinforcement* received for each.

material self (James) Part of self that represents one's body and family composition.

matriarchal (psychoanalysis) Mother- or female-dominated perspective adopted by Horney and other feminists in response to Freud's male-dominated theory.

mental Pertaining to the mind.

mesomorphic (Sheldon) Muscular body type with specific personality correlates.

meta-analysis Any set of rules used to systematically combine and evaluate a collection of research outcomes on a single topic.

metatraits (Baumeister) The trait of having or not having a particular trait.

methodological behaviorism An approach that emphasizes objectivity, direct observation of phenomena, precise definitions, and controlled experimentation (cf. *radical behaviorism*).

midlife crisis (Jung) The crisis people in their late 30s through the middle 40s experience when they come to realize that many of their goals have been set by others.

mirroring (Kohut) Individual's sense of self is derived through interactions with other people, each adequately "reflecting" the other by responding appropriately to them.

model An exemplar of behavior from which others may learn by observing.

modeling Performing a behavior that may be learned by observers.

modeling cues Specific components of another's (the *model's*) behavior that may bring about changes in the behavior of the observer.

monoamines A class of chemicals, a particular subset of *neurotransmitters.*

monozygotic (identical) Twins that develop from a single ovum-and-sperm pair.

mood-congruent bias The tendency to process information about past experiences selectively, in a way that is consistent with present mood.

mood disorders Conditions characterized by a deviation from normal (euthymic) mood.

moral Pertaining to distinctions between right and wrong.

moral anxiety (Freud) Experience of guilt or shame resulting from an *id-superego* conflict (cf. *neurotic anxiety, objective anxiety*).

mother (Jung) Archetype with dual nature that may be elicited by any "mothering" figure or symbol; part of the collective unconscious.

motivational types Patterns of behavior associated with clusters of motives instead of with a single motive.

motive A desire to satisfy a particular need (cf. *need*).

motive to avoid success (Horner) *Anxiety* about the negative consequences of success.

multifactorial Characteristics that result from the interaction between specific combinations of *genes* and environmental factors.

multiple consistent models Two or more *models* who display the same or similar behavior in response to a particular situation.

multivariate approaches Ways of studying personality that examine many variables simultaneously.

mutation Deviations or alterations in genetic material.

mutual dependency Object relations idea that represents a more mature form of interpersonal relationships involving reciprocity rather than unidirectional (infantile) dependence.

narrative A description in story form.

naturalistic observation Research involving the observation of a subject in a natural environment or setting.

natural killer cells A class of *leukocytes.*

need (Murray) A tendency to seek or produce particular effects or temporary end states.

negative correlation A relationship between two variables in which high scores on one variable occur with low scores on the other and vice versa (cf. *positive correlation*).

negative reinforcement Removal of an aversive stimulus contingent on the performance of a desired response, which results in an increase in the likelihood of the response (cf. *positive reinforcement*).

negative transference Feelings of *displacement* that the patient has toward the psychoanalyst that take the form of hatred, jealousy, or disgust.

Negative Valence (Tellegen and Waller) One of the "big seven" personality dimensions pertaining to the domains of anxiety, depression, and hostility.

neglectful parenting Parenting that lacks both adequate involvement with the children and adequate supervision.

neurochemistry Chemical actions in the nervous system.

neuroleptics Another term for *antipsychotics.*

neuromodulators Chemical messengers of the nervous system that spread more than *neurotransmitters* but less globally than *hormones.*

neuron A nerve cell.

neuroses A generic term for mental disorders that generally affect people in a limited sphere of their lives; symptoms include *anxiety,* depression, and physical complaints.

neurotic anxiety (Freud) Unrealistic fear or vague apprehension resulting from an *id-ego* conflict (cf. *moral anxiety, objective anxiety*).

Neuroticism (Eysenck) The personality dimension that includes a disposition toward unrealistic fear and emotional instability.

neurotransmitter A chemical "messenger" released by a *presynaptic neuron* that exerts an effect on *postsynaptic neurons.*

nocebo effect "Voodoo" that occurs when the *conditioned stimulus (CS)* becomes associated with a common stimulus related to illness or death (UCS), and the victim actually dies as a result.

nocturnal enuresis The inability of persons older than 4 years to suppress urination while sleeping.

nominations Persons offered by peers, teachers, or family members as examplars of a characteristic of interest.

nomothetic Pertaining to people in general (cf. *idiographic*).

nomothetic approach Research aimed at delineating general rules that apply to all people.

noncore role (Kelly) A role a person plays that is peripheral or unimportant in his or her life (cf. *core role*).

nonrapid eye movement period See *NREM period.*

nonverbal constructs (Kelly) *Constructs* for which people do not have verbal labels but that can potentially be verbalized.

normal autism In Mahler's *object relations* theory, the first phase of development in which the infant is completely within itself, oblivious to an external world.

normal distribution The pattern of scores formed when a large sample, plotted as a graph, produces a bell-shaped curve.

normal symbiosis In Mahler's *object relations* theory, the second phase of development in which the infant is fused with the mother and does not distinguish between self and nonself.

normative sample data A large number of scores gathered for the purpose of describing the distribution against which individual scores can be compared.

norms Quantified information about the responses and range of responses that characterize large samples of subjects for a particular assessment instrument.

NREM (nonrapid eye movement) period Stage 1 sleep not associated with dreaming (cf. *REM period*).

nuclear family A family consisting of the father, mother, and all of the dependent children of the union.

object Psychoanalytic term for person (see *object relations*).

objective Any experience or observation that can be shared with others.

objective anxiety (Freud) Fear from a realistic, external threat (cf. *moral anxiety, neurotic anxiety*).

objective reality An event about which a number of observers agree.

object relations Psychoanalytic term for interpersonal relations.

object relations theorists Those who emphasize interpersonal issues and the concept of self, especially as they develop during the first 2 years of life.

object representations In *object relations* theories, the cognitive representations one has of oneself and others.

observational learning The process by which the behavior of one person is changed through observing the behavior of another (rather than through direct experience, as in *classical* and *operant conditioning*).

obsessions Excessive and persistent worry.

obsessive-compulsive disorder (OCD) A psychological disorder characterized by excessive and persistent worry *(obsessions)* and ritualistic, repetitive behaviors *(compulsions)*.

Oedipus complex (Freud) The conflict in the *phallic stage* involving the child's *unconscious* wish to have sexual relations with the opposite-sex parent and at the same time do away with the same-sex parent.

openness (McCrae and Costa) A personality factor including a disposition toward originality, creativity, independence, and daring.

operant conditioning Learning process in which a behavior is strengthened or weakened by its consequences.

operationally defined The translation of a variable of interest into directly observable and measurable terms for the purpose of direct study.

oral character (psychoanalysis) Adult behavior pattern that results from *fixation* at the *oral stage*.

oral eroticism Pleasure from sucking and taking things in through the mouth during the early part of the *oral stage*.

oral sadism Pleasure from biting and chewing in the later part of the *oral stage;* begins with the eruption of teeth.

oral stage Freud's first *psychosexual stage* of development (first year of life) in which *libido* is centered in the mouth area.

organismic valuing process (Rogers) Process by which the *self-actualization tendency* evaluates experiences as maintaining or enhancing the person.

organization of personality (Freud) Personality is organized in several layers of structure and function.

ought self (Higgins) Refers to how people think they should be; similar to Freud's concept of the *superego*.

outcome expectation (Bandura) One's estimate that an action will result in a particular outcome.

overcorrection *Behavior therapy* for reducing undesirable behaviors in which the client first corrects the negative effects of a maladaptive behavior and then intensively practices an alternative, adaptive behavior.

overindulgence (Freud) When an individual is so satisfied in a particular stage of personality development that he or she is reluctant to move on to the next stage.

overt behavior Behavior that can be observed directly by others (cf. *covert behavior*).

overt self-instruction (Meichenbaum) A client performs a *target behavior* while stating aloud the required steps and strategy for success.

ovum Female *gamete,* or egg cell.

panic disorder Episodes of intense fear, often accompanied by palpitations, sweating, nausea, and dizziness.

paradigm A shared set of assumptions and orientation that directs research activity and interpretations.

paradigmatic behaviorism Broad model of psychology in the tradition of methodological behaviorism developed by Staats.

paradoxical sleep Phase of Stage 1 sleep in which the person is both active and relaxed; associated with dreaming; same as *REM period.*

parasympathetic nervous system One subsystem of the nervous system that acts to conserve energy and resources by slowing internal systems.

parenting styles Ways of parenting that vary along two dimensions: acceptance-involvement and strictness-supervision.

parsimonious The characteristic of explaining a phenomenon with the fewest possible assumptions or principles.

parsimony Refers to simplicity or conciseness.

partial penetrance In genetics, a gene for a characteristic that is only rarely displayed in phenotypes because it is most often overridden by the influence of other genes or environmental influences.

partial schedule of reinforcement Another term for *intermittent schedule of reinforcement.*

participant modeling The combination of a therapist's live *modeling* and *prompting* with closely supervised practice by the client.

patriarchal (psychoanalysis) Father- or male-dominated view that (according to feminists) inherently bias Freud's theories.

patriarchal biases Feminists argue that the male-centered perspective of psychoanalytic theory compromises research on gender differences and perpetuates and justifies male dominance.

patterned individuality (Allport) The assumption that each person has a unique inner organization of motives, traits, and personal style.

peak experience (Maslow) Intensely fulfilling and meaningful experience.

pedigree analysis Tracks the incidence of a characteristic throughout a family line.

penetrance The degree to which the presence of a particular gene predicts the appearance of the characteristic phenotype dictated by that gene.

penis envy (Freud) Woman's desire to be like a man; part of the *Electra complex.*

P-E-N model (Eysenok) A model of personality that suggests there are three primary factors that differentiate individuals: Psychoticism, Extraversion, and Neuroticism.

perceived self-efficacy (Bandura) People's beliefs that they can successfully execute behavior required to produce a desired outcome, which is partially independent of one's actual ability.

perceptual defense *Unconscious* mechanism that keeps a person from experiencing threatening ideas.

perceptual distortion (Rogers) Changing how one perceives an experience to make it consistent with one's self-concept.

performance accomplishments (Bandura) One source of efficacy expectations.

peripheral nervous system All nerves extending beyond the range of the *central nervous system.*

permeability (Kelly) Degree to which a construct is able to interpret new experiences.

persona The role adopted by an actor and represented by a mask worn for performance. The word *personality* was derived from the term.

personal construct (Kelly) An approach to personality that deals with how people interpret and anticipate the events in their lives and thereby develop unique personalities.

personal construct approach (Kelly) An approach within the Representational Strategy wherein the processes by which individuals come to anticipate events in their lives is viewed as the foundation of *personality.*

personal constructs (Mischel) Probability estimates about the outcome of a particular course of action in a specific situation.

personality The unique combination of characteristics which combine to determine how individuals respond to their social and physical environment. More specific definitions vary by theorists.

personality change Refers to planned changes in response to personality problems, usually synonymous with psychotherapy.

personality coefficient (Mischel) Term coined to describe the small *correlation* (between .20 and .30) that is typically found when any personality dimension measured by a questionnaire is related to another type of measure of the "same" characteristic.

personality disorders Diagnoses made when personality traits are inflexible and maladaptive, causing either significant functional impairment or subjective distress.

personality profile The resulting graphic image produced by plotting scores from a personality assessment device on a specialized graph based on existing *normative data.* This yields an image that can readily be understood in terms of typical and deviant scores.

personality psychology The branch of psychology concerned with developing theories and conducting empirical research on the functioning of the individual as a totality.

personality traits Dispositions as they appear in older children, adolescents, and adults that probably have a learned component (cf. *temperament traits*).

personality types (Eysenck) Normally distributed dimensions on which all people differ.

personal life story A consistent and coherent *narrative* about the self that influences future thoughts and behavior as well as representation of past events.

personal space The amount of physical space maintained around a person that is generally inaccessible to others.

personal unconscious (Jung) Part of the mind containing images that one is not immediately aware of but that one can easily become aware of; parallel concept to Freud's *preconscious.*

person-centered approach (Rogers) Extension of the principles of *client-centered therapy* to other endeavors, such as education and international relations.

personifications (Sullivan) Mental representations of self and others that can be narrow, representing particular aspects of people, so that each *object* can have multiple representations.

person-situation debate The argument about whether personality dimensions or situational variables are the more important determinant of behavior.

person variables (Bandura) Thoughts and feelings that influence behavior.

person variables (Mischel) The relatively enduring cognitive and behavioral attributes of an individual.

phallic character type (psychoanalysis) Adult behavior pattern that results from *fixation* at the *phallic stage.*

phallic stage Freud's third *psychosexual stage* of development (ages 4 to 5) in which *libido* is centered in the genital area; *Oedipus complex* occurs in this stage.

phenomenological knowledge (Rogers) Understanding another person from that person's unique perspective.

phenotype Visible characteristics resulting from the presence of specific genetic material.

phenylketonuria (PKU) Genetic inability to properly metabolize phenylalanine, often resulting in mental retardation.

phobia Strong, irrational fear of a particular situation or object.

phototherapy Therapy involving exposure to bright or artificial light on a regular basis.

physical aggression Behavior intended to physically harm someone.

pituitary gland Body organ that controls the secretion of *hormones* by other glands, sometimes called the "master gland."

placebo An inert substance or therapeutically empty treatment (which nonetheless often results in therapeutic change).

plans Steps and strategies devised to achieve one or more *goals.*

pleasure principle (Freud) Immediate discharge of intrapsychic tension; the principle by which the *id* operates (cf. *reality principle*).

polygenic Characteristics that are influenced by at least two pairs of *genes* acting in combination.

polygraph Measures of multiple physiological responses of the *sympathetic nervous system.*

population In research, the complete set of people of interest, from which a smaller set (a *sample*) is selected for direct study.

positive correlation A relationship between two variables in which high scores on one variable occur with high scores on the other, and low scores on one occur with low scores on the other (cf. *negative correlation*).

positive regard (Rogers) Esteem in the form of acceptance, respect, sympathy, warmth, or love.

positive regard from others (Rogers) *Positive regard* that comes exclusively from other people (i.e., not oneself).

positive reinforcement Presentation of a stimulus contingent on the performance of a desired response, which results in an increase in the likelihood of the response (cf. *negative reinforcement*).

positive self-regard (Rogers) *Positive regard* that has been internalized and thus comes directly from the self and not from external sources.

positive transference Feelings of *displacement* that the patient has toward the psychoanalyst that take the form of love, respect, and admiration.

Positive Valence (Tellegen and Waller) One of the "big seven" personality dimensions pertaining to the domain of self-esteem.

positron emission tomography (PET) Measures metabolic activity of structures of the brain.

possible selves (Markus and Nurius) Abstract mental representation of the type(s) of person one might become—these may be positive and motivate striving, or negative and motivate behaviors in other opposing directions.

post-Freudian Psychoanalytic theories and practices that are based on Freud's but deviate from them in varying degrees (cf. *Freudian*).

postsynaptic neuron Nerve cell that receives input via *neurotransmitters* from an adjacent *neuron.*

power (Winter) A person's ability or capacity to produce intended effects on the behavior or emotions of someone else.

powerful others control Belief that personal outcomes are caused by other people.

practicing (Mahler) The subphase between 9 and 18 months of age, when infants explore their environments by crawling, climbing, and walking.

preconscious (Freud) Part of the mind that contains information that one is not immediately aware of but that one can easily become aware of.

precursor chemicals Substances used in the production of other chemicals and *neurotransmitters.*

prediction The ability to accurately anticipate a person's future behavior.

predictive efficiency (Kelly) How well a construct anticipates events; the measure of the validity of a *construct.*

predisposition Genetic tendency to develop a particular characteristic or disorder, given certain environmental and social experiences.

Premack principle A lower-frequency behavior will increase if it is made contingent on a higher-frequency behavior.

press (Murray) An environmental circumstance that influences behavior.

presynaptic neuron A nerve cell that transmits messages to adjacent neurons by the release of *neurotransmitters* into the *synapse.*

preverbal constructs (Kelly) *Constructs* that consist of physiological, kinesthetic, and emotional patterns rather than verbal labels.

primary anxiety (Freud) Intense, negative experience in infants resulting from a *need* that is not immediately satisfied.

primary drives (Miller and Dollard) Motivation coming from the biological *needs* of the individual.

primary needs (Murray) *Needs* of biological origin, representing the physiological requirements of the organism.

primary process (Freud) *Id* process that reduces intrapsychic tension by producing a mental image of an object that will satisfy the *need* (cf. *secondary process*).

problem-solving therapy (D'Zurilla and Goldfried) Teaching general problem-solving skills to help alleviate the presenting problem and give the client skills to apply to future problems.

projection *Defense mechanism* in which a person attributes threatening impulses to another person (e.g., "I don't want to kill you; you want to kill me").

projective hypothesis Assumption that when people are forced to impose meaning on an ambiguous stimulus, the response will reflect significant aspects of their personalities; basis for projective techniques.

projective identification In *object relations* theories, the three-stage process whereby a person actually causes another to play out the role of his or her own "bad self."

projective techniques Indirect personality assessment procedures that present subjects with ambiguous stimuli (e.g., an inkblot) on which they must impose meaning.

prompting Reminding or instructing a person to perform a behavior so that it can be *reinforced.*

proprium (Allport) Self-like central organizing mechanism that provides a sense of unity, wholeness, and consistency.

prototype Typical case or example; possessing all of the central characteristics of its class.

pseudomemories Reported memories of events that were not actually directly witnessed or experienced.

psychic energy (Freud) Unitary energy source for all psychological functions.

psychoactive drugs Another term for *psychotherapeutic drugs.*

psychoanalysis Three common meanings: theory of personality, approach to research, and procedures for changing personality. All three were originally developed by Freud and subsequently extended and modified by other psychoanalysts.

psychodynamic Another term for *psychoanalytic.*

psychological behaviorism Another term for *paradigmatic behaviorism.*

psychological situation (Rotter) The existing circumstances from each individual's perspective.

psychoneuroimmunology The study of the relationship between the nervous system and immune functioning.

psychopathology The study of deviant behavior.

psychopharmacology The treatment of psychological symptoms through the use of medications.

psychosexual (Freud) Describing the stages of personality development; referring to the belief that each stage is a new manifestation of the sexual drive.

psychosexual stages (Freud) Periods in one's life representing the development of the *libido* (sexual drive); specifically, the *oral, anal, phallic,* and *genital stages.*

psychosis A state involving prominent delusions, hallucinations, or both.

psychosocial Interpersonal factors related to psychological functioning.

psychosocial stages Periods proposed by *post-Freudians* (e.g., Erikson, Sullivan) that represent the development of social behaviors (cf. *psychosexual stages*).

psychosurgery Surgery to correct or alleviate psychological problems.

psychotherapeutic drugs Pharmacologic agents used to treat psychological disorders.

psychotic Characterized by impaired functioning and loss of reality contact, delusions, and hallucinations.

Psychoticism (Eysenck) The dimension of personality that includes a disposition toward psychosis and psychopathy.

psychotropic drugs Another term for *psychotherapeutic drugs.*

punishment A consequence that reduces the likelihood of future occurrence of the behavior that preceded it; usually an aversive consequence.

pyknic (Kretschner) Plump body type associated with a manic-depressive personality.

Q-data (Cattell) Information about a person gathered from questionnaires and interviews.

Q-sort Assessment procedure in which people make comparative judgments of statements about themselves.

qualitative Relating to quality or type (opposed to amount); data usually derived from interviews or observations where the phenomena of interest are described, rather than tallied.

radical behaviorism The position that psychology should be concerned only with objective environmental events (stimuli) and overt behaviors (responses) (cf. *methodological behaviorism*).

random assignment Designating treatment groups for subjects in such a way that every subject has an equal likelihood of belonging to any group at the outset.

range of convenience (Kelly) Events that a construct is able to predict.

rapid eye movement period See *REM period.*

rapprochement (Mahler) A balance between dependence and independence from one's mother that is necessary for normal development.

ratings A method of personality assessment in which observational data are gathered indirectly through the reports of individuals who know the person well.

rational Based on reasoning and logic, as opposed to observation.

rational approach Reliance on subjective methods for studying personality, such as discussion, argument, popular opinion, and a general appeal to "reason."

rational-emotive therapy (RET) Ellis's version of *cognitive restructuring* therapy.

rationalization *Defense mechanism* in which a person *unconsciously* finds a sensible reason or "excuse" for performing or thinking about an unacceptable behavior.

ratio schedule of reinforcement A pattern of *reinforcement* in which the reinforcer is received after a certain number of responses have been made.

reaction formation *Defense mechanism* involving overemphasis on acting or thinking in ways opposite to a threatening impulse.

reactivity The tendency for the frequency of a response to change merely because it is being observed and recorded.

reality principle (Freud) Process of postponing tension reduction until an appropriate situation or object in the external world is found; the principle by which *ego* operates (cf. *pleasure principle*).

receptive character (Fromm) Adult behavior pattern that develops from being raised in an environment that fostered the attitude of expecting to receive (cf. *exploitative character*).

recessive A gene for a *phenotype* that is displayed only in *homozygous* individuals; that is, the phenotype will not result when paired with other different genes.

reciprocal altruism A concept from *sociobiology* referring to the idea that helping others increases the likelihood of receiving help when needed.

reflex action (Freud) At a primitive level, *id* reduces tension by immediately responding to internal and external irritations (e.g., sneezing, blinking, coughing).

regional cerebral blood flow (rCBF) Measures volume of blood flow to the *cerebral cortex* in order to assess metabolic activity.

regression (psychoanalysis) *Defense mechanism* in which the person repeats a behavior that led to satisfaction in an earlier stage of development.

reinforcement The process that occurs whenever an event that follows a behavior (i.e., a consequence) increases the likelihood that the behavior will be repeated.

reinforcement therapies *Behavior therapies* using the principle of *reinforcement* to increase adaptive behaviors that are being used too infrequently.

reinforcement value (Rotter) A person's subjective preference for a given *reinforcer* relative to other possible reinforcers in a given situation.

reinforcers Consequences of a behavior that increase its frequency.

reintegration (Rogers) A reverse of the process of fragmentation in which consistency between experience and *self-concept* is restored.

relational propositions The formal statements that describe the relationship among *theoretical constructs.*

reliability Measure of the "repeatability" or stability of a test or measure; prerequisite for *validity.*

REM (rapid eye movement) period Phase of Stage 1 sleep associated with dreaming; also called *paradoxical sleep.*

remarried families (stepfamilies) Families that include previously married adults (or involved partners) and the children from one or more previous unions.

repetition compulsion In psychoanalytic theory, the recurrence of common themes, symbols, or maladaptive behaviors that indicate unresolved (usually unconscious) *conflict.*

Representational Strategy An orientation in the study of personality based on the idea that people represent their environments and experiences mentally and that these abstract representations guide their actions.

representative A primary criterion of good research is that the sample adequately resembles the population to which the results will be generalized.

repression The most basic *defense mechanism,* completely excluding from consciousness a threatening experience.

resistance Conscious or unconscious processes that impede the progress of therapy.

respondent behavior Behavior that is elicited by an identifiable environmental stimulus.

response acquiescence The tendency to agree with personality test items, regardless of their content.

response biases The tendency to respond to test items in certain ways, regardless of their content (e.g., always choosing the first option).

response cost Removal of a valued item or privilege, contingent on the performance of an unwanted behavior.

response deviation The tendency to answer personality test items in an uncommon direction.

response sets Characteristic and consistent ways of responding to personality test items, regardless of what they say, taken to reflect distortion (cf. *response styles*).

response styles Characteristic and consistent ways of responding to personality test items, regardless of what they say, taken to reflect an underlying *disposition* (cf. *response sets*).

restatement of content (Rogers) *Client-centered therapy* technique in which the therapist rephrases what the client says (cf. *clarification of feelings*).

retest reliability Degree to which the same test (or an equivalent form) administered more than once yields the same basic results.

retrospective reports Accounts of events in the past—the previous day or even decades ago—provided by subjects or observers. Their credibility depends heavily on the delay between events and reporting, as well as on a variety of other factors.

reuptake A process of reabsorption of *neurotransmitters* from the *synapse* by the *presynaptic neuron* for storage and reuse.

reversal Research technique whereby treatment is stopped in order to reinstate pretreatment *(baseline)* circumstances.

role In the theatrical metaphor of the self, socially defined part the self plays when interacting with various others (mother, employer, teacher, friend).

role construct (Kelly) A *construct* that one uses to understand the demands of a particular social *role.*

Role Construct Repertory Test (Rep Test) Assessment device developed by Kelly for finding the *constructs* a person uses to construe other people.

role expectancy Behaviors believed to be characteristic of people when fulfilling socially defined categories (roles such as mother, teacher, or son).

Rorschach inkblots The most popular *projective technique;* subjects describe what they see in ambiguous, nearly symmetrical figures.

safety needs (Maslow) Needs for physical well-being and psychological security.

sample Relatively small group of people drawn from a much larger group *(population)* to study phenomena occurring in the population.

scatter diagram A graphic representation of the *correlation* between two variables; the stronger the relationship, the more the points approach a straight diagonal line.

schedule of reinforcement The rate or time interval at which desired responses are reinforced.

schema (Piaget) Organized mental "structures" that filter incoming information.

schematic (Markus) Refers to the state of possessing a *schema* for a particular type of information, or personal characteristic.

schizophrenia Chronic condition marked by psychosis, disturbed thought processes, and impaired functioning.

scientific approach A commitment to using *empirical* research methods to test and validate theories.

scientific theory An explanation for a phenomenon that uses both *theoretical constructs* and *relational propositions.*

scripts In the theatrical metaphor of the self, the social prescription for each *role* the self plays.

secondary disposition (Allport) A trait that manifests itself in only a few areas of personality.

secondary drives (Miller and Dollard) Motivation that has developed through association with *primary drives.*

secondary needs (Murray) *Needs* that have been learned.

secondary process (Freud) *Ego* process that reduces intrapsychic tension by problem solving and dealing directly with external reality (cf. *primary process*).

secure attachment An appropriate and strong child-parent bond.

secure base (Ainsworth) Any *object* that serves the protective needs of a child and when present and available allows the child's exploration of the surrounding environment without undue distress.

security operations (Sullivan) Term for processes undertaken to ensure ongoing contact and relationships with significant others and to reduce anxiety generated by the threat of loss of contact (e.g., *delusion of unique individuality*).

seduction theory (Freud) The idea that early sexual assaults or encounters are the root of neuroses expressed later in life.

seizures Abnormal electrical activity in the brain.

self The existing images and representations individuals have of their own functioning and characteristics.

self-actualization tendency (Maslow, Rogers) Unique, inborn inclination to behave in ways that result in maintaining and enhancing the person; leads people to become all that they can be.

self-complexity (Linville) Number of different self-concepts that a person has and the degree to which they overlap.

self-concept (self) How one views oneself, including how one actually views oneself (real self) and one's *ideal self.*

self-determination (Deci) Activities engaged in by personal choice or inclination are pursued more vigorously, and with more dedication and enthusiasm than those compelled by external forces or demands (i.e., *controlled activities*).

self-efficacy (Bandura) People's convictions that they can successfully execute the behavior required to produce a desired outcome in a particular situation.

self-enhancement Maintaining self-esteem by selectively attending to favorable information.

self-esteem (James) Degree of personal success relative to personal aspirations and goals. Feelings of self-worth derived from personal accomplishments.

self-esteem (Maslow) Desire for doing well by oneself and the accompanying feelings of worthwhileness and competence (cf. *esteem from others*).

self-handicapping Behaving in such a way as to minimize the likelihood of success at a task; this works ironically to protect self-esteem by allowing for external explanations in the event of actual failure.

self-instructional training (Meichenbaum) A cognitive-behavior *therapy* procedure that teaches clients to effectively plan and execute adaptive behaviors.

self-modeling Form of *symbolic modeling* in which clients serve as their own *models* via videotaped performances.

self-monitoring Degree and ways in which people observe their own behavior and present themselves to others.

selfobjects Mental representations of an individual's own characteristics, roles, and functioning.

self-regulatory system or plan Person's self-imposed rewards and personal goals.

self-report personality inventory A questionnaire containing a large number of questions about people, to which respondents answer for themselves.

self-schema (Markus) Mental representations of the type of person one is that influence all aspects of mental processing and behavior.

self-statements The soundless, mental speech that arises at the instant that people think, plan, or solve problems in their minds.

self-talk Another term for *self-statements.*

sensation seeking (Zuckerman) The tendency to actively pursue novel stimuli and experiences.

separation (Mahler) The process whereby the child achieves intrapsychic distinctiveness from the mother.

separation-individuation phase In Mahler's *object relations* theory, the third phase of development in which the person achieves independence from the mother and has a clear sense of self and nonself.

serotonin *Neurotransmitter* associated with aggression.

serotonin turnover Measure of *serotonin* activity in the brain.

setting events Those conditions that, when present, increase the likelihood of occurrence of specific behaviors. Thirst, for example, is a setting event for drinking, whereas the presence of water may act as a *discriminative stimulus* for drinking.

sex-linked Characteristics that occur at different rates in the two sexes, suggesting the 23rd chromosome pair as the likely site of the relevant gene or genes.

sex-typed In reference to gender roles, people who conform closely to the stereotypic traits of their own sex.

sex-type undifferentiated In reference to gender roles, individuals who possess few of the characteristics typical of *either* sex.

sexual drive (Freud) One of Freud's proposed *dual drives* that motivates all human behavior, see also *libido.*

Shadow, The (Jung) Archetype that represents the dark side in each of us; part of the collective unconscious.

shaping *Reinforcing* progressively closer approximations to the desired behavior.

signal anxiety (Freud) Discomfort that warns the *ego* to institute *defense mechanisms* to prevent the intense experience of *primary anxiety.*

single photon emission computerized tomography (SPECT) Tracks single-photon-emitting isotopes in the brain to examine the influence of mental operations on brain activity.

single-parent family A family consisting of only one adult and children.

single-subject design *Idiographic* approach employed by researchers; usually applied to animal models and *operant*-based treatments on people.

single-subject reversal Research design that compares a subject's behavior in periods in which a treatment is presented with periods in which it is withdrawn (reversed).

situational cues The location and context where *target behaviors* are likely to occur and which may serve to elicit the behavior.

situational specificity A given behavior may be restricted to a particular setting or set of circumstances.

skill deficits The condition in which a person does not know how to perform certain appropriate or adaptive behaviors.

sleep deprivation Restriction of the sleep-wake cycle to prevent or minimize sleep time.

slow to warm up As pertains to the *temperament type* called *sociability,* refers to children who are initially reluctant to approach new people, but who gradually become more willing over time.

sociability An early temperament type that appears related to the adult domain of *Extraversion.*

social capital Family relations and community organizations, which affect the child's cognitive and social development.

social cognitive approach An approach within the Representational Strategy that views the mental representations of self, others, and interpersonal relations as central to the study of *personality.*

social constructions Environmentally driven consensual dictates of appropriate behavior.

social desirability The tendency to answer personality test items in the most socially accepted direction, irrespective of whether such answers are correct for the respondent.

socialization The set of events and processes by which we acquire the beliefs and behaviors of the particular social group into which we are born.

social learning (Bandura and Walters) An approach that views personality as acquired through *conditioning, modeling,* and the family and cultural environment.

social models (Dollard and Miller) In *observational learning,* behavioral examples that influence how an observer behaves, acts, and thinks.

social roles All of the behaviors and attitudes construed as appropriate for a specific, socially defined group or status.

social self (James) Part of the self containing our beliefs about others' perceptions of us.

sociobiology The study of the evolutionary basis of social behavior.

somatic nervous system Nerves throughout the body that convey information from the body and sense organs up to the *central nervous system.*

somatotonia (Sheldon) One of three basic temperaments.

somatyping (Sheldon) A procedure for assessing physique by assigning scores on three dimensions of physical characteristics (endomorphy, mesomorphy, and ectomorphy).

source trait (Cattell) The underlying dispositions that determine behavior, often identified by factor analysis.

species In biology, a level of classification of organisms into groups characterized by some distinguishing features from other types of organisms.

specific expectancy (Rotter) A person's subjective estimate of the chances of obtaining a particular outcome by performing a particular behavior.

specific locus of control Individual expectations of personal control in a particular situation.

sperm Male sex cell, or *gamete.*

sperm competition A process by which sperm contributed by different males all seek to fertilize the ovum.

spiritual self (James) Aspect of self consisting of our deepest emotions and desires.

splitting In *object relations* theories, the mental separation of objects into their "good" and "bad" aspects.

spontaneous recovery In *classical conditioning,* the return of a *conditioned response* after *extinction.*

stabilizing selection Species with greater variability have a greater chance of surviving and reproducing in changing environments, thus variability within species is adaptive and may be favored over uniformity.

stable Attributions about the cause of an event that reflect consistency (e.g., natural skill).

state Temporary personality condition.

state anxiety A transient condition of the organism characterized by subjective feelings of apprehension and heightened autonomic nervous system activity.

statistical approach Determining the importance of *dispositions* by applying statistical procedures to data from a large group of people.

statistical significance An estimate of the likelihood that a particular research finding (e.g., a difference between two groups or a *correlation* between two variables) occurred by chance; by convention, a result must have a chance likelihood of less than 5 in 100 to be called statistically significant.

statistical test Mathematical test used to determine *statistical significance.*

stepfamilies Another term for *remarried families.*

steroid hormones Sex *hormones* associated with male aggression.

stimulus control Behavior that occurs only when certain environmental circumstances *(discriminative stimuli)* are present.

stimulus control procedures *Operant conditioning* techniques that use *setting events* and *discriminative stimuli* to bring behavior under stimulus control.

strategy Any of the four broad approaches (Psychoanalytic, Dispositional, Environmental, or Representational to the study of personality.

stress inoculation training (Meichenbaum) A cognitive behavior therapy that prepares clients to deal with stress-inducing events by teaching them self-control and coping skills and then having them rehearse these skills while they are gradually exposed to stressors.

stress moderators Variables that inhibit or exaggerate the health effects of stress on individuals.

striving for superiority (Adler) The fundamental human motive, it arises as the inevitable response to initial feelings of inferiority.

subjective experience Another term for *subjective reality.*

subjective knowledge Knowledge based on a single individual's personal experience and cannot be directly verified by others.

subjective reality Each individual's personal experience of an event.

sublimation *Defense mechanism* in which unacceptable desires are unconsciously channeled into socially acceptable outlets.

substantive Palpable, having solid mass, important, existing of its own, independent of other factors.

superego (Freud) Aspect of the personality incorporating ideals and the moral standards of one's parents and culture (cf. *ego, id*).

suppression *Conscious* forgetting of threatening thoughts; not a Freudian *defense mechanism* because it operates consciously.

surface traits (Cattell) Clusters of *overt behavior* that seem to go together but do not necessarily have a common cause (cf. *source traits*).

symbol A verbal or pictorial representation that stands for something else.

symbolic modeling The indirect observation of the behavior of *models,* such as in movies, by reading, or through oral descriptions of another person's behaviors.

symbolization The process through which threatening objects or ideas are represented by nonthreatening ones.

sympathetic nervous system Subsystem of the nervous system that prepares the body for energy expenditure by speeding some organs and systems.

synapse The small gap between neurons where *neurotransmitters* are released to influence surrounding *neurons.*

systematic desensitization (Wolpe) A *behavior therapy* technique based on counterconditioning; the client is gradually exposed to increasingly anxiety-evoking stimuli while making a response that is essentially incompatible with *anxiety* (e.g., relaxation).

systematic observation A *scientific method* of observing behavior in precisely defined circumstances, time periods, or situations for the purpose of *objective* measurement.

target behaviors In *behavior therapy,* the specific behaviors that the client and therapist are trying to encourage, eliminate, or modify.

T-data (Cattell) Information gained from putting subjects in objective test situations without telling them which aspects of their behavior are being observed or evaluated.

temperament types *Dispositions* that are present at birth, stable across time, and pervasive in their influence (cf. *personality traits*).

temporal consistency (Mischel) Behavior that remains consistent and stable over time in the same or similar situations.

temporal cues Identifying the time of the target behavior as an antecedent for therapy designed to change the behavior.

temporal precedence Sequence of occurrence—specifically, in science a cause must occur before its presumed effect.

termination The final stage of therapy, in which progress is reviewed and the therapist and the patient or client separate.

testability How well and how easily a theory can be subjected to *empirical* validation.

testosterone Male *hormone (androgen);* associated with sexual arousal and aggression.

tests Assessment devices for which *normative data* are available.

thanatos Another term for *aggressive drive.*

theatrical metaphor Characterization of the self as the sum of the different roles played in life.

Thematic Apperception Test (TAT) A *projective technique* consisting of pictures about which respondents must make up stories.

theoretical approach Determining the importance of *dispositions* by looking to a particular *theory.*

theoretical constructs The basic terms and building blocks of a *theory;* they do not actually exist but are invented to describe or explain phenomena.

theory A proposed explanation that serves to direct and drive research.

theory of natural selection Based on Darwin's idea that chance genetic variations producing adaptive reproductive and survival advantages will increasingly characterize a species over time.

theory of the four temperaments Theory of personality proposed by Hippocrates that predicts personality types by four humors (blood, black bile, yellow bile, and phlegm) that correspond with the four elements.

therapeutic alliance A cooperative relationship between patient and therapist.

third-variable problem When two variables are correlated, neither may cause the other, but rather another (third) variable may account for both variables (cf. *directionality problem*).

threat (Rogers) Feelings that result from becoming aware of incongruity between one's experience and *self-concept.*

time-limited Short-term therapy, such as interpersonal therapy, that specifies in advance a maximum treatment period.

time out (from positive reinforcement) Withdrawing a client's access to positive reinforcers for a brief, preset period immediately after an unwanted behavior occurs.

time series designs Any procedure that evaluates behavior over time. Time series data can be based on a single subject and collected over changing environmental circumstances.

token economy A systematically controlled environment in which clients earn tokens for performing various behaviors; the tokens can later be exchanged for tangible reinforcers and privileges.

tolerance As related to drug dependence or addiction, refers to the need for increasingly large doses to achieve the same effect over time or repeated use.

trait An enduring personality characteristic, or *disposition.*

trait anxiety The *disposition* to respond with anxiety to situations that are perceived as threatening.

trait elements Elements from which traits *(factors)* are derived by using *factor analysis.*

transference Feelings a patient has for a psychoanalyst that are *displacements* from the patient's past. Working through transference is critical in psychoanalytic psychotherapy.

triadic reciprocal determinism (Bandura) The theoretical assumption that personality develops through a continuing interaction among person, behavior, and environmental factors.

tryptophan Precursor of the *neurotransmitter serotonin.*

twin study method A procedure used to assess the degree to which a *disposition* is *heritable* by contrasting identical and fraternal twins.

type Broad grouping of personality characteristics that tend to co-occur.

Type A behavior pattern A pattern of responding characterized by a high competitive drive coupled with a continuous rush to meet deadlines ("hurry sickness"); it is predictive of later heart attacks (cf. *Type B behavior pattern*).

Type B behavior pattern A pattern of responding characterized by an easygoing and relaxed manner (cf. *Type A behavior pattern*).

types Broadest categories of people according to similar characteristics.

unconditional positive regard (Rogers) Esteem *(positive regard)* that does not depend on the person's behaviors and is thus nonevaluative.

unconditional positive regard from others (Rogers) *Unconditional positive regard* that comes exclusively from other people.

unconditional positive self-regard (Rogers) *Unconditional positive regard* that has been internalized and thus comes directly from the self.

unconditioned response (UCR) In *classical conditioning,* the response elicited by an *unconditioned stimulus* (cf. *conditioned response*).

unconditioned stimulus (UCS) In *classical conditioning,* a stimulus that naturally or automatically elicits a particular response.

unconscious Part of the mind containing information of which the person has no knowledge. For Freud, most of personality is unconscious.

understanding Comprehension of, or the ability to explain, a process.

undesired self-concept Personality characteristics that one considers undesirable.

undoing *Defense mechanism* involving restitution for an unacceptable act.

unified Separate parts coming together to make a whole.

unstable In reference to causal attributions, the belief that an event is due to an inconsistent or fluctuating condition (e.g., amount of practice).

urine alarm method Therapy technique for treating *nocturnal enuresis.* The alarm awakens the child when he or she begins to urinate.

validity The extent to which a test or measure taps what it is intended to measure.

value The worth that is placed on a possible outcome of a course of action.

variable-interval schedule A *schedule of reinforcement* in which the individual is reinforced for the first response made after a period of time that varies randomly around a specified time value.

variable-ratio schedule A *schedule of reinforcement* in which the number of responses required for reinforcement varies randomly around a particular number of responses.

variables Factors, characteristics, or events that may assume a range of values.

varieties Strains of organisms within a *species* with distinguishing features.

ventricles Fluid-filled spaces in the brain.

verbal aggression Speech that is directed toward hurting someone.

verbal persuasion (Bandura) One source of *efficacy expectations.* Often the most readily available form of efficacy expectations as it is easily delivered by others in the person's environment.

vicarious consequences Rewards and punishments administered to a *model* that influence the observer's subsequent likelihood of performing the modeled behavior.

vicarious experience Information about the *efficacy* of a behavior that the subject is provided by observing a *model* engage in the behavior.

vicarious extinction The elimination of fear and anxiety in clients by the process of observing *models* who successfully deal with anxiety-evoking situations without incurring negative consequences.

vicarious punishment An observed consequence received by a *model* that is perceived by the observer as negative or undesirable.

vicarious reinforcement An observed consequence received by a *model* that is perceived by the observer as positive or desirable.

vicarious reward An observed consequence received by a *model* that is perceived by the observer as positive or desirable.

viscerotonia (Sheldon) One of three basic temperaments.

visual representation The *dream work* process whereby abstract wishes, urges, and ideas are translated into concrete pictures or images.

wish fulfillment (Freud) Satisfying a desire through a mental image rather than in reality; part of *primary process.*

working self-concept The specific mental representation of the self that is currently mentally available and operative.

young male syndrome Human males are most aggressive among themselves when they are competing for mates.

zygote The earliest stage of embryonic development, the resulting form from the union of two *gametes.*

Bibliography

Abraham, K. (1927). The influence of oral eroticism on character formation. In K. Abraham (Ed.), *Selected papers on psychoanalysis.* London: Hogarth.

Abramson, H., Houts, A. C., & Berman, J. S. (1990, June). *The effectiveness of medical and psychological treatments for childhood enuresis.* Paper presented at the meeting of the Society for Psychotherapy Research, Wintergreen, VA.

Abromowitz, E. S., Baker, A. H., & Fleischer, S. F. (1982). Onset of depressive psychiatric crises and the menstrual cycle. *American Journal of Psychiatry, 139,* 475–478.

Abu, M., & Hashem, E. (1995). Some personality correlates in a group of drug addicts. *Personality and Individual Differences, 19,* 649–653.

Achamamba, B., & Kumar, K. G. (1989). I-E locus of control and job satisfaction among the workers of public and private sector undertaking. *Journal of the Indian Academy of Applied Psychology, 15,* 83–86.

Adalbjarnardottir, S. (1995). How schoolchildren propose to negotiate: The role of social withdrawal, social anxiety, and locus of control. *Child Development, 66,* 1739–1751.

Adamec, R. (1975). The behavioral basis of prolonged suppression of predatory attack in cats. *Aggressive Behavior, 1,* 297–314.

Adams-Webber, J. (1989). Some reflections on the "meaning" of repertory grid responses. *International Journal of Personal Construct Psychology, 2,* 77–92.

Adams-Webber, J. (1990). Personal construct theory and cognitive science. *International Journal of Personal Construct Psychology, 3,* 415–421.

Addad, M. (1987). Neuroticism, extraversion and meaning of life: A comparative study of criminals and non-criminals. *Personality and Individual Differences, 8,* 879–883.

Addis, M. E. (1993). Learning in the trenches: A student's perspective on the cognitive versus radical debate. *The Behavior Therapist, 16,* 55–56.

Adler, A. (1964). *Social interest: A challenge to mankind.* New York: Putnam (Capricorn Books).

Adler, A. (1973). *Superiority and social interest: A collection of later writings* (H. L. Ansbacher & R. R. Ansbacher, Eds.). New York: Viking Press.

Ahadi, S. A., & Rothbart, M. K. (in press). Temperament, development, and the Big Five. In C. F. Halberson, G. A. Kohnstamm, & R. P. Martin (Eds.), *The developing structure of temperament and personality from infancy to adulthood.* Hillsdale, NJ: Erlbaum.

Ainslie, R. C. (1989). Masters of the universe: Children's toys as reflections of contemporary psychoanalytic theory. *Journal of the American Academy of Psychoanalysis, 17,* 579–595.

Ainsworth, M., Blehar, M., Waters, E., & Wall, S. (1978). *Patterns of attachment.* Hillsdale, NJ: Lawrence Erlbaum.

Akbarian, S., Bunney, W. E., Jr., Potkin, S. G., Wigal, S. B., Hagman, J. O., Sandman, C. A., & Jones, E. G. (1993). Altered distribution of nicotinamide-adenine dinucleotide phosphate-diaphorase cells in frontal lobe of schizophrenics implies disturbances of cortical development. *Archives of General Psychiatry, 50,* 169–177.

Akbarian, S., Vinuela, A., Kim, J. J., Potkin, S. G., Bunney, W. E., Jr., & Jones, E. G. (1993). Distorted distribution of nicotinamide-adenine dinucleotide phosphate-diaphorase neurons in temporal lobe of schizophrenics implies anomalous cortical development. *Archives of General Psychiatry, 50,* 178–187.

Aker, R. M., & Panter, A. T. (1988). Extraversion and the ability to decode nonverbal communication. *Personality and Individual Differences, 9,* 965–972.

Aldwin, C., & Revenson, T. A. (1987). Does coping help? A reexamination of the relationship between coping and mental health. *Journal of Personality and Social Psychology, 53,* 337–348.

Alexander, C. N., Rainforth, M. V., & Gelderloos, P. (1991). Transcendental meditation, self-actualization, and psychological health: A conceptual overview and statistical meta-analysis [Special issue: Handbook of self-actualization]. *Journal of Social Behavior and Personality, 6,* 189–248.

Alexander, M. J., & Higgins, E. T. (1993). Emotional trade-offs of becoming a parent: How social roles influence self-discrepancy effects. *Journal of Personality and Social Psychology, 65,* 1259–1269.

Allen, M. K., & Liebert, R. M. (1969). Effects of live and symbolic deviant modeling cues on adoption of a previously learned standard. *Journal of Personality and Social Psychology, 11,* 253–260.

Allport, G. W. (1937). *Personality: A psychological interpretation.* New York: Holt, Rinehart & Winston.

Allport, G. W. (1943). *Becoming: Basic considerations for a psychology of personality.* New Haven, CT: Yale University Press.

Allport, G. W. (1961). *Pattern and growth in personality.* New York: Holt, Rinehart & Winston.

Allport, G. W. (1966). Traits revisited. *American Psychologist, 21,* 1–10.

Alter-Reid, K., Gibbs, M. S., Lachenmeyer, J. R., Sigal, J., & Massoth, N. A. (1986). Sexual abuse of children: A review of the empirical findings. *Clinical Psychology Review, 6,* 249–266.

Altman, S. A. (1962). A field study of the sociobiology of rhesus monkey, *Makacca mulatta. Annals of the New York Academy of Sciences, 102,* 338–435.

Altshuler, L. L., Casanova, M. F., Goldberg, T. E., & Kleinman, J. E. (1990). The hippocampus and parahippocampus in schizophrenic, suicide, and control brains. *Archives of General Psychiatry, 47,* 1029–1034.

American Psychiatric Association (1994). *Diagnostic and statistical manual of mental disorders* (4th ed.). Washington, DC: Author.

American Psychiatric Association. (1987). *Diagnostic and statistical manual of mental disorders* (3rd ed., rev.). Washington, DC: Author.

American Psychological Association Ethics Committee. (1992). APA's code of ethics and conduct and principles of psychologists. *American Psychologist, 47,* 1597–1611.

Amsterdam, J. D., Winokur, A., Dyson, W., Herzog, S., Gonzalez, F., Rott, R., & Kopprowski, H. (1985). Borna disease virus. *Archives of General Psychiatry, 42,* 1093–1096.

Anastasi, A. (1976). *Psychological testing* (4th ed.). New York: Macmillan.

Anastasi, A. (1988a). *Psychological testing* (6th ed.). New York: Macmillan.

Anastasi, A. (1988b). Self-report inventories. In *Psychological testing.* New York: Macmillan.

Anderson, J. W. (1988). Henry A. Murray's early career: A psychobiographical exploration. *Journal of Personality, 56,* 139–171.

Anderson, W. J. (1989). Family therapy in the client-centered tradition: A legacy in the narrative mode [Special issue: Person-centered approaches with families]. *Person-Centered Review, 4,* 295–307.

Andersen, S. M., & Cole, S. W. (1990). "Do I know you?": The role of significant others in general social perception. *Journal of Personality and Social Psychology, 59,* 384–399.

Andreasen, N. C., Rezai, K., Alliger, R., Swayze, V. W., II, Flaum, M., Kirchner, P., Cohen, G., & O'Leary, D. S. (1992). Hypofrontality in neuroleptic-naive patients and in patients with chronic schizophrenia. *Archives of General Psychiatry, 49,* 943–958.

Ansbacher, H. L., & Ansbacher, R. R. (1956). *The individual psychology of Alfred Adler: A systematic presentation in selections from his writings.* New York: Harper & Row.

Antill, J. K., Russell, G., Goodnow, J. J., & Cotton, S. (1993). Measures of children's sex typing in middle childhood. *Australian Journal of Psychology, 45,* 25–33.

Anzieu, D. (1986). *Freud's self-analysis.* Madison, CT: International Universities Press.

Arcaya, J. M., & Gerber, G. L. (1990). An object relations approach to the treatment of child abuse. *Psychotherapy, 27,* 619–626.

Arcus, D., & Kagan, J. (1995). Temperament and craniofacial variation in the first two years. *Child Development, 66,* 1529–1540.

Argyle, M., & Lu, L. (1990). The happiness of extraverts. *Personality and Individual Differences, 11,* 1011–1017.

Arkowitz, H. (1991). Introductory statement: Psychotherapy integration comes of age. *Journal of Psychotherapy Integration, 1,* 1–3.

Arkowitz, H. (1992). Integrative theories of therapy. In D. K. Freedheim (Ed.), *The history of psychotherapy: A century of change.* Washington, DC: American Psychological Association.

Arlow, J. A., & Brenner, C. (1988). The future of psychoanalysis. *Psychoanalytic Quarterly, 57,* 1–14.

Asarnow, J. R., & Callan, J. W. (1985). Boys with peer adjustment problems: Social cognitive processes. *Journal of Consulting and Clinical Psychology, 53,* 80–87.

Aserinsky, E., & Kleitman, N. (1953). Regularly occurring periods of eye motility, and concomitant phenomena, during sleep. *Science, 118,* 273–274.

Ashkanasy, N. M., & Gallois, C. (1987). Locus of control and attributions of academic performance of self and others. *Australian Journal of Psychology, 39,* 293–305.

Atkinson, J. W. (Ed.). (1958). *Motives in fantasy, action, and society.* Princeton, NJ: Van Nostrand.

Atkinson, J. W., & Litwin, G. H. (1960). Achievement motive and test anxiety conceived as motive to approach success and motive to avoid failure. *Journal of Abnormal and Social Psychology, 60,* 52–63.

Atkinson, J. W., & McClelland, D. C. (1948). The projective expression of needs, II. The effect of different intensities of the hunger drive on thematic apperception. *Journal of Experimental Psychology, 38,* 643–658.

Atkinson, M., & Violato, C. (1994). Neuroticism and coping with anger: The transsituational consistency of coping responses. *Personality of Individual Differences, 17,* 769–782.

Austin, J. T., & Vancouver, J. B. (1996). Goal constructs in psychology: Structure, process, and content. *Psychological Bulletin, 120,* 338–375.

Azrin, N. H., Sneed, T. J., & Foxx, R. M. (1973). Dry bed: A rapid method of eliminating bedwetting (enuresis) of the retarded. *Behaviour Research and Therapy, 11,* 427–434.

Azrin, N. H., Sneed, T. J., & Foxx, R. M. (1974). Dry-bed training: Rapid elimination of childhood enuresis. *Behaviour Research and Therapy, 12,* 147–156.

Azrin, N. H., Thienes-Hontos, P., & Besalel-Azrin, V. (1979). Elimination of enuresis without a conditioning apparatus: An extension by office instruction of the child and parents. *Behavior Therapy, 10,* 14–19.

Bacciagaluppi, M. (1989). Erich Fromm's views on psychoanalytic "technique." *Contemporary Psychoanalysis, 25,* 226–243.

Badalamenti, A. F. (1988). Freud and the fall of man. *Journal of Religion and Health, 27,* 23–61.

Bagby, R. M., Joffe, R. T., Parker, J. D. A., Kalemba, V., & Harkness, K. L. (1995). Major depression and the five-factor model of personality. *Journal of Personality Disorders, 9,* 224–234.

Bagby, R. M., Parker, J. D. A., & Taylor, G. J. (1991). Reassessing the validity and reliability of the MMPI alexithymia scale. *Journal of Personality Assessment, 56,* 238–253.

Bailey, J. M., Gaulin, S., Agyei, Y., & Gladue, B. A. (1994). Effects of gender and sexual orientation on evolutionarily relevant aspects of human mating psychology. *Journal of Personality and Social Psychology, 66,* 1081–1093.

Bakan, D. (1988). Some thoughts on reading Blight's article: "Can psychology reduce the risk of nuclear war?" *Journal of Humanistic Psychology, 28,* 59–61.

Baker, R. R., & Bellis, M. A. (1995). *Human sperm competition: Copulation, masturbation and infidelity.* London: Chapman & Hall.

Balasubramaniam, V., & Kanaka, T. S. (1976). Hypothalamotomy in the management of aggressive behavior. In T. P. Morley (Ed.), *Current controversies in neurosurgery.* Philadelphia: Saunders.

Bandura, A. (1965). Influence of models' reinforcement contingencies on the acquisition of imitative responses. *Journal of Personality and Social Psychology, 1,* 589–595.

Bandura, A. (1969). Social-learning theory of identificatory processes. In D. A. Goslin (Ed.), *Handbook of socialization theory and research.* Chicago: Rand McNally.

Bandura, A. (1984). Recycling misconceptions of perceived self-efficacy. *Cognitive Therapy and Research, 8,* 231–255.

Bandura, A. (1986a). From thought to action: Mechanisms of personal agency. *New Zealand Journal of Psychology, 15,* 1–17.

Bandura, A. (1986b). *Social foundations of thought and action: A social cognitive theory.* Englewood Cliffs, NJ: Prentice-Hall.

Bandura, A. (1989a). Human agency in social cognitive theory. *American Psychologist, 44,* 1175–1184.

Bandura, A. (1989b). Perceived self-efficacy in the exercise of personal agency. *The Psychologist: Bulletin of the British Psychological Society, 10,* 411–424.

Bandura, A. (1990). Perceived self-efficacy in the exercise of control over AIDS infection. *Evaluation and Program Planning, 13,* 9–17.

Bandura, A. (1991). Self-efficacy mechanism in physiological activation and health-promoting behavior. In J. Madden (Ed.), *Neurobiology of learning, emotion and affect.* New York: Raven Press.

Bandura, A. (1992a). Exercise of personal agency through the self-efficacy mechanism. In R. Schwarzer (Ed), *Self-efficacy: Thought control of action.* Washington, DC: Hemisphere.

Bandura, A. (1992b, April). *Perceived self-efficacy in cognitive development and functioning.* Paper presented at the annual meeting of the American Education Research Association, San Francisco.

Bandura, A. (1992c). Self-efficacy mechanisms in psychobiologic functioning. In R. Schwarzer (Ed.), *Self-efficacy: Thought control of action.* Washington, DC: Hemisphere.

Bandura, A. (1995). Comments on the crusade against the causal efficacy of human thought. *Journal of Behavioral Therapy and Experimental Psychiatry, 26,* 179–190.

Bandura, A. (1996). Failures in self-regulation: Energy depletion or selective disengagement? *Psychological Inquiry, 7,* 20–24.

Bandura, A., Adams, N. E., & Beyer, J. (1977). Cognitive processes mediating behavioral change. *Journal of Personality and Social Psychology, 35,* 125–139.

Bandura, A., Barbaranelli, C., Caprara, G. V., & Pastorelli, C. (1996a). Mechanisms of moral disengagement in the exercise of moral agency. *Journal of Personality and Social Psychology, 71,* 364–374.

Bandura, A., Barbaranelli, C., Caprara, G. V., & Pastorelli, C. (1996b). Multifaceted impact of self-efficacy beliefs on academic functioning. *Child Development, 67,* 1206–1222.

Bandura, A., & Mischel, W. (1965). Modification of self-imposed delay of reward through exposure to live and symbolic models. *Journal of Personality and Social Psychology, 2,* 698–705.

Bandura, A., O'Leary, A., Taylor, C. B., Gauthier, J., & Gossard, D. (1987). Perceived self-efficacy and pain control: Opioid and nonopioid mechanisms. *Journal of Personality and Social Psychology, 53,* 563–571.

Bandura, A., & Walters, R. H. (1963). *Social learning and personality development.* New York: Holt, Rinehart & Winston.

Bandura, A., & Wood, R. (1989). Effect of perceived controllability and performance standards on self-regulation of complex decision making. *Journal of Personality and Social Psychology, 56,* 805–814.

Baradell, J. G. (1990). Client-centered case consultation and single-case research design: Application to case management. *Archives of Psychiatric Nursing, 4,* 12–17.

Barash, D. P. (1986). *The hare and the tortoise: Culture, biology, and human nature.* New York: Penguin.

Barling, J., Bluen, S., & Moss, V. (1991). Type A behavior and marital dissatisfaction: Disentangling the effects of achievement striving and impatience-irritability. *Journal of Psychology, 124,* 311–319.

Barnard, D. (1984). The personal meaning of illness: Client-centered dimensions of medicine and health care. In R. F. Levant & J. M. Shlien (Eds.), *Client-centered therapy and the person-centered approach: New directions in theory, research, and practice.* New York: Praeger.

Barnet, H. S. (1990). Divorce stress and adjustment model: Locus of control and demographic predictors. *Journal of Divorce, 13,* 93–109.

Barnette, E. L. (1989). Effects of a growth group on counseling students' self-actualization. *Journal for Specialists in Group Work, 14,* 202–210.

Barr, C. E., Mednick, S. A., & Munk-Jorgensen, P. (1990). Exposure to influenza epidemics during gestation and adult schizophrenia. *Archives of General Psychiatry, 47,* 869–874.

Barratt, B. B., & Starus, B. S. (1994). Toward postmodern masculinities. *American Imago, 51,* 37–67.

Barrett, M. (1992). Psychoanalysis and feminism: A British sociologist's view. *Signs, 17,* 444–466.

Barrick, M. R., & Mount, M. K. (1991). The big five personality dimensions and job performance: A meta-analysis. *Personnel Psychology, 44,* 1–26.

Barrineau, P. (1992). Person-centered dream work. *Journal of Humanistic Psychology, 32,* 90–105.

Barris, B. P. (1990). Affirming the "personal" in PCT [Review of *Working with people: Clinical uses of personal construct psychology*]. *International Journal of Personal Construct Psychology, 3,* 249–256.

Basham, K. (1992). Resistance and couple therapy. *Smith College Studies in Social Work, 62,* 243–264.

Bass, E., & Davis, L. (1988). *The courage to heal: A guide for women survivors of child sexual abuse.* New York: Harper & Row.

Bassler, M., Krauthauser, H., & Hoffmann, S. O. (1992). A new approach to the identification of cognitive conflicts in the repertory grid: An illustrative case study. *International Journal of Personal Construct Psychology, 5,* 95–111.

Baucom, D. H., & Epstein, N. (1990). *Cognitive-behavioral marital therapy.* New York: Brunner/Mazel.

Baudry, F. (1988). Character, character type, and character organization. *Journal of the American Psychoanalytic Association, 37,* 655–686.

Baumeister, R. F. (1989a). The optimal margin of illusion. *Journal of Social and Clinical Psychology, 8,* 176–189.

Baumeister, R. F. (1989b). The problem of life's meaning. In D. M. Buss & N. Cantor (Eds.), *Personality psychology: Recent trends and emerging directions.* New York: Springer-Verlag.

Baumeister, R. F. (1991). On the stability of variability: Retest reliability of metatraits. *Personality and Social Psychology Bulletin, 17,* 633–639.

Baumeister, R. F., & Leary, M. R. (1995). The need to belong: Desire for interpersonal attachments as a fundamental human motivation. *Psychological Bulletin, 117,* 497–529.

Baumeister, R. F., & Tice, D. M. (1988). Metatraits. *Journal of Personality, 56,* 571–598.

Baumrind, D. (1967). Child care practices anteceding three patterns of preschool behavior. *Genetic Psychology Monographs, 75,* 43–83.

Baumrind, D. (1971). Current patterns of parental authority. *Developmental Psychology Monographs, 4,* 1–103.

Beail, N. (Ed.). (1985). *Repertory grid technique and personal constructs: Applications in clinical and educational settings.* London: Croom Helm.

Beail, N., & Parker, S. (1991). Group fixed-role therapy: A clinical application. *International Journal of Personal Construct Psychology, 4,* 85–95.

Bear, D. M., & Fedio, P. (1977). Quantitative analysis of interictal behavior in temporal lobe epilepsy. *Archives of Neurology, 34,* 454–467.

Beck, A. T. (1976). *Cognitive therapy and the emotional disorders.* New York: International Universities Press.

Beck, A. T. (1984). Cognitive approaches to stress. In R. Woolfold & P. Lehrer (Eds.), *Principles and practice of stress management.* New York: Guilford.

Beck, A. T. (1989). *Love is never enough.* New York: Harper & Row (Perennial Library).

Beck, A. T. (1993). Cognitive therapy: Past, present, and future. *Journal of Consulting and Clinical Psychology, 61,* 194–198.

Beck, A. T., & Emery, G. (1985). *Anxiety disorders and phobias: A cognitive perspective.* New York: Basic Books.

Beck, A. T., & Freeman, A. (1989). *Cognitive therapy of personality disorders.* New York: Guilford.

Beck, A. T., & Weishaar, M. (1989). Cognitive therapy. In A. Freeman, K. M. Simon, L. E. Beutler, & H. Arkowitz (Eds.), *Comprehensive handbook of cognitive therapy.* New York: Plenum.

Beckham, E. E., & Watkins, J. T. (1989). Process and outcome in cognitive therapy. In A. Freeman, K. M. Simon, L. E. Beutler, & H. Arkowitz (Eds.), *Comprehensive handbook of cognitive therapy.* New York: Plenum.

Beh, H. C. (1989). Achievement motivation and the end-effect. *Perceptual and Motor Skills, 68,* 799–805.

Bein, J., Anderson, D. E., & Maes, W. R. (1990). Teacher locus of control and job satisfaction. *Educational Research Quarterly, 14,* 7–10.

Bell, L., & Schniedewind, N. (1989). Realizing the promise of humanistic education: A reconstructed pedagogy for personal and social change. *Journal of Humanistic Psychology, 29,* 200–223.

Bell, R. A., Summerson, J. H., & Konen, J. C. (1995). Racial differences in psychosocial variables among adults with non-insulin-dependent diabetes mellitus. *Behavioral Medicine, 21,* 69–73.

Bem, S. L. (1972). *Psychology looks at sex roles: Where have all the androgenous people gone?* Paper presented at the UCLA Symposium on Sex Roles, Los Angeles.

Bem, S. L. (1974). The measurement of psychological androgyny. *Journal of Consulting and Clinical Psychology, 42,* 155–162.

Bem, S. L. & Lenny, E. (1976). Sex typing and the avoidance of cross-sex behavior. *Journal of Personality and Social Psychology, 33,* 48–54.

Bemporad, J. R. (1988). Psychodynamic treatment of depressed adolescents. *Journal of Clinical Psychiatry, 49,* 26–31.

Benes, F. M., & Bird, E. D. (1987). An analysis of the arrangement of neurons in the cingulate cortex of schizophrenic patients. *Archives of General Psychiatry, 44,* 608–616.

Benesch, K. F., & Page, M. M. (1989). Self-construct systems and interpersonal congruence. *Journal of Personality, 57,* 139–173.

Benet, V., & Waller, N. G. (1995). The big seven factor model of personality description: Evidence for its cross-cultural generality in a Spanish sample. *Journal of Personality and Social Psychology, 69,* 701–718.

Benjamin, J. (1988). *The bonds of love: Psychoanalysis, feminism, and the problem of domination.* New York: Pantheon.

Bennett, M. (1996). Men's and women's self-estimates of intelligence. *Journal of Social Psychology, 136,* 411–412.

Bennett, P. (1993). Critical clitoridectomy: Female sexual imagery and feminist psychoanalytic theory. *Signs, 18,* 235–259.

Berenbaum, S. A., & Hines, M. (1992). Early androgens are related to childhood sex-typed toy preferences. *Psychological Science, 3,* 203–206.

Bergeman, C. S., Chipuer, H. M., Plomin, R., Pedersen, N. L., McClearn, G. E., Nesselroade, J. R., Costa, P. T., & McCrae, R. R. (1993). Genetic and environmental effects on openness to experience, agreeableness, and conscientiousness: An adoption/twin study. *Journal of Personality, 61,* 159–179.

Bergeman, C. S., Plomin, R., McClearn, G. E., Pederson, N. L., & Friberg, L. T. (1988). Genotype-environment interaction in personality development: Identical twins reared apart. *Psychology and Aging, 3,* 399–406.

Berger, R. J., & Oswald, I. (1962). Eye movements during active and passive dreams. *Science, 137,* 601.

Bergman, A., & Ellman, S. (1985). Margaret S. Mahler: Symbiosis and separation-individuation. In J. Reppen (Ed.), *Beyond Freud: A study of modern psychoanalytic theorists.* Hillsdale, NJ: Analytic Press.

Bernard, M. E., & DiGiuseppe, R. (1989). Rational-emotive therapy today. In M. E. Bernard & R. DiGiuseppe (Eds.), *Inside rational-emotive therapy: A critical appraisal of the theory and therapy of Albert Ellis.* San Diego: Academic Press.

Berry, D. S., & Brownlaw, S. (1989). Were the physiognomists right? *Personality and Social Psychology Bulletin, 15,* 266–279.

Bertrand, S., & Masling, J. M. (1969). Oral imagery and alcoholism. *Journal of Abnormal Psychology, 74,* 50–53.

Berzonsky, M. D. (1989). The self as a theorist: Individual differences in identity formation. *International Journal of Personal Construct Psychology, 2,* 363–376.

Berzonsky, M. D. (1990). Self-construction over the life span: A process perspective on identity formation. In G. J. Neimeyer & R. A. Neimeyer (Eds.), *Advances in personal construct psychology* (Vol. 1). Greenwich, CT: JAI Press.

Best, D. L., House, A. S., Barnard, A. E., & Spicker, B. S. (1994). Parent-child interactions in France, Germany, and Italy: The effects of gender and culture. *Journal of Cross-Cultural Psychology, 25,* 181–193.

Bettelheim, B. (1976). *The uses of enchantment.* New York: Knopf.

Biglan, A. (1993). Recapturing Skinner's legacy to behavior therapy. *The Behavior Therapist, 16,* 3–5.

Bigoness, W. J., Keef, K. M., & Du Bose, P. B. (1988). Perceived goal-difficulty, locus of control, and performance ratings. *Psychological Reports, 63,* 475–482.

Bion, W. R. (1965). Transformations. In *Seven serpents: Four works by Wilfred R. Bion.* New York: Jason Aronsen, (1977).

Birns, B. (1965). Individual differences in human neonates' responses to stimulation. *Child Development, 36,* 249–256.

Birns, B., & Meyer, S. L. (1993). Mothers' role in incest: Dysfunctional women or dysfunctional theories? *Journal of Child Sexual Abuse, 2,* 127–133.

Bjorkqvist, K. (1994). Sex differences in physical, verbal, and indirect aggression: A review of recent research. *Sex Roles, 30,* 177–188.

Bjorkqvist, K., Lagerspetz, K. M. J., & Kaukiainen, A. (1992). Do girls manipulate and boys fight? Developmental trends in regard to direct and indirect aggression. *Aggressive Behavior, 18,* 117–127.

Black, C., Bucky, S. & Wilder-Padilla, F. (1986). Interpersonal and emotional consequences of being an adult child of an alcoholic. *International Journal of the Addictions, 21,* 213–231.

Blake, J. (1989). Number of siblings and educational attainment. *Science, 245,* 32–36.

Blanck, G., & Blanck, R. (1974). *Ego psychology: Theory and practice.* New York: Columbia University Press.

Blaney, N. T. (1990). Type A, effort to excel, and attentional style in children: The validity of the MYTH. *Journal of Social Behavior and Personality, 5,* 159–182.

Blatt, S. J., & Lerner, H. (1983). Investigations in the psychoanalytic theory of object relations and object representations. In J. Masling (Ed.), *Empirical studies of psychoanalytic theories.* Hillsdale, NJ: Erlbaum.

Blight, J. G. (1988). Can psychology help reduce the risk of nuclear war? Reflections of a "Little Drummer Boy" of nuclear psychology. *Journal of Humanistic Psychology, 28,* 7–58.

Bloch, D. (1989). Freud's retraction of his seduction theory and the Schreber case. *The Psychoanalytic Review, 76,* 185–201.

Block, J. (1965). *The challenge of response sets.* New York: Appleton-Century-Crofts.

Block, J. (1995a). A contrarian view of the five-factor approach to personality description. *Psychological Bulletin, 117,* 187–215.

Block, J. (1995b). Going beyond the five factors given: Rejoinder to Costa and McCrae (1995) and Goldberg and Saucier (1995). *Psychological Bulletin, 117,* 226–229.

Block, J. H. (1983). Differential premises arising from differential socialization of the sexes: Some conjectures. *Child Development, 54,* 1335–1354.

Bloom, H. (Ed.). (1987). *The interpretation of dreams.* New York: Chelsea House.

Blume, E. S. (1990). *Secret survivors: Uncovering incest and its aftereffects in women.* New York: Ballantine.

Bly, R. (with W. Booth, Ed.). (1988). *A little book on the human shadow.* New York: Harper & Row.

Bode, L., Ferszt, R., & Czech, G. (1993). Borna disease virus infection and affective disorders in man. *Archives of Virology* (Suppl. 7), 159–167.

Bode, L., Riegel, S., Lange, W., & Ludwig, H. (1992). Human infections with Borna disease virus: Seroprevalence in patients with chronic diseases and healthy individuals. *Journal of Medical Vironlogy, 36,* 309–315.

Bohan, J. S. (1993). Regarding gender: Essentialism, constructionism, and feminist psychology. *Psychology of Women Quarterly, 17,* 5–21.

Bohart, A. C. (1990). Psychotherapy integration from a client-centered perspective. In G. Lietaer, J. Rombauts, & R. Van Balen (Eds.), *Client-centered and experiential psychotherapy in the nineties.* Leuven, Belgium: Leuven University Press.

Bohart, A. C. (1991a). Empathy in client-centered therapy: A contrast with psychoanalysis and self psychology. *Journal of Humanistic Psychology, 31,* 34–48.

Bohart, A. C. (1991b). The missing 249 words: In search of objectivity. *Psychotherapy, 28,* 497–503.

Boklage, C. E. (1977). Schizophrenia, brain asymmetry development, and twinning: Cellular relationship with etiological and possibly prognostic implications. *Biological Psychiatry, 12,* 19–35.

Bolger, N., Foster, M., Vinokur, A. D., & Ng, R. (1996). Close relationships and adjustment to a life crisis: The case of breast cancer. *Journal of Personality and Social Psychology, 70,* 283–294.

Bolger, N., & Schilling, E. A. (1991). Personality and the problems of everyday life: The role of neuroticism in exposure and reactivity to daily stressors. *Journal of Personality, 59,* 355–386.

Bolger, N., & Zuckerman, A. (1995). A framework for studying personality in the stress process. *Journal of Personality and Social Psychology, 69,* 890–902.

Bolla-Wilson, K., Robinson, R. G., Starkstein, S. E., Boston, J., & Price, T. R. (1989). Lateralization of dementia of depression in stroke patients. *American Journal of Psychiatry, 146,* 627–634.

Bonarius, H. (1984). Personal construct psychology: Reappraisal of basic theory and its application. In H. Bonarius, G. Van Heck, & N. Smid (Eds.), *Personality psychology in Europe: Theoretical and empirical developments.* Lisse: Swets & Zeitlinger.

Boone, C., De Brabander, B., Gerits, P., & Willeme, P. (1990). Relation of scores on Rotter's I-E scale to short-term and long-term control expectancies and fatalism. *Psychological Reports, 66,* 1107–1111.

Boose, J. H. (1985). A knowledge acquisition program for expert systems based on personal construct psychology. *International Journal of Man-Machine Studies, 23,* 495–525.

Booth-Kewley, S., & Vickers, R. R., Jr. (in press). Associations between major domains of personality and health behavior. *Journal of Personality.*

Bootzin, R. R. (1985). Insomnia. In M. Hersen & C. G. Last (Eds.), *Behavior therapy casebook.* New York: Springer.

Bordages, J. W. (1989). Self-actualization and personal autonomy. *Psychological Reports, 64,* 1263–1266.

Borkenau, P. (1988). The multiple classification of acts and the big five factors of personality. *Journal of Research in Personality, 22,* 337–352.

Bornstein, R. F., & Masling, J. (1985). Orality and latency of volunteering to serve as experimental subjects: A replication. *Journal of Personality Assessment, 49,* 306–310.

Boscolo, P., & de Bernardi, B. (1992). Writing as a meaningful activity. *International Journal of Personal Construct Psychology, 5,* 341–353.

Boss, M. W., & Taylor, M. C. (1989). The relationship between locus of control and academic level and sex of secondary school students. *Contemporary Educational Psychology, 14,* 315–322.

Botella, L. (1991). Psychoeducational groups with older adults: An integrative personal construct rationale and some guidelines. *International Journal of Personal Construct Psychology, 4,* 397–408.

Bottome, P. (1957). *Alfred Adler: A portrait from life.* New York: Vanguard.

Bouchard, T. J., Lykken, D. T., McGue, M., Segal, N. L., & Tellegen, A. (1990). Sources of human psychological differences: The Minnesota study of twins reared apart. *Science, 250,* 223–228.

Bouchard, T. J., & McGue, M. (1990). Genetic and rearing environmental influences on adult personality: An analysis of adult twins reared apart. *Journal of Personality, 58,* 263–292.

Boudin, H. M. (1972). Contingency contracting as a therapeutic tool in decelerating amphetamine use. *Behavior Therapy, 3,* 602–608.

Bouffard-Bouchard, T., Parent, S., & Larivee, S. (1991). Influence of self-efficacy on self-regulation and performance among junior and senior high-school age students. *International Journal of Behavioral Development, 14,* 153–164.

Boy, A. V. (1990). The therapist in person-centered groups. *Person-Centered Review, 5,* 308–315.

Bozarth, J. D. (1984). Beyond reflection: Emergent modes of empathy. In R. F. Levant & J. M. Shlien (Eds.), *Client-centered therapy and the person-centered approach: New directions in theory, research, and practice.* New York: Praeger.

Bozarth, J. D. (1990). The evolution of Carl Rogers as a therapist [Special issue: Fiftieth anniversary of the person-centered approach]. *Person-Centered Review, 5,* 387–393.

Bozarth, J. D. (1991). Person-centered assessment. *Journal of Counseling and Development, 69,* 458–461.

Bozarth, J. D., & Brodley, B. T. (1991). Actualization: A functional concept in client-centered therapy [Special issue: Handbook of self-actualization]. *Journal of Social Behavior and Personality, 6,* 45–59.

Bozarth, J. D., & Shanks, A. (1989). Person-centered family therapy with couples [Special issue: Person-centered approaches with families]. *Person-Centered Review, 4,* 280–294.

Bradbury, T. N., & Miller, G. A. (1985). Season of birth in schizophrenia: A review of evidence, methodology, and etiology. *Psychological Bulletin, 98,* 569–594.

Brafford, L. J., & Beck, K. H. (1991). Development and validation of a condom self-efficacy scale for college students. *Journal of American College Health, 39,* 219–225.

Bramel, D. (1963). Selection of a target for defensive projection. *Journal of Abnormal and Social Psychology, 66,* 318–324.

Brand, C. R., & Egan, V. (1989). The "Big Five" dimensions of personality? Evidence from ipsative, adjectival self-attributions. *Personality and Individual Differences, 10,* 1165–1171.

Brandon, J. E., & Loftin, J. M. (1991). Relationship of fitness to depression, state and trait anxiety, internal health locus of control, and self-control. *Perceptual and Motor Skills, 73,* 563–568.

Brandstadter, J. (1992). Personal control over development: Implications of self-efficacy. In R. Schwarzer (Ed.), *Self-efficacy: Thought control of action.* Washington, DC: Hemisphere.

Brannigan, G. G., Hauk, P. A., & Guay, J. A. (1991). Locus of control and daydreaming. *Journal of Genetic Psychology, 152,* 29–33.

Brant, J. (1988, March). Typecasting. *Outside,* pp. 33–35.

Bray, J. H. (1988). Children's development during early remarriage. In E. M. Hetherington & J. D. Arasteh (Eds.), *Impact of divorce, single parenting and stepparenting on children.* Hillsdale, NJ: Erlbaum.

Breger, L., & McGaugh, J. L. (1966). Learning theory and behavior therapy: A reply to Rachman and Eysenck. *Psychological Bulletin, 65,* 170–173.

Breier, A., Buchanan, R. W., Elkashef, A., Munson, R. C., Kirkpatrick, B., & Gellad, F. (1992). Brain morphology and schizophrenia: A magnetic resonance imaging study of limbic prefrontal cortex, and caudate structures. *Archives of General Psychiatry, 49,* 921–926.

Brennan, T. P., & Piechowski, M. M. (1991). A developmental framework for self-actualization: Evidence from case studies. *Journal of Humanistic Psychology, 31,* 43–64.

Breuer, J., & Freud, S. (1955). Studies in hysteria. In J. Strachey (Ed. and Trans.), *The standard edition of the complete psychological works of Sigmund Freud* (Vol. 2). London: Hogarth. (Original work published, 1893–1895).

Brickman, B. (1988). Psychoanalysis and substance abuse: Toward a more effective approach. *Journal of the American Academy of Psychoanalysis, 16,* 359–379.

Briggs, S. R. (1989). The optimal level of measurement for personality constructs. In D. M. Buss & N. Cantor (Eds.), *Personality psychology: Recent trends and emerging directions.* New York: Springer-Verlag.

Briggs, S. R., Cheek, J. M., & Buss, A. H. (1980). An analysis of the Self-Monitoring Scale. *Journal of Personality and Social Psychology, 38,* 679–686.

Brokaw, D. W., & McLemore, C. W. (1991). Interpersonal models of personality and psychopathology. In D. G. Gilbert & J. J. Connolly (Eds.), *Personality, social skills, and psychopathology: An individual differences approach.* New York: Plenum.

Bronstein, P. (1994). Patterns of parent-child interaction in Mexican families: A cross-cultural perspective. *International Society for the Study of Behavioral Development, 17,* 423–446.

Brown, J. D. (1991). Accuracy and bias in self-knowledge. In C. R. Snyder & D. F. Forsyth (Eds.), *Handbook of social and clinical psychology: The health perspective.* New York: Pergamon Press.

Brown, J. D. (1993). Motivational conflict and the self: The double-bind of low self-esteem. In R. F. Baumeister (Ed.), *Self-esteem: The puzzle of low self-regard.* New York: Plenum.

Brown, J. D., & Smart, S. A. (1991). The self and social conduct: Linking self-representations to prosocial behavior. *Journal of Personality and Social Psychology, 60,* 368–375.

Brown, N. O. (1959). *Life against death.* New York: Random House.

Brown, P., Perry, L., & Harburg, E. (1977). Sex role attitudes and psychological outcomes for black and white women experiencing marital dissolution. *Journal of Marriage and the Family, 39,* 549–561.

Brown, R. (1965). *Social psychology.* New York: Free Press.

Bruhn, A. R. (1990). Cognitive-perceptual theory and the projective use of autobiographical memory. *Journal of Personality Assessment, 55,* 95–114.

Bruner, J. S. (1956). A cognitive theory of personality. *Contemporary Psychology, 1,* 355–356.

Buchsbaum, M. S., & Haier, R. J. (1987). Functional and anatomical brain imaging: Impact on schizophrenia research. *Schizophrenia Bulletin, 13,* 115–132.

Buchsbaum, M. S., Haier, R. J., Potkin, S. G., Nuechterlein, K., Bracha, H. S., Katz, M., Lohr, J., Wu, J., Lottenberg, S., Jerabek, P. A., Trenary, M.,

Tafalla, R., Reynolds, C., & Bunney, W. E., Jr. (1992). Frontostriatal disorder of cerebral metabolism in never-medicated schizophrenics. *Archives of General Psychiatry, 49,* 935–942.

Buie, J. (1988, November). Psychoanalysis barriers tumble: Settlement opens door to non-MDs. *APA Monitor,* pp. 1, 15.

Buie, J. (1989a, January). Questions linger in analysis settlement. *APA Monitor,* p. 18.

Buie, J. (1989b, January). Traditional analysis may be changing. *APA Monitor,* p. 19.

Bullock, W. A., & Gilliland, K. (1993). Eysenck's arousal theory of introversion-extraversion: A converging measures investigation. *Journal of Personality and Social Psychology, 64,* 113–123.

Bullough, V. L., & Ruan, F. F. (1994). Marriage, divorce, and sexual relations in contemporary China. *Journal of Comparative Family Studies, 25,* 383–393.

Bunch, J. M., & Schneider, H. G. (1991). Smoking-specific locus of control. *Psychological Reports, 69,* 1075–1081.

Burack, C. (1995a). Mind-mending and theory building: Lesbian feminism and the psychology question. *Feminism and Psychology, 5,* 495–510.

Burack, C. (1995b). True or false: The stratified self in lesbian feminist theory. *Feminism and Psychology, 5,* 329–344.

Burbank, V. K. (1994). Cross-cultural perspectives on aggression in women and girls: An introduction. *Sex Roles, 30,* 169–175.

Burke, M., Noller, P., & Caird, D. (1992). Transition from practitioner to educator: A repertory grid analysis. *International Journal of Personal Construct Psychology, 5,* 159–182.

Burke, R. J. (1988). Type A behavior, occupational and life demands, satisfaction, and well-being. *Psychological Reports, 63,* 451–458.

Burnham, J. C. (1968). Historical background for the study of personality. In E. F. Borgatta & W. W. Lambert (Eds.), *Handbook of personality theory and research.* Chicago: Rand McNally.

Burnstein, E., Crandall, C., & Kitayama, S. (1994). Some neo-Darwinian decision rules for altruism: Weighing cues for inclusive fitness as a function of the biological importance of the decision. *Journal of Personality and Social Psychology, 67,* 773–789.

Buros, O. K. (Ed.). (1965). *The sixth mental measurements yearbook.* Highland Park, NJ: Gryphon Press.

Buros, O. K. (Ed.). (1972). *The seventh mental measurements yearbook.* Highland Park, NJ: Gryphon Press.

Burr, V., & Butt, T. (1989). A personal construct view of hypnosis. *British Journal of Experimental and Clinical Hypnosis, 6,* 85–90.

Burwick, S., & Knapp, R. R. (1991). Advances in research using the Personal Orientation Inventory [Special issue: Handbook of self-actualization]. *Journal of Social Behavior and Personality, 6,* 311–320.

Buss, A. H. (1989). Personality as traits. *American Psychologist, 44,* 1378–1388.

Buss, A. H., & Plomin, R. (1984a). *A temperament theory of personality development* (Rev. ed.). New York: Wiley.

Buss, A. H., & Plomin, R. (1984b). *Temperament: Early developing personality traits.* Hillsdale, NJ: Erlbaum.

Buss, A. H., Plomin, R., & Willerman, L. (1973). The inheritance of temperaments. *Journal of Personality, 41,* 513–524.

Buss, D. M. (1985). Human mate selection. *American Scientist, 73,* 47–51.

Buss, D. M. (1988). The evolution of human intrasexual competition: Tactics of mate attraction. *Journal of Personality and Social Psychology, 54,* 616–628.

Buss, D. M. (1989). Sex differences in human mate preferences: Evolutionary hypotheses tested in 37 cultures. *Behavioral and Brain Sciences, 12,* 1–49.

Buss, D. M., & Craik, K. H. (1985). Why not measure that trait? Alternative criteria for identifying important dispositions. *Journal of Personality and Social Psychology, 48,* 934–946.

Buss, D. M., & Schmitt, D. P. (1993). Sexual strategies theory: An evolutionary perspective on human mating. *Psychological Review, 100,* 204–232.

Butcher, J. N. (1979). Use of the MMPI in personnel selection. In J. N. Butcher (Ed.), *New developments in the use of the MMPI.* Minneapolis: University of Minnesota Press.

Butcher, J. N., Graham, J. R., Dahlstrom, W. G., & Bowman, E. (1990). The MMPI-2 with college students. *Journal of Personality Assessment, 54,* 1–15.

Butler, G., Fennell, M., Robson, P., & Gelder, M. (1991). Comparison of behavior therapy and cognitive behavior therapy in the treatment of generalized anxiety disorder. *Journal of Consulting and Clinical Psychology, 59,* 167–175.

Byravan, A., & Ramanaiah, N. V. (1995). Structure of the 16 PF fifth edition from the perspective of the five-factor model. *Psychological Reports, 76,* 555–560.

Byrnes, K. D., & Lester, D. (1995). The imposter phenomenon in teachers and accountants. *Psychological Reports, 77,* 350.

Cacioppo, J. T., Petty, R. E., Feinstein, J. A., & Jarvis, B. G. (1996). Dispositional differences in cognitive motivation: The life and times of individuals varying in need for cognition. *Psychological Bulletin, 119,* 197–253.

Cain, D. J. (1989). From the individual to the family [Special issue: Person-centered approaches with families]. *Person-Centered Review, 4,* 248–255.

Cain, D. J. (1990a). Celebration, reflection and renewal: 50 years of client-centered therapy and beyond [Special issue: Fiftieth anniversary of the person-centered approach]. *Person-Centered Review, 5,* 357–363.

Cain, D. J. (1990b). Further thoughts about nondirectiveness and client-centered therapy. *Person-Centered Review, 5,* 89–99.

Caldwell, M. A., & Peplau, L. A. (1982). Sex differences in same-sex friendship. *Sex Roles, 8,* 721–732.

Caliso, J. A., & Milner, J. S. (1994). Childhood physical abuse, childhood social support, and adult child abuse potential. *Journal of Interpersonal Violence, 9,* 27–44.

Camp, B. W., & Bash, M. A. S. (1981). *Think aloud: Increasing social and cognitive skills—A problem-solving program for children (primary level).* Champaign, IL: Research Press.

Campbell, D. T., & Fiske, D. W. (1959). Convergent and discriminant validation by the multitrait-multimethod matrix. *Psychological Bulletin, 56,* 81–105.

Campbell, J. (1988). *The power of myth.* New York: Doubleday.

Campbell, J. D., & Lavallee, L. F. (1993). Who am I? The role of self-concept confusion in understanding the behavior of people with low self-esteem. In R. F. Baumeister (Ed.), *Self-esteem: The puzzle of low self-regard.* New York: Plenum.

Campbell, J. D., Trapnell, P. D., Heine, S. J., Katz, I. M., Lavallee, L. F., & Lehman, D. R. (1996). Self-concept clarity: Measurement, personality correlates, and cultural boundaries. *Journal of Personality and Social Psychology, 70,* 141–156.

Canary, D. J., Cunningham, E. M., & Cody, M. J. (1988). Goal types, gender, and locus of control in managing interpersonal conflict. *Communication Research, 15,* 426–446.

Cantor, D. W., & Bernay, T. (1988). *Psychology of today's women: New psychoanalytic visions.* Hillsdale, NJ: Analytic Press.

Cantor, N. (1990). From thought to behavior: "Having" and "doing" in the study of personality and cognition. *American Psychologist, 45,* 735–750.

Cantor, N., & Kihlstrom, J. F. (1987). *Personality and social intelligence.* Englewood Cliffs, NJ: Prentice-Hall.

Cantwell, D. P. (1972). Psychiatric illness in the families of hyperactive children. *Archives of General Psychiatry, 27,* 414–417.

Caputi, M. (1993). The maternal metaphor in feminist scholarship. *Political Psychology, 14,* 309–329.

Caputi, P., Breiger, R., & Pattison, P. (1990). Analyzing implications grids using hierarchical models. *International Journal of Personal Construct Psychology, 3,* 77–90.

Carlton, D. E., & Skowronski, J. J. (1994). Savings in the relearning of trait information as evidence for spontaneous inference generation. *Journal of Personality and Social Psychology, 66,* 840–856.

Carnelley, K. B., Pietromonaco, P. R., & Jaffe, K. (1994). Depression, working models of others, and relationship functioning. *Journal of Personality and Social Psychology, 66,* 127–140.

Carr, E. G. (1993). Behavior analysis is not ultimately about behavior. *The Behavior Analyst, 16,* 47–49.

Carr, E. G. (1994). Emerging themes in the functional analysis of problem behavior. *Journal of Applied Behavior Analysis, 2,* 393–399.

Carr, E. G. (1996). The transfiguration of behavior analysis: Strategies for survival. *Journal of Behavioral Education, 6,* 263–270.

Carroll, L. (1987). A study of narcissism, affiliation, intimacy, and power motives among students in business administration. *Psychological Reports, 61,* 355–358.

Carson, R. C. (1989). Personality. *Annual Review of Psychology, 40,* 227–248.

Carter, M., Day, W. K., & Francis, L. J. (1996). Personality and attitude toward Christianity among committed adult Christians. *Personality and Individual Differences, 20,* 265–266.

Cartwright, D., DeBruin, J., & Berg, S. (1991). Some scales for assessing personality based on Carl Rogers' theory: Further evidence of validity. *Personality and Individual Differences, 12,* 151–156.

Cartwright, D., & Mori, C. (1988). Scales for assessing aspects of the person. *Person-Centered Review, 3,* 176–194.

Cartwright, R. D., & Ratzel, R. (1972). Effects of dream loss on waking behaviors. *Archives of General Psychiatry, 27,* 277–280.

Carver, C. S. & White, T. L. (1994). Behavioral inhibition, behavioral activation, and affective responses to impending reward and punishment: The BIS/BAS Scales. *Journal of Personality and Social Psychology, 67,* 319–333.

Cashdan, S. (1973). *Interactional psychotherapy: Stages and strategies in behavioral change.* New York: Grune & Stratton.

Cashdan, S. (1988). *Object relations therapy: Using the relationship.* New York: Norton.

Caspi, A., Elder, G. H., & Bem, D. J. (1988). Moving away from the world: Life-course patterns of shy children. *Developmental Psychology, 24,* 824–831.

Castorina, M., & Mancini, F. (1992). Construct system as a knowing system. *International Journal of Personal Construct Psychology, 5,* 271–293.

Cattell, R. B. (1965). *The scientific analysis of personality.* Baltimore: Penguin.

Cattell, R. B. (1979). *Personality and learning theory* (Vol. 1). New York: Springer.

Cattell, R. B., & Kline, P. (1977). *The scientific analysis of personality and motivation.* New York: Academic Press.

Cattell, R. B., & Warburton, F. W. (1967). *Objective personality and motivation tests: A theoretical introduction and practical compendium.* Urbana: University of Illinois Press.

Celiberti, D. A., Alessandri, M., Fong, P. L., & Weiss, M. J. (1993). A history of the behavioral treatment of autism. *The Behavior Therapist, 16,* 127–132.

Celuch, K., & Slama, M. (1995). "Getting along" and "getting ahead" as motives for self-presentation: Their impact on advertising effectiveness. *Journal of Applied Social Psychology, 25,* 1700–1713.

Centerwell, B. S. (1989). Exposure to television as a cause of violence. In G. Comstock (Ed.), *Public communication and behavior* (Vol. 2). San Diego: Academic Press.

Cernovsky, Z. Z. (1988). A failure of the MMPI validity scale to detect random responding. *Psychological Reports, 62,* 930.

Cervone, D. (1989). Effects of envisioning future activities on self-efficacy judgments and motivation: An availability heuristic interpretation. *Cognitive Therapy and Research, 13,* 247–261.

Chambers, W. V. (1985). Personal construct integrative complexity and the credulous approach. *Psychological Reports, 57,* 1202.

Chambless, D. L., & Gillis, M. M. (1993). Cognitive therapy of anxiety disorders. *Journal of Consulting and Clinical Psychology, 61,* 248–260.

Charlop, M. H., & Milstein, J. P. (1989). Teaching autistic children conversational speech using video modeling. *Journal of Applied Behavior Analysis, 22,* 275–285.

Chase, M. H., & Morales, F. R. (1990). The atonia and myoclonia of active (REM) sleep. *Annual Review of Psychology, 41,* 557–584.

Cheyne, J. A. (1971). Effects of imitation of different reinforcement combinations to a model. *Journal of Experimental Child Psychology, 12,* 258–269.

Chia, R. C., Wuensch, K. L., Childers, J., Chuang, C., Cheng, B., Cesar-Romero, J., & Nava, S. (1994). A comparison of family values among Chinese, Mexican, and American college students. *Journal of Social Behavior and Personality, 9,* 249–258.

Chiang, H., & Maslow, A. H. (Eds.). (1977). *The healthy personality: Readings* (2nd ed.). New York: Van Nostrand.

Chiari, G., Mancini, F., Nicolo, F., & Nuzzo, M. L. (1990). Hierarchical organization of personal construct systems in terms of the range of convenience. *International Journal of Personal Construct Psychology, 3,* 281–311.

Chiu, C., Hong, Y., Mischel, W., & Shoda, Y. (1995). Discriminative facility in social competence: Conditional versus dispositional encoding and monitoring-blunting of information. *Social Cognition, 13,* 49–70.

Chodorow, N. (1989). *Feminism and psychoanalytic theory.* New Haven: Yale University Press.

Chodorow, N. J. (1995). Gender as a personal and cultural construction. *Signs, 20,* 516–544.

Christianson, S. A. (1992). Do flashbulb memories differ from other types of emotional memories? In E. Winograd & U. Neisser (Eds.), *Affect and accuracy in recall: Studies of "flashbulb" memories.* New York: Cambridge University Press.

Churchland, P. M., & Churland, P. S. (1990). Could a machine think? *Scientific American, 262,* 32–37.

Clair, S., & Preston, J. M. (1990). Integration in personal constructs of television. *International Journal of Personal Construct Psychology, 3,* 377–391.

Clark, M. M., Abrams, D. B., Niaura, R. S., Eaton, C. A., & Rossi, J. S. (1991). Self-efficacy in weight management. *Journal of Consulting and Clinical Psychology, 59,* 739–744.

Clarke, S. G., & Haworth, J. T. (1994). 'Flow' experience in the daily lives of sixth-form college students. *British Journal of Psychology, 85,* 511–523.

Cloninger, C. R. (1987). A systematic method of clinical description and classification of personality variants: A proposal. *Archives of General Psychiatry, 44,* 573–588.

Coan, R. W. (1991). Self-actualization and the quest for the ideal human. [Special issue: Handbook of self-actualization]. *Journal of Social Behavior and Personality, 6,* 127–136.

Cohen, D. (1987). *The development of play.* New York: New York University Press.

Cohen, S., & Syme, S. L. (Eds.). (1985). *Social support and health.* San Diego, CA: Academic Press.

Cohen, S., & Wills, T. A. (1985). Stress, social support, and the buffering hypothesis. *Psychological Bulletin, 98,* 310–357.

Colarusso, C. A., & Nemiroff, R. A. (1979). Some observations and hypotheses about the psychoanalytic theory of adult development. *International Journal of Psycho-Analysis, 60,* 59–71.

Coleman, J. (1990). *Foundations of social theory.* Cambridge, MA: Bellknap Press.

Coleman, J. S. (1988). Social capital in the creation of human capital. *American Journal of Sociology, 94,* 95–120.

Coles, R. (1989). *The call of stories: Teaching and the moral imagination.* Boston: Houghton Mifflin.

Collett, P. (1971). On training Englishmen in the non-verbal behavior of Arabs: An experiment in inter-cultural communication. *International Journal of Psychology, 6,* 209–215.

Colligan, R. C., & Offord, K. P. (1987). The MacAndrew alcoholism scale applied to a contemporary normative sample. *Journal of Clinical Psychology, 43,* 291–293.

Colligan, R. C., & Offord, K. P. (1988). The risky use of the MMPI hostility scale in assessing risk for coronary heart disease. *Psychosomatics, 29,* 188–196.

Colligan, R. C., Osborne, D., Swenson, W. M., & Offord, K. P. (1984). The aging MMPI: Development of contemporary norms. *Mayo Clinic Proceedings, 59,* 377–390.

Collins, N. L., & Reed, S. J. (1990). Adult attachment, working models, and relationship quality in dating couples. *Journal of Personality and Social Psychology, 58,* 644–663.

Comer, R. J. (1992). *Abnormal psychology.* New York: Freeman.

Comrey, A. L. (1973). *A first course in factor analysis.* New York: Academic Press.

Cone, A. L., & Owens, S. K. (1991). Academic and locus of control enhancement in a freshman study skills and college adjustment course. *Psychological Reports, 68,* 1211–1217.

Conley, J. J. (1984). Longitudinal consistency of adult personality: Self-reported psychological characteristics across 45 years. *Journal of Personality and Social Psychology, 47,* 1325–1333.

Constantinople, A. (1973). Masculinity-femininity: An exception to a famous dictum? *Psychological Bulletin, 80,* 389–407.

Conway, M., & Giannopoulos, C. (1993). Dysphoria and decision making: Limited information use for evaluations of multiattribute targets. *Journal of Personality and Social Psychology, 64,* 613–623.

Cooke, D. K., Sims, R. L., & Peyrefitte, J. (1995). The relationship between graduate student attitudes and attrition. *The Journal of Psychology, 129,* 677–688.

Coolidge, F. L., Becker, L. A., DiRito, D. C., Curham, R. L., Kinlaw, M. M., & Philbrick, P. B. (1994). On the relationship of the five-factor personality model to personality disorders: Four reservations. *Psychological Reports, 75,* 11–21.

Cooper, A. M. (1985). Will neurobiology influence psychoanalysis? *American Journal of Psychiatry, 142,* 1395–1402.

Cooper, A. M. (1990). The future of psychoanalysis: Challenges and opportunities. *Psychoanalytic Quarterly, 54,* 177–196.

Cooper, H., Okamura, L., & McNeil, P. (1995). Situation and personality correlates of psychological well-being: Social activity and personal control. *Journal of Research in Personality, 29,* 395–417.

Cooper, S. H. (1988). Recent contributions to the theory of defense mechanisms: A comparative view. *Journal of the American Psychoanalytic Association, 37,* 865–891.

Corcoran, K., & Fischer, J. (1987). *Measures for clinical practice.* New York: The Free Press.

Corda, M. G., Blaker, W. D., Mendelson, W. B., Guidotti, A., & Costa, E. (1983). Beta-carbolines enhance shock-induced suppression of drinking in rats. *Proceedings of the National Academy of Sciences, U.S.A., 80,* 2072–2076.

Costa, P. T., & McCrae, R. R. (1988a). From catalog to classification: Murray's needs and the five-factor model. *Journal of Personality and Social Psychology, 55,* 258–265.

Costa, P. T., & McCrae, R. R. (1988b). Personality in adulthood: A six-year longitudinal study of self-reports and spouse ratings on the NEO personality inventory. *Journal of Personality and Social Psychology, 54,* 853–863.

Costa, P. T., & McCrae, R. R. (1990). Personality disorders and the five factor model of personality. *Journal of Personality Disorders, 4,* 362–371.

Costa, P. T., & McCrae, R. R. (1992). *NEO-PI-R professional manual.* Odessa, FL: Psychological Assessment Resources.

Costa, P. T., & McCrae, R. R. (1992a). Normal personality assessment in clinical practice: The NEO Personality Inventory. *Psychological Assessment: A Journal of Consulting and Clinical Psychology, 4,* 5–13.

Costa, P. T., & McCrae, R. R. (1992b). Reply to Eysenck. *Personality and Individual Differences, 13,* 861–865.

Costa, P. T., & McCrae, R. R. (1995a). Domains and facets: Hierarchical personality assessment using the revised NEO personality inventory. *Journal of Personality Assessment, 64,* 21–50.

Costa, P. T., & McCrae, R. R. (1995b). Primary traits of Eysenck's P-E-N system: Three-and-five-factor solutions. *Journal of Personality and Social Psychology, 69,* 308–317.

Costa, P. T., & McCrae, R. R. (1995c). Solid ground in the wetlands of personality: A reply to Block. *Psychological Bulletin, 117,* 216–220.

Costa, P. T., & McCrae, R. R. (1997).

Costa, P. T., McCrae, R. R., & Dye, D. (1991). Facet scales for agreeableness and conscientiousness: A revision of the NEO Personality Inventory. *Personality and Individual Differences, 12,* 887–898.

Costa, P. T., & Widiger, T. A. (1994). Summary and unresolved issues. In P. T. Costa & T. A. Widiger (Eds.), *Personality disorders and the five-factor model of personality.* Washington, DC: American Psychological Association.

Cote, J. E., & Levine, C. G. (1989). An empirical test of Erikson's theory of ego identity formation. *Youth & Society, 20,* 388–415.

Cottraux, J. (1990). "Cogito ergo sum": Cognitive-behavior therapy in France. *the Behavior Therapist, 13,* 189–190.

Courtney, A. E., & Whipple, T. W. (1983). *Sex stereotyping in advertising.* Lexington, MA: Lexington Books.

Cowen, E. L., Work, W. C., Hightower, A. D., Wyman, P. A., Parker, G. R., & Lotyczewski, B. S. (1991). Toward the development of a measure of perceived self-efficacy in children. *Journal of Clinical Child Psychology, 20,* 169–178.

Craighead, W. E. (1990a). The changing nature of behavior therapy. *Behavior Therapy, 21,* 1–2.

Craighead, W. E. (1990b). There's a place for us: All of us. *Behavior Therapy, 21,* 3–23.

Craigie, F. C., Jr., & Houde, K. A. (1992). Religious involvement in behavior therapy training. *the Behavior Therapist, 15,* 59–81.

Crain, W. C. (1980). *Theories of development.* Englewood Cliffs, NJ: Prentice-Hall.

Cramer, P. (1987). The development of defense mechanisms. *Journal of Personality, 55,* 597–614.

Cramer, P., & Gaul, R. (1988). The effects of success and failure on children's use of defense mechanisms. *Journal of Personality, 56,* 729–742.

Crandall, R., & Jones, A. (1991). Issues in self-actualization measurement. [Special issue: Handbook of self-actualization] *Journal of Social Behavior and Personality, 6,* 339–344.

Crandall, V. J., Dewey, R., Katkovsky, W., & Preston, A. (1964). Parents' attitudes and behaviors and grade-school children's academic achievement. *Journal of Genetic Psychology, 104,* 53–66.

Crawford, C. J. (1994). Parenting practices in the Basque Country: Implications of infant and childhood sleeping location for personality development. *Ethos, 22,* 42–82.

Crawford, H. J., & Strapp, C. M. (1994). Effects of vocal and instrumental music on visuospatial and verbal performance as moderated by studying preference and personality. *Personality and Individual Differences, 16,* 237–245.

Crevier, D. (1993). *AI.* New York: Basic Books.

Crick, N. R., & Dodge, K. A. (1994). A review and reformulation of social information-processing mechanisms in children's social adjustment. *Psychological Bulletin, 115,* 74–101.

Cronbach, L. J. (1949). Statistical methods applied to Rorschach scores: A review. *Psychological Bulletin, 46,* 393–429.

Crystal, D. S., Chen, C., Fuligni, A. J., Stevenson, H. W., Hsu, C., Ko, H., Kitamura, S., & Kimura, S. (1994). Psychological maladjustment and academic achievement: A cross-cultural study of Japanese, Chinese, and American high school students. *Child Development, 65,* 738–753.

Csikszentmihalyi, M. (1990). *Flow: The psychology of optimal experience.* New York: Harper & Row.

Culp, R. E., Culp, A. M., Osofsky, J. D., & Osofsky, H. J. (1991). Adolescent and older mothers' interaction patterns with their six month old infants. *Journal of Adolescence, 14,* 195–200.

Cummins, P. (1992). Reconstruing the experience of sexual abuse. *International Journal of Personal Construct Psychology, 5,* 355–365.

Cummins, R. C. (1988). Perceptions of social support, receipt of supportive behaviors, and locus of control as moderators of the effects of chronic stress. *American Journal of Community Psychology, 16,* 685–700.

Cunningham, A. J., Lockwood, G. A., & Cunningham, J. A. (1991). A relationship between perceived self-efficacy and quality of life in cancer patients. *Patient Education and Counseling, 17,* 71–78.

Cutrona, C. E., Cole, V., Colangelo, N., Assouline, S. G., & Russell, D. W. (1994). Perceived parental social support and academic achievement: An attachment theory perspective. *Journal of Personality and Social Psychology, 66,* 369–378.

Cutter, H. S. G., Boyatzis, R. E., & Clancy, D. D. (1977). The effectiveness of power motivation training in rehabilitating alcoholics. *Journal of Studies on Alcohol, 38,* 131–141.

Dabbs, J. M., Jr., Jurkovic, G. J., & Frady, R. L. (1991). Salivary testosterone and cortisol among late adolescent male offenders. *Journal of Abnormal Child Psychology, 19,* 469–478.

Dabbs, J. M., Frady, R. L., Carr, T. S., & Besch, N. F. (1987). Saliva testosterone and criminal violence in young adult prison inmates. *Psychosomatic Medicine, 49,* 174–182.

Dabbs, J. M., Jr., & Morris, R. (1990). Testosterone, social class, and antisocial behavior in a sample of 4,462 men. *Psychological Science, 1,* 209–211.

Daecon, T. W. (1992). Brain-language coevolution. In J. A. Hawkins & M. Gell-Mann (Eds.), *The Evolution of Human Languages.* Reading, MA: Addison-Wesley.

Dahlstrom, W. G. (1980). Screening for emotional fitness: The Jersey City case. In W. G. Dahlstrom & L. Dahlstrom (Eds.), *Basic readings on the MMPI: A new selection on personality measurement.* Minneapolis: University of Minnesota Press.

Daly, M., & Wilson, M. (1990). Killing the competition: Female/female and male/male homicide. *Human Nature, 1,* 81–107.

Damon, A. (1955). Physique and success in military flying. *American Journal of Physical Anthropology, 13,* 217–252.

Daniels, D., & Plomin, R. (1984). Origins of individual differences in infant shyness. *Developmental Psychology, 21,* 118–121.

Daniels, M. (1988). The myth of self-actualization. *Journal of Humanistic Psychology, 28,* 7–38.

Dapcich-Miura, E., & Hovell, M. F. (1979). Contingency management of adherence to a complex medical regimen in an elderly heart patient. *Behavior Therapy, 10,* 193–201.

Dardenne, B., & Leyens, J. (1995). Confirmation bias as a social skill. *Personality and Social Psychology Bulletin, 21,* 1229–1239.

Daro, D. (1988). *Confronting child abuse.* New York: Free Press.

Darwin, C. (1952). The origin of species by means of natural selection and The descent of man and selection in relation to sex. In R. M. Hutchins (Ed.), *Great Books of the Western World* (Vol. 49). Chicago: William Benton.

Dattilio, F. M., & Padesky, C. A. (1990). *Cognitive therapy with couples.* Sarasota, FL: Professional Resource Exchange.

Davey, G. C. L. (1989a). Dental phobias and anxieties: Evidence for conditioning processes in the acquisition and modulation of a learned fear. *Behaviour Research and Therapy, 27,* 51–58.

Davey, G. C. L. (1989b). UCS revaluation and conditioning models of acquired fears. *Behaviour Research and Therapy, 27,* 521–528.

Davidson, R. J. (1984). Affect, cognition, and hemispheric specialization. In C. E. Izard, J. Kagan, & R. B. Zajonc (Eds.), *Emotions, cognition, & behavior.* Cambridge: Cambridge University Press.

Davidson, R. J. (1992). Prolegomenon to the structure of emotion: Gleanings from neuropsychology. *Cognition and Emotion, 6,* 245–268.

Davidson, R. J., Ekman, P., Saron, C. D., Senulis, J. A., & Friesen, W. V. (1990). Approach-withdrawal and cerebral asymmetry: Emotional expression and brain physiology I. *Journal of Personality and Social Psychology, 58,* 330–341.

Davis, C., & Cowles, M. (1988). A laboratory study of temperament and arousal: A test of Gale's hypothesis. *Journal of Research in Personality, 22,* 101–116.

Davis, J., Lockwood, L., & Wright, C. (1991). Reasons for not reporting peak experiences. *Journal of Humanistic Psychology, 31,* 86–94.

Davis, L. (1991). Murdered memory. *In Health, 5,* 79–84.

Davis, L. J., Colligan, R. C., Morse, R. M., & Offord,

K. P. (1987). Validity of the MacAndrew scale in a general medical population. *Journal of Studies on Alcohol, 48,* 202–206.

Davis, P. J., & Schwartz, G. E. (1987). Repression and the inaccessibility of affective memories. *Journal of Personality and Social Psychology, 52,* 155–166.

Davison, G. C., & Neale, J. M. (1974). *Abnormal psychology: An experimental-clinical approach.* New York: Wiley.

Davison, G. C., Robins, C., & Johnson, M. K. (1983). Articulated thoughts during simulated situations: A paradigm for studying cognition in emotion and behavior. *Cognitive Therapy and Research, 7,* 17–40.

Dean, P. R., & Edwards, T. A. (1990). Health locus of control beliefs and alcohol-related factors that may influence treatment outcomes. *Journal of Substance Abuse Treatment, 7,* 167–172.

Deaux, K. (1985). Sex and gender. *Annual Review of Psychology, 36,* 49–81.

De Bruyn, E. E. J., Delsing, M. J. M. H., & Welten, M. (1995). The EPQ-R (Junior): A Dutch replication study. *Personality and Individual Differences, 18,* 405–411.

DeCarvalho, R. J. (1990a). The growth hypothesis and self-actualization: An existential alternative. *Humanistic Psychologist, 18,* 252–258.

DeCarvalho, R. J. (1990b). A history of the "Third Force" in psychology. *Journal of Humanistic Psychology, 30,* 22–44.

DeCarvalho, R. J. (1991a). Abraham H. Maslow (1908–1970): An intellectual biography. *Thought, 66,* 32–50.

DeCarvalho, R. J. (1991b). *The founders of humanistic psychology.* New York: Praeger.

DeCarvalho, R. J. (1991c). The humanistic paradigm in education. *Humanistic Psychologist, 19,* 88–104.

Deci, E. L. (1975). *Intrinsic motivation.* New York: Plenum.

Deci, E. L., & Ryan, R. M. (1980). The empirical exploration of intrinsic motivational processes. In L. Berkowitz (Ed.), *Advances in experimental social psychology* (Vol. 13). New York: Academic Press.

Deci, E. L., & Ryan, R. M. (1987). The support of autonomy and the control of behavior. *Journal of Personality and Social Psychology, 53,* 1024–1037.

Deci, E. L., & Ryan, R. M. (1991). A motivational approach to self: Integration in personality. In R. Dienstbier (Ed.), *Nebraska symposium on motivation: Perspectives on motivation* (Vol. 38, pp. 237–288). Lincoln, NE: University of Nebraska Press.

Deci, E. L., & Ryan, R. M. (1995). Human autonomy: The basis for true self-esteem. In M. Kernis (Ed.), *Efficacy, agency, and self-esteem.* New York: Plenum.

Deffenbacher, J. L., & Suinn, R. M. (1988). Systematic desensitization and the reduction of anxiety. *The Counseling Psychologist, 16,* 9–30.

Degler, C. N. (1991). *In search of human nature: The decline and revival of Darwinism in American social thought.* New York: Oxford University Press.

De la Fuente, J. M., Lotstra, F., Goldman, S., Biver, F., Luxen, A., Bidaut, L., Stanus, E., & Mendlewicz, J. (1994). Temporal glucose metabolism in borderline personality disorder. *Psychiatry Research: Neuroimaging, 55,* 237–245.

Delmonte, M. M. (1989). Existentialism and psychotherapy: A constructivist perspective. *Psychologia: An International Journal of Psychology in the Orient, 32,* 81–90.

Delmonte, M. M. (1990). George Kelly's personal construct theory: Some comparisons with Freudian theory. *Psychologia: An International Journal of Psychology in the Orient, 33,* 73–83.

DeLongis, A., Folkman, S., & Lazarus, R. S. (1988). The impact of daily stress on health and mood: Psychological and social resources as mediators. *Journal of Personality and Social Psychology, 54,* 486–495.

Delprato, D. J., & Midgley, B. D. (1992). Some fundamentals of B. F. Skinner's behaviorism. *American Psychologist, 47,* 1507–1520.

Dement, W. C. (1964). Experimental dream studies. In J. H. Masserman (Ed.), *Science and psychoanalysis: Scientific proceedings of the Academy of Psychoanalysis.* New York: Grune & Stratton.

Dement, W. C. (1965). An essay on dreams: The role of physiology in understanding their nature. In *New directions in psychology* (Vol. 2). New York: Holt, Rinehart & Winston.

Dement, W. C., & Kleitman, N. (1957). The relation of the eye movements during sleep to dream activity: An objective method for the study of dreaming. *Journal of Experimental Psychology, 53,* 339–346.

Dement, W. C., & Wolpert, E. (1958). The relation of eye movements, body motility, and external stimuli to dream content. *Journal of Experimental Psychology, 55,* 543–553.

Denton, R. E., & Kampfe, C. M. (1994). The relationship between family variables and adolescent substance abuse: A literature review. *Adolescence, 29,* 475–495.

DePaulo, B. M. (1992). Nonverbal behavior and self-presentation. *Psychological Bulletin, 111,* 203–243.

Depue, R. A., & Iacono, W. G. (1989). Neurobehavioral aspects of affective disorders. *Annual Review of Psychology, 40,* 457–492.

de-Raad, B., & Szirmak, Z. (1994). The search for the "Big Five" in a non-Indo-European language: The Hungarian trait structure and its relationship to the EPQ and the PTS. Special issue: The Big Five model of personality in Europe. *European Review of Applied Psychology, 44,* 17–24.

DeRubeis, R. J., & Beck, A. T. (1988). Cognitive therapy. In K. S. Dobson (Ed.), *Handbook of cognitive-behavioral therapies.* New York: Guilford.

DeRubeis, R. J., & Beck, A. T. (1988). Cognitive therapy. In K. S. Dobson (Ed.), *Issues and approaches in personal construct theory.* Orlando, FL: Academic Press.

DeSilvestri, C. (1989). Clinical models in RET: An advanced model of the organization of emotional and behavioral disorders. *Journal of Rational-Emotive and Cognitive-Behavior Therapy, 7,* 51–58.

Diamond, C. T. P. (1983). The use of fixed role treatment in teaching. *Psychology in the Schools, 20,* 74–82.

Diamond, C. T. P. (1990). Recovering and reconstruing teachers' stories. *International Journal of Personal Construct Psychology, 3,* 63–76.

DiClemente, C. C., Fairhurst, S. K., Velasquez, M. M., Prochaska, J. O., Velicer, W. F., & Rossi, J. S. (1991). The process of smoking cessation: An analysis of precontemplation, contemplation and preparation stages of change. *Journal of Consulting and Clinical Psychology, 59,* 295–304.

Die, A. H., Seelbach, W. C., & Sherman, G. D. (1987). Achievement motivation, achieving styles, and morale in the elderly. *Psychology and Aging, 2,* 407–408.

Diener, E., & Larsen, R. J. (1984). Temporal stability and cross-situational consistency of affective, behavioral, and cognitive responses. *Journal of Personality and Social Psychology, 47,* 871–883.

Dienstbier, R. A. (1989). Arousal and physiological toughness: Implications for mental and physical health. *Psychological Review, 96,* 84–100.

Digman, J. M. (1989). Five robust trait dimensions: Development, stability, and utility. *Journal of Personality, 57,* 195–214.

Digman, J. M. (1990). Personality structure: Emergence of the five-factor model. *Annual Review of Psychology, 41,* 417–440.

Digman, J. M., & Inouye, J. (1986). Further specification of the five robust factors of personality. *Journal of Personality and Social Psychology, 50,* 116–123.

Dijkstra, A., De Vries, H., & Bakker, M. (1996). Pros and cons of quitting, self-efficacy, and the stages of change in smoking cessation. *Journal of Consulting and Clinical Psychology, 64,* 758–763.

DiMascio, A., Weissman, M. M., Prusoff, B. A., Neu, C., Zwilling, M. & Klerman, G. L. (1979). Differential symptom reduction by drugs and by psychotherapy in acute depression. *Archives of General Psychiatry, 36,* 1450–1456.

Dimen, M. (1995). The third step: Freud, the feminists, and postmodernism. *American Journal of Psychoanalysis, 55,* 303–319.

Dinnerstein, D. (1977). *The mermaid and the minotaur: Sexual arrangement and human malaise.* New York: Harper & Row.

Dobson, K. S. (1989). A meta-analysis of the efficacy of cognitive therapy for depression. *Journal of Consulting and Clinical Psychology, 57,* 414–419.

Doganis, G., Theodorakis, Y., & Bagiatis, K. (1991). Self-esteem and locus of control in adult female fitness program participants. *International Journal of Sport Psychology, 22,* 154–164.

Doherty, W. J. (1983). Impact of divorce on locus of control orientation in adult women: A longitudinal study. *Journal of Personality and Social Psychology, 44,* 834–840.

Doherty, W. J., & Baldwin, C. (1985). Shifts and stability in locus of control during the 1970s: Divergence of the sexes. *Journal of Personality and Social Psychology, 48,* 1048–1053.

Doi, K. (1985). The relation between the two dimensions of achievement motivation and personality of male university students. *Japanese Journal of Psychology, 56,* 107–110.

Doleys, D. M. (1977). Behavioral treatment of nocturnal enuresis in children: A review of the recent literature. *Psychological Bulletin, 84,* 30–54.

Dollard, J., & Miller, N. E. (1950). *Personality and psychotherapy.* New York: McGraw-Hill.

Dollinger, S. J., & Orf, L. A. (1991). Personality and performance in "personality": Conscientiousness and openness. *Journal of Research in Personality, 25,* 276–284.

Domino, G., & Affonso, D. D. (1990). A personality measure of Erikson's life stages: The Inventory of Social Balance. *Journal of Personality Assessment, 54,* 576–588.

Donaldson, M. (1978). *Children's minds.* New York: Norton.

Dornic, S., & Ekhammar, B. (1990). Extraversion, neuroticism, and noise sensitivity. *Personality and Individual Differences, 11,* 989–992.

Downs, A. F. D., Rosenthal, T. L., & Lichstein, K. L. (1988). Modeling therapies reduce avoidance of bathtime by the institutionalized elderly. *Behavior Therapy, 19,* 359–368.

Dowrick, P. W. (1991). *Practical guide to using video in the behavioral sciences.* New York: Wiley.

Draycott, S. G., & Kline, P. (1995). The Big Three or the Big Five—the EPQ-R vs the NEO-PI: A research note, replication and elaboration. *Personality and Individual Differences, 18,* 801–804.

Drell, W. K. (1988). Countertransference and the obese patient. *American Journal of Psychotherapy, 62,* 77–85.

Duckworth, J. C. (1991). The Minnesota Multiphasic Personality Inventory-2: A review. *Journal of Counseling and Development, 69,* 564–567.

Duncan, R. C., Konefal, J., & Spechler, M. M. (1990). Effect of neurolinguistic programming training on self-actualization as measured by the Personal Orientation Inventory. *Psychological Reports, 66,* 1323–1330.

Dunn, J., & Kendrick, C. (1981). The arrival of a sibling: Changes in patterns of interaction between mother and first-born child. *Annual Progress in Child Psychiatry and Child Development,* 362–379.

Dunnett, G. (Ed.). (1988). *Working with people: Clinical uses of personal construct psychology.* New York: Routledge.

Dunning, D., Meyerowitz, J. A., & Holzberg, A. (1989). Ambiguity and self-evaluation: The role of idiosyncratic definitions in self-serving assessments of ability. *Journal of Personality and Social Psychology, 57,* 1082–1090.

DuPreez, P. D. (1977). *Kelly's "matrix of decision" and the politics of identity.* Paper presented at the Second International Conference on Personal Construct Psychology,

Oxford University. Cited in Adams-Webber, J. R. (1979). *Personal construct theory: Concepts and applications.* Chichester, England: Wiley.

Dush, D. M., Hirt, M. L., & Schroeder, H. E. (1989). Self-statement modification in the treatment of child behavior disorders: A meta-analysis. *Psychological Bulletin, 106,* 97–106.

Dutton, D., Saunders, K., Starzomski, A., & Bartholomew, K. (1994). Intimacy-anger and insecure attachment as precursors of abuse in intimate relationships. *Journal of Applied Social Psychology, 24,* 1367–1386.

Dweck, C. S., & Leggett, E. L. (1988). A social-cognitive approach to motivation and personality. *Psychological Review, 95,* 256–273.

Dyk, P. H., & Adams, G. R. (1990). Identity and intimacy: An initial investigation of three theoretical models using cross-lagged panel correlations. *Journal of Youth and Adolescence, 19,* 91–110.

Dykman, B. M., & Abramson, L. Y. (1990). Contributions of basic research to the cognitive theories of depression. *Personality and Social Psychology Bulletin, 16,* 42–57.

D'Zurilla, T. (1965). Recall efficiency and mediating cognitive events in "experimental repression." *Journal of Personality and Social Psychology, 37,* 253–256.

D'Zurilla, T. (1986). *Problem-solving therapy.* New York: Springer.

D'Zurilla, T., & Goldfried, M. R. (1971). Problem solving and behavior modification. *Journal of Abnormal Psychology, 78,* 107–126.

D'Zurilla, T., & Nezu, A. (1982). Social problem-solving in adults. In D. Kendall (Ed.), *Advances in cognitive-behavioral research and therapy* (Vol. 1). New York: Academic Press.

Eagle, M. N. (1984). *Recent developments in psychoanalysis: A critical evaluation.* New York: McGraw-Hill.

Eagle, M. N., & Wolitzky, D. L. (1985). The current status of psychoanalysis. *Clinical Psychology Review, 5,* 259–269.

Eastman, C., & Marzillier, J. S. (1984). Theoretical and methodological difficulties in Bandura's self-efficacy theory. *Cognitive Therapy and Research, 8,* 213–229.

Eaton, W. O., & Enns, L. R. (1986). Sex differences in human motor activity level. *Psychological Bulletin, 100,* 19–28.

Eaton, W. O., & Yu, A. P. (1989). Are sex differences in child motor activity level a function of differences in maturational status? *Child Development, 60,* 1005–1011.

Ebersole, P., & Humphreys, P. (1991). The short index of self-actualization and purpose in life. *Psychological Reports, 69,* 550.

Eckardt, M. H. (1991). Feminine psychology revisited: A historical perspective. *American Journal of Psychoanalysis, 51,* 235–243.

Edelson, E. (1990). *Genetics and Heredity.* (The Encyclopedia of Health) New York: Chelsea House.

Eden, D., & Kinnar, J. (1991). Modeling Galatea: Boosting self-efficacy to increase volunteering. *Journal of Applied Psychology, 76,* 770–780.

Edwards, A. L. (1953). *Manual for Edwards Personal Preference Schedule.* New York: Psychological Corporation.

Edwards, A. L. (1957). *The social desirability variable in personality research.* New York: Dryden.

Edwards, A. L. (1970). *The measurement of personality traits by scales and inventories.* New York: Holt, Rinehart & Winston.

Edwards, A. L., & Edwards, L. K. (1991). The first-factor loadings of the MMPI factor scales. *Bulletin of the Psychonomic Society, 29,* 229–232.

Edwards, N. (1987). The unconscious ego-ideal and analytic group psychotherapy. *Group, 2,* 165–176.

Egeland, J. A., Gehrhard, D. S., Pauls, D. L., Sussex, J. N., Kidd, K. K., Allen, C. R., Hostetter, A. M., & Housman, D. E. (1987). Bipolar affective disorder linked to DNA markers on chromosome 11. *Nature, 325,* 783–787.

Ehrhardt, A. A. (1985). The psychobiology of gender. In A. S. Rossi (Ed.), *Gender and the life course.* New York: Aldine.

Eifert, G. H., & Evans, I. M. (Eds.). (1990). *Unifying behavior therapy: Contributions of paradigmatic behaviorism.* New York: Springer.

Eisenburg, N., Fabes, R. A., Murphy, B., Karbon, M., Maszk, P., Smith, M., O'Boyle, C., & Suh, K. (1994). The relations of emotionality and regulation to dispositional and situational empathy-related responding. *Journal of Personality and Social Psychology, 66,* 776–797.

Ekman, P., Friesen, W. V., & Bear, J. (1984, May). International language of gestures. *Psychology Today,* pp. 64–69.

Elder, G. H., & MacInnis, D. J. (1983). Achievement imagery in woman's lives from adolescence to adulthood. *Journal of Personality and Social Psychology, 45,* 394–404.

Elkin, (1994). The NIMH treatment of depression collaborative research program: Where we began and where we are. In A. E. Bergin, & S. L. Garfield (Eds.), *Handbook of Psychotherapy and Behavior Change* (4th ed.). New York: Wiley.

Ellenberger, H. F. (1970). *The discovery of the unconscious: The history and evolution of dynamic psychiatry.* New York: Basic Books.

Ellinwood, C. (1989). The young child in person-centered family therapy [Special issue: Person-centered approaches with families]. *Person-Centered Review, 4,* 256–262.

Ellis, A. (1962). *Reason and emotion in psychotherapy.* New York: Lyle Stuart.

Ellis, A. (1985). Expanding the ABCs of RET. In M. J. Mahoney & A. Freeman (Eds.), *Cognition and psychotherapy.* New York: Plenum.

Ellis, A. (1989). Comments on my critics. In M. E. Bernard & R. DiGiuseppe (Eds.), *Inside rational-emotive therapy: A critical appraisal of the theory and therapy of Albert Ellis.* San Diego: Academic Press.

Ellis, A. (1993). Reflections on rational-emotive therapy. *Journal of Consulting and Clinical Psychology, 61,* 199–201.

Ellis, A., & Bernard, M. E. (1985). What is rational-emotive therapy (RET)? In A. Ellis & R. M. Grieger (Eds.), *Handbook of rational-emotive therapy.* New York: Springer.

Ellis, A., & Dryden, W. (1987). *The practice of rational-emotive therapy.* New York: Springer.

Ellis, B. (1992). Satanic ritual abuse and legal ostension. *Journal of Psychology and Theology, 20,* 274–277.

Ellis, J. B. (1994). Children's sex-role development: Implications for working mothers. *Social Behavior and Personality, 22,* 131–136.

Ellis, J. B. & Range, L. M. (1988). Femininity and reasons for living. *Educational and Psychological Research, 8,* 19–24.

Elms, A. C. (1988). Freud as Leonardo: Why the first psychobiography went wrong. *Journal of Personality, 56,* 19–40.

Emmons, R. A., & Diener, E. (1986). Situation selection as a moderator variable of response consistency and stability. *Journal of Personality and Social Psychology, 51,* 1013–1019.

Emmons, R. A., & McAdams, D. P. (1991). Personal strivings and motive dispositions: Exploring the links. *Personality and Social Psychology Bulletin, 17,* 648–654.

Endler, N. S. (1989). The temperamental nature of personality. *European Journal of Personality, 3,* 151–165.

Engstrom, I. (1991). Family interaction and locus of control in children and adolescents with inflammatory bowel disease. *Journal of the American Academy of Child and Adolescent Psychiatry, 30,* 913–920.

Epstein, S. (1966). Some theoretical considerations on the nature of ambiguity and the use of stimulus dimensions in projective techniques. *Journal of Consulting Psychology, 30,* 183–192.

Epting, F. R., & Nazario, A. (1987). Designing a fixed role therapy: Issues, techniques, and modifications. In R. A. Neimeyer & G. J. Neimeyer (Eds.), *Personal construct therapy casebook.* New York: Springer.

Erdelyi, M. H. (1974). A new look at the new look: Perceptual defense and vigilance. *Psychological Review, 81,* 1–25.

Erdelyi, M. H. (1985). *Psychoanalysis: Freud's cognitive psychology.* New York: W. H. Freeman.

Erhardt, A. A., & Baker, S. W. (1974). Fetal androgens, human central nervous system differentiation, and behavioral sex differences. In R. C. Friedman, R. M. Rickard, & R. L. Van de Wiele (Eds.), *Sex differences in behavior.* New York: Wiley.

Ericksen, M. K., & Sirgy, M. J. (1989). Achievement motivation and clothing behavior: A self-image congruence analysis. *Journal of Social Behavior and Personality, 4,* 307–326.

Erikson, E. H. (1950). *Childhood and society.* New York: Norton.

Erikson, E. H. (1954). The dream specimen of psychoanalysis. *Journal of the American Psychoanalytic Association, 2,* 5–56.

Erikson, E. H. (1963). *Childhood and society* (2nd ed.). New York: Norton.

Erikson, E. H. (1968). *Identity, youth, and crisis.* New York: Norton.

Essig, T. S., & Russell, R. L. (1990). Analyzing subjectivity in therapeutic discourse: Rogers, Perls, Ellis and Gloria revisited. *Psychotherapy, 27,* 271–281.

Evans, F. J. (1974). The placebo response in pain reduction. In J. J. Bonica (Ed.), *Advances in neurology* (Vol. 4). New York: Raven Press.

Evans, F. J. (1985). Expectancy, therapeutic instructions, and the placebo response. In L. White, B. Tursky, & G. E. Schwartz (Eds.), *Placebo: Theory, research, and mechanisms.* New York: Guilford.

Evans, P. (1989). *Motivation and emotion.* New York: Routledge.

Evans, R. G. (1982). Skill versus chance tasks: Comparison of locus of control, defensive externality, and persistence. *Personality and Social Psychology Bulletin, 8,* 129–133.

Ewart, C. K. (1991). Social action theory for a public health psychology. *American Psychologist, 46,* 931–946.

Ewart, C. K. (1992). The role of physical self-efficacy in recovery from heart attack. In R. Schwarzer (Ed.), *Self-efficacy: Thought control of action.* Washington, DC: Hemisphere.

Exner, J. E. (1986). *The Rorschach: A comprehensive system,* (Vol. 1, Rev. ed.). New York: Riley.

Eysenck, H. J. (1952). *The scientific study of personality.* London: Routledge and Kegan Paul.

Eysenck, H. J. (1963). *Uses and abuses of psychology.* Baltimore: Penguin.

Eysenck, H. J. (1967). *The biological basis of personality.* Springfield, IL: Charles C Thomas.

Eysenck, H. J. (1975). *The inequality of man.* San Diego: EdITS/Educational & Industrial Testing Service.

Eysenck, H. J. (1982). *Personality genetics and behavior.* New York: Praeger.

Eysenck, H. J. (1985). Incubation theory of fear/anxiety. In S. Reiss & R. R. Bootzin (Eds.), *Theoretical issues in behavior therapy.* Orlando, FL: Academic Press.

Eysenck, H. J. (1991). Dimensions of personality: 16, 5, or 3 criteria for a taxonomic paradigm. *Personality and Individual Differences, 12,* 773–790.

Eysenck, H. J. (1992). Four ways five factors are *not* basic. *Personality and Individual Differences, 13,* 667–673.

Eysenck, H. J. (1995). How valid is the Psychoticism scale? A comment on the Van Kampen critique. *European Journal of Personality, 9,* 103–108.

Eysenck, H. J., & Eysenck, M. W. (1985). *Personality and individual differences: A natural science approach.* New York: Plenum.

Eysenck, H. J., & Eysenck, S. B. G. (1991). *Manual for the EPQ-R.* Sevenoaks, England: Hodder and Stoughton.

Eysenck, S. B. G., & Haapasalo, J. (1989). Cross-cultural comparisons of personality: Finland and England. *Personality and Individual Differences, 10,* 121–125.

Eysenck, S. B. G., & Long, F. Y. (1986). A cross-cultural comparison of personality in adults and children: Singapore and England. *Journal of Personality and Social Psychology, 50,* 124–130.

Eysenck, S. B. G., & Tambs, K. (1990). Cross-cultural comparison of personality: Norway and England. *Scandinavian Journal of Psychology, 31,* 191–197.

Facklam, M., & Facklam, H. (1979). *From cell to clone.* New York: Harcourt Brace Jovanovich.

Fairbairn, W. R. D. (1952). *Psychoanalytic studies of the personality.* London: Tavistock Publications and Routledge & Kegan Paul.

Falbo, T., & Polit, D. F. (1986). Quantitative review of the only child literature: Research evidence and theory development. *Psychological Bulletin, 100,* 176–189.

Faulkender, P. J. (1991). Does gender schema mediate between sex-role identity and self-actualization? *Psychological Reports, 68,* 1019–1029.

Fehr, B. J. (1977). *Visual interactions in same and interracial dyads.* Unpublished master's thesis, University of Delaware.

Fehr, B. J. (1981). *The communication of evaluation through the use of interpersonal gaze in same and interracial female dyads.* Unpublished doctoral dissertation, University of Delaware.

Feinberg, R. A. (1990). The social nature of the classical conditioning phenomena in people: A comment on Hunt, Florsheim, Chatterjee, & Kernan. *Psychological Reports, 67,* 331–334.

Feingold, A. (1992). Gender differences in mate selection preference: A test of the parental investment model. *Psychological Bulletin, 112,* 125–139.

Feixas, G. (1992). A constructivist approach to supervision: Some preliminary thoughts. *International Journal of Personal Construct Psychology, 5,* 183–200.

Fekken, G. C., & Holden, R. R. (1992). Response latency evidence for viewing personality traits as schema indicators. *Journal of Research in Personality, 26,* 103–120.

Felton, B., & Kahana, E. (1974). Adjustment and situationally bound locus of control among institutionalized aged. *Journal of Gerontology, 29,* 295–301.

Fenichel, O. (1945). *The psychoanalytic theory of neurosis.* New York: Norton.

Fernandez-Ballesteros, R., & Staats, A. W. (1992). Paradigmatic behavioral assessment, treatment and evaluation: Answering the crisis in behavioral assessment. *Advances in Behaviour Research and Therapy, 14,* 1–28.

Festinger, L. (1957). *A theory of cognitive dissonance.* Stanford, CA: Stanford University Press.

Fichter, M. M., & Noegel, R. (1990). Concordance for bulimia nervosa in twins. *International Journal of Eating Disorders, 9,* 255–263.

File, S. E., Pellow, S., & Braestrup, C. (1985). Effects of the beta-carboline, FG7142, in the social interaction test of anxiety and the holeboard: Correlations between behaviour and plasma concentrations. *Pharmacology Biochemistry & Behavior, 22,* 941–944.

Finchilescu, G. (1995). Setting the frame: Gender and psychology. *South African Journal of Psychology, 25,* 133–139.

Finell, J. S. (1987). A challenge to psychoanalysis: A review of the negative therapeutic reaction. *Psychoanalytic Review, 74,* 487–515.

Finkelhor, D. (1979). *Sexually victimized children.* New York: Free Press.

Finkelhor, D., & Dziuba-Leatherman, J. (1994). Victimization of children. *American Psychologist, 49,* 173–183.

Finkelhor, D., Hotaling, G., Lewis, I. A., & Smith, C. (1990). Sexual abuse in a national survey of adult men and women: Prevalence, characteristics, and risk factors. *Child Abuse and Neglect, 14,* 19–28.

Fischer, M. (1973). Genetic and environmental factors in schizophrenia. *Acta Psychiatrica Scandinavica.* (Suppl. 238).

Fisher, D. D. V. (1990a). Emotional construing: A psychobiological model. *International Journal of Personal Construct Psychology, 3,* 183–203.

Fisher, D. D. V. (1990b). Emotions: Adaptive standards and/or primitive constructs: A reply to Mascolo and Mancuso. *International Journal of Personal Construct Psychology, 3,* 223–230.

Fisher, S. (1973). *The female orgasm.* New York: Basic Books.

Fisher, S., & Greenberg, R. P. (1977). *The scientific credibility of Freud's theories and therapy.* New York: Basic Books.

Flett, G. L., Blankstein, K. R., & Hewitt, P. L. (1991). Factor structure of the short index of self-actualization. [Special issue: Handbook of self-actualization]. *Journal of Social Behavior and Personality, 6,* 321–329.

Flett, G. L., Hewitt, P. L., Blankstein, K. R., & Mosher, S. W. (1991). Perfectionism, self-actualization, and personal adjustment [Special issue: Handbook of self-actualization]. *Journal of Social Behavior and Personality, 6,* 147–160.

Flink, C., Boggiano, A. K., & Barrett, M. (1990). Controlling teaching strategies: Undermining children's self-determination and performance. *Journal of Personality and Social Psychology, 59,* 916–924.

Floderus-Myrhed, B., Pedersen, N., & Rasmuson, S. (1980). Assessment of heritability for personality based on a short form of the Eysenck Personality Inventory. *Behavior Genetics, 10,* 153–162.

Fodor, E. M. (1984). The power motive and reactivity to power stresses. *Journal of Personality and Social Psychology, 47,* 853–859.

Fonagy, P., & Moran, G. S. (1990). Studies in the efficacy of child psychoanalysis. *Journal of Consulting and Clinical Psychology, 58,* 684–695.

Fontaine, K. R. (1994). Personality correlates of sexual risk-taking among men. *Personality and Individual Differences, 17,* 693–694.

Ford, D. Y., & Harris, J. J. (1990). On discovering the hidden treasure of gifted and talented black children. *Roeper Review, 13,* 27–32.

Ford, J. G. (1991a). Inherent potentialities of actualization: An initial exploration. *Journal of Humanistic Psychology, 31,* 65–88.

Ford, J. G. (1991b). Rogerian self-actualization: A clarification of meaning. *Journal of Humanistic Psychology, 31,* 101–111.

Forsman, L. (1989). Parent-child gender interaction in the relation between retrospective self-reports on parental love and current self esteem. *Scandinavian Journal of Psychology, 30,* 275–283.

Forston, R. F., & Larson, C. U. (1968). The dynamics of space: An experimental study in proxemic behavior among Latin Americans and North Americans. *Journal of Communication, 18,* 109–116.

Fosshage, J. L. (1987). New vistas on dream interpretation. In M. L. Glucksman & S. L. Warner (Eds.), *Dreams in new perspective: The royal road revisited.* New York: Human Sciences.

Foster, S. L., & Cone, J. D. (1986). Design and use of direct observation. In A. R. Ciminero, K. S. Calhoun, & H. A. Adams (Eds.), *Handbook of behavioral assessment* (2nd ed.). New York: Wiley.

Foucault, M. (1980). *Herculine Barbin* (Richard McDougall, Trans.). New York: Pantheon.

Fox, M. L., & Dwyer, D. J. (1995). Stressful job demands and worker health: An investigation of the effects of self-monitoring. *Journal of Applied Social Psychology, 25,* 1973–1995.

Fox, N. A. (1989). Psychophysiological correlates of emotional reactivity during the first year of life. *Developmental Psychology, 25,* 364–372.

Foxx, R. M., Martella, R. C., & Marchand-Martella, N. E. (1989). The acquisition, maintenance, and generalization of problem-solving skills by closed head-injured adults. *Behavior Therapy, 20,* 61–76.

Francis, L. J. (1997). Coopersmith's model of self-esteem: Bias toward the stable extravert? *Journal of Social Psychology, 137,* 139–142.

Francis, L. J., & Jones, S. H. (1996). Social class and self-esteem. *Journal of Social Psychology, 136,* 405–406.

Fredrickson, R. (1992). *Repressed memories: A journey to recovery from sexual abuse.* New York: Simon & Schuster.

Freeman, S. C. (1990). C. H. Patterson on client-centered career counseling: An interview. *Career Development Quarterly, 38,* 291–301.

French, E. G., & Lesser, G. S. (1964). Some characteristics of the achievement motive in women. *Journal of Abnormal and Social Psychology, 68,* 119–128.

French, T., & Fromm, E. (1964). *Dream interpretation.* New York: Basic Books.

Freud, A. (1958). Adolescence. *Psychoanalytic Study of the Child, 13,* 255–278.

Freud, A. (1966). *The ego and the mechanisms of defense* (Rev. ed.). New York: International Universities Press.

Freud, A. (1966). *The writings of Anna Freud* (Vol. 2). New York: International Universities Press.

Freud, S. (1901). *The psychopathology of everyday life.* New York: W. W. Norton.

Freud, S. (1953). The interpretation of dreams. In J. Strachey (Ed. and Trans.), *The standard edition of the complete psychological works of Sigmund Freud* (Vols. 4 and 5). London: Hogarth. (Original work published 1900)

Freud, S. (1955). Analysis of a phobia in a five-year-old boy. In J. Strachey (Ed. and Trans.), *The standard edition of the complete psychological works of Sigmund Freud* (Vol. 10). London: Hogarth. (Original work published 1909)

Freud, S. (1957a). On the history of the psycho-analytic movement. In J. Strachey (Ed. and Trans.), *The standard edition of the complete psychological works of Sigmund Freud* (Vol. 14). London: Hogarth. (Original work published 1914)

Freud, S. (1957b). Repression. In J. Strachey (Ed. and Trans.), *The standard edition of the complete psychological works of Sigmund Freud* (Vol. 14). London: Hogarth Press. (Original work published 1915)

Freud, S. (1959). Character and anal eroticism. In J. Strachey (Ed. and Trans.), *The standard edition of the complete psychological works of Sigmund Freud* (Vol. 9). London: Hogarth. (Original work published 1908)

Freud, S. (1961a). *The interpretation of dreams* (J. Strachey, Ed. and Trans.). New York: Science Editions. (Original work published 1900)

Freud, S. (1961b). Two encyclopedia articles. In J. Strachey (Ed. and Trans.), *The standard edition of the complete psychological works of Sigmund Freud* (Vol. 18). London: Hogarth. (Original work published 1923)

Freud, S. (1963). Introductory lectures on psychoanalysis. In J. Strachey (Ed. and Trans.), *The standard edition of the complete psychological works of Sigmund Freud* (Vol. 16). London: Hogarth. (Original work published 1916–1917)

Freud, S. (1964a). An outline of psychoanalysis. In J. Strachey (Ed. and Trans.), *The standard edition of the complete psychological works of Sigmund Freud* (Vol. 23). London: Hogarth. (Original work published 1940)

Freud, S. (1964b). Femininity. In J. Strachey (Ed. and Trans.), *The standard edition of the complete psychological works of Sigmund Freud* (Vol. 22). London: Hogarth. (Original work published 1933)

Freud, S. (1965). *New introductory lectures on psychoanalysis.* New York: Norton. (Original work published 1933)

Freud, S., & Jung, C. G. (1974). *The Freud/Jung letters* (W. McGuire, Ed.). Princeton, NJ: Princeton University Press.

Friedman, H. S., & Booth-Kewley, S. (1987). Personality, Type A behavior, and coronary heart disease: The role of emotional expression. *Journal of Personality and Social Psychology, 53,* 783–792.

Friedman, H. S., Hall, H. S., & Harris, M. J. (1985).

Type A behavior, nonverbal expressive style, and health. *Journal of Personality and Social Psychology, 48,* 1299–1315.

Friedman, L. (1989). Hartmann's "ego psychology and the problem of adaptation." *Psychoanalytic Quarterly, 58,* 526–550.

Friedman, M., & Rosenman, R. H. (1974). *Type A behavior and your heart.* London: Wildwood House.

Friedrich, J. (1988). The influence of locus of control on students' aspirations, expectations, and information preferences for summer work. *Journal of College Student Development, 29,* 335–339.

Fristad, M. A. (1988). Assessing social desirability in family self-report. *Perceptual and Motor Skills, 66,* 131–137.

Froman, R. D., & Owen, S. V. (1989). Infant care self-efficacy. *Scholarly Inquiry for Nursing Practice, 3,* 199–211.

Fromm, E. (1947). *Man for himself: An inquiry into the psychology of ethics.* New York: Holt, Rinehart & Winston.

Fromm, E. (1955). *The sane society.* New York: Holt, Rinehart & Winston.

Fromm, E. (1963). *The art of loving.* New York: Bantam.

Frosh, S. (1987). *The politics of psychoanalysis: An introduction to Freudian and post-Freudian theory.* New Haven, CT: Yale University Press.

Funder, D. C. (1991). Global traits: A Neo-Allportian approach to personality. *Psychological Science, 2,* 31–39.

Funder, D. C., & Block, J. (1989). The role of ego-control, ego-resiliency, and IQ in delay of gratification in adolescence. *Journal of Personality and Social Psychology, 56,* 1041–1050.

Furnham, A. (1988). *Lay theories of behaviour: Everyday understanding of problems in the social sciences.* New York: Pergamon Press.

Furnham, A., & Brewin, C. R. (1990). Personality and happiness. *Personality and Individual Differences, 11,* 1093–1096.

Furnham, A., & Medhurst, S. (1995). Personality correlates of academic seminar behaviour: A study of four instruments. *Personality and Individual Differences, 19,* 197–208.

Gackenbach, J. (Ed.). (1987). *Sleep and dreams: A sourcebook.* New York: Garland.

Gallagher, D. J. (1990). Extraversion, neuroticism and appraisal of stressful academic events. *Personality and Individual Differences, 11,* 1053–1057.

Gallego-Mere, A. (1989). The manifest content of dreams. *American Journal of Psychoanalysis, 49,* 95–103.

Gallimore, R., Goldenberg, C. N., & Weisner, T. S. (1993). The social construction and subjective reality of activity settings: Implications for community psychology. *American Journal of Community Psychology, 21,* 537–559.

Galton, F. (1884). Measurement of character. *Fortnightly Review, 42,* 179–185.

Gao, Y., Waters, E., & Crowell, J. (1997). *Is it easier for a secure person to use and to serve as a secure base?* Poster session presented at the biennial meeting of the Society for Research in Child Development, Washington, DC.

Gangestad, S., & Snyder, M. (1985). To carve nature at its joints: On the existence of discrete classes in personality. *Psychological Review, 92,* 317–349.

Garcia, J. & Koelling, R. A. (1966). Relation of cue to consequence in avoidance learning. *Psychonomic Science, 4,* 123–124.

Garcia, J., McGowan, B. D., & Green, K. F. (1972). Biological constraints on learning. In A. H. Black & W. F. Prokasy (Eds.), *Classical conditioning II: Current research and theory.* New York: Appleton-Century-Crofts.

Garcia, M. E., Schmitz, J. M., & Doerfler, L. A. (1990). A fine-grained analysis of the role of self-efficacy in self-initiated attempts to quit smoking. *Journal of Consulting and Clinical Psychology, 58,* 317–322.

Garden, A. (1991). The purpose of burnout: A Jungian interpretation. *Journal of Social Behavior and Personality, 6,* 73–93.

Gardiner, J. K. (1992). Psychoanalysis and feminism: An American humanist's view. *Signs, 17,* 437–454.

Gardner, B. T., & Gardner, R. A. (1989). Beyond Pavlovian classical conditioning. *Behavioral and Brain Sciences, 12,* 143–144.

Gardner, H. (1985). *The mind's new science: A history of the cognitive revolution.* New York: Basic Books.

Garfield, S. L., & Bergin, A. E. (Eds.). (1985). *Handbook of psychotherapy and behavior change* (3rd ed.). New York: Wiley.

Garn, S. M., & Gertler, M. M. (1950). An association between type of work and physique in an industrial group. *American Journal of Physical Anthropology, 8,* 387–397.

Garratt, G. A., Baxter, J. C., & Rozelle, R. M. (1981). Training university police in black-American nonverbal behaviors. *Journal of Social Psychology, 113,* 217–229.

Gattuso, S. M., Litt, M. D., & Fitzgerald, T. E. (1992). Coping with gastrointestinal endoscopy: Self-efficacy enhancement and coping style. *Journal of Consulting and Clinical Psychology, 60,* 133–139.

Gay, P. (1988). *Freud: A life for our time.* New York: Norton.

Gay, P. (1989). *The Freud reader.* New York: Norton.

Gaylin, N. L. (1989). The necessary and sufficient conditions for change: Individual versus family therapy. [Special issue: Person-centered approaches with families]. *Person-Centered Review, 4,* 263–279.

Gaylin, W. (1987). *Rediscovering love.* New York: Penguin.

Gecas, V. (1989). The social psychology of self-efficacy. *Annual Review of Sociology, 15,* 291–316.

Gedo, J. E. (1979). *Beyond interpretation.* New York: International Universities Press.

Geen, R. G. (1984). Preferred stimulation levels in introverts and extraverts: Effects on arousal and performance. *Journal of Personality and Social Psychology, 46,* 1303–1312.

Geer, J. H. (1968). A test of the classical conditioning model of emotion: The use of nonpainful aversive stimuli as unconditioned stimuli in a conditioning procedure. *Journal of Personality and Social Psychology, 10,* 148–156.

Geer, J. H., Davison, G. C., & Gatchel, R. I. (1970). Reduction of stress in humans through nonveridical perceived control of aversive stimulation. *Journal of Personality and Social Psychology, 16,* 731–738.

Geisler, C. (1986). The use of subliminal psychodynamic activation in the study of repression. *Journal of Personality and Social Psychology, 51,* 844–851.

Geiss, S. K., & O'Leary, K. D. (1981). Therapist ratings of frequency and severity of marital problems: Implications for research. *Journal of Marital and Family Therapy, 7,* 515–520.

Geissler, T., & Kelly, I. W. (1994). Bulimic symptomatology and personality factors in a nonclinical sample: A replication. *Psychological Reports, 75,* 224–226.

Gendlin, E. T. (1988). Carl Rogers (1902–1987). *American Psychologist, 43,* 127–128.

Georgiou, A., & Bradley, C. (1992). The development of a smoking-specific locus of control scale. *Psychology and Health, 6,* 227–246.

Gibbons, F. X. (1990). Self attention and behavior: A review and theoretical update. In M. P. Zanna (Ed.), *Advances in experimental social psychology* (Vol. 23). New York: Academic Press.

Gifford, F. (1990). Genetic traits. *Biology and Philosophy, 5,* 327–347.

Gilbert, P., & Allen, S. (1994). Assertiveness, submissive behaviour, and social comparison. *British Journal of Clinical Psychology, 33,* 295–306.

Gilligan, C. (1982). *In a different voice: Psychological theory and women's development.* Cambridge, MA: Harvard University Press.

Gillis, J. R., Rogers, R., & Dickens, S. E. (1990). The detection of faking bad response styles on the MMPI. *Canadian Journal of Behavioral Science, 22,* 408–416.

Gladstone, R. (1990). Psychology versus philosophy. *American Psychologist, 45,* 782.

Glass, D. C. (1977). Stress, behavior patterns and coronary disease. *American Scientist, 65,* 177–187.

Glenn, J. (1987). Freud, Virgil, and Aeneas: An unnoticed classical influence on Freud. *American Journal of Psychoanalysis, 47,* 279–281.

Glueck, S., & Glueck, E. (1950). *Unraveling juvenile delinquency.* New York: Commonwealth Fund.

Glueck, S., & Glueck, E. (1956). *Physique and delinquency.* New York: Harper & Row.

Glynn, S. M. (1990). Token economy approaches for psychiatric patients: Progress and pitfalls over 25 years. *Behavior Modification, 14,* 383–407.

Goffman, E. (1959). *The presentation of self in everyday life.* Garden City, NY: Doubleday.

Goldberg, L. (1982). From Ace to Zombie: Some explorations in the language of personality. In Speilberger, C. D., & Butcher, J. N. (Eds.), *Advances in Personality Assessment* (Vol. 1). Hillsdale, NJ: Erlbaum.

Goldberg, L. R. (1981). Language and individual differences: The search for universals in personality lexicons. In L. Wheeler (Ed.), *Review of personality and social psychology* (Vol. 2). Beverly Hills, CA: Sage.

Goldberg, L. R. (1990). An alternative "description of personality": The big-five factor structure. *Journal of Personality and Social Psychology, 59,* 1216–1229.

Goldberg, L. R. (1993a). The structure of personality traits: Vertical and horizontal aspects. In D. C. Funder, R. Parke, C. Tomlinson-Keasey, & K. Widaman (Eds.), *Studying lives through time: Personality and development.* Washington, DC: American Psychological Association.

Goldberg, L. R. (1993b). The structure of phenotypic personality traits. *American Psychologist, 48,* 26–34.

Goldberg, L. R., & Rosolack, T. K. (1994). The Big Five factor structure as an integrative framework: An empirical comparison with Eysenck's P-E-N model. In C. F. Halverson, Jr., G. A. Kohnstamm, & R. P. Martin (Eds.), *The developing structure of temperament and personality from infancy to adulthood.* Hillsdale, NJ: Erlbaum.

Goldberg, L. R., & Saucier, G. (1995). So what do you propose we use instead? A reply to Block. *Psychological Bulletin, 117,* 221–225.

Golden, G. K. (1987). Creativity: An object relations perspective. *Clinical Social Work Journal, 15,* 214–222.

Goldfried, M. R. (1992). Psychotherapy integration: A mid-life crisis for behavior therapy. *the Behavior Therapist, 15,* 38–42.

Goldfried, M. R., Greenberg, L. S., & Marmar, C. (1990). Individual psychotherapy: Process and outcome. *Annual Review of Psychology, 41,* 659–688.

Goldsmith, H. H. (1983). Genetic influences on personality from infancy to adulthood. *Child Development, 54,* 331–355.

Goldsmith, H. H., & Campos, J. J. (1990). The structure of temperamental fear and pleasure in infants: A psychometric perspective. *Child Development, 61,* 1944–1964.

Goldstein, E. (1992). *Confabulations.* New York: SIRS Books.

Goldstein, H., & Mousetis, L. (1989). Generalized language learning by children with severe mental retardation: Effects of peers' expressive modeling. *Journal of Applied Behavior Analysis, 22,* 245–259.

Goldwater, L., & Duffy, J. F. (1990). Use of the MMPI to uncover histories of childhood abuse in adult female psychiatric patients. *Journal of Clinical Psychology, 46,* 392–398.

Goleman, D. (1985, December 31). Scientists find city is a series of varying perceptions. *The New York Times,* pp. C1, C6.

Goleman, D. (1988, November 1). Narcissism looming larger as root of personality woes. *The New York Times,* pp. C1, C16.

Gollwitzer, P. M. (1990). Action phases and mind-sets. In E. T. Higgins & R. M. Sorrentino (Eds.), *Handbook of motivation and cognition: Foundations of social behavior* (Vol. 2). New York: Guilford.

Gonzalez, J. T., & Gonzalez, V. M. (1990). Initial

validation of a scale measuring self-efficacy of breast self-examination among low-income Mexican American women. *Hispanic Journal of Behavioral Sciences, 12,* 277–291.

Goodman, W. K., Price, L. H., Delgado, P. L., Palumbo, J., Krystal, J. H., Nagy, L. M., Rasmussen, S. A., Heninger, G. R., & Charney, D. S. (1990). Specificity of serotonin reuptake inhibitors in the treatment of obsessive-compulsive disorder. *Archives of General Psychiatry, 47,* 577–585.

Goodwin, J. S., Hunt, W. C., Key, C. R., & Samet, J. M. (1987). The effect of marital status on stage, treatment, and survival of cancer patients. *Journal of the American Medical Association, 258,* 3125–3130.

Gorkin, M. (1987). *The uses of countertransference.* Northvale, NJ: Aronson.

Gottesman, I. L., & Bertelson, A. (1989). Confirming unexpressed genotypes for schizophrenia. *Archives of General Psychiatry, 46,* 867–872.

Gottesman, I. L., & Prescott, C. A. (1989). Abuses of the MacAndrew alcoholism scale: A critical review. *Clinical Psychology Reviews, 9,* 223–242.

Grant, B. (1990). Principled and instrumental nondirectiveness in person-centered and client-centered therapy. *Person-Centered Review, 5,* 77–88.

Grasha, A. F. (1978). *Practical applications of psychology.* Cambridge, MA: Winthrop.

Gray, A., & Jackson, D. N. (1990). Individual differences in Type A behavior and cardiovascular responses to stress. *Personality and Individual Differences, 11,* 1213–1219.

Gray, C. (1992). Enterprise trainees' self-construals as entrepreneurs. *International Journal of Personal Construct Psychology, 5,* 307–322.

Gray, J. A. (1981). A critique of Eysenck's theory of personality. In H. J. Eysenck (Ed.), *A model for personality.* Berlin: Springer-Verlag.

Gray, J. A. (1982). *The neuropsychology of anxiety: An enquiry into the functions of the septo-hippocampal system.* New York: Oxford University Press.

Gray, J. A. (1987). Perspectives on anxiety and impulsivity: A commentary. *Journal of Research in Personality, 21,* 493–509.

Gray, J. A. (1991). The neuropsychology of temperament. In J. Strelau & A. Angleitner (Eds.), *Explorations in temperament: International perspectives on theory and measurement.* New York: Plenum.

Greeley, A. (1974). *Ecstasy: A way of knowing.* Englewood Cliffs, NJ: Prentice-Hall.

Green, D. (1988). Resisting the stigma of incest: An experiment in personal construct psychotherapy. *Journal of Adolescence, 11,* 299–308.

Green, D., & Kirby-Turner, N. (1990). First steps in family therapy: A personal construct analysis. *Journal of Family Therapy, 12,* 139–154.

Greenberg, J. R., & Mitchell, S. A. (1983). *Object relations in psychoanalytic theory.* Cambridge, MA: Harvard University Press.

Greene, B. (1993). Psychotherapy with African-American women: Integrating feminist and psychodynamic models. *Journal of Training and Practice in Professional Psychology, 7,* 49–66.

Greenglass, E. R., & Julkunen, J. (1989). Construct validity and sex differences in Cook-Medley hostility. *Personality and Individual Differences, 10,* 209–218.

Greenglass, E. R., & Julkunen, J. (1991). Cook-Medley hostility, anger, and the Type A behavior pattern in Finland. *Psychological Reports, 68,* 1059–1066.

Greenson, R. R. (1965). The working alliance and the transference neurosis. *Psychoanalytic Quarterly, 34,* 155–181.

Greenson, R. R. (1967). *The technique and practice of psychoanalysis.* New York: International Universities Press.

Greenson, R. R. (1974). Loving, hating, and indifference toward the patient. *International Review of Psychoanalysis, 1,* 259–266.

Grieser, C., Greenberg, R., & Harrison, R. H. (1972). The adaptive function of sleep: The differential effects of sleep and dreaming on recall. *Journal of Abnormal Psychology, 80,* 280–286.

Grolnick, W. S., & Ryan, R. N. (1989). Parent styles associated with children's self-regulation and competence in school. *Journal of Educational Psychology, 81,* 143–154.

Grossman, L. S., Haywood, T. W., Wasyliw, O., & Cavanaugh, J. L. (1990). Sensitivity of MMPI validity scales to motivational factors in psychological evaluations of police officers. *Journal of Personality Assessment, 55,* 549–561.

Grubrich-Simitis, I. (Ed.). (1987). *A phylogenetic fantasy: Overview of the transference neurosis.* Cambridge, MA: Harvard University Press.

Grünbaum, A. (1984). *The foundations of psychoanalysis: A philosophical critique.* Berkeley: University of California Press.

Guevremont, D. C., & Foster, S. L. (1993). Impact of social problem-solving training on aggressive boys: Skill acquisition, behavior change, and generalization. *Journal of Abnormal Child Psychology, 21,* 13–27.

Guevremont, D. C., Osnes, P. G., & Stokes, T. F. (1988). The functional role of verbalizations in the generalization of self-instructional training with children. *Journal of Applied Behavior Analysis, 21,* 45–55.

Guevremont, D. C., & Spiegler, M. D. (1990, November). *What do behavior therapists really do? A survey of the clinical practice of AABT members.* Paper presented at the meeting of the Association for Advancement of Behavior Therapy, San Francisco.

Guilford, J. P. (Ed.). (1954). *Psychometric methods* (2nd ed.). New York: McGraw-Hill.

Guisinger, S., & Blatt, S. J. (1994). Individuality and relatedness. Evolution of a fundamental dialectic. *American Psychologist, 49,* 104–111.

Gurtman, M. B. (1995). Personality structure and interpersonal problems: A theoretically-guided item analysis of the Inventory of Interpersonal Problems. *Assessment, 2,* 343–361.

Gustafson, S. B. (1994). Female underachievement and overachievement: Parental contributions and long-term consequences. *International Journal of Behavioral Development, 17,* 469–484.

Haaga, D. A. F. (1990). Gender schematic parapraxes in the articulated thoughts of ex-smokers. *Social Behavior and Personality, 18,* 261–266.

Haaga, D. A. F., & Stewart, B. L. (1992). Self-efficacy for recovery from a lapse after smoking cessation. *Journal of Consulting and Clinical Psychology, 60,* 24–28.

Haaga, D. A. F., & Stewart, B. L. (1993). Self-efficacy for recovery from a lapse after smoking cessation. *the Behavior Therapist, 16,* 77.

Haaken, J. (1995). The debate over recovered memory of sexual abuse: A feminist psychoanalytic perspective. *Psychiatry Interpersonal and Biological Processes, 58,* 189–198.

Hahlweg, K., & Markman, H. J. (1988). Effectiveness of behavioral marital therapy: Empirical status of behavioral techniques in preventing and alleviating marital distress. *Journal of Consulting and Clinical Psychology, 56,* 440–447.

Haidt, J., McCauley, C., & Rozin, R. (1994). Individual differences in sensitivity to disgust: A scale sampling seven domains of disgust elicitors. *Personality and Individual Differences, 16,* 701–713.

Haley, W. E., Roth, D. L., Coleton, M. I., & Ford, G. R. (1996). Appraisal, coping, and social support as mediators of well-being in black and white family caregivers of patients with Alzheimer's disease. *Journal of Consulting and Clinical Psychology, 64,* 121–129.

Hall, A. G., Hendrick, S. S., & Hendrick, C. (1991). Personal construct systems and love styles. *International Journal of Personal Construct Psychology, 4,* 137–155.

Hall, C. S., & Van de Castle, R. L. (1963). An empirical investigation of the castration complex in dreams. *Journal of Personality, 33,* 20–29.

Hall, E. T. (1963). A system for the notation of proxemic behavior. *American Anthropologist, 65,* 1003–1026.

Hall, E. T. (1966). *The hidden dimension.* New York: Doubleday.

Hall, J. A. (1978). Gender effects in decoding nonverbal cues. *Psychological Bulletin, 85,* 845–857.

Hall, R. V., Lund, D., & Jackson, D. (1968). Effects of teacher attention on study behavior. *Journal of Applied Behavior Analysis, 1,* 1–12.

Halpern, J. (1977). Projection: A test of the psychoanalytic hypothesis. *Journal of Abnormal Psychology, 86,* 536–542.

Hamilton, N. G. (1989). A critical review of object relations theory. *American Journal of Psychiatry, 146,* 1552–1560.

Hammen, C. (1988). Depression and cognitions about personal stressful life events. In L. B. Alloy (Ed.), *Cognitive processes in depression.* New York: Guilford.

Haney, C. J., & Long, B. C. (1995). Coping effectiveness: A path analysis of self-efficacy, control, coping, and performance in sport competition. *Journal of Applied Social Psychology, 25,* 1726–1746.

Hansson, R. O. (1977). Marternal employment and androgyny. *Psychology of Women Quarterly, 2,* 76–78.

Hardin, H. T. (1987). On the vicissitudes of Freud's early mothering: I. Early environment and loss. *Psychoanalytic Quarterly, 56,* 628–644.

Hardin, H. T. (1988a). On the vicissitudes of Freud's early mothering: II. Alienation from his biological mother. *Psychoanalytic Quarterly, 57,* 72–86.

Hardin, H. T. (1988b). On the vicissitudes of Freud's early mothering: III. Freiberg, screen memories, and loss. *Psychoanalytic Quarterly, 57,* 209–223.

Harkapaa, K., Jarvikoski, A., Mellin, G., Hurri, H., & Luoma, J. (1991). Health locus of control beliefs and psychological distress as predictors for treatment outcome in low-back pain patients: Results of a 3-month follow-up of a controlled intervention study. *Pain, 46,* 35–41.

Harmon-Jones, E., Simon, L., Psyzczynski, T., Solomon, S., & McGregor, H. (1997). Terror management theory and self-esteem: Evidence that increased self-esteem reduces mortality salience effects. *Journal of Personality and Social Psychology, 72,* 24–36.

Harrell, T. W. (1972). High earning MBAs. *Personnel Psychology, 25,* 523–530.

Harri-Augstein, S. (1985). Learning-to-learn languages: New perspectives for the personal observer. In D. Bannister (Ed.), *Issues and approaches in personal construct theory.* Orlando, FL: Academic Press.

Harrington, D. M., Block, J., & Block, J. H. (1987). Testing aspects of Carl Rogers's theory of creative environments: Child-rearing antecedents of creative potential in young adolescents. *Journal of Personality and Social Psychology, 52,* 851–856.

Harris, B. (1979). Whatever happened to little Albert? *American Psychologist, 34,* 151–160.

Harris, J. G., Jr. (1980). Nomovalidation and idiovalidation: A quest for the true personality profile. *American Psychologist, 35,* 729–744.

Hartley, D. E., & Strupp, H. H. (1983). The therapeutic alliance: Its relationship to outcome in brief psychotherapy. In J. Masling (Ed.), *Empirical studies of psychoanalytical theories* (Vol. 1). Hillsdale, NJ: Analytic Press.

Hartmann, H. (1951). Ego psychology and the problem of adaptation. In D. Rapaport (Ed. and Trans.), *Organization and pathology of thought: Selected sources.* New York: Columbia University Press.

Hartmann, H. (1958). *Ego psychology and the problem of adaptation.* New York: International Universities Press.

Hartmann, H. (1964). *Essays in ego psychology.* New York: International Universities Press.

Hartshorne, H., & May, M. A. (1928). *Studies in the nature of character* (Vol. 1). New York: Macmillan.

Hathaway, S. R., & Monachesi, E. D. (1952). The Minnesota Multiphasic Personality Inventory in the study of juvenile delinquents. *American Sociological Review, 17,* 704–710.

Hattie, J. (1992). *Self-concept.* Hillsdale, NJ: Erlbaum.

Hayashi, S., Kuno, T., Osawa, M., Shimizu, M., & Suetake, Y. (1992). The client-centered therapy and person-centered approach in Japan: Historical development, current status and perspectives. *Journal of Humanistic Psychology, 32,* 115–136.

Hayes, S. C., & Brownstein, A. J. (1986). Mentalism, behavior-behavior relations and a behavior analytic view of the purposes of science. *The Behavior Analyst, 9,* 175–190.

Haynes, P., & Ayliffe, G. (1991). Locus of control of behaviour: Is high externality associated with substance misuse? *British Journal of Addiction, 86,* 1111–1117.

Haynes, S. N., & Uchigakiuchi, P. (1993). Incorporating personality trait measures in behavioral assessment: Nuts in a fruitcake or raisins in a mai tai? *Behavior Modification, 17,* 72–92.

Hays, R. D., & Ellickson, P. L. (1990). How generalizable are adolescents' beliefs about pro-drug pressures and resistance self-efficacy? *Journal of Applied Social Psychology, 20,* 321–340.

Hazan, C., & Shaver, P. (1987). Romantic love conceptualizations as an attachment process. *Journal of Personality and Social Psychology, 52,* 511–524.

Hazan, C., & Shaver, P. R. (1994). Attachment as an organizational framework for research on close relationships. *Psychological Inquiry, 5,* 1–22.

Heath, A. C., Cloninger, C. R., & Martin, N. G. (1994). Testing a model for the genetic structure of personality: A comparison of the personality systems of Cloninger and Eysenck. *Journal of Personality and Social Psychology, 66,* 762–775.

Heath, A. C., Neale, M. C., Kessler, R. C., Eaves, L. J., & Kendler, K. S. (1992). Evidence for genetic influences on personality from self-reports and informant ratings. *Journal of Personality and Social Psychology, 63,* 85–96.

Heatherington, L., Crown, J., Wagner, H., & Rigby, S. (1989). Toward an understanding of social consequences of "feminine immodesty" about personal achievements. *Sex Roles, 20,* 371–380.

Heatherton, T. F., & Polivy, J. (1991). Development and validation of a scale for measuring state self-esteem. *Journal of Personality and Social Psychology, 60,* 895–910.

Heaven, P. C. (1988). Locus of control and attitudes toward authority among adolescents. *Personality and Individual Differences, 9,* 181–183.

Heaven, P. C. (1989). Economic locus of control beliefs and lay attributions of poverty. *Australian Journal of Psychology, 41,* 315–325.

Heaven, P. C. (1990). Suggestions for reducing unemployment: A study of Protestant work ethic and economic locus of control beliefs. *British Journal of Social Psychology, 29,* 55–65.

Heelan, P. A. (1983). *Space-perception and the philosophy of science.* Berkeley: University of California Press.

Helgason, A. R., Fredrikson, M., Dyba, T., & Steineck, G. (1995). Introverts give up smoking more often than extraverts. *Personality and Individual Differences, 18,* 559–560.

Helgeson, A. R., Fredrikson, M., Dyba, T., & Steineck, G. (1995). Introverts give up smoking more often than extraverts. *Personality and Individual Differences, 18,* 559–560.

Helgeson, V. S., & Sharpsteen, D. J. (1987). Perceptions of danger and affiliation situations: An extension of the Pollak and Gilligan versus Benton et al. debate. *Journal of Personality and Social Psychology, 54,* 727–733.

Heller, M. C., & Krauss, H. H. (1991). Perceived self-efficacy as a predictor of aftercare treatment entry by the detoxification patient. *Psychological Reports, 68,* 1047–1052.

Helmes, E., & Holden, R. R. (1986). Response styles and faking on the Basic Personality Inventory. *Journal of Consulting and Clinical Psychology, 54,* 853–859.

Helmreich, R. L., Spence, J. T., & Pred, R. S. (1988). Making it without losing it: Type A, achievement motivation, and scientific attainment revisited. *Personality and Social Psychology Bulletin, 14,* 495–504.

Heppner, P., Neal, G., & Larsen, L. (1984). Problem-solving training as prevention with college students. *Personnel and Guidance Journal, 62,* 514–519.

Herman, A., & Heesacker, M. (1991). A developing model of exploratory psychotherapeutic research: The process within the process. *International Journal of Personal Construct Psychology, 4,* 409–425.

Herman, J. L. (1992). *Trauma and recovery.* New York: Basic Books.

Hermans, H. J. M. (1988). On the integration of nomothetic and idiographic research methods in the study of personal meaning. *Journal of Personality, 56,* 785–812.

Herrnstein, R. J. (1970). On the law of effect. *Journal of the Experimental Analysis of Behavior, 13,* 243–266.

Hesse, M. B. (1963). *Models and analogies in science.* London: Sheed & Ward.

Hessing, D. J., Elffers, H., & Weigel, R. H. (1988). Exploring the limits of self-reports and reasoned action: An investigation of the psychology of tax evasion behavior. *Journal of Personality and Social Psychology, 54,* 405–413.

Hetherington, E. M. (1972). Effects of father absence on personality development in adolescent daughters. *Developmental Psychology, 7,* 313–326.

Hetherington, E. M. (1989). Coping with family transitions: Winners, losers, and survivors. *Child Development, 60,* 1–14.

Hetherington, E. M., Stanley-Hagan, M., & Anderson, E. R. (1989). Marital transitions: A child's perspective. *American Psychologist, 44,* 303–312.

Hewitt, P. L., & Genest, M. (1990). The ideal self: Schematic processing of perfectionistic contents in dysphoric university students. *Journal of Personality and Social Psychology, 59,* 802–808.

Hickey, P. (1993). Behavior therapy: Have we compromised too much? *the Behavior Therapist, 16,* 117–119.

Higgins, E. T. (1987). Self discrepancy: A theory relating self and affect. *Psychological Review, 94,* 319–340.

Higgins, E. T. (1990). Personality, social psychology, and person-situation relations: Standards and knowledge activation as a common language. In L. A. Pervin (Ed.), *Handbook of Personality: Theory and Research.* New York: Guilford.

Higgins, E. T., Bond, R. N., Klein, R., & Strauman, T. (1986). Self-discrepancies and emotional vulnerability: How magnitude, accessibility and type of discrepancy influence affect. *Journal of Personality and Social Psychology, 51,* 1–15.

Higgins, E. T., Rholes, W. S., & Jones, C. R. (1977). Category accessibility and impression formation. *Journal of Experimental Social Psychology, 13,* 141–154.

Higgins, E. T., Roney, C. J. R., Crowe, E., & Hymes, C. (1994). Ideal versus ought predilections for approach and avoidance: Distinct self-regulatory systems. *Journal of Personality and Social Psychology, 66,* 276–286.

Hill, G. J. (1989). An unwillingness to act: Behavioral appropriateness, situational constraint, and self-efficacy in shyness. *Journal of Personality, 57,* 871–890.

Hill, P. (1989). Behavioural psychotherapy with children. *International Review of Psychiatry, 1,* 257–266.

Hill, T., Lewicki, P., Czyzewska, M., & Boss, A. (1989). Self-perpetuating development of encoding biases in person perception. *Journal of Personality and Social Psychology, 57,* 373–387.

Hilsman, R., & Garber, J. (1995). A test of the cognitive diathesis-stress model of depression in children: Academic stressors, attributional style, perceived competence, and control. *Journal of Personality and Social Psychology, 69,* 370–380.

Hineline, P. N. (1992). A self-interpretive behavior analysis. *American Psychologist, 47,* 1274–1286.

Hinkley, K., & Andersen, S. M. (1996). The working self-concept in transference: Significant-other activation and self change. *Journal of Personality and Social Psychology, 71,* 1275–1279.

Hirschowitz, R. (1987). Behavioral and personality correlates of a need for power in a group of English-speaking South African women. *Journal of Psychology, 121,* 575–590.

Hjelle, L. A. (1991). Relationship of social interest to internal-external control and self-actualization in young women [Special issue: Social interest]. *Individual Psychology Journal of Adlerian Theory, Research and Practice, 47,* 101–105.

Hjelle, L. A., & Ziegler, D. J. (1981). *Personality theories: Basic assumptions, research, and applications* (2nd ed.). New York: McGraw-Hill.

Ho, A. P., Gillin, J. C., Buchsbaum, M. S., Wu, J. C., Abel, L., & Bunney, W. E. (1996). Brain glucose metabolism during non-rapid eye movement sleep in major depression: A positron emission tomography study. *Archives of General Psychiatry, 53,* 645–652.

Hobart, C. (1991). Conflict in remarriages. *Journal of Divorce and Remarriage, 15,* 69–86.

Hobson, J. A., & McCarley, R. W. (1977). The brain as a dream state generator: An activation-synthesis hypothesis of the dream process. *American Journal of Psychiatry, 134,* 1335–1438.

Hoffart, A., & Martinsen, E. W. (1990). Agoraphobia, depression, mental health locus of control, and attributional styles. *Cognitive Therapy and Research, 14,* 343–351.

Hoffart, A., & Martinsen, E. W. (1991). Mental health locus of control in agoraphobia and depression: A longitudinal study of inpatients. *Psychological Reports, 68,* 1011–1018.

Hoffer, A. (1985). Toward a definition of psychoanalytic neutrality. *Journal of the American Psychoanalytic Association, 33,* 771–795.

Hoffer, A., & Pollin, W. (1970). Schizophrenia in the NAS-NPC panel of 15,909 veteran twin pairs. *Archives of General Psychiatry, 23,* 469–477.

Hoffman, E. (1992, January/February). The last interview of Abraham Maslow. *Psychology Today, 89,* 68–73.

Hogan, J. (1989). Personality correlates of physical fitness. *Journal of Personality and Social Psychology, 56,* 284–288.

Hoge, R. D., Andrews, D. A., & Robinson, D. (1990). Patterns of child and parenting problems within six family types. *Canadian Journal of Behavioral Science, 22,* 99–109.

Holahan, C. J., Moos, R. H., Holahan, C. K., & Brennan, P. L. (1995). Social support, coping, and depressive symptoms in a late-middle-aged sample of patients reporting cardiac illness. *Health Psychology, 14,* 152–163.

Holden, G. (1991). The relationship of self-efficacy appraisals to subsequent health related outcomes: A meta-analysis. *Social Work in Health Care, 16,* 53–93.

Holden, G. W., Moncher, M. S., Schinke, S. P., & Barker, K. M. (1990). Self-efficacy of children and adolescents: A meta-analysis. *Psychological Reports, 66,* 1044–1046.

Holland, D. C., Dollinger, S. J., Holland, C. J., & MacDonald, D. A. (1995). The relationship between psychometric intelligence and the five-factor model of personality in a rehabilitation sample. *Journal of Clinical Psychology, 51,* 79–88.

Holland, J. G. (1992). B. F. Skinner (1904–1990). *American Psychologist, 47,* 665–667.

Hollander, E., DeCaria, C. M., Nitescu, A., Gully, R., Suckow, R. F., Cooper, T. B., Gorman, J. M., Klein, D. F., & Liebowitz, M. R. (1992). Serotonergic functions in obsessive-compulsive disorder. *Archives of General Psychiatry, 49,* 21–28.

Hollander, E. P. (1964). *Leaders, groups, and influence.* New York: Oxford University Press.

Hollon, S. D., Shelton, R. C., & Davis, D. D. (1993). Cognitive therapy for depression: Conceptual issues and clinical efficacy. *Journal of Consulting and Clinical Psychology, 61,* 270–275.

Holman, H. R., & Lorig, K. (1992). Perceived self-efficacy in the management of chronic disease. In R. Schwarzer (Ed.), *Self-efficacy: Thought control of action.* Washington, DC: Hemisphere.

Holmes, D. S. (1972). Repression or interference? A further investigation. *Journal of Personality and Social Psychology, 22,* 163–170.

Holmes, D. S. (1978). Projection as a defense mechanism. *Psychological Bulletin, 85,* 677–688.

Holmes, D. S. (1991). *Abnormal psychology.* New York: HarperCollins.

Holmes, D. S., McGilley, B. M., & Houston, B. K. (1984). Task-related arousal of Type A and Type B persons: Level of challenge and response specificity. *Journal of Personality and Social Psychology, 46,* 1322–1327.

Holmes, T. H., & Rahe, R. H. (1967). The social readjustment rating scale. *Journal of Psychosomatic Research, 11,* 213–218.

Holtzman, W. H. (1988). Beyond the Rorschach. *Journal of Personality Assessment, 52,* 578–609.

Holtzman, W. H., Thorpe, J. S., Swartz, J. D., & Herron, E. W. (1961). *Inkblot perception and personality: Holtzman Inkblot Technique.* Austin: University of Texas Press.

Honikman, B. (1976). Construct theory as an approach to architectural and environmental design. In P. Slater (Ed.), *Explorations of intrapersonal space* (Vol. 1). London: Wiley.

Hopper, R. B., & Kirschenbaum, D. S. (1985). Social problem solving and social competence in preadolescents: Is inconsistency the hobgoblin of little minds? *Cognitive Therapy and Research, 9,* 685–701.

Horley, J. (1988). Construal of events: Personal constructs versus projects. In F. Fransella & L. Thomas (Eds.), *Experimenting with personal construct psychology.* London: Routledge & Kegan Paul.

Horley, J. (1991). Values and beliefs as personal constructs. *International Journal of Personal Construct Psychology, 4,* 1–14.

Horne, J. (1988). *Why we sleep: The functions of sleep in humans and other mammals.* New York: Oxford University Press.

Horner, M. S. (1973). A psychological barrier to achievement in women: The motive to avoid success. In D. C. McClelland & R. S. Steele (Eds.), *Human motivation: A book of readings.* Morristown, NJ: General Learning Press.

Horney, K. (1939). *New ways in psychoanalysis.* New York: Norton.

Horton, G. E., & Brown, D. (1990). The importance of interpersonal skills in consultee-centered consultation: A review. *Journal of Counseling and Development, 68,* 423–426.

Houston, B. K. (1983). Psychophysiological responsivity and the Type A behavior pattern. *Journal of Research in Personality, 17,* 22–39.

Houts, A. C. (1991). Nocturnal enuresis as a biobehavioral problem. *Behavior Therapy, 22,* 133–151.

Houts, A. C., & Follette, W. C. (1992). Philosophical and theoretical issues in behavior therapy. *Behavior Therapy, 23,* 145–149.

Houts, A. C., & Liebert, R. M. (1984). *Bedwetting: A guide for parents and children.* Springfield, IL: Charles C Thomas.

Houts, A. C., Peterson, J. K., & Whelan, J. P. (1986). Prevention of relapse in Full-Spectrum Home Training for primary enuresis: A components analysis. *Behavior Therapy, 17,* 462–469.

Howard, J. H., Cunningham, D. A., & Rechnitzer, P. A. (1987). Personality and fitness decline in middle-aged men. *International Journal of Sport Psychology, 18,* 100–111.

Howard, R., & McKillen, M. (1990). Extraversion and performance in the perceptual maze test. *Personality and Individual Differences, 11,* 391–396.

Hudson, R. (1974). Images of the retailing environment: An example of the use of the repertory grid methodology. *Environment and Behavior, 6,* 470–495.

Huertas-Rodriguez, E. (1991). Cognitive techniques in human classical conditioning. *Journal of Psychophysiology, 5,* 5–10.

Hyland, M. E. (1988). Motivational control theory: An integrative framework. *Journal of Personality and Social Psychology, 55,* 642–651.

Hyland, M. E., Curtis, C., & Mason, D. (1985). Fear of success: Motive and cognition. *Journal of Personality and Social Psychology, 49,* 1669–1677.

Hyman, R. (1964). *The nature of psychological inquiry.* Englewood Cliffs, NJ: Prentice-Hall.

Ihilevich, D., & Gleser, G. C. (1986). *Defense mechanisms: Their classification, correlates and measurement with the Defense Mechanisms Inventory.* Owoso, MI: DMI Associates.

Ingold, C. H. (1989). Locus of control and use of public information. *Psychological Reports, 64,* 603–607.

Inwald, R. E., & Brockwell, A. L. (1991). Predicting the performance of government security personnel with the IPI and MMPI. *Journal of Personality Assessment, 56,* 522–535.

Isaacs, W., Thomas, J., & Goldiamond, I. (1960). Application of operant conditioning to reinstate verbal behavior in psychotics. *Journal of Speech and Hearing Disorders, 25,* 8–12.

Isabella, R. A., Belsky, J., & von Eye, A. (1989). Origins of moter-infant attachment: An examination of interactional synchrony during the infant's first year. *Developmental Psychology, 25,* 12–21.

Jacklin, C. N., Maccoby, E. E., & Doering, C. H. (1983). Neonatal sex-steroid hormones and timidity in 6–18 month-old boys and girls. *Developmental Psychobiology, 16,* 163–168.

Jackson, D. D. (Ed.). (1960). *The etiology of schizophrenia.* New York: Basic Books.

Jackson, D. N. (1976). *Jackson Personality Inventory manual.* Port Huron, MI: Research Psychologists Press.

Jackson, D. N. (1994). *Jackson Personality Inventory–Revised manual.* Port Huron, MI: Sigma Assessment Systems.

Jackson, D. N., & Messick, S. (1958). Content and style in personality assessment. *Psychological Bulletin, 55,* 243–252.

Jackson, T. T., Markley, R. P., Zelhart, P. F., & Guydish, J. (1988). Contributions to the history of psychology: XLV. Attitude research: George A. Kelly's use of polar adjectives. *Psychological Reports, 62,* 47–52.

Jacobson, N. S. (1985). The role of observational measures in behavior therapy outcome research. *Behavioral Assessment, 7,* 297–308.

Jacobson, N. S. (1989). The maintenance of treatment gains following social learning-based marital therapy. *Behavior Therapy, 20,* 325–336.

Jacobson, N. S. (1991, September). *Marital therapy: Theory and treatment considerations.* Workshop sponsored by the Rhode Island Psychological Association, Warwick, RI.

Jacobson, N. S. (1992). Behavioral couple therapy: A new beginning. *Behavior Therapy, 23,* 493–506.

Jaffe, L. S. (1990). The empirical foundations of psychoanalytic approaches to psychological testing. *Journal of Personality Assessment, 55,* 746–755.

Jaison, B. (1991). Experiential learning: Reflections on Virginia Satir and Eugene Gendlin. *Journal of Couples Therapy, 2,* 155–163.

James, W. (1890). *The principles of psychology* (2 vols.). New York: Holt, Rinehart, & Wilson.

Jankowicz, A. D. (1987). Whatever became of George Kelly? Applications and implications. *American Psychologist, 42,* 481–487.

Jankowicz, A. D. (1990). Applications of personal construct psychology in business practice. In G. J. Neimeyer & R. A. Neimeyer (Eds.), *Advances in personal construct psychology* (Vol. 1). Greenwich, CT: JAI Press.

Jay, S. M., Elliot, C. H., Ozolins, M., Olson, R. A., & Pruitt, S. D. (1985). Behavioral management of children's distress during painful medical procedures. *Behaviour Research and Therapy, 23,* 513–520.

Jenkins, S. R. (1987). Need for achievement and women's careers over 14 years: Evidence for occupational structure effects. *Journal of Personality and Social Psychology, 53,* 922–932.

Jenkins, S. R. (1996). Self-definition in thought, action, and life path choices. *Personality and Social Psychology Bulletin, 22,* 99–111.

Jennings, B. M. (1990). Stress, locus of control, social support, and psychological symptoms among head nurses. *Research in Nursing & Health, 13,* 393–401.

Jensen, L., Olsen, J., & Hughes, C. (1990). Association of country, sex, social class, and life cycle to locus of control in Western European countries. *Psychological Reports, 67,* 199–205.

Jensen, L., Huber, C., Cundick, B., & Carlson, J. (1991). Development of a self theory and measurement scale. *Journal of Personality Assessment, 57,* 521–530.

Jerusalem, M., & Schwarzer, R. (1992). Self-efficacy as a resource factor in stress appraisal processes. In R. Schwarzer (Ed.), *Self-efficacy: Thought control of action.* Washington, DC: Hemisphere.

John, I. D., & Soyland, A. J. (1990). What is the epistemic status of the theory of personal constructs? *International Journal of Personal Construct Psychology, 3,* 51–62.

John, O. P., Angleitner, A., & Ostendorf, F. (1988). The lexical approach to personality: A historical review of trait taxonomic research. *European Journal of Personality, 2,* 171–203.

John, O. P., Caspi, A., Robins, R. W., Moffit, T. E., & Stouthamer-Loeber, M. (1994). The "little five": Exploring the nomological network of the five-factor model of personality in adolescent boys. *Child Development, 65,* 160–178.

John, O. P., Hampson, S. E., & Goldberg, L. R. (1991). The basic level in personality-trait hierarchies: Studies of trait use and accessibility in different contexts. *Journal of Personality and Social Psychology, 60,* 348–361.

Johnson, E. E., Nora, R. M., Tan, B., & Bustos, N. (1991). Comparison of two locus of control scales in predicting relapse in an alcoholic population. *Perceptual and Motor Skills, 72,* 43–50.

Johnson, G. B. (1966). Penis envy or pencil needing? *Psychological Reports, 19,* 758.

Johnson, J. H., Butcher, J. N., Null, C., & Johnson, K. N. (1984). Replicated item level factor analysis of the full MMPI. *Journal of Personality and Social Psychology, 47,* 105–114.

Johnson, L. R., Magnani, B., Chan, V., & Ferrante, F. M. (1989). Modifiers of patient-controlled analgesia efficacy: I. Locus of control. *Pain, 39,* 17–22.

Johnson, S. B. (1980). Enuresis. In R. Daitzman (Ed.), Clinical behavior therapy and behavior modification. New York: Garland.

Jones, A., & Crandall, R. (1986). Validation of a short index of self-actualization. *Personality and Social Psychology Bulletin, 12,* 63–73.

Jones, D. C., & Houts, R. (1992). Parental drinking, parent-child communication, and social skills in young adults. *Journal of Studies on Alcohol, 53,* 48–56.

Jones, E. (1927). The early development of female sexuality. *International Journal of Psycho-Analysis, 8,* 459–472.

Jones, E. (1953). *The life and works of Sigmund Freud* (Vol. 1). New York: Basic Books.

Jorm, A. F. (1987). Sex differences in neuroticism: A quantitative synthesis of published research. *Australian and New Zealand Journal of Psychiatry, 21,* 501–506.

Josephs, L. (1988). A comparison of archaeological and

empathic modes of listening. *Contemporary Psychoanalysis, 24,* 282–300.

Jung, C. G. (1933). *Modern man in search of a soul* (W. S. Dell & C. F. Baynes, Trans.). New York: Harcourt Brace.

Jung, C. G. (1969). General aspects of dream psychology. In *The collected works of C. G. Jung* (Vol. 8). Princeton, NJ: Princeton University Press.

Jussim, L. (1991). Social perception and social reality: A reflection-construction model. *Psychological Review, 98,* 54–73.

Kagan, J., & Moss, H. A. (1960). *Birth to maturity.* New York: Wiley.

Kagan, J., & Reznick, J. S. (1986). Shyness and temperament. In W. H. Jones, J. M. Cheek, & S. R. Briggs (Eds.), *Shyness.* New York: Plenum.

Kagan, J., Reznick, J. S., & Snidman, N. (1987). The physiology and psychology of behavioral inhibition in children. *Child Development, 58,* 1459–1473.

Kagan, J., & Snidman, N. (1991a). Infant predictors of inhibited and uninhibited profiles. *Psychological Science, 2,* 40–44.

Kagan, J., & Snidman, N. (1991b). Temperamental factors in human development. *American Psychologist, 46,* 856–862.

Kagitcibasi, C., & Berry, J. W. (1989). Cross-cultural psychology: Current research and trends. In M. R. Rosenzweig & J. W. Porter (Eds.). *Annual review of psychology* (Vol. 40). (pp. 493–531). Palo Alto, CA: Annual Reviews.

Kahn, E. (1989). Heinz Kohut and Carl Rogers: Toward a constructive collaboration. *Psychotherapy, 26,* 555–563.

Kahn, J. S., Kehle, T. J., Jenson, W. R., & Clark, E. (1990). Comparison of cognitive-behavioral, relaxation, and self-modeling interventions for depression among middle-school students. *School Psychology Review, 19,* 196–211.

Kalat, J. W. (1995). *Biological psychology* (5th ed.). Pacific Grove, CA: Brooks/Cole.

Kaplan, H. I., & Saddock, B. J. (1991). *Synopsis of Psychiatry* (6th ed.). Baltimore: Williams & Wilkins.

Karnes, F. A., & McGinnis, J. C. (1995). Self-actualization and locus of control of gifted children in fourth through eighth grades. *Psychological Reports, 76,* 1039–1042.

Karylowski, J. J. (1990). Social reference points and accessibility of trait-related information in self-other similarity judgments. *Journal of Personality and Social Psychology, 58,* 975–983.

Katerndahl, D. A. (1991). Relationship between panic attacks and health locus of control. *Journal of Family Practice, 32,* 391–396.

Katz, J. O. (1984). Personal construct theory and the emotions: An interpretation in terms of primitive constructs. *British Journal of Psychology, 75,* 315–327.

Kavanagh, D. (1992). Self-efficacy and depression. In R. Schwarzer (Ed.), *Self-efficacy: Thought control of action.* Washington, DC: Hemisphere.

Kehle, T. J., Owen, S. V., & Cressy, E. T. (1990). The use of self-modeling as an intervention in school psychology: A case study of an elective mute. *School Psychology Review, 19,* 115–121.

Kelly, D., & Taylor, H. (1981). Take and escape: A personal construct study of car "theft." In H. Bonarius, R. Holland, & S. Rosenberg (Eds.), *Personal construct psychology: Recent advances in theory and practice.* New York: St. Martin's Press.

Kelly, G. A. (1955). *The psychology of personal constructs* (Vols. 1 and 2). New York: Norton.

Kelly, G. A. (1961). Suicide: The personal construct point of view. In N. L. Farberow & E. S. Schneidman (Eds.), *The cry for help.* New York: McGraw-Hill.

Kelly, G. A. (1966). A brief introduction to personal construct theory. In D. Bannister (Ed.), *Perspectives in personal construct theory.* London: Academic Press.

Kelly, G. A. (1969). Sin and psychotherapy. In B. Maher (Ed.), *Clinical psychology and personality: The selected papers of George Kelly.* New York: Wiley.

Kelly, G. A. (1980). A psychology of the optimal man. In A. W. Landfield & L. M. Leitner (Eds.), *Personal construct psychology: Psychotherapy and personality.* New York: Wiley.

Keltikangas-Jarvinen, L. (1990). Continuity of Type A behavior during childhood, preadolescence, and adolescence. *Journal of Youth and Adolescence, 19,* 221–232.

Keltikangas-Jarvinen, L., & Raikkonen, K. (1990). Type A factors as predictors of somatic risk factors of coronary heart disease in young Finns: A six year followup study. *Journal of Psychosomatic Research, 34,* 89–97.

Keltikangas-Jarvinen, L., & Raikkonen, K. (1993). Emotional styles and coping strategies characterizing the risk and non-risk dimensions of Type A behavior in young men. *Personality and Individual Differences, 14,* 667–677.

Kemp, S. (1988). Personality in ancient astrology. *New Ideas in Psychology, 6,* 267–272.

Kendall-Tackett, K. A., Williams, L. M., & Finkelhor, D. (1993). Impact of sexual abuse on children: A review and synthesis of recent empirical studies. *Psychological Bulletin, 113,* 164–180.

Kendon, A. (1987). On gesture: Its complementary relationship with speech. In A. W. Siegman & S. Feldstein (Eds.), *Nonverbal behavior and communication.* Hillsdale, NJ: Erlbaum.

Kendrick, D. T., & Funder, D. C. (1988). Profiting from controversy: Lessons from the person-situation debate. *American Psychologist, 43,* 23–34.

Kenny, V., & Delmonte, M. (1986). Meditation as viewed through personal construct theory. *Journal of Contemporary Psychotherapy, 16,* 4–22.

Kenrick, D. T., Sadalla, E. K., Groth, G., & Trost, M. R. (1990). Evolution, traits, and the stages of human courtship: Qualifying the parental investment model. *Journal of Personality, 58,* 97–116.

Kern, S. (1973). Freud and the discovery of child sexuality. *History of Childhood Quarterly, 1,* 117–141.

Kernberg, O. (1975). *Borderline conditions and pathological narcissism.* New York: Aronson.

Kernberg, O. (1976). *Object-relations theory and clinical psychoanalysis.* New York: Aronson.

Kernberg, O. (1987). Projection and projective identification: Developmental and clinical aspects. *Journal of the American Psychoanalytic Association, 35,* 795–819.

Kernis, M. H., Cornell, D. P., Sun, C., Berry, A., & Harlow, T. (1993). There's more to self-esteem than whether it is high or low: The importance of stability of self-esteem. *Journal of Personality and Social Psychology, 65,* 1190–1204.

Kessler, S. (1980). The genetics of schizophrenia: A review. *Schizophrenia Bulletin, 6,* 404–416.

Kety, S., Rosenthal, D., Wender, P. H., & Shulsinger, F. (1968). The types and prevalence of mental illness in the biological and adoptive families of adopted schizophrenics. In D. Rosenthal and S. Kety (Eds.), *The transmission of schizophrenia.* New York: Pergamon Press.

Keutzer, C. (1978). Whatever turns you on: Triggers to transcendent experiences. *Journal of Humanistic Psychology, 18,* 77–80.

Kimmel, H. D. (1989). The importance of classical conditioning. *Behavioral and Brain Sciences, 12,* 148–149.

King, A. C., Enrico, A. L., & Parsons, O. A. (1995). Eysenck's personality dimensions and sex steroids in male abstinent alcoholics and nonalcoholics: An exploratory study. *Biological Psychology, 39,* 103–113.

Kinney, P. J., & Williams, S. L. (1988). Accuracy of fear inventories and self-efficacy scales in predicting agoraphobic behavior. *Behaviour Research and Therapy, 26,* 513–518.

Kinsey, A. C., Pomeroy, W. B., Martin, C. E. (1948). *Sexual behavior in the human male.* Philadelphia: W. B. Saunders.

Kirkland, J., & Anderson, R. (1990). Invariants, constructs, affordances, analogies. *International Journal of Personal Construct Psychology, 3,* 31–39.

Kirkpatrick, L. A., & Davis, K. E. (1994). Attachment style, gender, and relationship stability: A longitudinal analysis. *Journal of Personality and Social Psychology, 66,* 502–512.

Kirschenbaum, H. (1991). Denigrating Carl Rogers: William Coulson's last crusade. *Journal of Counseling and Development, 69,* 411–413.

Klein, G. S. (1976). *Psychoanalytic theory: An exploration of essentials.* New York: International Universities Press.

Klein, S. B., & Kihlstrom, J. F. (1986). Elaboration, organization, and the self-reference effect in memory. *Journal of Experimental Psychology: General, 115,* 26–38.

Kleinknecht, R. A., & Bernstein, D. A. (1979). Short term treatment of dental avoidance. *Journal of Behavior Therapy and Experimental Psychiatry, 10,* 311–315.

Klerman, G. L., Weissman, M. M., Markowitz, J., Glick, I., Wilner, P. J., Mason, B., & Shear, M. K. (1994). Medication and psychotherapy. In A. E. Bergin & S. L. Garfield (Eds.), *Handbook of psychotherapy and behavior change* (4th ed.). New York: Wiley.

Klerman, G. L., Weissman, M. M., Rounsville, B. J., & Chevron, E. S. (1984). *Interpersonal psychotherapy of depression.* New York: Basic Books.

Kline, P. (1972). *Fact and fantasy in Freudian theory.* London: Methuen.

Kline, P. (1987). The experimental study of the psychoanalytic unconscious. *Personality and Social Psychology Bulletin, 13,* 363–378.

Kline, P., & Barrett, P. (1983). The factors in personality questionnaires among normal subjects. *Advances in Behaviour Research and Therapy, 5,* 141–202.

Klinger, E. (1995). Effects of motivation and emotion on thought flow and cognition: Assessment and findings. In P. E. Shrout & S. T. Fiske (Eds.). *Personality research, methods, and theory,* (pp. 257–270). Hillsdale, NJ: Erlbaum.

Klinger, E. (1966). Fantasy need achievement as a motivational construct. *Psychological Bulletin, 66,* 291–308.

Klion, R. E. (1988). Construct system organization and schizophrenia: The role of construct integration. *Journal of Social and Clinical Psychology, 6,* 439–447.

Klopfer, B., & Davidson, H. H. (1962). *The Rorschach technique: An introductory manual.* New York: Harcourt, Brace & World.

Kluckhohn, V., & Murray, H. A. (1953). Personality formation: The determinants. In C. Kluckhohn, H. Murray, & D. Schneider (Eds.), *Personality in nature, society, and culture.* New York: Knopf.

Kluft, R. P. (1991). Multiple personality disorder. In A. Tasman & S. M. Goldfinger (Eds.), *Review of Psychiatry* (Vol. 10). Washington, DC: American Psychiatric Press.

Knapp, P. H., Levin, S., McCarter, R. H., Wermer, H., & Zetzel, E. (1960). Suitability for psychoanalysis: A review of 100 supervised analytic cases. *Psychoanalytic Quarterly, 29,* 459–477.

Knapp, R. R. (1976). *Handbook for the Personal Orientation Inventory.* San Diego: EdITS Publishers.

Knowles, E. S., & Byers, B. (1996). Reliability shifts in measurement reactivity: Driven by content engagement or self-engagement? *Journal of Personality and Social Psychology, 70,* 1080–1090.

Koestner, R., Zuckerman, M., & Koestner, J. (1987). Praise, involvement, and intrinsic motivation. *Journal of Personality and Social Psychology, 53,* 383–390.

Kohnken, G., & Maass, A. (1988). Eyewitness testimony: False alarms on biased instructions? *Journal of Applied Psychology, 73,* 363–370.

Kohut, H. (1977). *The restoration of self.* New York: International Universities Press.

Kohut, H. (1984). *How does analysis cure?* Chicago: University of Chicago Press.

Kok, G., Den Boer, D. J., De Vries, H., Gerards, F., Hospers, H. J., & Mudde, A. N. (1992). Self-efficacy and attribution theory in health education. In R. Schwarzer (Ed.), *Self-efficacy: Thought control of action.* Washington, DC: Hemisphere.

Kok, G., de Vries, H., Mudde, A. N., & Strecher, V. J. (1991). Planned health education and the role of self-efficacy: Dutch research. *Health Education Research, 6,* 231–238.

Kolotkin, R. L., Revis, E. S., Kirkley, B. G., & Janick, L. (1987). Binge eating and obesity: Associated with MMPI characteristics. *Journal of Consulting and Clinical Psychology, 55,* 872–876.

Korabik, K., & Van Kampen, J. (1995). Gender, social support, and coping with work stressors among managers. *Journal of Social Behavior and Personality, 10,* 135–148.

Kores, R. C., Murphy, W. D., Rosenthal, T. L., Elias, D. B., & North, W. C. (1990). Predicting outcome of chronic pain treatment via a modified self-efficacy scale. *Behaviour Research and Therapy, 28,* 165–169.

Kosinski, J. N. (1970). *Being there.* New York: Harcourt Brace Jovanovich.

Kowalski, R. M. (1996). Complaints and complaining: Functions, antecedents, and consequences. *Psychological Bulletin, 119,* 179–196.

Krahe, B. (1989). Faking personality profiles on a standard personality inventory. *Personality and Individual Differences, 10,* 437–443.

Krampen, G. (1989). Perceived childrearing practices and the development of locus of control in early adolescence. *International Journal of Behavioral Development, 12,* 177–193.

Kremsdorf, R. B. (1985). An extension of fixed role therapy with a couple. In F. R. Epting & A. W. Landfield (Eds.), *Anticipating personal construct theory.* Lincoln: University of Nebraska Press.

Kretschmer, E. (1926). *Physique and character: An investigation of the nature of constitution and of the theory of temperament* (W. J. H. Sprott, Trans.). New York: Harcourt.

Kringlen, E., & Cramer, G. (1989). Offspring of monozygotic twins discordant for schizophrenia. *Archives of General Psychiatry, 46,* 873–877.

Kris, E. (1950). On preconscious mental processes. *Psychoanalytic Quarterly, 19,* 540–560.

Kruesi, M. J. P., Hibbs, E. D., Zahn, T. P., Keysor, C. S., Hamburger, S. D., Bartko, J. J., & Rapoport, J. L. (1992). A 2-year prospective follow-up of children and adolescents with disruptive behavior disorders. *Archives of General Psychiatry, 49,* 429–435.

Kuhn, T. S. (1970). *The structure of scientific revolutions* (2nd ed.). Chicago: University of Chicago Press.

Kurdek, L. A., & Schmitt, J. P. (1986). Relationship quality of partners in heterosexual married, heterosexual cohabitating, and gay and lesbian relationships. *Journal of Personality and Social Psychology, 51,* 711–720.

Kurzweil, E. (1994). Ambivalences among Freudians and feminists. *Journal of the American Academy of Psychoanalysis, 22,* 363–376.

Kutcher, S., & Marton, P. (1991). Affective disorders in first-degree relatives of adolescent onset bipolars, unipolars, and normal controls. *Journal of the American Academy of Child and Adolescent Psychiatry, 30,* 75–78.

Kvavilashvili, L. (1987). Remembering intention as a distinct form of memory. *British Journal of Psychology, 78,* 507–518.

Labouvie-Vief, G., & Gonda, J. (1976). Cognitive strategy training and intellectual performance in the elderly. *Journal of Gerontology, 31,* 327–332.

Lacan, J. (1966). The meaning of the phallus. In J. Mitchell & J. Rose (Eds.), *Feminine sexuality: Jacques Lacan and the ecole freudienne.* New York: Norton.

Lagarde, D., Laurent, J., Milhaud, C., Andre, E., Aubin, H. H., & Anton, G. (1990). Behavioral effects induced by beta CCE in free or restrained rhesus monkeys *(Macaca mulatta). Pharmacology Biochemistry & Behavior, 35,* 713–719.

Lamia, M. C. (1995). The defensive aspect of feminism and its resistance function in psychoanalysis. *Journal of Clinical Psychoanalysis, 4,* 343–359.

Landfield, A. W. (1980). The person as a perspectivist, literalist, and chaotic fragmentalist. In A. W. Landfield & L. M. Leitner (Eds.), *Personal construct psychology: Psychotherapy and personality.* New York: Wiley.

Landfield, A. W., & Epting, F. R. (1987). *Personal construct psychology: Clinical and personality assessment.* New York: Human Sciences Press.

Landino, R. A., & Owen, S. V. (1988). Self-efficacy in university faculty. *Journal of Vocational Behavior, 33,* 1–14.

Landsman, T., & Landsman, M. S. (1991). The beautiful and noble person: An existentialist phenomenological view of optimal human functioning [Special issue: Handbook of self-actualization]. *Journal of Social Behavior and Personality, 6,* 61–74.

Lang, A. R., Goeckner, D. J., Adesso, V. J., & Marlatt, G. A. (1975). Effects of alcohol on aggression in males. *Journal of Abnormal Psychology, 84,* 508–516.

Langer, E. J., & Abelson, R. P. (1974). A patient by any other name . . . "Clinician group difference in labeling bias." *Journal of Consulting and Clinical Psychology, 42,* 4–9.

Langlois, J. H., & Downs, A. C. (1980). Mothers, fathers and peers as socializing agents of sex-typed play behaviors in young children. *Child Development, 51,* 1237–1247.

Langs, R. (1987). Psychoanalysis as an Aristotelian science: Pathways to Copernicus and a modern-day approach. *Contemporary Psychoanalysis, 24,* 555–576.

Langs, R. (1988). Perspectives of psychoanalysis as a late arrival to the family of sciences. *Contemporary Psychoanalysis, 24,* 397–419.

LaPiere, R. T. (1934). Attitudes vs. actions. *Social Forces, 13,* 230–237.

Laqueur, Thomas. (1990). *Making sex: Body and gender from the Greeks to Freud.* Cambridge, MA: Harvard University Press.

Larkin, J. E. (1991). The implicit theories approach to the self-monitoring controversy. *European Journal of Personality, 5,* 15–34.

Larsen, R. J. (1984). Theory and measurement of affect intensity as an individual difference characteristic. *Dissertation Abstracts International, 85,* 2297B.

Larsen, R. J., & Ketelaar, T. (1989). Extraversion, neuroticism and susceptibility to positive and negative mood induction procedures. *Personality and Individual Differences, 10,* 1221–1228.

Larsen, R. J., & Ketelaar, T. (1991). Personality and susceptibility to positive and negative emotional states. *Journal of Personality and Social Psychology, 61,* 132–140.

Lauer, C., Reimann, D., Lund, R., & Berger, M. (1987). Shortened REM latency: A consequence of psychological strain? *Psychophysiology, 24,* 263–271.

Lavie, P., & Hobson, J. A. (1986). Origin of dreams: Anticipation of modern theories in the philosophy and physiology of the eighteenth and nineteenth centuries. *Psychological Bulletin, 100,* 229–240.

Lavin, N. I., Thorpe, J. G., Barker, J. C., Blakemore, C. B., & Conway, C. G. (1961). Behavior therapy in a case of transvestism. *Journal of Nervous and Mental Disease, 33,* 346–353.

Lawton, J. M., & Sanders, M. R. (1994). Designing effective behavioral family interventions for stepfamilies. *Clinical Psychology Review, 14,* 463–496.

Lax, R. F. (1995). Freud's views and the changing perspective on femaleness and femininity: What my female analysands taught me. *Psychoanalytic Psychology, 12,* 393–406.

Lee, T. F. (1993). *Gene future: The promise and perils of the new biology.* New York: Plenum.

Lee, V. L. (1988). *Beyond behaviorism.* Hillsdale, NJ: Erlbaum.

Lefcourt, H. M. (1982). *Locus of control: Current theory and research* (2nd ed.). Hillsdale, NJ: Erlbaum.

Lefcourt, H. M. (Ed.). (1981). *Research with the locus of control construct: Assessment methods* (Vol. 1). New York: Academic Press.

Lefcourt, H. M., Martin, R. A., Fick, C. M., & Saleh, W. E. (1985). Locus of control for affiliation and behavior in social interactions. *Journal of Personality and Social Psychology, 48,* 755–759.

Lefcourt, H. M., Martin, R. A., & Saleh, W. E. (1984). Locus of control and social support: Interactive moderators of stress. *Journal of Personality and Social Psychology, 47,* 378–389.

Leichtman, M. (1990). Developmental psychology and psychoanalysis: I. The context for a revolution in psychoanalysis. *Journal of the American Psychoanalytic Association, 38,* 915–950.

Lennox, R. D., & Wolfe, R. N. (1984). Revision of the Self-Monitoring Scale. *Journal of Personality and Social Psychology, 46,* 1349–1364.

Lent, R. W., & Hackett, G. (1987). Career self-efficacy: Empirical status and future directions. *Journal of Vocational Behavior, 30,* 347–382.

Lent, R. W., Lopez, F. G., & Bieschke, K. J. (1991). Mathematics self-efficacy: Sources and relation to science-based career choice. *Journal of Counseling Psychology, 38,* 424–430.

Lentz, T. L., Burrage, T. G., Smith, A. L., Crick, J., & Tignor, G. H. (1982). Is the acetylcholine receptor a rabies virus receptor? *Science, 215,* 182–184.

Leonard, H. L., Swedo, S. E., Rapoport, J. L., Koby, E. V., Lenane, M. C., Cheslow, D. L., & Hamburger, S. D. (1989). Treatment of obsessive-compulsive disorder with clomipramine and desipramine in children and adolescents. *Archives of General Psychiatry, 46,* 1088–1092.

LeShan, L. (1991, January/February). Ratting on psychologists. *Hippocrates,* pp. 71–75.

Lesser, G. S. (1973). Achievement motivation in woman. In D. C. McClelland & R. S. Steele (Eds.), *Human motivation: A book of readings.* Morristown, NJ: General Learning Press.

Lesser, G. S., Krawitz, R., & Packard, R. (1963). Experimental arousal of achievement motivation in adolescent girls. *Journal of Abnormal and Social Psychology, 66,* 59–66.

Lessler, K. (1964). Cultural and Freudian dimensions of sexual symbols. *Journal of Consulting Psychology, 28,* 46–53.

Lester, D., Castromayor, I. J., & Icli, T. (1991). Locus of control, depression, and suicidal ideation among American, Philippine, and Turkish students. *Journal of Social Psychology, 131,* 447–449.

Levant, R. F., & Shlien, J. M. (1987). *Client-centered therapy and the person-centered approach: New directions in theory, research, and practice.* New York: Praeger.

Levenson, E. A. (1988). The pursuit of the particular: On the psychoanalytic inquiry. *Contemporary Psychoanalysis, 24,* 1–16.

Levey, A. B., & Martin, I. (1991). Human classical conditioning: The status of the CS. *Integrative Physiology and Behavioral Science, 26,* 26–31.

Levine, F. J., & Slap, J. W. (1985). George S. Klein: Psychoanalytic empiricist. In J. Reppen (Ed.), *Beyond Freud: A study of modern psychoanalytic theorists.* Hillsdale, NJ: Analytic Press.

Levinson, D. J., Darrow, C. N., Klein, E. B., Levinson, M. H., & McKee, B. (1978). *The seasons of a man's life.* New York: Knopf.

Levis, D. J. (1985). Implosive theory: A comprehensive extension of conditioning theory of fear/anxiety to psychopathology. In S. Reiss & R. R. Bootzin (Eds.), *Theoretical issues in behavior therapy.* Orlando, FL: Academic Press.

Levy, L. H. (1970). *Conceptions of personality: Theories and research.* New York: Random House.

Lewinsohn, P. M., Mischel, W., Chaplin, W., & Barton, R. (1980). Social competence and depression: The role of illusory self-perceptions. *Journal of Abnormal Psychology, 89,* 203–212.

Lewis, C. A., & Maltby, J. (1995). Religiosity and personality among U.S. adults. *Personality and Individual Differences, 18,* 293–295.

Lewis, M. (1967). The meaning of a response, or why

researchers in infant behavior should be Oriental metaphysicians. *Merrill-Palmer Quarterly, 13,* 7–18.

Lewis, O. (1961). *The children of Sanchez: Autobiography of a Mexican family.* New York: Random House.

Liebert, R. M. (1973). Observational learning: Some social applications. In P. J. Elich (Ed.), *The fourth Western symposium on learning.* Bellingham: Western Washington State College.

Liebert, R. M. (1979). Moral development: A theoretical and empirical analysis. In G. J. Whitehurst & B. Zimmerman (Eds.), *The functions of language and cognition.* New York: Wiley.

Liebert, R. M., & Baron, R. A. (1972). Some immediate effects of televised violence on children's behavior. *Developmental Psychology, 6,* 469–475.

Liebert, R. M., & Fernandez, L. E. (1969). Vicarious reward and task complexity as determinants of imitative learning. *Psychological Reports, 25,* 531–534.

Liebert, R. M., & Fischel, J. E. (1990). The elimination disorders: Enuresis and encopresis. In M. Lewis & S. Miller (Eds.), *Handbook of developmental psychopathology.* New York: Plenum.

Liebert, R. M., & Liebert, L. L. (1995). *Science and behavior: An introduction to the methods of psychological research* (4th ed.). Englewood Cliffs, NJ: Prentice-Hall.

Liebert, R. M., & Ora, J. P., Jr. (1968). Children's adoption of self-reward patterns: Incentive level and method of transmission. *Child Development, 39,* 537–544.

Liebert, R. M., Poulos, R. W., & Rubinstein, E. A. (1975). Positive social learning. *Journal of Communication, 25,* 90–97.

Liebert, R. M., & Spiegler, M. D. (1970). *Personality: An introduction to theory and research.* Homewood, IL: Dorsey Press.

Liebert, R. M., & Spiegler, M. D. (1990). *Personality: Strategies and Issues* (6th ed.). Pacific Grove, CA: Brooks/Cole.

Liebert, R. M., & Sprafkin, J. (1988). *The early window* (3rd ed.). Elmsford, NY: Pergamon Press.

Liebert, R. M., Wicks-Nelson, R., & Kail, R. (1986). *Developmental psychology* (4th ed.). Englewood Cliffs, NJ: Prentice-Hall.

Lietaer, G. (1981). The client-centered approach in the seventies. Part I: A structured review of the literature. *Tijdschrift voor Psychotherapie, 7,* 81–102.

Lietaer, G. (1984). Unconditional positive regard: A controversial basic attitude in client-centered therapy. In R. F. Levant & J. M. Shlien (Eds.), *Client-centered therapy and the person-centered approach: New directions in theory, research, and practice.* New York: Praeger.

Lindzey, G., & Herman, P. S. (1955). Thematic Apperception Test: A note on reliability and situational validity. *Journal of Projective Techniques, 19,* 36–42.

Linville, P. T., (1985). Self-complexity and affective extremity: Don't put all your eggs in one cognitive basket. *Social Cognition, 3,* 94–120.

Linville, P. T. (1987). Self-complexity as a cognitive buffer against stress-related illness and depression. *Journal of Personality and Social Psychology, 54,* 663–676.

Little, B. R. (1989). Personal projects analysis: Trivial pursuits, magnificent obsessions, and the search for coherence. In D. M. Buss & N. Cantor (Eds.), *Personality psychology: Recent trends and emerging directions.* New York: Springer-Verlag.

Ljubin, T., & Ljubin, C. (1990). Extraversion and audiomotor reflex. *Personality and Individual Differences, 11,* 977–984.

Lloyd, C., & Chang, A. F. (1979). The usefulness of distinguishing between a defensive and a nondefensive external locus of control. *Journal of Research in Personality, 13,* 316–325.

Lochman, J. E. (1992). Cognitive-behavioral intervention with aggressive boys: Three-year follow-up and preventive effects. *Journal of Consulting and Clinical Psychology, 60,* 426–432.

Lochman, J. E., & Curry, J. F. (1986a). Effects of social problem-solving training and self-instruction training with aggressive boys. *Journal of Clinical Child Psychology, 15,* 159–164.

Lochman, J. E., & Curry, J. F. (1986b). Situational social problem-solving skills and self-esteem of aggressive and nonaggressive boys. *Journal of Abnormal Child Psychology, 14,* 605–617.

Locke, E. A., & Latham, G. P. (1990). *A theory of goal setting and task performance.* Englewood Cliffs, NJ: Prentice-Hall.

Loehlin, J. C. (1989). Partitioning environmental and genetic contributions to behavioral development. *American Psychologist, 44,* 1285–1292.

Loehlin, J. C. (1992). *Genes and environment in personality development.* Newbury Park, CA: Sage.

Loehlin, J. C., & Nichols, R. C. (1976). *Heredity, environment, and personality.* Austin: University of Texas Press.

Loehlin, J. C., Willerman, L., & Horn, J. M. (1987). Personality resemblance in adoptive families: A ten-year follow-up. *Journal of Personality and Social Psychology, 53,* 961–969.

Loevinger, J. (1994). Has psychology lost its conscience? *Journal of Personality Assessment, 62,* 2–8.

Loewenstein, R., Newmann, L. M., Schur, M., & Solnit, A. J. (Eds.). (1966). *Psychoanalysis—a general psychology: Essays in honor of Heinz Hartmann.* New York: International Universities Press.

Loftus, E. (1993). The reality of repressed memories. *American Psychologist, 48,* 518–537.

Loftus, E. F. (1997). Creating false memories. *Scientific American, 277,* 71–75.

Loos, V. E. (1991). Construing couples: The challenges of marital therapy. *International Journal of Personal Construct Psychology, 4,* 293–312.

Lorand, S. (1946). *Technique of psychoanalytic therapy.* New York: International Universities Press.

Lovaas, O. I. (1977). *The autistic child: Language development through behavior modification.* New York: Irvington.

Lovaas, O. I. (1987). Behavioral treatment and normal educational and intellectual functioning in young autistic children. *Journal of Consulting and Clinical Psychology, 55,* 3–9.

Lowe, R. C., & Wilczynski, M. (1994). A cross-cultural study of need for achievement in Italian and American children. *Psychological Reports, 75,* 590.

Lowing, P. A., Mirsky, A. F., & Pereira, R. (1983). The inheritance of schizophrenia spectrum disorders: A reanalysis of the Danish adoptee study plan. *American Journal of Psychiatry, 140,* 1167–1171.

Lowman, R. L., & Williams, R. E. (1987). Validity of self-ratings of abilities and competencies. *Journal of Vocational Behavior, 31,* 1–13.

Lubetsky, M. J. (1989). The magic of fairy tales: Psychodynamic and developmental perspectives. *Child Psychiatry and Human Development, 19,* 245–255.

Lubin, B., Wallis, R. R., & Paine, C. (1971). Patterns of psychological test usage in the United States: 1935–1969. *Professional Psychology, 2,* 70–74.

Luccock, M. P., & Salkovskis, P. M. (1988). Cognitive factors in social anxiety and its treatment. *Behaviour Research and Therapy, 26,* 297–302.

Luger, G. F. (1994). *Cognitive Science.* New York: Academic Press.

Lundberg, U., Westermark, O., & Rasch, B. (1990). Type A behaviour in pre-school children: Interrater reliability, stability over six months and subcomponents. *Scandinavian Journal of Psychology, 31,* 121–127.

Lundin, R. W. (1961). *Personality.* New York: Macmillan.

Lunenburg, F. C., & Cadavid, V. (1992). Locus of control, pupil control ideology, and dimensions of teacher burnout. *Journal of Instructional Psychology, 19,* 13–22.

Lutfiyya, Z. M. (1991). "A feeling of being connected": Friendships between people with and without learning difficulties. *Disability, Handicap and Society, 6,* 233–245.

Lynch, J. J. (1979). *The broken heart: The medical consequences of loneliness.* New York: Basic Books.

Lyon, J., & Gorner, P. (1995). *Altered fates: Gene therapy and the retooling of human life.* New York: Norton.

MacAndrew, C. (1965). The differentiation of male alcoholic outpatients from nonalcoholic psychiatric outpatients by means of the MMPI. *Quarterly Journal of Studies on Alcohol, 26,* 238–246.

Macaskill, G. T., Hopper, J. L., White, V., & Hill, D. J. (1994). Genetic and environmental variation in Eysenck Personality Questionnaire scales measured on Australian adolescent twins. *Behavior Genetics, 24,* 481–491.

MacDonald, K. (1995). Evolution, the five-factor model, and levels of personality. *Journal of Personality, 63,* 525–567.

MacDonald, K., & Parke, R. D. (1984). Bridging the gap: Parent-child play interaction and peer interaction competence. *Child Development, 55,* 1265–1277.

MacKinnon, D. W., & Dukes, W. F. (1962). Repression. In L. Postman (Ed.), *Psychology in the making.* New York: Knopf.

MacMillan, V., Guevremont, D. C., & Hansen, D. J. (1989). Problem-solving training with a multi-distressed abusive mother. *Journal of Family Violence, 3,* 69–81.

Macrae, C. N., Milne, A. B., & Bodenhausen, G. V. (1994). Stereotypes as energy-saving devices: A peek inside the cognitive toolbox. *Journal of Personality and Social Psychology, 66,* 37–47.

Maddi, S. (1989). *Personality theories: A comparative analysis* (6th ed.). Pacific Grove, CA: Brooks/Cole.

Magnusson, D. (1989). Personality research: challenges for the future. *European Journal of Psychology, 4,* 1–17.

Mahler, M. (1968). *On human symbiosis and the vicissitudes of individuation: Infantile psychosis* (Vol. 1). New York: International Universities Press.

Mahler, M., Bergman, A., & Pine, F. (1975). *The psychological birth of the infant: Symbiosis and individuation.* New York: Basic Books.

Mahoney, M. J. (1992, April). *Psychotherapy integration: Diversity, dynamics, and development.* Paper presented at the meeting of the Society for Exploration of Psychotherapy Integration, San Diego.

Mahoney, M. J. (1993a). Diversity and the dynamics of development in psychotherapy integration. *Journal of Psychotherapy Integration, 3,* 1–13.

Mahoney, M. J. (1993b). Introduction to special section: Theoretical developments in the cognitive psychotherapies. *Journal of Consulting and Clinical Psychology, 61,* 187–193.

Mahrer, A. R., Nadler, W. P., Stalikas, A., Schachter, H. M., & Sterner, I. (1988). Common and distinctive therapeutic change processes in client-centered, rational-emotive, and experimental psychotherapies. *Psychological Reports, 62,* 972–974.

Main, M., & Cassidy, J. (1988). Categories of response to reunion with the parent at age 6: Predictable from infant attachment patterns and stable over a 1-month period. *Developmental Psychology, 24,* 415–426.

Main, M., & Hesse, E. (1990). Parents' unresolved traumatic experiences are related to infant disorganized status: Is frightened and/or frightening parental behavior the linking mechanism? In M. T. Greenberg, D. Cicchetti, & E. M. Cummings (Eds.), *Attachment in the preschool years* (pp. 161–184). Chicago: University of Chicago Press.

Main, M., & Solomon, J. (1986). Discovery of an insecure/disorganized attachment pattern. In T. B. Brazelton & M. W. Yogman (Eds.), *Affective development in infancy.* Norwood, NJ: Ablex.

Mair, M. (1990). Telling psychological tales. *International Journal of Personal Construct Psychology, 3,* 121–135.

Major, B., Cozzarelli, C., Sciacchitano, A. M., Cooper, M. L., Testa, M., & Mueller, P. (1990). Perceived social support, self-efficacy, and adjustment to abortion. *Journal of Personality and Social Psychology, 59,* 452–463.

Malinowski, B. (1927). *Sex and repression in savage society.* London: Routledge & Kegan Paul.

Maltby, J. (1995). Personality, prayer, and church attendance among U.S. female adults. *Journal of Social Psychology, 135,* 529–531.

Mampunza, S., Verbanck, P., Verhaus, M., Martin, P., Paternot, J., Le Bon, O., Kornreich, C., Den Bulk, A., & Pelc, I. (1995). Cerebral blood flow in just detoxified alcohol dependent patients A 99 m Tc-HMPAO-SPECT study. *Acta Neurologica Belgica, 95,* 164–169.

Mancuso, J. C., & Shaw, M. L. G. (1988). *Cognition and personal structure: Computer access and analysis.* New York: Praeger.

Manicas, P. T., & Secord, P. F. (1983). Implications for psychology of the new philosophy of science. *American Psychologist, 38,* 399–413.

Manuck, S. B., Kaplan, J. R., & Clarkson, T. B. (1983). Social instability and coronary atherosclerosis in cynomolgus monkeys. *Neuroscience and Biobehavioral Reviews, 7,* 485–491.

Maqsud, M., & Rouhani, S. (1991). Relationships between socioeconomic status, locus of control, self-concept, and academic achievement of Batswana adolescents. *Journal of Youth and Adolescence, 20,* 107–114.

Marcus, D. M. (1988). Aspects of psychoanalytic cure. *Psychoanalytic Review, 75,* 231–243.

Marecek, J., & Hare-Mustin, R. T. (1991). A short history of the future: Feminism and clinical psychology. *Psychology of Women Quarterly, 15,* 521–536.

Mark, V. H., & Ervin, F. R. (1970). *Violence and the brain.* New York: Harper & Row.

Markman, K. D., Gavanski, I., Sherman, S. J., & McMullen, M. N. (1995). The impact of perceived control on the imagination of better and worse possible worlds. *Personality and Social Psychology Bulletin, 21,* 588–595.

Marks, I. (1978). Behavioral psychotherapy of adult neurosis. In S. L. Garfield & A. E. Bergin (Eds.), *Handbook of psychotherapy and behavior change: An empirical analysis* (2nd ed.). New York: Wiley.

Marks, I. (1981). *Cure and care of neuroses: Theory and practice of behavioral psychotherapy.* New York: Wiley.

Marks, I. M. (1987). *Fears, phobias, and rituals: Panic, anxiety and their disorders.* New York: Oxford University Press.

Marks, P. A., & Seeman, W. (1963). *An atlas for use with the MMPI: Actuarial description of abnormal personality.* Baltimore: Williams & Wilkins.

Markus, H. (1977). Self-schemata and processing information about the self. *Journal of Personality and Social Psychology, 35,* 63–78.

Markus, H. (1983). Self-knowledge: An expanded view. *Journal of Personality, 51,* 543–565.

Markus, H., & Nurius, P. (1986). Possible selves. *American Psychologist, 41,* 954–969.

Markus, H., & Wurf, E. (1987). The dynamic self-concept: A social psychological perspective. *Annual Review of Psychology, 38,* 299–337.

Markus, H., & Kitayama, S. (1991). Culture and the self: Implications for cognition, emotion, and motivation. *Psychological Review, 98,* 224–253.

Marlatt, G. A., & Rohsenow, D. J. (1980). Cognitive processes in alcohol use: Expectancy and the balanced placebo design. In N. K. Mellow (Ed.), *Advances in substance abuse: Behavioral and biological research.* Greenwich, CT: JAI Press.

Marsh, H. W. (1987). Masculinity, femininity and androgyny: Their relations to multiple dimensions of self-concept. *Multivariate Behavioral Research, 22,* 91–118.

Marsh, H. W. (1995). A Jamesian model of self-investment and self-esteem: Comment on Pelham (1995). *Personality and Social Psychology, 69,* 1151–1160.

Marsh, H. W. (1996). Positive and negative global self-esteem: A substantively meaningful distinction or artifactors? *Journal of Personality and Social Psychology, 70,* 810–819.

Marshall, G. N. (1991). A multidimensional analysis of internal health locus of control beliefs: Separating the wheat from the chaff? *Journal of Personality and Social Psychology, 61,* 483–491.

Marshall, G. N., Wortman, C. B., Wickers, R. R., Jr., Kusulas, J. W., & Hervig, L. K. (1994). The five-factor model of personality as a framework for personality-health research. *Journal of Personality and Social Psychology, 67,* 278–286.

Martens, B. K. (1990). A context analysis of contingent teacher attention. *Behavior Modification, 14,* 138–156.

Martens, B. K. (1992). Contingency and choice: The implications of matching theory for classroom instruction. *Journal of Behavioral Education, 2,* 121–137.

Martens, B. K., & Houk, J. L. (1989). The application of Herrnstein's law of effect to disruptive and on-task behavior of a retarded adolescent girl. *Journal of the Experimental Analysis of Behavior, 51,* 17–27.

Martens, B. K., Lochner, D. G., & Kelly, S. Q. (1992). The effects of variable-interval reinforcement on academic engagement: A demonstration of matching theory. *Journal of Applied Behavior Analysis, 25,* 143–151.

Martin, C. L. (1990). Attitudes and expectations about children with non-traditional and traditional gender roles. *Sex Roles, 22,* 151–165.

Martin, J. V., Cook, J. M., Hagen, T. J., & Mendelson, W. B. (1989). Inhibition of sleep and benzodiazepine receptor binding by a beta-carboline derivative. *Pharmacology Biochemistry & Behavior, 34,* 37–42.

Marusic, I., Bratko, D., & Zarevski, P. (1995). Self-reliance and some personality traits: Sex differences. *Personality and Individual Differences, 19,* 941–943.

Mascolo, M. F., & Mancuso, J. C. (1990). Functioning of epigenetically evolved emotions systems: A constructive analysis. *International Journal of Personal Construct Psychology, 3,* 205–222.

Masling, J. (Ed.). (1983). *Empirical studies of psychoanalytic theories* (Vol. 1). Hillsdale, NJ: Analytic Press.

Masling, J. (Ed.). (1985). *Empirical studies of psychoanalytic theories* (Vol. 2). Hillsdale, NJ: Analytic Press.

Masling, J., O'Neill, R., & Katkin, E. S. (1981). Orality and latency of volunteering to serve as experimental subjects. *Journal of Personality Assessment, 45,* 20–22.

Masling, J. (1960). The influence of situational and interpersonal variables in projective testing. *Psychological Bulletin, 56,* 65–85.

Masling, J., & Cohen, I. S. (1987). Psychotherapy, clinical evidence, and the self-fulfilling prophecy. *Psychoanalytic Psychology, 4,* 65–79.

Masling, J., Johnson, C., & Saturansky, C. (1974). Oral imagery, accuracy of perceiving others, and performance in Peace Corps training. *Journal of Personality and Social Psychology, 30,* 414–419.

Masling, J., Rabie, L., & Blondheim, S. H. (1967). Obesity, level of aspiration, and Rorschach and TAT measures of oral dependence. *Journal of Consulting Psychology, 31,* 233–239.

Masling, J., Weiss, L., & Rothschild, B. (1968). Relationships of oral imagery to yielding behavior and birth order. *Journal of Consulting and Clinical Psychology, 32,* 89–91.

Maslow, A. (1950). Self-actualizing people: A study of psychological health. *Personality, Symposium No. 1,* 11–34.

Maslow, A. (1954). *Motivation and personality.* New York: Harper & Row.

Maslow, A. (1955). Deficiency motivation and growth motivation. In M. R. Jones (Ed.), *Nebraska symposium on motivation* (Vol. 3). Lincoln: University of Nebraska Press.

Maslow, A. (1962). Lessons from the peak-experiences. *Journal of Humanistic Psychology, 2,* 9–18.

Maslow, A. (1963). Self-actualizing people. In G. B. Levitas (Ed.), *The world of psychology* (Vol. 2). New York: Braziller.

Maslow, A. (1966). *The psychology of science.* Chicago: Regnery.

Maslow, A. (1970). *Motivation and personality* (Rev. ed.). New York: Harper & Row.

Maslow, A. (1971). *The farther reaches of human nature.* New York: Viking Press.

Mason, A., & Blankenship, V. (1987). Power and affiliation motivation, stress, and abuse in intimate relationships. *Journal of Personality and Social Psychology, 52,* 203–210.

Masson, J. M. (1984). *The assault on truth: Freud's suppression of the seduction theory.* New York: Farrar, Straus & Giroux.

Masters, W. H., & Johnson, V. E. (1966). *Human Sexual Response.* London: J. & A. Churchill.

Mathieu, J. E. (1990). A test of subordinates' achievement and affiliation needs as moderators of leader path-goal relationships. *Basic and Applied Social Psychology, 11,* 179–189.

Matlin, M. W. (1994). *Cognition* (3rd ed.). New York: Harcourt Brace.

Matsumoto, D. (1997). *Culture and modern life.* Pacific Grove, CA: Brooks/Cole.

Matsumoto, D., & Kudoh, T. (1993). American-Japanese cultural differences in attributions of personality based on smiles. *Journal of Nonverbal Behavior, 17,* 231–243.

Matthews, G. (1989). The factor structure of the 16PF: Twelve primary and three secondary factors. *Personality and Individual Differences, 9,* 931–940.

Matthews, G., Dorn, L., & Glenson, A. I. (1991). Personality correlates of driver stress. *Personality and Individual Differences, 12,* 535–549.

Matthews, K. A. (1982). Psychological perspectives on the Type A behavior pattern. *Psychological Bulletin, 91,* 293–323.

Matthews, K. A., & Carra, J. (1982). Suppression of menstrual distress symptoms: A study of Type A behavior. *Personality and Social Psychology Bulletin, 8,* 146–151.

Matthews, K. A., Stoney, C. M., Rakaczky, C. J., & Jamison, W. (1986). Family characteristics and school achievements of Type A children. *Health Psychology, 5,* 453–467.

Mawson, A. R., & Jacobs, K. W. (1978). Corn, tryptophan, and homicide. *Journal of Orthomolecular Psychiatry, 7,* 227–230.

May, P. A., & Van Winkle, N. W. (1994). Durkheim's suicide theory and its applicability to contemporary American Indians and Alaska natives. In D. Lester (Ed.), *Emile Durkheim: Le suicide 100 years later.* Philadelphia: Charles Press.

May, R. (1967). Existential psychology. In T. Millon (Ed.), *Theories of psychopathology.* Philadelphia: W. B. Saunders.

Mayman, M. (1967). Object-representations and object relationships in Rorschach responses. *Journal of Projective Techniques and Personality Assessment, 31,* 17–24.

McAdams, D. P. (1985). *Power, intimacy, and the life story: Personological inquiries into identity.* Chicago: Dorsey Press.

McAdams, D. P. (1992). The five-factor model in personality: A critical appraisal. *Journal of Personality, 60,* 329–361.

McAdams, D. P., Lensky, D. B., Daple, S. A., & Allen, J. (1988). Depression and the organization of autobiographical memory. *Journal of Social and Clinical Psychology, 7,* 332–349.

McArthur, L. Z., & Eisen, S. V. (1976). Achievements of male and female storybook characters as determinants of achievement behavior by boys and girls. *Journal of Personality and Social Psychology, 33,* 467–473.

McAuley, E., & Courneya, K. S. (1992). Self-efficacy relationships with affective and exertion responses to exercise. *Journal of Applied Social Psychology, 22,* 312–326.

McCallum, M., & Piper, W. E. (1988). Psychoanalytically oriented short-term groups for outpatients: Unsettled issues. *Group, 12,* 21–32.

McCann, S. J. H., Stewin, L. L., & Short, R. H. (1990). Frightening dream frequency and birth order. *Individual Psychology, 46,* 304–310.

McClelland, D. C. (1965). Toward a theory of motive acquisition. *American Psychologist, 20,* 321–333.

McClelland, D. C. (1967). *The achieving society.* New York: Free Press.

McClelland, D. C. (1977). The impact of power motivation training on alcoholics. *Journal of Studies on Alcohol, 38,* 142–144.

McClelland, D. C. (1982). The need for power, sympathetic activation, and illness. *Motivation and Emotion, 6,* 31–61.

McClelland, D. C., Atkinson, J. W., Clark, R. A., & Lowell, E. I. (1976). *The achievement motive.* New York: Irvington. (Original work published 1953)

McClelland, D. C., Davis, W. N., Kalin, R., & Wanner, E. (1972). *The drinking man.* New York: Free Press.

McClelland, D. C., Koestner, R., & Weinberger, J. (1989). How do self-attributed and implicit motives differ? *Psychological Review, 96,* 690–702.

McClelland, D. C., & Winter, D. G. (1969). *Motivating economic achievement.* New York: Free Press.

McConachie, H. (1983). Fathers, mothers, siblings: How do they see themselves? In P. Mittler & H. McConachie (Eds.), *Parents, professionals and mentally handicapped people.* London: Croom Helm.

McConachie, H. (1985). How parents of young mentally handicapped children construe their role. In D. Bannister (Ed.), *Issues and approaches in personal construct theory.* Orlando, FL: Academic Press.

McCoy, M. M. (1977). A reconstruction of emotion. In D. Bannister (Ed.), *New perspectives in personal construct theory.* London: Academic Press.

McCoy, M. M. (1981). Positive and negative emotion: A personal construct theory interpretation. In H. Bonarius, R. Holland, & S. Rosenberg (Eds.), *Personal construct psychology: Recent advances in theory and practice.* New York: St. Martin's Press.

McCrae, R. R. (1987). Creativity, divergent thinking, and openness to experience. *Journal of Personality and Social Psychology, 52,* 1258–1265.

McCrae, R. R. (1990). Traits and trait names: How well is Openness represented in natural languages? *European Journal of Personality, 4,* 119–129.

McCrae, R. R. (1994). Openness to Experience: Expanding the boundaries of Factor V. *European Journal of Personality, 8,* 251–272.

McCrae, R. R. (1996). Social consequences of experiential openness. *Psychological Bulletin, 120,* 323–337.

McCrae, R. R., Bartone, P. T., & Costa, P. T. (1976). Age, anxiety, and self-reported health. *International Journal of Aging and Human Development, 7,* 49–58.

McCrae, R. R., & Costa, P. T. (1983). Social desirability scales: More substance than style. *Journal of Consulting and Clinical Psychology, 51,* 882–888.

McCrae, R. R., & Costa, P. T. (1985a). Comparison of the EPI and psychoticism scales with measures of the five-factor model of personality. *Personality and Individual Differences, 6,* 587–597.

McCrae, R. R., & Costa, P. T. (1985b). Updating Norman's "adequate taxonomy": Intelligence and personality dimensions in natural language and questionnaires. *Journal of Personality and Social Psychology, 49,* 710–721.

McCrae, R. R., & Costa, P. T. (1987). Validation of the five-factor model of personality across instruments and observers. *Journal of Personality and Social Psychology, 52,* 81–90.

McCrae, R. R., & Costa, P. T. (1989). Reinterpreting the Myers-Briggs Type Indicator from the perspective of the five-factor model of personality. *Journal of Personality, 57,* 17–40.

McCrae, R. R., & Costa, P. T. (1995). Positive and negative valence within the five-factor model. *Journal of Research in Personality, 29,* 443–460.

McCrae, R. R., & Costa, P. T. (1996). Toward a new generation of personality theories: Theoretical contexts for the five-factor model. In J. S. Wiggins (Ed.), *The five-factor model of personality: Theoretical perspectives.* New York: Guilford.

McCrae, R. R., & Costa, P. T. (1997). Personality trait structure as a human universal. *American Psychologist, 52,* 509–516.

McCrae, R. R., Costa, P. T., & Piedmont, R. L. (1993). Universal aspects of Chinese personality structure. In M. H. Bond (Ed.), *The handbook of Chinese psychology.* Hong Kong: Oxford University Press.

McDowell, J. J. (1982). The importance of Herrnstein's mathematical statement of the law of effect for behavior therapy. *American Psychologist, 37,* 771–779.

McDowell, J. J. (1988). Matching theory in natural human environments. *The Behavior Analyst, 11,* 95–109.

McFarland, R. A. (1953). *Human factors in air transportation.* New York: McGraw-Hill.

McFarland, S. G., & Sparks, C. M. (1985). Age, education, and the internal consistency of personality scales. *Journal of Personality and Social Psychology, 49,* 1692–1702.

McGaw, W. H., Rice, C. P., & Rogers, C. R. (1973). *The steel shutter.* La Jolla, CA: Film Center for Studies of the Person.

McGuffin, P., & Katz, R. (1989). The genetics of depression and manic-depressive disorder. *British Journal of Psychiatry, 155,* 294–304.

McGuire, W. J., & McGuire, C. V. (1988). Content and process in the experience of self. In L. Berkowitz (Ed.)., *Advances in experimental social psychology.* (Vol. 21). New York: Academic Press.

McGuire, W. J., & McGuire, C. V. (1996). Enhancing self-esteem by directed thinking tasks: Cognitive and affective positively asymmetries. *Journal of Personality and Social Psychology, 70,* 1117–1125.

McIntyre, J. J., & Teevan, J. J., Jr. (1972). Television violence and deviant behavior. In G. A. Comstock & E. A. Rubinstein (Eds.), *Television and social behavior* (Vol. 3). *Television and adolescent aggressiveness.* Washington, DC: U.S. Government Printing Office.

McKeachie, W. J. (1961). Motivation, teaching methods,

and college learning. In M. R. Jones (Ed.), *Nebraska symposium on motivation, 1961* (Vol. 9). Lincoln: University of Nebraska Press.

McKenna v. Fargo, 451 F. Suppl. 1355 (1978).

McKenzie, J. (1988). Three superfactors in the 16PF and their relationship to Eysenck's P, E and N. *Personality and Individual Differences, 9,* 843–850.

McKim, W. A. (1986). *Drugs and behavior.* Englewood Cliffs, NJ: Prentice-Hall.

McKusick, L., Coates, T. J., Morin, S. F., Pollack, L., & Hoff, C. (1990). Longitudinal predictors of reductions in high risk sexual behaviors among gay men in San Francisco: The AIDS behavioral research project. *American Journal of Public Health, 80,* 978–983.

McMains, M. J., Liebert, R. M., Hill, J. H., Spiegler, M. D., & Baker, E. L. (1969). Children's adoption of self-reward patterns: Verbalization and modeling. *Perceptual and Motor Skills, 28,* 515–518.

Mead, M. (1949). *Male and female.* New York: Morrow.

Mearns, D., & McLeod, J. (1984). A person-centered approach to research. In R. F. Levant & J. M. Shlien (Eds.), *Client-centered therapy and the person-centered approach: New directions in theory, research, and practice.* New York: Praeger.

Mednick, S. A., Machon, R. A., & Huttunen, M. O. (1990). An update on the Helsinki influenza project. *Archives of General Psychiatry, 47,* 292.

Meichenbaum, D. (1975). Enhancing creativity by modifying what subjects say to themselves. *American Educational Research Journal, 12,* 129–145.

Meichenbaum, D. (1985). *Stress inoculation training.* Elmsford, NY: Pergamon Press.

Meichenbaum, D. (1986). Cognitive-behavior modification. In F. H. Kanfer & A. P. Goldstein (Eds.), *Helping people change: A textbook of methods* (3rd ed.). Elmsford, NY: Pergamon Press.

Meichenbaum, D. (1991, February-March). *Cognitive behavioral therapy.* Workshop sponsored by the Institute for the Advancement of Human Behavior (Portola Valley, CA), Chicago.

Meichenbaum, D., Gilmore, B., & Fedoravicius, A. (1971). Group insight vs. group desensitization in treating speech anxiety. *Journal of Consulting and Clinical Psychology, 36,* 410–421.

Meichenbaum, D., & Goodman, J. (1971). Training impulsive children to talk to themselves: A means of developing self-control. *Journal of Abnormal Psychology, 77,* 115–126.

Melamed, B. G. (1979). Behavioral approaches to fear in dental settings. In M. Hersen, R. M. Eisler, & P. M. Miller (Eds.), *Progress in behavior modification* (Vol. 7). New York: Academic Press.

Melamed, B. G., & Siegel, L. J. (1975). Reduction of anxiety in children facing hospitalization and surgery by use of filmed modeling. *Journal of Consulting and Clinical Psychology, 43,* 511–521.

Meltzer, F. (1994). Final analysis? Psychoanalysis in the postmodern West. *Annual of Psychoanalysis, 22,* 29–36.

Mendelson, M. D. (1991). Transference: Theoretical conceptions and clinical approach. *Contemporary Psychoanalysis, 27,* 189–199.

Merrill, R. M., & Heathers, L. B. (1956). The relation of the MMPI to the Edwards Personal Preference Schedule on a college counseling center sample. *Journal of Consulting Psychology, 20,* 310–314.

Metzler, A. E., & Neimeyer, G. (1988). Vocational hierarchies: How do we count the ways? *International Journal of Personal Construct Psychology, 1,* 205–217.

Meuris, G. (1988). Carl Rogers (1902–1987): Une pedagogie centree sur la personne. [Carl Rogers (1902–1987): Client-centered education.] *Bulletin de Psychologie Scholaire et d'Orientation, 37,* 83–94.

Meyers, A., Mercatoris, M., & Sirota, A. (1976). Use of covert self-instruction for the elimination of psychotic speech. *Journal of Consulting and Clinical Psychology, 44,* 480–483.

Michels, R. (1988). The future of psychoanalysis. *Psychoanalytic Quarterly, 57,* 167–185.

Miller, C. (1991). Self-actualization and the consciousness revolution. [Special issue: Handbook of self-actualization]. *Journal of Social Behavior and Personality, 6,* 109–126.

Miller, K., & Treacher, A. (1981). Delinquency: A personal construct theory approach. In H. Bonarius, R. Holland, & S. Rosenberg (Eds.), *Personal construct psychology: Recent advances in theory and practice.* New York: St. Martin's Press.

Miller, L. (1989). On the neuropsychology of dreams. *Psychoanalytic Review, 76,* 375–401.

Miller, N. E. (1959). Liberalization of basic S-R concepts: Extensions to conflict behavior, motivation, and social learning. In S. Koch (Ed.), *Psychology: A study of a science* (Vol. 2). New York: McGraw-Hill.

Miller, N. E., & Dollard, J. (1941). *Social learning and imitation.* New Haven, CT: Yale University Press.

Miller, P. C., Lefcourt, H. M., Holmes, J. G., Ware, E. E., & Saleh, W. E. (1986). Marital locus of control and marital problem solving. *Journal of Personality and Social Psychology, 51,* 161–169.

Miller, T. Q., Smith, T. W., Turner, C. W., & Guijarro, M. L. (1996). Meta-analytic review of research on hostility and physical health. *Psychological Bulletin, 119,* 322–348.

Millis, K. K., & Neimeyer, R. A. (1990). A test of the Dichotomy Corollary: Propositions versus constructs as basic cognitive units. *International Journal of Personal Construct Psychology, 3,* 167–181.

Millon, T. (1969). *Modern psychopathology.* Philadelphia: Saunders.

Millon, T. (Ed.). (1967). *Theories of psychopathology.* Philadelphia: W. B. Saunders.

Mineka, S., Davidson, M., Cook, M., & Keir, R. (1984). Observational conditioning of snake fear in rhesus monkeys. *Journal of Abnormal Psychology, 93,* 355–372.

Minsky, R. (1994). Reaching beyond denial—sight and in-sight—a way forward? *Free-Association, 5,* 326–351.

Mirin, S. M., & Weiss, R. D. (1989). Genetic factors in the development of alcoholism. *Psychiatric Annals, 19,* 239–242.

Mischel, W. (1966). Theory and research on the antecedents of self-imposed delay of reward. In B. A. Maher (Ed.), *Progress in experimental personality research* (Vol. 3). New York: Academic Press.

Mischel, W. (1968). *Personality and assessment.* New York: Wiley.

Mischel, W. (1973). Toward a cognitive social learning reconceptualization of personality. *Psychological Review, 80,* 252–283.

Mischel, W. (1979). On the interface of cognition and personality: Beyond the person-situation debate. *American Psychologist, 34,* 740–754.

Mischel, W. (1980). George Kelly's anticipation of psychology: A personal tribute. In M. J. Mahoney (Ed.), *Psychotherapy Process.* New York: Plenum.

Mischel, W. (1984). Convergences and challenges in the search for consistency. *American Psychologist, 39,* 351–364.

Mischel, W. (1988). Review of conceptual foundations of behavioral assessment. *Behavioral Assessment, 10,* 1125–1128.

Mischel, W., & Baker, N. (1975). Cognitive appraisals and transformations in delay behavior. *Journal of Personality and Social Psychology, 31,* 254–361.

Mischel, W., & Ebbesen, E. (1970). Attention in delay of gratification. *Journal of Personality and Social Psychology, 16,* 329–337.

Mischel, W., Ebbesen, E., & Raskoff, A. (1971). *Cognitive and attentional mechanisms in delay of gratification.* Unpublished manuscript, Stanford University.

Mischel, W., & Moore, B. (1973). Effects of attention to symbolically presented rewards upon self-control. *Journal of Personality and Social Psychology, 28,* 172–179.

Mischel, W., & Moore, B. (1980). The role of ideation in voluntary delay for symbolically presented rewards. *Cognitive Therapy and Research, 4,* 211–221.

Mischel, W., & Peake, P. K. (1982). Beyond deja vu in the search for cross-situational consistency. *Psychological Review, 89,* 730–755.

Mischel, W., & Shoda, Y. (1994). Personality psychology has two goals: Must it be two fields? *Psychological Inquiry, 5,* 156–158.

Mischel, W., & Shoda, Y. (1995). A cognitive-affective system theory of personality: Reconceptualizing situations, dispositions, dynamics, and invariance in personality structure. *Psychological Review, 102,* 246–268.

Mischel, W., Shoda, Y., & Peake, P. K. (1988). The nature of adolescent competencies predicted by delay of gratification. *Journal of Personality and Social Psychology, 54,* 687–696.

Mischel, W., Shoda, Y., & Rodriguez, M. L. (1989). Delay of gratification in children. *Science, 244,* 933–938.

Mitchell, J. (1974a). On Freud and the distinction between the sexes. In J. Strouse (Ed.), *Women & analysis: Dialogues on psychoanalytic views of femininity.* New York: Grossman.

Mitchell, J. (1974b). *Psychoanalysis and feminism.* New York: Pantheon.

Mitchell, J. (1991). Deconstructing difference: Gender, splitting, and transitional space. *Psychoanalytic Dialogues, 1,* 353–357.

Mitchell, J. (1995). Psychoanalysis and feminism: 20 years on: Introduction. *British Journal of Psychotherapy, 12,* 73–77.

Mitroff, I. (1988). Comments on Blight's article. *Journal of Humanistic Psychology, 28,* 67–69.

Mittelman, W. (1991). Maslow's study of self-actualization: A reinterpretation. *Journal of Humanistic Psychology, 31,* 114–135.

Miura, I. T., Okamoto, Y., Kim, C. C., Chang, C., Steere, M., & Fayol, M. (1994). Comparisons of children's cognitive representation of number: China, France, Japan, Korea, Sweden, and the United States. *International Journal of Behavioral Development, 17,* 401–411.

Modell, A. H. (1984). *Psychoanalysis in a new context.* New York: International Universities Press.

Modell, A. H. (1988). The centrality of the psychoanalytic setting and the changing aims of treatment. *Psychoanalytic Quarterly, 57,* 577–596.

Mogil, J. S., Sternberg, W. F., & Liebeskind, J. C. (1993). Studies of pain, stress and immunity. In C. R. Chapman & K. M. Foley (Eds.), *Current and emerging issues in cancer pain: Research & practice.* New York: Raven Press.

Moldin, S. O., Reich, T., & Rice, J. P. (1991). Current perspectives on the genetics of unipolar depression. *Behavior Genetics, 21,* 211–242.

Moll, A. (1912). *The sexual life of the child.* New York: Macmillan.

Montag, I., & Levin, J. (1994). The five factor model and psychopathology in nonclinical samples. *Personality and Individual Differences, 17,* 1–7.

Montague, E. K. (1953). The role of anxiety in serial rote learning. *Journal of Experimental Psychology, 45,* 91–96.

Mooney, S. P., Sherman, M. F., & lo Presto, C. T. (1991). Academic locus of control, self-esteem, and perceived distance from home as predictors of college adjustment. *Journal of Counseling and Development, 69,* 445–448.

Moore, J. (1990). On the "causes" of behavior. *The Psychological Record, 40,* 469–480.

Moran, M. G. (1991). Chaos theory and psychoanalysis: The fluidic nature of the mind. *International Review of Psycho-Analysis, 18,* 211–221.

Morrill, A. C., Ickovics, J. R., Golubechikov, V. V., Beren, S. E., & Rodin, J. (1996). Safer sex: Social and psychological predictors of behavioral maintenance and change among heterosexual women. *Journal of Consulting and Clinical Psychology, 64,* 819–828.

Morris, B. S. (1949). Officer selection in the British Army, 1942–1945. *Occupational Psychology, 23,* 219–234.

Morris, M. W., & Murphy, G. L., (1990). Converging

operations on a basic level in event taxonomies. *Memory and Cognition, 18,* 407–418.

Morrison, J. R., & Stewart, A. M. (1971). A family study of the hyperactive child syndrome. *Biological Psychiatry, 3,* 189–195.

Moskowitz, D. S. (1994). Cross-situational generality and the interpersonal circumplex. *Journal of Personality and Social Psychology, 66,* 921–933.

Motley, M. T., & Baars, B. J. (1978). Laboratory verification of "Freudian" slips of the tongue as evidence of pre-articulatory semantic editing. In B. Ruken (Ed.), *Communication yearbook 2.* New Brunswick, NJ: Transaction.

Mowrer, O. H., & Mowrer, W. M. (1938). Enuresis: A method for its study and treatment. *American Journal of Orthopsychiatry, 8,* 436–447.

Muller, J. (1987). Lacan's view of sublimation. *American Journal of Psychoanalysis, 47,* 315–323.

Multon, K. D., Brown, S. D., & Lent, R. W. (1991). Relations of self-efficacy beliefs to academic outcomes: A meta-analytic investigation. *Journal of Counseling Psychology, 38,* 30–38.

Muran, J. C. (1991). A reformulation of the ABC model in cognitive psychotherapies: Implications for assessment and treatment. *Clinical Psychology Review, 11,* 399–418.

Muris, P., Jong, P. J. D., & Suvrijn, A. (1995). Monitoring, imagery, and perception of threat. *Personality and Individual Differences, 6,* 749–759.

Muris, P., & Merkelbach, H. (1996). The short version of the Defensive Style Questionnaire: Factor structure and psychopathological correlates. *Personality and Individual Differences, 20,* 123–126.

Murray, G. W., Hay, C. A., & Armstrong, S. M. (1995). Personality factors in seasonal affective disorder: Is seasonality an aspect of neuroticism? *Personality and Individual Differences, 19.*

Murray, H. A. (1936). Facts which support the concept of need or drive. *The Journal of Psychology, 3,* 27–42.

Murray, H. A. (1943). *The Thematic Apperception Test: Manual.* Cambridge, MA: Harvard University Press.

Murray, H. A. (1951). Uses of the Thematic Apperception Test. *American Journal of Psychiatry, 107,* 577–581.

Murray, H. A. (1962). *Explorations in personality.* New York: Science Editions.

Myers, I. (1962). *The Myers-Briggs Type Indicator.* Princeton, NJ: Educational Testing Service.

Narayanan, L., Menon, S., & Levine, E. L. (1995). Personality structure: A culture-specific examination of the five-factor model. *Journal of Personality Assessment, 64,* 51–62.

Neale, J. M. (1968). Personal communication.

Neale, J. M., & Liebert, R. M. (1986). *Science and behavior: An introduction to methods of research* (3rd ed.). Englewood Cliffs, NJ: Prentice-Hall.

Neale, J. M., & Weintraub, S. (1977). Personal communication.

Neary, R. S., & Zuckerman, M. (1976). Sensation seeking, trait and state anxiety, and the electrodermal orienting reflex. *Psychophysiology, 13,* 205–211.

Neher, A. (1991). Maslow's theory of motivation: A critique. *Journal of Humanistic Psychology, 31,* 89–112.

Neimeyer, G. J., & Hudson, J. E. (1985). Couples' constructs: Personal systems in marital satisfaction. In D. Bannister (Ed.), *Issues and approaches in personal construct theory.* Orlando, FL: Academic Press.

Neimeyer, G. J., & Neimeyer, R. A. (Eds.). (1990). *Advances in personal construct psychology* (Vol. 1). Greenwich, CT: JAI Press.

Neimeyer, R. A., Baker, K. D., & Neimeyer, G. J. (1990). The current status of personal construct theory: Some scientometric data. In G. J. Neimeyer & R. A. Neimeyer (Eds.), *Advances in personal construct psychology* (Vol. 1). Greenwich, CT: JAI Press.

Neisser, U. (1976). *Cognition and reality.* San Francisco: W. H. Freeman.

Neisser, U. (1988). Five kinds of self-knowledge. *Philosophical Psychology, 1,* 35–59.

Neisser, U. (1991). Two perceptually given aspects of the self and their development. *Developmental Review, 11,* 197–209.

Nelson, K. (1993). The psychological and social origins of autobiographical memory. *Psychological Science, 4,* 7–14.

Nesler, M. S., Tedeschi, J. T., & Storr, D. M. (1995). Context effects, self-presentation, and the self-monitoring scale. *Journal of Research in Personality, 29,* 273–284.

Nesse, R. M. (1990). The evolutionary function of repression and the ego defenses. *Journal of the American Academy of Psychoanalysis, 18,* 260–285.

Neuberg, S. L., & Newsom, J. T. (1993). Personal need for structure: Individual differences in the desire for simple structure. *Journal of Personality and Social Psychology, 65,* 113–131.

Newman, J. P., Wallace, J. F., Strauman, T. J., Skolaski, R. L., Oreland, K. M., Mattek, P. W., Elder, K. A., & McNeeley, J. (1993). Effects of motivationally significant stimuli on the regulation of dominant responses. *Journal of Personality and Social Psychology, 65,* 165–175.

Nezu, A. M., & D'Zurilla, T. J. (1989). Social problem solving and negative affective conditions. In P. C. Kendall & D. Watson (Eds.), *Anxiety and depression: Distinctive and overlapping features.* San Diego, CA: Academic Press.

Nezu, A. M., Nezu, C. M., & Perri, M. G. (1989). *Problem-solving therapy for depression: Theory, research, and clinical guidelines.* New York: Wiley.

Nichols, S. L., & Newman, J. P. (1986). Effects of punishment on response latency in extraverts. *Journal of Personality and Social Psychology, 50,* 624–630.

Nicholson, L. (1994). Interpreting gender. *Signs: Journal of Women in Culture and Society, 20,* 79–105.

Nicol, S. E., & Gottesman, I. I. (1983). Clues to the genetics and neurobiology of schizophrenia. *American Scientist, 71,* 398–404.

Nisbett, R. E., & Wilson, T. (1977). Telling more than we can know: Verbal reports on mental processes. *Psychological Review, 84,* 231–259.

Nishith, P., Mueser, K. T., & Gupta, P. (1994). Personality and hallucinogen abuse in a college population from India. *Personality and Individual Differences, 17,* 561–563.

Noesjirwan, J. (1977). Contrasting cultural patterns of interpersonal closeness in doctors' waiting rooms in Sydney and Jakarta. *Journal of Cross-Cultural Psychology, 8,* 357–368.

Noesjirwan, J. (1978). A laboratory study of proxemic patterns of Indonesians and Australians. *British Journal of Social and Clinical Psychology, 17,* 333–334.

Noller, P., Law, H., & Comrey, A. (1987). Cattell, Comrey, and Eysenck personality factors compared: More evidence for the five robust factors? *Journal of Personality and Social Psychology, 53,* 775–782.

Norcross, J. C., & Goldfried, M. R. (Eds.). (1992). *Handbook of psychotherapy integration.* New York: Basic Books.

Norman, W. T. (1963). Toward an adequate taxonomy of personality attributes: Replicated factor structure in peer nomination personality ratings. *Journal of Abnormal and Social Psychology, 66,* 574–583.

Novick, J. (1987). The timing of termination. *International Review of Psycho-Analysis, 14,* 307–318.

Nowicki, S., & Duke, M. P. (1974). A preschool and primary locus of control scale. *Developmental Psychology, 10,* 874–880.

Nowicki, S., & Duke, M. P. (1983). The Nowicki-Strickland life-span locus of control scales: Construct validation. In H. M. Lefcourt (Ed.), *Research with the locus of control construct:* Vol. 2. *Developments and social problems.* New York: Academic Press.

Nowicki, S., & Strickland, B. (1973). A locus of control scale for children. *Journal of Consulting and Clinical Psychology, 40,* 148–154.

Nutt, D. J. (1989). Altered central a2-adrenoceptor sensitivity in panic disorder. *Archives of General Psychiatry, 46,* 165–169.

O'Boyle, M. (1995). DSM-III-R and Eysenck personality measures among patients in a substance abuse programme. *Personality and Individual Differences, 18,* 561–565.

O'Connor, D., & Wolfe, D. M. (1991). From crisis to growth at midlife: Changes in personal paradigm. *Journal of Organizational Behavior, 12,* 323–340.

O'Connor, R. D. (1969). Modification of social withdrawal through symbolic modeling. *Journal of Applied Behavior Analysis, 2,* 15–22.

O'Donnell, C. R., Tharp, R. G., & Wilson, K. (1993). Activity settings as the unit of analysis: A theoretical basis for community intervention and development. *American Journal of Community Psychology, 21,* 501–520.

Oei, T. P. S., Evans, L., & Cook, G. M. (1990). Utility and validity of the STAI with anxiety disorder patients. *British Journal of Clinical Psychology, 29,* 429–432.

Ogden, T. (1982). *Projective identification and psychotherapeutic technique.* New York: Jason Aronson.

Ogden, T. H. (1987). The transitional Oedipal relationship in female development. *International Journal of Psycho-Analysis, 68,* 485–498.

Ogilvie, D. M. (1987). The undesired self: A neglected variable in personality research. *Journal of Personality and Social Psychology, 52,* 379–385.

Ogilvie, D. M. (1988, June). *Dreaded states and desired outcomes.* Paper presented at the meeting of the Society for Personology, Durham, NC.

O'Grady, K. E. (1988). The Marlowe-Crowne and Edwards social desirability scales: A psychometric perspective. *Multivariate Behavioral Research, 23,* 87–101.

O'Hare, D. P. A., & Gordon, I. E. (1976). An application of repertory grid technique to aesthetic measurement. *Perceptual and Motor Skills, 42,* 1183–1192.

O'Heron, C. A. & Orlofsky, J. L. (1990). Stereotypic and nonstereotypic sex role trait and behavior orientations, gender identity, and psychological adjustment. *Journal of Personal and Social Psychology, 58,* 134–143.

Oldroyd, D. (1986). *The arch of knowledge.* New York: Methuen.

O'Leary, A. (1990). Stress, emotion, and human immune function. *Psychological Bulletin, 108,* 363–382.

O'Leary, A. (1992). Self-efficacy and health: Behavioral and stress-physiological mediation. *Cognitive Therapy and Research, 16,* 229–245.

O'Leary, C. J. (1989). The person-centered approach and family therapy: A dialogue between two traditions [Special issue: Person-centered approaches with families]. *Person-Centered Review, 4,* 308–323.

O'Leary, E. (1989). The expression of disapproval by teachers and the maintenance of unconditional positive regard. *Person-Centered Review, 4,* 420–428.

Oliver, M. B., & Hyde, J. S. (1993). Gender differences in sexuality: A meta-analysis. *Psychological Bulletin, 114,* 29–51.

Orbach, S., & Eichenbaum, L. (1995). From objects to subjects. *British Journal of Psychotherapy, 12,* 89–97.

Orgler, H. (1963). *Alfred Adler: The man and his work.* New York: Putnam (Capricorn Books).

Orlofsky, J. L. (1979). Parental antecedents of sex-role orientation in college men and women. *Sex Roles, 5,* 495–512.

Ormel, J., & Schaufeli, W. B. (1991). Stability and change in psychological distress and their relationship with self-esteem and locus of control: A dynamic equilibrium model. *Journal of Personality and Social Psychology, 60,* 288–299.

Orpen, C. (1991). The work locus of control scale as a predictor of employee attitudes and behaviour: A validity study. *Psychological Studies, 36,* 67–69.

Ortmann, J., & Lunde, I. (1986). Psychiatric disorders in the relatives of probands with affective disorders. *Archives of General Psychiatry, 43,* 923–929.

Osgood, C. E., Suci, G. J., & Tannenbaum, P. H.

(1957). *The measurement of meaning.* Urbana: University of Illinois Press.

Osman, M. P., & Tabachnick, N. D. (1988). Introduction and survey of some previous views. *Psychoanalytic Review, 75,* 195–215.

OSS Assessment Staff. (1948). *Assessment of men.* New York: Holt, Rinehart & Winston.

Öst, L. G., & Hugdahl, K. (1985). Acquisition of blood and dental phobia and anxiety response patterns in clinical patients. *Behaviour Research and Therapy, 23,* 27–34.

Overholser, J. C. (1993). Idiographic, quantitative assessment of self-esteem. *Personality and Individual Differences, 14,* 639–646.

Oyserman, R., & Markus, H. R. (1990). Possible selves and delinquency. *Journal of Personality and Social Psychology, 59,* 112–125.

Ozer, D. J., & Reise, S. P. (1994). Personality assessment. *Annual Review of Psychology, 45,* 357–388.

Ozer, E. M., & Bandura, A. (1990). Mechanisms governing empowerment effects: A self-efficacy analysis. *Journal of Personality and Social Psychology, 58,* 472–486.

Padgett, D. K. (1991). Correlates of self-efficacy beliefs among patients with non-insulin dependent diabetes mellitus in Zagreb, Yugoslavia. *Patient Education and Counseling, 18,* 139–147.

Pais, J. (1979). Social-psychological predictors of adjustment for divorced mothers. *Dissertation Abstracts International, 39,* 5165. (University Microfilms No. 79-03460)

Pancoast, D. L., & Archer, R. P. (1988). MMPI adolescent norms: Patterns and trends across 4 decades. *Journal of Personality Assessment, 52,* 691–706.

Pancoast, D. L., & Archer, R. P. (1989). Original adult MMPI norms in normal samples: A review with implications for future developments. *Journal of Personality Assessment, 53,* 376–395.

Pani, M. K. (1991). Differences in locus of control and reading abilities among grade three children. *Psycho-Lingua, 21,* 9–12.

Paprota, M. (1988). *Real/undesired-self discrepancies and depression in male and female high school students.* Unpublished undergraduate honors thesis, Department of Psychology, Rutgers University.

Parcel, T. L., & Menaghan, E. G. (1993). Family social capital and children's behavior problems. *Social Psychology Quarterly, 56,* 120–135.

Parcel, T. L., & Menaghan, E. G. (1994). Early parental work, family social capital and early childhood outcomes. *American Journal of Sociology, 99,* 972–1009.

Pardes, H., Kaufmann, C. A., Pincus, H. A., & West, A. (1989). Genetics and psychiatry: Past discoveries, current dilemmas, and future directions. *American Journal of Psychiatry, 146,* 435–443.

Parker, K. C. H., Hanson, R. K., & Hunsley, J. (1988). MMPI, Rorschach, and WAIS: A meta-analytic comparison of reliability, stability, and validity. *Psychological Bulletin, 103,* 367–373.

Parkes, K. R. (1984). Locus of control, cognitive appraisal, and coping in stressful episodes. *Journal of Personality and Social Psychology, 46,* 655–668.

Parkes, K. R. (1986). Coping in stressful episodes: The role of individual differences, environmental factors, and situational characteristics. *Journal of Personality and Social Psychology, 51,* 1277–1292.

Parnell, R. W. (1953). Physique and choice of faculty. *British Medical Journal, 2,* 472–475.

Parnell, R. W. (1957). Physique and mental breakdown in young adults. *British Medical Journal, 1,* 1485–1490.

Passini, F. T., & Norman, W. T. (1966). A universal conception of personality structure? *Journal of Personality and Social Psychology, 4,* 44–49.

Patterson, C. H. (1990a). Involuntary clients: A person-centered view. *Person-Centered Review, 5,* 316–320.

Patterson, C. H. (1990b). On being client-centered [Special issue: Fiftieth anniversary of the person-centered approach]. *Person-Centered Review, 5,* 425–432.

Patton, M. Q. (1990). Humanistic psychology and humanistic research [Special issue: Human inquiry & the person-centered approach]. *Person-Centered Review, 5,* 191–202.

Paul, D. B., & Blumenthal, A. L. (1989). On the trail of little Albert. *The Psychological Record, 39,* 547–553.

Paunonen, S. V., & Jackson, D. N. (1996). The Jackson Personality Inventory and the five-factor model of personality. *Journal of Research in Personality, 30,* 42–59.

Paunonen, S. V., Jackson, D. N., Trzebinski, J., & Forsterling, F. (1992). Personality structure across cultures: A multimethod evaluation. *Journal of Personality and Social Psychology, 62,* 447–456.

Peabody, D., & Goldberg, L. R. (1989). Some determinants of actor structures from trait descriptors. *Journal of Personality and Social Psychology, 57,* 552–567.

Pearce-McCall, D., & Newman, J. P. (1986). Expectations of success following noncontingent punishment in introverts and extraverts. *Journal of Personality and Social Psychology, 50,* 439–446.

Pearson, G. L., & Freeman, F. G. (1991). Effects of extraversion and mental arithmetic on heart-rate reactivity. *Perceptual and Motor Skills, 72,* 1239–1248.

Pedersen, N. L., Plomin, R., McClearn, G. E., & Friberg, L. (1988). Neuroticism, extraversion and related traits in adult twins reared apart and reared together. *Journal of Personality and Social Psychology, 55,* 950–957.

Pederson, L. L., Strickland, C., & DesLauriers, A. (1991). Self-efficacy related to smoking cessation in general practice patients. *International Journal of the Addictions, 26,* 467–485.

Pekarik, E. G., Prinz, R. J., Liebert, D. E., Weintraub, S., & Neale, J. M. (1976). The Pupil Evaluation Inventory: A sociometric technique for assessing children's social behavior. *Journal of Abnormal Child Psychology, 4,* 83–97.

Pelham, B. W. (1995). Self-investment and self-esteem: Evidence for a Jamesian model of self-worth. *Journal of Personality and Social Psychology, 69,* 1141–1150.

Pellis, S. M., Obrien, D. P., Pellis, V. C., Teitelbaum, P., Wolgin, D. L., & Kennedy, S. (1988). Escalation of feline predation along a gradient from avoidance through "play" to killing. *Behavioral Neuroscience, 102,* 760–777.

Persky, V. M., Kempthorne-Rawson, J., & Shekele, R. B. (1987). Personality and the risk of cancer: 20-year follow-up of the Western Electric Study. *Psychosomatic Medicine, 49,* 435–449.

Person, E. S. (1988, March). Some differences between men and women: I. The passionate quest. *Atlantic Monthly,* pp. 71–74, 76.

Pervin, L. A. (1982). The stasis and flow of behavior: Toward a theory of goals. In M. M. Page & R. Dienstbier (Eds.), *Nebraska Symposium on Motivation* (Vol. 30). Lincoln: University of Nebraska.

Pervin, L. A. (1983). The stasis and flow of behavior: Toward a theory of goals. In M. M. Page (Ed.). *Personality: Current theory and research* (Nebraska Symposium on Motivation, Vol. 30, pp. 1–53). Lincoln: University of Nebraska Press.

Pervin, L. A. (1994). A critical analysis of current trait theory. *Psychological Inquiry, 5,* 103–113.

Peters, C. L., & Brown, R. D. (1991). The relationship of high school involvement, high school population size, and gender to college students' self efficacy beliefs. *College Student Journal, 25,* 473–481.

Peterson, L., & Ridley-Johnson, R. (1980). Pediatric hospital response to survey on prehospital preparation for children. *Journal of Pediatric Psychology, 5,* 1–7.

Peterson, L., Schultheis, K., Ridley-Johnson, R., Miller, D. J., & Tracy, K. (1984). Comparison of three modeling procedures on the presurgical and postsurgical reactions of children. *Behavior Therapy, 15,* 197–203.

Petri, H. L., & Mishkin, M. (1994). Behaviorism, cognitivism, and the neuropsychology of memory. *American Scientist, 82,* 30–37.

Phares, E. J. (1978). Locus of control. In H. London & J. E. Exner (Eds.), *Dimensions of personality.* New York: Wiley-Interscience.

Phares, E. J. (1979). Defensiveness and perceived control. In L. C. Perlmuter & R. A. Monty (Eds.), *Choice and perceived control.* Hillsdale, NJ: Erlbaum.

Phares, E. J. (1984). *Introduction to personality.* Columbus, OH: Charles E. Merrill.

Phelps, R. E., Huntley, D. K., Valdes, L. A., & Thompson, M. C. (1987). Parent-child interactions and child social networks in one-parent families. *Advances in Family Intervention, Assessment and Theory, 4,* 143–163.

Piacentini, J. C., Schaughency, E. A., & Lahey, B. B. (1985). Tantrums. In M. Hersen & C. G. Last (Eds.), *Behavior therapy casebook.* New York: Springer.

Pierce, J. V. (1961). *Sex differences in achievement motivation.* Quincy, IL: Quincy Youth Development Project.

Pigott, H. E., & Gonzales, F. P. (1987). The efficacy of videotape self-modeling to treat an electively mute child. *Journal of Clinical Child Psychology, 16,* 106–110.

Pihl, R. O., & Peterson, J. (1990). Inherited predisposition toward alcoholism: Characteristics of sons of male alcoholics. *Journal of Abnormal Psychology, 99,* 291–301.

Pincus, J. H. (1980). Can violence be a manifestation of epilepsy? *Neurology, 30,* 304–307.

Pinto, R. P., & Hollandsworth, J. G., Jr. (1989). Using videotape modeling to prepare children psychologically for surgery: Influence of parents and costs versus benefits of providing preparation services. *Health Psychology, 8,* 79–85.

Piper, W. E., Azim, H. F. A., Joyce, A. S., McCallum, M., Nixon, G. W. H., & Segal, P. S. (1991). Quality of object relations versus interpersonal functioning as predictors of therapeutic alliance and psychotherapy outcome. *Journal of Nervous and Mental Disease, 179,* 432–438.

Pittenger, D. J., & Pavlik, W. B. (1988). Analysis of the partial reinforcement extinction effect in humans using absolute and relative comparisons of schedules. *American Journal of Psychology, 101,* 1–14.

Pittenger, D. J., & Pavlik, W. B. (1989). Resistance to extinction in humans: Analysis of the generalized partial reinforcement effect. *Learning and Motivation, 20,* 60–72.

Pittenger, D. J., Pavlik, W. B., Flora, S. R., & Kontos, J. M. (1988). The persistence of learned behaviors in humans as a function of changes in reinforcement schedule and response schedules. *Learning and Motivation, 19,* 300–316.

Place, U. T. (1993). A radical behaviorist methodology for the empirical study of private events. *Behavior and Philosophy, 20,* 25–35.

Plaud, J. J. (1992). Should we take the "radical" out of "behaviorism"? Some comments about behavior therapy and philosophy. *the Behavior Therapist, 15,* 121–122.

Plomin, R. (1981). Ethnological behavioral genetics and development. In K. Immelmann, G. W. Barlow, L. Petrinovich, & M. Main (Eds.), *Behavioral development: The Bielefeld interdisciplinary project.* Cambridge: Cambridge University Press.

Plomin, R. (1986). Behavioral genetic methods. *Journal of Personality, 54,* 226–261.

Plomin, R., & Bergeman, C. S. (1991). The nature of nurture: Genetic influence on "environmental" measures. *Behavioral and Brain Sciences, 14,* 373–427.

Plomin, R., & Nesselroade, J. R. (1990). Behavioral genetics and personality change. *Journal of Personality, 58,* 191–220.

Plomin, R., Pedersen, N. L., McClearn, G. E., Nesselroade, J. R., & Bergman, C. S. (1988). EAS temperament during the last half of the life span: Twins reared apart and twins reared together. *Psychology and Aging, 3,* 43–50.

Poehlmann, J. A., & Fiese, B. H. (1994). The effects of divorce, maternal employment, and maternal social support on toddlers' home environments. In C. A. Everett (Ed.), *The economics of divorce: The effects on parents and children.* Binghamton, NY: Hawthorne.

Poidevant, J. M., Loesch, L. C., & Wittmer, J. (1991). Vocational aspirations and perceived self-efficacy of doctoral students in the counseling professions. *Counselor Education and Supervision, 30,* 289–300.

Polanyi, M. (1959). *The study of man.* Chicago: University of Chicago Press.

Pope, M., Denicolo, P., & de Bernardi, B. (1990). The teaching profession: A comparative view. *International Journal of Personal Construct Psychology, 3,* 313–326.

Popham, S. M., & Holden, R. R. (1991). Psychometric properties of the MMPI factor scales. *Personality and Individual Differences, 12,* 513–517.

Popper, K. R. (1959). *The logic of scientific discovery.* Hutchinson: London.

Porder, M. S. (1987). Projective identification: An alternative hypothesis. *Psychoanalytic Quarterly, 56,* 431–451.

Porter, L. M. (1987). *The interpretation of dreams: Freud's theories revisited.* Boston: Twayne.

Posada, G., Waters, E., Crowell, J., & Lay, K. L. (1995). Is it easier to use a secure mother as a secure base: Attachment Q-sort correlates of the Berkely Adult Attachment Interview. In E. Waters, B. Vaughn, G. Posada, & K. Kondo-Ikemura (Eds.), *Culture, caregiving, and cognition: Perspectives on secure base phenomena and attachment working models. Monographs of the Society for Research in Child Development, 60,* 133–145.

Posner, M. (1973). Coordination of internal codes. In W. Chase (Ed.), *Visual information processing.* New York: Academic Press.

Post, P., Stewart, M. A., & Smith, P. L. (1991). Self-efficacy, interest, and consideration of math/science and non-math/science occupations among Black freshmen. *Journal of Vocational Behavior, 38,* 179–186.

Postlethwaite, K., & Jaspars, J. (1986). The experimental use of personal constructs in educational research: The critical triad procedure. *British Journal of Educational Psychology, 56,* 241–254.

Power, M. J. (1991). Cognitive science and behavioural psychotherapy: Where behaviour was, there shall be cognition? *Behavioural Psychotherapy, 19,* 20–41.

Prager, K. J. (1986). Intimacy status: Its relationship to locus of control, self-disclosure, and anxiety in adults. *Personality and Social Psychology Bulletin, 12,* 91–109.

Premack, D. (1965). Reinforcement theory. In D. Levine (Ed.), *Nebraska symposium on motivation.* Lincoln: University of Nebraska Press.

Price, M. (1995). Gender talk: Discussion of Muriel Dimen's "Third Step." *American Journal of Psychoanalysis, 55,* 321–330.

Prince, P. N., & Hoffmann, R. F. (1991). Dreams of the dying patient. *Omega, 23,* 1–11.

Prociuk, T. J., & Breen, L. J. (1977). Internal-external control and information-seeking in a college academic situation. *Journal of Social Psychology, 101,* 309–310.

Purton, C. (1989). The person-centered Jungian. *Person-Centered Review, 4,* 403–419.

Putnam, F. W., Guroff, J. J., Sliberman, E. K., Barban, L., & Post, R. M. (1986). The clinical phenomenology of multiple personality disorder: Review of 100 recent cases. *Journal of Clinical Psychiatry, 47,* 285–293.

Quadrel, M. J., & Lau, R. R. (1989). Health promotion, health locus of control, and health behavior: Two field experiments. *Journal of Applied Social Psychology, 19,* 1497–1521.

Rachlin, H. (1976). *Behavior and learning.* San Francisco: W. H. Freeman.

Rachlin, H. (1977). Review of *Cognition and Behavior Modification* by M. J. Mahoney. *Journal of Applied Behavior Analysis, 10,* 369–374.

Rahim, M. A., & Psenicka, C. (1996). A structural equations model of stress, locus of control, social support, psychiatric symptoms, and propensity to leave a job. *Journal of Social Psychology, 136,* 69–84.

Ramond, C. K. (1953). Anxiety and task as determiners of verbal performance. *Journal of Experimental Psychology, 46,* 120–124.

Rangell, L. (1988). The future of psychoanalysis: The scientific crossroads. *Psychoanalytic Quarterly, 57,* 313–340.

Rao, N., Moely, B. E., & Lockman, J. J. (1987). Increasing social participation in preschool social isolates. *Journal of Clinical Child Psychology, 16,* 178–183.

Rapheal-Leff, J. (1995). Psychoanalysis and feminism. *British Journal of Psychotherapy, 12,* 84–88.

Raskin, R. N., & Hall, C. J. (1979). A Narcissistic Personality Inventory. *Psychological Reports, 45,* 590.

Raskin, R. N., & Hall, C. J. (1981). The Narcissistic Personality Inventory: Alternate form reliability and further evidence of construct validity. *Journal of Personality Assessment, 45,* 159–162.

Raskin, R. N., Novacek, J., & Hogan, R. (1991). Narcissistic self-esteem management. *Journal of Personality and Social Psychology, 60,* 911–918.

Rasmussen, S. A. (1985). Obsessive compulsive disorder in dermatologic practice. *Journal of the American Academy of Dermatology, 13,* 965–967.

Rathunde, K., & Csikszentmihalyi, M. (1993). Undivided interest and the growth of talent: A longitudinal study of adolescents. *Journal of Youth and Adolescence, 22,* 385–405.

Rawlings, D., & Carnie, D. (1989). The interaction of EPQ extraversion with WAIS subtest performance under timed and untimed conditions. *Personality and Individual Differences, 10,* 453–458.

Read, P. P. (1974). *Alive: The story of the Andes survivors.* Philadelphia: Lippincott.

Read, S. J., Jones, D. K., & Miller, L. C. (1990). Traits as goal-based categories: The importance of goals in the coherence of dispositional categories. *Journal of Personality and Social Psychology, 58,* 1048–1061.

Read, S. L., Miller, B. L., Mena, I., Kim, R., Itabashi, H., & Darby, A. (1995). SPECT in dementia: Clinical and pathological correlation. *Journal of the American Geriatrics Society, 43,* 1243–1247.

Reardon, R., & Doyle, S. M. (1995). The self-concept and reality judgements: Memory, memory monitoring, and internal-external correspondence. *Social Cognition, 13,* 1–24.

Rees, L. (1961). Constitutional factors and abnormal behavior. In H. J. Eysenck (Ed.), *Handbook of abnormal psychology.* New York: Basic Books.

Reinisch, J. M. (1981). Prenatal exposure to synthetic progestins increases potential for aggression in humans. *Science, 211,* 1171–1173.

Reis, H. T. (1990). The role of intimacy in interpersonal relations. *Journal of Social and Clinical Psychology, 9,* 15–30.

Reisner, M. F. (1989). The future of psychoanalysis in academic psychiatry: Plain talk. *Psychoanalytic Quarterly, 58,* 185–209.

Relke, D. M. (1993). Foremothers who cared: Paula Heimann, Margaret Little, and the female tradition of psychoanalysis. *Feminism and Psychology, 3,* 89–109.

Renik, O. (1990). The concept of transference neurosis and psychoanalytic methodology. *International Journal of Psycho-Analysis, 17,* 197–204.

Rescorla, R. A. (1988). Pavlovian conditioning: It's not what you think it is. *American Psychologist, 43,* 151–160.

Rescorla, R. A., & Wagner, A. R. (1972). A theory of Pavlovian conditioning: Variations in the effectiveness of reinforcement and nonreinforcement. In A. H. Black & W. F. Prokasy (Eds.), *Classical Conditioning II: Current Research and Theory,* New York: Appleton-Century-Crofts.

Resnik, S. (1987). *The theatre of the dream.* New York: Tavistock/Methuen.

Rhodewalt, F., Morf, C., Hazlett, S., & Fairfield, M. (1991). Self-handicapping: The role of discounting and augmentation in the preservation of self-esteem. *Journal of Personality and Social Psychology, 61,* 122–131.

Richard, L. S., Wakefield, J. A., & Lewak, R. (1990). *Personality and Individual Differences, 11,* 39–43.

Richard, R. L., & Jex, S. M. (1991). Further evidence for the validity of the Short Index of Self-Actualization [Special issue: Handbook of self-actualization]. *Journal of Social Behavior and Personality, 6,* 331–338.

Richards, P. S. (1994). Religious devoutness, impression management, and personality functioning in college students. *Journal of Research in Personality, 28,* 14–26.

Richardson, M. S. (1994). Agency/empowerment in clinical practice. *Journal of Theoretical and Philosophical Psychology, 14,* 40–49.

Richardson, R. C. (1990). The "tally argument" and the validation of psychoanalysis. *Philosophy of Science, 57,* 668–676.

Richaud de Minzi, M. C. (1991). A new multidimensional children's locus of control scale. *Journal of Psychology, 125,* 109–118.

Riemann, R. (1990). The bipolarity of personal constructs. *International Journal of Personal Construct Psychology, 3,* 149–165.

Riese, M. (1988). Temperament in full-term and preterm infants: Stability over ages 6-24 months. *Journal of Developmental and Behavioral Pediatrics, 9,* 6–11.

Riese, M. L. (1990). Neonatal temperament in monozygotic and dizygotic twins. *Child Development, 61,* 1230–1237.

Rigby, K., & Slee, P. T. (1987). Eysenck's personality factors and orientation toward authority among schoolchildren. *Australian Journal of Psychology, 39,* 151–161.

Ritter, B. (1969). Eliminating excessive fears of the environment through contact desensitization. In J. D. Krumboltz & C. E. Thoresen (Eds.), *Behavioral counseling: Cases and techniques.* New York: Holt, Rinehart & Winston.

Rivera, D., & Smith, D. D. (1988). Using a demonstration strategy to teach midschool students with learning disabilities how to compute long division. *Journal of Learning Disabilities, 21,* 77–81.

Rivers, I., & Smith, P. K. (1994). Types of bullying behaviour and their correlates. *Aggressive Behavior, 20,* 359–368.

Roazen, P. (1975). *Freud and his followers.* New York: Knopf.

Robbins, S. B. (1989). Role of contemporary psychoanalysis in counseling psychology. *Journal of Counseling Psychology, 36,* 267–278.

Roberson, R. (1989). Assessing personal work goals in the organizational setting: Development and evaluation of the Work Concerns Inventory. *Organizational Behavior and Human Decision Processes, 44,* 345–367.

Robert, R., Jansson, B., & Wager, J. (1989). Dreams of pregnant women: A pilot study. *Journal of Psychosomatic Obstetrics and Gynecology, 10,* 21–33.

Robin, A. L., & Foster, S. L. (1989). *Negotiating parent-adolescent conflict: A behavioral family systems approach.* New York: Guilford.

Robins, L. N. (1966). *Deviant children grown up: A sociological and psychiatric study of sociopathic personality.* Baltimore, MD: Williams & Wilkins.

Roche, S. M., & McConkey, K. M. (1990). Absorption: Nature, assessment, and correlates. *Journal of Personality and Social Psychology, 59,* 91–101.

Rock, I. (1983). *The logic of perception.* Cambridge, MA: MIT Press.

Rockland, L. H. (1989). Psychoanalytically oriented supportive therapy: Literature review and techniques. *Journal of the American Academy of Psychoanalysis, 17,* 451–462.

Rodriguez, M. L., Mischel, W., & Shoda, Y. (1989). Cognitive person variables in the delay of gratification of older children at risk. *Journal of Personality and Social Psychology, 57,* 358–367.

Roger, D., & Morris, J. (1991). The internal structure of the EPQ scales. *Personality and Individual Differences, 12,* 759–764.

Rogers, C. (1954). Towards a theory of creativity. *ETC: A Review of General Semantics, 11,* 249–260.

Rogers, C. R. (1942). *Counseling and psychotherapy.* Boston: Houghton Mifflin.

Rogers, C. R. (1951). *Client-centered therapy: Its current practice, implications, and theory.* Boston: Houghton Mifflin.

Rogers, C. R. (1959). A theory of therapy, personality, and interpersonal relationships, as developed in the client-centered framework. In S. Koch (Ed.), *Psychology: A study of a science* (Vol. 3). New York: McGraw-Hill.

Rogers, C. R. (1961). *On becoming a person.* Boston: Houghton Mifflin.

Rogers, C. R. (1963). The concept of the fully functioning person. *Psychotherapy: Theory, Research, and Practice, 1,* 17–26.

Rogers, C. R. (1964). Toward a science of the person. In T. W. Wann (Ed.), *Behaviorism and phenomenology.* Chicago: University of Chicago Press.

Rogers, C. R. (1965). *Client-centered therapy.* Boston: Houghton Mifflin.

Rogers, C. R. (1973). Some new challenges. *American Psychologist, 28,* 379–387.

Rogers, C. R. (1974). In retrospect: Forty-six years. *American Psychologist, 29,* 115–123.

Rogers, C. R. (1975). Empathic: An unappreciated way of being. *Counseling Psychologist, 5,* 2–10.

Rogers, C. R. (1979). The foundations of the person-centered approach. *Education, 100,* 98–107.

Rogers, C. R. (1980). *A way of being.* Boston: Houghton Mifflin.

Rogers, C. R. (1983). *Freedom to learn for the 80s.* Columbus, OH: Charles E. Merrill.

Rogers, C. R., & Dymond, R. F. (Eds.). (1954). *Psychotherapy and personality change.* Chicago: University of Chicago Press.

Rogers, C. R., & Ryback, D. (1984). One alternative to nuclear planetary suicide. In R. F. Levant & J. M. Shlien (Eds.), *Client-centered therapy and the person-centered approach: New directions in theory, research, and practice.* New York: Praeger.

Rohde-Dachser, C. (1992). Do we need a feminist psychoanalysis? *Psychoanalysis and Contemporary Thought, 15,* 241–259.

Rohsenow, D. J., & Marlatt, G. A. (1981). The balanced placebo design: Methodological considerations. *Addictive Behaviors, 6,* 107–122.

Rokeach, M., & Kliejunas, P. (1972). Behavior as a function of attitude-toward-object and attitude-toward-situation. *Journal of Personality and Social Psychology, 22,* 194–201.

Rokke, P. A., al-Absi, M., Lall, R., & Oswald, K. (1991). When does a choice of coping strategies help? The interaction of choice and locus of control. *Journal of Behavioral Medicine, 14,* 491–504.

Romi, S., & Itskowitz, R. (1990). The relationship between locus of control and type of aggression in middle-class and culturally deprived children. *Personality and Individual Differences, 11,* 327–333.

Romney, D. M. (1990). Thought disorders in the relatives of schizophrenics: A meta-analytic review of selected published studies. *Journal of Nervous and Mental Disease, 178,* 481–486.

Rorschach, H. (1921). *Psychodiagnostik.* Bern and Leipzig: Ernst Bircher Verlag.

Rose, R. J., Koskenvuo, M., Kaprio, J., Sarna, S., & Langinvainio, H. (1988). Shared genes, shared experiences, and similarity of personality: Data from 14,288 adult Finnish co-twins. *Journal of Personality and Social Psychology, 54,* 161–171.

Rosen, C. M. (1987). The eerie world of reunited twins. *Discover, 8,* 36–46.

Rosenberg, S. (1977). New approaches to the analysis of personal constructs in person perception. In J. K. Cole & A. W. Landfield (Eds.), *Nebraska symposium on motivation, 1976* (Vol. 24). Lincoln: University of Nebraska Press.

Rosenblatt, A. D. (1988). Envy, identification, and pride. *Psychoanalytic Quarterly, 57,* 56–71.

Rosenfarb, I. S. (1992). Review of unifying behavior therapy: Contributions of paradigmatic behaviorism by G. H. Eifert & I. M. Evans (Eds.). *Child and Family Behavior Therapy, 13,* 73–75.

Rosenhan, D. L., & Seligman, M. E. P. (1984). *Abnormal psychology.* New York: Norton.

Rosenman, R. H., Brand, R. J., Jenkins, C. D., Friedman, M., Straus, R., & Wurm, M. (1975). Coronary heart disease in the Western Collaborative Group Study: Final follow-up experience of 8 years. *Journal of the American Medical Association, 233,* 872–877.

Rosenthal, D., Moore, S., & Flynn, I. (1991). Adolescent self-efficacy, self-esteem and sexual risk-taking. *Journal of Community and Applied Social Psychology, 1,* 77–88.

Rosenthal, R. (1979). The "file drawer problem" and tolerance for null results. *Psychological Bulletin, 86,* 638–641.

Rosenwald, G. C. (1972). Effectiveness of defenses against anal impulse arousal. *Journal of Consulting and Clinical Psychology, 39,* 292–298.

Rosolack, T. K., & Hampson, S. E. (1991). A new typology of health behaviours for personality-health predictions: The case of locus of control. *European Journal of Personality, 5,* 151–168.

Ross, C. A., Miller, S. D., Reagor, P., Bjornson, L., Fraser, G. A., & Anderson, G. (1990). Structured interview data on 102 cases of multiple personality disorder from four centers. *American Journal of Psychiatry, 147,* 596–601.

Ross, M. (1989). Relation of implicit theories to the construction of personal histories. *Psychological Review, 96,* 341–357.

Rotenberg, V. S. (1988). Functional deficiency of REM sleep and its role in the pathogenesis of neurotic and psychosomatic disturbances. *Pavlovian Journal of Biological Science, 23,* 1–3.

Roth, P. A. (1991). Truth in interpretation: The case

of psychoanalysis. *Philosophy of the Social Sciences, 21,* 175–195.

Rothbaum, F., & Weisz, J. R. (1994). Parental caregiving and child externalizing behavior in nonclinical samples: A meta-analysis. *Psychological Bulletin, 116,* 55–74.

Rotter, J. B. (1954). *Social learning and clinical psychology.* Englewood Cliffs, NJ: Prentice-Hall.

Rotter, J. B. (1966). Generalized expectancies for internal versus external control of reinforcement. *Psychological Monographs, 80,* 1–28.

Rotter, J. B. (1981). The psychological situation in social learning theory. In D. Magnusson (Ed.), *Toward a psychology of situations: An interactional perspective.* Hillsdale, NJ: Erlbaum.

Rotter, J. B. (1982). *The development and application of social learning theory.* New York: Praeger.

Rounsaville, B. J., Weissman, M. M., & Prusoff, B. A. (1979). Process of psychotherapy among depressed women with marital disputes. *American Journal of Orthopsychiatry, 49,* 505–510.

Rowe, D. C. (1994). *The limits of family influence: Genes, experience and behavior.* New York: Guilford.

Royce, J. R., & Powell, A. (1983). *Theory of personality and individual differences: Factors, systems, and processes.* Englewood Cliffs, NJ: Prentice-Hall.

Rubin, J. Z., Provenzano, F. L., & Luria, Z. (1974). The eye of the beholder: Parents' views on sex of newborns. *American Journal of Orthopsychiatry, 44,* 512–519.

Rudnytsky, P. L. (1987). *Freud and Oedipus.* New York: Columbia.

Ruggiero, K. M., & Taylor, D. M. (1997). Why minority group members perceive or do not perceive the discrimination that confronts them: The role of self-esteem and perceived control. *Journal of Personality and Social Psychology, 72,* 373–389.

Ruiz-Caballero, J. A., & Bermudez, J. (1995). Neuroticism, mood, and retrieval of negative personal memories. *Journal of General Psychology, 122,* 29–35.

Rule, W. R. (1991). Self-actualization: A person in positive movement or simply an esteemed personality characteristic? [Special issue: Handbook of self-actualization]. *Journal of Social Behavior and Personality, 6,* 249–264.

Runco, M. A., Ebersole, P., & Mraz, W. (1991). Creativity and self-actualization. [Special issue: Handbook of self-actualization]. *Journal of Social Behavior and Personality, 6,* 161–167.

Runyan, W. M. (1983). Idiographic goals and methods in the study of lives. *Journal of Personality, 51,* 413–437.

Runyan, W. Mck. (Ed.). (1988). *Psychology and historical interpretation.* New York: Oxford University Press.

Rushton, J. P. (1988). Genetic similarity, mate choice, and fecundity in humans. *Ethology and Sociobiology, 9,* 329–335.

Rushton, J. P. (1989). Genetic similarity, human altrusim, and group selection. *Behavioral and Brain Sciences, 12,* 503–559.

Rushton, J. P., Russell, R. J. H., & Wells, P. A. (1985). Personality and genetic similarity theory. *Journal of Social and Biological Structures, 8,* 63–86.

Russell, R. J. H., & Wells, P. A. (1994). Predictors of happiness in married couples. *Personality and Individual Differences, 17,* 313–321.

Russo, D. C. (1990). A requiem for the passing of the three-term contingency. *Behavior Therapy, 21,* 153–165.

Ryan, J. (1995). Diversity and psychoanalysis. *British Journal of Psychotherapy, 12,* 78–80.

Ryan, J. J., Dei, X. Y., & Zheng, L. (1994). Psychological test usage in the People's Republic of China. *Journal of Psychoeducational Assessment, 12,* 324–330.

Rychlak, J. F. (1990). George Kelly and the concept of construction. *International Journal of Personal Construct Psychology, 3,* 7–19.

Rychlak, J. F. (1991). *Artificial intelligence and human reason: A teleological critique.* New York: Columbia University Press.

Rychlak, J. F. (1995). A teleological critique of modern cognitivism. *Theory and Personality, 5,* 511–531.

Rychlak, J. F., Barnard, S., Williams, R. N., & Wollman, N. (1989). The recognitions and cognitive utilization of oppositionality. *Journal of Psycholinguistic Research, 10,* 135–152.

Sabbe, B. G. (1991). Clientgerichte partnerrelatietherapie: het model van Auckenthaler. [Client-centered marital therapy: Auckenthaler's model.] *Tijdschrift voor Psychotherapie, 17,* 224–233.

Sackeim, H. A. (1983). Self-deception, self-esteem, and depression: The adaptive value of lying to oneself. In J. Masling (Ed.), *Empirical studies of psychoanalytical theories* (Vol. 1). Hillsdale, NJ: Analytic Press.

Safran, J. (1990, November). Cognitive therapy for depression: An examination of the process of change in light of recent developments in interpersonal theory. In A. M. Hayes (Chair), *A comparison of three psychotherapies for depression: The search for mechanisms of change.* Symposium presented at the meeting of the Association for Advancement of Behavior Therapy, San Francisco.

Safran, J. D., & Myran, J. C. (1995). The therapeutic alliance. *In Session, 1,* 1–92.

Sagan, E. (1988). *Freud, women, and morality: The psychology of good and evil.* New York: Basic Books.

Saklofske, D. F., Kelly, I. W., & Janzen, B. L. (1995). Neuroticism, depression, and depression proneness. *Personality and Individual Differences, 18,* 27–31.

Salmon, P. (1988). *Psychology for teachers: An alternative approach.* London: Hutchinson.

Sampson, E. E. (1989). The challenge of social change for psychology: Globalization and psychology's theory of the person. *American Psychologist, 44,* 914–921.

Sand, R. (1988). Early nineteenth century anticipation of Freudian theory. *International Review of Psycho-Analysis, 15,* 465–479.

Sanday, P. (1981). The sociocultural context of rape: A cross-cultural study. *Journal of Social Issues, 37,* 5–27.

Sanderman, R., & Ranchor, A. V. (1994). Stability of

personality traits and psychological distress over six years. *Perceptual and Motor Skills, 78,* 89–90.

Sandin, B., Chorot, P., & Fernández-Trespalecios, J. L. (1989). Pavlovian conditioning and phobias: The state of the art. In P. M. G. Emmelkamp, W. T. A. M. Everaerd, F. Kraaimaat, & Y. M. J. M. van Son (Eds.), *Fresh perspectives on anxiety disorders.* Amsterdam: Swets & Zeitlinger.

Sanford, N. (1963). Personality: Its place in psychology. In S. Koch (Ed.), Psychology: A study of a science. Study II, Vol. 5. *The process areas, the person, and some applied fields: Their place in psychology and science.* New York: McGraw-Hill.

Sanford, R. N., Adkins, M. M., Miller, R. B., & Cobb, E. A. (1943). Physique, personality, and scholarship. *Monographs of the society for research in child development, 7.*

Sappington, A. A. (1990). Recent psychological approaches to the free will versus determinism issue. *Psychological Bulletin, 108,* 1–11.

Sarason, I. G., Sarason, B. R., & Pierce, G. R. (1990). Anxiety, cognitive interference, and performance. *Journal of Social Behavior and Personality, 5,* 1–18.

Sarnoff, C. (1976). *Latency.* New York: Aronson.

Sarnoff, I., & Corwin, S. M. (1959). Castration anxiety and the fear of death. *Journal of Personality, 27,* 374–385.

Savage-Rumbaugh, E. S., Murphy, J., Sevcik, R. A., Brakke, K. E., Williams, S. L., & Rumbaugh, D. M. (1993). Language comprehension in ape and child. *Monographs of the Society for Research in Child Development, 58.*

Saxe, G. N., Vasile, R. G., Hill, T. C., Bloomingdale, K., & van der Kolk, B. A. (1992). SPECT imaging and multiple personality disorder. *Journal of Nervous and Mental Disease, 180,* 662–663.

Sayers, J. (1991). *Mothers of psychoanalysis.* New York: Norton.

Scarr, S., & McCartney, K. (1983). How people make their own environments: A theory of genotype/environment effects. *Child Development, 54,* 424–435.

Schaefer, W. S., & Bayley, N. (1963). Maternal behavior, child behavior, and their intercorrelations from infancy through adolescence. *Monographs of the Society for Research in Child Development, 28,* 1–27.

Schafer, R. (1950). Review of *Introduction to the Szondi Test: Theory and practice* by S. Deri. *Journal of Abnormal and Social Psychology, 45,* 184–188.

Schaffer, H. R., & Emerson, P. E. (1964). Patterns of response to physical contact in early human development. *Journal of Child Psychology and Psychiatry, 5,* 1–13.

Schaller, G. (1963). *The mountain gorilla.* Chicago: University of Chicago Press.

Scharff, D. E., & Scharff, J. S. (1987). *Object relations family therapy.* Northvale, NJ: Aronson.

Schiaffino, K. M., Revenson, T. A., & Gibofsky, A. (1991). Assessing the impact of self-efficacy beliefs on adaptation to rheumatoid arthritis. *Arthritis Care and Research, 4,* 150–157.

Schimek, J. G. (1983). The construction of the transference: The relativity of the "here and now" and the "there and then." *Psychoanalysis and Contemporary Thought, 6,* 435–456.

Schlinger, H. D., Jr. (1992). Theory in behavior analysis: An application to child development. *American Psychologist, 47,* 1396–1410.

Schloss, P. J., Smith, M., Santora, C., & Bryant, R. (1989). A respondent conditioning approach to reducing anger responses of a dually diagnosed man with mild mental retardation. *Behavior Therapy, 20,* 459–464.

Schmukler, A. G., & Garcia, E. E. (1989). Special symbols in early female Oedipal development: Fantasies of folds and spaces, protuberances and concavities. *International Journal of Psycho-Analysis, 71,* 297–300.

Schnake, M. E., & Dumler, M. P. (1990). Use of vicarious punishment to offset effects of negative social cues. *Psychological Reports, 66,* 1299–1308.

Schramm, W., Lyle, J., & Parker, E. (1961). *Television in the lives of our children.* Stanford, CA: Stanford University Press.

Schretlen, D. (1988). The use of psychological tests to identify malingered symptoms of mental disorder. *Clinical Psychology Review, 8,* 451–476.

Schretlen, D. (1990). A limitation of using the Wiener and Harmon obvious and subtle scales to detect faking on the MMPI. *Journal of Clinical Psychology, 46,* 782–786.

Schretlen, D., & Arkowitz, H. (1990). A psychological test battery to detect prison inmates who fake insanity or mental retardation. *Behavioral Sciences and the Law, 8,* 75–84.

Schroeder, M. L., Wormworth, J. A., & Livesley, W. J. (1992). Dimensions of personality disorder and their relationships to the Big Five dimensions of personality. *Psychological Assessment, 4,* 47–53.

Schwaber, E. A. (1990). Interpretation and the therapeutic action of psychoanalysis. *International Journal of Psycho-Analysis, 71,* 229–240.

Schwarz, N. (1990). Feelings as information: Informational and motivational functions of affective states. In E. T. Higgins and R. M. Sorrentino (Eds.), *Handbook of motivation and cognition: Foundations of social behavior* (Vol. 2). New York: Guilford.

Schwarzer, R. (1992a). Self-efficacy in the adoption and maintenance of health behaviors: Theoretical approaches and a new model. In R. Schwarzer (Ed.), *Self-efficacy: Thought control of action.* Washington, DC: Hemisphere.

Schwarzer, R. (Ed.). (1992b). *Self-efficacy: Thought control of action.* Washington, DC: Hemisphere.

Scrull, T. K., & Wyer, R. S., Jr. (1979). The role of category accessibility in the interpretation of information about persons: Some determinants and implications. *Journal of Personality and Social Psychology, 37,* 1660–1672.

Searle, J. R. (1990). Is the brain's mind a computer program? *Scientific American, 262,* 25–31.

Sears, R. R. (1943). *Survey of objective studies of psychoanalytic concepts.* New York: Social Science Research Council, Bulletin 51.

Sedikides, C. (1992). Changes in the valence of the self as a function of mood. In M. S. Clark (Ed.), *Emotion and social behavior.* Newbury Park, CA: Sage.

Sedikides, C. (1993). Assessment, enhancement, and verification determinants of the self-evaluation process. *Journal of Personality and Social Psychology, 65,* 317–338.

Sedikides, C., & Skowronski, J. J. (1995). On the sources of self-knowledge: The perceived primacy of self-reflection. *Journal of Social and Clinical Psychology, 14,* 244–270.

Seeman, J. (1984). The fully functioning person: Theory and research. In R. F. Levant & J. M. Shlien (Eds.), *Client-centered therapy and the person-centered approach: New directions in theory, research, and practice.* New York: Praeger.

Seeman, J. (1991). "Person-centered assessment": Reaction. *Journal of Counseling and Development, 69,* 462.

Segall, M. E., & Wynd, C. A. (1990). Health conception, health locus of control, and power as predictors of smoking behavior change. *American Journal of Health Promotion, 4,* 338–344.

Seligman, M. E. P. (1971). Phobias and preparedness. *Behavior Therapy, 2,* 307–320.

Sewell, K. W., Adams-Webber, J., Mitterer, J., & Cromwell, R. L. (1992). Computerized repertory grids: Review of the literature. *International Journal of Personal Construct Psychology, 5,* 1–23.

Shane, M. (1977). A rationale for teaching analytic technique based on a developmental orientation and approach. *International Journal of Psycho-Analysis, 58,* 95–108.

Shannon, B. (1990). Why are dreams cinematographic? *Metaphor and Symbolic Activity, 5,* 235–248.

Shapiro, M. A. (1991). Memory and decision processes in the construction of social reality. *Communication Research, 18,* 3–24.

Sharp, M. J., & Getz, J. G. (1996). Substance use as impression management. *Personality and Social Psychology Bulletin, 22,* 60–67.

Shaver, K. G., & Tarpy, R. M. (1993). *Psychology.* New York: Macmillan.

Shear, H. J., & Kundrat, S. L. (1987). Providing conditions to help clients outgrow disturbing dreams. *Psychotherapy, 24,* 363–367.

Sheehy, G. (1976). *Passages: Predictable crises of adult life.* New York: Dutton.

Sheehy, G. (1981). *Pathfinders.* New York: Morrow.

Sheldon, W. H. (1942). *The varieties of temperament: A psychology of constitutional differences.* New York: Harper & Row.

Sheldon, W. H. (1954). *Atlas of man: A guide for somatotyping the adult male at all ages.* New York: Harper & Row.

Shell, D. F., Murphy, C. C., & Bruning, R. H. (1989). Selfefficacy and outcome expectancy mechanisms in reading and writing achievement. *Journal of Educational Psychology, 81,* 91–100.

Shelton, S. H. (1990). Developing the construct of general self-efficacy. *Psychological Reports, 66,* 987–994.

Sherrill, C., Gench, B., Hinson, M., Gilstrap, T., Richir, K., & Mastro, J. (1990). Self-actualization of elite blind athletes: An exploratory study. *Journal of Visual Impairment and Blindness, 84,* 55–60.

Sherwood, G. G. (1979). Classical and attributive projection: Some new evidence. *Journal of Abnormal Psychology, 88,* 635–640.

Sherwood, M. (1969). *The logic of explanation in psychoanalysis.* New York: Academic Press.

Shimp, T. A., Stuart, E. W., & Engle, R. W. (1991). A program of classical conditioning experiments testing variations in the conditioned stimulus and context. *Journal of Consumer Research, 18,* 1–12.

Shoda, Y., & Mischel, W. (1996). Toward a unified, intra-individual dynamic conception of personality. *Journal of Research in Personality, 30,* 414–428.

Shoda, Y., Mischel, W., & Peake, P. K. (1990). Predicting adolescent cognitive and self-regulatory competencies from preschool delay of gratification: Identifying diagnostic conditions. *Developmental Psychology, 26,* 978–986.

Shoda, Y., Mischel, W., & Wright, J. C. (1989). Intuitive interactionism in person perception: Effects of situation-behavior relations on disopositional judgments. *Journal of Personality and Social Psychology, 56,* 41–53.

Shoda, Y., Mischel, W., & Wright, J. C. (1994). Intra-individual stability in the organization and patterning of behavior: Incorporating psychological situations into the idiographic analysis of personality. *Journal of Personality and Social Psychology, 67,* 674–687.

Shopshire, M. S., & Craik, K. H. (1994). The five factor model of personality and the DSM-III-R personality disorders: Correspondence and differentiation. *Journal of Personality Disorders, 8,* 41–52.

Shostrom, E. L. (1963). *Personal Orientation Inventory.* San Diego: EdITS/Educational & Industrial Testing Service.

Shostrom, E. L. (1964). An inventory for the measurement of self-actualization. *Educational and Psychological Measurement, 24,* 207–218.

Shostrom, E. L. (1974). *Manual for the Personal Orientation Inventory.* San Diego: EdITS/Educational & Industrial Testing Service.

Shostrom, E. L., Knapp, L. F., & Knapp, R. R. (1976). *Actualizing therapy: Foundations for a scientific ethic.* San Diego: EdITS/Educational & Industrial Testing Service.

Showers, C. (1992a). Compartmentalization of positive and negative self-knowledge: Keeping bad apples out of the bunch. *Journal of Personality and Social Psychology, 62,* 1036–1049.

Showers, C. (1992b). Evaluatively integrated thinking

about characteristics of the self. *Personality and Social Psychology Bulletin, 18,* 719–729.

Shulman, D. G. (1990a). The investigation of psychoanalytic theory by means of the experimental method. *International Journal of Psycho-Analysis, 71,* 487–498.

Shulman, D. G. (1990b). Psychoanalysis and the quantitative research tradition. *Psychoanalytic Review, 77,* 245–261.

Shuptrine, F. K., Bearden, W. O., & Teel, J. E. (1990). An analysis of the dimensionality and reliability of the Lennox and Wolfe reversed self-monitoring scale. *Journal of Personality Assessment, 54,* 515–522.

Shuter, R. (1977). A field study of nonverbal communication in Germany, Italy, and the United States. *Communication Monographs, 44,* 298–305.

Siegel, A., & Pott, C. B. (1988). Neural substrates of aggression and flight in the cat. *Progress in Neurobiology, 31,* 261–283.

Siegel, S. (1985). Drug anticipatory responses in animals. In L. White, B. Tursky, & G. E. Schwartz (Eds.), *Placebo: Theory, research, and mechanisms.* New York: Guilford.

Siegel, S., & Ellsworth, D. W. (1986). Pavlovian conditioning and death from apparent overdose of medically prescribed morphine: A case report. *Bulletin of the Psychonomic Society, 24,* 278–280.

Siegert, M. B. (1990). Reconstruction, construction, or deconstruction: Perspectives on the limits of psychoanalytic knowledge. *Contemporary Psychoanalysis, 26,* 160–170.

Siegler, I. C., Zonderman, A. B., Barefoot, J. C., Williams, R. B., Costa, P. T., & McCrae, R. R. (1990). Predicting personality in adulthood from college MMPI scores: Implications for follow-up studies in psychosomatic medicine. *Psychosomatic Medicine, 52,* 644–652.

Sigurdson, J. F., & Gudjonsson, G. H. (1995). *Nordic Journal of Psychiatry, 49,* 33–38.

Silver, E. J., Bauman, L. J., & Ireys, H. T. (1995). Relationships of self-esteem and efficacy to psychological distress in mothers of children with chronic physical illness. *Health Psychology, 14,* 333–340.

Silverman, L. H. (1983). The subliminal psychodynamic activation method: Overview and comprehensive listing of studies. In J. Masling (Ed.), *Empirical studies in psychoanalysis* (Vol. 1). Hillsdale, NJ: Erlbaum.

Simonton, O. C., Mathews-Simonton, S., & Creighton, J. L. (1980). *Getting well again.* New York: Bantam.

Simpson, J. A. (1990). Influence of attachment styles on romantic relationships. *Journal of Personality and Social Psychology, 59,* 971–980.

Singer, J. L. (1985). Transference and the human condition: A cognitive-affective perspective. *Psychoanalytic Psychology, 2,* 189–219.

Singer, J. L. (1988). Psychoanalytic theory in the context of contemporary psychology: The Helen Block Lewis memorial address. *Psychoanalytic Psychology, 5,* 95–125.

Singh, B. G., & Verma, O. P. (1990). Cultural differences in locus of control beliefs in two Indian societies. *Journal of Social Psychology, 130,* 725–729.

Singh, D. (1993). Adaptive significance of female physical attractiveness: Role of waist-to-hip ratio. *Journal of Personality and Social Psychology, 65,* 293–307.

Siskind, D. (1987). An example of preverbal determinants in a classical analysis. *Clinical Social Work Journal, 15,* 361–367.

Sitharthan, T., & Kavanagh, D. J. (1991). Role of self-efficacy in predicting outcomes from a programme for controlled drinking. *Drug and Alcohol Dependence, 27,* 87–94.

Sizemore, C. C., & Huber, R. J. (1988). The twenty-two faces of Eve. *Individual Psychology Journal of Adlerian Theory, Research and Practice, 44,* 53–62.

Skinner, B. F. (1938). *The behavior of organisms.* New York: Appleton-Century-Crofts.

Skinner, B. F. (1953). *Science and human behavior.* New York: Macmillan.

Skinner, B. F. (1956). A case history in scientific method. *American Psychologist, 11,* 221–233.

Skinner, B. F. (1974). *About behaviorism.* New York: Knopf.

Skinner, B. F. (1989). The origins of cognitive thought. *American Psychologist, 44,* 13–18.

Skinner, E. (1992). Perceived control: Motivation, coping, and development. In R. Schwarzer (Ed.), *Self-efficacy: Thought control of action.* Washington, DC: Hemisphere.

Slade, L. A., & Rush, M. C. (1991). Achievement motivation and the dynamics of task difficulty choices. *Journal of Personality and Social Psychology, 60,* 165–172.

Slater, M. D. (1989). Social influences and cognitive control as predictors of self-efficacy and eating behavior. *Cognitive Therapy and Research, 13,* 231–245.

Slavin, M. O. (1990). The dual meaning of repression and the adaptive design of the human psyche. *Journal of the Academy of Psychoanalysis, 18,* 307–341.

Slife, B. D., Stoneman, J., & Rychlak, J. F. (1991). The heuristic power of oppositionality in an incidental-memory task: In support of the construing process. *International Journal of Personal Construct Psychology, 4,* 333–346.

Sloan, E. P., Fenton, G. W., Kennedy, N. J. S., & MacLennan, J. M. (1995). Electroencephalography and single photon emission computed tomography in dementia: A comparative study. *Psychological Medicine, 25,* 631–638.

Smeraldi, E., Kidd, K. K., Negri, F., Heimbuch, R., & Melica, A. M. (1979). Genetic studies of affective disorders. In J. Obiols, C. Ballus, E. Gonzalez Monclus, & J. Pujol (Eds.), *Biological psychiatry today.* Amsterdam: Elsevier/North Holland Biomedical Press.

Smith, D. A., & Andresen, J. J. (1988). Shadows in dreams. *Contemporary Psychoanalysis, 24,* 46–60.

Smith, G. E., Gerrard, M., & Gibbons, F. X. (1997). Self-esteem and the relation between risk behavior and perceptions of vulnerability to unplanned pregnancy in college women. *Health Psychology, 16,* 137–146.

Smith, J. E., Stefan, C., Kovaleski, M., & Johnson, G. (1991). Recidivism and dependency in a psychiatric population: An investigation with Kelly's dependency grid. *International Journal of Personal Construct Psychology, 4,* 157–173.

Smith, M. B. (1988). The wrong drummer: A reply to Blight. *Journal of Humanistic Psychology, 28,* 62–66.

Smith, M. B. (1990). Humanistic psychology. *Journal of Humanistic Psychology, 30,* 6–21.

Smith, R. E. (1973). The use of humor in the counterconditioning of anger responses: A case study. *Behavior Therapy, 4,* 576–580.

Smith, T. W., & Anderson, N. B. (1986). Models of personality and disease: An interactional approach to Type A behavior and cardiovascular risk. *Journal of Personality and Social Psychology, 50,* 1166–1173.

Smith, T. W., & Frohm, K. D. (1985). What's so unhealthy about hostility? Construct validity and psychosocial correlates of the Cook and Medley Ho Scale. *Health Psychology, 4,* 503–520.

Smith, T. W., & Pope, M. K. (1990). Cynical hostility as a health risk: Current status and future directions. *Journal of Social Behavior and Personality, 5,* 77–88.

Snow, M. E., Jacklin, C. N., & Maccoby, E. E. (1983). Sex-of-child differences in father-child interaction at one year of age. *Child Development, 54,* 227–232.

Snyder, C. R. (1990). Self-handicapping processes and sequelae: On the taking of a psychological dive. In R. L. Higgins, R. R. Snyder, & S. Berglas (Eds.), *Self-handicapping: The paradox that isn't.* New York: Plenum.

Snyder, C. R., & Larson, G. R. (1972). A further look at student acceptance of general personality interpretations. *Journal of Consulting and Clinical Psychology, 38,* 384–388.

Snyder, F. (1965). The organismic state associated with dreaming. In N. W. Greenfield (Ed.), *Psychoanalysis and current biological thought.* Madison: University of Wisconsin Press.

Snyder, M. (1974). The self-monitoring of expressive behavior. *Journal of Personality and Social Psychology, 30,* 526–537.

Snyder, M. (1989). The relationship enhancement model of couple therapy: An integration of Rogers and Bateson [Special issue: Person-centered approaches with families]. *Person-Centered Review, 4,* 358–383.

Snyder, M., & Ickes, W. (1985). Personality and social behavior. In G. Lindzey & E. Aronson (Eds.), *The handbook of social psychology* (Vol. 2). New York: Random House.

Snyder, W. U. (1947). *Casebook of non-directive counseling.* Boston: Houghton Mifflin.

Sokolov, A. N. (1972). *Inner speech and thought.* New York: Plenum.

Solas, J. (1992). Ideological dimension implicit in Kelly's theory of personal constructs. *International Journal of Personal Construct Psychology, 5,* 377–391.

Soldz, S., Budman, S., Demby, A., & Merry, J. (1995). The relation of defensive style to personality pathology and the big five personality factors. *Journal of Personality Disorders, 9,* 356–370.

Solomon, K. E., & Annis, H. M. (1990). Outcome and efficacy expectancy in the prediction of post-treatment drinking behaviour. *British Journal of Addiction, 85,* 659–666.

Solomon, L. N. (1988). On being a sociotherapist in policy-land: A commentary on James Blight's article. *Journal of Humanistic Psychology, 28,* 70–72.

Solomon, S., Greenberg, J., & Pyszczynski, T. (1991a). A terror management theory of social behavior: The psychological functions of self-esteem and cultural worldview. In M. P. Zanna (Ed.), *Advances in experimental social psychology* (Vol. 2). New York: Academic Press.

Solomon, S., Greenberg, J., & Pyszczynski, T. (1991b). Terror management theory of self-esteem. In C. R. Snyder & D. Forsyth (Eds.), *Handbook of social and clinical psychology: The health perspective.* New York: Pergamon.

Sorrentino, R. M., & Field, N. (1986). Emergent leadership over time: The functional value of positive motivation. *Journal of Personality and Social Psychology, 50,* 1091–1099.

Spector, P. E. (1988). Development of the work locus of control scale. *Journal of Occupational Psychology, 61,* 335–340.

Spence, D. P. (1984). *Narrative truth and historical truth: Meaning and interpretation in psychoanalysis.* New York: Norton.

Spence, J. T., & Helmreich, R. L. (1978). *Masculinity and femininity: Their psychological dimensions, correlates and antecedents.* Austin: University of Texas Press.

Spence, J. T., Helmreich, R. L., & Pred, R. S. (1987). Impatience versus achievement strivings in the Type A behavior pattern: Differential effects on students' health and academic achievement. *Journal of Applied Psychology, 72,* 522–528.

Spence, J. T., Helmreich, R., & Stapp, J. (1974). The personal attributes questionnaire: A measure of sex-role stereotypes and masculinity-femininity. *JSAS Catalog of Selected Documents in Psychology, 4,* 43. (Ms. no. 617).

Spiegler, M. D. (1983). *Contemporary behavioral therapy.* Palo Alto, CA: Mayfield.

Spiegler, M. D. (1985, August). *Treating guilt within the framework of personal construct theory.* Paper presented at the International Congress on Personal Construct Theory, Cambridge, England.

Spiegler, M. D. (1989). *Transference in everyday life.* Unpublished manuscript, Providence College.

Spiegler, M. D. (1991). Satir's formula for therapeutic endurance: The wonderful human being myth. *Journal of Couples Therapy, 2,* 165–167.

Spiegler, M. D., & Agigian, H. (1977). *The Community*

Training Center: An educational-behavioral-social systems model for rehabilitating psychiatric patients. New York: Brunner/Mazel.

Spiegler, M. D., & Davison, G. C. (1989, April). *What therapists tell clients: Implications for psychotherapy integration and ethical practice.* Paper presented at the Fifth Annual Conference of the Society for the Exploration of Psychotherapy Integration, Berkeley, CA.

Spiegler, M. D., & Guevremont, D. C. (1993). *Contemporary behavior therapy* (2nd ed.). Pacific Grove, CA: Brooks/Cole.

Spiegler, M. D., & Liebert, R. M. (1970). Some correlates of self-reported fear. *Psychological Reports, 26,* 691–695.

Spiegler, M. D., & Weiland, A. (1976). The effects of written vicarious consequences on observers' willingness to imitate and ability to recall modeling cues. *Journal of Personality, 44,* 260–273.

Spielberger, C. D., & Gorsuch, R. L. (1966). *Mediating processes in verbal conditioning: Report of United States Public Health Service Grants MH-7229, MH-7446, and HD-947.* Unpublished manuscript, Vanderbilt University.

Spielman, A. J., Saskin, P., & Thorpy, M. J. (1987). Treatment of chronic insomnia by restriction of time in bed. *Sleep, 10,* 45–56.

Spoont, M. R. (1992). Modulatory role of serotonin in neural information processing: Implications for human psychopathology. *Psychological Bulletin, 112,* 330–350.

Squire, L. R. (1992). Declarative and nondeclarative memory: Multiple brain systems supporting learning and memory. *Journal of Cognitive Neuroscience, 4,* 232–243.

Staats, A. W. (1986). Behaviorism with a personality: The paradigmatic behavioral assessment approach. In R. O. Nelson & S. C. Hayes (Eds.), *Conceptual foundations of behavioral assessment.* New York: Guilford.

Staats, A. W. (1989a). Paradigmatic behaviorism's theory of intelligence: A third-generation approach to cognition. *Psicothema, 1,* 7–24.

Staats, A. W. (1989b). Unificationism: Philosophy for the modern disunified science of psychology. *Philosophical Psychology, 2,* 143–164.

Staats, A. W. (1990). Paradigmatic behaviorism and intelligence: Task analysis? Technical plan? or Theory? *Psicothema, 2,* 7–24.

Staats, A. W. (1991). Unified positivism and unification psychology: Fad or new field? *American Psychologist, 46,* 899–912.

Staats, A. W. (1993a). Personality theory, abnormal psychology, and psychological measurement: A psychological behaviorism. *Behavior Modification, 17,* 8–42.

Staats, A. W. (1993b). Why do we need another behaviorism such as paradigmatic behaviorism? *the Behavior Therapist, 3,* 64–68.

Staats, A. W., & Burns, G. L. (1981). Intelligence and child development: What intelligence is and how it is learned and functions. *Genetic Psychology Monographs, 104,* 237–301.

Staats, A. W., & Burns, G. L. (1982). Emotional personality repertoire as cause of behavior: Specification of personality and interaction principles. *Journal of Personality and Social Psychology, 43,* 873–881.

Staats, A. W., & Burns, G. L. (1992). The psychological behaviourism theory of personality. In *Modern personality psychology: Critical reviews and new directions.* New York: Harvester Whatsheaf.

Staats, A. W., & Eifert, G. H. (1990). The paradigmatic behaviorism theory of emotions: Basis for unification. *Clinical Psychology Review, 10,* 539–566.

Stagner, R. (1976). Traits are relevant: Theoretical analysis and empirical evidence. In N. S. Endler & D. Magnusson (Eds.), *Interactional psychology and personality.* Washington, DC: Hemisphere.

Starkstein, S. E., & Robinson, R. G. (1986). Cerebral lateralization in depression. *American Journal of Psychiatry, 143,* 1631.

Starkstein, S. E., Vasquez, S., Merello, M., Teson, A., Petracchi, M., & Leiguarda, R. (1995). A SPECT study of Parkinsonism in Alzheimer's disease. *Journal of Neuropsychiatry and Clinical Neurosciences, 7,* 308–313.

Staw, B. M., & Ross, J. (1985). Stability in the midst of change: A dispositional approach to job attitudes. *Journal of Applied Psychology, 70,* 469–480.

St. Clair, M. (1986). *Object relations and self psychology: An introduction.* Pacific Grove, CA: Brooks/Cole.

Steele, C. M. (1988). The psychology of self-affirmation: Sustaining the integrity of the self. In L. Berkowitz (Ed.). *Advances in experimental and social psychology.* (Vol. 21). New York: Academic Press.

Steele, R. S. (1979). Psychoanalysis and hermeneutics. *International Review of Psycho-Analysis, 6,* 389–411.

Steele, R. S. (1985). Paradigm lost: Psychoanalysis after Freud. In C. E. Buxton (Ed.), *Points of view in the modern history of psychology.* New York: Academic Press.

Steele, R. S. (1986). Deconstructing histories: Toward a systematic criticism of psychological narratives. In T. Sarbin (Ed.), *Psychology and narrative.* New York: Praeger.

Stein, G. L., Kimiecik, J. C., Daniels, J., & Jackson, S. A. (1995). Psychological antecedents of flow in recreational sport. *Personality and Social Psychology Bulletin, 21,* 125–135.

Steinberg, L., Lamborn, S. D., Darling, N., Mounts, N. S., & Dornbusch, S. M. (1994). Over-time changes in adjustment and competence among adolescents from authoritative, authoritarian, indulgent, and neglectful families. *Child Development, 65,* 754–770.

Steinmark, S. W., & Borkovec, T. D. (1974). Active and placebo treatment effects on moderate insomnia under counterdemand and positive demand instructions. *Journal of Abnormal Psychology, 83,* 157–163.

Stelmack, R. M. (1990). Biological bases of extraversion: Psychophysiological evidence. *Journal of Personality, 58,* 293–311.

Stelmack, R. M. (1991). Advances in personality theory

and research. *Journal of Psychiatric Neuroscience, 16,* 131–138.

Stelmack, R. M., & Stalikas, A. (1991). Galen and the humour theory of temperament. *Personality and Individual Differences, 12,* 255–263.

Stephan, C., & Linder, H. B. (1985). Suicide, an experience of chaos or fatalism: Perspectives from personal construct theory. In D. Bannister (Ed.), *Issues and approaches in personal construct theory.* Orlando, FL: Academic Press.

Stewart, A. E., & Barry, J. R. (1991). Origins of George Kelly's constructivism in the works of Korzybski and Moreno. *International Journal of Personal Construct Psychology, 4,* 121–136.

Stewart, V., & Stewart, A. (1982). *Business applications of repertory grid.* London: McGraw-Hill.

Stiles, T. C., & Götestam, K. G. (1989). The role of automatic negative thoughts in the development of dysphoric mood: An analogue experiment. *Cognitive Therapy and Research, 13,* 161–170.

Stiles, T. C., Schröder, P., & Johansen, T. (1993). The role of automatic thoughts and dysfunctional attitudes in the development and maintenance of experimentally induced dysphoric mood. *Cognitive Therapy and Research, 17,* 71–82.

St. Mary, S., & Russo, T. J. (1991). A self-efficacy scale for chemical dependency in adolescence. *Psychology: A Journal of Human Behavior, 27,* 62–68.

Stolorow, R. D. (1988). Transference and the therapeutic process. *Psychoanalytic Review, 75,* 245–254.

Stoneman, Z., Brody, G. H., & MacKinnon, C. E. (1986). Same-sex and cross-sex siblings: Activity choices, roles, behavior, and gender stereotypes. *Sex-Roles, 15,* 495–511.

Storr, A. (1988). *Solitude: A return to the self.* New York: Free Press.

Storr, A., & Kermode, F. (Eds.). (1973). *C. J. Jung.* New York: Viking.

Stotland, S., & Zuroff, D. C. (1991). Relations between multiple measures of dieting self-efficacy and weight change in a behavioral weight control program. *Behavior Therapy, 22,* 47–59.

Stotland, S., Zuroff, D. C., & Roy, M. (1991). Situational dieting self-efficacy and short-term regulation of eating. *Appetite, 17,* 81–90.

Strano, D. A., & Dixon, P. N. (1990). The comparative feeling of inferiority index. *Individual Psychology, 46,* 29–42.

Strassburger, L. A., Rosen, L. A., Miller, C. D., & Chavez, E. L. (1990). Hispanic-Anglo differences in academic achievement: The relationship of self-esteem, locus of control and socioeconomic level with grade-point average in the USA. *School Psychology International, 11,* 119–124.

Strauman, T. J., & Higgins, E. T. (1987). Automatic activation of self-discrepancies and emotional syndromes: When cognitive structures influence affect. *Journal of Personality and Social Psychology, 53,* 1004–1014.

Strean, H. S. (1985). *Resolving resistances in psychotherapy.* New York: Wiley.

Strelau, J. (1987). The concept of temperament in personality research. *European Journal of Personality, 1,* 107–117.

Strickland, B. R. (1977). Internal-external control of reinforcement. In T. Bass (Ed.), *Personality variables in social behavior.* Hillsdale, NJ: Erlbaum.

Strickland, B. R. (1978). Internal-external expectancies of health-related behaviors. *Journal of Consulting and Clinical Psychology, 46,* 1192–1211.

Strickland, B. R. (1979). Internal-external expectancies and cardiovascular functioning. In L. C. Perlmuter & R. A. Monty (Eds.), *Choice and perceived control.* Hillsdale, NJ: Erlbaum.

Strickland, B. R. (1989). Internal-external control expectancies: From contingency to creativity. *American Psychologist, 44,* 1–12.

Striker, G., & Gold, J. (Eds.). (1993). *Comprehensive handbook of psychotherapy integration.* New York: Plenum.

Stropes-Roe, M., & Cochrane, R. (1990). The child-rearing values of Asian and British parents and young people: An inter-ethnic and inter-generational comparison in the evolution of Kohn's 13 qualities. *British Journal of Social Psychology, 29,* 149–160.

Strupp, H. H. (1967). *An introduction to Freud and modern psychoanalysis.* Woodbury, NY: Barron's.

Stuart, E. W., Shimp, T. A., & Engle, W. W. (1987). Classical conditioning of consumer attitudes: Four experiments in an advertising context. *Journal of Consumer Research, 14,* 334–349.

Stuart, R. B. (1980). *Helping couples change: A social learning approach to marital therapy.* New York: Guilford.

Stumpf, H. (1993). The factor structure of the Personality Research Form: A cross-national evaluation. *Journal of Personality, 61,* 27–48.

Stumphauzer, J. S. (1972). Increased delay of gratification in young prison inmates through imitation of high-delay peer-models. *Journal of Personality and Social Psychology, 21,* 10–17.

Sullivan, H. S. (1953). *The interpersonal theory of psychiatry.* New York: Norton.

Sulloway, F. J. (1979). *Freud, biologist of the mind.* New York: Basic Books.

Suls, J., David, J. P., & Harvey, J. H. (1996). Personality and coping: Three generations of research. *Journal of Personality, 64,* 711–735.

Sutton, W. S. (1991). Hypnocounselling: A client-centered way of tuning into the subconscious. *Australian Journal of Clinical Hypnotherapy and Hypnosis, 12,* 7–20.

Sutton-Smith, B., & Rosenberg, B. G. (1970). *The sibling.* New York: Holt, Rinehart, & Winston.

Swan, G. E., & MacDonald, M. L. (1978). Behavior

therapy in practice: A national survey of behavioral therapists. *Behavior Therapy, 9,* 799–807.

Szasz, T. S. (1960). The myth of mental illness. *American Psychologist, 15,* 113–118.

Tamminga, C. A., Thaker, G. K., Buchanan, R., Kirkpatrick, B., Alphs, L. D., Chase, T. N., & Carpenter, W. T. (1992). Limbic system abnormalities identified in schizophrenia using positron emission tomography with fluorodeoxyglucose and neocortical alterations with deficit syndrome. *Archives of General Psychiatry, 49,* 522–530.

Tanner, J. M. (1955). *Growth at adolescence.* Springfield, IL: Charles C Thomas.

Tarter, R. E. (1988). Are there inherited behavioral traits that predispose to substance abuse? *Journal of Consulting and Clinical Psychology, 56,* 189–196.

Tauber, M. A. (1979). Parental socialization techniques and sex differences in children's play. *Child Development, 50,* 981–988.

Taylor, J. A. (1953). A personality scale of manifest anxiety. *Journal of Abnormal and Social Psychology, 48,* 285–290.

Taylor, J. A., & Spence, K. W. (1952). The relationship of anxiety level to performance in serial learning. *Journal of Experimental Psychology, 44,* 61–64.

Taylor, M. (1991). How psychoanalytic thinking lost its way in the hands of men: The case for feminist psychotherapy. *British Journal of Guidance and Counselling, 19,* 93–103.

Taylor, M. C., & Hall, J. A. (1982). Psychological androgyny: Theories, methods, and conclusions. *Psychological Bulletin, 92,* 347–366.

Taylor, S. E., & Brown, J. D. (1988). Illusion and well-being: A social psychological perspective on mental health. *Psychological Bulletin, 103,* 193–210.

Taylor, S. E., Neter, E., & Wayment, H. A. (1995). Self-evaluation processes. *Personality and Social Psychology Bulletin, 21,* 1278–1287.

Tellegen, A. (1985). Structure of mood and personality and their relevance to assessing anxiety, with an emphasis on self-report. In A. H. Tuma & J. D. Maser (Eds.), *Anxiety and the anxiety disorders.* Hillsdale, NJ: Erlbaum.

Tellegen, A. (1991). Personality traits: Issues of definition, evidence, and assessment. In W. M. Grove & D. Cicchetti (Eds.). *Thinking clearly about psychology* (Vol. 2). Minneapolis: University of Minnesota Press.

Tellegen, A. (1993). Folk concepts and psychological concepts of personality and personality disorder. *Psychological Inquiry, 4,* 122–130.

Tellegen, A., Lykken, D. T., Bouchard, T. J., Wilcox, K. J., Segal, N. L., & Rich, S. (1988). Personality similarity in twins reared apart and together. *Journal of Personality and Social Psychology, 54,* 1031–1039.

Tellegen, A., & Waller, N. G. (1987). Reexamining basic dimensions of natural language trait descriptors. 95th annual meeting of the American Psychological Association. (Abstract).

Tellegen, A., & Waller, N. G. (in press). Exploring personality through test construction: Development of the Multidimensional Personality Questionnaire. In J. M. Cheek & E. M. Donahue (Eds.), *Handbook of personality inventories.* New York: Plenum.

Terry, D. J., & O'Leary, J. E. (1995). The theory of planned behaviour: The effects of perceived behavioural control and self-efficacy. *British Journal of Social Psychology, 34,* 199–220.

Tesauro, G. (1994). TD-gammon, a self-teaching backgammon program, achieves master-level play. *Neurai Computation, 6,* 215–219.

Teti, D. M., & Gelfand, D. M. (1991). Behavioral competence among mothers of infants in the first year: The mediational role of maternal self-efficacy. *Child Development, 62,* 918–929.

Thase, M. E., Bowler, K., & Harden, T. (1991). Cognitive behavior therapy of endogenous depression: Part 2: Preliminary findings in 16 unmedicated inpatients. *Behavior Therapy, 22,* 469–477.

Thase, M. E., Simons, A. D., Cahalane, J. F., & McGeary, J. (1991). Cognitive behavior therapy of endogenous depression: Part 1: An outpatient clinical replication series. *Behavior Therapy, 22,* 457–467.

Thibodeau, R., & Aronson, E. (1992). Taking a closer look: Reasserting the role of the self-concept in dissonance theory. *Personality and Social Psychology Bulletin, 18,* 591–602.

Thigpen, C. H., & Cleckley, H. (1954). A case of multiple personality. *Journal of Abnormal and Social Psychology, 49,* 135–151.

Thigpen, C. H., & Cleckley, H. M. (1957). *The three faces of Eve.* New York: McGraw-Hill.

Thomas, A., & Chess, S. (1977). *Temperament and development.* New York: Brunner/Mazel.

Thomas, A., Chess, S., & Birch, H. G. (1970). The origin of personality. *Scientific American, 223,* 102–109.

Thomas, H. F. (1988). Keeping person-centered education alive in academic settings. *Person-Centered Review, 3,* 337–352.

Thomas, L., & Cooper, P. (1980). Incidence and psychological correlates of intense spiritual experiences. *Journal of Transpersonal Psychology, 12,* 75–85.

Thomaz, M. F., & Gilbert, J. K. (1989). A model for constructivist initial physics teacher education. *International Journal of Science Education, 11,* 35–47.

Thompson, C. M. (1941). The role of women in this culture. *Psychiatry, 4,* 1–8.

Thompson, C. M. (1942). Cultural pressures in the psychology of women. *Psychiatry, 5,* 331–339.

Thompson, C. M. (1943). Penis envy in women. *Psychiatry, 6,* 123–125.

Thompson, C. M. (1950). Cultural pressures in the psychology of women. In P. Mullahy (Ed.), *A study of interpersonal relations.* New York: Hermitage Press.

Thompson, C. M. (1957). *Psychoanalysis: Evolution and development.* New York: Grove.

Thompson, T. (1987). Resistance and preoedipal object relations. *Clinical Social Work Journal, 15,* 342–348.

Thorne, A. & Gough, H. (1991). *Portraits of Type: An MBTI research compendium.* Palo Alto, CA: Consulting Psychologists Press.

Throne, J. M. (1992). Understanding Skinner. *American Psychologist, 47,* 1678.

Thurman, P. J., Jones-Saumty, D., & Parsons, O. A. (1990). Locus of control and drinking behavior in American Indian alcoholics and non-alcoholics. *American Indian and Alaska Native Mental Health Research, 4,* 31–39.

Tice, D. M. (1992). Self-concept change and self-presentation: The looking glass self is also a magnifying glass. *Journal of Personality and Social Psychology, 63,* 435–451.

Tice, D. M., & Baumeister, R. F. (1990). Self-esteem, self-handicapping, and self-presentation: The strategy of inadequate practice. *Journal of Personality, 58,* 443–464.

Tinsley, B. J., & Holtgrave, D. R. (1989). Maternal health locus of control beliefs, utilization of childhood preventive health services, and infant health. *Journal of Developmental and Behavioral Pediatrics, 10,* 236–241.

Tjeltveit, A. C. (1989). The ubiquity of models of human beings in psychotherapy: The need for rigorous reflection. *Psychotherapy, 26,* 1–10.

Tobin, S. A. (1991). A comparison of psychoanalytic self psychology and Carl Rogers's person-centered therapy. *Journal of Humanistic Psychology, 31,* 9–33.

Torgersen, S. (1985). Heredity differentiation of anxiety and affective neuroses. *British Journal of Psychiatry, 146,* 530–534.

Torgerson, S. (1990). Comorbidity of major depression and anxiety disorders in twin pairs. *American Journal of Psychiatry, 147,* 1199–1202.

Torrey, E. F., Rawlings, R., & Waldman, I. N. (1988). Schizophrenic births and viral diseases in two states. *Schizophrenia Research, 1,* 73–77.

Toshima, M. T., Kaplan, R. M., & Ries, A. L. (1992). Self-efficacy expectancies in chronic obstructive pulmonary disease rehabilitation. In R. Schwarzer (Ed.), *Self-efficacy: Thought control of action.* Washington, DC: Hemisphere.

Tracy, L. (1990). Treating factor interpretations as hypotheses. *Social Behavior and Personality, 18,* 309–326.

Trice, A. D. (1990). Adolescents' locus of control and compliance with contingency contracting and counseling interventions. *Psychological Reports, 67,* 233–234.

Trice, A. D., & Hackburt, L. (1989). Academic locus of control, type A behavior, and college absenteeism. *Psychological Reports, 65,* 337–338.

Trivers, R. L. (1971). Parental investment and sexual selection. In B. Campbell (Ed.), *Sexual selection and the descent of man.* Chicago: Aldine.

Trivers, R. L. (1972). Parental investment and sexual selection. In B. Campbell (Ed.), *Sexual selection and the descent of man: 1871–1971* (pp. 136–179). Chicago: Aldine.

Trott, J. (1991). The grade five syndrome. *Cornerstone, 20,* 16–18.

Trull, T. J. (1992). DSM-III-R personality disorders and the five-factor model of personality: An empirical comparison. *Journal of Abnormal Psychology, 101,* 553–560.

Trull, T. J., & Sher, K. J. (1994). Relationship between the five-factor model of personality and Axis I disorders in a nonclinical sample. *Journal of Abnormal Psychology, 103,* 350–360.

Tryon, W. W. (1990). Why paradigmatic behaviorism should be retitled psychological behaviorism. *The Behavior Therapist, 13,* 127–128.

Tucker, R. K., & Dyson, R. (1991). Factor structure of the short form measure of self-actualization in a Black sample. *Psychological Reports, 69,* 871–877.

Turk, D., Meichenbaum, D., & Genest, M. (1983). *Pain and behavioral medicine.* New York: Guilford.

Turkel, A. R. (1988). Money as a mirror of marriage. *Journal of the American Academy of Psychoanalysis, 16,* 525–535.

Turkel, S. (1988). Artificial intelligence and psychoanalysis: A new alliance. *Journal of the American Academy of Arts and Sciences, 117,* 241–268.

Turkkan, J. S. (1989a). Classical conditioning beyond the reflex: An uneasy rebirth. *Behavioral and Brain Sciences, 12,* 161–179.

Turkkan, J. S. (1989b). Classical conditioning: The new hegemony. *Behavioral and Brain Sciences, 12,* 121–179.

Turkkan, J. S., & Brady, J. V. (1985). Mediational theory of the placebo effect: Discussion. In L. White, B. Tursky, & G. E. Schwartz (Eds.), *Placebo: Theory, research, and mechanisms.* New York: Guilford.

Turner, R. M. (1990, November). *The utility of psychodynamic techniques in the practice of cognitive behavior therapy.* Workshop presented at the meeting of the Association for Advancement of Behavior Therapy, San Francisco.

Turner, S. M., Beidel, D. C., & Nathan, R. S. (1985). Biological factors in obsessive-compulsive disorders. *Psychological Disorders, 97,* 430–450.

Tuttman, S. (1988). Psychoanalytic concepts of "the self." *Journal of the American Academy of Psychoanalysis, 16,* 209–219.

Tversky, A. (1977). Features of similarity. *Psychological Review, 84,* 327–352.

Tyler, F. B., Dhawan, N., & Sinha, Y. (1989). Cultural contributions to constructing locus of control attributions. *Genetic, Social, and General Psychology Monographs, 115,* 205–220.

Ulanov, A., & Ulanov, B. (1987). *The witch and the clown: Two archetypes of human sexuality.* Wilmette, IL: Chiron Publications.

Ulrich, R. E., Stachnik, T. J., & Stainton, N. R. (1963). Student acceptance of generalized personality interpretations. *Psychological Reports, 13,* 831–834.

Unger, R. K. (1979). Towards a redefinition of sex and gender. *American Psychologist, 34,* 1085–1094.

University of Minnesota. (1982). *User's guide for the Minnesota Report.* Minneapolis: National Computer Systems.

Valenzuela, A., & Dornbusch, S. M. (1994). Familism and social capital in the academic achievement of Mexican origin and Anglo adolescents. *Social Science Quarterly, 75,* 18–36.

Valliant, G. E. (1971). Theoretical hierarchy of adaptive ego mechanisms. *Archives of General Psychiatry, 24,* 107–118.

Valliant, G. E. (1977). *Adaptation to life.* Boston: Little, Brown.

Valliant, G. E., & Valliant, C. O. (1990). Determinants and consequences of creativity in a cohort of gifted women. *Psychology of Women Quarterly, 14,* 607–616.

Van-Buren, J. (1985). Postmodernism: Feminism and the deconstruction of the feminine: Kristeva and Irigary. *American Journal of Psychoanalysis, 55,* 231–243.

Van de Castle, R. L. (1971). *The psychology of dreaming.* Morristown, NJ: General Learning Press.

Van den Hout, M. A., & Merckelbach, H. (1991). Classical conditioning: Still going strong. *Behavioural Psychotherapy, 19,* 59–79.

Veenhoven, R. & Verkuyten, M. (1989). The well-being of only children. *Adolescence, 24,* 155–166.

Velting, D. M., & Liebert, R. M. (1997). Predicting three mood phenomena from factors and facets of the NEO-PI. *Journal of Personality Assessment, 68,* 164–171.

Vermorel, M. (1990). The drive *[trieb]* from Goethe to Freud. *International Review of Psycho-Analysis, 17,* 249–256.

Vernon, D. T. A. (1974). Modeling and birth order in responses to painful stimuli. *Journal of Personality and Social Psychology, 29,* 794–799.

Veroff, J. (1957). Development and validation of a projective measure of power motivation. *Journal of Abnormal and Social Psychology, 54,* 1–8.

Veroff, J., Atkinson, J. W., Feld, S. C., & Gurin, G. (1960). The use of thematic apperception to assess motivation in a nationwide interview study. *Psychological Monographs, 74* (12, Whole No. 499).

Veroff, J., Reuman, D., & Feld, S. (1984). Motives in American men and women across the adult life span. *Developmental Psychology, 20,* 1142–1158.

Viney, L. L. (1990). Psychotherapy as shared reconstruction. *International Journal of Personal Construct Psychology, 3,* 437–456.

Volkmer, R. E., & Feather, N. T. (1991). Relations between Type A scores, internal locus of control and test anxiety. *Personality and Individual Differences, 12,* 205–209.

Vollhardt, L. T. (1991). Psychoneuroimmunology: A literature review. *American Journal of Orthopsychiatry, 61,* 35–47.

Von Bergen, C. W. (1995). Locus of control. *Psychological Reports, 76,* 739–746.

Von Hippel, W., Jonides, J., Hilton, J. L., & Narayan, S. (1993). Inhibitory effect of schematic processing on perceptual encoding. *Journal of Personality and Social Psychology, 64,* 921–935.

Von Hooff, J. A. R. A. M. (1967). The facial displays of the catarrhine monkeys and apes. In D. Morris (Eds.), *Primate Ethology.* London: Weidenfeld and Nicolson.

Waddell, M. (1995). Psychoanalysis and Feminism. *British Journal of Psychotherapy, 12,* 81–84.

Waddington, J. L. (1989). Sight and insight: Brain dopamine receptor occupancy by neuroleptics visualized in living schizophrenic patients by positron emission tomography. *British Journal of Psychiatry, 154,* 433–436.

Wade, T., Tiggemann, M., Heath, A. C., & Abraham, S. (1995). EPQ-R personality correlates of bulimia nervosa in an Australian twin population. *Personality and Individual Differences, 18,* 283–285.

Wagner, H. N., Weinberger, D. R., Kleinman, J. E., Casanova, M. F., Gibbs, C. J., Gur, R. E., Hornykiewicz, O., Huhar, M. J., Pettegrew, J. W., & Seeman, P. (1988). Neuroimaging and neuropathology. *Schizophrenia Bulletin, 14,* 383–397.

Wagner, T. (1988, June 12). Does father always know best? *New York Times Magazine,* pp. 18, 20.

Walker, B. M. (1990). Construing George Kelly's construing of the person-in-relation. *International Journal of Personal Construct Psychology, 3,* 41–50.

Walker, B. M. (1992). Values and Kelly's theory: Becoming a good scientist. *International Journal of Personal Construct Psychology, 5,* 259–269.

Walker, C. E., Milling, L. S., & Bonner, B. L. (1988). Incontinence disorders: Enuresis and encopresis. In D. K. Routh (Ed.), *Handbook of pediatric psychology.* New York: Guilford.

Wallace, E. R. (1986). The scientific status of psychoanalysis: A review of Grunbaum's *The foundations of psychoanalysis. Journal of Nervous and Mental Disease, 174,* 379–386.

Waller, K. V., & Bates, R. C. (1992). Health locus of control and self-efficacy beliefs in a healthy elderly sample. *American Journal of Health Promotion, 6,* 302–309.

Waller, N. G. (in press). Evaluating the structure of personality. In C. R. Cloninger (Ed.), *Personality and psychopathology.* Washington, DC: American Psychiatric Press.

Wallerstein, R. S. (1988). One psychoanalysis or many? *International Journal of Psycho-Analysis, 69,* 5–21.

Wallerstein, R. S. (1989). Psychoanalysis and psychotherapy: An historical perspective. *International Journal of Psycho-Analysis, 70,* 563–591.

Wallis, R., & Kleinke, C. L. (1995). Acceptance of external versus internal excuses by an externally or internally oriented audience. *Basic and Applied Social Psychology, 17,* 411–420.

Walsh, S. M. (1991). Employee assistance and the helping professional: The more things change, the more they stay the same. *Employee Assistance Quarterly, 7,* 113–118.

Walters, G. D., & Greene, R. L. (1988). Differentiating

between schizophrenic and manic inpatients by means of the MMPI. *Journal of Personality Assessment, 52,* 91–95.

Wang, A. Y., & Richarde, R. S. (1988). Global versus task-specific measures of self-efficacy. *The Psychological Record, 38,* 533–541.

Ward, S. E., Leventhal, H., & Love, R. (1988). Repression revisited: Tactics used in coping with a severe health threat. *Personality and Social Psychology Bulletin, 14,* 735–746.

Waring, E. M. (1990). Self-disclosure of personal constructs. *Family Process, 29,* 399–416.

Warner, M. S. (1989). Empathy and strategy in the family system [Special issue: Person-centered approaches with families]. *Person-Centered Review, 4,* 324–343.

Warner, S. L. (1987). Manifest dream analysis in contemporary practice. In M. L. Glucksman & S. L. Warner (Eds.), *Dreams in new perspective: The royal road revisited.* New York: Human Sciences.

Warren, W. (1989). Personal construct theory and general trends in contemporary philosophy. *International Journal of Personal Construct Psychology, 2,* 287–300.

Warren, W. G. (1990). Is personal construct psychology a cognitive psychology? *International Journal of Personal Construct Psychology, 3,* 393–414.

Warren, W. G. (1991). Rising up from down under: A response to Adams-Webber on cognitive psychology and personal construct psychology. *International Journal of Personal Construct Psychology, 4,* 43–49.

Warren, W. G. (1992). Personal construct theory and mental health. *International Journal of Personal Construct Psychology, 5,* 223–237.

Warren, W. G., & Parry, G. (1981). Personal constructs and death: Some clinical refinements. In H. Bonarius, R. Holland, & S. Rosenberg (Eds.), *Personal construct psychology: Recent advances in theory and practice.* New York: St. Martin's Press.

Waschull, S. B., & Kernis, M. H. (1996). Level and stability of self-esteem as predictors of children's intrinsic motivation and reasons for anger. *Personality and Social Psychology Bulletin, 22,* 4–13.

Wasik, B. (1984). *Teaching parents effective problem solving: A handbook for professionals.* Unpublished manuscript, University of North Carolina, Chapel Hill.

Waters, E., Kondo-Ikemura, K., Posada, G., & Richters, J. (1990). Learning to love: Mechanisms and milestones. In M. Gunner & L. A. Sroufe (Eds.), *Minnesota Symposia on Child Psychology, 23.* Hillsdale, NJ: Erlbaum.

Waters, E., Merrick, S. K., Albersheim, L., & Treboux, D. (1995). From the Strange Situation of the Adult Attachment Interview: A 20-year longitudinal study of attachment security in infancy and early adulthood. In J. A. Crowell & E. Waters (Chairs), *Is the parent-child relationship a prototype of later love relationships? Studies of attachment and working models of attachment.* Symposium conducted at the biennial meeting of the Society for Research in Child Development, Indianapolis, IN.

Watson, D., & Hubbard, B. (1996). Adaptational style and dispositional structure: Coping in the context of the Five-Factor Model. *Journal of Personality, 64,* 737–774.

Watson, J. B. (1914). *Behavior: An introduction to comparative psychology.* New York: H. Holt.

Watson, J. B. (1919). *Psychology from the standpoint of a behaviorist.* Philadelphia: Lippincott.

Watson, J. B. (1924). *Behaviorism.* New York: W. W. Norton.

Watson, J. B., & Rayner, R. (1920). Conditioned emotional reactions. *Journal of Experimental Psychology, 3,* 1–14.

Watson, O. M., & Graves, T. D. (1966). Quantitative research in proxemic behavior. *American Anthropologist, 68,* 971–985.

Watson, P. J., Morris, R. J., & Hood, R. W. (1990). Intrinsicness, self-actualization, and the ideological surround. *Journal of Psychology and Theology, 18,* 40–53.

Watson, W. E., Doster, J., & Michaelsen, L. K. (1990). Individual and group meaning: Exploring the reciprocal relation. *International Journal of Personal Construct Psychology, 3,* 231–248.

Watzlawick, P. (Ed.). (1984). *The invented reality.* New York: Norton.

Weaver, J. B., III, Walker, J. R., McCord, L. L., & Bellamy, R. V., Jr. (1996). Exploring the links between personality and television remote control device use. *Personality and Individual Differences, 20,* 483–489.

Webb, W. B. (1982). Sleep and biological rhythms. In W. B. Webb (Ed.), *Biological rhythms, sleep, and performance.* New York: Wiley.

Wegner, D. M. (1994). Ironic processes of mental control. *Psychological Review, 101,* 34–52.

Weidner, G., & Matthews, K. A. (1978). Reported physical symptoms elicited by unpredictable events and the Type A coronary-prone behavior pattern. *Journal of Personality and Social Psychology, 36,* 1213–1220.

Weinberger, D. R. (1987). Implications of normal brain development for the pathogenesis of schizophrenia. *Archives of General Psychiatry, 44,* 660–669.

Weiner, B. (1990). Attribution in personality psychology. In L. A. Pervin (Ed.), *Handbook of personality: Theory and Research.* New York: Guilford.

Weinrach, S. G. (1990). Rogers and Gloria: The controversial film and the enduring relationship. *Psychotherapy, 27,* 282–290.

Weisberg, P., & Waldrop, P. B. (1972). Fixed-interval work habits of Congress. *Journal of Applied Behavior Analysis, 5,* 93–97.

Weiss, A. S. (1987). Shostrom's Personal Orientation Inventory: Arguments against its basic validity. *Personality and Individual Differences, 8,* 895–903.

Weiss, A. S. (1991). The measurement of self-actualization: The quest for the test may be as challenging as the search for the self [Special issue: Handbook of self-actualization]. *Journal of Social Behavior and Personality, 6,* 265–290.

Weiss, R. S. (1979). The emotional impact of marital separation. In G. Levinger & O. C. Moles (Eds.),

Divorce and separation: Context, causes, and consequences. New York: Basic Books.

Weisse, C. S. (1992). Depression and immunocompetence: A review of the literature. *Psychological Bulletin, 111,* 475–489.

Weissman, M. M., Gershon, E. S., Kidd, K. K., Prusoff, B. A., Leckman, J. F., Dibble, E., Hamovit, J., Thompson, D., Pauls, D. L., & Guroff, J. J. (1984). Psychiatric disorders in the relatives of probands with affective disorders. *Archives of General Psychiatry, 41,* 13–21.

Weissman, M. M., Myers, J. K., & Thompson, W. D. (1981). Depression and its treatment in a U.S. urban community, 1975–1976. *Archives of General Psychiatry, 38,* 417–421.

Weissman, M. M., Prusoff, B. A., DiMascio, A., Neu, C., Goklaney, M., & Klerman, G. L. (1979). The efficacy of drugs and psychotherapy in the treatment of acute depressive episodes. *American Journal of Psychiatry, 136,* 555–558.

Weitzman, B. (1967). Behavior therapy and psychotherapy. *Psychological Review, 74,* 300–317.

Weitzmann, E. (1961). A note on the EEG and eye movements during behavioral sleep in monkeys. *EEG Clinical Neurophysiology, 13,* 790–794.

Welch, D. C., & West, R. L. (1995). Self-efficacy and mastery: Its application to issues of environmental control, cognition, and aging. *Developmental Review, 15,* 150–171.

Wender, P. H., Kety, S. S., Rosenthal, D., Schulsinger, F., Ortmann, J., & Lunde, I. (1986). Psychiatric disorders in the biological and adoptive families of individuals with affective disorders. *Archives of General Psychiatry, 43,* 923–929.

Weston, D. (1988). Transference and information processing. *Clinical Psychology Review, 8,* 161–179.

Westen, D. (1991a). Cognitive-behavioral interventions in the psychoanalytic psychotherapy of borderline personality disorders. *Clinical Psychology Review, 11,* 211–230.

Westen, D. (1991b). Social cognition and object relations. *Psychological Bulletin, 109,* 429–455.

Wetzler, S., & Marlowe, D. (1990). "Faking bad" on the MMPI, MMPI-2, and Millon-II. *Psychological Reports, 67,* 1117–1118.

White, J., Davison, G. C., Haaga, D. A. F., & White, K. (1992). Cognitive bias in the articulated thoughts of depressed and nondepressed psychiatric patients. *Journal of Nervous and Mental Disease, 180,* 77–81.

White, J., Joseph, S., & Neil, A. (1993). Religiosity, psychoticism, and schizotypal traits. *Personality and Individual Differences, 19,* 847–851.

White, L., Tursky, B., & Schwartz, G. E. (Eds.). (1985). *Placebo: Theory, research, and mechanisms.* New York: Guilford.

White, L. K. & Booth, A. (1985). The quality and stability of remarriages: The role of stepchildren. *American Sociological Review, 50,* 689–698.

White, R. W. (1959). Motivation reconsidered: The concept of competence. *Psychological Review, 66,* 297–333.

White, R. W. (1960). Competence and the psychosexual stages of development. In M. R. Jones (Ed.), *Nebraska symposium on motivation, 1960* (Vol. 8). Lincoln: University of Nebraska Press.

White, R. W. (1963). *Ego and reality in psychoanalytic theory: Psychological issues* (Monograph No. 11). New York: International Universities Press.

White, R. W. (1976). *The enterprise of living: A view of personal growth* (2nd ed.). New York: Holt, Rinehart & Winston.

Whitley, B. E. (1983). Sex role orientation and self-esteem: A critical meta-analytic review. *Journal of Personality and Social Psychology, 44,* 765–778.

Whitson, E. R., & Olczak, P. V. (1991). The use of the POI in clinical situations: An evaluation [Special issue: Handbook of self-actualization]. *Journal of Social Behavior and Personality, 6,* 291–310.

Wicker, A. W. (1971). An examination of the "other variables" explanation of attitude-behavior inconsistency. *Journal of Personality and Social Psychology, 19,* 18–30.

Wickramasekera, I. (1985). A conditioned response model of the placebo effect: Predictions from the model. In L. White, B. Tursky, & G. E. Schwartz (Eds.), *Placebo: Theory, research, and mechanisms.* New York: Guilford.

Widiger, T. A., & Trull, R. J. (1992). Personality and psychopathology: An application of the five-factor model. *Journal of Personality, 60,* 363–393.

Wiedenfeld, S. A., O'Leary, A., Bandura, A., Brown, S., Levine, S., & Raska, K. (1990). Impact of perceived self-efficacy in coping with stressors on components of the immune system. *Journal of Personality and Social Psychology, 59,* 1082–1094.

Wildstein, A. B., & Thompson, D. N. (1989). Locus of control, expectational set, and problem solving. *Perceptual and Motor Skills, 68,* 383–388.

Wilhite, S. C. (1990). Self-efficacy, locus of control, self-assessment of memory ability, and study activities as predictors of college course achievement. *Journal of Educational Psychology, 82,* 696–700.

Wilkinson, S. M. (1991). Penis envy: Libidinal metaphor and experiential metonym. *International Journal of Psycho-Analysis, 72,* 335–346.

Willerman, L. (1975). *Individual and group differences.* New York: Harper's College Press.

Willerman, L., & Plomin, R. (1973). Activity level in children and their parents. *Child Development, 44,* 854–858.

Williams, D. E., & Page, M. M. (1989). A multidimensional measure of Maslow's hierarchy of needs. *Journal of Research in Personality, 23,* 192–213.

Williams, R. B., Barefoot, J. C., & Shekelle, R. B. (1985). The health consequences of hostility. In M. Chesney & R. Rosenman (Eds.), *Anger and hostility in cardiovascular and behavioral disorders* (pp. 173–185). Washington, DC: Hemisphere.

Williams, R. B., Jr., Friedman, M., Glass, D. C., Herd, J. A., & Schneiderman, N. (1978). Mechanisms linking behavioral and pathophysiological processes. In T. M. Dembroski, S. M. Weiss, J. L. Shields, S. G. Haynes, & M. Feinleib (Eds.), *Coronary-prone behavior.* New York: Springer-Verlag.

Williams, S. L. (1992). Perceived self-efficacy and phobic disability. In R. Schwarzer (Ed.), *Self-efficacy: Thought control of action.* Washington, DC: Hemisphere.

Williams, S. L., & Kinney, P. J. (1991). Performance and nonperformance strategies for coping with acute pain: The role of perceived self-efficacy, expected outcomes, and attention. *Cognitive Therapy and Research, 15,* 1–19.

Williams, S. L., & Zane, G. (1989). Guided mastery and stimulus exposure treatments for severe performance anxiety in agoraphobics. *Behaviour Research and Therapy, 27,* 237–245.

Wilmut, I., Schnieke, A. E., McWhir, J., Kind, A. J., & Campbell, K. H. S. (1997). Viable offspring derived from fetal and adult mammalian cells. *Nature, 385,* 810–813.

Wilson, E. O. (1975). *Sociobiology: The new synthesis.* Cambridge: Harvard University Press.

Wilson, G. (1986). The behaviour therapy of W. S. Gilbert. *the Behavior Therapist, 2,* 32–34.

Wilson, G. T. (1982). Clinical issues and strategies in the practice of behavior therapy. In C. M. Franks, G. T. Wilson, P. C. Kendall, & K. D. Brownell (Eds.), *Annual review of behavior therapy: Theory and practice* (Vol. 8). New York: Guilford.

Wilson, G. T. (1984). Fear reduction methods and the treatment of anxiety disorders. In C. M. Franks, G. T. Wilson, P. C. Kendall, & K. D. Brownell (Eds.), *Annual review of behavior therapy: Theory and practice* (Vol. 10). New York: Guilford.

Wilson, G. T., O'Leary, K. D., & Nathan, P. (1992). *Abnormal psychology.* Englewood Cliffs, NJ: Prentice-Hall.

Wilson, M., & Daly, M. (1985). Competitiveness, risk-taking, and violence: The young male syndrome. *Ethology and Sociobiology, 6,* 59–73.

Wilson, T. D., & Capitman, J. A. (1992). The effects of script availability on social behavior. *Personality and Social Psychology Bulletin, 8,* 11–19.

Winell, M. (1987). Personal goals: The key to self-direction in adulthood. In M. E. Ford & D. H. Ford (Eds.), *Humans as self-constructing living systems: Putting the framework to work* (pp. 261–287). Hillsdale, NJ: Erlbaum.

Wingerson, L. (1990). *Mapping our genes: The genome project and the future of medicine.* New York: Dutton.

Wink, P., & Gough, H. G. (1990). New narcissism scales for the California Psychological Inventory and MMPI. *Journal of Personality Assessment, 54,* 446–462.

Winnicott, D. W. (1971). *Playing and reality.* London: Tavistock Publications.

Winson, J. (1985). *Brain and psyche: The biology of the unconscious.* New York: Anchor/Doubleday.

Winter, D., Baker, M., & Goggins, S. (1992). Into the unknown: Transitions in psychiatric services as construed by clients and staff. *International Journal of Personal Construct Psychology, 5,* 323–340.

Winter, D. A. (1990a). *Personal construct theory in clinical practice.* London: Routledge.

Winter, D. A. (1990b). Therapeutic alternatives for psychological disorder: Personal construct psychology investigations in a health service setting. In G. J. Neimeyer & R. A. Neimeyer (Eds.), *Advances in personal construct psychology* (Vol. 1). Greenwich, CT: JAI Press.

Winter, D. G. (1967). *Power motivation in thought and action.* Unpublished doctoral dissertation, Harvard University.

Winter, D. G. (1968). Need for power in thought and action. *Proceedings of the 76th Annual Convention of the American Psychological Association, 3,* 429–430.

Winter, D. G. (1972). The need for power in college men: Action correlates and relationship to drinking. In D. C. McClelland, W. N. Davis, R. Kalin, & E. Wanner (Eds.), *The drinking man.* New York: Free Press.

Winter, D. G. (1973). *The power motive.* New York: Free Press.

Winter, D. G. (1987a). Enhancement of an enemy's power motivation as a dynamic of conflict escalation. *Journal of Personality and Social Psychology, 52,* 41–46.

Winter, D. G. (1987b). Leader appeal, leader performance, and the motive profiles of leaders and followers: A study of American presidents and elections. *Journal of Personality and Social Psychology, 52,* 196–202.

Winter, D. G. (1988). The power motive in women and men. *Journal of Personality and Social Psychology, 54,* 510–519.

Winter, D. G., & Barenbaum, N. B. (1985). Responsibility and the power motive in women and men. *Journal of Personality, 53,* 335–355.

Winter, D. G., & Carlson, L. A. (1988). Using motive scores in the psychobiographical study of an individual: The case of Richard Nixon. In D. P. McAdams & R. L. Ochberg (Eds.), *Psychobiography and life narratives.* Durham, NC: Duke University Press.

Winter, D. G., Hermann, M. G., Weintraub, W., & Walker, S. G. (1991). The personalities of Bush and Gorbachev at a distance: Follow-up on predictions. *Political Psychology, 12,* 457–464.

Wolk, S., & Kurtz, J. (1975). Positive adjustment and involvement during aging and expectancy for internal control. *Journal of Consulting and Clinical Psychology, 43,* 173–178.

Wolpe, J. (1958). *Psychotherapy by reciprocal inhibition.* Stanford, CA: Stanford University Press.

Wolpe, J. (1978). Cognition and causation in human behavior and its therapy. *American Psychologist, 33,* 437–446.

Wolpe, J. (1989). The derailment of behavior therapy: A tale of conceptual misdirection. *Journal of Behavior Therapy and Experimental Psychiatry, 20,* 3–15.

Wolpe, J., & Lazarus, A. A. (1966). *Behavior therapy*

techniques: A guide to the treatment of neurosis. New York: Pergamon Press.

Wolpe, J., & Rachman, S. (1960). Psychoanalytic "evidence": A critique based on Freud's case of Little Hans. *Journal of Nervous and Mental Diseases, 130,* 135–148.

Wolpe, J., & Rowan, V. C. (1988). Panic disorder: A product of classical conditioning. *Behaviour Research and Therapy, 26,* 441–450.

Wolpe, J., & Rowan, V. C. (1989). Classical conditioning and panic disorder: Reply to Sanderson and Beck. *Behaviour Research and Therapy, 27,* 583–584.

Wood, J. V., Taylor, S. E., & Lichtman, R. R. (1985). Social comparison and adjustment to breast cancer. *Journal of Personality and Social Psychology, 49,* 1169–1183.

Wood, R., & Bandura, A. (1989). Impact of conceptions of ability on self-regulatory mechanisms and complex decision making. *Journal of Personality and Social Psychology, 56,* 407–415.

Woodruffe, C. (1985). Consensual validation of personality traits: Additional evidence and individual differences. *Journal of Personality and Social Psychology, 48,* 1240–1252.

Worchel, P. (1955). Anxiety and repression. *Journal of Abnormal and Social Psychology, 51,* 201–205.

Worobey, J. (1986). Convergence among assessments of temperament in the first month. *Child Development, 57,* 47–55.

Wright, J., & Mischel, W. (1982). Influence of affect on cognitive social learning variables. *Journal of Personality and Social Psychology, 43,* 901–914.

Wright, J., & Mischel, W. (1986). *Predicting cross-situational consistency: The role of person variables and situation requirements.* Unpublished manuscript, Columbia University.

Wright, J. C., & Mischel, W. (1987). A conditional approach to dispositional constructs: The local predictability of social behavior. *Journal of Personality and Social Psychology, 53,* 1159–1177.

Wright, L. (1988). The Type A behavior pattern and coronary heart disease. *American Psychologist, 43,* 2–14.

Wrightsman, L. S. (1969). Wallace supporters and adherence to "law and order." *Journal of Personality and Social Psychology, 13,* 17–22.

Wylie, R. C. (1968). The present status of self theory. In E. F. Borgatta & W. W. Lambert (Eds.), *Handbook of personality theory and research.* Chicago: Rand McNally.

Yates, B. T., & Mischel, W. (1979). Young children's preferred attentional strategies for delaying gratification. *Journal of Personality and Social Psychology, 37,* 286–300.

Young-Bruehl, E. (1994). What theories women want. *American Imago, 51,* 373–396.

Zachariah, R. (1996). Predictors of psychological well-being of women during pregnancy: Replication and extension. *Journal of Social Behavior and Personality, 11,* 127–140.

Zajonc, R. B. (1976). Family configuration and intelligence: Variations in scholastic aptitude scores parallel trends in family size and the spacing of children. *Science, 192,* 227–236.

Zajonc, R. B., & Markus, G. B. (1975). Birth order and intellectual development. *Psychological Review, 82,* 74–88.

Zajonc, R. B., & Markus, H. (1985). Affect and cognition: The hard interface. In C. E. Izard, J. Kagan, & R. Zajonc (Eds.), *Emotions, cognition, and behavior* (pp. 73–102). New York: Cambridge University Press.

Zaleski, Z., Eysenck, S., & Eysenck, H. (1995). *Personality and Individual Differences, 18,* 677–679.

Zayas, L. H. (1988). Thematic features in the manifest dreams of expectant fathers. *Clinical Social Work Journal, 16,* 282–296.

Zeldow, P. B., Daugherty, S. R., & Clark, D. C. (1987). Masculinity, femininity and psychosocial adjustment in medical students: A 2-year follow-up. *Journal of Personality Assessment, 51,* 3–14.

Zeldow, P. B., Daugherty, S. R., & McAdams, D. P. (1988). Intimacy, power, and psychological well-being in medical students. *Journal of Nervous and Mental Disease, 176,* 182–187.

Zeller, A. (1950). An experimental analogue of repression, II. The effect of individual failure and success on memory measured by relearning. *Journal of Experimental Psychology, 40,* 411–422.

Zeller, A. (1951). An experimental analogue of repression, III. The effect of induced failure and success on memory measured by recall. *Journal of Experimental Psychology, 42,* 32–38.

Zettle, R. D., & Hayes, S. C. (1987). Component and process analysis of cognitive therapy. *Psychological Reports, 61,* 939–953.

Zetzel, E. (1956). Current concepts of transference. *International Journal of Psycho-Analysis, 37,* 369–376.

Zhurbin, V. I. (1991). The notion of psychological defense in the conceptions of Sigmund Freud and Carl Rogers. *Soviet Psychology, 29,* 58–72.

Zimmerman, B. J. (1990). Self-regulating academic learning and achievement: The emergence of a social cognitive perspective. *Educational Psychology Review, 2,* 173–201.

Zimmerman, B. J., & Bandura, A. (1994). Impact of self-regulatory influences on writing course attainment. *American Education and Research Journal, 31,* 845–862.

Zipursky, R. B., Lim, K. O., Sullivan, E. V., Brown, B. W., & Pfefferbaum, A. (1992). Widespread cerebral gray matter volume deficits in schizophrenia. *Archives of General Psychiatry, 49,* 195–205.

Zucker, R. A., Manosevitz, M., & Lanyon, R. I. (1968). Birth order, anxiety, and affiliation during a crisis. *Journal of Personality and Social Psychology, 8,* 354–359.

Zuckerman, M. (1983). The distinction between trait and state scales is not arbitrary: Comment on Allen and Potkay's "On the arbitrary distinction between traits and states." *Journal of Personality and Social Psychology, 44,* 1083–1086.

Zuckerman, M. (1991). *Psychobiology of personality.* Cambridge: Cambridge University Press.

Zuckerman, M. (1994). Sensation seeking and impulsivity: A marriage of traits made in biology? In W. McCown, J. Johnson, & M. Shure (Eds.), *The impulsive client: Theory, research and treatment* (pp. 69–89). Washington, DC: American Psychological Association.

Zuckerman, M. (1995). Good and bad humors: Biochemical bases of personality and its disorders. *Psychological Science, 5,* 325–332.

Zuckerman, M., Knee, C. R., Kieffer, S. C., Rawsthorne, L., & Bruce, L. M. (1996). Beliefs in realistic and unrealistic control: Assessment and implications. *Journal of Personality, 64,* 435–464.

Zuckerman, M., & Neeb, M. (1979). Sensation seeking and psychopathology. *Psychiatry Research, 1,* 255–264.

Zuroff, D. C. (1994). Depressive personality styles and the five-factor model of personality. *Journal of Personality Assessment, 63,* 453–472.

NAME INDEX

T

U

V

W

Subject Index

D

E

F

Demonstration Materials

The following pages are perforated for easy removal.

Weight (pounds)
Height (inches)

RANK	NAME	NUMBER OF ADJECTIVES USED	PERVASIVENESS				PERCENTAGE OF SIMILARITY
			ALMOST ALWAYS 4	FRE-QUENTLY 3	OCCA-SIONALLY 2	RARELY 1	
	Self						
Know best 1st							%
2nd							%
3rd							%
4th							%
Know least 5th							%
	Σ = Sum (total)	$\Sigma =$	$\Sigma =$	$\Sigma =$	$\Sigma =$	$\Sigma =$	
	M = Mean	$M =$	%	%	%	%	

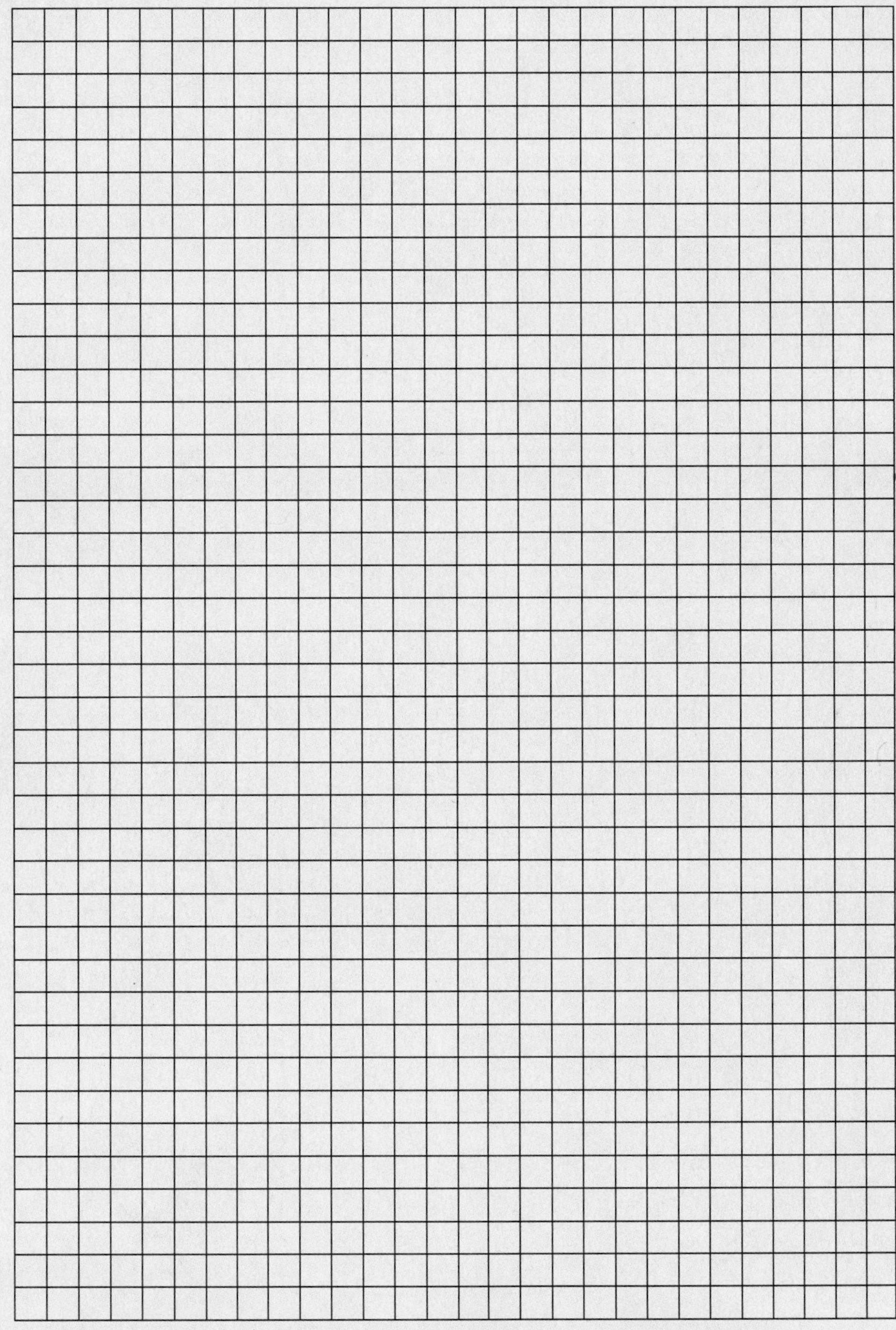

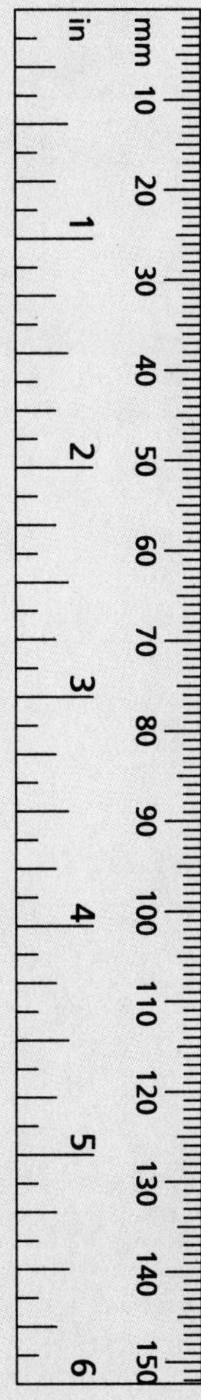
mm
10
20
30
40
50
60
70
80
90
100
110
120
130
140
150
in
1
2
3
4
5
6

1. I like to study.	2. I prefer socializing with people my own age.	3. Success is important to me.	4. I am religious.
5. I dislike crude language.	6. I take good care of my body.	7. I am sensitive to other people's needs.	8. I think it is okay to get drunk occasionally.
9. I prefer to save money than to spend it.	10. I am concerned with how I look.	11. I am organized.	12. I enjoy being alone.
13. I have high standards for my work.	14. I think it is important to obey the law.	15. My family is important to me.	16. I like meeting new people.